Also by Jim McKairnes

The Sheep Is What Makes It Funny:
From Philadelphia to CBS, How I Found Myself in Television

103 Ways to Get Into TV (By 102 Who Did, Plus Me)

103 Ways to Get Into TV: The Sequel

ALL IN THE DECADE

70 Things About 70s TV
That Turned Ten Years
Into A Revolution

Jim McKairnes

\<jmck\>

for Matt McNamee (1993-2017) ...

... and with thanks to Temple University's School of Media and Communication for the support of this course as part of its 2014 curriculum

INTRODUCTION

In the very first week of the very first year of an entirely new decade — the 1970s — these were among the episodes of TV that aired in prime-time:

"When Darrin is conflicted between a business trip to Japan and staying at home with his new baby, mother-in-law Endora splits him into two people." (*Bewitched* January 1 1970)

"Marcia wants to nominate her new Dad as Father of the Year." (*The Brady Bunch* January 2 1970)

"Billie Joe brings her new boyfriend home to Hooterville to meet the family." (*Petticoat Junction* January 3 1970)

"Steve Douglas gets cast in daughter Dodie's school play as a tree." (*My Three Sons* January 3 1970)

"Lassie is struck by a car while saving a child and now appears to have amnesia." (*Lassie* January 4 1970)

"A circus midget and new widower struggle to deal with the prejudice of the town's banker." (*Bonanza* January 4 1970)

"Craig's high-school club initiation scavenger hunt includes a candelabra that he borrowed from Liberace, which Lucy tries to return, with disastrous results." (*Here's Lucy* January 5 1970)

"Miss Kitty and her horse are taken hostage, and Marshall Dillon sets out to rescue them." (*Gunsmoke* January 5 1970)

"Julie is held hostage by a disturbed man who mistakes her for the daughter of a woman he wants to punish for insulting him." (*The Mod Squad* January 6 1970)

"Jim tries to quash Debbie's attempts to get into the newspaper business once and for all." (*The Debbie Reynolds Show* January 6 1970)

In the very last week of the very last year of the 1970s, these were among the episodes of TV that aired in prime-time:

"Billie researches an article on the suicide of teenagers." (*Lou Grant* December 24 1979)

"A visit to a restaurant at a nudist colony is featured." (*Real People* December 26 1979)

"Gary and Valene Ewing move to Knots Landing and get acquainted with their new neighbors – including a drunken teenaged daughter who's wreaking havoc on her parents' marriage." (*Knots Landing* December 27 1979)

"Danny and Polly continue to grapple with their inter-racial romance; Chester begs wife Jessica for another chance after she discovers his infidelity; high-school senior Billy is thrown an 18th birthday by the teacher he is sleeping with." (*Soap* December 27 1979)

"Barney assigns a female detective to investigate a dentist who has a history of sexually assaulting sedated patients." (*Barney Miller* December 27 1979)

"Disc-jockey Johnny Fever awakens in the middle of the night convinced that God is talking to him." (*WKRP in Cincinnati* December 31 1979) more of all of it was unfolding "in living color" helped to re-draw some of the lines. Lucy and Ed Sullivan and Jack Benny and Sheriff Dillon were sharing space these days with Uhura and the Smothers Brothers.

By time the 1970s arrived, TV was a full-fledged adolescent. And like any teen, it had one foot inside the world it knew and the other out in the new world it wanted to explore. Rebelliousness and curiosity led to transition – from concrete thinking and rules-adhering to abstract thinking and rules-breaking, from acceptance to rejection, from passive to active learning, from conventional to experimental, from dependence to semi-autonomy, from indirect experience to immersion, and from looking and listening to seeing and hearing.

If still tethered in a child-like way to its roots of radio -- *Dragnet*, *Gunsmoke*, Ed Sullivan, Walt Disney, Lucy were each still on the air at the beginning of the decade -- TV was beginning to show an un-earthing of its roots. In the 1970s, TV looked around and saw change underway in real life and knew it had to reflect it. Be a part of it. What the nightly news was covering was something prime-time television could not ignore.

The transition was a halting one.

> Some shows began to reflect the new cultural landscape, but most continued to ignore it. *That Girl* (ABC, 1966–71), an old-fashioned show about a single woman living and working in the big city—with the help of her boyfriend and her "daddy"—aired on the same schedule as *The Mary Tyler Moore Show* (CBS, 1970–77), a new-fashioned comedy about a single woman making it on her own. In the same week, one could watch *The Lawrence Welk Show* (ABC, 1955–71), a 15-year-old musical variety program that featured a legendary polka band, and *Rowan and Martin's Laugh-In* (NBC, 1968–73), an irreverent new comedy-variety show plugged into the 1960s counterculture. (*Encyclopedia Britannica*, "The Relevance Movement")

Clearly between January 1970 and December 1979 something ab
TV changed.

The something was everything.

In large part that's because so did the people making it. The 197
more or less marked the arrival *in* TV of the first generation raised
it -- producers and writers, network and studio executives, dreame
and decision makers. A collective that along with select risk-takir
long-timers seemed to realize that at this point TV's reach could an
should extend further than its thus-far self-limiting grasp.

Developed in the 1920s and officially unveiled at the 1939 World's Fai
in New York (fairly or not by NBC head David Sarnoff, as chiefly hi
creation alone), television began as a business in the 1940s. Its earl
thinking was as black-and-white as its programming: Schedules were
filled with shows imported from radio: already working and popular
star-driven sitcoms and variety shows, easy-to-digest panel shows,
genre series like cop shows and westerns. *Dragnet*, Lucy, *Gunsmoke.*
Close your eyes and the radio's still on.

These were safe broad strokes for a curious new experiment -- an
infancy of adherence (to what was already working) and limitation (to
what was already allowed) that lasted through the 1950s as the industry
settled in and TV took off. Even the drama showcases that led to the
decade being christened as television's Golden Age were adaptations
of the established live-theater format.

With the 1960s, the TV that had been thus far crawling began to walk,
tentatively at first, as toddlers do when first stepping outside the safety
and structure of what is known. Convention and formula still reigned,
but some sitcoms became a bit more sophisticated and layered (*The
Dick Van Dyke Show, The Many Loves of Dobie Gillis, Green Acres*); some
families became bit less conventional (*The Andy Griffith Show, Bonanza*),
some dramas took on a bit more shading (*The Defenders, Dr. Kildare, Ben
Casey*); some casts were a bit less all-white (*I Spy, East Side West Side*);
some authority groups were a bit less all-male (*Julia, Star Trek*). That

more of all of it was unfolding "in living color" helped to re-draw some of the lines. Lucy and Ed Sullivan and Jack Benny and Sheriff Dillon were sharing space these days with Uhura and the Smothers Brothers.

By time the 1970s arrived, TV was a full-fledged adolescent. And like any teen, it had one foot inside the world it knew and the other out in the new world it wanted to explore. Rebelliousness and curiosity led to transition – from concrete thinking and rules-adhering to abstract thinking and rules-breaking, from acceptance to rejection, from passive to active learning, from conventional to experimental, from dependence to semi-autonomy, from indirect experience to immersion, and from looking and listening to seeing and hearing.

If still tethered in a child-like way to its roots of radio -- *Dragnet*, *Gunsmoke*, Ed Sullivan, Walt Disney, Lucy were each still on the air at the beginning of the decade -- TV was beginning to show an un-earthing of its roots. In the 1970s, TV looked around and saw change underway in real life and knew it had to reflect it. Be a part of it. What the nightly news was covering was something prime-time television could not ignore.

The transition was a halting one.

> Some shows began to reflect the new cultural landscape, but most continued to ignore it. *That Girl* (ABC, 1966–71), an old-fashioned show about a single woman living and working in the big city—with the help of her boyfriend and her "daddy"—aired on the same schedule as *The Mary Tyler Moore Show* (CBS, 1970–77), a new-fashioned comedy about a single woman making it on her own. In the same week, one could watch *The Lawrence Welk Show* (ABC, 1955–71), a 15-year-old musical variety program that featured a legendary polka band, and *Rowan and Martin's Laugh-In* (NBC, 1968–73), an irreverent new comedy-variety show plugged into the 1960s counterculture. (*Encyclopedia Britannica*, "The Relevance Movement")

Clearly between January 1970 and December 1979 something about TV changed.

The something was everything.

In large part that's because so did the people making it. The 1970s more or less marked the arrival *in* TV of the first generation raised *on* it -- producers and writers, network and studio executives, dreamers and decision makers. A collective that along with select risk-taking long-timers seemed to realize that at this point TV's reach could and should extend further than its thus-far self-limiting grasp.

Developed in the 1920s and officially unveiled at the 1939 World's Fair in New York (fairly or not by NBC head David Sarnoff, as chiefly his creation alone), television began as a business in the 1940s. Its early thinking was as black-and-white as its programming: Schedules were filled with shows imported from radio: already working and popular star-driven sitcoms and variety shows, easy-to-digest panel shows, genre series like cop shows and westerns. *Dragnet*, Lucy, *Gunsmoke*. Close your eyes and the radio's still on.

These were safe broad strokes for a curious new experiment -- an infancy of adherence (to what was already working) and limitation (to what was already allowed) that lasted through the 1950s as the industry settled in and TV took off. Even the drama showcases that led to the decade being christened as television's Golden Age were adaptations of the established live-theater format.

With the 1960s, the TV that had been thus far crawling began to walk, tentatively at first, as toddlers do when first stepping outside the safety and structure of what is known. Convention and formula still reigned, but some sitcoms became a bit more sophisticated and layered (*The Dick Van Dyke Show*, *The Many Loves of Dobie Gillis*, *Green Acres*); some families became bit less conventional (*The Andy Griffith Show*, *Bonanza*), some dramas took on a bit more shading (*The Defenders*, *Dr. Kildare*, *Ben Casey*); some casts were a bit less all-white (*I Spy*, *East Side West Side*); some authority groups were a bit less all-male (*Julia*, *Star Trek*). That

TABLE OF CONTENTS

REALISM

FEMINISM

INDIVIDUALISM

Carter Wins By Wide Margin

ELVIS PRESLEY DIES AT 42

'Peace with honor'
POWs to be freed within 60 days

BLACKOUT!
LIGHTNING HITS

MASS SUICIDES IN GUYANA CULT
Report 300 dead found at site

'NO ONE IS SAFE' FROM SON OF SAM

Incident at Three Mile Island

Viking 2 Lander Settles On Mars And Sends Signal

PATTY HEARST ARRESTED
Don't Shoot, I'll Go With You; FBI Grabs Her & 3 in Frisco

NIXON RESIGNS
HE URGES A TIME OF 'HEALING'; FORD WILL TAKE OFFICE TODAY

TEST-TUBE BABY GIRL

JIMMY CARTER: 'IF KENNEDY RUNS I'LL WHIP HIS ASS'

POPE PAUL DIES AT AGE 80
Cardinals Called To Rome To Elect Successor
9 Days Of Mourning With Body

Occupation of Wounded Knee Is Ended

Oxygen-starved spacemen battle way round moon

CRIPPLED APOLLO IN 'LIFE OR DEATH' RACE FOR HOME

A Lonely Life Ends on Elvis Presley Boulevard

THE GUARDIAN

Thatcher foot in No. 10 door
'Two nations'

PAUL IS QUITTING THE BEATLES

SECRETARIAT!
Sweeps Triple Crown With A Record-Smashing Belmont

Aaron Hits 715th, Pa

Iran students mob embassy

Associated Press
Iranian students occupied the U.S.
Embassy...

BILLIE JEAN KING OUTLIBS THE LIP

FORD TO CITY: DROP DEAD
Vows He'll Veto Any Bail-Out

EGYPT AND ISRAEL SIGN FORMAL TREATY, ENDING A STATE OF WAR AFTER 30 YEARS; SADAT AND BEGIN PRAISE CARTER'S ROLE

3 Astronauts' Lives Hang on LM; Chance of Safe Return 'Excellent'

Apr 10 1970	The Beatles break-up is official
Apr 22 1970	First Earth Day celebration
Jun 13 1971	The Pentagon Papers published
Jan 25 1972	Shirley Chisolm to run for President
Jun 17 1972	Break-in at the Watergate's DNC
Feb 27 1973	Occupation begins at Wounded Knee
Oct 10 1973	Vice-President Spiro T. Agnew resigns
Oct 17 1973	Arab oil-embargo begins
Feb 4 1974	Heiress Patricia Hearst in kidnapped
Apr 8 1974	Hank Aaron breaks Ruth's record
Aug 9 1974	President Richard M. Nixon resigns
Apr 4 1975	Gates and Allen found Microsoft
Sep 3 1976	*Viking II* lands on Mars
May 23 1977	Janet Guthrie an Indy 500 first
Jul 13 1977	New York City blackout
Aug 16 1977	Elvis Presley dies at 42
Jul 25 1978	birth of the first test-tube baby
Sep 17 1978	Camp David Peace Accords signed
Nov 18 1978	918 people die at Jonestown in Guyana
Mar 28 1979	Partial meltdown at Three Mile Island
Nov 4 1979	Militants seize U.S. Embassy in Iran
Dec 3 1979	Stampede at Cincinnati Who concert
Dec 25 1979	Soviet troops invade Afghanistan

REALISM

"Your whole generation's afraid of sex."

-- Gloria Stivic
All in the Family

On May 4 1970, as a mass protest-rally against the Vietnam War unfolded on the campus of Ohio's Kent State University, members of the National Guard were called in to quell the disturbance and ended up shooting into the crowd. Four unarmed college students were killed, and nine others were injured. "The killing ... at Kent State, followed soon after by the murder of two black students at Jackson State in Mississippi, awakened profound anxieties in American society," writes Peter N. Carroll in *It Seemed Like Nothing Happened: American in the 1970s.* "Never in the twentieth century had the nation been so divided."

It was a reality of the only-four-months-old decade -- a nation divided as it hadn't been in a hundred years. By war, by politics, by outlook, by beliefs, by generation. It was also a reality that TV was beginning to acknowledge. Not just by covering it as part of the nightly news but by reflecting it in scripted prime-time programming. The world was changing. TV was changing with it.

It had little choice.

The change had actually begun, in increments, the previous decade, with a handful of TV projects developed for and mindful of a rising subset of younger and more influential (and more consumer-spending) voices. Two projects that then arrived as part of the new decade's first TV season pushed the change along further -- one, *Mary Tyler Moore*, a bit accidently, coming in quietly through prime-time's back door; the other, *All in the Family*, more noisily, blasting through the front, knocking it off its hinges. In big ways and small, as seen in these shows

1

and in the changes in storytelling and characterizations that each fostered, TV entertainment was becoming more real and less defined. Its dramas and its sitcoms, its on-screen parents and its kids, its doctors and lawyers and cops and doctors and politicians ... were more and more being presented as complex people involved in sometimes unresolved stories dealing with relevant situations.

> The 1970–71 season was the last season for a number of series that had defined the old television landscape, including *The Ed Sullivan Show*, *The Lawrence Welk Show*, *The Red Skelton Show*, *The Andy Williams Show*, and *Lassie*, all of which had been on the air since the 1950s or earlier. *(britannica.com)*

In the news and on the streets, as Bruce J. Schulman notes in *The Seventies: The Great Shift in American Culture, Society, and Politics*, "[W]hile students fought for various reforms, they primarily struggled against something: the established order."

So did many of the people involved in and on TV.

ABC Afterschool Special
1972-97 ABC
(1)

ABC

Long before the phrase *a very special episode* became a go-to TV joke for a show that begins to take itself too seriously with a change-of-pace issue-oriented episode (we're looking at you, "Bicycle Man" episode of *Diff'rent Strokes*), ABC introduced an entire series devoted to the concept: a once-a-month hour-long drama called *ABC Afterschool Special*, about and for young viewers and usually focusing on a social issue of specific interest to them.

In developing the afternoon franchise, designed as a bit of educational programming to air during those hours of a student's day between end-of-school and dinnertime, ABC was targeting an audience that had little of their own original TV to watch. (The afternoon window mostly opened to adult-oriented soaps, local news, and syndicated talk-shows.) But what was envisioned as noble began with a stumble: The debut installment of *ABC Afterschool Special* on October 4 1972 was an adaptation of the 1955 novel *The Last of the Curlews*, about "the last male Eskimo curlew, his search for a mate, and the problems they face as they make the treacherous migration from the high arctic tundra to Argentina." And it was animated.

Not an auspicious beginning.

With time and the right source material, though, as well as with a realization that while the purpose was education the specials themselves needn't look like homework, the franchise became a much-admired and widely viewed and much talked-about TV habit for young viewers. Having young and relatable (live-action) faces proved key. Kristy McNichol, Jodie Foster, Lance Kerwin, Moose Drier, Melissa Sue Anderson, Kim Richards, Scott Baio, Robbie Rist, and Eric Scott – each TV up-and-comers in the early 1970s -- were among the actors cast in lead roles. Each of their faces became the face of an episode and of an issue, its hook in an era when celebrities were rarely seen outside of their established personae. For balance and credibility, if not added publicity, older more established actors were featured as well. This roster ran from John Gielgud to Butterfly McQueen.

It was the topics that made *ABC Afterschool Special* stand out, though, pushing the afternoon-programming envelope. By later standards, they would seem to represent a mix of the tired and tame; but in the 1970s, particular in the early 1970s when targeting kids tended to mean luring them to watch Saturday-morning cartoons, programming that dealt with divorce, alcoholism, abusive parenting, bullying, mental illness, physical and emotional disability, the racial divide, gender roles, and the Big Three (drinking, drugs, and sex) was considered beyond daring. To explore them with teen stars for teen audience? On daytime television? More daring still.

But the anthology, a mix of established fiction and non-fiction titles, as well as original concepts, stared down the occasional controversy and plowed though. (Later episodes would present still-meatier stories on teen pregnancy and suicide.)

The imprimatur of what became its "brand" enabled the *Afterschool* specials to pull it all off. And they did it with what became the franchise's creative signature -- memorable repeatable titles. Such as:

"Reading Writing and Reefer"
"It Must Be Love 'Cause I Feel So Dumb"
"My Dad Lives in A Downtown Hotel"

These headed a list that came to include:

"Have You Ever Been Ashamed of Your Parents?"
"The Woman Who Willed a Miracle"
"The Day the Senior Class Got Married"
"Which Mother Is Mine?"
"She Drinks a Little"
and
"High School Narc."

TV Guide

The ABC Afterschool Special introduced young viewers to politics, to classical music, and to literature, making entertainment of subjects such as Shakespeare that would otherwise drive most 15-year-olds from a classroom. (**Fun Fact**: the writers of the 1973 outing called *William: The Life, Works and Times of William Shakespeare* were Ruth Prawler Jhabvala and James Ivory, who would go on to Oscar-winning

5

fame with the Merchant-Ivory films of the 1980s and 1990s). Among the directors who worked on the franchise in its early years were future prime-time-TV names such as Larry Elican (who directed 18 episodes in total), Arthur Allen Seidelman (five episodes), Thomas Schlamme (*The West Wing*), feature-film-directors-to-be Robert Mandel (F/X) and Jeremey Paul Kagan (Henry Winkler's 1977 HEROES), as well as a gallery of actors-turned-directors including Peter Horton, Anson Williams, Kevin Hooks, Beau Bridges, Richard Masur, Tom Skerritt, and, at a time when not many women were considered for episodic-TV directing assignments, Lee Grant, Joan Van Ark, and Melissa Gilbert. The franchise also featured two episodes each from pioneering prime-time directors Joanne Lee and Joan Darling.

Throughout its 25 years on the air, *ABC Afterschool Special* won 51 Daytime Emmys and multiple Peabody and Humanitas awards. Its "very special episode" approach would indeed come to be both overused and much maligned as TV evolved, but that this children's show did it first, that a network would turn over even an hour one afternoon each quarter to explore issues affecting teenagers, seems to make it worthy of mention and emphasis. The project helped to define the 1970s as one in which television was both aware of and spoke to headlines and changing ideas of the day. It set a standard that each of the other networks tried to copy, with varying degrees of success. And in the process, it opened up dialogues for parents and children on subject matters that were rarely even touched on in prime-time, even among adults.

TV Guide

"A Case of Rape"
February 20 1974 NBC
(2)

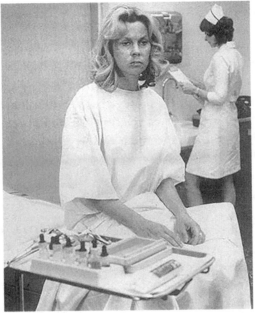

NBCUniversal

The idea of a movie made exclusively for television dates back to the early 60s (1964's *See How they Run* is generally recognized as the first). In large part it was conceived as an alternative to the expensive licensing of big-screen movies for little-screen broadcasts. TV was increasingly becoming a nationwide pull, and movies were seen as equal parts attractive options for viewing and effective prime-time fillers or the networks. (There were several other reasons the genre cropped up, but this was a key one.)

It wasn't until the late 1960s and early 1970s, though, that the made-for-TV-movie became important projects in their own rights, first as regularly scheduled genre stories (romance, sci-fi, period, comedy, thriller) and then as powerful event-programming chess-pieces for a network's playing board. They also served as showcases for actors looking to break free of well-entrenched personae or for producers and writer to explore new-to-TV social issues like euthanasia or divorce or alcoholism.

"The popularity of the format in the 1970s coincided with a renewed focus on crime in the United States, as well as second-wave feminism," writes Jennifer Wallis in her 2017 essay "Rape on the Small Screen," published in *The Historian*. "Tackling rape was high on the agenda of institutions like the National Center for the Prevention and Control of Rape, with significant efforts being made to debunk rape myths and highlight the pervasiveness of victim-blaming in the legal system. These discussions about rape were readily incorporated into the TV movie."

One in particular.

After her ABC hit series *Bewitched* left the air in 1972 after eight years, Elizabeth Montgomery set about shedding herself of the image that light-hearted fantasy sitcom had left her with -- that of a feisty, young, funny, nose-twitching witch -- with a succession of made-for-television movies that were more grounded in every way.

First, in 1973, came the price-on-her-head western *Mrs. Sundance*, playing off the pop-culture wake of the big-screen 1969 blockbuster BUTCH CASSIDY AND THE SUNDANCE KID. The following season, she left *Bewitched* behind for good with what became one of the most controversial movies of the decade, "A Case of Rape," TV's first frank depiction of both the rape-act itself and of the re-victimization that can often follow during the criminal prosecution process, especially at that time.

Based on real events, "A Case of Rape" featured Montgomery as a woman attacked twice by the same assailant, four days apart. That the first rape goes unreported is what prompts the second, during which the woman is also critically beaten. When this latter assault is reported, it's compounded by the way the woman is treated by police. (*New York Times* TV critic John J. O'Conner wrote in his 1974 review that the film demonstrated the reality that "the experience of bringing charges against the rapist can be as harrowing as and even more personally destructive than the crime itself.") The case leads to the arrest and prosecution of her attacker, but as was becoming the case with TV movies at the time, in which reality-reflecting shades of gray were being introduced into once black-and-white scripted content, the man is acquitted of all crimes at his trial.

"A Case of Rape" was raw by any standards but certainly for 1974 in its on-screen depiction of the woman's second rape and beating. NBC even had reservations about including it after viewing the scene. But lead actress Montgomery wielded considerable clout in prime-time in the early 1970s, and reports were that she threatened to leave the project if the scene were cut. (NBC aired the film as shot, the scene intact, though with a viewer warning; some advertisers withdrew their support as a result.) Just as powerful was what the woman says to her attacker after his acquittal: "If you ever come near me again, I'll kill you."

Viewer tune-in for the film was huge, its message of victim re-victimization applauded. "The main point was neatly and valuably underlined: that although the incidence of rape is rising faster than any other crime of violence, the rickety structure of old laws would appear to protect the accused more than the victim," wrote O'Conner. "Along the way, the production also managed to tweak the ethics of lawyers. The defense lawyer seemed less concerned with her client's guilt or innocence than with brilliant technical maneuvers."

Emmy-nominated later that year (for Montgomery and for director Boris Sagal and editor Richard Brackan), "A Case of Rape" is credited with initiating a dialogue in the 1970s about how sexual-assault victims are treated. Considered the first true-to-life "issue"-oriented TV-movie, it also opened the doors for what would become a 1970s staple, the frank and sometimes graphic exploration of controversial topics and current events, from Charles Manson to the Holocaust.

For good or ill, the movie also served as inducement for other well-known TV actors to take on projects that would expand or smash well-entrenched small-screen images, from *Brady Bunch* alumna Eve Plumb starring as a prostitute in "Dawn: Portrait of a Teenage Runaway" (1976) to Susan Dey as a child abuser in "Mary Jane Harper Cried Last Night" (1977) and from Dennis Weaver as a wife-beater in "Battered" (1977) to Carol Burnett playing a Vietnam soldier's grieving mother in "Friendly Fire" (1979). A year after "A Case of Rape," Montgomery herself would smash her twitching good-wife image once again by starring as an axe-murderer in "The Legend of Lizzie Borden" (which in turn pushed TV-movies as far as they'd ever gone in terms of violence and nudity, if not a co-mingling of the two).

NBCUniversal

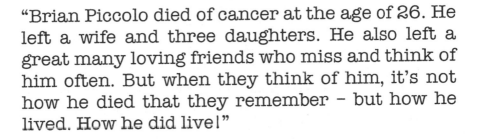

"Brian Piccolo died of cancer at the age of 26. He left a wife and three daughters. He also left a great many loving friends who miss and think of him often. But when they think of him, it's not how he died that they remember – but how he lived. How he did live!"

-- Chicago Bears Coach George Halas
"Brian's Song"

All in the Family
"Meet the Bunkers"
January 12 1971 CBS
(3)

> Because the main character...expressed views which
> are not socially desirable, viewers might feel required
> to criticize him, even if deep down they identify with
> him. It is for this reason that we are somewhat less sure
> of our prediction for this program than is usually the
> case and caution you that, although we think it unlikely,
> the   program   may   be   a   worthwhile   entry.
> CONCLUSION: A less than average share of audience
> is indicated for this series.

-- CBS *All in the Family* Program Testing
April 7 1970

Likely one of the funniest things about the landscape-shifting TV
sitcom *All in the Family* – funny/strange, that is (although somewhat
funny/ha-ha and a bit funny/ironic) – is that the cutting-edge New
York-set show made its 1971 debut directly following an episode of
Hee-Haw, the kind of old-school TV show it would end up kicking to
the prime-time curb.

Hard as it is to imagine: Archie Bunker from Queens had Grandpa
Jones from Kornfield Kounty as a lead-in. Even harder to imagine: He
needed him.

Sony

Though it has become the stuff of TV legend through the decades, the fact remains that as *All in the Family* neared that January 1971 debut, CBS wasn't all that sure what it had with the new show. It was written and executed like a stage-play; it featured course language and in-fighting among members of a struggling blue-collar family; and the family itself was headed by an unlikeable and unrepentant bigot. (By comparison, TV's Number One sitcom at the time was *Here's Lucy*.) Plus, the first episode talked openly about sex. As in the act itself. And it had already been rejected twice, with other actors in the starring roles, by another network.

So the network was hedging its bets by scheduling it after the crowd-pleasing *Hee-Haw*. It hedged them even further when, in one of those curious decisions made in network television (during any era), it inserted a laughtrack under the comedy's main-title sequence, which featured co-leads Carroll O'Connor and Jean Stapleton singing "Those Were the Days." This was evidently done in an effort to clue in viewers that little-known Stapleton was singing *in character* as atonal Edith Bunker and was *supposed* to sound funny. It was a TV first.

All that, plus a cautionary disclaimer that preceded the premiere:

WARNING:
The program you are about to see is *All in the Family*. It seeks to throw a humorous spotlight on our frailties, prejudices, and concerns. By making them a source of laughter, we hope to show -- in a mature fashion -- just how absurd they are.

America had been warned.

All in the Family, as was the case with 1970s-shows-to-come *Sanford and Son* and *Three's Company*, was adapted from a British sitcom – here, called *Till Death Do Us Part*. But, as creator/writer/producer Norman Lear has told it, the American version he put together and shepherded through a long birthing process, about the marriage of Edith and Archie Bunker (and the home they shared with their married daughter and her opinionated husband) was very much inspired by the lives of his own parents.

The gestation was indeed a lengthy one: Commissioned by ABC in 1968 as *Justice for All*, about the life and times of Archie Justice, a pilot was shot and then rejected by the network, after which it commissioned a second pilot, with a new cast. Retitled *Those Were the Days*, it, too, was rejected. "Funny but impossible to air" was the consensus at ABC about the unconventional comedy, writes Lear in his 2014 memoir *Even This I Get To Experience*.

Enter CBS, a network then looking to change its image as purveyor of safe and formulaic TV (especially sitcoms, the genre that was long its mainstay and which at the time included *Mayberry RFD*, *Here's Lucy*, *The Doris Day Show*, *The Beverly Hillbillies*, *Green Acres*, *Family Affair*, *My Three Sons*, and *Gomer Pyle, USMC*). The network was also growing mindful, as was much of the TV business, that demographics were becoming more important in prime-time -- that bragging rights were beginning to come from not just overall household ratings but from the breakdown of that whole number into *kinds* of audiences (age, gender, status).

Lear's show gave a hint that it would speak to non-traditional younger viewers in a way its current line-up was not. So CBS gave the producer as a third pass at the show. Another pilot was shot, with another version of its four-member cast. The newly titled *All in the Family*, featuring the four stars who'd make the characters their own over the course of the coming decade, was the result.

In his book, Lear recalls that for the January 1971 debut, CBS and its affiliated stations across the country hired dozens of additional telephone operators to handle the "tsunami of protest" the network expected over the precedent-breaking show. Which proved unnecessary. "The torrent turned out to be more of a trickle," writes Lear. "Not that there weren't questions of taste raised, and some severe condemnation, but most of that came from establishment professionals, the people who run research and do focus groups and are paid by the media and academia to tell us at any given hour who we are and what we are thinking." It was, CBS programming chief Perry Lafferty would say decades later in a *Newsday* interview, "like putting a toe in the water to see how far we could go."

The first-episode review, in *The Hollywood Reporter:*

> Billed as adult social satire ... *All in the Family* is either going to be instant smash or instant disaster. Unfortunately for Bud Yorkin and Norman Lear, who based this on the British series *Till Death Do Us Part*, the latter is more likely to occur. The majority of television viewers will find this show tasteless, crude, and very unfunny.

In reality, it took a while for the majority of television viewers to find it at all, hiding as it was after *Hee-Haw* and opposite established competitive programming. But *All in the Family* picked up Emmy Award attention that May (it won Outstanding Comedy, Outstanding New Comedy, and Outstanding Lead Actress in a Comedy;) and subsequently picked up viewers during summer rerun season, when the people who'd heard about but not seen it started watching to see all the fuss. And it continued picking them up when the second season began, soon becoming TV's highest-rated series, a ranking it kept for five straight seasons, which was a first for any show of any genre. (*I Love Lucy* reigned for five years in the 1950s, but not consecutively.)

Essentially a weekly four-character play about a family battling the changing times and each other, predicated on the exploration of day-to-day life rather than a situation of the week, *All in the Family* became a landmark ground-shifting TV-shaping megahit.

As Lear and countless others have said through the decades, it simply cannot be overstated how different TV was in 1971 when *All in the Family* arrived. (That it broke ground in such a benign category as the first TV show to feature the sound of a flushing toilet gives an indication.) It featured TV's first anti-hero sitcom-lead in the narrow-minded and boorish Archie Bunker, and it spotlighted weekly conflict among its characters that was rooted in the very generational conflict dividing the nation in real life. Its scripted debates and arguments and discussions mirrored those heard in homes across the country. And started new ones, too – about gender roles and women's rights, about sexualized violence and sex itself, about politics and crime and racism and xenophobia, about Vietnam and religion. As of 1971, prime-time television was no longer an escape from reality: It *was* reality. One of those rare TV projects generating coverage not just on the entertainment pages of newspapers but on their front pages. *All in the Family* offered a topicality never before seen on scripted TV.

The Norman Lear creation didn't just push the envelope, "it sealed and stamped it as well," wrote Kara Kovalchik in a 2015 *Mental Floss* appreciation. "But viewers kept tuning in week after week to see stories about previously taboo topics, such as menopause, rape, homosexuality, and race relations." At a time of middle-class crusade, when, according to *Staying Alive: The 1970s and the Last Days of the Working Class,* "the multifaceted resurrection of blue-collar America resonated in commercial popular culture from Nashville to Hollywood," the country had found a spokesperson in working-class Archie Bunker. The comedy was mined from characters rather than situations, specifically how characters responded to and dealt with things viewers themselves were dealing with.

With its stage-like presentation on a stage-like single set and with heavy-dialogue scenes that ran well past the length of TV's usual give-and-take talk-and-run dialogue, and with a flatter duller and more realistic look courtesy of being recorded on tape (like daytime dramas) rather than film (like most of scripted TV), *All in the Family* ended up being an amalgam of innovations. Overnight, the medium that only recently had become fully broadcast in color was now dealing in shades of comedic gray. With *All in the Family*, both CBS and prime-time began a transition from broad strokes to fine lines, informing most all TV that followed.

Lasting eight-and-a-half years, nine seasons, and 208 episodes, the comedy won more accolades of more kinds – Emmys, Humanitas, Christopher, Writers Guild and Directors Guild awards, craft awards-- than any series to date. It became the first TV series for which all principal members of its cast won acting Emmys. (Only one other show, *The Golden Girls*, has ever managed the feat.) Decades removed from its premiere, it's still listed by the Writers Guild of America as one of the best-written shows in the medium's history. Wrote Claudia Luther in her 2013 obituary for Jean Stapleton, the show marked the beginning "of sitcoms as a forum for political family warfare."

All in the Family changed TV as it changed the country. "Lear …is to be congratulated for finally giving television the relevance it has called for," *The Hollywood Reporter* observed in its 1971 review.

(**Fun Fact**: At one point early in the development process, according to his memoir, Lear pitched the idea of playing Archie to Mickey Rooney, and he only got as far as describing Archie as "a bigot who uses words like 'spade'" before Rooney interrupted him. "Norm, they're going to kill you, shoot you dead in the street." Even Carroll O'Conner was dubious about the show's prospects when he ended up being cast. He reportedly told Lear that CBS would cancel *All in the Family* inside of six weeks.)

Sony

"Any woman who chooses to behave like a full human being should be warned that the armies of the status quo will treat her as something of a dirty joke."

-- Gloria Steinem
December 1971

An American Family
January 11-March 29 1973 PBS
(4)

Scripted television told it, PBS showed it. And early on, too.

"While audiences laughed at the Bunkers in conflict and *Ms.* Magazine published a liberated marriage contract," Peter N. Carroll notes in *It Seemed Like Nothing Happened: America in the 1970s*, "the broadcast on public television of a documentary series … captured national attention by its raw exposure of a pervasive crisis in domestic relations." The crisis was divorce. The series was *An American Family*.

PBS / WNET

It was a daring proposal from the start: A documentary crew would move in to a family's home and record every moment of its various members' daily lives, alone or with each other or among outside friends and colleagues. Beyond that? No real plan, no real script. Twenty years before *Seinfeld* made a running joke of being "a show about nothing" *An American Family* was pitched as just that.

All three broadcast networks passed. *Cinema verite*, the new fly-on-the-wall approach to non-fiction filmmaking since the late 1950s -- "truthful cinema" -- just wouldn't cut it as a TV series, went the thinking. It wasn't something viewers turned to weekly television for. There were no characters to follow, to root for. TV, they said, was news and talk and public affairs and sports and kids' shows and variety shows. It was scripted series with fictional characters. Documentaries? They were one-off specials from a network's News division -- and with specific themes, at that.

Not so fast, said PBS. The fledging public television network gave it a go, after which a subject family was selected – the Pat and Bill Loud family of Santa Barbara, California. Married parents, five teenaged children. And with cameras then placed most everywhere in their middle-class home, shooting began in the spring of 1971.

Midway through the seven-month shoot, though, the show about nothing became the show about *everything* when matriarch Pat Loud, selected for the series as representative of the average American housewife and mother, announced to her husband that .... she wanted a divorce. (It wasn't part of what little plan there was for the show.) And producers, originally faced with packing up both the equipment and the idea, decided to keep the cameras rolling. *An American Family* was to be about the American family, after all -- the *changing* American family.

For seven months in 1971, the cameras recorded it all, not just a crumbling union (which was enough) but also the routine comings and goings of seven people sharing a house and a life and a name. Bill's busy job, Pat's increasing *ennui*, the school and social lives of five adolescents -- chief among them eldest Lance, who during the shoot both turn 20 and came out as gay, marking a second Now What? moment for producers. Was Lance's sexuality relevant? Would it be acceptable to viewers? By shooting's end, Pat and Bill Loud were living apart, and Lance was off to New York, hoping to find himself.

The unprecedented 12-part *An American Family* premiered on PBS a little more than a year later, on January 11 1973, almost two years to the day since the premiere on broadcast television of the equally unprecedented *All in the Family*. The result was just as seismic, if only on a public-TV scale: Tune-in was sizeable and looked to grow. Which it did. For twelve weeks on Thursday nights that winter, the series took root, the Louds took off, and viewers took sides. About the Loud marriage, about the Loud off-spring and the ways they were parented, about the obvious disconnect between the generations that the family represented -- and especially about how or even if an affluent white family from Santa Barbara represented a typical American family. Viewers couldn't get enough of the Louds and of their unfolding, even unraveling, daily lives.

Beyond the issue of how or whether the show represented America, however, was the more critical issue (to the Loud family, as the drama played out) of how it represented *them*. Or, as the Louds would hurriedly come to position it when their private drama became more and more public fodder, how the series *mis*represented them. Even in the viral-less social-media-free days of 1973, it did not take long for TV viewers to weigh in on how much they had come to dislike, even despise, some or all of Louds. The Louds became daily talking points, and the talk was mostly negative.

Six weeks into the series, the family took defensive measures by agreeing to appear, as a group, on the popular afternoon Dick Cavett talk-show, to defend themselves as victims of selective post-production editing. By mid-March, on the eve of the final episode, the Louds were on the cover of *Newsweek* alongside a cover-line that read: "The Broken Family."

An American Family wrapped up it broadcast that spring with the Loud divorce (already official a year earlier), after which each of the family members went on about their lives, life as unusual thanks to their TV fame. Pat Loud wrote a memoir. Lance Loud became a gay icon, *en route* to a public career of many stripes, including a journalist and performer and all-around "personality."

In the decades since, multiple retrospectives of the groundbreaking TV project have aired, including one in 2003 on the 30th anniversary that paid tribute to Lance, who died in December 2001 at age 50 from complications of AIDS and hepatitis-C. (Lance Loud had a well-documented and self-confessed 20-year crystal-meth addiction.) One of his final wishes was that his parents reunite, which after his death they did. In 2011, HBO aired a scripted take on the PBS experiment called *Cinema Verite*, starring Oscar nominee Diane Lane as Pat Loud. Equal parts meta and ironic, it chronicled the entirety of the project from inception through the mid-shoot bombshell to the PBS airing and its aftermath.

As TV's first *verite* series (300 hours of raw footage were recorded), *An American Family* -- note the use of lower-case type in the print ads -- introduced a re-working of non-fiction TV. The genre was as old as TV itself, but its new form was all about "lifting the lid" and showing the *verite* of life. Its pockmarks and blemishes. Its success paved the way for the arrival of the weekly non-fiction series *Real People* on NBC in 1979, which in turn led to ABC's *That's Incredible* a year later. MTV's *Real World* and the *Real Housewives* franchise weren't far behind.

An American Family also became the TV show through which the country came to meet its first out-and-proud gay person. Lance Loud had his flaws and virtues, his supporters and his detractors, but in the spring of 1973, four years after Stonewall and nine months before the American Psychiatric Association (APA) removed *homosexuality* from its Diagnostic and Statistical Manual of Mental Disorders (DSM), Lance Loud put a face to a mystery and a real person to a punchline. (Delisted to "disturbance," it wasn't until 1987 that homosexuality was removed from the DSM completely.) He, and his *American Family*, began the changing of minds and of a culture fully 23 years before Ellen DeGeneres did as much with her sitcom.

TV in 1973 had its first gay lead.
And first real-life divorce.
And PBS was, for about two months, the hottest network on TV. Which was a first for it, in turn.

The value of *An American Family* -- as a documentary, as a TV project, and a social experiment – has been debated for decades. But in

2002, nearly 30 years after it aired, the show placed 32nd on *TV Guide*'s list of "50 Greatest TV Shows of All Time." The laughably memorable exchange heard in the series' eighth episode between Pat Loud and husband Bill when she announced her plans to divorce him (Pat: "You know there's a problem" … Bill: "What's your problem?") was selected as one of the top moments in TV history.

An American Family spoke to how *the* American family was being recalibrated in the early part of the new decade, as much due to inevitability as erosion. The news of the early months of 1973 (when it aired) was *Roe v. Wade*, inflation, Wounded Knee, Watergate, Vietnam prisoners of war, a mass shooting in New Orleans, and a growing fear of a gas shortage. War, peace and politics. Us versus them; you against me. The Louds' breakdown was not unlike the country's.

Barney Miller
1975-82 ABC
(5)

If recognized or remembered for nothing other than its casting, *Barney Miller* would stand out as one of the most important shows in TV history.

The ensemble sitcom about the fictional detective denizens of New York City's 12th Precinct premiered in 1975 with what was likely the most diverse cast ever to be assembled up to that time, with a Hispanic, an Asian, and an African-American among the members of a squad that also featured such varied white faces as that of an aging curmudgeon, a proud Pole, and the Jewish precinct leader (played by Hal Linden) for whom the series was titled. (A civilian gay character who'd appear occasionally through the run of the show showed up as early as episode two, and a female detective was added to the ranks six episodes later.)

It represented a new kind of reality-based prime-time for the 70s -- an ethnically mixed New York City that even *Friends* would be unfamiliar with 20 years in the future.

Barney Miller was significantly more than the sum of its parts, however. As realistic a portrait of an urban police force as there'd ever been (albeit within the confines of a sitcom), *Barney Miller* quickly proved itself to be one of the smartest and best-written series of the decade, moving the sitcom ball considerably downfield with a deft blending of humor and pathos as it covered crime in the Big City.

It began life as a mid-season replacement during ABC's 1974-75 season, borne of a pilot called *The Life and Times of Barney Miller* that aired in August 1974, starring Tony-winner Linden. The pilot was considered a failure, but producers and ABC liked the general idea behind the show and Linden, so the busted pilot was re-fashioned as *Barney Miller*. (Character actor Abe Vigoda was the only supporting cast member kept around for the reincarnation). New cast members included Gregory Sierra, Jack Soo, Ron Glass, Max Gail, and Linda Lavin as the later-added female detective.

ABC / Sony / Four D

The oft-cerebral and subversive social commentary that was *Barney Miller* marked a significant departure from earlier cop sitcoms from *The Andy Griffith Show* to *Car 54, Where Are You?* It took time to catch on with ABC viewers, hampered by ABC's scheduling it against CBS's Top Ten drama *The Waltons* on an already troubled Thursday night. But within a year, paired with a hit (*Welcome Back, Kotter*), it soon settled in as an audience favorite, continuing to win over viewers and critics alike as the seasons went by, even as original cast members left (Sierra, Vigoda) or died (Soo, in 1979) and new detectives (Steve Landesberg, Ron Carey) arrived.

Producer Danny Arnold, who came out of 1950s variety programming and went on to write for *Bewitched* in the 1960s (and who won an Emmy for 1969's clever but short-lived *My World and Welcome to It*), created and oversaw *Barney Miller* with Ted Flicker. Like a handful of stage-like sitcoms of the early 1970s, *Barney Miller* played out on essentially just one set -- here the precinct squad room -- where multiple storylines inter-connected. (Shot in front of an audience in its first few seasons, the show, notorious for marathon all-night tapings, ultimately abandoned the live-audience format.)

Unlike the broad and cartoon-like sitcoms in vogue and much more popular at the time – especially on parent network ABC, then reigning supreme with *Mork & Mindy* and *Laverne & Shirley* and *Three's Company* -- *Barney Miller* was arid-dry. It offered nuanced depictions of the characters behind the crimes and the weary seen-it-all frustrated-with-the-system cops. Its comedy and commentary were more subtle, even as other series were (rightly) hailed as groundbreaking for their own. *Barney Miller* quietly folded into its episodes explorations of ageism, anti-Semitism, feminism, sexism – and pretty much any other -*ism* the country was dealing with at the time.

The show also cultivated a sort of repertory company of guest actors for recurring civilian roles, most notably Jack De Leon and Ray Stewart as a pair of gay men who frequently showed up at the 12th Precinct. If the actors played them as flamboyant and stereotypical, especially by modern-day standards, the characters nonetheless represented a sizeable step in the prime-time depiction of homosexuality as a lifestyle rather than an affliction. Their appearances were few but important.

Barney Miller won multiple writing and directing awards in its eight seasons, winning the Emmy as TV's Best Comedy in 1982 for its final year. It innovated with complex characterizations and razor-shop comedic observations about the human condition. It was never ranked higher than 16th place for any of its seasons, but it had a loyal and appreciative audience. It also had a rabid fan base among real-life cops, one of whom, Lucas Miller (no relation), paid tribute to the series in a 2004 *New York Times* essay:

> Many police officers maintain that the most realistic police show in the history of television was the sitcom *Barney Miller*, far more so than that father of reality TV, *Cops*. The action was mostly off screen, the squad room the only set, and the guys were a motley bunch of

character actors who were in no danger of being picked for the N.Y.P.D. pin-up calendar. But they worked hard, made jokes, got hurt and answered to their straight-man commander. For real detectives, most of the action does happen off screen, and we spend a lot of time back in the squad room writing reports about it. Like *Barney Miller*'s squad, we crack jokes at one another, at the cases that come in, and at the crazy suspect locked in the holding cell six feet from the new guy's desk. Life really is more like *Barney Miller* than *NYPD Blue*, but our jokes aren't nearly as funny.

Neither Danny Arnold nor Ted Flicker had another successful TV series.

"There is a special niche in memory where a child places his parents. A place in time where they are never younger, never older -- a time when they are changeless. For me that memory is of many years ago, and no matter what came after, they are forever young."

-- Narrator [as John "John-Boy" Walton, Jr., writing in his journal]
The Waltons

The Body Human
1977- 84 CBS
(6)

It was a simple project, with a basic aim. *The Body Human* was an umbrella title for a series of CBS News specials that aired in prime-time over the course of several years beginning in the late 1970s. They focused on issues related to human biology, such as reproduction and gender differences and human endurance. Science-based and executed with an educational bent, celebrated for using then-new video technology, the franchise brought to prime-time a welcome frankness that bespoke the era.

And as such, like much of TV in the 1970s, it was not without controversy. The biggest flare-up came with an installment that aired in May 1979, simply called "The Sexes." *New York Times* critic John J. O'Connor noted in his advance review that the aim of the broadcast was to celebrate modern medicine with "some superb photography, which provides the most solid justification for the series [and] explicit descriptions of various sexual functions," but which would also likely "stimulate the negative gland secretions of those watchful citizens who want books like 'Slaughterhouse-Five' removed from their schools and libraries."

It did. CBS ended up airing "The Sexes" with an advisory and with plenty of protest.

CBS

29

Looked at in retrospect, *The Body Human* seemed to make possible most of the prime-time science-based documentaries that would follow in the 1980s and beyond. It made biology relatable and accessible, especially as it expanded the field of topics to be covered, among them childbirth ("The Miracle Months") and the circulatory system ("Red River").

It won multiple Emmys throughout its run, as the year's Outstanding Informational Special. And in 1978 it was given the prestigious Peabody Award for excellence in broadcasting in the wake of a celebrated outing called "The Vital Connection," about the link between the brain and the nervous system. The Peabody citation:

> The world of the human brain has rarely been so graphically displayed and explained as in "The Vital Connection." Written with an excellence too rarely seen in television by Dr. Robert E. Fuisz, M.D., directed by Robert Elfstrom and produced by Alfred R. Kelman under the capable guiding hand of executive producer Tom Moore, this excursion into the world of miracle surgery has brought acclaim to the CBS Television Network and to all who had a part.

"Duel"
November 13 1971 ABC
(7)

Though there are questions as to how true the legend (one perhaps propelled by the director himself in interviews throughout his long career), the story is that as an L.A. film-school student in the 1960s Steven Spielberg would, every so often, sneak onto the city's Universal Studios backlot for a bit of self-advanced cinema education.

True or not, the tale dovetails with the facts: Spielberg did have an unpaid internship at Universal back when he was in school at Cal State (having been turned down by USC due to less-than-stellar grades); and at some point during this association Universal president Sid Sheinberg was impressed enough by an experimental short-film that Spielberg directed that he offered him a seven-year contract there -- making Spielberg, at 23, the youngest director ever signed to a long-term deal at a movie studio.

His one-off assignments there were for episodes of Universal's many network TV dramas, among them *Night Gallery*, *Owen Marshall Counselor at Law* and *Marcus Welby, M.D.* He also directed the first regular episode of the detective series *Columbo*, which had begun as a made-for-TV movie in the 1960s and went on to be part of the *NBC Mystery Movie* franchise. This, in turn, led to the assignment to direct a TV movie called "Duel," which effectively launched his big-screen film career.

Based on a script by iconic sci-fi/fantasy writer Richard Matheson, "Duel" was essentially a two-character thriller -- the two characters being 1) a man (Dennis Weaver) alone behind the wheel of a car, and 2) a Peterbilt 218 tanker-truck, its driver never seen or identified, which suddenly and inexplicably begins menacing him on the deserted back-roads of California. The result is a ninety-minute literal do-or-die game of chicken, the ultimate modern-age test of man against machine. (Weaver's character in the movie is, in fact, named "Mann.")

NBCUniversal

For a TV-movie, especially in the genre's embryonic days of the very early 1970s, "Duel" is a master-work of suspense. What will become Spielberg's cinematic techniques and trademark flourishes are seen in their early forms: the track-in and sideways-tracking shots, the killer-point-of-view shots, the spatial playfulness and sometimes disorienting camera angles, the close-ups and the quick edits that ratchet the tension. (The film won a 1972 Emmy for its sound editing.)

The movie is a knot of discomfort with very little relief -- and very little dialogue -- as its lens frames a lone man fighting for survival behind the wheel of his car, with no help to be found. It'll be summed up later in the 1970s, after Spielberg's big-screen movie career takes off, as "JAWS on wheels" – each a high-wire test of nerves involving a depersonalized killing machine threatening human lives without reason except for bloodlust and the thrill of the kill.

Critically hailed when it aired in the fall of 1971, "Duel" became a benchmark of sorts for small-screen projects to come. Its two-character format, dated only by Mann's car and its well-used AM-radio, has kept it a frequent go-to both for thrill-ride viewing and academic analysis. In *TV (The Book)*, a 2016 compendium written with Alan

Sepinwall, Matt Zoller Seitz names it the greatest American TV-movie ever made, writing that "almost fifty years after its initial broadcast, this stripped-down, subtly mythic action thriller retains a good deal of its power."

"Duel" did for sure launch Steven Spielberg's movie-making career -- he'd direct two more TV movies at Universal before getting his first shot at feature films in 1974 with THE SUGARLAND EXPXRESS, which was followed a year later by JAWS. It left behind a new standard for the small-screen movie as more than just a piece of network scheduling.

It showed that a made-for-TV-movie could be a stand-alone and entertaining piece of competitive programming rather than just a prime-time slot-filler. And that in the right hands it could even rival big-screen projects. In fact, following its successful TV broadcast "Duel" was released overseas as a feature film.

(**Spoiler Alert**: In Spielberg's *Mann v. machine*, machine lost.)

Family
"Rites of Friendship"
December 28 1976 ABC
(8)

ABC / Sony

Mega-producer Aaron Spelling's output for the ABC network in the 1970s -- he made a dozen weekly series and more than 60 TV movies – was such that by decade's end it was being disparaged as "Aaron's Broadcasting Company." Most of his success in the decade, which included long-running hits from *Charlie's Angels* to *Fantasy Island* to *The Love Boat*, was categorized as fluff -- light-hearted action or escapist fantasy or even well-meaning but libido-driven melodrama. Unrealistic stuff.

Yet Spelling's work did occasionally have weight, for which he likely deserved more respect than he was given throughout the entirety of his career, so enormous were the fluff pieces. Included among these projects are the little-seen but sensitively crafted 1979 drama *Friends*, about the coming-of-age of three 11-year-olds, each of a different background, and the highly rated Emmy-winning TV movie "The Boy in the Plastic Bubble" (1976), starring new sitcom star John Travolta in a break-out dramatic role. (Spelling would finally get significant industry respect much later in his producing career with the acclaimed 1989 TV-movie "Day One," which won an Emmy as Best Drama/Comedy Special.)

In the early months of 1976, as cartoon-level Spelling series *The Rookies* and *S.W.A.T.* were making him famous (and rich), but before *Charlie's Angeles* arrived to make him more of each, a new Spelling show appeared as part of ABC's mid-season schedule that was about as far away from his stock-in-trade as thought possible at the time. Introduced as a six-episode mini-series, *Family* was a first-of-its-kind contemporary nuclear-family drama, focusing on the upper-middle-class Lawrence family of Pasadena, California. It would become the producers' most critically hailed series. And it would change – if not create -- a genre in the process.

Until 1976, most family centered TV shows were relegated to the half-hour sitcom form, from *Father Knows Best* in the early 1950s to *The Courtship of Eddie's Father* in the late 1960s. Hour-long dramas were chiefly the reserve of law enforcers or doctors or office workers. If they centered on families, they tended to be in westerns such as *Bonanza* and *The Big Valley*.

And while the 1970s saw family dramas fleshed out a bit, taking on the complications of having and raising children, these were period pieces: *Little House on the Prairie* was set in 1870s Minnesota, and *The Waltons* took place in 1930s Virginia. Popular and well-executed, they didn't speak directly to 1970s America.

Family changed that. Starring Sada Thompson and James Broderick as Doug and Kate Lawrence, with Kristy McNichol, Gary Frank, and Meredith Baxter (then -Birney) portraying offspring Buddy, Willie, and Nancy, who ranged in age from adolescent to young adult., it was a contemporary series with topical-for-the-era themes, drawing its drama from the well of the family dynamic itself and how it intersected with the changing times both inside of and outside the home.

It pulled prime-time into a believable modernity, dealing with intra-family conflict in a way brand-new to TV and taking on problems and issues that were being hammered out in real life by real families during a critical decade: gender equality, abortion, infidelity, independence, identity, marriage. It tackled TV taboos of the day like divorce and casual sex. It explored real-world struggles associated with cancer and alcoholism and aging. All with a frankness and direct-ness rarely if ever seen in a one-hour drama.

If anything, in the days of much more highly rated dramas such as *The Waltons* and *The Rockford Files*, *Family* was a bit of an art-house project, given its penchant for teetering on self-reflection and emotional introspection. But also given its pedigree: Spelling's fellow producers were stage and film director Mike Nichols and noted playwright Jay Presson Allen.

The first episode, in fact, titled "The Best Years," directed by rising filmmaker Mary Rydell, bears this out, predicated on the arrival back home of 20-something daughter Nancy after she finds her husband in bed with another woman, precipitating discussions about how their children were raised. (For comparison, among the most-watched one-hour dramas the week it aired were *The Bionic Woman*, *The Six Million Dollar Man*, and *Starsky & Hutch*.)

One scene in the pilot finds 40-something parents Doug and Kate Lawrence in a heated post-dinner kitchen debate about their eldest daughter's marital plight, which escalates into a then-timely (for 1976) discussion about female identity and motherhood. Kate Lawrence, who has established herself in the episode thus far as the every-woman voice of reason, attempts to explain how the tying of the two concepts can frequently feel like the tying of a noose around a woman's neck. That often even a much-wanted pregnancy can be paired with regret and a desire to be free of burden.

"If I got rid of a baby every time I thought I didn't want it, we wouldn't have much of a family," she confesses to her husband.

His response is that she can't possibly mean what she's saying.

"Don't presume to tell me what I mean!" she fires back. Then:

> I'm 46 years old. I've borne three children. Some of the times of those pregnancies I wanted out. It's the body that makes the baby and hangs on to it for nine months. Why can't men understand sometimes women just want *out*! My god, when I found out I was pregnant with Buddy, I even got as far as tracking down an abortionist. Why can't you understand? Eventually I wanted all of them. Now I can't imagine life without them. But sometimes...sometimes...just for a minute ...I didn't.

It's a fearless monologue new to the world of prime-time scripted TV but not to real world that TV was trying to catch up with and to reflect. The sentiments spoke to a time and a movement, when half the country was petitioning for legal recognition. For acknowledgement. For understanding.

When will men understand that sometimes a woman just wants *out*?

Family broke ground with nearly every one of its 86 episodes from 1976 to 1980, if not with its storylines than with its careful approach to presenting how real people -- real family members – communicate and feel. Or not. Helping when they can; admitting when they can't. All of which came on display in a seminal and controversial episode called "Rites of Friendship" that aired during the show's first year. Credited to writers Bethel Leslie, Gerry Day and Lawrence Konner, it focused on late-teens son Willie, who to his dismay discovers that longtime best-friend Zeke is gay. It's a new scenario for him, as it was for scripted TV.

Willie rejects Zeke upon finding out about him, after which he grows sullen and argumentative at home, pushing his family away. As the story progresses, against a backdrop of Zeke having been rousted in a gay-bar raid, which both precipitates and worsens his revelation, Willie's father finds himself having to console and question a hurting child whose anger he can't approve of, about a topic he himself does not understand. In a pivotal scene, he confesses that he's unsure what Willie should do or how he should act around Zeke -- a confession notable for what seems to be a new and frank approach to parenting, as well as an infusion of humor to soften and distract from the tough-love lesson-learning underway.

> **Doug Lawrence**: I wish you'd tell me what's been going on. I can't believe your cruelty to Zeke was deliberate.

> **Willie**: It was.

> **DL**: Why?

> **W:** I don't know....Zeke says that I was scared to death. That inside I had the same feelings that he did. ... I mean, sure when I was fourteen I had what I guess you'd call a 'crush' on Richie Oakhurst.

> **DL:** [chuckling] When I was that age it was Steve Pevney.

> **W:** [thinking, then incredulous]: Mr. *Pevney*? The guy who owns the shoe store?

> **DL:** The same. It's normal at that age. A lot of young boys and young girls have those feelings. I can't believe you don't know that.

> **W:** Listen, I've read the same books that everyone else has.

> **DL:** If that's what's bothering you, I think you're using it as an excuse.

W: You do?

DL: I think finding out about Zeke made you furious. You felt betrayed. That you've never really had a friendship at all.

W: That's right … That's right … Zeke and I have been best friends ever since we were seven years old. He was the one person that I figured I could tell everything to, and that he told me everything. Now after all these years I find out he hast been honest with me? I mean it's not so great when you find out that the person you figure your best friend is a total stranger.

DL: It's not as simple as that. Think of the turmoil Zeke has been going through. I bet he's wanted to try to tell you a hundred times. He had a lot to lose, if you couldn't, or wouldn't, understand. He was right.

In an online appreciation of "Rites of Friendship" decades later, writer Terrence Moss observed:

> It's not riveting. It's not melodramatic or over-the-top. It's just a well-written and well-acted episode of a well-written and well-acted show. Simple as that. And I'm always fascinated by how the topic of homosexuality was handled on television before it was more widely accepted to do so. If this episode of *Family* is any indication, it was with a lot more grace, truth and dignity that the standard tropes the writing of such episodes fall back on today. Go figure. [*terrencemoss.blogspot.com*]

"Rites of Friendship" was supposed to be *Family*'s first full-season premiere, in September 1976, coming off a critically acclaimed mini-series season that spring. But ABC executives, nervous about the content, pushed it back to air during the low-rated often-ignored "dark week" between Christmas and New Year's Day, when fewer viewers would likely mean fewer to take notice (or to protest to advertisers). Still, it aired, which is significant in itself for the mid-1970s. And it showed that TV could handle mature and adult and relevant taboo topics -- ones that were becoming more important in the country -- with sensitivity and care. For the episode, Glenn Jordan won a Directors Guild of America (DGA) Award in the 60-minute category.

ABC / Sony

Family was nominated for 17 Emmys during its four-year run, including three times as Best Drama. Kristy McNichol and Gary Frank and Sada Thompson each won acting Emmys. The show was also a nominee multiple times for the distinguished Humanitas Prize, with Jay Presson Allen winning for writing the provocative "Best Years" pilot episode.

The series left the air in 1980 as a new decade began, having carved out a piece of small-screen history as the family drama that elevated the form, paving the way for other like-minded ensembles that explored topical and emotional issues of their own days as a country and its people continue to change, such as *Eight is Enough* in 1977 and then in later years *thirtysomething* (1987) and *7th Heaven* (1996).

"I'm not going to comment on a third-rate burglary attempt."

-- White House press secretary Ron Ziegler
June 1972

"Helter Skelter"
April 1-2 1976 CBS
(9)

TV Guide

A half-decade removed from what were called the Murders of the Century and then their corresponding Trial of the Century a few years later – and at the height of the FCC-mandated "Family Hour," no less, which put the TV industry on notice about the airing of violence in prime-time – "Helter Skelter" came to CBS as a four-hour two-part movie that compelled a nation as much as the crime it recounted.

The movie was based on the 1974 best-seller of the same name written by Curt Gentry and Manson prosecutor Vincent Bugliosi, which chronicled the events surrounding the August 1969 murders of pregnant actress Sharon Tate and four others in Bel Air, California, as well as those of Leno LaBianca and wife Rosemary in the L.A. suburb of Los Feliz the following night. A bloody and seemingly random killing spree, involving the vicious stabbing death of eight-months pregnant Hollywood star, it riveted America as it frightened metropolitan Los Angeles. Few details were spared in the CBS re-telling, which seemed to create a New Normal for how violence in general and murder in particular could be depicted on TV during the Decade of Change. Which is to say -- graphically.

NBC's made-for-TV movie *Born Innocent* of just 20 months earlier, which precipitated the imposition of the Family Hour, was one thing: A teen-in-crisis movie, it positioned itself as a film that would Make a Difference in the lives of young people. ABC's bloodletting a year after that with *The Legend of Lizzie Borden* was historical in nature, set a century earlier. And it was speculative at that. It, too, aired with a certain remove when it came to its brutality.

But "Helter Skelter" was a few-holds-barred look at a contemporary real-life massacre, still casting a specter over the country, depicting savage events and the people behind them who seemed to flirt with insanity. It had little to offer other than a shocking story. Which it did on CBS in 1976 as a TV-movie, too. An avalanche of viewers watched, becoming the highest-rated made-for-TV movie *ever*, on *any* network, with an astounding 60 share for its two-hour conclusion. (Sixty percent of TVs turned on at the time the film aired were tuned in to CBS.)

Skillfully made and acted, "Helter Skelter" turned real-life crime into big TV business, the more shocking the better. After it aired, each of the three broadcast networks went in search of other horrific crimes to document or other depraved stories to tell, preferably in mini-series form, for the coming TV season.

Among its projects: "21 Hours At Munich" (about the 1972 Summer Olympic massacre), "Victory at Entebbe" (about the Israeli commandos' real-life hostage-freeing raid on Uganda's airport in 1976), "Sybil" (about what was purported to be the real-life case of a young woman who emerged from a childhood of tortuous abuse at the hand of her mother with 19 separate personalities), "The Disappearance of Aimee" (about the unexplained real-life four-week disappearance of evangelist Aimee Semple McPherson in 1926), "Tail Gunner Joe" (about the life of controversial U.S. Senator Joseph McCarthy), and "The Amazing Howard Hughes." ("Holocaust" was another year away.)

CBS re-made "Helter Skelter" in 2004, but it found that lightning could strike just once in the same place. The film fizzled. The original had become that indelible in the 28 years since its broadcast. As had Steve Railsback's performance as deranged and maniacal Charles Manson. The 1976 film was Railsback's third acting job, and it forever altered the trajectory of his career, seemingly for the worse: So convincing and compelling was he as Manson, that though he would act steadily in the coming decades he never shook the connection.

A 2004 *Los Angeles Times* piece mused that " 'Helter Skelter' actor Steve Railsback wonders if playing mass murderer Charles Manson ruined his career." Wrote Rachel Abramowitz, "[a]fter 'Helter Skelter' he was offered every psychopathic killer that Hollywood could drag out from under a rock."

From a sanguine Railsback in her piece:

> This town is a town in which you can get pigeonholed. They say, 'He can do craziness.' I didn't do it. I turned them all down. This town figures, he must not be able to do anything else, which is a load of crap. I'm an actor.

"It was one of those parts," Railsback's onetime agent said. "There was such negativity around Manson that the actor might suffer with it."

(**Not-So-Fun-Fact**: Scenes in the film of the LaBianca murders were shot in the victims' actual house in L.A.'s Los Feliz community.)

"Holocaust"
April 16-19 1978 NBC
(10)

Having proven itself a new kind of ratings-magnet and attention-grabber, first with "QBVII" and then in the next few years with "Rich Man, Poor Man" and "Roots" and "Jesus of Nazareth," the TV mini-series got its most serious upgrade in the spring of 1978 with "Holocaust." It marked TV's first attempt at chronicling the atrocity in this form. And in the process, it broke down most all of TV's decades-long taboos connected to violence (and nudity).

NBCUniversal

"Holocaust" was, of course, a difficult sell for a commercial television project. Gerald Green's script would explore key events that led up to World War II and then to the Holocaust itself, which it would recount in detail, grounded in the fictional story of a family of German Jews. But NBC committed to running it, over the course of four nights in one week, totaling nine-and-a-half hours.

Veteran actors of the era, each with TV-friendly faces (among them Fritz Weaver, Rosemary Harris and Sam Wanamaker), were hired to head a large cast that also included newcomer Meryl Streep, eight months from her big-screen breakthrough in THE DEER HUNTER, and James Woods, a young TV-actor himself a year away from his own breakthrough in THE ONION FIELD. Filming took place on location in West Berlin and Austria – including, for some scenes, at the latter's Mauthhausen concentration camp. The first two parts were devoted to the "gathering storm," with the third and the fourth parts to the more intense scenes of extermination and their aftermath.

Reviews were mixed when "Holocaust" was broadcast, with critics admiring the scope and ambition of the mini-series as well as its capacity for conveying the horrors of the events within the constraints of television -- but left wanting by the story of the fictional family at its core.

As could be expected about a film that tackles non-fiction, especially those of this nature, "Holocaust" was alternately attacked and applauded in various corners of the world -- by historians and academics, by Germans and Poles and Jews. Some criticized it for trivializing a tragedy; others praised it for shedding light on a dark chapter of humanity.

Writing in *The New York Times* upon its premiere, activist and Holocaust survivor Elie Weisel slammed the project:

> The story is gripping, the acting competent, the
> message compelling—and yet. The calculated brutality
> of the killers, the silent agony of the victims, the

indifference of the outside world—this TV series will show what some survivors have been trying to say for years and years. And yet something is wrong with it. Something? No: everything.

Untrue, offensive, cheap: as a TV production, the film an insult to those who perished and to those who survived. In spite of its name, this "docu-drama" is not about what some of us remember as the Holocaust.

Washington Post TV critic Tom Shales, on the other hand, offered this appraisal on the same date:

Television, the good news machine, departs from its role as national comforter tonight when NBC begins the four-night telecast of "Holocaust," a 9 1/2 hour filmed drama on one of the most discomforting of all possible topics: Nazi persecution and extermination of Jews in the 1930s and '40s. It is hard to imagine television drama more demanding or rewarding.

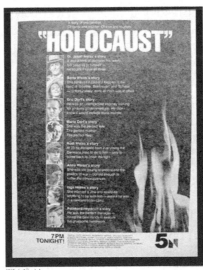

TV Guide

No matter the opinion of it as drama or as history, "Holocaust" was a skillful and needle-moving effort that provided for the first time in a longform TV project an unsparing look at a horrific piece of world history. As noted by the Museum of Broadcast Communication:

> Most obviously, this nine-and-a-half-hour, four-part series may be compared to "Roots," which aired on ABC a year earlier and on which [its] director, Marvin Chomsky, has worked. Like "Roots'" saga of American slavery, "Holocaust'"s story of Jewish suffering before and during World War II apparently flew in the face of network programming wisdom, which advised against presenting tales of virtually unrelieved or inexplicable misery ... NBC estimated after the 1979 rebroadcast that as many as 220 million viewers in the United States and Europe had seen the series. (*museum.tv*)

"Holocaust" was nominated for 15 Emmy awards, dominating the 1978 ceremony. It won eight -- for directing (Chomsky), writing (Green), and for stars Michael Moriarty, Blanche Baker and Streep. It was also named Best Limited Series. In addition, it received a 1978 Peabody Award, the prestigious honor selectively given each year "to spotlight instances of how electronic media can teach, expand, our horizons, defend the public interest, or encourage empathy with others."

The mini-series set yet another new standard for the television movie as the genre continued to evolve throughout the 1970s, from "My Sweet Charlie" to "Roots" and beyond. It continued to show that the changing medium could tackle a changing world, that it could handle weighty if not shocking material with sensitivity and that it could explore the human condition in ways that perhaps feature films could or would not. Wrote Shales in 1978:

> For years, TV has taken subjects that seemed to defy sugar-coating and turned them into mind snacks - subjects like death, for instance, depicted as everything

from cute to noble but never quite ghastly. The people who made "Holocaust" are shrewd dramatists, and they tell absorbing, interwoven stories about fictitious, believable people that hold one's interest through almost every minute of the 450-minute film, but they have not - to their great credit - minimized or trivialized the reality of horror against which these lives are led...

Every American should see "Holocaust." It is the most powerful film ever made for television.

James at 15
1977-78 NBC
(11)

Not perfect, not revolutionary, not always deliriously urgent, *James at 15* is still the most respectable new entertainment series of the season. Consistently, it communicates something about the state of being young, rather than just communicating that it wishes to lure young viewers. And if it romanticizes adolescence through the weekly trials and triumphs of its teen-age hero, at least it does so in more ambitious, inquisitive and authentic ways than the average TV teeny-bop.

-- Tom Shales
The Washington Post December 15 1977

Shales' review above was written in support of an episode of *James at 15* that aired halfway through the series' first and only season, one that focused on how the teenager at the center of the show deals with the death of his best friend. Outside of an *ABC Afterschool Special*, feelings and emotions were not the stuff of typical TV at the time, but *James at 15* had already proven deft at it. "Ronald Rubin's script is perceptive to the rhythms and moods of youthful friendships and to the privileged isolation of the adolescent," wrote Shales. Young James' dealing with the tragedy marks it "a believable personal victory."

Perceptive and believable were the hallmarks of *James at 15*.

Long before *My So-Called Life* and *Party of Five* came along in the 1990s, and at a time when TV was finally beginning to recognize teenagers as young adults rather than older children, the 1977 drama dared to represent a contemporary teenager's real thoughts and feelings. Starring Lance Kerwin, a teenager himself, it was about James Hunter and his coming-of-age at a time after his family's cross-country move from Portland to Boston, where his professor-father had taken a new job. The episodes focused on James as he tried to settle in both to a

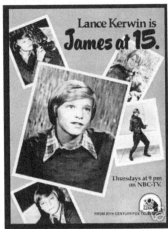

NBC /20th Century Fox Television

new school and a new life, supplemented by his many big-thinking adolescent daydreams. (In Walter Mitty fashion, some of those daydreams came to life on screen.)

The series began with a two-hour movie of the same name, written by novelist Dan Wakefield, which aired on NBC without much expectation on Labor Day 1977. It ended up being the highest-rated program of the week. A series order was immediately struck, hurried to air by the end of October to help prop up the NBC Thursday-night line-up, which had collapsed upon the start of the season in September. (Five weeks in, a hodgepodge of programming had already been scheduled on the night, including boxing, baseball, and the brand-new-and-doomed series *The Man from Atlantis* and *The Richard Pryor Show*.)

If the series version of *James* did not meet with the kind of stellar ratings that the movie did, it nonetheless settled in with what future TV standards would classify as a loyal cult audience, fortified by a TV rarity -- near-unanimous praise and support from critics.

But even that was not enough, as viewership lagged throughout the winter opposite CBS's longtime and still popular *Hawaii Five-0* and ABC's rising comedy *Barney Miller*. Not helping: a change in executive producers and backstage fighting between writer/creator Wakefield and NBC.

The behind-the-scenes drama reached a critical point in February with what was planned to be a special episode of the series in which James would lose his virginity. It was happen on his birthday, thus ameliorating NBC's concerns about depicting a 15-year-old having sex; but this would necessitate a title change for the struggling series (and too soon into its run, felt by some).

In the end, it was thought that both "events" -- the act and the title change -- would shore up the show's profile, so the episode got under way. But as soon as it did Wakefield pushed back against NBC's insistence that the words "birth control" in its script be replaced by the more benign "being responsible." He also strongly disagreed with the network's call that James, in the wake of his first sexual experience, exhibit remorse for having gone through with it. So the producer left the episode and quit the show. Each went on without him.

Dogged by a bit of controversy and advertiser skittishness, the *James at 16* episode entitled "The Gift" aired on February 9, 1978. But not even the well-publicized storyline nor its associated backstage drama -- nor the new title -- could make the necessary difference for the show. Ratings were just as unimpressive. *James* just never could recover its movie-of-the-week momentum from the previous September. It was pulled from NBC's line-up in March and officially cancelled soon after, running out its five unaired episodes that June.

Decades later, the drama series is still held in high regard -- as much for what it was as a TV show as for what it did for TV in general. *James at 15* stands as a noteworthy and important next-step in prime-time, allowing for the normalization of the teen experience. In the 1990s, *Dawson's Creek* creator Kevin Williamson cited the show as a major influence on that drama, itself applauded for its own realistic depiction of teen lives. "*Dawson's Creek* came out of my desire to do 'James at 15' for the '90s," he said. "[That drama] was ... way ahead of its time."

Norman Lear
(12)

"It was a bifurcated life," writes Norman Lear of his younger years, in his 2014 memoir *Even This I Get To Experience*. From ages nine to twelve, he lived with relatives while his father served time in jail. "There was the reality I was actually living, which I could do nothing about. And then there was the reality that was a product of my need and imagination. That was what I showed to the world..."

It's this reality -- that product of his need and imagination - that seemed to go on to inform Lear's adult life and career. The result would be his position as the most influential producer in television history.

Producers Guild of America

Norman Milton Lear was born on July 27, 1922. He became a household name 48 years and five months later, when *All in the Family*, the sitcom he created and developed and later watched as it changed the world, premiered on CBS. Though he lived multiple lives both before that sitcom (World War II combat veteran, door-to-door salesman, public-relations executive, joke-writer for Martin & Lewis, Oscar-nominated screenwriter) and after (film producer, studio head, political activist, business leader), it's still the landmark success that was that series for which he'd always remain best-known and with which he'd always be most associated.

All in the Family, like *Sanford and Son* and *Three's Company*, which proceeded it in the 1970s, was a reworking of a 1960s British series. (*Sanford and Son* came from *Steptoe and Son*; *Three's Company* came from *Man About the House*.) But as Lear has indicated through the years, the American version of Britain's *Till Death Do Us Part* that he put together in the late 1960s after buying rights to the format was very much inspired by the union of his own parents.

It told of the marriage of Edith and Archie Bunker, and the Queens, New York, home they shared with their 20-something newlywed daughter and her opinionated husband, who, as sitcoms would have it, was an out-and-proud liberal to his new father-in-law's staunch myopic conservative.

Whatever the history, though, its gestation was a lengthy one, spanning three years.

Originally developed for ABC under the title *Justice For All*, about the life and family of Archie Justice (for which role the network had envisioned the likes of Jack Warden, Tom Bosley, or Jackie Gleason, among others, before it eventually hired Carroll O'Connor), it became *Those Were the Days* when ABC passed on the first pilot and ordered a second, complete with a new supporting cast.

When a nervous ABC passed again, CBS, looking for an image change for its somewhat staid and traditional schedule, picked it up and shot a third pilot, with still more cast changes. This one, titled *All in the Family* and starring the O'Connor, Jean Stapleton, Sally Struthers, Rob, premiered on January 12 1971.

Within six months, the bold and unconventional *All in the Family* was the biggest hit in TV. And within a year, Lear's production company was the busiest in town. First out of the post-*Family* gate was *Sanford and Son*, premiering on NBC in January 1972. It became the first modern black sitcom to crack Nielsen's Top Ten. It was followed that fall by an *All in the Family* spin-off, *Maude*, which courted the kind of controversy its landmark parent show could only dream of when within two months of its premiere it was condemned by the Catholic Church over an episode about abortion.

Good Times, another spin-off – this one of *Maude* – came next, exposing prime-time to the Chicago projects for the first time, followed by, in 1975, *The Jeffersons* (a third *All in the Family* spin-off, which featured TV's first inter-racial couple), *One Day at a Time* (TV's first sitcom success predicated on divorce), and then the syndicated second-wave feminism satire *Mary Hartman Mary Hartman* (which in addition to its revolutionary creative content re-wrote the rules of TV syndication).

Rolled out over the course of five years, these seven series yielded a collective 1400 episodes, amounting to *51 seasons* of television. (This does not count the various Lear productions that made it to air in those five years but failed to find an audience.) In that half-decade, Lear and company rewired television writing for generations of future storytellers.

If this period marked Lear's most prolific, such that it later saw him part of the freshman class of inductees when the Television Academy Hall of Fame was founded in 1984, the years that followed found Lear just as if not more involved in affecting future generations through his advocacy and producing enterprises.

He established The People for the American Way in 1981 to take on the rising strength of the Christian right and Moral Majority. His production company produced TV movies and specials, among them *I Love Liberty* (1982), as well as big-screen films such as THE SURE THING, STAND BY ME, THE PRINCESS BRIDE, and FRIED GREEN TOMATOES. He staged a minor prime-time comeback in the early 1990s with the socially-bent sitcoms *Sunday Dinner, The Powers That Be*, and *704 Hauser*. And then he managed another reinvention 20 years later, in a new century, when at age 95 he took to the new world of streaming content with a Latino-infused re-working of his 1970s classic *One Day at a Time* for Netflix.

But it's Norman Lear's prolific output in the 1970s for which he is still best known and most associated -- sitcoms that pulled TV from its infancy and guided it through adolescence into adulthood. Sitcoms that entertained as they told stories about family (his) and the human condition (ours). Sitcoms that changed a business as they changed and made history.

"We have bet with our lives that we could change the course of Oglala history on this reservation and the history of the rest of Indian America."

-- Russell Means
Wounded Knee February 1973

Lou Grant
1977-82 CBS
(13)

> [T]he 1970s offered a different kind of drama. It was during the 1970s that the results of the major social movements of the previous two decades became concrete in American communities and in Americans' daily lives.
>
> -- Beth L. Bailey, David R. Farber
> *America in the 70s*

Were it not for its pedigree – and for its loose connection at the time to a journalism *zeitgeist*, all about exposing the forces that affect Americans' daily lives – the newspaper drama *Lou Grant*, about the inner workings of the fictional *Los Angeles Tribune*, would likely have been cancelled before the end of its first low-rated season.

Viewers didn't exactly flock to watch the show when it premiered in September 1977, unsure at first what to make of it. Technically a spin-off of the just-ended and popular *Mary Tyler Moore* sitcom, *Lou Grant* was a drama -- and a hard-hitting one at that. And while it featured Edward Asner in a continuation of his familiar gruff-but-lovable role from that long-running hit, for which he'd won two Emmys as a supporting character, the new show wasn't about showcasing the comic side of either the character or the actor playing him.

Plus, *Lou Grant* arrived facing a more basic issue: There'd just never been a successful TV series about the running of a newspaper.

Like, ever.

CBS / 20th Century Fox Television

But with seven years' equity in the Lou Grant character and a belief in the show, if not a long-standing relationship with its producers, CBS gave *Lou Grant* the time it needed to take root and to take off. And there really was a belief in its journalism trendiness: ALL THE PRESIDENT'S MEN, about the investigative reporting that had brought down the Nixon presidency (and which had caused a spike in journalism-school enrollment in the mid-1970s), had won four Oscars earlier in 1977.

Between the timing and the trending, *Lou Grant* finished out the 1977-78 TV season as one of its best-reviewed new shows, which led to six Emmy nominations that summer, including one for Best Drama. The result was indeed increased awareness and ratings, and in its second season *Lou Grant* become an official hit for CBS. And it continued a change in TV storytelling as it directed its attention to those "major social movements of the previous two decades [that] became concrete in ... Americans' daily lives."

As early as its first episode, in fact, entitled "Cophouse," *Lou Grant* positioned itself as a show that would re-work some of the rules of the one-hour drama genre in service of those major social moments, in both small ways (humor-laced drama, fostering the advent of a new genre to be called *dramedy*) and large (controversial subject matter). "Cophouse" focused on the uncovering of and the debate over how to report an underage-girls sex scandal involving the Los Angeles Police Department.

It marked a fairly wide right-turn from only months earlier when the Lou Grant character was zinging jokes at half-wit employee Ted Baxter on *Mary Tyler Moore*.

With the possible exceptions of three series (*Police Story, James at 15, Family*), no drama among the more than three dozen airing in the fall of 1977 was writing about contemporary life the way *Lou Grant* was. With *Lou Grant*, TV began to show that unlike the well-ordered life of prime-time's past, life in the 1970s could be messy. And hard to know about, deal with, report on.

First-season episodes came to explore the gender wars, Nazism, senility on the judicial bench, abuse of mental-health patients, battered women, homelessness, prostitution, government spying, prescription addiction, and disparities in inner-city education, as well as examinations of basic journalism practices. They also tread on then-current-events topics such as NCAA violations, religious cults, nuclear-industry whistleblowing, and prisoner-torture in Central America.

The show asked questions, not always getting answers. It exposed problems, not always leading to solutions. Elsewhere in prime-time, crimes were being solved and punishment was being meted out (in *Charlie's Angels, Baretta, Starsky & Hutch, The Rockford Files, Columbo*); the world was being saved from disaster (in *The Bionic Woman, The Six Million Dollar Man*); and space and new life-forms were being explored (in *Project UFO, The Man From Atlantis, The Incredible Hulk*), as history was being recounted (*The Black Sheep Squadron, Young Dan'l Boone*). But *Lou Grant* was covering the news. The day's news. Our news.

Four years before *Hill Street Blues* and then a host of other dramas would be rightly credited with re-drawing the hard lines of episodic drama (dark humor, unresolved storylines, flawed characters and anti-heroes, controversial topics), *Lou Grant* had already began erasing them.

Controversy of a whole different kind in the 1980s (off-screen, involving Asner's liberal politics) may have contributed to the show's cancellation after just five seasons, but the five seasons it had were significant both in their reach and grasp.

Because of the writing of the fictional newspaper drama *Lou Grant*, real-life women came to know about the medical condition known as DES Daughters ("Inheritance"); senility on the judicial bench was explored ("Judge"); whistleblowing at unsafe nuclear power-plants was exposed, a year before Three Mile Island and four years before the release of *Silkwood* ("Poison"); and the unknown or not-yet-talked-about physical risks associated with professional football were spotlighted ("Violence").

Journalism itself became a noble even heroic profession thanks to *Lou Grant*. The show was nominated for a total of 56 Emmy awards (nine for its writing), winning 13. Twice, it won the Emmy as TV's Best Drama. It was also nominated for 14 Writers Guild awards.

(**Fun Fact**: Each episode of *Lou Grant* had a single-word title, modeled after the single-word "slug" title applied to newspaper articles in production in old-school newsrooms.)

M*A*S*H
"Sometimes You Hear the Bullet"
January 28 1973 CBS
(14)

M*A*S*H* loyalists seem to fall into two camps -- one that claims the sitcom's best years were its first three seasons, when it was mostly a punchline-heavy satire akin to the Robert Altman film on which it was based, and the other that says its later seasons were its best, when it incorporated, often in experimental and heavy-handed ways, social commentary.

Both claims have merit, and each can be strongly argued. But one episode of the show in particular so straddles the line between the two opinions that it usually ends up seen by both sides as one of the best of the show's 11-year run.

Airing midway through its first season, "Sometimes You Hear the Bullet" became the episode that illustrated the folly of war, the limitations of doctors, the inevitability of death. It also announced that *M*A*S*H**, a new show for a new decade, about the lives of those who staff a medical hospital near the front lines of the Korean conflict in the 1950s, was a contemporary storytelling force to be reckoned with.

The episode centers on the arrival in camp of a reporter-friend of lead character Dr. Benjamin "Hawkeye" Pierce, there to research an article he's calling *You Never Hear the Bullet*, about how on the lines of combat – unlike the way in which battle scenes are depicted in the movies -- death can come with no warning. That unlike in the movies, a soldier in real combat can never hear coming the bullet that ends his life.

But when the reporter himself turns up on Hawkeye's operating table a few days into the visit -- a victim of enemy fire -- he tells Hawkeye in what become his dying words that he'd actually heard the bullet coming at him after all, just like in the movies. A scene follows that finds camp commander Henry Blake discovering Hawkeye crying over the loss his friend -- a reaction the surgeon realizes he's never had for the many deaths he's seen during his tour of duty thus far. Which saddens him further. Blake attempts to offer consolation:

CBS / 20th Century Fox Television

Blake: Look, all I know is what they taught me in Command School. There are certain rules about a war. And Rule Number One is young men die. And Rule Number Two is doctors can't change Rule Number One.

It's a heavy moment for a show that until then could be comedic to the point of farce. (Among *M*A*S*H** fans, the "Rule Number One/Rule Number Two" speech went on to be one of the series' most oft-repeated lines.)

"Sometimes You Hear the Bullet" served to remind that unlike most medical shows since the dawn of television in the 1940s, *M*A*S*H** was going to be about making and breaking the rules -- about life and death in prime-time TV and about the doctors and nurses who were up to their bloody arms in each. On TV in the 1970s, sometimes healers will fail; sometimes good people will die; and sometimes you'll hear the bullet.

As the 1972-73 TV season unfolded, with TV comedies still in large part about side-stepping reality (*Here's Lucy, The Doris Day Show, The Partridge Family, The Brady Bunch*) M*A*S*H* demonstrated with each episode that such an approach was no longer realistic. That TV was becoming about confronting or at least acknowledging rather than sidestepping issues – even if through the allegory the show often offered. And that TV, like life, could often exhibit both comedy and drama in the same beat.

It was one of two new series of the 1972-73 TV season -- the other being *Maude* (both on CBS) -- that would go on to trade heavily in that concept. Taken with other freshman hits such as *The Bob Newhart Show* and *Bridget Loves Bernie*, as well as other series introduced since 1970, from *Mary Tyler Moore* to *The Odd Couple* to *All in the Family* to *Sanford and Son* to *The Corner Bar*, it was evident that the sitcom as a genre had morphed, now about relatable people experiencing real life and real situations, making viewers think as much as making them laugh.

(**Fun Fact**: "Sometimes You Hear the Bullet" aired immediately following an episode of the largely forgotten 1971-74 sitcom *The New Dick Van Dyke Show* that was about marijuana use in the home.)

Written by Carl Kleinschmitt, "Sometimes You Hear the Bullet" was plainly anti-war at a time when the stance could create ripples of controversy and make networks nervous. It was nominated for a Writers Guild Award as one of the year's best sitcom episodes. It also marked the first time that the M*A*S*H* doctors lost a patient (albeit a civilian).

"They're All Gone"
Jim McKay, 1972 Summer Olympics
September 6 1972 ABC
(15)

ABC

It's known as the "They're All Gone" speech -- the on-air announcement that veteran ABC Sports commentator Jim McKay had to make on September 6 1972 while onsite covering the Munich Summer Olympics, about the deaths of nine Israeli Olympic team members who'd been taken hostage a day earlier in the Olympic Village. They'd been murdered by their captors, members of the Palestinian terror group Black September (an offshoot of the PLO), as the group sought escape from Germany.

The nine dead athletes were among eleven taken in the Village raid. (Two others were killed at the attack unfolded.) As the face of ABC's Olympic coverage, McKay had ended up on the air for 16 hours, tracking the unfolding drama, and it fell to him to report its tragic ending. In doing so, a revolutionary day in sports was marked. The

Olympics and their coverage were never to be the same, stained by the blood of politics. And McKay, already an ABC legend, became a world figure.

Born in Philadelphia, Jim McKay began his career in the 1940s as a police reporter for *The Baltimore [Evening] Sun*, giving up the job in 1947 to switch over to work at a newly created TV station run by the paper's owner, where he'd perform various duties.

In 1950 he joined CBS, where he hosted a variety series, but McKay came to gravitate more and more to sports journalism. He covered football beginning in 1956 and then in 1960 was sent to Rome to cover the Summer Olympics. He moved over to ABC after that, where among other assignments, including ABC's coverage of the Olympics, he became the man behind its *Wide World of Sports*, a role he'd have for 37 years.

As Bob Costas was for NBC during that network's 12 Olympics from 1992 to 2016, Jim McKay was the face of the Games for ABC throughout the 1960s and 1970s. So by default he became the face of the unfolding Munich hostage-crisis, too, as soon as the news broke -- the kidnapping, the ransom demand, the negotiations, the agreement to offer the terrorists safe passage out of Germany to Cairo, and the carnage that followed at the local airport during a botched rescue effort, during which the captors were also killed. McKay was fed updates on the unfolding tragedy from ABC Sports' Roone Arledge while on the air, via an earpiece:

> We just got the final word ... you know, when I was a kid my father used to say, 'Our greatest hopes and our worst fears are seldom realized.' Our worst fears have been realized tonight. They have now said there were eleven hostages; two were killed in their rooms this morn-- yesterday morning, nine were killed at the airport tonight. They're all gone.

Despite the fact that he'd walked away from news assignments in 1947, Jim McKay earned an Emmy Award for his hours-long news reporting of what became known as the Munich Massacre. For his calm during a terrorist storm. He also won a Sports Emmy, as well as the George Polk Memorial Award. (In the course of his career, he won 13 Emmys total.)

He stayed with ABC for the rest of his broadcast career, though in a bit of a valedictory lap in 2002 he appeared on NBC during its coverage of the Salt Lake City Olympics. It marked his final Olympics appearance.

When Jim McKay died in 2008, there was much about his career to highlight, but his official obituary and the many tributes that followed focused on his role at and contribution to the Munich Games.

> Jim McKay, the venerable and eloquent sportscaster thrust into the role of telling Americans about the tragedy at the 1972 Munich Olympics, has died. (Associated Press)

Jim McKay, the sportscaster who brought the "thrill of victory and the agony of defeat" into U.S. homes as the longtime host of *ABC's Wide World of Sports* and who anchored the network's coverage of the terrorist killings of 11 Israeli athletes at the 1972 Summer Olympics, died Saturday at his farm in Monkton, Md. (*The Philadelphia Inquirer*)

On September 6 1972, Jim McKay had already been on air for 16 hours, anchoring ABC's coverage of the Israeli Olympians taken hostage by Palestinian gunmen, when he heard the news in his earpiece. Visibly shaken, he reported the results of the botched rescue of the hostages by German police at Munich airport. 'Tonight, our worst fears have been realized,' he said. 'They're all gone.' … Those simple words have been etched into the collective memory of the horror of Munich, but by the time he uttered them, McKay, who has died at age 86, had already established himself as an American sportscasting legend. (*The Guardian*)

Jim McKay elegantly covered competitions from badminton to barrel jumping. Yet he may best be remembered for that grim day at the Munich Olympics when he broke the news with three simple words: "They're all gone." (*American Sportscasters Online*)

In a 2012 interview with *The Hollywood Reporter*, CBS Sports President Sean McManus, McKay's son, who as a child had accompanied McKay to Germany for the Games, recalled the Munich events of 40 years earlier. (Born Jim McManus, the elder McKay changed his name at the outset of his career.)

I was with my father, either in the control room or by his side off in the wings, for the entire day. Roone [Arledge], as he often did, made a gut decision and said, 'I'm going to put McKay in the chair,' not certain whether he would stay in the chair or whether they would change anchors throughout the day. But my father didn't get up from that chair for 16 hours.

The entire day's coverage was live, with conflicting reports coming in. At one point, all the athletes had been rescued; at one point, they had all been killed. Ironically, as awful as that day was, and as terrible as the circumstances were, it was the one event that catapulted my father from being a relatively well-known sports commentator to a national figure. On the other end of things, even more importantly, people like the parents of Israeli weightlifter David Berger [who were watching from] Shaker Heights, Ohio, were trying to figure out if their son was dead or alive. And my father knew that.

When finally Roone said it's been confirmed, I could see it in my father's face, a combination of exhaustion and sadness and a knowledge that he had to report objectively and professionally what happened.

My father used that line from his own dad: 'In life, your greatest fears and your greatest hopes are seldom realized. Our worst fears have been realized tonight ...' He would use that line with me often, before big athletic events or when things didn't go as well as I would have liked them to. So it was pretty emotional for me to hear that.

He didn't realize -- and nobody realized, I think -- the impact this story would have on the American public. Terrorism was something that America just had not dealt with. The idea of masked gunmen kidnapping athletes was something that was so foreign to the consciousness. Now we are familiar with terrorism and kidnappings and bombings and massacres, but in those days it was just unheard of. So I don't think he realized how many people were watching him and what a huge, huge national event it was.

It's the Berger perspective that McKay himself recalled in *Jim McKay: My Life in My Words*, a 2003 HBO documentary that aired five years before his death: "I know my eyes were heavy with sorrow, and I knew what I must say."

The Munich Massacre changed the Olympics and sports broadcasting as a whole, blurring the lines between news and sports and entertainment, as the 1968 Games in Mexico had started to do. No longer mere games, sports were now targets for exploitation, offering masses of crowds and live TV. (Author Thomas Harris has said that he was inspired by the events in Munich to write the terrorism-centered BLACK SUNDAY, about a bombing at the Super Bowl, which later became a 1977 film.) Jim McKay became the face of that change, and while it played out on TV in the way Vietnam had been coming into American living rooms, McKay's composure helped to calm the storm and to put a face on tragedy. In 1993, *TV Guide* named McKay the best sports broadcaster of the 1970s.

Credited with uttering the first words ever heard on TV in Baltimore (when the medium began in that city in 1947), Jim McKay became the last word in sports broadcasting for an entire country.

"The Police Story: Stakeout" (aka "Slowboy")
March 20 1973 NBC
(16)

From the rise of anti-heroes to the incorporation of darker and more morally ambiguous material, the changes that were creeping into big-screen movies in the early 1970s (as detailed in Peter Biskind's *Easy Riders, Raging Bulls: How the Sex-Drugs-and-Rock 'N' Roll Generation Saved Hollywood*) were showing up on television, too.

The hard-right angles of traditional cop stories, for example, were beginning to bow: Police work was no longer seen in absolutes; its officers were no longer the paragons of justice-for-all they'd long been presented to be; and the bad guys were sometimes seen as better than the good ones, if the two groups could be distinguished at all. It was an evolution that began to come about late in the 1960s, in large part at the hands of cop-turned-novelist Joseph Wambuagh.

The son of an East Coast policeman, Wambuagh had joined the L.A.P.D. in 1960, just out of the Marines, rising quickly through the ranks to detective sergeant. He began to write about his work in the late 1960s while still in uniform. In 1971, he published *The New Centurions*, a mostly plotless examination of the professional and personal tolls of police work. It became a best-seller. In it and his follow-up novels *The Choirboys* and *The Blue Knight*, Wambaugh wrote of police-officer protagonists who were shaded with dimension and often very flawed.

In March 1973, at the height of his celebrity (and a year before he retired from the force), Wambaugh brought his image of the modern cop to NBC in a made-for-TV movie he created called "The Police Story."

Written by E. Jack Neuman, it starred Vic Morrow as the head of an elite L.A.P.D. unit who skirts the law in his pursuit of a particularly dangerous criminal. The movie's success spawned a weekly series that fall called *Police Story*, an anthology about the public duties and private lives of cops (different ones each week). The mix of stories and protagonists and experiences spoke to the changing depictions of law enforcement on TV. (The anthology format often allowed for episodes that served as *de facto* pilots for new series; three episodes led to separate NBC series -- *Joe Forrester*, *David Cassidy-Man Undercover*, and *Police Woman*.) David Gerber, one of the more prolific guiding forces of the 1970s, produced.

NBC / Sony

The un-sanitized approach to criminal justice was one of the reasons that led to *Police Story* being hailed by *The Complete Directory of Prime Time Network and Cable TV Shows* as "one of the more realistic police series to be seen on television."

In 1976, the series won the Emmy as Best Dramatic series. More critical to the decade and to prime-time, *Police Story* took the TV cop from the pedestal of virtue to a new reality that would be fleshed out in decades to come by *Hill Street Blues* and *NYPD Blue*.

Wambaugh as author went on to other best-selling novels before turning to non-fiction with *The Onion Field*, *Echoes in the Darkness*, and *The Blooding*, each about especially heinous real-life murders. In 2006 he reverted to fiction with the first of a five-volume series about cops working out of L.A.'s Hollywood Division precinct, called *Hollywood Station*.

(**Fun Fact**: The first regularly scheduled episode of *Police Story* in the fall of 1973 was directed by John Badham, who'd go on to direct the popular feature films SATURDAY NIGHT FEVER, WARGAMES, and BLUE THUNDER.)

Real People
1979-1984 NBC
(17)

> Dismissed as hokey and tacky by most critics but adored by its fans, "Real People" probably speaks more intimately than any other television show to the average viewer who so rarely sees his life reflected on the situation comedies, police dramas and steamy serials that dominate prime time.

> -- Tony Schwartz
> *New York Times* May 6 1982

The decade that began with a celebration of real people on PBS – in the documentary series *An American Family* – concluded on NBC in much the same way, with *Real People*, a non-fiction series launched in April of 1979. Long before something called "reality TV" became a prime-time staple, it stood out a newcomer to programming, observed at the time as a new-fangled reimagining of the fading variety-series genre.

NBC / George Schlatter Productions

Real People, shot in front of a live studio audience (broadcast live in its early episodes, too), with a roster of six quasi-familiar names as on-stage hosts, revolved around featured "segments" about everyday people who had unusual jobs or stories. That was the sum total of its premise. It likely says as much if not more about NBC's woeful prime-time schedule in the late 1970s and early 1980s (*The Misadventures of Sherriff Lobo* to *Hello Larry, Buck Rogers in the 25th Century* to *Here's Boomer* to *Pink Lady and Jeff*) that the series was regularly the network's most-watched show.

As Dan Snierson noted in a 20-years-on piece for *Entertainment Weekly* in 1997:

> NBC's cheeky-cheery "variety" hour turned TV conventions upside down, or at least backward: It spun its cameras around 180 degrees, transforming common folk into celebrities. Peppered with Velveeta banter from its hosts and reporters ... *Real People* highlighted stories that fell through the cracks between network-news and circus-freak shows. Says executive producer George Schlatter, who also created *Rowan & Martin's Laugh-In*, "We celebrated overlooked accomplishments and ordinary people who overcame obstacles."

The *New York Times*, for the Schwartz piece, framed the show as "Heartland vs. Hollywood":

> *Real People*, in its fourth season, is indeed about real people, but with a relentlessly upbeat emphasis on the overlooked - war veterans, the handicapped, the elderly - and the inventively outrageous - the fellow who is building a spaceship from used auto-parts, the gorilla who watches television, the society of bald men. ... Mr. Schlatter, who may be the least-cynical man in Hollywood, is by turns carnival barker, patriot, populist and proselytizer. ... "This show," he says, "is about letting people know that their opinions are important, that people just like them are interesting and attractive. I'm for the little guy, the underdog."

It seems worth noting (or worth reminding) that, despite popular lore, reality programming itself – as a genre -- didn't start in 1979 with *Real People*. Or even with *An American Family* six years earlier. Non-fiction TV began when TV itself did. It was an inexpensive form of storytelling when TV was an experiment not yet proven worthy of the high expenditures that can come with scripted dramatic content and high-wattage casting.

The first recognized regularly scheduled TV season (1946-47) was chock full of what would be classified today as reality shows, from dance-and-music shows to quiz-and-panel shows and from gardening series to interview shows. Decades later, it was the *focus* that started to change (with both *An American Family* and *Real People*) -- from uplifting *Queen for a Day*-type format that celebrated regular people to a *verite* warts-and-all freak-show that "exposed" them.

Regardless, within a year of its launch, *Real People* was joined at or near the top of the Nielsen ratings by ABC's *That's Incredible*, about ordinary people who did extraordinary things. Michael McKenna, in his 2015 book called *Real People and the Rise of Reality Television*, refers to the NBC hit as the "prototypical and most influential program in the first wave of reality programming" of the 1980s.

Variations on the real-people theme did permeate the decade, some of which lasted and some of which did not. But the reality genie was out of its bottle. MTV's *Real World* took it to the next level starting 1992. Unscripted weekly television series, real people playing to the camera to shock and to self-aggrandize, was becoming a commodified presence that would influenced if not change TV as few other genres had.

That *Real People* created the genre that ultimately unleashed the hounds from 21st century hell -- from *16 and Pregnant* to *Rock of Love with Bret Michaels* -- should not be held against it.

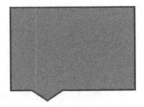

"Oh -- you wear it belted"

-- Mary Campbell, to adult son Jodie,
upon discovering him wearing her dress
Soap

SCARED STRAIGHT
1979 syn
(18)

SCARED STRAIGHT is one of the most innovative and controversial projects to come out of the 1970s.

Directed by then-newcomer Arnold Shapiro, who'd go on to produce the CBS reality show *Rescue 911* a decade later, SCARED STRAIGHT was a big-screen documentary released in 1978. It showcased an innovative outreach program being offered, in which young offenders were taken to a high-security facility -- Rahway Prison in North Jersey -- for extended group talk-sessions with some of its lifer convicts, who told them about the realities of their incarcerated lives. A reality that portends the youths' own if they continued on their errant ways.

Equal parts shock therapy and tough love, SCARED STRAIGHT documented two such lengthy sessions. "The visitors, cocky before arriving, are herded into cells and given a glimpse of what confinement truly means," wrote John J. O'Conner's in his 1979 *New York Times* review.

> They are ridiculed by the prisoners. Finally, taken to a special room and then locked in, they meet the men face to face ... They are told about despair, loneliness, homosexuality, rape, constant struggles for survival. The language is tough, crude, at times brutal. Gradually, the youthful arrogance of the visitors disappears; the smiles begin to fade. They are bullied and threatened. "Take something from my family," one convict warns, "and I'll be waiting for you." Or: "I'll take one eye out and squash it." By session's end, the visitors are sitting in stunned silence. Several have tears in their eyes.

The language is blistering and raw, making full use of the *verite* approach to filmmaking that had become the norm of the 1970s. The project won an Oscar as the year's Best Documentary.

Arnold Shapiro Productions

What makes the project part of the TV revolution, though, is that it actually came to TV a year later, as a one-hour syndicated special in the spring of 1979. And it aired raw and unedited, trimmed only for time, marking not only a first for such a non-fiction piece on commercial television but the first time the words *fuck* and *shit* were heard as well. (Some stations aired the program without commercials.) And another TV levee had been breached.

For good or ill, the prime-time television of *I Love Lucy* and *Happy Days*, the communications innovation introduced as a bit of a reprieve from much of life's ugliness, was now welcoming the ugliness into the home, broadcasting it as an evening entertainment option. The decade was ending with a look that was significantly different than the look it had when it began.

TV's airing of SCARED STRAIGHT also spawned a cottage industry of small-screen sequels and "inspired-by" projects that made going to prison just another prime-time escape.

"Sybil"
November 14-15 1976 NBC
(19)

NBCUniversal / Warner Bros.

Sally Field won scores of acting awards over the course of her long career, including two Academy Awards and three Emmys, for a wealth of performances that showed a range of ability. But if the only job the actress ever had was portraying the title character in the landmark four-hour 1976 movie *Sybil*, she'd likely still be regarded as one of Hollywood's most towering figures.

Broadcast on NBC during a season the network devoted to the increasingly more popular mini-series format, *Sybil* was based on Flora Rheta Schrieber's 1973 best-seller of the same name, which told what it reported to be the true story of a woman with 19 separate personalities, among them a French sophisticate, an infant, and two young boys, in addition to the core personality of Sybil Dorsett (Field). Fellow Oscar-winner Joanne Woodward co-starred as the real-life psychiatrist who took on Sybil as a patient with hopes of healing the young woman's stunning fracture.

The sordid and shocking assault experienced by Sybil and uncovered as the cause of her disorder -- abuse at the hands of a deranged mother -- went on to become a frequent TV-movie trope. But it was a first for 1976: Even in a time of such extraordinary change on TV, to depict the emotional and sexual torture of a child, as *Sybil* did in brief though unsparing detail, was unprecedented.

The two-part film aired with a network advisory, but no caution could mitigate the bleak and harrowing childhood flashbacks connected to Sybil's story, made all the more so given the pronouncements both upon the publication of the book and the airing of the mini-series, that they were all true. (In subsequent decades, the tale of Sybil Dorsett would be revealed as largely, though not entirely, fictional).

Like a handful of other TV movies in the middle years of the 1970s – *Born Innocent, Helter Skelter, Mary Jane Harper Cried Last Night –Sybil,* despite its arrival around the same time that the Family Viewing Hour was causing a re-think about what was appropriate on television, pushed the TV-movie envelope to a tearing point.

Years later, it remains an uncomfortable viewing experience. But it remains an important TV benchmark, as a project that put a spotlight on the oft-hidden social issue of child abuse, and a milestone in the evolution of the TV-movie format, and for Field's revelatory performance as she slips into and out of multiple and distinct "others" throughout a corrosive four hours.

The uninterrupted near-sixteen-minute sequence that marks the film's finale, during which Sybil Dorsett meets and then integrates each of her separate identities into a core single "Sybil" identity (the others are seen on screen as separate selves), offers a masterclass in acting.

The movie, its script, and Field each were awarded Emmy Awards in 1977. *Sybil* was also honored with a 1977 Peabody Award as "a truly outstanding dramatic program," its nominating committee offering this assessment:

> When all the elements of skillful writing, sensitive direction and extraordinary performances are adroitly blended, the result is sheer magic. It is not possible to give credit to all those who brought *Sybil* to completion, but the remarkable performance of Sally Field and the warmth and compassion of Joanne Woodward's characterization made this a film to remember – a work of artistry and intelligence.

NBCUniversal / Warner Bros.

Taxi
1978-82 ABC / 1982-83 NBC
(20)

Ostensibly a star-vehicle for leading-man Judd Hirsch -- a stage star, his name came above the title in the opening credits -- *Taxi* instead became the breakout ensemble hit of the 1978-79 television season, on its way to recognition as one of TV's best-ever ensemble sitcoms.

It became most celebrated, in fact, *because* of that ensemble, brought together by producers James L. Brooks, Stan Daniels, David Davis, and Ed. Weinberger as their first joint venture (called the John Charles Walters company) after leaving the ranks of MTM Enterprises, where each worked on the recently ended *Mary Tyler Moore* and other noted comedies from the esteemed mini-studio.

Paramount

From *The Encyclopedia of Television*:

> To launch their new venture, they looked back to an
> idea that Brooks and Davis had previously considered
> with MTM: the daily life of a New York City taxi

company. From MTM head Grant Tinker they purchased the rights to the newspaper article that had initiated the concept and began producing this new show at Paramount for ABC. They brought a few other MTM veterans along for the ride, including director James Burrows and writer/producers Glen and Les Charles. Although *Taxi* certainly bore many of the trademark signs of 'quality television' as exemplified by MTM, other changes in style and focus distinguished this from an MTM product. After working on the middle-class female-centered worlds of *The Mary Tyler Moore Show, Rhoda*, and *Phyllis* for years, the group at John Charles Walters wanted to create a program focusing on blue-collar male experience.

Taxi was about a group of everymen (and one everywoman) working as drivers for the fictional Sunshine Cab Company in New York City. Sunshine's Manhattan garage provided the primary setting for the show, from which the cabs and their drivers were dispatched and where the group, with Hirsch's character as leader, sat around in between shifts to commiserate about their somewhat-lacking mundane lives.

"While *The Mary Tyler Moore Show* proudly proclaimed that 'you're going to make it on your own,'" notes *TV.com*, "the destitute drivers of *Taxi* were doomed to perpetual failure; the closest any of them came to happiness was [lead character Alex] Reiger's content acceptance of his lot in life--to be a cabby."

Taxi did not court controversy or tackle issues, nor did it push envelopes or rely on story arcs or move mountains in any significant way. It did not traffic so much in specific characters' "journeys" so much as it documented their mostly ordinary lives. *Taxi* just *was*. Funny. Entertaining. Relatable. And well-cast and well-written.

Taxi can actually be seen as TV's first organic sitcom, sprung from things that just *were*, with most of its (especially early) episodes as much about day-to-day life of just loitering in the Sunshine Cab garage as anything else. The characters in the series seemed to have dimension and an existence that belied the cameras trained on them -- those rare TV characters that viewers could imagine going about their lives outside of the half-hour seen each week. Like, in fact, the characters in *Mary Tyler Moore,* those in *Taxi* seem to have lives that unfolded whether we were there to watch or not. Such is how well-drawn and well-realized they were.

Week in and out, *Taxi* was hailed at one of prime-time's best. That came to include three consecutive Emmys as Outstanding Comedy. With success and clout came the confidence to offer more cerebral or experimental storylines, such as one that turns a satirical eye on the TV industry ("Jim Joins the Network") or one that addressed midlife *ennui* ("Vienna Waits") or one into which was threaded a then-still-risky gay storyline ("Elaine's Strange Triangle").

The show's success, as described by The Museum of Broadcast Communications, "was due to its excellent writing, [James] Burrows' award-winning directing using his innovative four-camera technique, and its largely unknown but talented cast."

> Danny DeVito's Louie DePalma soon became one of the most despised men on television--possibly the most unredeemable and worthless louse of a character ever to reside on the small screen. Andy Kaufman's foreign mechanic Latka Gravas provided over-the-top comedy within an ensemble emphasizing subtle character humor ... In the second season Christopher Lloyd's Reverend Jim Ignatowski was added to the group as television's first drugged-out '60s burn-out character. But Lloyd's Emmy-winning performance created in Jim more than just a storehouse of fried brain cells; he established a deep, complex humanity that moved far beyond mere caricature.

Taxi was also a curiosity: After two years in Nielsen's Top 20 and three for which it was named TV's best comedy, ABC cancelled it in 1982. Right after, though, another network – NBC – rescued it, giving it a fifth season, in its same Thursday night timeslot. (HBO apparently bid for the show, as well, in an effort to dive into original-programming waters, but it lost out to NBC.)

After that lone extra season, NBC cancelled it as well, and *Taxi* was permanently garaged. Its producers went on to greater fame with yet another example of what were beginning to be called *workplace ensembles* – this one the mother of them all, *Cheers*, which would last eleven seasons.

"*Taxi* will be best remembered as the ancestral bridge between two of the most successful sitcoms of all time: *The Mary Tyler Moore Show* and *Cheers*" (*tv.com*). Perhaps if it came to air after the success of *Cheers* or even instead of it, it, too, would have had a longer life. *Married … with Children* and *Murphy Brown* and *Friends* each ran twice that length.

Perhaps, too, *Taxi* was either just too good for its day or well ahead of its time, when much of the sitcom universe it orbited in (*Alice*, *Archie Bunker's Place*, *One Day at a Time*, *The Jeffersons*, *Three's Company*, *Too Close for Comfort*, *The Facts of Life*) was fairly conventional and formulaic.

At the time of its cancellation in 1982, ABC certainly was having more success with lighthearted less-demanding TV shows like *Dynasty* and *The Love Boat* and *TJ Hooker*. Still, every single new sitcom it introduced the following 1982-83 season – those than effectively replaced *Taxi* on the network – failed. (**Not-So-Fun-Fact**: This was the year that ABC chose to renew *Joanie Loves Chachi* over *Taxi*.)

But as surely as those who watched *Taxi* know what a yellow traffic-light means, they know that the show stood out as one of the best at a time of bests, a great next step in the 1970s evolution of the sitcom genre that had begun eight years before its premiere (with *Mary Tyler Moore*) -- a premiere assessed this way by *The Hollywood Reporter* in September 1978:

Often as not, it's said the true magical moments on TV occur quite by accident; and often as not, that's true. Which is why a show like *Taxi* is so rare. Not only does it have magic, it is completely under control, making one believe that week after week, we will continue to be treated to ensemble comedy performances at their near best.

WKRP in Cincinnati
1978-82 CBS
(21)

WKRP in Cincinnati sits atop that small mountain of short-lived series almost too good for broadcast TV -- so good that it was likely doomed by it. Wickedly sly. Subversively smart. Expertly cast. Funny as hell. And ultimately ill-managed by caretaker CBS, which scheduled it in twelve different timeslots throughout just four seasons, to the point of cancellation after just 90 episodes at a time when even a semi-decent show could amass twice that.

Gary Sandy starred. He portrayed the new Program Director hired at struggling radio-station WKRP -- that its call letters spelled *crap* was indicative of its standing in the broadcast community -- which has converted to an all-rock format in one last attempt at finding a listening audience, much to the chagrin and confusion of its otherwise always confused station-manager (Gordon Jump).

Another in the valued workplace comedies that had come to populate the prime-time schedule in the 1970s, moving the *sit* of sitcoms from the home to the office, it featured the requisite odd-ball regulars (played by Tim Reid, Frank Bonner, Jan Smithers, Loni Anderson, and Richard Sanders -- new faces, all -- and Howard Hesseman.) But it challenged TV tropes as it incorporated them with oft-dramatic storylines and upended casting conventions. The presumed brainless blonde receptionist at the station was in effect nearly running the place; the buffoonish and clueless newsman tended to have the last laugh; the self-inflating Sales executive masked a savvy that belied the white belt crowning his polyester pants.

If the show stumbled out of the gate both in terms of execution and ratings, almost mortally wounded by that bad CBS scheduling, by early 1979 *WKRP* had found the smoother groove it would operate in throughout its all-too-short run. At heart, it was a comedy about how the radio business in general worked and about how WKRP in particular ran (or how each sometimes didn't). But its scripts were infused with both overt and covert commentary about media and society.

When such topics were still considered novel and/or risky to explore, *WKRP* featured a gay storyline as early as its third episode and a Vietnam-desertion story before the end of its first season. It went on to press radio-business hot-buttons like corporate formatting, listener boycotts, payola, call-in advice shows, and censorship. It took a sizeable swipe at the powerful and ubiquitous and feared (for its day) Moral Majority. And in 1982 it weighed in on current-events headlines with an episode inspired by the Janet Cooke fake-story scandal that had just rocked *The Washington Post*.

In December of 1979, when eleven people were killed and 26 others injured at a real-life Cincinnati concert headlined by The Who – an accident borne of panic and what was then the default use of festival or open seating at the city's Riverfront Coliseum – *WKRP* quickly put together an episode that incorporated the tragedy into a storyline that found station employees wracked with guilt in the days after the concert, due to their part in promoting it on-air.

As the episode approached its airdate soon after, CBS's Cincinnati affiliate threatened to preempt it, claiming it trivialized the tragedy. But according to news reports of the time, the affiliate head changed his mind after he previewed the episode. Called "In Concert," written by staffer Steve Kampmann and directed by Linda Day, it aired on February 11 1980.

From a 2014 DW Dunphy essay in *UltimateClassicRock.com*, titled "How *WKRP in Cincinnati* Covered The Who's Concert Tragedy":

> Neither the details of this horrible incident – nor the history of sitcoms itself – indicated that it would make good TV comedy fodder. ...After all, network situation comedies aren't typically known for tackling controversial current events. There are "very special episodes" that will hit upon a broad topic, but when it comes to focusing on a difficult moment ripped from the headlines, the format understandably often can't handle the balance of comedy and the shock of the real...But *WKRP* broke from that pattern a few months after the Riverfront tragedy, when an episode titled "In Concert"– addressed the deadly stampede head on. ... [I]f the "In Concert" episode stands for nothing else, it at least has the honor of saying this: 35 years ago when things got real, right in the backyard of its fictional setting, *WKRP in Cincinnati* did not flinch.

The episode sealed WKRP's reputation as one of the decade's best "thinking" sitcoms.

A pair of other episodes later in the show's run did much the same, though with different tones: "Real Families" parodied the then-just blossoming reality-television trend, and "Venus and the Man," featured station DJ (and former teacher) Venus Flytrap reaching out to a bored student considering dropping out of high school with a challenge that if the deejay can teach him the basic elements of the atom in a single five-minute lecture the young man will stick with his studies.

The spectacularly written three-minute scene that followed stands out as one of the sitcom's – if not TV's – best. The live audience at the taping applauded when it concluded. (**Spoiler Alert**: Venus succeeds.) Director Rod Daniel was nominated for an Emmy for the episode, and *WKRP* creator High Wilson won the prestigious Humanitas Award for his script.

The most famous of all 90 *WKRP in Cincinnati* episodes, however, is one that features its most quoted line. It was its first-season Thanksgiving episode titled "Turkeys Away." (Incongruously, the episode aired the night before Halloween.)

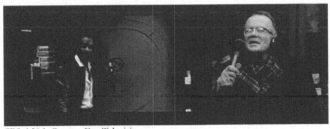

CBS / 20th Century Fox Television

In it, WKRP station manager Arthur Carlson hatches a holiday promotion that leads to live turkeys being dropped from a helicopter over downtown Cincinnati, covered live by earnest old-school station-newsman Les Nessman.

Unaware of the planned stunt, Nessman's melodramatic coverage from below -- "Oh, the humanity!" he screams on-air, as one bird after another is dropped to its death -- only reinforces the macabre incident. It all leads to the classic line delivered back at the station in its aftermath, by WKRP's mortified and misinformed station-manager (which will be repeated by comedy fans for generations every Thanksgiving thereafter):

"As God as my witness, I thought turkeys could fly."

"*WKRP* dealt with many topical issues related to broadcasting-advertiser pressure, inter-office competition, and the all-too-real problem of listeners taking on-air personalities seriously," *televisonheaven.com* relates. "But even with serious subjects, the show never lost its sense of humor."

That the announced last-ever original episode of *WKRP in Cincinnati* was ranked # 7 the week it aired in the spring of 1982, and that during the entirety of the summer rerun season that followed, left to air in the same timeslot each week, *WKRP* consistently ranked in the Top Ten, suggested that the show could have and should have had a longer life if better cared for by its network. Perhaps some of its best episodes were ahead.

CBS / 20th Century Fox Television

WKRP In Cincinnati
(MTM)

CONCEPT:
WKRP, a floundering Cincinnati radio station which plays old-time hits, undergoes a sudden change when Andy Travis is hired as the new Program Director. A likable young man with strong convictions, he updates the station to a rock 'n' roll format despite resistance from Arthur Carlson, WKRP's blustery manager. However, Arthur's mother, who owns the station, backs Andy -- provided he increases profits. Comedic situations arise as Andy strives for improved ratings and acceptance by the station's offbeat employees. With Andy at the helm, laughs and the beat of today's music fill the airwaves from WKRP IN CINCINNATI.

PRODUCER/WRITER:
HUGH WILSON
(The Tony Randall Show)

DIRECTOR:
JAY SANDRICH
(Soap, The Mary Tyler Moore Show, Rhoda, Phyllis)

CAST:
Andy Travis...............................GARY SANDY
Arthur Carlson............................GORDON JUMP
Jennifer Marlowe..........................LONI ANDERSON
Bailey Quarters...........................JAN SMITHERS
Herb Tarlek...............................FRANK BONNER
Les Nessman...............................RICHARD SANDERS
Venus Flytrap.............................TIM REID
Johnny Sunshine...........................HOWARD HESSEMAN

GUEST CAST:
Lillian Carlson...........................SYLVIA SIDNEY

PRODUCTION DATA:
Taped before a live audience at KTLA on March 28, 1978.

From CBS archives: the Development sheet listing WKRP as a potential new 1978 series.

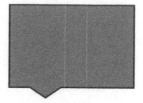

"You come in here with a skull full of mush. And, if you survive, you leave thinking like a lawyer."

-- Professor Charles Kingsfield
The Paper Chase

The White Shadow
1978-81 CBS
(22)

TV's first ensemble drama to feature a mostly black cast, *The White Shadow* was also the first successful drama to come from acclaimed MTM Enterprises, one of the 1970s' premiere suppliers of sitcoms (*Mary Tyler Moore, The Bob Newhart Show, Rhoda, WKRP in Cincinnati*). It stands with ABC's *Room 222* of the 1960s as one of very few TV series in the medium's early history that offered a realistic representation of the high-school experience.

Ken Howard starred, playing an NBA player who in forced retirement takes a job as a basketball coach at an inner-city L.A. high school. There, he so stands out among the multi-ethnic faces on the team that he earns his colorful nickname of the White Shadow. (Reportedly, the concept and title for the series came from Howard's own high-school basketball days, when he was in fact the only white player on its starting line-up, which netted him that same joking nickname.) Episodes revolved around his coaching and the team's playing, but they incorporated the various characters' school and social lives, as well. As well as the day-to-day of the high school itself.

CBS / 20th Century Fox Television

The series emerged seemingly out of nowhere in November of 1978, brought off the bench by CBS early in its new season to fortify an already troubled Monday line-up. It didn't have a big-name star, nor did it tap into any sort of apparent thirst among viewers for school-set or sports-related dramas. (The call that season was for new shows that could cash in on the nation's undying interest in any of four things: STAR WARS, *Charlie's Angels*, one-hour comedies like *The Love Boat*, SATURDAY NIGHT FEVER / GREASE.)

Doing what TV had been doing more of in the 1970s, *The White Shadow* brought the changing world of adolescence to the changing world of prime-time. Topics came to include STDs, homosexuality, racism, substance abuse, and mental and physical disabilities. But in keeping with its studio's trademark, *The White Shadow* also wove threads of humor throughout its stories.

The show was strong; the MTM Enterprises auspices helped; and the drama settled in as a modest hit for CBS for the next three years, with critics responding favorably. Also helping was a roster of then mostly new producer and writers working on the series, each of whom would go on to acclaimed dramas of the 1980s and 1990s, including creator Bruce Paltrow (*St. Elsewhere*), the writing team of Joshua Brand and John Falsey (*St. Elsewhere, A Year in the Life, Northern Exposure, I'll Fly Away, The Americans*), and producers Mark Tinker (*St. Elsewhere, NYPD Blue, Deadwood*) and Scott Brazil (*Hill Street Blues, The Shield*).

Of note is that among the large ensemble cast of actors portraying the students, three -- Kevin Hooks, Timothy Van Patten, and Thomas Carter -- went on to award-winning careers as TV directors.

The White Shadow ended in 1981, leaving behind a respected legacy for work done in front of and behind the camera and for introducing a realistic one-hour high-school drama in a medium still reliant on the stalwart arenas of crime and medicine. When chief architect Bruce Paltrow died in 2008, sports columnist Bill Simmons acknowledged the loss this way:

One of my favorite people died Thursday. Since he affected my life, I thought you needed to know about him…

Back in 1978, Paltrow created my favorite TV show, *The White Shadow*. Created it from scratch. Thought up the characters. Gave them names and histories. Gave them a premise. Wrote the pilot episode. Slapped his imprint on every facet of the show. And it became the only meaningful sports-related TV show of my lifetime.

Like anything else, you had to be there. For instance, when you watch those old *Saturday Night Live* reruns from the 70s, the ones they show on E!, you can't help but think to yourself, 'We *really* thought this stuff was groundbreaking?' Well, it was. You had to be there. They were pushing boundaries, crossing lines, pulling things that no one had ever seen. We were just along for the ride.

The White Shadow was like that, too. Back in the 70s, most African-American characters on TV were relegated to sitcoms, and only under mitigating circumstances…As for dramas, African-Americans appeared mostly as criminals, pimps, drug dealers, and thugs … Then *The White Shadow* came along…It felt like they created [it] just for me…It knocked me over like a ton of bricks. (*espn.com*)

In 2016, *Atlantic* writer Nell Beram wrote this:

I realize it's tedious for you to read a list of the "real-life" subjects that *The White Shadow* tackled in its fifty-four episodes—racism, alcoholism, drugs and overdosing, wrongful incarceration, gang violence, family violence, student violence against teachers, student sex with teachers, teen pregnancy, teen death, STDs, homosexuality, inter-racial dating, autism, and so on—but I must list them in order to make this point: *The White Shadow*, which began its prime-time run on CBS in 1978, usually got there first.

American television has always tried to keep pace with the direction of film, which by the 1970s had given Technicolor romances the kiss-off in favor of gritty realism courtesy of so-called New Hollywood. It was now time for America to see the inner city without punch lines—we had *Welcome Back, Kotter* for those—by way of television's first prime-time drama with a predominantly black cast.

Watching *The White Shadow* today, it's impossible not to think of season four of *The Wire*, which centers on Baltimore's crumbling public schools and a failed white cop's skittish attempt at a new career as a teacher. It's also impossible not to sorrowfully marvel that, nearly forty years on, "White Shadow" doesn't seem dated outside its sneakers and shorty-short gym shorts: we're still talking about what a wreck inner-city schools are, what a blight to the community drugs are, what a tragedy urban violence is.

And nearly forty years on, broadcast television is still waiting for that next realistic high-school drama, especially one with a predominantly minority cast.

"From out there on the moon, international politics looks so petty. You want to grab a politician by the scruff of the neck and drag him a quarter of a million miles out and say, 'Look at that, you son of a bitch.'"

-- *Apollo 14* astronaut Edgar Mitchell
April 8 1974

FEMINISM

"I thank you, MS magazine. You taught me everything I know."

-- Rhoda Morgenstern
Rhoda

Reproductive rights. Gender equality. *Title IX*. Helen Reddy and Loretta Lynn. Kate Millet and Gloria Steinem. The ERA. NOW. The 1970s was a bubbling, often scalding, soup of women's issues, topics, concerns, controversies and challenges. In the home, on the streets, around the corner, across the country -- to be female was to be caught up in a white-water rapids of change. Up and down the TV dial (back when there was such a thing), prime-time was trying to keep pace. Sometimes, it even set it.

Until the 1970s, scripted TV entertainment largely followed a patriarchal familial model. Families consisted of a married working father and housewife mother, with a Protestant level acceptable number of children. The father worked outside the home; the mother, inside. Where she often was seen wearing dresses and heels.

Those few females who did work outside the home worked as support personnel (housekeepers, secretaries) or as part of the caring professions (nurses, teacher). And of these, the single ones, from Eve Arden's *Our Miss Brooks* to *The Brady Bunch*'s Alice Nelson, even to the equal-to-men-ish career gals like Sally Rogers in *The Dick Van Dyke Show* or Ann Marie in *That Girl* or widowed fulltime nurse *Julia* ... either pined for or relied on a man. (Only in the far-off future of *Star Trek*, as envisioned by Gene Roddenberry in the 1960s, were there full-time workers who happened to be women rather than women who worked outside the home.)

Then feminism and the counter-culture and evolution collided, leading to what can only be summed up in the broadest of terms as new thoughts on gender and gender roles. New thoughts that trickled down and on to TV and into prime-time – though there often was speculation about which came first. Did fictional working women Ann Marie and Mary Richards lead to more real-life women taking on careers? Or were they merely reflections of what was already happening in the country? Was *Maude* the cause of more women finding their voices or the result of it?

Long credited with championing the Single Career Women, *Mary Tyler Moore*'s iconic Mary Richards became an icon by default: Originally the character was to be a divorcee, but CBS said no. Still, she was part of an important triumvirate of female characters introduced in the single 1970-71 TV season that were both cause and result, influence and influencer. The faces of feminism for a new decade, if not for the whole movement.

Thirtysomething Mary Richards, who arrived in September, along with twentysomething Gloria Stivic and her fortysomething mother Edith Bunker (both from *All in the Family*, which arrived the following January) collectively represented the evolving female population in the country: the working girl *en route* to career woman, the out-and-proud protest-leading young feminist, and the fulltime homemaker reevaluating both her role and her worth.

Second-wave feminism had come ashore in prime-time.

"The Battle of the Sexes"
September 20 1973 ABC
(23)

How to explain a joke that became history?

In September of 1973, with feminist movement in the United States at full boil, a tennis match between one of the sport's rising female players (Billie Jean King) and one of its male elder statesmen (Bobby Riggs), aired in prime-time. Dubbed the Battle of the Sexes, it became a defining moment not just for athletics but also for an epoch. The Battle was, in fact, part of a war.

A top-ranked tennis player in the 1940s, Bobby Riggs was a self-confessed hustler who had spent much of his post-1950s retirement in the corporate world. But he remained active on the sidelines of tennis, playing in the occasional seniors' tournament. In 1973, in a bid for reinvention or attention (or both), 55-year-old Riggs began to make disparaging public remarks about women in his sport, just as the field was gaining traction and attention of its own. He touted men's superiority to women at the game (if not in life). He openly challenged any of tennis's top women, including Billie Jean King, to a match in order to prove his point in front of the world. King declined.

Top-ranked Margaret Court did not.

On May 13 1973 -- Mother's Day -- Court met Riggs in a match so lopsided that it ended up being referred to as the Mother's Day Massacre. She lost 6-2 6-1. And Riggs beamed, triumphant in what he thought was proof of male dominance in this and all sports.

He taunted King and, by extension, the women's movement in its aftermath. He kept at her with his challenge to meet on the court, until finally, for the good of womankind (and some promotion for women's tennis and women's sports in general, only a few years after the passage of *Title IX*), King accepted Riggs' challenge. A September date was set for a $100,000 winner-take-all showdown, to be held in Houston's Astrodome.

Between the sense of revenge needed after Court's drubbing and Riggs' expertise in self-promotion, not to mention the times it was to be played in and the decision to play it in an arena billed as The Eighth Wonder of the World (when it opened a few years earlier), "the match quickly became a media circus," writes Bruce J. Schulman in his book *The Seventies: The Great Shift in American Culture, Society, and Politics.* "ABC paid the event's promoters more than $700,000 for broadcast rights, and the network collected over $1 million in advertising fees from sponsors, both records for an event of this kind."

The build-up to the meeting was nothing short of a frenzy, escalating from a competitive sports outing to a showdown to a global entertainment event. That it would serve as a referendum on the entire women's movement made it a cultural touchstone, to boot. Astrodome tickets were impossible to find. Home viewing parties were set up.

On match night, Riggs and King each entered the arena gladiator style – carried in to blaring music as a crowd of 30,000 erupted, in appreciation or with blood-lust. (Pick one.) Color commentary from the broadcast booth, especially from master sports-showman Howard Cosell, contributed to the carnival atmosphere. Then the glitter settled, and a tennis match began. Riggs never stood a chance. The 55-year-old proved to be all-show to 29-year-old King's all-business. In front of a viewing audience estimated at a whopping 90 million, King won 6-4, 6-3, 6-3.

Equal parts tennis victory, moral victory, symbolic victory. Gender

EQUAL RIGHTS AMENDMENT

"MEN AND WOMEN SHALL HAVE EQUAL RIGHTS THROUGH-OUT THE UNITED STATES AND EVERY PLACE SUBJECT TO ITS JURISDICTION."

The passage of this Amendment has been found necessary to secure compliance with the provisions of the Constitution guaranteeing equality in all things as well as in voting, most of all equality in the struggle for a living.

So-called "protective" laws do not protect. They are only prohibitive and restrictive. They are not and never can be uniform, universal, or permanent in any degree. Class legislation is unconstitutional, and is contrary to the fundamental principles of Democracy. The Constitution guarantees the inalienable right to life, liberty and the pursuit of happiness, with EQUAL RIGHTS TO ALL AND SPECIAL PRIVILEGES TO NONE, regardless of race, color, creed, sex or station in life.

The passage of the **EQUAL RIGHTS AMENDMENT** would bring about:

(1.) Equal Pay for Equal Work;

(2.) Equal Opportunities in Professions, Industries, Schools and Universities;

(3.) Equal Representation in Government and Equal Citizenship Rights;

(4.) Equal Control of Children, Property and Earnings;

(5.) Equal Right to Make Contracts in All States and Equality before the Law.

The Passage of the Equal Rights Amendment Is a Short Cut to the Inevitable

A symbol of the 1970s, the Equal Rights Amendment actually was introduced in 1923 in the wake of the adoption of the 19th Amendment in 1920.

equality, at least as decried by Riggs and his supporters, was no longer a punchline.

The ABC network won, too, profiting from a highly rated and in-demand sporting event – a primitive early look at and encouraging referendum on the concept of pay-per-view. Plus, along with *Monday Night Football* in 1970 and baseball's World Series in 1971, the Battle of the Sexes demonstrated that live sports on prime-time TV could wrestle up a crowd as large as a sitcom or a drama. As the Olympic Games had been proving as well, athletics could be commodified. As of the Battle of the Sexes, networks didn't have to wait four years at a time to do.

Bobby Riggs made the most of his renewed 1970s celebrity in the aftermath of the match, making TV and personal appearances, publicly acknowledging the errors of his chauvinistic thinking. He consistently swatted down rumors of having thrown the match for financial gain, and he maintained a friendship with Billie Jean King until his death in 1995.

"King's victory marked a watershed in the expansion of women's' athletics in the United States," writes Schulman. "But the Battle of the Sexes dramatized far more than women's achievement in sport. It also signaled the arrival of the women's movement as a broad cultural force."

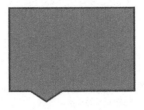

"The hardest decision I have to make each day is whether to play checkers in the park or go down to the Safeway and watch them unload melons."

-- Grandpa Larkin
Mary Hartman, Mary Hartman

Barbara Walters Moves to ABC
October 4 1976 ABC
(24)

> Barbara Walters yesterday accepted an offer of $1 million a year over the next five years to become a major personality of ABC News and the co-anchor, with Harry Reasoner, of *The Evening News*. She will thus become the world's highest-paid newscaster and the first woman ever to present the evening news over a major television network.
>
> -- *The New York Times* April 23 1976

Against the backdrop of what was summed up as the women's liberation movement, the 1970s unfolded with a series of firsts for women, from the first woman to ride in the Kentucky Derby (Diane Crump, 1970) to the first woman ordained as a rabbi in the United States by a rabbinical seminary (Sally Jane Priesand, 1972) to the first female Fortune 500 CEO (Katherine Graham, 1972), first woman fully elected a U.S. governor (Ella Grasso, 1974, Connecticut), first woman to serve as Secretary of HUD (Carla Hills, 1975), and first American female airline captain (Emily Howell Warner, Frontier Airlines, 1976).

On television, the firsts rolled by, as well. Among the most famous (or infamous, depending) was NBC's *Today Show* host Barbara Walters' move in 1976 from the female-focused morning-show "ghetto" to ABC's evening news broadcast -- male turf since the dawn of TV news itself. It was of course a game-changer for female journalists and for the media industry as a whole, given the salary that'd be paid for the new gig and how the figure made its way into the headlines that trumpeted the deal.

"It was not in my nature to be courageous, to be the first," Walters recalls in her 2008 memoir *Audition* (perhaps marking the first-ever use of the term *humble-brag*).

> The money didn't bowl me over. I was already making close to that amount at NBC. It was the historic offer to become the first female co-anchor of a network news program. A woman doing the network news was unheard of and certainly not something I had ever considered. The prestigious position had always been a male bastion, and the prevailing thought was that news about politics, wars, and natural disasters would not be taken seriously if delivered by a woman.

Like all moves and all firsts, Barbara Walters' did not come without complications and heartache. One in particular. Its name was Harry Reasoner.

Harry Reasoner was the sole anchor at the time of the ABC news broadcast. Despite the fact that it consistently placed third to those of CBS and NBC, Reasoner saw no need for any changes to the program nor any reason to share the anchor role with anyone, let alone with a woman. And especially not Barbara Walters. Once the deal was struck (without his say-so or involvement), he saw less of a need to hide

ABC

a displeasure over it that bordered on contempt. So ... he didn't. So much so that by the time Walters officially joined him at the anchor desk six months later for the newly christened *ABC Evening News* – following a summer of hype (over her move) and coverage (of his contempt) -- they resembled, as one critic described it, "a couple set up for an awkward blind date that they guy didn't want to be on."

The new team ended that first broadcast on personal notes of sorts, acknowledging the drum-beating for Walters' historical first: She promised a watchful eye on women's issues; he joked that she had four minutes more airtime during the broadcast. He wasn't entirely joking.

After a huge first-night tune-in that left the CBS and NBC news shows trailing in the ratings, the revamped ABC broadcast settled back into third place. Where it largely stayed. And Walters, according to her memoir, settled into her role as newsroom pariah, viewed as unwanted company among Reasoner and his loyalists.

Bad blood and hostility could be seen and felt off- and on-air, she remembers. Walters writes that at a public function soon after, she was called a "flop" directly to her face by a noted magazine editor. Still, the pair went on co-anchoring, with Walters also hosting prime-time interview specials for ABC, as mandated by her deal with the network. (Highly-rated, the specials simultaneously reinforced ABC's belief in her as a ratings draw and Reasoner's dismissal of Walters as more a personality than news anchor.)

The Reasoner/Walters union lasted about 18 months. In mid-1978, Harry Reasoner opted to leave ABC News to return to longtime home CBS, which he'd left for ABC back in 1970; Walters moved over to ABC's new prime-time news magazine *20/20*. The network's evening news broadcast was then re-invented, yet again, as *World News Tonight*, with a triumvirate of men (Frank Reynolds, Peter Jennings, and first black network-news anchor Max Robinson) deskbound in three different cities.

But the short-lived TV news marriage, coming when it did, was and still is seen as, in Walters' own words in 1976, "a breakthrough for all of us in journalism." The network news ceiling had been breached, and, as was beginning to be the case in print media, too, the lines between what women and men reported on, between that which was considered women's news and men's, were disappearing.

Here's how *The Huffington Post* framed it in 2014, upon Walters' retirement from television in her 80s:

> Barbara Walters, who is retiring after 50 years in television today, has had the kind of career that sends writers to their thesauruses, scrambling around to find another synonym for 'legendary' or 'pioneering' or 'iconic.' The scope of her professional life is nearly impossible to sum up coherently. But let's try.
>
> Television news looks the way it does today in large part because of her. She was one of the first people to so fully fuse journalism and celebrity, often looming larger in her interviews than the people she was talking to. And, most importantly, women are taken seriously on TV because people like her battled their way through a deeply sexist world. Walters was the first, and, because she triumphed, there will never be another like her...
>
> ... While it's uncertain what she'll do with the rest of her life, what is clear is that her career will never be replicated. The media world is too fractured for anyone to hold the spotlight in the way that she did. The audience appetite for in-depth interviews has waned. And the barriers are no longer there to be broken, because she already broke them.

Its headline: "How Barbara Walters Changed Everything."

"I fear this progress is being retarded by a strange and strident voice that professes to speak for all women everywhere. This small band of bra-less bubbleheads."

-- Senator Jennings Randolph (D-WV)
August 26 1970

Charlie's Angels
1976-81 ABC
(25)

ABC / Sony

Movement, schmovement. When it came to the fight for women's rights in the 1970s, one new TV show stood out with the liberation of little more than underwear.

"When the show was Number Three," said *Charlie's Angels* Farrah Fawcett in a 2006 interview with *The Independent*, "I figured it was our acting. When it got to be Number One, I decided it could only be because none of us wears a bra."

Charlie's Angels meant well. It did seem to want to be speaking to a new age -- a movie-turned-series that did seem to be borne of some kind of mandate.

In the early-to-mid 1970s, when nearly 40 percent of the three networks' prime-time schedules were made up of made-for-TV movies, ABC regularly used its own to sample interest in potential new series. Or even to air outright pilots. *Kung-Fu*, *The Love Boat*, and *Starsky & Hutch*, to name a few, all began their series lives as 90-minute ABC movies. *Charlie's Angels*, too -- one of its most popular, about three policewomen (at a time when that itself was a novelty) recruited by a never-to-be seen Beverly Hills millionaire to work for him as private detectives.

Ratings were heavenly when the mindless caper-movie aired in the spring of 1976, and a series version was quickly ordered for the coming season. It in turn became that TV rarity known as a *runaway hit* – a new show that debuts in the Top Ten and never leaves.

Looking back, there seems to be two reasons why the less-than-intellectually demanding *Charlie's Angels* became the phenomenon it did: 1) it was the right TV show at the right time, featuring strong independent women being paid to do what was traditionally a man's work; 2) the three female lead characters rarely wore bras.

As Fawcett herself indicated, this second theory can't be too easily dismissed. After all, in the summer of 1976, as the drums were beating for the new show, hyped during ABC's broadcast of the Montreal Olympics, a revealing swimsuit poster of the actress sold seven million copies, the best-selling poster *ever*. (Some later reports have the figure topping out at 12 million.) It served as the perfect appetizer for the series to come.

Whatever the root cause, the first-season success of *Charlie's Angels* was staggering. Co-stars Fawcett, Kate Jackson, and Jaclyn Smith became the most famous actresses on the planet. That the drama was airing on white-hot ABC just as the network had dethroned longtime Nielsen king CBS to become the country's Number One TV network didn't hurt.

Once titled *Alley Cats, Charlie's Angels* was very much seen as a feminist marker, despite a title that conveyed both ownership and diminutization and "cases" for the fully trained cops-turned-detectives that more often than not found them using their looks to solve the crimes. And despite the fact that the Angels' work often meant going undercover in the fashion business or the beauty-pageant business or the roller-derby business or the day-spa business -- each requiring scenes of minimal wardrobe.

Two steps forward, one step back.

Beyond the obvious visual lure, though, a considerable part of the show's appeal was its simplicity and silliness. Its camp. An Angel rides a skateboard to collar a perp; the Angels go undercover on the stock-car-racing circuit; the Angels investigate poltergeists at a gothic mansion.

In the show's most infamous (and highest-rated) first-year episode -- entitled "Angels in Chains" -- the Angels go undercover at a Southern women's penal farm that happens to front for a local prostitution enterprise. Lesbian prison security, a soft-speaking-yet lethal female warden, prison chain-gangs overseen by sunglass-wearing guards, bloodhounds used to track escapees. One TV critic observed that he didn't think it possible for one lone TV show to incorporate every single trope ever created for women-in-prison stories.

For all the wrong reasons, it's likely one of the most entertaining TV episodes of the entire decade, especially when keeping in mind how co-star Jaclyn Smith defended the series years later. "Critics said that as actresses we were sexually exploited," she said in an interview. "But it was a nursery rhyme."

Farrah Fawcett left *Charlie Angels* after a single season to capitalize on her stratospheric new fame, heading into the movies. (Nothing came of it.) The show weathered this and other defections over the course of four more seasons, never really re-capturing that freshman-year frenzy. It was cancelled in 1981, with Smith the lone original Angel left standing.

The cancellation seemed fair: The show had tired, and it was a new decade when women tackling "a man's job" (especially in law enforcement) was less a novelty to build a series around. (Two weeks after its final episode in June 1981, Sandra Day O'Connor was chosen to be the first female Supreme Court Justice, which seemed to frame the notion of giggling crime-solving "angels" in a new light.)

But the show had left its mark. As was the case with lesser-TV-lights that got there two years ahead of it (*Police Woman* and *Get Christie Love*),

Charlie Angels showed that women could both be cops *in* a TV drama and serves as sole leads *on* a TV drama – both longtime male bastions. It was done. What's next?

(The answer, arriving four months later, is *Cagney & Lacey*, which wasn't ever about what its leads worse. Or didn't wear.)

An early promotional still for Charlie's Angels, *because, well, they were detectives.*

Mary Hartman, Mary Hartman
1976-77 syn
(26)

The achievement that was *Mary Hartman Mary Hartman* is that it aired at all. Only the name behind it — that of Norman Lear, the most powerful man in television at the time it was developed -- got it there. That, and, perhaps, the times itself.

A five-times-a-week soap-opera parody rejected by all three broadcast networks in 1975, *Mary Hartman, Mary Hartman* was sold door-to-door (local- TV-station-to-local-TV-station) instead, on the strength of Lear's name and on a below-budget presentation cobbled together for its innovative concept. A mere 65 of the country's 200-plus TV markets signed on to air it, later at night, but it was enough to get *Mary Hartman, Mary Hartman* launched in January 1976. And overnight, it answered a question that America didn't even know it had asked:

Five years into the revolutionary decade of shocking TV change, what else do you have?

Louise Lasser starred. Then known mostly for sitcom guest appearances and for roles in five early Woody Allen films (the two were married from 1966 to 1970), Lasser portrayed Midwestern middle-aged housewife and mother Mary Hartman. She set the tone for the new series in its very first scene, which showed her standing in the kitchen of her suburban tract-home, mop in hand, admiring the just-cleaned-and-shiny kitchen floor -- and then crestfallen when her visiting younger sister points out that the shine she's so proud of is actually a waxy build-up.

It marks only the latest of Mary's many life disillusions, as it reveals the debate raging in the nation in 1976 between those who saw the shine in society and those who saw the waxy yellow build-up.

Sony

The series' first week alone cast its spotlight on Mary's unhappy marriage, her husband's impotence, a local killing spree (of both people and goats), the revelation that Mary's father is a neighborhood flasher, and a policeman who falls in love with Mary -- all of it orbiting around Mary's kitchen in suburban Fernwood, Ohio, the shining symbol of her disappointment, the hub of her *ennui*, and the intersection of her relationships with her blah blue-collar husband, their bitterly resentful young daughter, her brain-addled parents, and Mary's aspiring country-music-singing best-friend.

And right away -- for thirty minutes a night, five nights a week, watching in the later hours on low-profile local stations – viewers somehow related. And watched. It was a series about nothing in particular but which in its navel-gazing nothingness seemed to be saying everything about the changing status of the American family, if not America itself.

That, plus saying something about how easy it is to drown in a bowl of chicken soup.

Pitched and delivered as a parody of daytime soap-operas, the show, as was becoming more common in the 1970s, worked on multiple layers. "*Mary Hartman Mary Hartman* ... used serialization and a blend of humor and pathos ... to tell its stories of life after the sexual revolution, and it resulted in a TV sex comedy that embraced sexual change instead of denying its significance," notes Elana Levine in *Wallowing in Sex*. "[Its] brand of sex-themed humor was a surprise hit because the show was different from most TV sex comedy, not only in its distribution and its narrative structure, but also in its tone, style, and subject matter ... Lear constructed the show as a commentary on class and gender politics in the era of the sexual revolution, in other words as a newer more radical version of his hit CBS sitcoms."

Mary Hartman, Mary Hartman – the title came from Lear's memory that characters in daytime soap-operas of old tended to call out to one another by saying a name twice -- became one of the three most buzzed-about new shows of the new Bicentennial year, up there with the infinitely more conventional *Laverne & Shirley* and *The Bionic Woman*.

Within two months, Lasser was on the cover of *Rolling Stone*, followed by *Newsweek* ("Mary Hartman: TV's Newest Craze"), *Soap Opera Digest* ("Mary Hartman's Two Men") *TV Guide* ("How 'Mary Hartman' Beat the System"), and, of course, *People*, with the requisite life-in-turmoil angle ("How She Survives Despite a Grueling Show and the Drug Bust").

The melodramatic *People* cover-line was no press fabrication. *Mary Hartman, Mary Hartman*'s five-days-a-week production schedule had very much become grueling by the end of its first frenzied wildly popular *zeitgeist*-tipping season in the summer of 1976. The cliff-hanging season finale was both allegorical and revelatory.

In it, Mary Hartman is invited to be a guest on a nationally popular TV talk-show (hosted by then real-life talk-show host David Susskind) as a representative of "the typical American housewife," but during her appearance she suffers a nervous breakdown. Though Lasser would say years later that she always thought that Mary's breakdown "was America's breakdown," the scene came off so painfully real that it seemed to be documenting a real break from reality for the actress herself.

Lasser did have a drug problem at the time, and amid all the hubbub of the end of the first season in the early summer of 1976 she was arrested for possession. The following month she hosted the season finale of the *other* big-headline hit of the 1975-76 TV season, *NBC's Saturday Night* (not yet titled *Saturday Night Live,*)

The week leading up to the live show was reported to be a rough one for all those involved in the variety show, and Lasser became the first host ever to be banned from returning. The pair of back-to-back dramas found the show with a bit of a black mark to go with its accolades. And even this early on, the speculation was that perhaps *Mary Hartman, Mary Hartman* might fade sooner than most new shows.

But buoyed either by the press and the growing attention of all kinds, *Mary Hartman, Mary Hartman* returned in the fall of 1976 with more stations carrying it -- and with the show's outlandish-meter striking new heights. The second season opened with Mary's post-breakdown hospitalization, during which recovery she's (somehow) invited to be a television Nielsen family, yielding all kinds of *meta* storytelling techniques decades before the term became its own TV sub-genre.

Meanwhile, storylines back home unfolded around Fernwood's popular juvenile televangelist Jimmy Joe Jeter (who'll be accidentally electrocuted in his bathtub when a TV falls into the water), UFOs, stolen plutonium, sex and the Bible, a religious housing development planned for the area called Condos for Christ, spouse-battering and child abuse, as well as the familiar daytime go-tos of amnesia, alcoholism, and suicide. Not to mention Sasquatch, Gore Vidal, and

Merv Griffin. Along the way, perhaps due to her new role as official Nielsen TV watcher, Mary finds her mental health deteriorating. As, it seemed, might have Lasser: She made it as far as the end of Season Two, whereupon she left the show. And inside of two years, Mary Hartman – the person, the series, the social phenomenon – was no more.

For its first (and best) season, *Mary Hartman, Mary Hartman* was nominated for three Emmys -- for Lasser, for the writers, and for the show itself. Odd fish that it was, though – a five-times-a-week syndicated satire that ran off-network and outside of prime-time – each of the three nominations came under the category of Special Classification. No matter: Writers Ann Marcus, Jerry Adelman, and Daniel Gregory Browne won Emmys for the show's bold pilot. (Co-star Mary Kay Place, who played Mary's best-friend singer Loretta Hagars, went on to score a real hit single called "Baby Boy" and an album that ended up nominated for a Grammy.)

Decades after its brief run, *Mary Hartman, Mary Hartman* still makes many TV Best-of and Cult Favorite lists. The chicken-soup-drowning episode that aired early on is still hailed as one of TV's funniest (half-) hours. And Louise Lasser's on-air breakdown is remembered by critics as a landmark performance.

The show made history during a history-making decade. Few then or since have been able to weave together so deftly, and with such subversion, such singular threads as impotence and infidelity and teenaged rebellion and senior dementia into such a bolt of existentialism. *Mary Hartman, Mary Hartman* was likely TV's first dramatic sitcom.

Its contribution to the 1970s revolution involved more than just what it showed, however, but also how it showed it. At a time when women were rarely front nor center in the behind-the-scenes TV ranks, *Mary Hartman, Mary Hartman* was a series created by two women (Ann Marcus and Gail Parent), often directed by a woman (Joan Darling), and which featured five women (Peggy Goldman, Lynn Phillips,

Cynthia Santillo, Mara Lideks, Eugenie Ross-Leming) as part of its sizable writing staff. *Mary Hartman, Mary Hartman* blazed trails both on- and off-screen.

(**Fun Fact**: Co-star Mary Kay Place, who won an Emmy as Best Supporting Actress for *Mary Hartman, Mary Hartman's* second and final season, was previously nominated for an Emmy as a writer: She and future TV showrunner Linda Bloodworth-Thomason were nominated for writing the 1974 episode of M*A*S*H* called "Hot Lips and Open Arms.")

Time Inc.

Mary Tyler Moore
1970-77 CBS
(27)

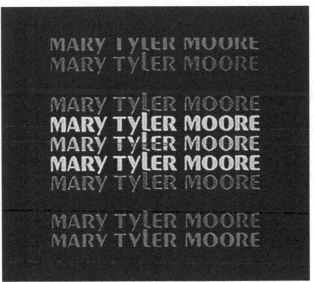

CBS / 20th Century Fox Television

For decades after it left the air in 1977, on various anniversaries of its premiere or upon the death of one of its cast, and especially in the many tributes that accompanied its star's death in January of 2017, *Mary Tyler Moore* was championed as the TV show that brought the liberation movement into American living-rooms. Which it kinda did. But it wasn't by design.

Feminism is not what got the show on the air in 1970. While certainly part of the culture and conversation at the time, the movement was not what *Mary Tyler Moore* was created to service or to tap into. It was created to showcase Mary Tyler Moore, who, four years after the end of *The Dick Van Dyke Show*, the popular sitcom on which she'd co-starred from 1961 to 1966, CBS wanted back on its schedule. Buoyed by the ratings for a 1969 special that reunited her with her onetime co-star called "Dick Van Dyke and the Other Woman", the network offered Moore her own series, to start in the fall of 1970.

Famously, early on in the show's development CBS nixed plans to have the actress's new Mary Richards character be a divorcee, which actually would have been much more with the times and would have made that social statement. In a 2017 essay in *The Hollywood Reporter*, co-creator Allan Burns, who wrote the pilot script with James L. Brooks, explained what happened:

> It's hard to believe, but in 1970 that was a controversial idea. Mary loved the idea, [MTM head] Grant [Tinker] loved the idea. Both of them were divorced and understood it, but the network had a sort of cardiac episode. We were summoned to New York, to the office of Mike Dann, who was then the head of programming for CBS. He was a long-termer, the entity you had to go to, hard-nosed. He did not like what we had proposed and in fact called upon a research guy who was in the meeting with us.

> They were really ready for the two of us, and we were relatively inexperienced. We thought we were ready for their objections to divorce, because we said everybody is touched by divorce and it gives us an awful lot of possibilities story-wise. They clearly were not happy. We had gone to New York accompanied by Arthur Price, who was Mary's manager and the vice president of MTM, and when the meeting was over, and Jim and I were dismissed, [Dann] turned to Arthur and said, "Tell Grant to get rid of these clowns."

> We said, "OK, if they won't do divorce, what can we do that would explain an attractive 30-year-old woman without a relationship?" We came up with the notion that this woman is coming off a long-term relationship with a guy at the Mayo Clinic. They were somewhat

satisfied; as long as they had gotten rid of the divorce idea, maybe they would tolerate us a little longer. And that's what the first show was really about: a woman having to give up her small-town life in Rochester, Minn. The main title sets up the whole thing.

So...Mary Richards was single, not divorced, on her own for the first time in a new city. As such, she'd need a job. She applied for one as a secretary. Not much about it was revolutionary. Marlo Thomas had been portraying a single working female since 1966 on her own sitcom on ABC, called *That Girl*. What tipped the scale, however, was that in her interview for that secretarial job Mary Richards was instead offered -- or comically backed into -- a position as associate producer.

So whereas around the TV dial Marlo Thomas's character was a struggling actress who ended up relying on her father and boyfriend day to day and the female lead of the *Julia* sitcom was nurse and the women in *Room 222* were teachers and *Here's Lucy* Lucille Carter was a secretary -- Mary Richards arrived on the air in 1970 as management. On top of that, her new life in her new city also came to involve a new best friend (Rhoda Morgenstern) who herself was a single career-woman, and neither of their lives necessarily revolved around men.

And a new image for women had indeed arrived: single, alone, working, content.

CBS / 20th Century Fox Television

Speaking to and *de facto* symbolic of a feminist movement, yes. But not necessarily the cause of one. Even star Mary Tyler Moore would spending the rest of her career somewhat downplaying the Mary Richards characters as feminist flag-waver. *Mary Tyler Moore* did, however, directly change TV.

It did so with a combination of three factors. The first is that while it was built around a single star, it featured a company of equals who starred with her. (The ensemble approach became an MTM Enterprises hallmark.) The second is that it marked the beginning of a new-ish kind of sitcom that would offer more *com* that *sit* in its weekly formula, its laughs mined from characters with ongoing lives and stories rather than from a situation or a complication of the week.

And the third is that *Mary Tyler Moore* wasn't about Mary Richards' job or new apartment or being single but rather about Mary Richards as a person. There seemed a difference. (Plus, as *All in the Family* would do starting a few months later, *Mary Tyler Moore* made multi-camera comedies, those shot in front of and for a live studio audience, popular again. Of the more than two dozen sitcoms on the air in the 1969-70 TV season, just three were filmed in front of an audience. By 1975, the number had grown to more than 20.)

Mary Tyler Moore had a well-documented rocky development in the months leading up to its debut on September 19 1970. And it actually received some only lukewarm reviews for both its pilot and first few episodes. But it gradually became one of the most acclaimed and respected comedies of the 1970-71 season.

Its cast – Lou (Edward Asner) and Murray (Gavin MacLeod) and Ted (Ted Knight) as Mary's newsroom colleagues and Rhoda (Valerie Harper) and Phyllis (Cloris Leachman) as her off-hours girlfriends – was matched by a writing and production staff that either in experience or vision came to represent a new kind of TV, writing stories about characters rather than writing a sitcom. (Georgia Engel joined the cast in 1972; Betty White, in 1973.) It lasted seven seasons and 168 episodes, setting Emmy Award records with a total of 67 nominations during its run and an unheard-of 29 total wins.

It won in the Best Supporting Actress category for six straight years (among Harper, Leachman, White), five times in the Best Supporting Actor category (three for Asner and two for Knight) and picked up Emmys for writing-of-the-year five times out of seven seasons. Mary Tyler Moore herself won four Emmys for the series, which was named Outstanding Comedy three years in a row (1975-77).

It also holds claim to what *The New York Times* called the funniest half-hour in television history -- the October 1975 episode called "Chuckles Bites the Dust," written by David Lloyd, about the accidental death of the station clown and the laughs had at his expense both after it's announced and then during his funeral.

Mary Tyler Moore and *Mary Tyler Moore* did come to imbue Mary Richards with a sense of the female empowerment that women were looking for and more frequently finding in real life. In large part this came as a result of what was happening backstage at the show, where its real revolution was playing out, as Hope Reese noted in her 2013 *Atlantic* essay "The Real Feminist Impact of *The Mary Tyler Moore Show* Was Behind the Scenes," in which she discusses Jennifer Keisha Armstrong's then-just-released book *Mary and Lou and Rhoda and Ted: And All the Brilliant Minds Who Made* The Mary Tyler Moore Show *a Classic.*

> [I]t was the women behind the scenes, Armstrong argues, who were role models for women who wanted to start a career. It was the first time in television history when a woman's perspective was not only highly regarded, but crucial to the success of the show *The Mary Tyler Moore Show*, which Armstrong calls "TV's first truly female-dominated sitcom" ...

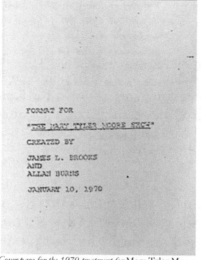

Cover page for the 1970 treatment for Mary Tyler Moore.

In its seven seasons, the show was directed four times by women, including Joan Darling (Emmy-nominated for the darkly comedic "Chuckles Bites the Dust," which reportedly its go-to male directors refused to helm, given its material) and many of its more significant episodes were written by women, among them Marilyn Suzanne Miller, who'd go on to win multiple Emmys for writing *Saturday Night Live* and *The Tracey Ullman Show*, and Treva Silverman, who won an Emmy as Writer of the Year in 1974 (a since-discontinued Emmy category) for "The Lou and Edie Story," an episode that marked the first time a divorce played out in a prime-time sitcom. (Silverman's win also marked the first time in Emmy history that a woman won a writing Emmy on her own rather than as part of a writing team.)

The women's movement was never the point of *Mary Tyler Moore*, but it ended up being a strong party to and beneficiary of it. The show help to change women's lives in its depiction of a successful independent woman, and it changed prime-time, too, in soft-stroke ways rather than through controversy, using its Everyperson Best Friend / Girl Next Door formula to introduce themes from extramarital sex and divorce to homosexuality and religion. Again, Reese:

America was in the middle of the women's rights movement; *The Feminine Mystique*, released in 1963, urged women to envision work outside the home, touching a nerve for housewives. The Pill became available to all women, regardless of marital status, in 1972. And more and more women were earning degrees and setting off to find jobs. Still, workplaces were dominated by men.

So, when Mary Tyler Moore's character Mary Richards, single and 30, moved to Minneapolis and started working as associate producer at the WJM-TV, she did something that no female character on television had done before. (*theatlantic.com*)

Not insignificantly, *Mary Tyler Moore* left a comedy legacy, as well. When Emmy-winning Lloyd (of "Chuckles Bites the Dust" fame) died in 2009, Mark Harris noted the loss in *Entertainment Weekly* in a way the not many comedies in TV history have earned, saying of Lloyd: "His DNA survives in almost every contemporary sitcom...but also in the instincts of every comedy writer who pushes the envelope not for shock value but for honesty."

(**Fun Fact**: Though it borders on besmirching a sainted figure, it should be pointed out that, as was slyly revealed in the 1972 episode entitled "You've Got a Friend," good-girl single career woman Mary Richards was ... on the Pill.)

Maude
"Maude's Dilemma"
November 14 and 21 1972 CBS
(28)

Condemned by the United States Catholic Conference to the extent
that church sermons across the country the week it aired instructed
congregants not to watch, "Maude's Dilemma" upped the ante in the
poker-game of shock-and-awe that was 1970s TV. The rule-bending
convention-shattering *All in the Family*, which had premiered just 20
months earlier and from which the new comedy was spun, paled in
comparison. "Maude's Dilemma" took on the most inflammatory
domestic issue in the United States – abortion.

The two-part episode aired a full two months before the landmark *Roe
v. Wade* Supreme Court decision was handed down in January 1973,
granting women reproductive rights and further dividing the nation.
More boldly, the Norman Lear-produced show tackled the topic in just
its tenth episode – unheard of even by latter-day standards for a brand-
new series.

TV Guide   Sony

It focused on what happens when the outspoken tough-talking four-times-married women's-liberation supporter Maude Findley (Bea Arthur) unexpectedly finds herself, at 47, pregnant, and, after careful consideration, opts to have an abortion. The first half aired on November 14 1972, 34 days after re-arguments began in *Roe*. *Maude* producer Rod Parker, in a 1992 *Chicago Tribune* article marking the episode's 20th anniversary, recalled the irony that initially producers hadn't even considered the idea of an abortion for the show.

"The group Zero Population Growth announced they were giving a $10,000 prize for comedies that had something to do with controlling population," he said, "so everyone came in [to the *Maude* writers' room] with ideas for vasectomies." Given the central character, though, as well as the fact that the show was a by-product of a real-life social tumult, it was determined that an expected pregnancy for Maude would be more with keeping with the times.

"As you would expect," writes executive producer Norman Lear in his 2014 memoir *Even This I Get To Experience*, "[CBS] Program Practices fought our touching the subject ... [but its] initial 'no way' turned into a 'go ahead' when I [said] we would write in a good friend who had four kids, was pregnant with a fifth that she could not afford emotionally or economically, yet for whom an abortion was out of the question – and who didn't understand how Maude could see it any other way."

If CBS acquiesced, many in the country did not: The episode met with fierce protests and complaints. But the controversy fueled awareness of and curiosity for the already highly rated series. Each part of the two-part "Maude's Dilemma" ranked in the week's Top Ten.

(**Fun Fact**: Part One of the abortion episodes aired against the much more easily digested *Bonanza* on NBC. Make of it whatever you will that the western that night was about what happens when Little Joe is given a beautiful black stallion for his birthday but ends up having to sacrifice it.)

131

Remembers Lear:

> Two Illinois affiliates, in Champagne and Peoria, refused to air the shows – the first time any CBS station had rejected any episode of a continuing series. Things escalated considerably when [the abortion] episodes were due to be rerun in August. The expanding Religious Right, energized by the Supreme Court's *Roe v. Wade* decision, went to town. Zealots across the country made thousands of phone calls; seventeen thousand similarly worded letters of protest were received by CBS; hundreds in the South and Midwest picketed their local TV stations; and in New York City protestors lay down in front of William Paley's car as the chairman of CBS was driving into his network's garage. Thirty-nine affiliates declined to air the reruns, and, most telling of all, not one corporate sponsor bought commercial time on those broadcasts.

25 C.B.S. Affiliates Won't Show 'Maude' Episodes on Abortion

By ALBIN KREBS   AUG. 14, 1973

Lost in some of the legacy that is "Maude's Dilemma" is that the two-part installment was written by a game-changer herself, Susan Harris, who played no small part in the entirety of 1970s prime-time revolution.

Having broken in as a TV writer during the male-dominated 1960s on light-hearted series like *The Courtship of Eddie's Father*, *Love American Style*, and *The Partridge Family* (one of the producers of which, Paul Junger Witt, would later become both her business partner and husband), she graduated to more realistic fare with scripts for *All in the Family* before being hired for spin-off *Maude*. She went on to create *Soap* (1977) and *The Golden Girls* (1985). Oddly, her script for "Maude's

132

Dilemma" was passed over for 1973 Emmy recognition, perhaps in part because of its hot-potato status. Also a bit unsung: "Maude's Dilemma" director Bill Hobin, who was nonetheless nominated for the prestigious DGA Award (losing to Gene Reynolds for the *M*A*S*H** pilot).

Years removed from its original airing, the episode would likely still divide, as the issue of abortion continues to do. Which is both understandable and too bad. Much can be learned from "Maude's Dilemma."

The issue it explores is carefully and sensitively handled, and the associated controversy is succinctly addressed in its final scene, between Maude and husband Walter, behind the closed door of their bedroom. It bespeaks what came to be the Supreme Court's decision in January 1973. And it makes one of the most powerfully written episodes of TV in the 1970s just as powerful in the 21st century.

> **Maude**: "Just tell me, Walter, that I'm doing the right thing, not having the baby."

> **Walter:** "For you, Maude. For me. In the privacy of our own lives, you're doing the right thing."

Time Inc.

"We have forgotten how to be good guests, how to walk lightly on the earth as its other creatures do."

-- Barbara Ward
Only One Earth: The Care and Maintenance of a Small Planet 1972

One Day at a Time
1975-84 CBS
(29)

By way of writer Melissa Camacho in the "What Parents Need to Know" column of *CommonSenseMedia.org*, a present-day look back at a seminal 1970s sitcom, forty years on:

> Parents need to know that *One Day at a Time* (1975–1984) is a comedy that addresses the issues that were contemporary in its time, mainly relating to women and female adolescence. It's milder than some of today's TV sitcoms, but it's still a bit strong for younger viewers thanks to some mature themes including divorce, sex, virginity, birth control, drug use, and suicide, just to name a few. Whole-family watching can definitely open up doors for communicating about some of these issues with tweens and teens.

One Day at a Time was one of two new series to arrive at the start of the 1975-76 TV season about the trending concept of a newly divorced woman. Both it and *Fay* were heralded for that reason. Alas, only *One Day at a Time* made it all the way through the season: *Fay*, which actually made it to air first, was cancelled by NBC after just three episodes. That the former came with Norman Lear's name affixed meant interest and tune-in were all but guaranteed.

Sony

135

Bonnie Franklin headed the cast as Ann Romano, newly single mother of two teenaged daughters (Mackenzie Phillips and Valerie Bertinelli), each of whom represented a different shade of acceptance of parents who divorce. (Phillips as older daughter Julie was angry and defiant; Bertinelli as younger Barbara was people-pleasing and naive). The pilot found the trio moving to a new town, post-split, blazing new and (for Ann, anyway) independent paths.

Early episodes revolved around Ann Romano's new roles – as a single parent, as a 17-years-married woman trying to get her first real job at age 34, as someone re-entering the dating scene for the first time since high school. The show seemed to speak to viewers.

Helped by a cushy timeslot following *M*A*S*H*, One Day A Time* became a breakout hit for CBS. And with success came ambition and desire that the series do and be about more. (Reportedly, star Bonnie Franklin became unhappy with the show after the first season, insisting upon more creative input.)

The second season opened with a strong and near-unprecedented four-part story, in which elder daughter Julie runs away to live with a boyfriend -- no forwarding information provided. It comes to a head with a tough-love showdown when the teen is finally tracked down and then tells her mother that she'll return home only if certain conditions are met that allow for her independence. "Okay, Julie," says Ann, weighing the offer. "Don't come home."

Because it was a Norman Lear show, *One Day at a Time* did indeed come to explore all the requisite 1970s issues of sexual expression and gender disparity and teen angst -- including suicide, drugs, cults, and unplanned pregnancy -- each of which was woven into an otherwise conventionally comedic domestic (and eventually workplace) sitcom. *Social realism*, it was called. Ann Romano's divorce-lawyer-boyfriend and her ex-husband, regular characters on the show when it premiered, were eventually phased out, the series having secured a weekly berth in the Top Ten with just its three core female players making their ways in the world, alone together, aided and sometimes irritated by the comic-relief superintendent of their apartment building (Pat Harrington, Jr., who won an Emmy for the role).

Future seasons tackled Ann's growing career and social circle and the post-school lives of the young daughters. Each of the three developed multiple romances, and each married at some point throughout the show's long run. Ann Romano, in fact, ultimately re-married twice, in what seemed to be an effort to mine new storylines for a show who original *raison d'être* had faded in the early 1980s.

One Day at A Time ended in 1984 a markedly different sitcom that the one it began as nearly a decade earlier. After 209 episodes, it was much more conventionally sitcom-y than revolutionary. The concept of a TV show predicated on a divorced single parent had long since lost its novelty. Its protagonist had become just another working woman, her children grown and out of the house.

But the show had made its mark, leaving the air that summer as a TV series that that had put its stamp on a decade that was about, among other things, the rise of female empowerment. It was both cause and effect of the women's liberation movement, in fact, having been developed originally in the 1960s by actress and single-mother Whitney Blake, about her own life trying to raise a daughter in a turbulent decade. (The real-life daughter was actress Meredith Baxter, who'd go on to star in *Family* and *Family Ties*). For whatever reasons, the idea reportedly languished until Norman Lear's company bought it in 1974 and developed it as *One Day At a Time*.

In some ways one of TV's first 'dramedys,' … "*One Day at a Time* [did not] shy away from difficult themes, its warts and all portrayal of contemporary life, especially of women's lives," as celebrated by The Museum of Broadcast Television. "The series helped expand the dimensions and role of U.S. television comedy."

HELLO, ANN!

(T.A.T. Communication Co.)

CONCEPT: Ann, a free-lance nurse, has been married for 17 of
                   her 34 years and has recently awakened to the fact that
                   there must be more to life than a three bedroom home.
                   She is fond of her husband, who loves her, but she must
                   find out who she is. In the series, she has separated
                   from her husband and has left the small town of Clinton,
                   Indiana to move to an apartment in Indianapolis. Her
                   15-year-old daughter soon joins her. Now there are two
                   females, both on the verge of discovery and womanhood.
                   The husband remains in the picture from time to time,
                   but, in the main, it is the story of mother and daughter
                   growing up together. Ann's upstairs neighbor, Gail, is
                   the editor of the Clinton Police Department's house
                   organ. The women's lives are complicated by the amorous
                   building superintendent.

EXECUTIVE PRODUCER: NORMAN LEAR
                      (All In The Family, Maude, The Jeffersons, Good Times)

PRODUCER: ALLAN MANINGS
                   (Good Times)

DIRECTOR: JOAN DARLING
                   JIM DRAKE
                   (Love Of Life, Calucci's Department, Candid
                   Camera)

WRITERS: NORMAN LEAR
                   (All In The Family)
                   ALLAN MANINGS
                   (Lily Tomlin Special)

SCRIPT CONSULTANTS: DON NICHOLL, MICHAEL ROSS, BERNIE WEST
                      (All In The Family)

CAST: Ann Benton.................. BONNIE FRANKLIN
                   Julie Benton................ MACKENZIE PHILLIPS
                   Gail........................ MARCIA RODD
                   Superintendent.............. GABE DELL

From CBS archives: An entry in the 1975 Development Report, first version of One Day at a Time, when it had a different title, a best friend for its lead -- and no sign of a second daughter.

Rhoda
"Rhoda's Wedding"
October 28 1974 CBS
(30)

It was a national cultural happening that ended up a costly creative mistake. So much so that nearly 20 years after it happened an episode of *Murphy Brown* referenced it in a scene between TV journalist Murphy and colleague Jim Dial, when she confesses to him her secret pregnancy and her plans to keep and raise the baby alone.

"Oh, good Lord!" exclaims the often-histrionic Dial. "This could be the worst decision anyone's made in television since Rhoda's wedding."

But it really was a national cultural happening.

For four years beginning in 1970, the TV character known as Rhoda Morgenstern had been the wise-cracking tough-talking perennially self-deprecating overweight under-wed upstairs neighbor to Mary Richards on *Mary Tyler Moore*. As played by Valerie Harper, Rhoda had become Mary's -- and then in many ways viewers' -- best friend and confidante.

She'd all but stolen most of her scenes opposite the more together Mary Richards, with an earthy and practical and relatable toughness and messiness that (naturally) masked deep insecurity. In doing so, Harper had won three Emmys for the role. A spin-off series for her character, less commonplace in the day than it would become, seemed inevitable. And it came to pass amid great fanfare in 1974.

Rhoda found New York native Rhoda Morgenstern back home in Manhattan, making a new life nearby to her sister and parents -- and as of the eighth episode with a husband. (She'd met Joe Gerard in the premiere episode.) Which is where the show went wrong before it really had a chance to begin: While it premiered to high hopes and higher ratings, finishing its first season as a freshman hit with ratings

20th Century Fox Television

higher than parent-show *Mary Tyler Moore*, interest and ratings started to wane in Season Two as Rhoda herself settled in as a bit of ... a bore.

As it turned out, viewers liked the overweight single underdog Rhoda Morgenstern more than a slimmed-down happily married Mrs. Gerard. The show's jokes started going more towards supporting characters, who had more threads to pull. In Season Three, Joe and Rhoda separated, and they were divorced within a year. *Rhoda* limped along from there, ending with a bit of a whimper during an abbreviated fifth season. It marked the end of a once-promising show and popular TV character.

But what a bang of a beginning, leading to that cultural happening.

After those four years as an always unlucky bridesmaid, Rhoda Morgenstern arrived in *Rhoda* as a confident champ whose time had come. She'd spent her 20s as an educated and independent career woman, living and (mostly) enjoying life on her own.

Now in her 30s, with the admiration of millions, she'd found and grabbed the brass ring of romance, on her own terms and in her own way. In 1974, at the height of a movement that championed female independence and equality, Rhoda Morgenstern had come to define it. It was even she who approached future husband Joe for a first date, and then it was she, in *Rhoda*'s sixth episode, who proposed marriage. (Jim Dial would likely see these twin facts as red flags.) So the marriage,

Rhoda's ultimate triumph, was to be nothing less than a TV event, not only for longtime fans of the character but also for women in general.

That *Rhoda* premiered at Number One on September 9 -- a first for a new show -- created a huge TV snowball that moved rapidly downhill as the opener led to an introduction that led to a courtship and then engagement. By the time of the October 28 wedding, the TV world was dressed and ready. CBS's planned nuptials was the place to be that night. ("Let's go over to Rhoda's wedding quick," said *Monday Night Football* commentator Howard Cosell at the start of that night's Steelers-Falcons game on rival ABC, acknowledging the elephant in the room. "The chicken liver is getting rancid.")

20th Century Fox Television

The one-hour episode set a new standard for TV publicity, not to mention sitcom length. (Many half-hour comedies dating back to *I Love Lucy* had multi-part episodes that aired over separate weeks, but few if any had ever been given a full hour of prime-time for a single episode.) A must-see event, it spawned at-home wedding-parties and, in a pre-delayed-viewing era, led to viewers' plans rearranged or cancelled to accommodate their being there.

Some reports were that people away from their homes for whatever reasons scrambled to find the nearest TV at 9pm so that they could watch the event with the rest of nation. (CBS even reported that during the week leading up to the wedding gifts were sent by viewers to the soundstage where the series was shot.)

The episode, which included most all the *Mary Tyler Moore* cast members as guests at the wedding, was equal parts funny and poignant, drawing on many familiar TV-wedding tropes -- the best-friend-sidekick as maid-of-honor, the last-minute mix-up, the delayed start to the ceremony, the hyper-stressed mother-of-the-bride, the self-written vows.

In the end it set a viewing record of more than 50 million people – the highest-rated sitcom episode since the birth of Little Ricky on *I Love Lucy* in 1953 and the highest-rated episode of any TV show in the 1970s until *Roots* aired in 1977.

20th Century Fox Television

Viewers did stay with the show (and the marriage) through the highly rated season, as the snowball kept rolling (the honeymoon, the search for a place to live, the talk of having children). It culminated with Harper winning a fourth Emmy Award, this time as Lead Actress in a Comedy, edging out competitor Mary Tyler Moore. But then the freshman-year frenzy died down and viewer interest began to fizzle. The writing soon appeared on the wall that the marriage was a mistake.

But the happening that was "Rhoda's Wedding" in 1974 was a TV phenomenon. An unusual referendum on the growing women's movement, it was also a statement about the power of TV, the power of women on TV, the power of women who watch TV.

Even if Jim Dial ended up being right, *Rhoda* still has that.

"Politics has gone from the age of Camelot when all things are possible to the age of Watergate when all things are suspect."

-- U.S. Representative William Hungate (D-MO)
1975

INDIVIDUALISM

"How come we overcame and nobody told me?"

-- Florence Johnston
The Jeffersons

It started out as a TV jingle for a soft-drink and became an anthem of co-existence.

"I'd Like to Buy the World a Coke" was borne of an off-the-cuff idea conceived by an executive at Coca Cola's advertising agency in the late 1960s and then shared with some British songwriters. The Brits then took the idea, turned to a previously recorded melody they had and adapted it to fit new lyrics that incorporated the executive's idea and, most important, Coca-Cola's new slogan -- "It's the real thing." An ad-campaign was born.

The TV commercial that followed – a location-shoot that at $250,000 became the most expensive in advertising history -- secured a legacy. It showed close-ups of dozens of young faces, reflecting various ethnicities from around the globe, Coca-Cola bottles in hand, singing a song that began with the lyrics "I'd like to teach the world to sing, in perfect harmony." The minute-long spot concluded with a sweeping helicopter shot of the assemblage and an on-screen message:

> On a hilltop in Italy,
> We assembled young people
> From all over the world...
> To bring you this message
> From Coca-Cola Bottlers
> All over the world.
> It's the real thing. Coke.

It became the most popular commercial in the country. So much so that that its song was released as a radio single (minus the brand reference), first by a studio-assembled group christened The Hillside Singers and then by a popular British group known as The New Seekers. Both versions became massive hits on the 1972 charts, with the latter eventually selling 12 million copies.

Added to a musical landscape that already featured "Everyday People" in 1968 and Cat Stevens' "Peace Train" (which charted during the same 1971 fall), "I'd Like to Teach the World to Sing" tapped into a seismic cultural shift: Society was changing and its population was diversifying, with young faces leading the charge. As people we were one, and we were also individuals.

Black Power, Asian Power, post-Stonewall gay rights would soon be joined by post-Wounded Knee Native-American rights, by Italian-Americans and Irish-Americans and Polish-Americans celebrating and affirming and defending their own individual identities, even by older Americans, led and energized by a new hero named Maggie Kuhn, founder of the Gray Panthers.

The long-held belief of the United States being a melting pot was being exposed as more concept than reality. There was not much melting going on in the 1970s.

On television, the black-and-white images of the 1950s and 1960s were being replaced by those in full color – slowly and incrementally but certainly. (Gene Roddenbery's *Star Trek* envisioned such a daring future as far back as 1966, with various ethnicities and both genders working as equals in leadership roles.)

If Asians were still bowing servants, they were becoming more integral to lives of those they served, along the lines of Mrs. Livingston (on *The Courtship of Eddie's Father*), or more respected along the lines of Kwai Chang Caine (in *Kung Fu*), rather than relegated to the comic relief they'd long been, along the lines of *Bonanza*'s Hop Sing.

If women were still subservient in the workplace, reporting to men, they were at least being seen in management (*Mary Tyler Moore*) and authority roles (*Police Woman*, *Get Christie Love!*) as much as they were seen in the caring professions of nurse and teacher (*Julia*, *Room 222*). Moreover, if they were "still" single in their 30s, the lifestyle represented less a problem to be solved (Sally Rogers in *The Dick Van Dyke Show*) than an opportunity to be appreciated (Carol Traynor of *Maude*, Willona Woods of *Good Times*).

African-Americans were still largely relegated to comedic and supporting roles, but at least they were no longer exclusively roles as domestics or support personnel. They now ranged from business owners (*Sanford and Son*) to college students (Lionel Jefferson of *The Jeffersons*) to police officers (*The Mod Squad*, *The Rookies*).

As for gays and lesbians, the last bastion of 1970s isolation? Most were still Central Casting stereotypes, with both the individuals and their presumed lives still used as punchlines. But there was at least some presence where there once was none. There was acknowledgement and awareness where there once was secrets and shadows. And landmark stories were just around the corner. For them and other minorities.

This was TV in the 1970s: An attempt to acknowledge if not celebrate the reality that the population of the country was made up of many different kinds of people -- many of whom watched TV. There were increasingly more attempts to move away from the default prime-time presentation of nuclear middle-class suburb-dwelling white families. Radio was singing it, newspapers were reporting it, the evening news was broadcasting it, and advertisers were drinking it up.

It was, after all, the real thing.

"The Autobiography of Miss Jane Pittman"
January 31 1974 CBS
(31)

In the 1970s, there seemed to be two ways that a TV movie signaled itself as a Very Important Movie: The first is that it was three hours long, taking up its network's entire nightly schedule; the second is that aired "with limited commercial interruption," usually one or two "pods" of commercials rather than the usual seven or eight. (There was a third way, of sorts: If a movie were advertised with a *Parental Advisory* warning, it was likely Important, but probably more for content-related reasons than anything else.)

Running for two hours but with just one commercial break, *The Autobiography of Miss Jane Pittman* was a Very Important Movie for 1974. Adapted from the 1971 best-selling novel by Ernest Gaines, it chronicled the black experience from the Civil War to Civil Rights through the eyes of Jane Pittman, a centenarian witness to it all.

Its scope alone – as exploration of a country's culture over the course of a century – certainly made it Important. But it also made it a sizeable risk for network TV at the time, given that most movies made for television tended to stick to proven genre formulas (crime, romance, horror, science-fiction). Socially relevant material was scarce; biographical movies were few and tended to focus on real people; so-called *black movies* were fewer still.

On top of this, the racial issues that were to be depicted on-screen in the historical *Miss Jane Pittman* were still an uncomfortable reality that that still stirred up pockets of animus when explored on TV. So the question was, Who'll watch?

In her role as a woman recalling the story of her life at its end for a visiting and inquisitive reporter, Cicely Tyson ages from 23 to 110. Her journey dates back to a childhood of slavery in the South and then winds through history, from Reconstruction through the Industrial Age past the turn of the century and on to the Depression and two World Wars -- Jane growing up as the country does. All punctuated by memories of what it was to be black as it did.

If hers is not an easy story to hear about (or see depicted), Jane reminds that it was more daunting to live. But if conventional thinking in network TV at the time was that hers was too real a story to tell, and that white audiences in particular wouldn't be interested, conventional thinking, as is often the case, was wrong. Tune-in for *The Autobiography of Miss Jane Pittman* was enormous.

Against a backdrop of a black population seeking and seizing its racial identity in general and on television, the film was a landmark must-see TV. It also met with (mostly) rapturous acclaim, winning nine Emmy Awards, including two for Tyson herself as Lead Actress in a Movie and in the since-eliminated category Actress of the Year. John Korty also won as Best Director, and a pair of rising special-effects technicians who'd go on to even greater renown -- Stan Winston (ALIENS, TERMINATOR 2: JUDGMENT DAY, JURASSIC PARK) and Rick Baker (AN AMERICAN WEREWOLF IN

LONDON, THE NUTTY PROFESSOR) -- won for the make-up design that aged Tyson through nine decades.

Praise for the film was not unanimous, though. Some in the black community condemned it as a white view of the black experience, given that both the director behind the film and Pittman's on-screen interviewer were white. Writing in *Black World*, Alvin Ramsey dismissed the project as "insidious propaganda" and lamented that black history "was again filtered through that white lens that is constructed to keep Black truth from passing through with integrity." (His was a lamentation that would become more common as the 1970s unfolded and as black culture developed its own voices.)

Still, three years before *Roots* and not all that many years removed from when black faces were not even welcome in prime-time, a made-for-TV movie about the black experience was a major accomplishment, if only because it kept race in the national dialogue. And its sizeable tune-in belied convention that 1970s viewers would not flock to "black stories," leveling a path that led to *Roots* itself.

Few who saw the movie then, who have seen it since, or who will watch it in the future, can deny the power of and universal message behind the wordless sequence that marks the finale of *The Autobiography of Miss Jane Pittman*, when its century-old narrator's journey comes to an end with a slow but steely unassisted approach to a public water-fountain once labeled WHITE ONLY for a cool and symbolic sip.

CBS

Bewitched
"Sisters at Heart"
December 24 1970 ABC
(32)

Sony

On the list of people and projects in the trenches of a TV revolution, the fantasy sitcom *Bewitched* seems an odd inclusion. Yet in 1970, at the very dawn of the decade of change (even *All in the Family* had not yet come on the air), the innocuous sitcom about the modern-day marriage between a witch and mortal took aim at convention and fired off a critical early shot.

Begun in 1964 on the forefront of a mini-trend of fantasy-coms like *My Favorite Martian, I Dream of Jeannie,* and *The Munsters* (not to mention the Edsel of them all, *My Mother the Car*), *Bewitched* starred Elizabeth Montgomery as Samantha Stephens, new bride to New York ad-exec husband Darrin Stephens (Dick York).

After a meet-cute introduction and a whirlwind romance in the pilot, the two marry and settle into idyllic suburban green-front-lawn life. But there's a hitch: On their honeymoon, Samantha confesses to Darrin that she's actually a "real broom-riding, house-haunting, cauldron-stirring witch." Eight seasons of sitcom hijinks thus commence.

In its early years, *Bewitched* offered shades of adult-level modern-age sophistication, along the lines of big-screen rom-coms in vogue at the time – young marrieds, white-collar hard-working men, supportive and often stay-at-home suburban wives (albeit of the witch/mortal classification here).

But it soon came to rely less on the sophistication as the seasons went on, with more on the mayhem-producing witchcraft practiced at exasperated husband Darrin's expense, especially by Samantha's eccentric extended family of witches. So much so that after five seasons or so, the sitcom, always well-crafted, devolved into a sort of live-action cartoon, with episodes about UFOs, storybook characters and historical figures come to life, mistaken identities, unsuspecting adults (and even children) transformed into animals, and anthropomorphized bed-warmers.

Beyond a single reference to UNICEF in a 1969 episode and a bit of commentary about the 17th-century witch trials during a multi-episode visit to Salem in 1970, *Bewitched* never really addressed the world around it, let alone social issues. With one notable exception.

In a December 1970 episode, during its seventh and penultimate season and at a time when it seemed its producers felt the country needed it, the fluff-sitcom that was *Bewitched* tackled the reality of racism. And what got it to air made it even more remarkable.

Called "Sisters at Heart," the episode was spun from an actual class of Los Angeles tenth-graders. Earlier that year, Marcella Saunders, then a young English teacher at L.A.'s inner-city Thomas Jefferson High School, contacted several Hollywood TV productions, looking for a way to use television as a means of connecting her TV-watching students to the benefits of reading and writing. *Bewitched* star Elizabeth Montgomery and producer William Asher (also Montgomery's husband at the time) responded to Saunders with an invitation to bring her class to the set of their show, where they'd spend the day watching parts of it made.

And as a thank-you following that visit, the students collaborated on an idea for a *Bewitched* episode, which producers accepted and had staffer Barbara Avedon shape into a script. "Sisters at Heart" became its 1970 Christmas show.

It threaded two separate storylines into a single whole, about acceptance. One story focused on how the Stephens' (white) 7-year-old daughter Tabitha and her best (black) girlfriend wished they were real sisters, leading to witch-in-training Tabitha conjuring a spell that made them look alike; the other focused on ad-exec Darrin dealing with a big-pockets client whom he discovers to be a big-time bigot.

The episode serviced the show's by-then cartoon-y mandate (the spell that Tabitha conjures results in black spots on her white face and white spots on her black girlfriend's face), but it also offered some social-awareness storytelling when Darrin calls his client-to-be on his racism, indicating that he'd rather lose millions from his business than endorse intolerance. One scene, designed to make the client reflect on his own racism, even featured white members of the *Bewitched* cast in blackface.

The episode, which concludes with the now-woke client apologizing for his prejudiced ways, aired on ABC on Christmas Eve. Its end-credits read: "Story by 5th Period English – Room 309 Thomas Jefferson High School," and the names of all 26 of Marcella Saunders' students were listed on-screen. Fifth graders with a TV credit!

Even while running out of creative steam towards the end of its long run, *Bewitched* was far from a low-rated show, especially in what was then still a three-network universe. So its audience still numbered in the tens of millions. Those who tuned in on this December Thursday night saw a TV show taking a chance to make a difference, which more and more of those on and in TV would come to do this decade. Television, as envisioned by longtime social activist Elizabeth

Montgomery, the real-life power behind *Bewitched*, could and should get involved.

Sony

Shed of her Samantha Stephens persona, in fact, the actress appeared on-screen as herself first to introduce and then to provide a coda for the special episode, saying "Sisters at Heart" evokes "the true spirit of Christmas ...conceived in the image of innocence and filled with truth."

She thanked the show's sponsor (Oscar Mayer), and, at the dawn of the new decade and in a nod to the turbulent times, she wished viewers "a happy and peaceful new year." She emphasized the word *peaceful*.

Hailed by critics and educators, "Sisters at Heart" was given the Emmy Governor's Award in 1971. Montgomery, who died in 1995, always cited it as her favorite of the 254 *Bewitched* episodes produced from 1964 to 1972.

Sony

"I didn't hear you say that. Because it isn't possible. It's inhuman to serve the same food, day after day. The Geneva Convention prohibits the killing of our taste buds! I simply cannot eat the same food every day! Fish! Liver! Day after day! I've eaten a river of liver and an ocean of fish!"

-- Benjamin 'Hawkeye' Pierce
M*A*S*H*

Chico and the Man
"Pilot"
September 13 1974 NBC
(33)

> Despite the revitalization of ethnic culture in the Seventies, equally strong voices advocated the rapid abandonment of minority values and urged full integration into the American mainstream. For minority peoples struggling for recognition and the redress of historical grievances, this tension between traditionalists and assimilationists constituted a central and unresolved dilemma.
>
> -- Peter N. Carroll
> *It Seemed Like Nothing Happened: America in the 1970s*

The new-world change that *Chico and the Man* represented for television was evident before even a frame of the first episode was seen, by way of its main-titles sequence. As it opened the show on premiere night, it opened viewers' eyes to a whole different side of contemporary American life. That side was the barrios of East Los Angeles.

NBC / Warner Bros.

Prior to the 1970s, most of the main-title sequences for sitcoms did little more than list the names of the actors in the cast. They weren't all that visually creative (*I Love Lucy*, *Leave It to Beaver*, *Father Knows Best*). Even as some came to offer more interesting visuals or even animation in the 1960s, like those for *Bewitched* or *My Favorite Martian* or *I Dream of Jeannie* or *The Munsters*, they were still more about reinforcing a premise than "telling a story."

Even the iconic tripping-over-the-living-room-ottoman opening for *The Dick Van Dyke Show* or the fishing-hole opening of *The Andy Griffith Show*, which set nice tones, said little about what their respective sitcoms were actually *about*.

Two comedies of the late 1960s stand out as examples of when the approach to main-titles started to change, recalibrating the template as a means of exploring narrative, setting scenes, even tapping emotions. *That Girl* (1966-71) and *Room 222* (1969-74), each on ABC, used their openings to establish locations -- to make their settings themselves parts of or characters in the shows.

These main-titles showcased context, taking viewers inside the locations and inside the shows. (Or at least dropping them off at their very specific locales.) These and a smattering of other series that bridged into the 1970s represented a new wave of sitcom that would change not just what TV said but what it did and how it looked.

All in the Family gave viewers a tour of New York City before taking them to the Bunkers' Queens doorstep. *Mary Tyler Moore* showed its heroine leaving one city (and job and group of friends) on her way to a new life in a different one (where she found a different job and different group of friends). Goodbye to the old and hello to the news. *Sanford and Son* offered up a glimpse of a somewhat-grimy Watts and the junkyard therein where its title characters called home. More and more, main-titles were about the grounding of TV characters in everyday life. Maybe even like our own.

Among the unsung names behind that grounding of reality, for a short while anyway, is James Komack. A former actor, he came to prominence behind the scenes as producer and writer of the NBC sitcom *The Courtship of Eddie's Father* (1969-72). His main-title sequence for that show, in fact, is probably better remembered than either him or the comedy itself: Each week opened with its father-and-son co-stars (Bill Bixby and Brandon Cruz) walking together, often along the California coastline, as young Eddie asks his father different questions about life and the elder man tries in earnest to offer answers.

The short snippets then led into the main titles (with their modern font) backed by Harry Nilsson's "Best Friend" theme song. The sequence spelled out the premise of the show as a soft-hearted exploration of a parent-and-child relationship in today's world.

Komack's biggest TV hit, and likely his most notable contribution to a changing culture, came with his third series a few years later, in 1974, *Chico and the Man*. It paired veteran actor Jack Albertson with rising young stand-up comedian Freddie Prinze. And its main titles, featuring images of those barrios, had a different message to spread: Times had changed, and there was more to America in the 1970s that the white TV faces of the past 20 years and their suburban homes.

> Because there's good in every one /
> And a new day has begun /
> You can see the morning sun if you try /
>
> And I know /
> Things will be better /
> I know they will for Chico and The Man.

Just as the blue-collar movement had yielded Archie Bunker and women's liberation had created *Maude*, a Brown Pride movement was moving across the landscape. And *Chico and the Man* had arrived to tell its stories. Boyle Heights, Lincoln Heights, El Sereno -- welcome to the barrio. The main-titles lifted a curtain to all of it.

A rare Latino breakthrough in the entertainment business of the early 1970s, Freddie Prinze had a meteoric rise to TV fame, cast in the series at age 20. (That his fall came so soon thereafter -- suicide at 22 -- makes his story and legacy even more remarkable.) Komack had already been developing the idea of a Latino-oriented sitcom (reportedly at one point for Cheech & Chong) when he and the rest of the country caught wind of Prinze after his headline-making debut on *The Tonight Show* in December 1973. Prinze was just 19.

The appearance served as *de facto* career benediction from the country's reigning comedy king, *Tonight Show* host Johnny Carson. Komack turned to Prinze as his new star.

He'd play the charming job-seeking hustler Chico Rodriguez, who talks his way into the East L.A. garage-shop business -- and life -- of a crusty old-school and world-weary Ed Brown (Albertson). After which a fractious but loving father-son-type relationship is formed.

As Chico, Prinze essentially portrayed himself; and much of his stand-up material found its way into his dialogue. It was a role, observed Dan Epstein in a 2015 remembrance for *Rolling Stone*, that "fed off his streetwise stage persona and fit him like a glove."

Chico and the Man, with its generation-gap premise that pit a had-enough white senior against a young and optimistic minority upstart, really did reflect that larger Brown Pride picture in the country, especially in Los Angeles, where a real-life culture gap was widening as Latino identity was growing.

Widowed and alone, white Ed Brown had become an embittered small-business owner who, in the show's pilot, is angry at how both his city and his neighborhood had changed -- and had changed his business and lifestyle. (Shades of TV's most infamous character of the day, Archie Bunker.) Stubbornly refusing to change with the times, he's none too accepting or friendly when he discovers Rodriguez squatting in his garage-shop; he anoints him with the derogatory "Chico" nickname. (It's a term that would never fly in the prime-time of the future.)

Ed represented the *then* to Chico's *now*. With this simple pairing, an era was addressed, a premise was established, and a hit show was launched.

Chico and the Man's ratings were indeed huge. NBC was flush. Critical and Emmy favor were bestowed. And then just as quickly... the hit show was grounded. Midway through its third season, on January 28 1977, Prinze, experiencing more fame and with more career opportunities than he probably ever dreamed possible, but also with mental-health and drug issues that compromised it all, shot himself in the head at his Los Angeles apartment. He died the following day. He was just 22. (Some in his circle contend the death was accidental, yet police and others report that Prinze left a suicide note.)

NBC / Warner Bros.

Seven episodes of *Chico and the Man*'s 21-episode third season were left hanging in the balance -- four filmed and waiting to be aired, three others written and waiting to be shot. NBC broadcast one of the ready-four the week following Prinze's death. It pre-empted the show the week after that, and then it aired the remaining three as scheduled over the course of the next three weeks. (The last episode to feature Freddie Prinze aired March 4 1977, ironically titled "Ed Talks to God" -- though it related not to Chico but to Ed Brown's unwillingness to celebrate yet another birthday.)

With that, Freddie Prinze and his short brass-ring life came to a close: The three Chico-less episodes that followed were filmed and broadcast under a death pall, and the third season of *Chico and the Man* wrapped up on April 8 1977. Which is where anyone would be forgiven for assuming that such marked the final season of the sitcom as a whole, too, given that its lead, whose character's name is in the title, had just committed suicide.

Which is where anyone would be wrong.

Demonstrating the kind of wisdom rarely seen outside of TV's executive suites -- and in an effort to hang on even to a trace of an important money-making weekly series rather than start from scratch launching a new one to replace it -- NBC renewed *Chico and the Man* in the spring of 1977 and studio Warner Bros. went forward with for a fourth season.

As a replacement for the handsome and cocky 20-something Chico Rodriguez, it cast an unknown acting-novice 12-year-old (Gabriel Melgar) as Mexican orphan named Raul, whom Ed Brown finds hiding in his garage and decides to adopt. The reported (bizarre but era-appropriate) rationale for keeping the title (and thus the show): "They're all named Chico." (Melgar was born in Tijuana; Prinze, half-Puerto Rican and half Hungarian, was born in New York.) Ratings for the revised show come fall were nil. Both the Man and the new Chico were gone by Christmas 1977.

From luck to talent to timing to chance, many factors and many people seem to have made for the brief success that was *Chico and the Man* from September 1974 though January 1977. But it was Freddie Prinze that made it such a huge success. In the process, it was Prinze who brought Brown Pride to prime-time, making Latino/Hispanic happen on TV in a way America had not seen since Cuban-born Desi Arnaz came to CBS in 1951. (And rarely seen since.)

He put a face on an ethnicity that rarely appeared on TV. He and producer James Komack made accessible life in Boyle Heights and similar other barrio communities around the country. They made them *ordinary*, just more swatches of the American fabric. From the opening credits of its first episode in September of 1974 through to the final episode to feature Prinze two years and six months later, *Chico and the Man* moved the ethnicity needle for network television and welcomed to prime-time a whole new sub-culture.

It would be 40 years before TV fully embraced it, at least according to a 2016 piece written by Ellie Kauffman for Mic Network called "It's 2016 and Latino Representation on TV Is Finally Starting to Reflect Reality." But in the 1970s, Freddie Prinze started it. He left a legacy that belies his brief life. It can only be imagined what else he would have done and what other work he would have left had he lived past age 22.

A poignant reflection in *Time* magazine on February 7 1977, a week after Prinze's death:

> He seemed to have everything going for him. Playing a wisecracking Chicano hustler in an East Los Angeles garage, he starred in NBC's three-year-old hit series *Chico and the Man*. He had just signed a multiyear $1 million contract with Las Vegas' Caesars Palace. He was negotiating film deals with Warners and Universal. He had filled in for Johnny Carson on *The Tonight Show*; more such appearances were in the works. And at the age of 22, he attained one of the highest status roles in show business when he performed for the incoming President at last month's Inaugural Gala ...

Yet something was terribly wrong in the life of comedian Freddie Prinze. After a few games of backgammon at his TV producer's home late last week, he returned to his $695-a-month apartment in the plush Beverly Comstock Hotel. Depressed, he called his parents and his psychiatrist. He told them he was going to kill himself. His secretary and his business manager, Marvin Snyder, had come over to cheer him up. Then, with Snyder still present, Prinze hung up the phone after talking with his estranged wife Katherine, reached down into the sofa's cushions, pulled out a small automatic pistol, placed it to his temple and fired. The bullet passed straight through his head. Police found a note that said he could not go on any longer. After a day in the hospital, he succumbed.

It was such a quick end to such a quick career. The son of a Puerto Rican mother and a Hungarian father, Prinze had used his wit to survive among the teen-age toughs in the Latino section of Manhattan's Upper West Side. Disarming his foes with switchblade-sharp one-liners, he avoided the fighting he hated. At the High School for Performing Arts, Prinze's ability to twit his own background—the comedic formula he never abandoned—earned him star status in the boys' room, where he would try out his routines. His ethnic-based act worked on New York's club circuit too, which led to his first national appearance on the Jack Paar show. Then, in December 1973, his stand-up routine on *The Tonight Show* thrust him into the big leagues: he had caught the eye of James Komack, who was casting his generation-and ethnic-gap sitcom. With *Chico* a winner, Prinze had reached the top.

But the fast trip left the sensitive Prinze off balance. A close friend, comedian David Brenner, explains: "There was no transition in Freddie's life. It was an explosion. It's tough to walk off a subway at age 19 and then step out of a Rolls-Royce the next day. He was in a lifestyle that's very unusual for a 22-year-old." Producer Komack, 20 years his elder, became a close confidant. Says he: "Freddie saw nothing around that would satisfy him. He would ask me, 'Is this what it is? Is this what it's all about?' He'd say, 'I can't go out now, I can't walk around.' " The hokiness of Hollywood fame got to him too. He would say, 'Even my friendships are related to ratings.'"

Some friends suggest that the breakup of his marriage in December [1976] was the source of his last bout of despondency. Though he did suffer over the divorce and worried about his ten-month-old son, those closest to Prinze minimize the domestic problem ... Noted Prinze's TV costar, Jack Albertson: "A combination of things had him down. On the set he would sometimes retreat into himself. But he would recover. He would joke, have fun, kibitz around. Then the next day he would be depressed again." Says Komack: "His real despondency, whether he could articulate it or not, concerned the questions: 'Where do I fit in? Where is my happiness?' I would tell him, 'God, Freddie, your happiness is right here. You're a star.' He'd say, 'No, that's not happiness for me anymore.' "

Prinze liked to tell interviewers that the Chico character "is very close to me. He comes out an optimist, very ambitious and hardworking. He's made something of a life that could have made him bitter." But for one of the most singular escape stories in ghetto history, escape was not enough.

The Crying Indian
1971
(34)

It's probably the most famous tear in American history: Iron Eyes Cody, an actor in Native American garb, paddles a birch-bark canoe on water that seems, at first, tranquil and pristine, but that becomes increasingly polluted along his journey. He pulls his boat ashore and walks toward a bustling freeway. As the lone Indian ponders the polluted landscape, a passenger hurls a paper bag out a car window. The bag bursts on the ground, scattering fast-food wrappers all over the Indian's beaded moccasins. In a stern voice, the narrator comments: "Some people have a deep, abiding respect for the natural beauty that was once this country. And some people don't." The camera zooms in on Iron Eyes Cody's face to reveal a single tear falling, ever so slowly, down his cheek.

-- Finis Dunaway
Chicago Tribune November 21 2017

The "most famous tear in American history" was part of a 1971 public service announcement known as "the Crying Indian spot." It made its TV debut in April, on the first anniversary of Earth Day, which itself had come about as a response to a 1969 oil spill off the coast of Santa Barbara, California. (The environmental movement as a whole in the United States had been slowly fermenting since the end of World War Two, pushed along further and with more intensity after the 1962 publication of Rachel Carson's *Silent Spring.*)

Created by the Marstellar, Inc., advertising agency and sponsored by the non-profit organization Keep America Beautiful (formed in 1953),

Keep America Beautiful, Inc.

the campaign literally put a face on the burgeoning anti-pollution movement, in conjunction with the simple and repeatable slogan "People start pollution. People can stop it." It led to widespread local, regional, and national anti-littering efforts on its way to winning two Clio Awards for Best in Advertising, securing a legacy as one of the best-known ads in TV history.

But separate and apart from the commercial's effectiveness and popularity – and beyond the controversies that it stirred about both whether its star Iron Eyes Cody was in fact Native American and what the Keep America Beautiful organization's true motivations and politics were – is the fact that with the Crying Indian spot the *idea* of being Native American, of there being a Native American population in the United States, was re-affirmed, if not, to some, introduced.

In clear language and visuals, over and over again, the concept was displayed to tens of millions of TV viewers whose awareness was limited to black-and-white western series and the Grand Canyon episode of *The Brady Bunch*. (No shade on the latter: While that 1970 outing of the derided sitcom did fall back on some Indian tropes, it's to be commended for introducing a young Native-American boy who not only mocks the young Brady kids' attempts to stereotype, he also has ambitions to become an astronaut.)

The Crying Indian was depicted not as a caricature (totem-pole shaman or monosyllabic peacekeeper or savage warrior) but as a fellow resident of the country -- *of* it, not outside of or foreign to it. The Native American population now had a face – and a face that conveyed heart and emotion, at that.

For many, Iron Eyes Cody as the Crying Indian was the first sympathetic and relatable Indian they'd ever seen. The days of Tonto seemed over. (That so were the days of the TV western as of the 1970s helped.)

The PSA wasn't created to be part of a cultural movement, but it aired as the Native American population in the United States was protesting and rebelling in an effort to reclaim a culture and a birthright. To champion an individuality in a decade of multi-culturalism. It was the right spot at the perfect time, benefiting two movements at once.

Sacheen Littlefeather and Wounded Knee were only around the corner.

The Flip Wilson Show
1970-74 NBC
(35)

Fourteen years before comedian Flip Wilson's variety show successfully premiered on NBC, singer Nat King Cole had a series on the same network that sank inside of a single season because it couldn't find a national advertiser. The world of 1970 was considerably and finally different from that of the late 1950s.

The Flip Wilson Show was a smash, the first successful variety series ever to star a black performer.

Wilson, an Air Force vet and onetime San Francisco bellhop, had begun doing stand-up and sketch comedy in the 1950s. Throughout the 1960s, he found himself a regular at the famed Apollo Theater in Harlem, and he was also a frequent guest on various TV quiz and talk shows.

"Part of the first wave of black comedians to break the color line, he arrived during the sociocultural crack in time we call the mid-1960s," wrote Robert Lloyd in his 2013 review of Kevin Cook's *Flip: The Inside Story of TV's First Black Superstar*.

Later in the decade, after a series of appearances on the both the long-running CBS staple *The Ed Sullivan Show* and the new NBC hit *Rowan and Martin's Laugh-In* -- and proceeding the release of his fourth comedy album (*The Devil Made Me Buy This Dress*, 1970) and his first solo TV special – Wilson was offered his own series.

The Flip Wilson Show premiered on September 17 1970, in a timeslot that had it competing with markedly different fare (*Family Affair*, *Bewitched*, and *The Jim Nabors Hour*). It quickly became NBC's highest-rated show, eclipsing even *Laugh-In*, marking unprecedented ground-breaking success for a black performer. Wilson shook up the staid

NBC / SFM

variety-show genre in the process, too: His show was performed in the round, rather than utilizing the standard proscenium staging; and musical guests were featured that aggressively went after the more-and-more important younger demographic -- among them Diana Ross, The Osmonds and The Jackson 5, Sha-Na-Na, and Roberta Flack. (Older more traditional viewers weren't forsaken, though: Lena Horne, Ella Fitzgerald, and Bing Crosby made appearances.) Few series at the time showcased as many black acts.

Two recurring comedic sketches became popular signature pieces – Wilson as Reverend Leroy, of the Church of What's Happening Now, and Wilson in drag as feminist icon Geraldine Jones, a modern woman with a boyfriend named Killer and with expressions such as "The devil made me do it!" and "What you see is what you get!" Each became national catchphrases. If the comedian courted feminist backlash with the cartoonish Jones character, which he did, audiences loved and embraced her nonetheless. (Wilson as a performer though would never escape Geraldine, even decades after the show left the air.)

Flip Wilson's TV show was NBC's highest-rated series for two straight years before losing favor upon the arrival of timeslot competitor *The Waltons* in 1972. The rural Depression-era drama started big itself, and its second and most-popular season became *Flip Wilson*'s last.

A contributing factor to its demise was the waning appeal of variety-series format itself, as scripted TV was growing up and getting bolder, moving beyond the medium's familiar roots. His reign was brief but significant: it may not have represented the generation-gap anarchy that variety-series like *Rowan and Martin's Laugh-In* or *The Smothers Brothers Comedy Hour* did, but it breathed new life to prime-time, introducing it to black faces. Wilson won two Emmy Awards in doing so.

Wilson was part of that phalanx of black faces marching into TV across all genres (Bill Cosby, Diahann Carroll, Redd Foxx, Clarence Williams III, Lloyd Haynes, Denise Nicholas), paving the way for more to follow in the 1970s and beyond. When he died in 1998, the obituaries noted his legend as the first black person in a solo starring role in TV's Top Ten.

"Free To Be ... You and Me"
March 11 1974 ABC
(36)

Marlo Thomas, daughter of 1950s TV superstar Danny Thomas, was born into television. So much so that in her 20s she ended up the lead of her own sitcom. But it came about with a bit of a struggle.

TV Guide

In an interview years later, Thomas, a longtime women's rights advocate, said she remembered being courted by each of the networks, whose representatives pitched a handful of potential series ideas. But each of the ideas was for a series that featured her as "the daughter of somebody or the wife of somebody or the secretary of somebody."

She said she eventually went to the networks' powers-that-be and dared to ask: "Have you ever considered doing a show where the *girl* is the somebody?" *That Girl* (1966-71, ABC), about young Ann Marie, eking out a living on her own in Manhattan as an actress, was the result. In it, Thomas starred not only as the *somebody* at the center of the show, that someone was an independent and single "career-women" who was pursuing life and job first and then husband and family after, if at all.

It was a TV first, four years before Mary Richards blazed a trail of feminism on *Mary Tyler Moore*. (That Thomas' character did so while still being referred to as a *girl* and with the constant involvement of a boyfriend and a nearby father to save or advise her -- which wasn't the case with Mary Richards -- was just a factor of the times.)

Both *That Girl* and Marlo Thomas (she also produced the show, another rarity) proved to be a significant piece of the larger female-empowerment puzzle being pieced together in the country and on TV. When the series ended in 1971, with the Ann Marie character still unmarried (though engaged), Thomas continued to represent: The activist became a familiar face on the literal front lines of the women's movement, as a frequent marcher for the cause and as among those women calling for ratification of the Equal Rights Amendment.

In 1972, the passion led to her conceiving and producing a children's project called *Free to Be ... You and Me* in conjunction with the just-formed Ms. Foundation for Women, of which Thomas was a founder. The project involved both a vinyl album and an illustrated book, each of which featured well-known people sharing stories about empowerment and the right for a person to be anything he or she wants to be.

The actress said the idea for the project was borne of an attempt to buy a book on the topic as a gift for her young niece; finding none, she decided to create her own.

The album, with songs like "It's Okay to Cry" and "Sisters and Brothers" and "William's Doll," sold half a million copies.

Two years later, a TV adaptation of *Free To Be...You and Me* expanded on the message, featuring still more famous faces and incorporating then-cutting-edge animation for a one-hour special that spun stories about gender stereotypes and individualism. ABC aired it on March 11

1974, to high ratings and considerable acclaim as an important TV show at an important time in the country.

It went on to win both Emmy and Peabody awards, too, with the voting board of the latter calling it "very warm, very human, and very rewarding" as well as "an imaginative program of quality entertainment which could well set the standard for programming of this type for years to come." The simple and small show, rarely seen or referred to decades later, had a basic message for a complicated time: It's okay to be whoever and whatever you are.

"Free to be" became a default expression that would carry the project into the future in the mind of those many who watched (and listened) and in the culture it helped to change.

Free to Be ... You and Me informed a decade, resonated for a generation, and created a legacy for Marlo Thomas.

ABC / Marlo Thomas / Free to Be Productions/ Ms. Foundation

Good Times
1974 -1979 CBS
(37)

A TV rarity, *Good Times* was a spin-off of a spin-off -- borne of *Maude* in 1974, which itself came from *All in the Family* in 1972. Actress Esther Rolle was the connecting link. She portrayed Maude's housekeeper Florida Evans, then continued in the role as the character moved to Chicago for her own series, as mother of three (Jimmie Walker, BernNadette Stanis, Ralph Carter) and wife of strong-willed and proud husband James (John Amos).

Good Times entered the prime-time sweepstakes representing something that TV had never seen: a hit sitcom about a nuclear African-American family. Another first: It was set in the projects (presumably Chicago's famous Cabrini-Green, though it was never named). So its success was not guaranteed when it premiered in January 1974.

Not helping was that CBS scheduled it on a troubled Friday night, where the network hadn't had so much as a pulse for five years, and then inexplicably paired it there with a new and already failing western saddled with the unfortunate title of *Dirty Sally*. (**Fun Fact**: A spin-off itself, *Dirty Sally* is the only show ever to come out of the longtime classic *Gunsmoke*.) All this, plus the competition on the other networks -- the established *Sanford and Son* and *The Brady Bunch*.

What *Good Times* did have, though, was *Maude*'s equity and Norman Lear's name. Which was sufficient. The show premiered big that January and got bigger as the months went on. It finished out its first (partial) season as a Top 20 show.

Mining laughs from what was essentially a poverty existence in a housing project would seem a challenge. But in his 2014 memoir *Even This I Get to Experience*, Lear writes, "[W]e were determined that the family …. would deal with the reality of their world — gangs, drugs, crime, poverty, etc." And as was being proven with Lear's other sitcoms *All in the Family* and *Sanford and Son,* if audiences could relate, then they could laugh. And many people related to the Florida Evans family and to *Good Times.*

Helping to ground the sitcom were its co-creators: Mike Evans, who had played next-door neighbor Lionel Jefferson on *All in the Family* since that show's 1971 premiere, and Eric Monte, a Chicago native who had lived in Cabrini-Green as a child. (Monte was also one of the writers of the controversial 1974 animated THE NINE LIVES OF FRITZ THE CAT and in 1975 wrote COOLEY HIGH, the film that would become the inspiration for both the ABC sitcom *What's Happening!!* in 1976 and the CBS drama *The White Shadow* in 1978.)

The youngest of the three Evans children in the series, 11-year-old Michael, a preternatural black activist nicknamed by his father as "the Militant Midget," was the go-to character for many of those socio-political references about black history or the black experience. Reportedly, the strategy was that the insights and indictments of a racist society would sound less threatening to white audiences if they came out of a child's mouth.

At its core, though, *Good Times* was about a loving family unit that just happened to be black.

In its second year, *Good Times* was upgraded to a better timeslot and started to benefit from worth of mouth. Ratings increased. But, as can happen with success, from *Good Times* came big problems. Pressures mounted both in front of and behind the cameras to make the series still more relevant as a means of servicing its "responsibility" to the black community. Scripts became scrutinized. Egos became inflated. Plus, co-star Jimmie Walker, with his animated-like rubbery physique and his strutting play-to-the-back-row performance as eldest Evans child J.J., had started to break out as the most popular cast member, eclipsing the roles of lead actors Esther Rolle and John Amos.

Sony

Plots began focusing more on if not encouraging his mugging shuck-and-jive caricature, replete with a go-to expression -- "Dy-no-mite!" -- that was fast becoming a national viewer catch-phrase. (It was Walker's version of Fonzie's "A-a-a-yyyyy.") The expression was feeding more of his scene and the audiences at the live tapings were eating it up and cheering it on.

That Walker was a stand-up comedian at the same time that stand-ups-turned sitcom stars like Freddie Prinze and Gabe Kaplan were in TV vogue supported the producers'/network's decision to focus on the J.J. character. But Rolle and Amos reportedly felt marginalized and that the big-eyed J.J. character was fast becoming an offensive black stereotype. To them, the show was devolving into something at odds with the socially-conscious project they each signed on for.

The discontent came to a head as *Good Times* ended its third season in 1976, leading to John Amos leaving the show and producers announcing that his character would be killed off.

Good Times opened the 1976-77 season with mother Florida Evans grieving her late husband. (Her "Damn! Damn! Damn!" meltdown scene would become a YouTube favorite in later decades.) The sitcom just sort of limped along from there, with Walker's mugging and preening "Dy-no-mite!"'s central to the show.

The result was too much for Rolle. She lamented being in show that fostered a stereotype of the strong single black mother raising a family alone in the projects. When the season was over, she quit, too, calling the character of J.J. a bad role-model for young black men. In an interview, Rolle let loose about the character. "He's eighteen and he doesn't work," she observed. "He can't read or write. He doesn't think. The show didn't start out to be that. Little by little, with the help of the artist, I suppose, because they couldn't do that to me, they have made J.J. more stupid, and they have enlarged the role."

Still, the sitcom remained popular enough for CBS to renew it for yet another season, during which it would showcase three parent-less teenagers. (It was explained that mother Florida Evans had re-married and relocated to the Southwest.) Longtime next-door neighbor Willona Woods (Ja'net DuBois), once a supporting character, assumed a starring role in the series as its now *de facto* matriarch.

Once again, *Good Times* made it through the season, but the absence of a mother character, as well as the loss of original star Rolle, hit it hard. So much so that when it concluded CBS convinced the actress to return to the show with the promise that the character of J.J. would be toned down.

It paved the way for a sixth season (1978-79), though by this time *Good Times* was running on legacy and goodwill. The once relevant and highly rated sitcom, which started out as a loud-and-proud social statement, ended with a bit of a formula sitcom whisper in the summer of 1979.

But when it did, it left a prime-time that was in a markedly different state than when it arrived five-and-a-half years earlier. Black families had established themselves as part of prime-time, no longer anomalies. The decade was closing out with three all-black series that at one point or another had found a perch in Nielsen's Top Ten. (The others were *Sanford and Son* and *The Jeffersons*).

And a new one coming five years hence, the Huxtables of *The Cosby Show*, would change TV forever.

Sony   *TV Guide*

Hot l Baltimore
January-April 1975 ABC
(38)

Lanford Wilson

By 1975, producer Norman Lear all-but owned prime-time television, having reinvented it in 1971 with *All in the Family* and then going on to launch four more hits in as many years on two separate networks. His name attached could get just about any new show on the air, which he proved in 1975 when a series adaptation of the Lanford Wilson's then-daring 1973 off-Broadway play *Hot l Baltimore* came to ABC.

Hot l Baltimore, like the stage play, was set in the lobby of Maryland's rundown Hotel Baltimore. (It was so run-down that a burnt-out *e* in its neon sign out front never got fixed.) The hotel offered both temporary and permanent quarters to a disparate group of tenants and guests -- young and old, black and white, male and female -- that included a pair of prostitutes, an illegal immigrant, and, in a TV first, a gay couple.

This resulted in another first: *Hot L Baltimore*, promoted in advance of its premiere as "another Norman Lear milestone," was the first sitcom whose *trailers* included a viewer warning ("Due to mature subject matter, parental judgement and discretion are advised").

The caution only added to the outcry that was building before it even aired. "ABC was absolutely bombarded with viewer mail protesting the subject matter," notes *crazyaboutTV.com*.

Unfortunately, not even the negative hype could prevent *Hot l Baltimore* from being a fast flop when it premiered in January 1975, marking the producer's first post-*Family* sitcom failure. ABC found it impossible to get traction for it on a night owned by NBC (*Sanford and Son, Chico and the Man, The Rockford Files, Police Woman*). (CBS wasn't fairing much better.)

Had the ratings even been middling, ABC would likely have stuck with the series, if only for the prestige that came with the producer's name. They actually stuck with it longer than anyone expected, given the protests and headaches from its own Standards and Practices people.

Still, even with just thirteen episodes, *Hot l Baltimore* left a significant footprint. After three years of baby steps -- a 1972 summer replacement sitcom with TV's first regularly occurring gay character (*The Corner Bar*), a 1972 movie-of-the-week about an adult gay relationship (*That Certain Summer*), a 1973 episode of *Mary Tyler Moore* that casually reveals a guest-character's sexuality, and a 1973 PBS special that featured a pair of gay men in the ensemble cast (*Steambath*) -- the short-lived sitcom proved a giant leap for prime-time in its featuring two men in a gay relationship as part of its core storyline.

If their sexuality was the point of their roles rather than incidental to them (that advancement was coming), *Hot l Baltimore* nonetheless inched the gay-needle forward. Future series with gay characters would no longer have to walk the "first-ever" social plank. In 1976, *The Nancy Walker Show*, another short-lived Lear comedy for ABC, featured a gay character in a role that was considerably larger than any gay character's had been(even if his sexuality was never really explored). And a year after that Billy Crystal's Jodie Dallas arrived in *Soap* as an everyman character who just happened to be gay. (Though he stumbled out of the gate at first, Jodie Dallas marked the first time a gay character was part of a hit series.)

Segments of both the viewing and non-viewing American public still fought back during these late 70s TV seasons. Objections were still raised, and protests were still made. Gay storylines and characters were still rare, and gay stereotypes were still a common fallback. It would still be 20 years before *Ellen* made gay cool and *Will & Grace* made it a non-issue. But the rainbow ceiling had cracked, thanks to a run-down hot l in Baltimore.

ABC / Sony

The Jeffersons
1975-85 CBS
(39)

Sony

As racial barriers continued to fall on the small screen in the 1970s, with more black (and other minority) faces showing up in more movies and series and specials, there still seemed a sense that series with black casts were "black shows" that began and ended with the being of black. Covert (or even sometimes overt) stereotyping by way of series premises didn't help the case.

Sanford and Son, for instance, however much adapted from a British format, featured two black men who worked (and lived in) a junkyard, itself located in what had become the infamous L.A. neighborhood of Watts (infamous as in race riots of 1965). Of course. *Good Times* was set in the Chicago projects, and its pilot revolved around its core family facing eviction for lack of rent payment. Of course. *That's My Mama* (1974-75) took place in what network notes described as "the African American section" of Washington D.C., featuring a rotund widowed black woman in the title role of "Mama." Of course. (This mama was not to be confused with the even-more rotund divorced black mother who'd show up two years later at the center of *What's Happening!!*. Set in Watts. Of course.)

D.C., Watts, Chicago. The Projects, junk-dealers, poverty. It was as though *black* was shorthand for *rough life*, telegraphed to all who watched. And it all sort of smacked of prime-time segregation by association. *The Jeffersons* changed that.

A fourth spin-off of *All in the Family*, *The Jeffersons* showed up in 1975 to offer a different and much brighter picture for and of black America, where, for good or ill, the being black part eventually was a non-issue.

It focused on hard-working George and Louise Jefferson -- for years the next-door-neighbors to white Archie and Edith Bunker of Queens, New York -- who celebrate the growing success of their dry-cleaning business by moving to the affluent Upper East Side of Manhattan. The pilot episode was nicely planted in an episode of *All in the Family*, still TV's Number One show, and as the Jeffersons settled in to their deluxe apartment in the sky, *The Jeffersons* did the same in Nielsen's Top Ten. And TV had it first "black" series not predicated on struggle. At least not a racial or economic one.

The Jeffersons real struggle was a cultural one, involving a tried-and-true fish-out-of-water formula right out of *The Beverly Hillbillies*, here about the once-poor family that *happens* to be black (rather than *because* they were) fitting in among the always wealthy. In fact, beyond the premise-setting early episodes that transitioned the characters away from *All in the Family* and a catchy theme-song that each week reminded how it "took a whole lot of trying just to get up that hill," the sitcom actually rose and fell on cartoonish oft-buffoonish George Jefferson struggling to fit in anywhere, with anyone.

The Jeffersons ended up being just plain funny and relatable to all, which seems to have been what made it last as long as it did. If it did deal with race in America, it did so primarily early on, in its first two seasons, when the move to Manhattan was a thread used to weave commentary about leaving identity behind and "Uncle Toms" and "passing." But even then, it didn't so in the headline-making way that *All in the Family* did. In fact, George's racism, so evident and strident on *All in the Family* when he was introduced on that show as a black counterpart to white Archie Bunker, was toned down in the spin-off, made more comical than confrontational. (He didn't mean it the way Archie did, it turns out.)

Beyond this, traditional sitcom convention prevailed, with stories about intra-family conflict and outside-world misunderstandings and insult-slinging in both arenas. Even the occasional "very special episodes" -- George or Louise reflecting upon or revisiting their less-affluent past, son Lionel's alcohol-fueled fears of success -- seemed to orbit more on the human condition, not necessarily racial ones.

But race does connect in a substantial way to the legacy of *The Jeffersons*: It was the first show in television history to feature an inter-racial couple as part of its core cast. Tom and Helen Wills, the parents of son Lionel Jefferson's girlfriend Jenny and upstairs-neighbors to George and Louse in their East Side high-rise, were played by white Franklin Cover and black Roxie Roker.

Barely eight years after *Loving v. Virginia*, a prime-time TV show on a major broadcast network featured a longtime and happily married inter-racial couple.

Another TV taboo smashed.

TV's first non-struggling nuclear black family and TV's longest-running black show when it went off the air in 1985 (it ran longer than the sitcom it was spun from), *The Jeffersons* marked the transition from "black shows" to TV series that happened to feature a black cast. (America was years away from *The Cosby Show*, which in many ways made race all-but-irrelevant on TV.) Never nominated in the writing or directing categories for any of its 253 episodes, it won just two Emmys over the course of eleven seasons (for videotaping editing and for star Isabel Sanford as Best Lead Actress, the first win ever in the category for a black woman).

"*The Jeffersons'* use of confrontational humor and candid commentary that helped ease the discussion of topics like race and class on American television (and beyond) is the cornerstone of the show's lasting legacy," observed *The Huffington Post* after the death of star Sherman Hemsley in 2012 (" 'The Jeffersons': How Sherman Hemsley and the Sitcom Changed the Landscape of American Television"). "Its characters opened doors for future black actors, and its success proved that African American sitcoms did, in fact, resonate with general audiences."

Sony

Marcus Welby, M.D.
"The Other Martin Loring" February 20 1973 ABC
"The Outrage" October 8 1974 ABC
(40)

If TV viewers in the 1970s were to be asked to name the least controversial or even most innocent shows on the air, chances are good that the ABC medical drama *Marcus Welby, M.D.* would top the list. Not only was it sanctioned by the American Medical Association, it starred onetime *Father Knows Best* actor Robert Young in the title role of a physician who still makes house-calls. Each week, the series opened with a main-title sequence that showed the smiling face of benevolent Dr. Welby the first thing a recovery-room patient sees coming out of anesthesia. The message: *You're better; I'm here.*

But *Marcus Welby*'s wholesome reputation belied its weekly reach. Airing from 1969 to 1976, it offered up a fairly progressive approach to medicine, unafraid of taking on issues of the day. Two of the series' 169 episodes, in particular, showed that like it or not (and many did not) the world was changing.

As many 1970s series did, *Marcus Welby, M.D.* started out as a movie-of-the-week. It aired in March of 1969, called *A Matter of Humanities*, about a longtime Santa Monica-based family-practitioner who takes on a "brash" fresh-from-medical-school young partner (James Brolin) to ease his caseload.

The differing approaches to medicine that made up their now-joint practice -- reflective of their different eras of training -- set up the premise for the movie and then the series that came from it that fall. (A familiar TV-storytelling model of the late 1960s and early 1970s, the old guard/new generation hook was also employed for *Ironside, Medical Center, The F.B.I., The Streets of San Francisco,* and *Barnaby Jones.*)

From the start, *Marcus Welby. M.D.* indicated it was to be a medical drama set in a new age for both TV and medicine: Not all its illnesses would have a treatment, let alone a cure; not all patients would survive; physical maladies would often involve emotional or even psychiatric components; and medical authorities would be seen as fallible.

TV Guide

In addition, the series would be exploring many outside-TV-convention topics, which over the course of its long run would come to include menopause, birth defects, sexual dysfunction, mental retardation, and substance abuse, as well as hot-button issues of the day that ranged from abortion and faith-healing and plastic surgery to eating disorders and a parent's right to withhold treatment for a child. Patients would run the demographic gamut as well, nodding to the times by ranging from hippies and drug-addicts to Native-Americans and Vietnam veterans.

In all, it was a far cry from what had been the traditional TV-doctor series. (Reportedly, the early 1960s medical hit *Dr. Kildare* had written episodes about birth-control and venereal disease, though due to network objections they were never produced.) In the hands of kindly and wise and compassionate Dr. Marcus Welby, however, it was accepted and embraced. *Marcus Welby M.D.* became a Top Ten fixture in its freshman season, and then TV's number-one show in year two.

But the pill of progress is a sometimes-bitter one to swallow. One two separate episodes that came midway through its seven-year run on ABC – one in 1973 and another in 1974 – *Marcus Welby, M.D.* addressed the hottest of hot-button current-events issues. And twice the show was burned.

The 22nd episode of the show's fourth season, titled "The Other Martin Loring," found Welby taking on the case of a 50-ish married man who comes to him with complaints of stress and fatigue -- symptoms of a mask, Welby finds out, used by a functioning alcoholic who's also dealing with a crumbling marriage and depression. And, it comes to be revealed, a life in hiding as a gay man. Which is where the episode ran into trouble.

In it, after finding out the man's secret and in what he sees as an attempt to deal with his health issues, Welby suggests to the depressed patient that perhaps he's just *afraid* that he's gay rather than *actually* gay. But that consultation leads to a failed suicide attempt, which in turns sends the man to a psychiatrist at Welby's suggestion, all the better to put him back on the road to a "normal" marital life.

ABC / NBCUniversal

Reportedly, the script for "The Other Martin Loring" was leaked a month ahead of the episode's scheduled airdate, including to advocates from the gay community, increasing in numbers nationwide since the Stonewall Rebellion in New York of four years earlier. They lodged a complaint against ABC over the story's portrayal of homosexuality as an abnormality to be cured.

A meeting with network executives followed, and, as reported in *The Prime Time Closet: A History of Gays and Lesbians on TV*, an advanced screening of the completed episode was arranged, presumably to off-set publicity. But gay supporters who saw it denounced it as "medically unsound … and demoralizing to homosexuals" -- especially in its scenes that feature the character of Martin Loring describing himself as "loathsome and degrading" and summing up his life as "a hollow fraud."

Network executives offered to remove the offending lines for the upcoming broadcast (though reportedly they were kept in for future airings ins reruns and syndication), but protesters failed in their larger demand that ABC revise or even withhold the entire episode. As a result, demonstrations were set up outside the network's New York headquarters four days before the episode was to air, with another held in Los Angeles on the actual day of air at ABC offices and at the Los Angeles County Medical Association.

"The Other Martin Loring" aired that night as scheduled and promoted, its storyline intact of Dr. Welby suggesting if not encouraging his gay patient to resist his homosexual impulses for the sake of his health and the respect of his son.

Eighteen months later, another episode, this one the fifth of *Welby*'s sixth season, ended up in the social crosshairs. Called "The Outrage," its story focused on an 11-year-old boy raped by his male science-teacher. Its own various threads involved the boy's shame, the married teacher's threats against him to remain silent about the abuse, and the victim's parents' "shock and disgust" over what happened to their son.

In one conversation, the father even asks his son, "Wasn't there something you could have done [to stop it]?"

The focus of an investigative story in *The Advocate* a month before it aired (as recounted in *The Prime Time Closet*), the script for the episode featured a scene between the boy's father and a police officer that included the following conversation:

> **George**: I thought this was – the kind of thing that might happen in prison – or one of those bars but –

> **[Investigating Officer] Buchanan**: Nah – those weird bars have got enough problems as it is -- our garden variety homosexual, this isn't his game – let me tell you something.

Once again, ABC provided the script to gay-rights advocates in advance of production. Once again, they protested, here over what was felt to be the linking of child molestation with homosexuality and effeminacy, despite the fact that the repeat-offender rapist in the episode is presented as heterosexual. (The 11-year-old boy is reassured after his assault that he's "still a man.")

"The Outrage" reportedly went through multiple versions over multiple months -- the father/policeman scene was altered -- but gay-rights supporters still objected, since the episode would still include a scene in which the offending teacher threatens the student ("Do I really have to draw pictures for you to know what other people are going to think about you [if you tell]?"). But ABC stood its ground, even trumpeting the episode's "social value."

Unlike "The Other Martin Loring," which went from awareness to complaints to air in a relatively brief time, "The Outrage" had courted webs of controversy for months, since early summer 1974. By time it aired, it had come to ensnare the ABC network, its body of affiliates, the increasingly more cohesive and media-savvy gay community, the

National Association of Broadcasters (NAB), the American Federation of Teachers (AFT), the American Psychiatric Association (APA) and even the AFL-CIO.

Further, that it was scheduled to run a month before the 1974 mid-term elections, some of which pivoted on issues of discrimination based on sexual-orientation, meant the show had become a political hot-potato, too. (Sample local newspaper headline from October 5: "Quiet Old Dr. Marcus Welby Stirs National Controversy.") Demonstrations were planned in cities across the country for its day of broadcast.

As a consequence, some advertisers told ABC they wanted no part of the episode, and some of the network's affiliates announced that the episode would air with a parental advisory. Seventeen refused to air it at all.

ABC / NBCUniversal

Unusual for a series well into its run, critics weighed in, too, about everything from the specific episode's quality (**Spoiler Alert:** They hated it) to over-arching issues of prior restraint, freedom of speech, and pressure-group tactics. In his *New York Times* column on the Sunday before "The Outrage" aired, John J. O'Conner wrote that the whole affair could be summed up as "Powerful Networks Versus Increasingly Powerful Pressure Groups." (A lesbian-themed episode of NBC's new hit drama *Police Woman* called "Flowers of Evil" was also caught up in the controversy, especially in connection with one scene in which the title character says to a lesbian, "I understand what a love like yours can do to a person.") The episode came and went as scheduled.

At the end of the day, what seems most remarkable about the "The Outrage" is not the gay text but the frankness with which the 11-year-old's rape is discussed, regardless of perpetrator. The episode opens with the boy's mother discovering his bloody sheets, which leads to her taking him to Welby. And as the story continues it's established that the young victim will require surgery to correct the physical damage inflicted during the assault. In 1974, this kind of writing just didn't happen. Yet here it did.

Each of the two controversial episodes of *Marcus Welby, M.D.* did what much of TV did throughout the decade: They pushed the prime-time envelope to see how far TV could go in trying to reflect a changing world calling for and expecting it; and in various forms and with varying degrees of success it showed that prime-time stories could and should reflect the many different people watching them.

Medical Center
"The Fourth Sex"
September 8 and 15 1975 CBS
(41)

James Daley
as
Dr. Paul Lochner

Chad Everett
as
Dr. Joe Gannon

CBS

A year after the iconic and long-running family sitcom *The Brady Bunch* was cancelled in 1974, actor Robert Reed, who'd headed the cast as patriarch Mike Brady and who reportedly had a fractious relationship with its producer over what Reed felt was a project that didn't service his skills as actor, apparently made up for lost creative time.

In the two-part season premiere of the seventh and final season of the popular CBS medical drama *Medical Center*, he guest-starred as a patient who entered the hospital a man and left a woman. Called "The Fourth Sex," the episode marked yet another TV fist for the 1970s -- the first show to deal with and depict the consequences of what was then called sex-change surgery.

In the 1970s, the idea behind the procedure was chiefly tied to the name Christine Jorgensen, the New York-born World War II-serving George Jorgensen who in a series of surgeries beginning in 1951 became and lived the rest of her 62 years as a woman.

A celebrated figure, Jorgensen published an autobiography in 1967 and for much of the next decade appeared on the lecture circuit to talk about her unusual life. (She was also an occasional entertainer and actress.) In 1970, she famously had a dust-up with Vice-President Spiro T. Agnew in the wake of what she felt were disparaging remarks he'd made about her -- thus making her transgenderism front-page news all over again for a new generation.

CBS

Around the same time, in the fall of 1969 -- the night following the premiere of *Marcus Welby, M.D.* on ABC, in fact -- the new TV series *Medical Center* premiered on CBS. Chad Everett and James Daly co-starred, playing the requisite young-blood/old-school pair, here two surgeons at a Los Angeles-based university-affiliated hospital. (**Fun Fact**: First guest-patient on the show was played by O.J. Simpson.)

Like *Welby, Medical Center* demonstrated from the start that it would not shy away from storylines that reflected a changing medical field and a changing country, including those dealing with drug and alcohol abuse, child abuse, emotional disorders, politics of war, homelessness and abortion. (These were explored in the first season alone.) It, too, would end up blazing the trail for the modern medical drama. But with "The Fourth Sex," *Medical Center* pushed TV's limit.

The episode embraced the conventions of prime-time melodrama as it eschewed them. In it, having come to the hospital for the surgery, Reed's character, a world-famous surgeon himself, is at first denied the procedure by the hospital's board. His dreams are crushed. It falls to Everett as the forward-thinking and sympathetic Dr. Joe Gannon to make an impassioned case in support of the operation and his colleague, to hospital staff as well as to the patient's wife and son, each wrestling with feelings of betrayal.

The surgery is then approved, and the patient undergoes the procedure that transforms him from a man to a woman. (Of course, the transformation is achieved in remarkably short TV-friendly order, belying the lengthy reality of re-assignment surgery, which can take months, if not years.) Before leaving the hospital, she is afforded a benediction of sorts from her former angry wife, who offers supportive wishes. Then Reed, in full make-up and wardrobe, is seen leaving the hospital, as a woman, in search of the rest of her life.

If the "The Fourth Sex" took both medical and emotional short-cuts in fitting its storyline into the confines of episodic TV -- even as part of an expanded two-parter -- it neither exploited nor made light of it, either. The dialogue about the procedure was frank and maturely written; and the performances were effective, particularly Reed's, which ably conveyed internal anguish before the surgery and then nervous relief after. That *Medical Center* took on the subject and then took such care in presenting it is almost not to be believed. That it did so 40 years before Caitlyn Jenner, tackling questions then that would become front-page news in 2015, seems historic.

Robert Reed came out of what he felt were five years of *Brady Bunch* servitude with a vengeance, earning an Emmy nomination, his first, for his performance in "The Fourth Sex," the first of three nominations in a single two-year span. (The same year that he was nominated for *Medical Center* he was also nominated for his supporting role in the mini-series *Rich Man Poor Man*; a year later he was nominated for his performance in *Roots*.)

A private man who by some accounts dealt with his own internal anguish as a closeted gay actor in Hollywood, Reed died in 1992. He was just 59.

Christine Jorgenson, in comments made before she herself died of cancer in 1989, summed up her life by saying that she gave the sexual revolution "a good swift kick in the pants." In its own way, the two-part episode of *Medical Center* called "The Fourth Sex" did the same for prime-time television.

CBS

"Kunta Kinte, behold the only thing greater than yourself!"

> -- Omoro, lifting newborn son Kunta Kinte to the skies
> *Roots*

"My Sweet Charlie"
January 20 1970 NBC
(42)

One of the unsung pioneers of 1970s television was director Lamont Johnson, responsible for three seminal TV films in the early years of the decade: "That Certain Summer" (1972), a milestone exploration of an adult gay romance; "The Execution of Private Slovik" (1974), an Emmy-nominated drama about the first American court-martialed and executed for desertion since the Civil War; and "My Sweet Charlie," about a relationship between a white teenaged girl and a black adult male, broadcast against the backdrop of heightened racial tension in the United States. Together, the three set a tone for how topical material would be addressed in 1970s television. Especially *My Sweet Charlie*.

Based on the David Westheimer book, set during the Civil Rights movement of the early 1960s, "My Sweet Charlie" starred Al Freeman, Jr., as black attorney from the North on the run in the South after being unjustly accused of murder and Patty Duke as a bigoted white teen who's run away from home after finding herself pregnant. The pair end up seeking refuge in the same isolated and deserted Gulf Coast cottage, and, after considerable initial hostilities, form a relationship as each turns to the other for survival.

NBC

That the film aired barely two years after the assassination of Martin Luther King, a year after James Earl Ray pleaded guilty to shooting King, and a month after the chairman of the Illinois Black Panther Party was assassinated (not to mention amid a tide of ongoing college-campus race-riots and barely three years after the Supreme Court's *Loving v. Virginia* ruling) hints at the tinderbox that it was dropped into. Scenes of Duke's character recoiling in horror after discovering "a nigger" in her hideaway did not help.

It was filmed in Texas in the summer of 1968, shortly after the deaths of both King and Robert Kennedy. And it met with hostility from the start: Duke was harassed at her hotel, and rumors were planted that suggested the movie's two stars were having an affair. Ultimately, Texas governor John Connelly called on local police to help keep the peace during filming.

When it aired in January 1970, despite or because of the storyline "My Sweet Charlie" was a ratings hit. It achieved the biggest audience to date for a made-for TV film, on any network. Later that year it was nominated for eight Emmys, including one each for its lead actors and for both director Johnson and writers Richard Levinson and William Link. Its writers and director won. (The award-winning Johnson/Levinson/Link trio would go on to "That Certain Summer" and "The Execution of Private Slovik.")

Then as today, topicality was considered not just a sizable risk for TV to take, it represented a sizeable step as well: It brought to scripted prime-time issues of the day that were being covered on the evening news. TV was beginning to cast its considerable spotlight on important topics, even (or especially) ones that were dividing a nation. "My Sweet Charlie" is still help up and celebrated today as an important work for each generation that it's bequeathed to.

Roots
January 23-30 1977 ABC
(43)

Though pointed out many times through the decades, it still seems of worthy of note: The epic and justly acclaimed 1977 mini-series *Roots* owes much of its well-earned legacy to … the weather.

Airing over the course of eight consecutive nights on ABC, the project did benefit from massive publicity, and it did premier to impressive ratings that continued to grow each night as its serialized story unfolded. So stellar numbers for its finale were predicted and expected.

But few imagined just how stellar as the days counted down and as a record-cold January (snow fell on both Miami and parts of the Bahamas on January 20) came to a head over the month's final weekend, with an East Coast blizzard (as much as 100 inches of snow in some regions) that trapped about a third of the country inside their homes with little to do but watch TV. Which in turn meant that when the TV show that everyone had been talking about that week concluded on Sunday January 30, it ended up with a mind-boggling 77 audience share, amounting to nearly 100 people.

Half the country watched *Roots'* two-hour conclusion.

Time Inc.

Of all the shows that TV had aired in its first 30 years, "none can compare to the tsunami-like impact ... *Roots* had," wrote Josef Adalian in a 2016 retrospective. "It wasn't just the biggest event of the week or the season: Up until that point, *Roots* was the top-rated TV production the medium had ever produced. And nearly 40 years later, no other television movie or mini-series has surpassed its reach."

Based on Alex Haley's 1976 best-selling and culture-stirring *Roots: The Saga of An American Family*, in which the author chronicled his family history from the early slave-trade era though Reconstruction, *Roots* came along at a critical time in a decade that was devoting itself to ethnic identity and self-exploration.

ABC invested a substantial sum of $6 million (approximate 2018 value: $26 million) in producing the 12-hour project, pairing an unknown (LeVar Burton, in the key starring role of ancestor Kunta Kinte) with a roster of familiar African-American actors (John Amos, Cicely Tyson, Louis Gossett, Leslie Uggams, Richard Roundtree) to populate the many branches of the Haley family tree. Scores of TV-friendly white performers of the day (from Sandy Duncan to Edward Asner to Robert Reed) were added to the cast to ensure cross-audience appeal, if not to make more inviting such an inflammatory TV-movie topic.

Chicago Tribune

205

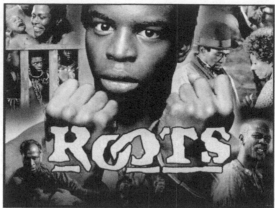

TV Guide / ABC

Despite the financial investment, there were reservations at the top about who, if anyone, would actually sit down to watch an eight-part movie about slavery. ABC executives debated how and when to run it -- once a week for 12 weeks? two hours a week for six? high-profile or low-profile time of year? in Sweeps or out?

At issue: Would a poor first-night tune-in cripple the network for as long as it took to run the mini-series out, and if so should it be broadcast as quickly as possible to get it over with?

In the end, the network opted for a sort of Hail Mary-play -- all twelve hours of *Roots* would air over the course of a single week (Sunday to Sunday, eight consecutive nights) in the lower-stakes month of January, before the start of the critical February Sweeps period. Which in the end, of course, is what made the project a social phenomenon.

ABC executives are on record saying that after the ratings came in for the first night's airing, a collective exhale could be heard in its halls. They knew ratings would only grow from there, as mini-series tended to do. But few inside or outside the network could have foreseen what the week actually became.

Word-of-mouth excitement, front-of-newspaper coverage, talk-show and news-broadcast chatter, on the streets and in the schools and at the office -- the subject was *Roots*. In an era before recorded or delayed viewing was a thing, some restaurants and shops and entertainment venues closed at night that week. Social engagements were re-scheduled. Las Vegas gaming tables were reported to be clearing out and New York movie-theaters going empty come the start of prime-time. Coast to coast, everyone everywhere was tuning in to *Roots*.

And then the Blizzard of 1977 descended in time for its final three nights, after five nights of snowballing interest, sealing its fates. History *became* history.

Months later, *Roots* made history again when it was nominated for an unprecedented 37 Emmy Awards (a never-broken record). It won nine at the ceremonies on September 11, including Outstanding Limited Series, Outstanding Directing, Outstanding Writing, as well as acting trophies for Edward Asner, Louis Gossett, Jr., and Olivia Cole. (Ten other cast members were nominated, another record.)

Director John Erman won the Directors Guild of America award, and the mini-series also went on to win both the Peabody and the Christopher awards.

In the aftermath of the streaking comet that was *Roots*, the cultural conversation about race and identity that started with the 1976 publication of Haley's book ... accclerated. The legacy of slavery and the black experience in the country since became a national conversation.

If the Black Power movement of the 1960s was about addressing identity (*negro* had become *black*), which paved the way for the publication and acceptance of the book itself, *Roots* the TV mini-series exacerbated that as at the same time it stirred white consciousness about black culture.

When 1977 began, the Civil Rights Act was not yet 14 years old; the Watts riots and the assassination of Martin Luther King, Jr., were still fresh in mind; Shirley Chisholm's 1972 presidential run was seen as a one-off; whites of a certain generation were still using the term *colored*; and there was no Obama, no Oprah, no BET, no *Cosby Show*. Even with the progress made to date on TV by the mid-1970s, the notion of being black in America was relegated to five broad sitcoms (*All in the Family, Sanford and Son, Good Times, That's My Mama, The Jeffersons*) and a handful of TV movies (*My Sweet Charlie, The Autobiography of Miss Jane Pittman*).

There was little to nothing by way of black drama series, unless allowing for the short-lived and bordering-on-caricature *Shaft* or *Get Christie Love!*, which few were. Then came *Roots*, which changed ... everything. Mass audiences were not only available for serious black storytelling, they were also interested in it. It pulled the Hollywood curtain back on a wide range of black faces, too (even if, as *Roots* and *Good Times* actor John Amos would later observe, the interest in hiring them went only so far for only so long).

The floodgates for TV mini-series opened wider in its wake, too, lasting longer, having first made a mark a year earlier (on the same network) with the 12-hour *Rich Man, Poor Man*. More historical long-forms were ordered, including *Holocaust* (due the following spring), *Centennial* (due the following fall), and a seven-part *Roots* sequel called *Roots: The Next Generations* (due late winter 1979).

More significant, as was being seen in more and more projects since *All in the Family* arrived in 1971 to introduce new content to TV, *Roots* made television itself important. It gave it credibility. It showed that it can *about* something. Something to involve one's self in, not just watch. It can be that vehicle for change that was envisioned for it at the turn of the decade. A *means*, not just an end.

In the decades since its historic airing, many in the black community (and many academic and critics and historians in and outside of it), have tried to explain the significance of *Roots*, its impact on black culture, on themselves personally, on society as a whole from economic, artistic, familiar, and cultural points-of-view. No less a TV titan than Oprah Winfrey herself has devoted a good deal of her airtime through the years to honoring it as well. The simple explanation seems to be that when he established his legacy, Alex Haley helped black America establish its own. Because of TV. And a snowstorm. In the eyes of most people who follow TV and pop culture, *Roots* remains the medium's most significant piece of programming in its history.

"More than half the population of the United States," writes Bruce J. Schulman in *The Seventies: The Great Shift in American Culture, Society and Politics,* "watched at least some part of the eight-night mini-series. Haley's efforts to recover his family's heritage... transfixed the entire nation … Americans rediscovered their families, their ethnicity, their spirituality. They looked back – but almost exclusively at themselves."

Dramatic 'Roots' Of America

By Sander Vanocur

LeVar Burton (top, second from left), as Kunta Kinte, while above, Cicely Tyson, left, and Maya Angelou rejoice as Kinte is born.

'Roots' Getting a Grip on People Everywhere

By CHARLAYNE HUNTER-GAULT

Time Inc. / *The Washington Post* / *The New York Times*

209

Sanford and Son
1972-77 NBC
(44)

Sony

Seven years before the arrival of *Sanford and Son* on NBC, a light-hearted drama called *I Spy* on the same network made Bill Cosby the first black lead on a scripted prime-time drama -- an achievement somewhat mitigated by the fact that in it Cosby was paired with white actor Robert Culp. So he wasn't the sole lead.

Four years before the arrival of *Sanford and Son* on NBC, Diahann Carroll, also on the same network, became the first black female lead on a TV series. Here, too, though, the achievement was marked with the asterisk of a white co-lead (Lloyd Nolan, who played boss to her nurse).

Sanford and Son, on the other hand, which premiered as a mid-season replacement on NBC in January 1972, was the first hit sitcom to feature all-black leads (discounting the 1950s comedy *Amos & Andy*, which most do). Two black actors heading up their own show. And it wasn't just a hit: It was a Top Ten smash, the most successful sitcom in NBC's history to that date.

(**Fun Fact:** *Sanford and Son* was one of the large pieces of prime-time artillery used to take down perennially popular *The Brady Bunch*, which aired opposite it on ABC and which represented one of prime-time TV's final holdovers from the more-simple 1960s approach to family comedy.)

Like *All in the Family*, *Sanford and Son* was an adaptation of a 1960s British sitcom, here called *Steptoe and Son*, about a white father-and-son team who worked as proprietors of a junk store. Episodes focused on their intergenerational differences when it came to the store, their lives, and pretty much everything else.

NBC's iteration kept the same basic premise, pairing nightclub comic Redd Foxx, then 50, in his first TV series, with stage actor Demond Wilson playing his son. Episodes focused on their own loving and sparring relationship as junk dealers in the blighted Watts section of Los Angeles.

Crusty widower Fred Sanford was an outrageous anti-hero at odds with the world, a character along the lines of Archie Bunker, though Fred's vitriol was a bit more cartoonish and less topical. Bigger than life, he was often just plain cranky and caustic. But his antics helped make *Sanford & Son* the instant hit it became.

Storylines were routine and less-than-memorable -- "Fred fakes a robbery to cover up his careless destruction of his son's prized porcelain collection" "Lamont's daily haul of junk one day ends up including a briefcase full of cash" "Fred and Lamont are duped into smuggling stolen diamonds from Hawaii" -- but the Foxx-Wilson dynamic made the show funny. And made it work. It ranked sixth among all TV shows for the 1971-72 season, impressive for a mid-season replacement series. And it helped to further NBC's axis-tilt toward more relevant and diverse programming (begun in 1968 with *Rowan and Martin's Laugh-In*, supplemented by *The Flip Wilson Show* in 1970, with *Police Story* and *Chico and the Man* shortly to come).

Never an awards favorite, with a total of just seven Emmy nominations (no wins) throughout its long run, *Sanford and Son* remained popular into its sixth season, during which Redd Foxx was lured to ABC with the promise of his own solo variety show, which quickly sank. In 1980, the chastened star was invited back to NBC and to his most famous character for a revival series called *Sanford* (no *Son*). It, too, failed, perhaps indicating that Fred Sanford's outrageousness was not as novel or entertaining at the end of the decade as it was in its beginning. By 1980, TV itself had become as outrageous as Fred Sanford, if not more so.

Still, Redd Foxx and *Sanford* (with *Son*) made a difference. The lines may be more dotted than solid, but its success helped to make TV more receptive to the "black" programming to come in the decade. Helped in no small part by the names attached to it -- Bud Yorkin and Norman Lear, who'd hit pay-dirt a year earlier with *All in the Family* -- it paved the way for more black faces in American prime-time.

Sony

"Steambath"
May 4 1973 PBS
(45)

> Public distrust of the political leadership represented only the tip of a massive iceberg of discontent…The problems of confidence and credibility extended far beyond questions of willful dishonesty, touched the most basic foundations of American culture. The loss of faith in doctors and lawyers, the skepticism about corporate leaders, the omnipresent distrust of politicians – all produced a spreading disillusionment about the competence of the dominant institutions of society…By the mid-Seventies, this crisis of confidence leaped quickly from the projections of speculative science to the bastions of education to the definition of life itself."

-- Peter N. Carroll
It Seemed Like Nothing Happened: American in the 1970s

> Journeys of discovery became commonplace in the Seventies. The personal odysseys of white ethnics, the elderly, racial minorities, and ecologists also fed into a widespread religious revival.

-- Bruce J Schulman
The Seventies: The Great Shift in American Culture, Society and Politics

The total number of people who actually watched it on air could probably fit inside a single football stadium, with many seats left empty. But still: It aired. In 1973, it aired.

God and gays and Valerie Perrine's not-insignificant breasts met up in a TV steambath in 1973. And more small-screen taboos toppled.

Based on Bruce Jay Friedman's 1970 off-Broadway satire about a disparate group of the newly dead awaiting word on their after-fates in a public gym that's doubling as a celestial way-station -- and where God is it Puerto Rican janitor -- *Steambath* came to the scene at a time when individuality was growing in importance and spiritually was in a state of flux. (*Time*'s famous April 8 1966 cover story: "Is God Dead?".)

The result was as much a looking within as above for both explanation and salvation. And led to Friedman, a Jewish-born former men's-magazine editor-turned-writer, addressing the changing tide with this his second play, predicated on the arrival at the bath of a newcomer named Tandy who's at first unsure of where he is (or why) and then upon realizing what's happened to him lapses into a sizeable review of his life and death.

And frankly, as least according to the group of souls waiting alongside him there in purgatory-adjacent, life had a whole lot of explaining to do.

Steambath's arch approach to and commentaries on religion and mortality -- not to mention its language, leading-lady nudity and healthy infusion of gay text, including but not limited to a pair of effeminates singing and line-kicking their ways through a song called "The Fabulous Fags of Steambath" -- found it in scalding hot water almost from the start of its stage run.

It lasted only a few months, but it said what it had to say and made an impression at a time when rebellion and the questioning of authority was very much in the *zeitgeist*. (**Fun Fact**: In the Off-Broadway production, Anthony Perkins starred as Tandy, opposite Hector Elizondo as the steambath janitor.) So much so that in 1973 it was adapted for (public) television as part of a project called Hollywood Television Theater, a stage-to-screen anthology series broadcast from 1970 to 1978 and produced by PBS's Los Angeles affiliate KCET.

TV-friendly Bill Bixby, who'd most recently been seen in the warm family sitcom *The Courtship of Eddie's Father* (1969-72) was cast as

Tandy, heading an ensemble that featured, among others, Neil Simon-film-favorite Herb Edelman, Kenneth Mars (who'd just co-starred in the Barbra Streisand film WHAT'S UP, DOC?), Valerie Perrine (who'd made her film debut in 1972's SLAUGHTERHOUSE-FIVE and was a year away from a Best Actress nomination for the Dustin Hoffman drama LENNY), and, as God the attendant, rising star Jose Perez.

(**Another Fun Fact**: According to Friedman, he didn't know of any of the TV names that were being suggested for the role of Tandy, so he petitioned his 12-year-old son for help in selecting an actor from among a given list; the son chose Bixby.)

As was the case with the stage-play, most of the characters in the PBS adaptation were depicted sitting around the steamroom, draped in towels – or, in the case of new arrival Tandy, white briefs and dress-shirt -- commiserating about life and wondering their futures.

Their colorful language was toned down for the small screen, but TV's *Steambath* was still replete with jabs at religion and with debates about the nature of existence itself. It still featured enough of its only female character's breasts to be shocking for TV in 1973. And it still offered the dark-mood-puncturing line-kicking performance of the self-described "Fabulous Fags." For those afforded the chance to see it, that is.

The reality is that *Steambath*'s content drew brays of protests from those concerned that it was airing on the same channel that brought *Sesame Street* and *Mr. Rogers' Neighborhood* to their kids. The controversy that ensued resulted in just 23 of the network's affiliated stations broadcasting it.

But broadcast it was. And *Steambath*'s content and language and peek-a-boo nudity conspired with a handful of other prime-time projects of its day to force the child that was TV to become an adult.

It showed that television can offer a home for arts-y programming. And with its inclusion of an out-and-proud gay couple, it also made a

PBS / KCET

significant contribution to the cause of individualism in a decade pivoting on it. (Less of a big deal on the New York stage in the 1970s, homosexuality was still a shocking and considerable taboo for a national television audience.)

As minorities were coming to realize, acknowledgement on TV begat awareness, which begat conversation. Even baby steps are moves forward. (As for the fact that much of the project's comedy was mined from the incredible notion that God was a minority? Chalk that up to the times, too.)

A mere flickering flame in the conflagration that was prime-time in the 1970s, *Steambath* more than anything helped to singe expectations about what should and could air on TV. Not just in terms of language or nudity or format but also in terms of topics and thoughts. As *M*A*S*H** and *Maude* had started to do upon their premieres on CBS the previous September, and as more scripted shows were doing in general (and would continue to do on all three networks as the decade progressed), *Steambath* brought to TV the idea of *ideas* – that TV, scripted TV, designed as entertainment, could be *about* things. It could spark dialogue and debate.

The lead character of Tandy in *Steambath* is equal parts confused by and rebellious over his fate, a fate that everyone faces at some point. He provokes important questions that are seen as worth asking during questioning times: What is life about? What is *God* about? Does in fact God even exist and if not is there even a point to any of what we do if not?

TV in the 1970s, as so few even well-meaning and big-picture-thinking series had done in the 1950s and 1960s, was incorporating the concept of *thinking*. (A memorable and seemingly important exception from the black-and-white era: a 1964 episode of *The Dick Van Dyke Show* called "The Life and Love of Joe Coogan," which casually but effectively explored the subjects of religion and of religious calling when one of Laura Petrie's old boyfriends shows up as a priest.) The 1970s opened the door to material that dared to question, even to provoke.

Both Friedman and *Steambath* spoke to a questioning nation, at a time when the questions were many. Each was nominated for a 1973 Emmy.

> Even after the censors got done with the script, "Steambath" still is a big step for TV to take ... (It) questions every belief you ever held.
>
> -- Anthony La Camera
> *The Boston Herald* April 15 1973

(**A Third Fun Fact**: The executive producer of *Steambath* was Norman Lloyd, who went on to co-star as Dr. Daniel Auschlander on *St. Elsewhere* from 1982-1988.)

Soul Train
1971-2006 syn
(46)

In 1967, a Chicago personality named Don Cornelius switched from his job in radio over to one in local TV, where he ended up as host of a series of live concerts in the area that spotlighted high-school singers. He called the traveling show "The Soul Train." In 1970, he brought the concept to his TV station as a live weekday-afternoon series. "The show debuted in the middle of a magnificent era of black music and fashion, and it quickly challenged its venerable Saturday-morning colleague, *American Bandstand,* in the ratings," recounted Jake Austin in a 2008 piece for *The Chicago Reader.* Within a year, it was syndicated around the country. It went on to last 35 years.

Cornelius watched *American Bandstand* growing up: "I saw dancing," he said in a 1995 Associated Press interview, "and I knew black kids can dance better; and I saw white artists, and I knew black artists make better music; and if I saw a white host and I knew a black host could project a hipper line of speech." In fact categorized in its early years (understandably at first though perhaps unfairly in sum) as "the black *American Bandstand,*" *Soul Train* was envisioned by Cornelius as a TV show that acknowledged and celebrated African-American culture, especially its R&B, Soul, and Gospel musical roots.

It was an innovative and near-unprecedented vision for a TV show, tapping into a black identity movement. As it grew in popularity, it gained the attention of the black community and attracted some of the biggest black singers of the day to appear as guest performers.

As was the case with *Bandstand,* though, when people tuned in, it wasn't just to see a favorite singer. "They tuned in to see their favorite dancers come down the *Soul Train* line," noted Ericka Blount Danois in her book *Love, Peace, and Soul: Behind the Scenes of America's Favorite Dance Show.* They continued to do so for generations.

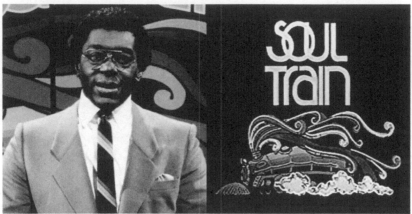

Don Cornelius Productions / Tribune Entertainment

Soul Train became the longest-running syndicated entertainment show in TV history, until *Entertainment Tonight* eclipsed it in 2016. (Cornelius stepped down as host in 1993, but he continued to serve as the show's executive producer through the end of its run.)

"It's impossible to overstate the show's influence, especially considering its longevity," wrote Stephen Deusner in a 2014 appreciation for *pitchfork.com*. "Weathering every pop trend from funk to disco to new wave to new jack swing, it is a vivid chronicle of black popular culture in the late 20th century." Deusner called it "a singular institution in American pop culture that presented black culture -- fashion, dance, politics -- in a positive light."

Soul Train, he pointed out, "showed blacks coming together in joyous celebration, and it's impossible to discount the impression that would have made on viewers of any age or color." It influenced multiple generations and became a sort of mother ship for several black-based entertainment specials and series – a brand that lasted past the show's cancellation in 2006 and even its host's death in 2012, and which as recently as 2013 came to include a Soul Train Cruise as part of the Holland American line.

A 2010 VH1 Rock Docs examined its influence and legacy in *Soul Train: The Hippest Trip in America,* narrated by Terrence Howard. In a loose spin-off to that called *The Hippest Trip in America: Soul Train and the Evolution of Culture and Style,* Nelson George writes, "Inspired by the civil rights movement, [Don Cornelius] saw a space for black joy on television."

"That Certain Summer"
November 1 1972 ABC
(47)

ABC / NBCUniversal

In her *New York Times* review, Marilyn Beck called it "one of the finest pieces of drama you'll see this year on large or small screen." Charles Champlin of the *Los Angeles Times* said, "It is the best movie for TV I have yet seen . . . a film which would do honor to any size screen." Others viewed it "a giant step for television" (*New York* magazine) and evidence that with its broadcast "Television grows up" (*TV Guide*).

The giant step was *That Certain Summer*, a made-for-ABC movie that for the first time in TV history and at a time when *homosexuality* was still considered a disorder presented a romantic relationship between two adult men. Three years after what became known as the Stonewall Rebellion set a new course for gay culture in 1969, *That Certain Summer* changed it for TV.

The movie focuses on a long-divorced man in his 40s (played by Hal Holbrook) who while living with a partner (Martin Sheen) is faced with having to explain his post-married life for the first time to his now 14-year-old son (Scott Jacoby), about to visit him for vacation. The turmoil that results jeopardizes both relationships as the concept of sexuality is examined.

When TV was still more Dodge City than it was San Francisco, it was a daring proposal. Which its writers (Richard Levinson and William Link) discovered when they pitched it to NBC, where their popular series *Columbo* was a hit and where they had a production deal.

NBC "had no intention of okaying a movie in which homosexuality was treated as a fact of life, one explored with sympathy and understanding," according to notes from The Paley Center for Media. Fortunately, "the executive in charge of ABC's TV-movie division, Barry Diller, was deeply moved by the script and quickly green-lighted the project." (ABC was in the vanguard of the TV-movie genre at the time.) To placate nervous sponsors, dialogue was written for lead actor Hal Holbrook that incorporated what could be described as an opposing viewpoint on the subject of homosexuality. It came as part of a powerful monologue in the film's pivotal father-son discussion.

> A lot of people – most people I guess – think it's wrong. They say it's a sickness. They say it's something that has to be cured. I don't know. I do know it isn't easy. If I had a choice, it's not something I'd pick for myself. But it's the only way I can live … Does that change me so much? I'm still your father … I've lied to myself for a long time. Why should I lie to you? It's funny, I never talked about this with my own father. I should have. He knew. At least, I think he knew. But we could never sit down, even approach it. And he died. I know how you feel. You may not believe that, but I do. Nick, the hardest time I've ever had was accepting it myself. Can you at least try to understand? Please?

"Amazingly, Standards & Practices tried to get the writers to remove Holbrook's simple declaration to his son that he and his partner 'love each other,' but Levinson and Link fought that battle and the line stayed in" (*paleycenter.org*).

Homosexuality is something people never talk about. If they did, this family would never have to face...

THAT CERTAIN SUMMER

Starring Hal Holbrook, Hope Lange, Martin Sheen, Scott Jacoby, A World Premiere Wednesday Movie of the Week 8:30pm 7 11

ABC /NBCUniversal

Holbrook explained decades later that it was the universal truth in the script -- the story of a man suffering from pain and loss -- that transcended its gay storyline and which led to his decision to accept what was then considered a risky role for an actor. He even credited the divorce he was going through at the time for informing his performance.

Co-star Martin Sheen, who was at the height of his leading man status in both film and TV in the early 1970s, recalled in a 2007 interview that those in his circle were concerned about the movie damaging his career. "I'd robbed banks and kidnapped children and raped women and murdered people, you know, in any number of shows," he told *The Dallas Voice*. "Now I was going to play a gay guy and that was like considered a career ender. Oh, for Christ's sake! What kind of culture do we live in?"

(**Not So Fun Fact**: 1968 Oscar-winner Cliff Robertson was offered and rejected outright the lead role that went to Holbrook; according to co-writer Link, on the *emmyTVlegends.org* website, the actor said he'd "sooner play Hitler.")

That Certain Summer ends with a level of sadness verging on hopelessness for its characters: The father-son relationship is changed, and the partners' relationship is ended. Such is 1972. It will be take many years and many movies before homosexuals are allowed to be happy on TV.

But throughout the film the very concept of a gay relationship is thoughtfully and carefully examined. That the film was made at all marked a small miracle. That it was broadcast -- not everywhere: some ABC affiliates preempted it in its entirety, fearing viewer backlash -- a more sizeable one.

It went on to win a Golden Globe award as the year's best TV movie and the Directors Guild Award for Lamont Johnson. It was also nominated for seven Emmys, including Outstanding Single Program of the Year and Outstanding Writing for a Drama. Scott Jacoby, who co-starred as the young son, was named Best Supporting Actor in a Drama.

That Certain Summer is remembered generations after its broadcast – ones that have seen gay characters evolve from hidden victims to legally married spouses – as a landmark in television programming.

In a 2014 salute, The Paley Center for Media noted: "Over the years many have spoken of the program as a life-changing one, meaning that television had done its job, educating and enlightening a select few and giving others a little bit of hope."

PBS

CBS

COMMERCIALISM

"This is HBO, the Home Box Office. Premium Subscription Television from Time-Life."

-- HBO original identifier
November 1972 to August 1975

Television entered the 1970s as a clearly defined three-network advertiser-driven business – those three networks representing the chief ways for most Americans to get programming and those advertisers representing the chief ways for networks to generate revenue.

Television ended the 1970s as an ill-defined-and rapidly changing no-longer-just-three-network and no-longer-purely-advertiser-driven business – part of an entertainment empire that included a strengthening and competitive public television service (PBS), newly arrived so-called superstations (TBS, WGN), cable broadcasting outlets (from CBN to ESPN), subscription services (HBO and Showtime), pay-per-view programming, and emerging technology that would allow for self-elected viewing of all of it by way of videocassette recorders (VCRs).

So finite was the programming business at the start of the decade that local TV stations actually shut down through the night and awakened again at sunrise. So different was the business at the end of the decade that 24/7 programming (The Cable News Network) was just seven months away.

Throughout the 1970s, the creative structure of the TV business was morphing as well. More and more TV writers were also becoming producers of and the powers behind TV. Mini-studios like Lorimar and MTM Enterprises, aided by regulatory changes, were supplying increasingly more content to the networks, sometimes more than the traditional suppliers such as Paramount Television or 20ᵗʰ Century Fox Television. Local TV markets were turning to more of their own content to air ---- either produced by them or independently purchased for them -- rather than having to rely primarily on that which was provided to them.

Sports and non-fiction and mini-series, late-night and early-morning TV? In. Cigarette advertising? Out. Along with the advertising money connected to it, which since the 1940s had helped pay for TV programming. (In 1970, the last year tobacco ads were allowed on TV, the industry received 65% of the tobacco industry's $314 million advertising budget.) Also out, as in *really* out: gay people and women's breasts, as TV got more and more daring about who and what it dealt with. Which gave more people more reasons to issue more complaints about more programming.

Television was still an industry for millions that made billions, but it was increasingly in the hands of corporations and conglomerates rather than those of the men who helped to sire and then raise it, who unveiled it at the 1939 World's Fair, introduced it as a commercial enterprise in July of 1941. Television was on the way to its status as an entertainment industrial complex. Big business, with big business concerns.

In the 1970s, prime-time hours shortened, government reach lengthened, and the TV highway widened.

"Born Innocent" / The Family Hour
September 10 1974 NBC / 1975-76
(48)

NBC

"As the 1970s proceeded," writes Elana Levine in *Wallowing in Sex: The New Sexual Culture of 1970s American Television*, "the made-for-TV movie was quickly becoming a major site for television's representation of sex and a major focus of regulatory inquiry. One movie in particular ...

would feature strongly in the TV industry's main effort at self-regulation."

The movie was *Born Innocent*. And decades removed from its first airing, it still stands as the go-to reference in any discussion about how and when TV officially crossed some sort of line as far as the images and words it broadcast.

Born Innocent is TV's missing link – the project that came along and then came to represent the difference between what the medium was and what it became.

Linda Blair starred. The actress had just been nominated for an Academy Award for her supporting role as the 14-year-old at the center of THE EXORCIST (1973). In *Born Innocent*, she portrayed a troubled and rebellious teen who as a ward of the court is sentenced to a girls detention center in a last-ditch effort to scare her straight. But there in the facility, of course, she finds daily life to be just as perilous as her life on the outside.

Thirty minutes into the film, she's gang-raped by her fellow teen inmates in the communal shower, pinned to the tile floor as the hardened group's leader violates her with the handle of a plunger.

Even by latter-day standards, the intense and graphic scene is difficult to watch. In 1974, it made viewers and TV-guardians apoplectic. That the film itself aired beginning at 8pm (EST) made things worse.

TV Guide

Shockwaves of outrage and protest were felt across the TV landscape and around the country. "[Y]oung people's exposure to 'deviant' sexual violence ... was at the heart of the protest," notes Levine. "But it was more than one movie at the heart of the reaction. It was ... everything. *Born Innocent* just gave people something specific to focus on."

That *everything* is what TV had become for so many since *All in the Family* arrived in 1971 to change the rules about TV content. Three years after that sitcom's hate-speech and exploration of adult topics, two years after *Maude's* abortion and *That Certain Summer's* homosexual romance, one year after *Steambath* and its nudity and its Fabulous Fags and its questioning of the very existence of God ... the word rang out: Enough.

Enough of the R-rated situations.
Enough of the violence.
Enough of the course language.
Enough of the liberal attitudes.
Enough of the violence and other material against which children's eyes and ears must be shielded.
Just.
Enough.

Special-interest groups set the industry in their crosshairs and got attention from those outside it. (The fact that much of the protesting was mass-produced and involved political opportunism seems worth remembering.) The result: the Federal Communications Commission (FCC), the government agency that oversees broadcast television, stepped in and The Family Viewing Hour came out -- a new policy mandating that the first hour of the prime-time every night is to be set aside for "family friendly" programming, effective with the start of the 1975-76 TV season. (The new policy was actually a complex construct that came out of a labyrinthine maze made up of the FCC, the Industry Code of Practices department of the National Association of Broadcasters, and the presidents of NBC, ABC, and CBS.)

The Family Viewing Hour was met with immediate push-back in the television business, which was financially and artistically threatened by its mandate (if not just put off by the interference). Regarding the former, it meant that in adhering to it the three broadcast networks were faced with having to re-position some of their most successful shows just to fit the clock – a less-than-scientific approach to the usually carefully considered practice of network Scheduling.

Specifically, that meant Number One network CBS was forced to find a different timeslot for its adult-skewing Saturdays-at-8pm *All in the Family*, which was not only its Number One show but the highest-rated show on all of television. Such a switch might not just imperil the show, it might also threaten CBS as a whole, given that the show's success in its long-held Saturday berth was key to success not just on the rest of the night but for its entire prime-time week and, by extension, entire season.

Plus it meant finding that new timeslot for *All in the Family*, bumping from whatever slot it ended up in yet another perhaps long-running series. And who was to know if each series' constituency would follow it to a new timeslot? An entire network's fortunes could hang in the domino-effects balance. And that was just one show on one network.

In addition, under the Family Hour mandate, proposals for potential new series at each of the networks would now have to be evaluated in terms of where and how (and if) they would rank on the "family-friendly" index. A good idea from good auspices might not be good enough to get it on the air. It was an approach to Development that backed both creatives and studio executives into a bit of a tight and ill-fitting box. TV writers in particular viewed the new regulation as one that violated their artistic expressions and, consequently, one that affected their abilities to earn a living. Negative reaction from Hollywood's rank-and-file was loud and fierce.

Still, beginning with the new TV season in September of 1975, the Family Hour took effect. *All in the Family* was indeed one of its casualties – TV's highest-profile show, long associated with Saturday night viewing (often and ironically appointment-viewing for the entire family) was re-located to Monday at 9pm opposite ABC's ratings juggernaut *Monday Night Football.*

For its part, ABC was forced to move its hard-charging often-violent police drama *The Rookies* from its well-established Monday-at-8pm timeslot to Tuesdays at 9pm. (Both series were well into their respective runs, so a bit of attrition was to be expected as they aged, but as a result of the moves *All in the Family*'s 30 Nielsen rating for 1974-75, when it aired on Saturday, slipped to a 22 rating after two seasons on Monday night; CBS's hold on Saturdays and its status as TV's Number One network were gone by 1977; and *The Rookies*, a Top 20 series going into the 1975-76 season, was cancelled at the end of it.)

The family-friendly programming that aired from 8pm to 9pm across all three networks included: returning shows *The Waltons, Little House on the Prairie, Cher, The Six Million Dollar Man, Happy Days, Good Times, Welcome Back Kotter, The Bionic Woman, Tony Orlando and Dawn, Sanford and Son*; and new series *Doc, The Montefuscos, When Things Were Rotten*, and *The Family Holvak*. (Oddly, returning ABC sitcom *Barney Miller*, new ABC sitcom *On the Rocks*, and new NBC sitcom *Fay*, each of which featured adult content, aired in the 8pm hour on their respective nights.)

The disapproving Hollywood rank-and-file fought back, even as the Family Hour rolled out. Fighting both for survival and on free-speech principles, writers and producers were merciless in their attacks on and mockery of what they saw as ham-handed politically motivated government efforts to curb creativity with labeling and by self-important declarations that the country's children needing a "safe-haven" at night when they sat down to their TVs.

Chief among the protesters was Norman Lear, who enlisted his *All in the Family* cast to shoot a video lampooning the Family Hour, with the quartet singing a revised version of their series' popular "Those Were the Days" theme song, retitled "These Are the Days." (Recorded on the Bunker family's living-room set, the spoof was apparently meant for private viewing but became well-known and well-viewed around Hollywood anyway.)

> Television's' grown up now,
> No one needs a marriage vow,
> Folks go to the toilet now,
> These are the days.
> Single girls can take the pill,
> Robert can propose to Bill,
> And we can all say prune juice and toosh and potty out loud,
> These are the days.
> We can show my pregnancy,
> John-Boy can have VD,
> Plus a quick vasectomy (after 9 o'clock),
> These are the days.

Lear saw the new policy as an infringement on creative freedom as guaranteed by the First Amendment. Together with the Writers Guild of America and other industry organizations, he filed suit. In short: In the Fall of 1976 the Family Viewing Hour was declared null-and-void by the District Court, effective with the 1977 TV season. (**Fun Fact**: It was lifted just in time for the arrival of satirical and very-adult sitcom *Soap,* which ABC scheduled in the post-9pm hours regardless.)

The Family Hour was likely headed to null-and-void status before long anyway, as beyond the token relocation of a few high-profile series to

How a Shower Scene Changed Television History (Guest Blog)

Yahoo / Oath Inc.

appease the attention-seeking wavers of decency flags there was no real logic to the mandate, nor was there a clear way to enforce it. Exactly what made a show "family friendly viewing"? Who decided the criteria? Could words like *hell* or *damn* be heard and yet still be classified family-friendly for all and by all? Could 8pm dramas not address current events?

Would news specials or nature documentaries -- educational efforts, about, say, sex -- have to be scheduled in the later hours of a network's schedule? Wouldn't there inevitably and always be *some* one or *some* group that took issue with *some* content? And who or what exactly would decide what for whom -- and to whom would complaints be taken? Local stations? The networks? The FCC? A monitoring agency?

The Family Viewing Hour was about many things — changing times, generational differences, government overreach, parental outrage, good intentions, bad judgment, and a plunger. Though it invoked an actual need (accountability), it wasn't based in any kind of reality nor thought out fully. It called to mind Supreme Court Justice Potter Stewart's infamous 1964 *Jacobellis v. Ohio* definition of obscenity ("I know it when I see it"), but when push came to shove in the mid-1970s no one seemed to have an actionable definition for *inappropriate* nor for a knowing of what to do once they saw it.

For those who lived through it, "the Family Hour" was and always will remain the default joke to be heard in TV executive suites when the conversation -- and the question -- turns to *going too far*.

As for the film that started it all? The shower scene that led to TV being scrubbed clean? TV being TV, NBC re-broadcast it (!) a year later, in October of 1975, just weeks into the start of the Family Viewing Hour. The offending rape sequence was edited. And the film itself aired beginning at 9pm. (**Fun Fact**: The second airing of *Born Innocent* ran against the famous "Chuckles Bites the Dust" episode of the *Mary Tyler Moore* sitcom.)

So connected is *Born Innocent* to derision, though, that the film has seldom been broadcast anywhere since the 1970s. (**Spoiler Alert:** It's also just not very good.) That it also led to a real-life crime and then court case -- ten days after it aired, a 9-year-old girl was gang-raped with a soda-bottle by a group of minors who later confessed that they were inspired to commit the act by *Born Innocent* -- probably hasn't helped. (NBC was sued; and in 1981, in the case of *Olivia N. v. the National Broadcasting Company*, it was held not liable for the attack.)

Born Innocent was part of a triptych of endangered-teenaged-girl TV-movies that Linda Blair starred in for NBC in the immediate aftermath of her EXORCIST fame, when TV movies were proliferating (especially ones hung on the peg of a well-known person in a role at odds with viewers' perceptions). The other two were *Sarah T: Portrait of a Teenaged Alcoholic*, which aired in February 1975 and was one of a long line of "*Portrait of ...*" exploitation movies on NBC in the 1970s *(...of a Stripper, ...of a Teenaged Runaway, ... of a Mistress)*, and *Sweet Hostage*, which was broadcast later that same year.

Together, for good or ill, the schlocky derivative trio did their shares in advancing the prime-time-content ball further down the TV field. Only *Born Innocent*, however, changed TV as a commercial medium, leading to government intervention and, in the process, spotlighting the strength of citizen advocacy.

The film and the movement it inspired remain one of the small-screen most explosive periods during an already explosive era.

"The fact is that our country hasn't been working very well."

-- Rep. Morris Udall (R-AZ)
Democratic National Convention July 1976

Bridget Loves Bernie
1972-73 CBS
(49)

It was the highest-rated first-year TV show ever to be cancelled. Tied for fifth place at the end of the 1972-73 season, it was done in by what passed for controversy at the time:

What happens when a Catholic marries a Jew?

> ... Rabbi Wolfe Kelman, executive vice-president of the Rabbinical Assembly of America, called the show "an insult to some of the most sacred values of both the Jewish and Catholic religions," and said the Synagogue Council of America and the Catholic and Protestant churches had been asked to voice protest ... Jewish groups are assailing the intermarriage-can-be-beautiful theme of *Bridget Loves Bernie*.
>
> -- *Daily News Bulletin*, Jewish Telegraphic Agency
> October 24 1972

Meredith Baxter and David Birney co-starred in the lighter-than-air comedy, as New York newlyweds negotiating both their first year of marriage and the union it formed between their distinctly different families. This being 1972, "distinctly different" meant that one family (hers) is well-to-do Irish-Catholic and the other (his) is working-class Jewish.

It was the brainchild of veteran TV writer Bernard Slade, who'd written for *Bewitched* in the mid-1960s and then created *The Flying Nun* in 1967. (He based the new series very loosely on the 1940s film ABIE'S IRISH ROSE, based on the early 20th century hit of the same name, which had already been made into a film in 1928.) And as TV controversy went in the 1970s, one would think that the discussion in the first ten

TV Guide

minutes of its pilot -- about birth control and pre-marital sex, involving a joking Catholic priest, no less -- would have lit more of a fuse.

Yet it was solely the show's interfaith-marriage that was at issue, as even among the more reform-minded a union outside the faith was not an insignificant matter in the Jewish religion.

But street protests, boycotts, and bomb threats?

Bridget Loves Bernie was assailed from the start. So as it took off in the ratings upon its premiere (sample joke, one character to another in response to a silly question: "Is the Pope Catholic?") and as it kept audiences coming back through that fall and winter (sample storylines: "Confusion and chaos reign when Catholic Bridget runs a Jewish delicatessen" and "Bridget and Bernie reach the holiday season unsure of whether to celebrate Christmas or Hanukkah"), *Bridget Loves Bernie* continued to be seen as a broadside against the Jewish faith. One that had to be addressed and stopped.

"A campaign aimed at forcing the Columbia Broadcasting System to take the program off the air entirely is now under way," reported *The*

New York Times on February 7 1973, further quoting Rabbi Balfour Brickner of the Commission on Interfaith Activities as saying:

> The program treats intermarriage, one of the gravest problems facing Jews today, not only as an existent phenomenon but one that should be totally accepted. … We've had to grapple with our consciences, but in the end, faced with CBS's shocking insensitivity to the religious beliefs of six million Americans, we've had to draw the line here. We've tried to negotiate with CBS to take the show off the air, and failing that, remove from it those aspects offensive to Jews.

Network representatives, for their parts, were baffled. "Though CBS had employed Jewish and Catholic religious advisers on the series, network executives apparently had not anticipated the pressure they were to get from Jewish clergy," writes Katherine C. Montgomery in *Target: Prime Time: Advocacy Groups and the Struggle Over Entertainment.*

CBS found itself in the position of defending a hit series that most of the country was watching, but which a significant minority was protesting. (The Catholics were otherwise occupied at the time with *Maude*'s abortion.)

The whole season was fraught with headaches and a withering spotlight. As it wound down, CBS caved to the controversy. The network announced in March 1973 that *Bridget Loves Bernie*, its highest-rated new show and one of TV's highest-rated series period, would not be renewed for a second season.

CBS president Bob Wood made a point of saying that the decision was in no way due to the trouble that surrounded the sitcom but rather because the freshman show had not been holding on to the huge viewing audience that preceded it on the Saturday-night schedule (*All in the Family*, TV's Number One series). To renew it, he suggested, would be to jeopardize the rest of its winning Saturday night line-up.

In fairness, the numbers did bear this out, but not to degree that seemed to warrant cancellation of a Top Five show. And *Bridget Loves Bernie* was hardly the only series on the network that failed to match the ratings of the series that preceded it: The *Here's Lucy* audience dropped from that of lead-in *Gunsmoke,* and *The Bob Newhart Show* audience dropped from *Mary Tyler Moore*'s. CBS did appear to punt.

Two positive elements were borne of the religious war of 1972-1973, though. The first is that *M*A*S*H**, also introduced in the fall of 1972, replaced *Bridget Loves Bernie* on Saturday night when the 1973-74 season began. This not only turned that first-year show into a hit, it also led to the formation of a powerhouse lineup that season that forever would be held as the best single night of TV in the history of TV -- comprised of *All in the Family, M*A*S*H*, Mary Tyler Moore, The Bob Newhart Show,* and *The Carol Burnett Show,* acclaimed and award-winners all.

The second positive fall-out was the continued immersion into prime-time television of Jewish characters, which were mostly sidelined since the start of TV, helped along by the arrival of the Rhoda Morgenstern character on *Mary Tyler Moore* in 1970.

A third possible benefit that came from the show: *Bridget Loves Bernie* lead actors Meredith Baxter and David Birney fell in love while making the sitcom and married in 1974. Bridget really did love Bernic.

(**Not-So-Fun Fact**: They divorced 15 years later.)

Bridget Loves Bernie was widely watched but not particularly liked, certainly not by the critics. No one seemed to lament it as one of those series of the decade that was Gone Too Soon. But in its one single year on the air, over the course of its 24 not-exactly memorable episodes, the sitcom made a bit of TV history. Because of it, prime-time opened up to still more non-WASP-y characters. Real-world diversity was continuing to be the watchword of 1970s TV.

The Frost/Nixon Interviews
May 1977 syn
(50)

The political if not cultural importance of the 1977 David Frost/Richard Nixon interviews was documented at length in the 2006 Broadway play *Frost/Nixon* and then again in the play's 2008 Oscar-nominated film adaptation. Both showed how a disgraced U.S. President – the country's first to resign from office -- came back into the spotlight in 1977 after three years in exile, and how in the process they reinvented the career of longtime-but-by-then-fading British journalist David Frost.

What the four-part broadcast did for the TV industry, though, was just as noteworthy, if less obvious. The Frost/Nixon interviews demonstrated that a TV project didn't have to come from or even be broadcast on a major television network to be widely viewed. Their success seemed to set the stage for TV content to be valued as content alone, platform be damned.

The idea was all Frost's. Having reportedly thought of securing a Nixon interview as soon as the former President resigned in August 1974, the British journalist engaged in protracted negotiations with the Nixon team over the course of subsequent years, until in 1977 a deal was struck when Nixon came out of hiding. (That Frost represented a friendlier interrogator helped.)

With a mountain of legal bills (and with a new memoir to sell), President Nixon wanted to be paid for his first post-resignation interviews, which Frost agreed to. But the result of that agreement was that his sit-down with the former President would not be airing on the major U.S. networks, due to standard journalism practices of never paying for news. The Frost team instead enlisted a marketing agency to sell the project local market by local market around the country. A total of 145 stations signed on, essentially creating, if only for this project, a fourth commercial television network.

Culled down from 28 hours of conversation recorded over 12 days in March and April of 1977, four 90-minute interviews aired in May -- one a week for four weeks. Forty-five million people watched. The first installment alone had the largest viewing audience for a news or public-affairs program in TV history.

Together, they marked an unplanned but telling reinforcement of the value of syndication, the process of bringing original programming to stations directly rather than having the stations depend on their affiliated network for it and which was becoming more and more an industry thing at the time. The Frost-Nixon interviews showed there to be an audience available for non-network fare -- game shows and variety shows and talk shows and sitcoms and even public-affairs shows bought and aired on their own.

The new life that the project gave Nixon, in turn, as an elder statesman, lasted in one form or another until his death in 1994. The life it breathed into the TV business – expanding both opportunity and the landscape -- lived on.

Home Box Office, Inc. v. FCC
December 1977
(51)

In 1926 the Federal Radio Commission (FRC) was created to regulate radio use of public airwaves, as dictated by "the public interest, convenience, or necessity." Eight years later, the FRC was replaced by the Federal Communications Commission (FCC) upon the signing into law of the Communications Act of 1934 by President Franklin Roosevelt.

For most of the next 40 years, through the evolution of the radio business and then with the introduction and proliferation of the television business, the FCC oversaw all matters related to use of the public airwaves. In the 1960s and 1970s, this came to include matters related to the new area of cable television, too, especially as its own business grew and as the three major broadcast (non-cable) networks grew concerned in turn that cable would siphon off their audiences.

At the height of this concern, in 1975, the FCC stepped in, essentially declaring that cable networks could exhibit only certain types of programming -- and even then could so only under certain conditions.

Representatives of the fledgling cable industry, chief among them those behind Home Box Office, which had launched in 1972, fought back, in various lawsuits, against what they felt were unconstitutional rules. These ended up being consolidated in 1976 under *Home Box Office, Inc. v. FCC.*

The cable-industry's challenge: Taken together, the FCC orders of 1975 appeared "to regulate and limit the program fare cablecasters and subscription broadcast television stations may offer to the public for a fee set on a per-program or per-channel basis" (*law.justia.com*).

In December 1977, weaving into its decision previous media cases and such judicial concepts as *ex parte communication* and informal rule-making, the U.S. Court of Appeals for the District of Columbia Circuit struck down these FCC "anti-siphoning" policies, ruling that the FCC had exceeded its authority.

HBO had won.
So, too, had consumers, if not all of TV itself.

With *Home Box Office, Inc. v. FCC,* "The FCC was forced to recognize that cable operators had the right to make independent programming choices free of FCC interference," wrote Roger L. Sadler in his 2005 *Electronic Media Law.* "Subsequently, the ruling also opened the doors for other cable pay channels, which would soon result in a rapid growth of the cable industry." By the end of the 1970s, the television universe had expanded to include such non-broadcast-TV networks as

TBS, WGN, WOR, CBN, ESPN, C-Span, HBO, and Showtime. Within ten years, there were nearly 80 cable networks of one sort or another, attracting more than 50 million households, at which point the annual cable advertising revenues that had begun the decade at around $10 million had grown to $2 billion.

And, starting with the made-for-HBO film *The Terry Fox* in 1983 and Showtime's *The Paper Chase* revival in 1983 and *Brothers* sitcom in 1984, original programming on cable-TV was on its way to being an everyday consumer reality.

The *Kojak* Trial
Fall 1977
(52)

> Culture wars and echoes of culture wars stretch back
> to long before we bothered naming them. This could
> be seen as being on the cusp of that change when the
> fumes of '60s love and understanding were giving way
> to late '70s Me Generation ugliness. Evidenced by the
> curious 1977 case of 15-year-old Ronny Zamora.

-- Eugene S. Robinson
ozy.com November 8 2017

> If Ronny Zamora's lawyer has his way, Zamora will
> become the first person in history to be found not
> guilty of murder by reason of television.

-- Tom Shales
The Washington Post October 6 1977

Riding sidecar to the too-much-sex-and-violence-on-TV controversy
in the 1970s, which among other things yielded the Family Viewing
Hour in 1975, was a real-life criminal case that though largely forgotten
as the decades passed was just as critical to and important for the small-
screen revolution: the 1977 murder trial of 15-year-old Ronny Zamora.

In June 1977, on a bit of a teenaged dare, Ronny Zamora and 14-year-
old friend Darrell Agrella broke into the empty Miami Beach house of
Zamora's 82-year-old neighbor Elinor Haggart. They set about
ransacking and stealing from the house. When Haggart came home
unexpectedly and interrupted the crime in progress, Zamora, using a
gun the pair found among the woman's things, shot and killed her,

after which the teens resumed their burglarizing and finished by stealing Haggart's car. They then drove to Disney World.

Zamora and Agrella were soon arrested and charged with murder. During Zamora's trial -- the 15-year-old was tried as an adult -- defense attorney Ellis Rubin blamed television for the teen's actions. Specifically, he cited the excessive amounts of violence on television that Zamora had been exposed to since a child, leading to "prolonged, intense, involuntary, subliminal television intoxication."

To make his case, Rubin, a politician-turned-full-time-lawyer whose specialty was working on behalf of "the poor and the powerless who don't have a voice" and who'd already achieved a level of renown in the early 1970s as the lawyer who'd taken on the NFL in its local black-out policy, subpoenaed Telly Savalas. The actor was the star of the popular *Kojak* police series, one of Zamora's favorite shows. This, as the Florida Supreme Court had also recently approved the use of cameras in courtrooms. Thus making the trial a case of taking on TV on TV. (Described at the time as "unconventional," Rubin would later use nymphomania in his defense of a woman arrested for prostitution.)

For decades, the television industry had been under a social and legislative microscope for its (perceived) levels of entertainment programming violence and the potential influence of such on viewers.

The issue dated back to *The Untouchables*, the tommy-gun friendly crime-drama of the late 1950s that many saw both as ultra-violent in particular and not in the new medium's best interest as a whole. After the assassination of President John Kennedy in 1963, and then again in the wakes of the killings of Senator Robert Kennedy and Martin Luther King, Jr. in 1968, television came under further and more aggressive scrutiny, with studies commissioned and debates exchanged -- in Hollywood and on the streets and among politicians -- on the subject of how much violence on TV is too much violence and what if any are its effects.

No less an authority than the U.S. Surgeon General even entered the maelstrom. (**Not-So-Fun Fact**: The most tangible result of this late-1960s round of introspection seems to have been the 1969 cancellation of the CBS western *The Wild Wild West*.) Then, in 1974, came *Born Innocent* and the Family Viewing Hour. By now the hand-wringing, a generation old, revived every seven years or so, to little result, had reached satire-level: *NBC's Saturday Night* mocked it in a "Weekend Update" segment that featured clueless citizen commentator Emily Litella (Gilda Radner) asking, "What all this fuss I hear about sex and violins on television?"

But with what became known as "the *Kojak* trial," the television business itself was put on trial – in the national headlines and on the front pages in a way it never had been before.

NBCUniversal

Rubin's "TV intoxication" defense of Ronny Zamora held that years of TV-watching, specifically police shows (and especially *Kojak*), has caused a blurring of the lines in Zamora's eyes between fantasy and reality. That "through the excessive and long-continued use of this intoxicant, a mental condition of insanity was produced."

The lawyer brought in mental-health experts to testify on the influences of TV violence and on the application of *social learning theory* that holds that children can learn what they see and can develop conditioned reflexes as a result. This reflex, Rubin argued, was what led Zamora to shoot Haggart.

It was a theory refuted by prosecution experts, among them Dr. Charles Mutter, who contended:

> If this individual saw programs where people were killing, and that they became rewarded from this, and that this was a pleasant, pleasurable experience and they were only good consequences, they would get a

lot of money, they would get a lot of food, they would be praised, and he saw this repeatedly over and over again, then I think that would be conceivable. But that's not what happened, in fact, with him…

The defense's attempt to make TV violence part of the trial was "repeatedly rejected" by presiding judge Paul Baker, according to a 1977 report in *The Washington Post*. Inside and outside the courtroom, Rubin's strategy was ridiculed. (The actual defense plea was insanity.) *Kojak* star Telly Savalas, for his part, was ultimately released from having to testify for the defense.

Ronny Zamora was found guilty of murder and sentenced to life in prison, with added years for the related charges of burglary and assault. He appealed his conviction, blaming Ellis's unconventional and derided defense. But in 1987 a federal appeals court upheld the conviction.

He served 27 years before being released in 2004 at age 42, two years after he first became eligible for parole. Upon his release, he was deported to his native Costa Rica. (Daniel Agrella received three life terms for second-degree murder, robbery and burglary; he served seven years.)

Upon the conclusion of the *Kojak* Trial, "TV saw the 1970s — now awash in congressional hearings, national PTA resolutions, academic studies and the American Medical Association pegging televised violence an 'environmental hazard' — pull back from overwhelmingly violent televised content," wrote Eugene S. Robinson in a 2017 40th-anniversary reflection for *ozy.com*. At least for a few minutes, anyway. Nonetheless, the voice of accountability had now been raised to its loudest level.

In an interview he gave two years before his 2006 death, Ellis Rubin said, "I regret the defense didn't work [and] if I was allowed to introduce that today, there would have been a different result."

But thanks to his innovative approach to a murder defense, as well as a 12-month Florida experiment called cameras-in-the-courtroom, the television revolution continued. And in every sense it was being televised.

"There is no reason why anyone would want a computer in their home."

-- engineer Ken Olsen
World Future Society Convention 1977

Monday Night Football
1970-2005 ABC
(53)

Pro football in prime-time didn't begin with *ABC Monday Night Football* in the 1970s. Games were broadcast on a weekly basis as far back as 1953, on Saturday nights, courtesy of the long-forgotten Dumont network. But ABC made it a ratings and financial bonanza.

There were occasional games in prime-time after Dumont closed up 1955, on both CBS and NBC, throughout the 1960s. But in the later part of the decade NFL commissioner Pete Rozelle set out to bring football back to weekly TV, pitching the idea to all three broadcast networks. None saw the value, and each punted.

Eventually, though, last-place ABC bought in, as much for the possible up-side of tune-in as for fear that Rozelle would follow through on a threat he evidently made during those pitching rounds to sell the concept to individual stations if no network was interested -- which in the process would lure away some of its much-needed affiliates.

Roone Arledge, then head of ABC Sports, is said to have wanted *Monday Night Football* to be as much entertainment option for viewers as well as a sporting one – all the better to suit a more-demanding and less-wide-open audience, which had viewing options during prime-time. (Sunday afternoon games did not have the same level of competition.)

To that end, he called for an increase in the number of cameras to be used on and above the field for the Monday night games, as well as for heavy use of new on-air-graphics technologies and other innovations like Instant Replay. He also added a third man to the usual two-man announcers' booth, creating *de facto* "hosts" for the broadcasts. And he envisioned each week's airing to be tailored both for the calendar and for its location.

From Lee Henry in *TV Technology* in 2005:

> [T]here was an effort to bring the people-factor into play first. Most trucks today carry very long lenses because ABC lit a spark [then] with director Craig Janoff's style of "up close and personal." ... At one time, low end-zone cameras were an unnecessary extra. ABC's willingness to make them standard, as part of using more cameras on a game, meant field-level, "up-close" shots were possible despite two-thirds of a player's head being covered with a helmet. The risk of paying extra dollars for longer lenses and additional cameras was necessary for the viewer to see the face and the eyes of players. ... ABC also capitalized on cultural specials such as their Halloween telecasts by making pumpkin faces of their announce team. The network gave a special feel to each town, regularly showing city landmarks in and out of breaks, always using airships over the stadium to showcase the area as much as the game and finding a way for each Monday night to be an American experience in a city that most Americans probably had never visited. ... ABC tried to create a national entertainment experience; their tone and style set an expectation that if you were missing their telecast you were missing the national experience of the week.

ABC / NFL

The plan paid off: *Monday Night Football* – airing live coast-to-coast (leading to a bit of disruption among affiliates in its early days) -- kicked off on September 21 1970 (Jets v. Browns) and was an instant audience hit. Ratings kept up throughout the fall.

The NFL itself became a TV star. And the three-man hosting team of Keith Jackson, Howard Cosell, and Don Meredith proved to be as popular as the games themselves. (Each of the three became celebrities in their own rights as a result of their *Monday Night Football* exposure, with Cosell eventually getting his own ill-fated prime-time variety show in 1975 and Meredith taking on acting roles in such popular series as *Police Story*.) "The television equation was re-written forever," noted *The New York Times* in a 2005 reflection on the franchise.

Monday nights in America changed, both on-screen and in the culture, as the weekly game became a bigger and bigger draw. *Monday Night Football* seemed to be how many people began their weeks, at the national gathering spot called ABC. Movie attendance on Mondays dropped. "It became appointment television, with the interplay between the Cosell and Meredith providing almost as much entertainment as the play on the field" (*espn.com*).

The broadcast was often where the country got its breaking news, too. During a December 1980 outing between Miami and New England, it fell to Cosell to announce the shooting death that night of John Lennon -- a contribution that sports media-critic Milton Kent reflected on after the December 2010 death of Cosell colleague Don Meredith:

> [T]he confluence of the 30th anniversary of the shooting death of John Lennon this Wednesday - announced late in the fourth quarter of a Monday night game -- and the death Sunday of Don Meredith serves as a reminder that while the New England-Miami clash may have been just another football game, 'Monday Night Football' was no mere telecast.

With various combinations in the booth, *Monday Night Football* remained one of ABCs most reliably popular prime-time series for decades.

In 2005, as part of a different TV universe, it moved to ABC sister-network ESPN. But it left broadcast television as one of prime-time's longest-running TV franchises – alongside one-named juggernauts like Disney and Hallmark. It also made prime-time sports both profitable and popular. A year after it began back in 1970, NBC aired the first nighttime World Series game (Game 4 between the Pirates and the Orioles), on the way to a regular prime-time airing for just about all sports championship games.

From Henry:

> As the second longest running prime-time show in television after *60 Minutes*, its impact has helped define our industry's production style and has been a cultural maypole around which we reference other shows. ... If late night television has the likes of Paar, Carson and Letterman as legacy holders, sports television has ABC Sports' *Monday Night Football* as one of ours. ... However, in the same way Letterman, Leno and Conan are good comedians who benefited from the groundwork laid by Jack Paar and Johnny Carson, today's sports-as-entertainment style of television owes its due to ABC's *MNF*.

ABC/NFL

MTM Productions, Inc.
1970-1995
(54)

The company was merely named for her, Mary Tyler Moore always explained. In the same way a boat is christened in someone's honor. It was (then-husband) Grant Tinker and others who actually ran it, not she. Still, in many eyes, MTM the studio and Mary Tyler Moore the person were synonymous in the 1970s, especially as the sitcom she starred in and the studio that produced it became so influential.

MTM began as *Mary Tyler Moore* did in 1970: The studio was launched to produce the sitcom that was to mark the actress's return to series TV four years after the end of *The Dick Van Dyke Show* (another sitcom that set a standard for a decade and on which she starred as wife Laura Petrie).

It premiered on September 19 1970, and with *Mary Tyler Moore*'s success, MTM under Tinker went about developing other series that would follow its formula -- star-driven, script-focused sophisticated ensemble comedies set in a large cosmopolitan city that quietly serviced the real world. Launching one new sitcom after the next, the studio quickly established itself as one of the most successful developers of quality product in Hollywood. So much so that it became known as (and would become remembered to be) a "writers' factory"–the place where writers were left alone to write.

"It was *the* 'quality' company in the American television industry," according to *MTM: Quality Television*, a 1984 book that chronicles its history.

The studio was headquartered on the Studio City, California, production lot known as CBS Studio Center, where *Mary Tyler Moore* and most of the rest of its shows were shot. (Because MTM co-owned the facility at the time, the place came to be known as "the MTM lot," a moniker that came to stick.) Co-run by a quality-minded and protective factory manager in the form of former ad-man-turned-TV-executive Tinker, MTM was where TV writers were encouraged to write and to leave Tinker and his team in charge of the business and corporate ends. Including network interference.

Grant Tinker was famous for his support of writers and the creative process."[His] philosophy was essentially to hire talented people and give them the room and discretion to operate as they saw fit, while he kept studio brass from meddling with content and program development" (*pophistorydig.com*).

The process resulted in that succession of successful sitcoms that followed in the path of and mirrored respected first hit *Mary Tyler Moore* -- ones that placed a grounded central character (portrayed by a well-known lead actor) in a big-city work and/or home setting, where he or she would be surrounded by a supporting ensemble, in which relatable situations begat relatable comedy.

As observed in *museum.tv*, the MTM template was "television readily identifiable by its textured, humane, and contemporary themes and characters."

Mary Tyler Moore, The Bob Newhart Show, Rhoda, Phyllis, Paul Sand in Friends & Lovers, Doc, The Bob Crane Show, The Tony Randall Show, The Betty White Show were part of that succession of shows produced by

MTM from 1970 to 1977, its most prolific period. Star-focused but ensemble in nature. Topical without being trendy or dated. Comedy over situation, with humor derived as much from *how* and *why* something is said rather than merely *what* is said. Character-driven without caricature-leaning. (Of the entries that didn't last, such as *Phyllis*, it might be said they didn't because they failed to nail the importance of a grounded lead.)

In MTM comedies, jokes seemed to come from the characters, the speakers of the words, not the writer's pen. Smart, clever, but not obvious. (Prostitute's dryly delivered reply to naïve Mary Richards in *Mary Tyler Moore*, when asked why she'd been arrested: "Oh, I fell in love with a cop"... Model-handsome new patient's first-session presenting complaint to psychologist Dr. Bob Hartley in *The Bob Newhart Show*'s: "Dr. Hartley, you have no idea what it's like to be incredibly good-looking" ... Perennially overweight Rhoda Morgenstern, panicked at finding herself with a date for later that evening: "I have to lose 10 pounds by 8:30"... Pampered and spoiled Stephanie Vanderkellen to her emotionally wounded boyfriend after a lovers' spat clearly of her doing: "Okay, Michael, what's the least I can do to make this up to you – and I mean the *very* least"...)

Sly character-defining, character *expanding* and *enhancing* humor, as often as not mined from less-than-humorous circumstances. This was the MTM sitcom trademark. One TV critic of the day observed them as "warmedies."

Of the three biggest independent suppliers of sitcoms in the 1970s, those from Norman Lear (13 series on the air during the decade) pushed the envelope, those from Garry Marshall (10) pushed the hijinks, and MTM (20) pushed the warmth.

> By the mid 1970s, MTM had become a major force in TV, grossing more than $20 million a year. The *People* magazine of September 30th 1974 featured Mary on the cover with the tagline, "TV's Newest Tycoon." The MTM payroll by then included nearly 500 people,

and in that year the company had at least eight TV shows then in preparation or on the air – more prime-time series in fact than any of the "majors," except for Universal. And there was more to come. (*pophistorydig.com*)

In calendar year 1975 alone, MTM had nine series in production, on all three broadcast networks, including *Three for the Road*, its first one-hour drama. But neither it nor its other new or newer shows that year took off, as the prime-time tide seemed to be turning from Lear's and MTM's approaches to comedy to that of Marshall (*Happy Days*, *Laverne & Shirley*). The studio's last successful sitcom of the 1970s was the critically praised *WKRP in Cincinnati*, which ran from 1978 to 1982.

Success in the one-hour drama format did come later in the decade, though, with the *Mary Tyler Moore* spin-off newspaper drama *Lou Grant* and the high-school set *The White Shadow*. (The latter involved writers and producers who went on to ride the wave of MTM's biggest successes in the 1980s with the genre-redefining drama ensembles *Hill Street Blues* and *St. Elsewhere*, considered two of TV's finest hours and amassing an astounding 160 Emmy nominations during their collective runs.)

MTM Enterprises was also behind acclaimed TV movies of the day, among them *Just an Old Sweet Song* (1976) and the Emmy-nominated tear-jerkers *Something for Joey* (1977) and *First You Cry* (1978), Mary Tyler Moore's dramatic-TV-movie debut.

"MTM has produced what is arguably the most interesting and innovative collection of weekly series in the thirty-eight-year history of network television," wrote David Marc of the company's first 15 years in a 1984 issue of *The Atlantic*.

In the 1980s, with MTM head Grant Tinker having left his post to run the NBC network, the company suffered some executive-level behind-the-screens drama that resulted in a handful of staff firings or resignations. Though it had remarkable success in the decade with *Hill*

20th Century Fox Television

Street Blues and *St. Elsewhere*, as well as with *Remington Steele*, *Newhart*, and TV movies like *The Boy Who Drank Too Much*, it began to flounder as an independent supplier.

It effectively ended as such in 1988 when it was sold to UK-based TVS Entertainment, only to be sold again in the early 1990s. Regardless of ownership, by the 1990s MTM seemed to have become merely a grouping of familiar initials rather than the acclaimed writers' factory it was. It was a catalogue of once-popular TV shows at best. The last successful prime-time series from the studio was the minor Burt Reynolds sitcom *Evening Shade* (1990-94 CBS). The first season of NBC's *The Pretender* in 1996 and the only season of UPN's *Good News* in 1997 were the last network shows MTM produced. (**Fun Fact**: MTM was behind the original 1980s Broadway productions *Noises Off* and the Tony-winning revival of *Joe Egg*.)

The mini-studio known as MTM shut down in 1998. But it did so with an impressive legacy as the company that not only redefined the one-hour TV drama in the 1980s but, more important, the company that changed the 1970s as it changed the TV comedy form itself -- from situation comedy to contemporary character comedy.

And it accomplished the feat in the hands of a Who's Who of behind-the-scenes talent that would go on to continue to shape both the sitcom form and the medium as a whole. Among the many: James L. Brooks, Charlotte Brown, Sheldon Bull, Allan Burns, Glen and Les Charles, Stan Daniels, David Davis, Barton Dean, Bob Ellison, Lloyd Garver, Tom Patchett, Phoeff Sutton, Jay Tarses, Ed. Weinberger, and Hugh Wilson.

(The studio's stable of drama-series included behind-the-scenes names that went on to make their own difference in TV. Among this group: Steven Bochco, Joshua Brand, Robert Butler, Glenn Gordon Caron, Michael Gleason, Gary David Goldberg, Tom Fontana, Mark Frost, , Marshall Herskovitz, David Milch, Bruce Paltrow, and Dick Wolf.)

Simply, MTM Enterprises was a "comedy club and Triple-A baseball league," notes *MTM: Quality Television*. From its higher-profile hits alone, MTM amassed more than 300 Emmy nominations — 138 of which were for acting and an amazing 45 of which were for writing.

These resulted in 85 wins, marking MTM as the winner of more Emmy awards than any other independent company of its time. Beyond this, in 1981 alone the studio accounted for two of the three winning scripts and four of the nine finalists for the Humanitas Prizes, awarded yearly to the prime-time television programs judged to "most fully communicate human values."

The Muppet Show
1976-81 syn
(55)

The Jim Henson Company / ABC

It's a familiar story in the TV and film industries: An idea is pitched; it's rejected as being too different; the people behind it move ahead with the idea anyway; it ends up a huge hit.

Jim Henson's *The Muppet Show* is a classic example of that success-borne-of-rejection formula.

Thanks to his sprawling Muppet family, puppeteer Jim Henson found nationwide attention when the educational series *Sesame Street* started on public television in 1969. The Muppets were a big part of the success it soon found, and the popularity of both the show and the creatures became such that Henson feared both he and they would be forever stuck with the label *educational TV*. So he pursued other avenues to showcase the entertaining menagerie, which led to a pair of ABC specials, one in 1974 and the other in 1975, that were envisioned as pilots for a more mainstream not-necessarily educational all-Muppet shows.

But ABC went no further with Henson than the two specials. And CBS and NBC, then the only other TV networks, didn't show interest in a weekly Muppet show, either.

Undeterred, with the help of a longtime British TV producer (Lew Grade), Henson took his idea to the United Kingdom, where it was embraced, financed, put into production, and then aired as a weekly variety series there and around the world, including the United States, sold through syndication. Local stations, as it turned out, lined up to buy the *Muppet Show* that the TV networks didn't want.

The Muppet Show was an immediate hit when it came to American TV in the fall of 1976, on its way to becoming one of the most popular shows of any kind on all of television, network or otherwise. A half-hour variety show modeled on the song-dance-and-comedy revues of the early 20th-century vaudeville era, it was "hosted" by Kermit the Frog, the face of the extended family.

And while still threaded with the kind of juvenile mischief that had made the Muppets a favorite of the younger set, it offered the kind of subversive grown-up humor with which Henson wanted to be more associated. Each of the many Muppets were showcased at one point or another in the episodes, and each episode featured a well-known non-Muppet guest-star.

As *The Muppet Show* grew in popularity, it was seen as so cool a gig that celebrities clamored for a chance to be on it -- some of whom rarely if ever guest-starred on TV, from Charles Aznavour and Peter Sellers to Julie Andrews and Elton John.

The show remained a hit for five years, going head-to-head in various categories each season at the Emmys with the broadcast networks that had once rejected it. There, it was routinely singled out for its writing and directing; and in 1978 it even edged out perennial favorite *The Carol Burnett Show* and young upstart *Saturday Night Live* to be named Outstanding Comedy-Variety or Music Series.

With the win, it put the networks on notice that good ideas can come from anywhere. And that viewers are the ultimate judge of what's watchable. That it's content, not tradition, that can make a show succeed.

Outside of its creative achievements, *The Muppet Show* also joined forces with such disparate weekly programming attempts of the day such as *The World at War*, *Ozzie's Girls*, *Wayland Flowers and Madam*, *The Bobby Vinton Show*, and *Space: 1999*, not to mention nighttime editions of popular daytime game-shows, to demonstrate the increasing importance of original syndicated programming for local stations.

The Muppet Show led to a rise in syndication, which in turned helped to change the TV playing-field. Programming could come from and go to anywhere. (Shades of the OTT era to come in the next century.) More important, *The Muppet Show* represented a true-ism in TV that would serve as a guidepost thereafter for those with outside-the-box ideas: "Not here" doesn't have to mean "not anywhere."

Jim Henson died in 1990, but his unyielding belief in his idea created an empire of entertainment that has lived on for decades in TV, as well as in films, music, and the digital world.

"If a bullet should enter my brain, let that bullet destroy every closet door."

-- San Francisco politician / gay-rights activist Harvey Milk
(from a November 1977 tape-recording made
in the event of assassination)

NBC's Saturday Night / Saturday Night Live
1975-pres NBC
(56)

> The combined failures of the Vietnam War and
> Watergate (and by 1975, one could and should enlarge
> the list of national failures to include economic
> stagflation and the energy crisis) had led reporters and
> editors, as well as most Americans, to conclude that an
> attitude of fierce skepticism, even cynicism, about the
> honesty, competency, integrity, and even humanity of
> government officials was a mandatory defense against
> the knavery and policy failures the nation had endured.
>
> -- Beth L. Bailey, David R. Farber
> *America in the 70s*

Cynicism, meet *Saturday Night Live*.
Saturday Night Live, meet cynicism.

NBC / BroadwayVideo

Pop-culture-trivia fans know that for its first two seasons *Saturday Night Live* was actually called *"NBC's Saturday Night,"* due to it showing up at a time when the title *"Saturday Night Live"* had already been taken --

271

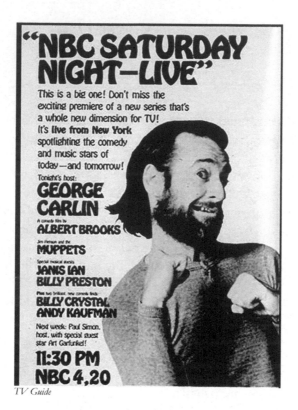

TV Guide

by ABC, for the new and heavily touted variety series *Saturday Night Live with Howard Cosell*. ("Saturday Night Dead" is how most critics greeted Cosell's show, a bone-headed TV idea if ever there was one; it limped along for just 18 episodes before ABC put it -- and viewers -- out of their misery in January of 1976.)

It actually wasn't until 1977, more than a year after Cosell's show left the air and two years into its own run, that NBC re-christened what had become its weekend hit *Saturday Night Live*, a name it would be known by for at least 40 more years. (Give or take, that's 40 times longer than Cosell's version.)

At a time when the variety-series genre was down to fumes – it had begun as TV itself did in 1946, and its last stalwart, CBS's *The Carol Burnett Show*, on the air since 1967, was in its home stretch -- *Saturday*

Night Live came along to reinvent it for a new generation, albeit it outside of prime-time. Its beginnings were much more humble if not mercenary: The show was originally conceived to address a need NBC had for late-night programming on the weekend, to match the success it was enjoying from Monday through Friday in late-night courtesy of *The Tonight Show.* (The network actually had been using reruns of *Tonight* on the weekend, which reportedly irked the Johnny Carson camp.)

They went the opposite way of Carson's mainstream show with a less-conventional series, opting for Saturday night, where it was presumed younger and hipper audiences were looking for something to watch.

Under the helm of producer Lorne Michaels, a Canadian who'd relocated to Los Angeles in the late 1960s and then broke into TV there as a writer (*The Beautiful Phyllis Diller Show, Rowan and Martin's Laugh-In*) before heading to New York, a cast of new-to-television young comic actors (to be called the Not Ready for Prime-Time Players) was assembled to serve as a repertory company for what would be a live weekly 90-minute comedy-and-music showcase -- each outing hosted by a different well-known person.

The mantra as the project was conceived and launched: young. Young cast, young or young-skewing hosts, young or young-skewing musical guests. All to get young viewers to show up at an imposing time with the promise or at list hint that the late hour allowed for fewer restrictions.

The premiere episode, on October 11 1975, fittingly featured as host anti-establishment icon George Carlin, whose anarchic persona set the opening-night tone. Musical guests were Janis Ian, known at the time for appearances on *The Midnight Special*, and Billy Preston.

Among the comedy sketches were ones that introduced the Talking Bees, a courtroom sketch, and a sketch called "Trojan Horse Home Security." In addition, rising young comedian Andy Kaufman performed, lip-syncing the *Mighty Mouse* theme. And Muppet creator

Jim Henson, then still trying to break out of his *Sesame Street* shackles, introduced a new collection of puppets in what would be a regular feature, called "The Land of Gorch." Finally, young filmmaker Albert Brooks also presented an original short film. (Like Henson and Kauffman, Brooks would be featured this first season only.)

In the weeks that followed, hosts included Rob Reiner, Paul Simon, Candice Bergen, and Lily Tomlin; and musical acts ranged from Randy Newman to Phoebe Snow to Loudon Wainwright III. The comedy was new and irreverent and involved what future generations would call *meta*, given its commentary on culture and television itself. An unconventional live TV series had landed in late-night, and NBC found itself with an enormous hit.

Two months in, on December 13, *NBC's Saturday Night* announced itself as much more than that, though. It showed with its seventh episode that it was a rules-breaking and convention-dismissing enormous hit. And it was hand-crafted for a new generation of TV watchers who wanted their TV to reflect their lives, which often meant making fun of … well … everything.

Richard Pryor hosted, and for the first time since its debut *Saturday Night* wasn't really live: Given Pryor's reputation, NBC had decided ahead of time that it would air this night with a seven-second delay. Soon after a mostly uneventful monologue, Pryor appeared in what would become the episode's and then the franchise's most famous sketch. He played a job-applicant being interviewed for a new position by a white hiring manager (Chevy Chase).

> **Manager**: Alright, Mr. Wilson, you've done just fine on the Rorschach. Your papers are in good order. Your file's fine. No difficulties with your motor skills. And I think you're probably ready for this job. We've got one more psychological test we always do here. It's just a Word Association. I'll throw you out a few words. Anything that comes to your mind, just throw back at

me, okay? It's kind of an arbitrary thing. Like, if I say "dog", you'd say...?

Mr. Wilson: Tree.

Interviewer: Tree. [nods head, prepares the test papers] ... Dog

Mr. Wilson: Tree.

Interviewer: Fast.

Mr. Wilson: Slow.

Interviewer: Rain.

Mr. Wilson: Snow.

Interviewer: White.

Mr. Wilson: Black.

Interviewer: Bean.

Mr. Wilson: Pod.

Interviewer [casually]: Negro.

Mr. Wilson: Whitey.

Interviewer: Tar-baby.

Mr. Wilson [silent, confused, unsure]: What'd you say?

Interviewer [repeating, casual]: Tar-baby.

NBC / *Broadway Video*

Mr. Wilson: Ofay.

Interviewer: Colored.

Mr. Wilson: Redneck.

Interviewer: Jungle-bunny.

Mr. Wilson [starting to get angry]: Peckerwood.

Interviewer: Burrhead.

Mr. Wilson: Cracker!

Interviewer [aggressive]: Spear-chucker.

Mr. Wilson: White trash!

Interviewer: Jungle-bunny!

Mr. Wilson: Honky!

Interviewer: Spade!

Mr. Wilson: Honky Honky!

Interviewer: [relentless, final bullet in his arsenal] Nigger!

Mr. Wilson: [immediate] "*Dead* honky!"

Interviewer: [quickly wraps up the interview] Okay, Mr. Wilson, I think you're qualified for this job. How about a starting salary of $5,000?

Mr. Wilson: Your mama!

Interviewer: [fumbling] Uh.. $7,500 a year?

Mr. Wilson: Your grandmama!

Interviewer: [desperate] $15,000, Mr. Wilson. You'll be the highest paid janitor in America. Just, don't... don't hurt me, please.

Mr. Wilson: Okay.

Interviewer: [relieved] Okay.

Mr. Wilson: You want me to start now?

Interviewer: Oh, no, no. that's alright. I'll clean all this up. Take a couple of weeks off, you look tired.

With this episode, *NBC's Saturday Night* took off, landed on a whole other level of television, and never returned. It became the It show for a new America and the must-see entry for a college-aged audience that became feverish with anticipation for each week's poking of the establishment bear.

As it moved on and kept testing the authority that surrounded it --
NBC's, the FCC's, convention's and society's -- it often waded in
shallow streams of easy not-so-subtle (but still taboo-smashing) sex
jokes. (Chevy Chase at the top of a "Weekend Update" segment, on
the phone with a presumed girlfriend, unaware he's on camera: "No,
no, you don't actually blow on it.")

But more often it dug deep over the years with commentary on topics
from the 2nd Amendment (a parody ad called "America! Show Us
Your Guns!") to high-fiber-cereal trends (a commercial for the new
product called "Colon Blow"). Few targets were in fact off-target,
including death.

In 1976, a popular French performer named Claudine Longet was
famously in the news for having shot and killed her boyfriend, a ski
champion named Spider Sabich. She claimed the death was an
accident, an explanation widely mocked in the media. A month later
Saturday Night parodied the event with a mock news report from "The
Claudine Longet Invitational Ski Tournament," showing footage of
one athlete after another toppling down a mountain at the sounds of
repeated rifle shots. ("Uh oh, folks, it looks as though Claudine Longet
has accidentally shot yet another skier.")

A year into the NBC hit, Chevy Chase, who'd become its breakout star
-- it was he who opened the show each week with its famous "Live!
From New York! It's *Saturday Night!*" -- left for a film career. With that,
and even with John Belushi becoming the new breakout star of the
show, *Saturday Night* became a bit more of an ensemble showcase. And
it grew even more popular.

In 1977, around the same time of its official title change to *Saturday
Night Live*, Bill Murray was added to the cast, after which
counterculture morphed into a sort of comedy anarchy. *Saturday Night
Live* was the hottest show on television.

These first five years of the franchise – made up of the lone season
with Chevy Chase and then the Belushi/ Murray years -- are generally

considered by fans and pundits as its best. This is the era that saw the rise of the Nerds, *The Coneheads*, *Samurai Warrior*, Bill Murray's lounge-singer Nick Winters, and King Tut. The era that featured guest hosts from Steve Martin to O.J. Simpson to "Anyone Can Host" winner Miskel Spillman. The era that saw musical guests from Jackson Browne to Elvis Costello to The Blues Bothers.

Provocative and shocking would continue to be the show's hallmarks for decades to come, but it's the timespan from 1975 to 1980 that saw *SNL* first raise its flag of defiance, which changed American humor as it changed broadcast TV.

The award-winning late-night NBC franchise – and franchise is what it became, launching spin-offs of its characters into films and stage for 40 years, fortifying its network's prime-time line-up when needed, becoming the poster-show for late-night humor -- saw comparable spikes (and many dips) in quality and popularity over the course of its record-setting weekend reign. It made stars as it made headlines; it was both the object and subject of countless pieces of social commentary.

It stands as both a milestone for network TV and a landmark for pop culture.

NBC/ Broadway Video

"Probably the biggest surprise of last night's [presidential] debates was when Jimmy Carter, to the confusion of everyone, revealed that, when the mood hits him, he likes to dress up like Eleanor Roosevelt."

-- Chevy Chase
"Weekend Update" *NBC's Saturday Night*

Operation Prime Time (OPT)
1976-87
(57)

As more and more local TV stations took interest in first-run programming in the 1970s – original TV series and specials purchased by and for local stations – a new idea came along that shook up the landscape, creating, for a while, a sort of alternative major network to compete with ABC, CBS, and NBC. Launched as much as a business venture as a creative one by producer Al Masini, it was called Operation Prime Time (OPT).

In 1976, working with fellow TV executive Rich Frank, Masini assembled a consortium of independent stations for the purpose of developing and producing and airing their own programming -- as a group. The wanted to work outside the longstanding network-TV advertising model that they felt yielded an unfair slice of the financial pie for producers. For its first project, OPT turned to a TV genre that had been fast becoming one of prime-time's most popular -- the mini-series.

The six-hour *Testimony of Two Men*, based on Taylor Caldwell sprawling 1968 best-seller, aired in May 1977 on 93 local U.S. stations. (**Fun Fact**: This was the same month that the syndicated David Frost-Richard Nixon interviews drew an audience of 45 million people, reinforcing the idea that programming did not have to come from and air on a network to be popular.)

The mini-series was slammed by critics -- *The New York Times* admired its "intention of providing a quality alternative to the embarrassment of mediocrities being churned out by the commercial networks" yet went on to point out that it failed miserably at doing so – but it was reasonably sampled by viewers and even scored an Emmy nomination (for Costuming). With it, OPT was in business.

Relying heavily on book titles, OPT put more mini-series into production, aiming to air them during what local stations around the country viewed as the critical Sweeps weeks in the months of May, July, November, and February.

Three were spun from John Jakes' historical novels, drafting off the winds of interest kicked up by Bicentennial celebrations around the country mid-decade: *The Bastard* (in May 1978 – which ended up courting controversy for its title alone), *The Rebels* (May 1979), and *The Seekers* (July 1979). These were followed by *A Woman Called* Golda (1982), starring Ingrid Bergman in what became her final performance, and *Sadat* (1983), headlined by new Oscar-winner Louis Gossett, Jr., as well as the sagas *Blood Feud* (1983) and *A Woman of Substance* (1984), based on Barbara Taylor Bradford's novel. (In 1980, OPT even produced and aired an animated holiday special, *Yogi's First Christmas*.)

Each met with diminishing viewer interest and ratings. By the 1980s, OPT projects were struggling to find audiences.

The consortium known as Operation Prime Time disbanded in 1987, when inside of just its ten years of existence the television business had changed drastically: HBO and Showtime were each filling up with original programming, FOX had been launched as an actual rather than *de facto* fourth broadcast network, and first-run syndication had gone from creative novelty to a business necessity that everyone on all levels had eyes on, not just prescient executives.

(Cable TV in general had established a beachhead in most all homes, sometimes even picking up cancelled network shows and making new episodes of each. No fewer than six broadcast-network TV shows in the 1980s were given new life this way.)

But Operation Prime Time really had foreseen it all. When Al Masini died in 2010, onetime business-partner Rich Frank remembered him as "one of the creative forces in the development of non-network programming and a key force in helping to move the industry away from a three-network environment."

The Prime Time Access /
Financial Interest in Syndication
Rules
1970
(58)

To know even a modicum of information about the complicated government regulations called the Prime Time Access Rule (PTAR) and the Financial Interest and Syndication Rules (Fin-Syn) is to understand key changes in the television business just as the 1970s began.

The Prime Time Access Rule, established in 1970, essentially shortened the number of hours each night given to the broadcast networks (ABC, CBS, and NBC) to air their programming on their affiliated stations -- the block of hours known as *prime-time*.

Before the ruling, the networks had access to three-and-a-half hours each night, from 7:30pm to 11pm (Eastern and Pacific). But in 1970, the FCC concluded that these 24 ½ hours given the networks each week represented too many hours and too much network control over what local stations aired (and what viewers watched).

The agency cut that amount by a half-hour each night, with the thinking being that local TV stations would have more time for their own programming, leading to what it hoped would be increased opportunities for local TV suppliers. Effective with the start of the 1971-72 television season, prime-time would begin at 8pm. (Sundays and Tuesdays were exempted, though the latter for just a year. Sunday held on to its 7:30pm start for an additional four years until 1975, when it was officially pushed *back* to a 7pm start.)

As of the 1975-76 season, each of the three networks had the same 22-hour schedule: Monday through Saturday 8-11pm, Sunday 7-11pm -- which became the default and permanent network TV prime-time schedule.

At the same time, the FCC also instituted a policy called the Financial Interest and Syndication Rules (Fin-Syn), which put a cap on the number of TV series that a broadcast network could both produce (read: own) and air, since to do so was to profit twice from the same product.

Without Fin-Syn, went the thinking, networks had incentives to keep even low-rated shows on the air, since they owned them, squeezing smaller TV studios out of business. Or at the least putting them at a severe disadvantage.

Both rules were issued as television and network profits were growing. The ultimate goal was to lessen what were perceived as network television strangleholds on the business. They delivered tangible and less-obvious, even unforeseen, results.

With PTAR, each of the networks lost a sizeable chunk of half-hours of programming from its weekly prime-time schedule, which led to the culling of existing shows and a reduction in the number of new ones. (At CBS, it led in part to what was a wholesale re-shuffling of its weekly slate and re-imagining of the network's image.) There was more competition now for fewer available timeslots. On the plus side, though, local stations found themselves with a sizeable chunk of extra time each week that they had to *fill*, resulting in increased local competition for more timeslots.

The rulings helped to accelerate the growth of first-run (original) syndicated programming chasing those extra minutes. As for Fin-Syn: Smaller Hollywood studios and other TV suppliers benefitted from a playing field that if not exactly leveled was a least re-landscaped in such a way that it afforded them more room to compete.

The two rules remained in effect until the 1990s, by which time the TV business had become bigger and more complex still -- six broadcast networks, a wealth of cable outlets and premium services, and a nascent streaming industry -- and they were re-thought and then eliminated.

Rich Man, Poor Man
February 1-March 15 1976 ABC
(59)

> We became household entities in hours. I was walking
> in New York after the third or fourth episode aired. I
> suddenly became aware that everybody was looking at
> me, pointing at me, trying to touch me. I don't think I
> left my hotel the rest of the week.
>
> -- *Rich Man, Poor Man* star Peter Strauss

QB VII (1974) may have been one of the first, and *Roots* (1977) was
certainly the most famous. But the sweeping and addictive *Rich Man,
Poor Man* in 1976 was what solidified the TV mini-series format as a
commercial and creative force, keeping viewers inside their homes for
two winter months, glued to ABC.

In the process, it opened the door to all the epic and influential mini-
series to come over the next five years, from *Roots* to *Holocaust* (1978)
to *Centennial* (1978) to *Shogun* (1980).

ABC / NBCUniversal

"In 1975, when there were basically three options for your average
family to find original programming, the mini-series was a

revolutionary idea ... It ushered in a new era of television, one that saw great triumphs" (*popdose.com*). The form came to prominence coincident with objections to envelope-pushing TV-movies such as NBC's *Born Innocent* (1974), resulting in a recalibration of the types of movie projects the networks were willing to air.

"Although individual films had been critically lauded from the earliest days of TV movies, it wasn't until the 1975-76 season (when the networks stayed away from the sex-themed films) that films produced for television began to be taken seriously on a wider scale," writes Elana Levine in *Wallowing in Sex: The New Sexual Culture of 1970s American Television.*

Rich Man, Poor Man was to be the widest attempt yet, a 12-hour adaptation of Irwin Shaw's 1969 novel that chronicled the turbulent lives of the Jordache family from World War 2 through the 1960s -- and through the lives of its good son/bad son archetypes Rudy (Peter Strauss) and Tom (Nick Nolte).

At the time, top-rated network ABC had proven adept at marketing, launching, and getting at least an initial audience for just about every one of its new projects, but *Rich Man, Poor Man* was a sizeable gamble both in content (a period drama) and length (an 8-part movie, essentially). "Everybody was very doubtful and skeptical about the form," remembered TV-movie head Brandon Stoddard in 1991 in *Entertainment Weekly*. "It was at a point in television's growth where it was risky."

The two-hour premiere shot to the top of the ratings on Sunday February 1, though, leading to its regular Monday timeslot the following night. *Rich Man, Poor Man* stayed in the Top Ten each of its successive weeks.

It marked an example of appointment viewing during the days when viewers either saw a show as it aired in a certain time-period or they didn't see it at all. Restaurants closed early on Monday nights; social engagements were re-scheduled. It seemed as if everyone everywhere was watching the Jordache story play out. *Rich Man, Poor Man* ended the 1975-76 TV season as the year's second most-viewed show on any network.

From the Museum of Broadcast Communications:

> The success of *Rich Man, Poor Man* hinged on the employment of several innovative techniques. The narrative struck a unique combination that contained the lavish film-style production values of prestigious special-event programming, while at the same time relying upon the "habit-viewing" characteristic of a weekly series. Also, by setting the plots in the historical context of such development as McCarthyism, the Korean War, campus riots, and the Civil Rights Movement, *Rich Man Poor Man* suggested larger circumstances than those usually found in a traditional soap-opera. However, the limited series also liberally took on a range of risqué melodramatic topics, including adultery, power struggles, and alcoholism. Another inventive concept introduced by *Rich Man, Poor Man* was the use of multiple, revolving guest stars throughout the series.

Rich Man, Poor Man was a TV blockbuster. Later that year, it was also an Emmy powerhouse, too, with a staggering 23 nominations, including one each for Peter Strauss and Nick Nolte as the Jordache brothers. It ended up winning four.

In a salute to the project 15 years after it aired, producer Harve Bennett said he believed at the time that that an immigrant family's struggle for success would captivate Americans. "We ran the first two hours for the cast and crew. At the end, everybody stood up and began chanting, 'More, more, more.' We knew we had a great piece of work."

And the TV industry had a new form of programming -- one associated with a "quality demographic" to boot, for which advertisers were willing to pay a high premium. *Roots* was a year away; *Holocaust* and *Centennial*, two years away. And beyond them a new decade would rise and fall on the form, with *Shogun, The Thorn Birds,* and *The Winds of War,* among others.

The Richard Pryor Show
September 13-October 20 1977 NBC
(60)

TV Guide

Like his contemporary George Carlin, the late Richard Pryor started his stand-up career in the early 1960s with both a look and an approach that was a bit more mainstream and conservative than his legacy would suggest. (Pryor had even had a guest-starring role on an episode of *The Partridge Family*.)

It was only after what he would later call a 1967 epiphany, followed by an immersion into the California counterculture two years after that, that the iconic "Richard Pryor" emerged. In short order, he began writing for TV and film -- winning an Emmy Award as part of the writing team behind the Lily Tomlin special *Lily* (1973) and co-writing BLAZING SADDLES (1974) with Mel Brooks.

As his star ascended, he took on movie roles (UPTOWN DATURDAY NIGHT, SILVER STREAK), and then he made late-night-TV history in December 1975 when he served as host of the new sketch series *NBC's Saturday Night* (its first black host) and famously appeared in what everyone would end up calling "the n------ sketch" with Chevy Chase.

By 1977, Pryor was a singular, popular, and often controversial full-on comedy brand. And amid much fanfare, he came to prime-time TV that year with his own NBC show. Inside of six months of its announcement, though, the comedian had gone from the network's biggest headline to its most troubling headache.

It all began with a one-hour special on NBC in May of that year, called *The Richard Pryor Special?* (the intentional question mark was perhaps a telling sign), that did well enough in the ratings the network followed it up with an announcement that Pryor would star in his own weekly series that fall. Which is when things started to go wrong. Because Pryor, for his part, was under the impression (or so he later said) that he'd be starring in a series of *specials* beginning that fall, not a weekly series. Let the conflict begin.

When whatever it actually was began pre-production that summer and Pryor discovered that the TV-series process involved getting creative notes about content from the network, he pushed back again, saying that his contract with NBC stipulated there'd be no interference or creative involvement. Communication between the sides soured.

(One has to wonder exactly what kind of relationship NBC thought it had gotten into, given that Pryor's two-most-recent albums were titled *That Nigger's Crazy* and *Bicentennial Nigger*.)

Back and forth went the squabbling between the camps, making headlines both inside and outside of Hollywood. Pryor threatened to leave. (The series had yet to premiere.) Then he balked and stuck around. Production resumed.

The show seemingly under control -- right around the same week *Time* featured a lengthy piece on Pryor, calling him a "New Black Superstar" (August 22 1977) -- the comedian began shooting the first episode. The plan: The show would open with a close-up of Pryor's face addressing the camera (and what would be revealed as a live audience in front of him), saying how happy he is to be hosting his own TV show and dismissing reports of behind-the-scenes fights and scoffing at those who he said told him that doing a network show would mean giving up his principles.

As he speaks, the camera slowly pulls back to reveal a full-body shot of Pryor, standing on stage nude (actually, wearing a flesh-colored body stocking) his genitalia missing (the stocking had a smoothed-over crotch). "Look at me -- I'm standing here naked," he says. "I've given up nothing."

NBC's reaction: No way. More fights and threats. More headlines.

NBC

"Pryor did not quit entirely but did announce the following ultimatum concerning censorship," writes David S. Silverman in *You Can't Air That: Four Cases of Controversy and Censorship in American Television Programming.* He said, "'If it's not resolved, if we can't find a reasonable means of dealing with it, then Tuesday night's [taping] will probably be the last.'" Pryor was also quoted as saying, "Everybody will say I'm crazy if I quit, that I'll be the crazy nigger who ran off from NBC, but this is stifling my creativity and I just can't work under those conditions."

The Richard Pryor Show premiered on September 13 with the inflammatory opening intact. Sort of. NBC had blurred the offending full-frame missing-genitalia shot, which of course was confusing for viewers, unsure what it was they were looking at and what it was the studio audience members were laughing at.

Of course, only some viewers in the country even had the chance to see it, confused or not: Some NBC stations pre-empted the premiere for their own programming, pushing Pryor to air in late-night; and some refused to air it all.

Pryor's outrage and troublemaking mushroomed. Controversial sketches were written; network notes were given and ignored. Fights erupted. Not helping: low ratings, even for the hyped debut and then certainly for subsequent episodes.

For whatever reason, NBC had scheduled *The Richard Pryor Show* opposite ABC's *Happy Days* and *Laverne and Shirley*, the two most popular shows on the air. (Why NBC even chose 8pm on any night is anyone's guess, given the concerns of the day about family-friendly viewing in the first hour of prime-time.) After four episodes, *The Richard Pryor Show* was gone forever.

Both NBC and Richard Pryor survived the ill-fated 1977 dust-up called *The Richard Pryor Show* – as did television itself, battered thought it was by the fracas. As to the variety series overall? As a genre? Not so much. Bigger TV names than Pryor's in the 1970s had tried and failed to keep the old-fashioned format alive – including Redd Foxx that same season. But the traditional variety show had been consumed by a new anarchic form of comedy and variety being seen in late-night on *NBC's Saturday Night*.

The irony is that it was Pryor's headline-making appearance on that show in 1975 that paved the way for NBC's offer for him to star in his own show.

Still, like Flip Wilson seven years before him, Richard Pryor, an African-American host of a weekly TV series in the 1970s, helped to widen TV's lanes for non-white faces. In 1978, the long-since-cancelled series was nominated for two Emmy Awards – for Outstanding Direction and for Outstanding Art Direction (which it won).

(**Fun Fact**: Among the regulars who appeared on *The Richard Pryor Show* were Sandra Bernhard, Edie McClurg, and Robin Williams.)

> [T]he NBC program gave the risqué Pryor the shot to give millions of Americans a glimpse into hilarious sketch comedy of varying formats, sociopolitical criticism, prototypical improvisation and gorgeous, historical expressions of blackness once a week. And he provided that … but for only four weeks, after which he pulled the plug on his own show, fed up with content restrictions. The battle of maintaining unfiltered blackness with television regulations and paranoid powers-that-be didn't start with Pryor. And while he helped other black vehicles get further along, he didn't end these challenges altogether, either. (*theroot.com*)

"It takes a lot of pain and love to raise a boy; maybe I gave so much to Rudy, there wasn't enough left over for you."

-- Mary Jordache, to son Tom
Rich Man, Poor Man

The Rural Purge
1971 CBS
(61)

> [A]t the end of the 1970–71 season not a single rural comedy was left on CBS, the network that had based much of its competitive dominance in the 1960s on that genre.
>
> -- *Encyclopedia Britannica*
> "The Relevance Movement"

> The network got rid of every show that had a tree in it.
>
> -- actor Tim Conway

It sounds like a joke, but it was a real thing. It really happened. In 1971, CBS really did take a whack at and cancel some of it most popular series simply because each was attracting the wrong kind of audience.

Green Acres. The Beverly Hillbillies. Hee-Haw. Mayberry RFD. The Jim Nabors Show. The New Andy Griffith Show. Each doing well in the ratings, but not among viewers in big cities, where in 1971 was where more and more of TV's advertising dollars were focused. Where more and more of the money came from that greased prime-time TV's wheels.

So ... gone. Dismissed. Cancelled.
It was called The Rural Purge.

(*The Glen Campbell Goodtime Hour*, a CBS variety show hosted by the country singer since 1969, would join them in the cancellation graveyard in 1972, having barely aired at all in its final 1971-72 season.)

And it wasn't just *where* the viewers were from that had begun to matter more but the *who* they were? How old. How smart. How sophisticated. How rich. How cool. When *Batman* aired on ABC from 1966 to 1968, it never cracked the Top 30 for any of its three seasons, but its ratings were strong with young urban viewers (back when "urban" meant city, years before the word would be co-opted by white TV and film executives to mean black) and ABC framed that as being popular with *cool* viewers. Along with a few of its other shows that did well with younger viewers, it gave the third-place network some bragging rights that converted into advertiser dollars.

The notion of "socio-economic" demographics began to grow in importance from there.

So with the new decade came new rules. And rural-appeal programming like *The Beverly Hillbillies*, while still popular even after nine seasons, just wouldn't cut it anymore. Nor would the rest of its CBS ilk. And for much the same reason neither would the network's *The Ed Sullivan Show*, TV's oldest of old-fashioned variety shows -- and one of TV's oldest-skewing. It, too, was shown the door in 1971.

(That the roots of *The Ed Sullivan Show* can be traced back to 1930s radio made its exit singularly symbolic of the adolescent rebellion that was prime-time in the 1970s.)

CBS / Sony

If it seemed like wholesale changes were afoot at CBS, they were. After all, the network had the hottest show on all of TV in 1971 – the New York-set, progressive-minded, young-demographic skewing, envelope-pushing *All in the Family*. Some of its line-up just didn't fit in with that audience profile, which was the one it was pushing. Seeing more value in. Envisioning generating more money from. Prime-time TV was transitioning into a whole new kind of ballgame with the surging *All in the Family*, and CBS -- in fact each of the broadcast networks -- both wanted and needed new players to flesh out that changing team.

The call was for real shows that featured real people and real situations. Character-comedy over *situation*-comedy. Programming that appealed to younger viewers living in big cities – Minneapolis or New York or Chicago, rather than Petticoat Junction. Programming that reflected the changing face of the country. And the changing faces within it.

From *The HBO Effect* by Dean J. DeFino: "Recognizing that they could attract higher-value advertisers to programs that appealed to the most desirable group-affluent, educated 18-49-year-olds, they began to offer more sophisticated programming, primarily in the form of socially conscious sitcoms."

At CBS in particular, the challenge, though, was to manage it all without alienating and then losing altogether those tens of millions of viewers who'd made it the country's most watched network since 1955. To court new viewers without losing longtime ones. (In 1992, NBC attempted a similar network-wide re-branding that was executed with the finesse of a record scratch; it cancelled some long-running series but then lost their viewers as well when it served up inferior replacements. Some in the industry jokingly refer to the era as the time when NBC cancelled its audience.)

CBS had begun the shift in the fall of 1970, at what *tvobscurities.com* calls the start of a "wave of relevancy." (*All in the Family* would not premiere until January 1971.)

Addressing the demographic trend already showcased by the success of NBC's *Rowan and Martin's Laugh-In* beginning in 1968 and then ABC's young-and-relevant *Room 222* in 1969 (not to mention its own recent college-skewing hit, *The Smothers Brothers Comedy Hour*), CBS seeded its fall 1970 schedule with a mix of new series -- some that it hoped would appeal to its core "C&D county" (smaller-town) audience, and some that invited younger and more-big-city viewers.

Some worked (*Mary Tyler Moore*, about a 30-year-old single woman working in TV news in Minneapolis); some did not (*Storefront Lawyers* and *The Interns* – each about a team of 20-something professionals in Los Angeles).

Then *All in the Family* showed up in January, its popularity cementing and then accelerating the transformation. Set in a Queens, New York rowhome, featuring both white and black faces, and exploring topics like sex and politics and the generation gap, it made history and re-made CBS. Out went "every show that had a tree in it." Concrete was in.

The Rural Purge was helped along by the 1970 FCC decree known as the Prime Time Access Rule (PTAR), which, effective with the start of the 1971-72 TV season, shortened the prime-time schedules for the three broadcast networks by a half-hour -- their 7:30pm (EST) starts would now be 8pm.

One of the by-products was a weekly loss of 150 minutes of programming that forced a trimming of network schedules and inventory. Whatever the impetus, CBS, the network that in 1970 was the home of *The Beverly Hillbillies, The Ed Sullivan Show, The Glen Campbell Goodtime Hour, Green Acres, Hee-Haw, The Jim Nabors Show, Lassie. Mayberry R.F.D., The New Andy Griffith Show, The Red Skelton Show*, and *Petticoat Junction* was inside of two years later the home of *All in the Family, The Bob Newhart Show, Bridget Loves Bernie, M*A*S*H*, Mary Tyler Moore, Maude*, and *The Sonny & Cher Comedy Hour* -- with hits from *Kojak* to *Good Times* to *The Jeffersons* on the docket and when old-school 1950s-era stalwarts like *Gunsmoke* and *Here's Lucy* were finally and literally history.

Dodge City and Hooterville just weren't where people of the 1970s were *at*, man.

It was a slow and careful turn of an enormous ship, but CBS managed it without alienating its core audience. It would remain TV's Number One network until 1975, when a whole other kind of audience shift found ABC on top for a change. (**Fun Fact**: The 1970 out-with-the-old/in-with-the-new-and-young approach wasn't limited to CBS. NBC and ABC each also unveiled 1970-71 line-ups that offered young(er) stars, more ethnically diverse casts and storylines, and more cosmopolitan settings. Some -- *The Flip Wilson Show, The Partridge Family* -- worked; others -- *The Young Lawyers*, a black-cast version of *Barefoot in the Park* -- did not.)

Socionomics Institute / CBS

CBS

Upstairs, Downstairs
1971-75 ITV / 1974-77 PBS
(62)

PBS / LWT

In the three-network TV universe of the 1970s, it took a special project to lure viewers away from the mainstream. *Upstairs, Downstairs* premiered on PBS when the public television network was all-but brand-new, known chiefly for *Sesame Street*. The British series became an American sensation.

Created by co-stars Jean Marsh and Eileen Atkins, and produced by the UK's LTV, the multi-generation story, set in Edwardian England, chronicled the lives of the aristocratic Bellamy family and the servants in its employ at the large family townhouse.

It unfolded over the course of five "series" (seasons, to American viewers), extending from 1903 to 1930 and featuring a large cast of regulars. It began airing in the U.S. in 1974 as part of the PBS anthology *Masterpiece Theatre*, which itself had premiered on the public

TV outlet in January 1971 to showcase British series and mini-series imports.

"*Upstairs, Downstairs* was the most extensive series on *Masterpiece Theatre* and brought a new and refreshing image of British television to many Americans whose only perception of British programming, not necessarily correct, was of ponderous adaptations of dated British literature" (*Encyclopedia of Television*).

Not only was it the first original production on *Masterpiece Theater* — written directly for TV rather than an adaptation of an existing text -- *Upstairs, Downstairs* was one of the first to be shot on videotape rather than film, verisimilitude being the watchword of the 70s.

As in the United Kingdom, the series was one of new decade's biggest and most transfixing hits in the United States. Sizable audiences opted for it over mainstream network fare on Sunday nights, and it ended up elbowing out network front-runners *Family*, *Police Story*, *The Waltons* and *Columbo* to win the Emmy as TV's Best Drama -- twice.

As much as anything, though, *Upstairs, Downstairs* helped put PBS on the prime-time map, showcasing it as home to more than just *Sesame Street* and *Mr. Rogers' Neighborhood*. It was a veritable fourth option on and as a result expanded the whole of the television landscape.

Its legacy has been felt for decades, most notably when PBS and *Masterpiece* introduced another highly viewed game-changer in 2010 seen as its generational successor, *Downton Abbey*. After the new show's successful first season, *The AV Club* paid a lengthy tribute to *Upstairs, Downstairs* to coincide with the long-awaited arrival on DVD of a complete set of episodes:

> Belying *Upstairs, Downstairs'* reputation as typically stodgy PBS *Masterpiece Theatre* material, the new 40th-anniversary complete-series collection reveals the show as an important missing link between the anthology dramas of the earliest days of television and the

serialized dramas that became popular in the years after it left the airwaves. Now it's easy to draw a direct line between the kinds of cumulative stories *Upstairs, Downstairs* told and the similar storylines on modern-day classics like *The Sopranos* and *Mad Men...*

Though the series was, in many ways, a typical soap about life among the manor-born, *Upstairs, Downstairs* broke new ground in a handful of intriguing ways. While other stories set in these sorts of homes often made characters of both the rich and their servants, no one did it to the degree that creators Jean Marsh (who also starred in the series as young maid Rose) and Eileen Atkins did. The show's sympathies defiantly begin with the servants, then expand to encompass seemingly everyone who's ever set foot inside the Bellamy house...

Upstairs, Downstairs also broke new ground on a storytelling level. The idea that relationships continued over time and that characters hopped between beds wasn't new—it was commonplace on most popular soap operas on both sides of the Atlantic—but *Upstairs, Downstairs* wedded this to clear-eyed, small-scale storytelling where events accumulated, until something that happened a handful of episodes ago would come back in devastating fashion a few episodes later. Every episode told its own story, creating something between a one-act play and a short story by someone like Evelyn Waugh, but those stories gradually added up to a greater portrayal ...

The series also indulged in surprisingly compelling— and surprisingly relevant to the modern day—political commentary about how little the rich could understand their servants' plight, and how working-class people were trapped by the lives into which they were born.

In a time when statistics about income disparity are increasingly discussed, the stratified social-caste system of *Upstairs, Downstairs* (a system the show's richest inhabitants refuse to admit exists) feels more contemporary than any other 40-year-old drama series…

Upstairs, Downstairs remains a wonderful example of how creative people can use the inherent limitations of television—from budget to the awkwardness of the episodic format—to tell stories with an almost novelistic sweep. By the time the series is over, plot twists have piled upon plot twists, the show has written out many former protagonists, and the writers have thoughtfully, thoroughly defined a few dozen people within the show's universe. It's tempting to write off older shows as "good for their time," but *Upstairs, Downstairs* isn't just good TV for the 1970s. It's good TV, period.

TV Guide / CBS

ESCAPISM

"Oh Barnes, you just get dumber and dumber every day."

-- J.R. Ewing, to arch-rival Cliff Barnes
Dallas

Maybe the TV academics are right: Maybe there was so much learning, so much *sturm und drang*, on television during the first half of the 1970s that by mid-decade viewers felt in need of a breather. a break from all the thinking and feeling and analyzing and internalizing that TV was forcing upon them.

Or maybe it was the arrival of the anti-violence Family Viewing Hour in D.C. Or of Fred Silverman at ABC. Or a need to get away from real-life stress after so many years of Vietnam and Watergate, crime and corruption, let alone amid rising divorce rates and cities in decay and New York in bankruptcy.

Whatever the reason(s), in and around 1975, TV viewers started turning to the tube as much for escape as illumination. Maybe even more. (Even the eye-opening 8-part history lesson that was *Roots* in 1977 had sweeping elements of adventure to it.) Prime-time TV started to become more a place for chilling out, for having a laugh, for taking a ride. The new "generation of seekers" wanted a break. The navel-gazing of *Kung Fu* was being replaced by the outdoor embrace in *The Life and Times of Grizzly Adams* and *Centennial*. I.Q. stated to become not so nearly appealing as T&A. Content became rife with silliness and fluff not seen since the early days of TV when both cars and horses talked.

After the 'turn toward relevance' in early-1970s sitcoms like *All in the Family* and *M*A*S*H**, another vein of more escapist sitcoms emerged in the mid-1970s.

Typified by ABC hits *Happy Days* and *Laverne & Shirley*, these programs offered an explicitly nostalgic emphasis on humor over social critique, reaching out to young audiences through physical humor and feel-good affirmation instead of targeting quality audiences through relevant issues of the time or satire. (*Genre and Television: From Cop Shows to Cartoons in American Culture*)

The concept of "almost anything goes" didn't go as far as it would in the 21st century, but still ... in 1975 it definitely started to take on a revised definition.

Almost Anything Goes
1975-76 ABC
(63)

ABC

For much of TV's early years, the broadcast networks generally operated on a year-round 39/13 prime-time schedule: 39 weeks of original in-season programming, followed by 13 weeks of out-of-season summer programming (mostly reruns).

The formula came to fluctuate through the years, and there were sporadic attempts at original scripted summer series; but television's default schedule basically boiled down to *new episodes during the school year / reruns when school was out*. (There was no real correlation between TV and academia: The concept of a TV season starting in September was more tied to the time of year that auto manufacturers rolled out their new car lines and their turns to the TV industry to buy commercial time to promote them, necessitating the kind of big audiences provided by fresh programming.)

By the early 1970s, the 39/13 formula was more 26/26. Original (new) episodes were spread out from September through March; reruns or specials or summer replacement shows (usually cheaper-to-produce variety shows) filled in the gap between seasons.

It's a cycle that worked fine in a less-competitive three-network universe, when reruns were still a draw. Sometimes it even worked to a network's advantage, as newer series that had gone un-sampled during the regular season, due either to stiff competition or lack of awareness, came to find an audience in reruns, against other reruns. (Best case example: *All in the Family*, which became a hit on its way to legend thanks to the new-but-low-rated show's exposure opposite reruns in the summer of 1971.)

Occasionally, there were also original scripted shows in the summer – be they leftover episodes of expiring series used as summer filler or rejected pilots from the most recent Development season or try-outs of less conventional shows to gauge audience interest (1972's *The Corner Bar* and 1978's *Free Country* are two examples).

But these were rare. Especially in the first half of the decade. By and large, summers were somewhat ... ignored. By the networks, if not always the viewers.

In the summer of 1975, ABC introduced an experimental new series called *Almost Anything Goes*, a variety series by way of what they network described as a family game-show. It was an adaptation of a popular UK game-show of the late 1960s and early 1970s called *It's a Knockout*, which itself was based on a French series from the early 1960s.

> This show almost defies description. Each week, three
> teams (each representing a particular USA town, and

consisting solely of members from the town) compete for money and prizes. The competitions vary from week to week, and include bizarre obstacle courses, pie throwing contests, swing relays, and other humorous, crazy contests (*imdb.com*).

For each of the first four weeks of its five-week run, *Almost Anything Goes* featured multiple teams, each from four sections making up the United States (North, South, East, West), squaring off against one another, with the winners from each region pitted against one another for a fifth-week series finale.

Then-popular sportscasters Charlie Jones, Lynn Shackelford, and former longtime L.A. disc-jockey-turned-TV-personality Dick Whittington called the action. (And quite seriously, too.)

Airing against negligible counter-programming, it was a late-summer hit for ABC. So much so that the network rushed to get it back in production for in-season airing when it found itself in need of a replacement for the new and quick failure that was *Saturday Night Live With Howard Cosell*. (That disaster was an idea so bad that it sort of qualifies as its own singular version of *Almost Anything Goes*).

However, as a regular season series, scheduled against real competition -- CBS's new runaway hit *The Jeffersons* and NBC's long-running stalwart *Emergency!* -- it didn't do nearly as well and was soon canceled.

However short-lived its success, though, *Almost Anything Goes* made its mark in and on 1970s TV, changing prime-time by demonstrating to the networks that an original summer series -- one not built around a familiar musical-variety act (which is what most summer replacements shows were at the time), so a cheaper one at that -- could attract an audience. They saw that viewers wanted new shows to watch between Memorial Day and Labor Day, not just reruns of even popular series. In the process it also provided significant new wick to the average-people-on-TV candle that had been lit two years earlier with PBS's admittedly different *An American Family*. *Real People* and *That's Incredible* weren't that far behind. *Almost Anything Goes* led to a genre and TV staple of exactly that.

The show also contributed to the building of the *TV franchise* concept, the idea that a hit idea can be diversified and multiplied, in the way that popular 1960s/1970s game-show *Hollywood Squares* showed when it begat two spin-off editions aimed at younger viewers. *Almost Anything Goes* morphed into both a children's show in 1977 (*Junior Almost Anything Goes*) and then a celebrities-contestant version not long thereafter (*All-Star Almost Anything Goes*). Each was short-lived.

(**Fun Fact**: The winning cities for each of the two seasons of *Almost Anything Goes* on ABC were Boulder City, Nevada and Chambersburg, Pennsylvania.)

I want to talk to you right now about a fundamental threat to American democracy ... I do not mean our political and civil liberties. They will endure. And I do not refer to the outward strength of America, a nation that is at peace tonight everywhere in the world, with unmatched economic power and military might ...The threat is nearly invisible in ordinary ways ... It is a crisis of confidence.

-- President Jimmy Carter
July 1979

Dallas
1978-91 CBS
(64)

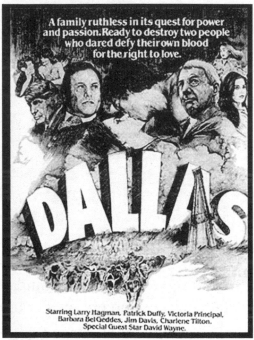

A family ruthless in its quest for power and passion. Ready to destroy two people who dared defy their own blood for the right to love.

Starring Larry Hagman, Patrick Duffy, Victoria Principal,
Barbara Bel Geddes, Jim Davis, Charlene Tilton.
Special Guest Star David Wayne.

TV Guide

Like a lot of long-running and culture-defining TV shows, from *The Dick Van Dyke Show* to *Seinfeld*, *Dallas* was a bit of a low-rated also-ran when it first showed up, in its case on Sunday nights in the spring of 1978 as a five-week fill-in for the expiring *Kojak* and *The Carol Burnett Show* series. Not a huge number of people noticed. (Long forgotten is that *Dallas* was conceived as just that five-week mini-series, the TV format of choice at the time.)

But CBS saw something in the new project from TV neophyte David Jacobs, and it ordered its return as a weekly series for the 1978-79 TV season. It was during this season, after bouncing around a bit on the network's flailing Saturday and Sunday schedules before ultimately finding a home on Friday, that *Dallas* started to catch on.

Dallas told the story of the powerful and wealthy Ewing family and its Ewing Oil empire headquartered at their Southfork Ranch of Dallas, Texas, a story rooted in rocky soil thanks to a longtime feud between the Ewings and the rival Barnes family. The first episode started out with the bombshell news that a marriage has taken place that unites both clans.

It was an old-fashioned soap-opera, infected with a 1970s-tuned coal-black heart, the first real hit soap since *Peyton Place* (1964-69). "When I created *Dallas*," wrote Jacobs in a 1990 *New York Times* reflection, "I did not anticipate [it] would still be on the air [today] ... [n]or could I have imagined the scale of *Dallas*'s success. A hit and a curiosity on every continent, *Dallas* at its peak seemingly transcended entertainment and became a worldwide sociological phenomenon. Even as the phenomenon was occurring, I was hard put to explain [it]."

The series had a large ensemble cast and featured multi-threaded storylines striking all the familiar soap-opera chords – heroes and villains, marriages and affairs, wealth and the thirst for more, disease and dysfunction, lovers and nemeses.

And at its core it had contemptible J.R. Ewing, gleefully played by TV-sitcom refugee Larry Hagman, chewing up and spitting out the scenery of his every scene. It offered characters to cheer for and to root against, stories to connect to and to be shocked by. The stakes were high, the stories rich, the power seductive and compelling-- struck from oil but exercised by position, with J.R. inevitably on top.

Within two years of its mini-series premiere, *Dallas* was a powerful national addiction fed by a weekly Friday-night must-see-it-live fix, which came to a head in the spring of 1980 with a third-season finale episode that showed Hagman's dastardly Ewing gunned down by an unseen assailant. Left bleeding on the carpet as the credits rolled.

Time Inc., CBS, Genesis Park, DC Comics

The cliff-hanging scene somehow connected with viewers in a way few series had ever done, leading to an unparalleled cultural frenzy that saw the entire known universe asking all summer long, "Who shot J.R.?" (To a lesser but still significant extent, the question "Does He Live?" was also being asked – borne as much from creative storytelling as the fact that now-worldwide-popular Hagman was bargaining for more money to return to the role and speculation was that the show's network and studio might kill J.R. off as a result.).

It all made for an excruciatingly long hiatus for the series -- and for viewers -- between its third and fourth seasons, further lengthened by a 1980 actors strike.

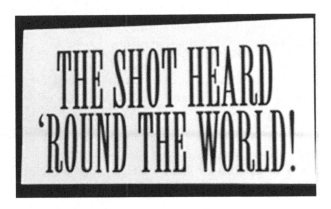

It worked out: The nearly eight-month wait for an answer played out over three episodes in November that saw record-shattering history-making Nielsen ratings as J.R.'s fate and killer were revealed. (Competitors ABC and NBC all-but phoned in each of their Fridays this month, airing feature films and news magazines against the tell-all episodes.) *Dallas* ended up the season's Number One show. It continued a long and mostly healthy run for the rest of the decade, eventually ending in 1991 after 13 years.

The simple experiment that was *Dallas* in the spring of 1978 changed everything. It changed CBS as a network, giving it the Number One show for three seasons, which it used to construct a fortress of a three-hour Friday-night block that walled in viewers week after week, season after season.

It changed the literal fortunes of those involved behind and in front of the camera, chief among them Hagman, who as he did in 1980 often held out for still-more money between seasons or between contracts, knowing (as *All in the Family*'s Carroll O'Connor demonstrated before him in the decade of TV-as-Big-Business) that there was no show without him. And it changed TV as a whole, making the nighttime soap-opera not only popular but an integral part of each networks'

Development for the better part of the next ten years (despite the fact that given their serialized nature, soaps were difficult to air in reruns and nearly impossible to syndicate when they were done). *Dallas* begot *Knots Landing* (CBS) in 1979, *Dynasty* (ABC) and *Flamingo Road* (NBC) and *Falcon Crest* (CBS) in 1981, and then a rasher of soap-themed series and mini-series for many seasons thereafter.

TV's approach to storytelling (story arcs) and character (anti-heroes and villains, especially women) and production (ensemble casts) each changed, in turn. More than anything, after *Dallas*'s "Who Shot J.R." earthquake, TV, in any format (even comedy), went in search the season-ending cliffhangers that would Get Everyone Talking. (Two of the best came from Dynasty: "Who's the Mystery Witness Behind the Black Veil?" in 1981 and "Who Survived the Moldavian Massacre?" in 1985.)

> "Who shot J. R.?" asked magazine covers, comedy sketch writers and titillated viewers. The world had to wait months -- until the fall season premiere on Nov. 21, 1980 -- to learn the [killer's identity]. What the television industry learned was the power of the cliffhanger season finale. An almost unfathomable 76 percent of all television viewers in the country tuned in to "Dallas" that night. Since then, season finales have never been the same. And this year there seems to be an even bigger epidemic than usual of cliffhangers, shocking revelations and dramatic wrap-ups ... Even Fox's animated series "The Simpsons" is getting into the act with its finale "Who Shot Mr. Burns?" Suspects include Homer, Bart, Lisa, Principal Skinner, Grampa Simpson, Smithers and Tito Puente.

> -- Andy Meisler
> *The New York Times* May 7 1995

But the genre also changed TV -- by making TV expensive. Expensive to produce, expensive to own, expensive to keep on the air in success, expensive to satisfy during actors' contract negotiations. It set precedents for star salaries, placing significant pavers on the path to million-dollar-paychecks-or else mentality that would plague the business in the very-near future.

Dallas reinvigorated TV, becoming a cultural touchstone even among those who didn't follow it. Or even watch TV. From J.R.'s evil grin to alcoholic Sue Ellen's quivering chin, from the shooting of its lead to its dismissal of entire badly-received season in the mid-1980s as a dream, it defined pop culture in a way few TV shows ever did or ever would do.

It rode a wave a Southernism that came ashore in the latter half the 1970s, evidenced from the rise of southern rock to the election of a President and from the opening of The Center for the Study of Southern Culture at the University of Mississippi to actor Burt Reynolds' *Gator / Smokey and the Bandit / Hooper* triptych.

In doing so, it also reinvigorated a piece of America: Dallas, the city, was said to welcome *Dallas,* the TV show, still reeling as it was from its association with the 1963 assassination of John Kennedy. Filmed on location in its early years, *Dallas* made the city stand for something more, even if that something more was avarice and adultery.

The "Who Shot J.R.?" resolution episode of *Dallas* (November 21, 1980) remains the second-most watched episode in the history of TV, behind only the 1983 finale of *M*A*S*H*.*

(**Spoiler Alert**: It was Kristin.)

Jiggle Television
1977
(65)

> "Jiggle TV" is a real thing, bro. Back in the 1970s, America began to tire of socially conscious television like "All in the Family," "Good Times," and "One Day at a Time," which made viewers feel bummed about poor people and minorities, so the struggling ABC network decided to lighten the mood with what TV critics termed "Jiggle Television." ... Basically, the elements of Jiggle TV are these: 1) A main character or characters who are women, 2) that wear revealing clothing, and that 3) contain uncomplicated plot lines that do not distract male viewers from the jiggle. (*uproxx.com*)

None of us remembers the TV series *Sugar Time!*

None of the people who wrote, produced, and acted in it remember *Sugar Time!*

Still, *Sugar Time!* is as good a place as any to start on the subject of Jiggle TV.

A sitcom created by James Komak, who'd distinguished himself in the early 70s as producer of both *The Courtship of Eddie's Father* and *Chico and the Man* and who then forsook innovation for commercialism with *Welcome Back Kotter*, *Sugar Time!* (the punctuation is part of the title, thanks) lived a very short life on ABC in 1977 and 1978. Eleven episodes total.

It told the story of an all-female rock group, appropriately called (wait for it) Sugar (no exclamation point). And it starred Barbi Benton, onetime (wait for it) *Playboy* Bunny and the longtime girlfriend of (wait for it) Playboy Enterprises founder Hugh Hefner.

Benton's notoriety by way of Hefner more or less sums up the concept of Jiggle TV, as *Sugar Time!* was virtually ... um ... built on its foundation and on the many images of the 20-something published as and after it happened. Look no further than the main-title sequence that features her bouncing on a trampoline and then galloping on a horse.

That the sitcom arrived on the air just as ABC had ascended to the top of the ratings with *Charlie's Angels* and *Three's Company* – a pair of shows known for the pairs they showed – officially announced what became known as the network's "T&A strategy." Programming that appealed because it featured beautiful woman whose breasts and buttocks tended to be on full display.

In turn, a bit of jealous snark, attributed to a jealous NBC executive, led to the label Jiggle TV.

> "The term was coined by a whiny-baby NBC exec, Paul Klein, slamming ... ABC. He was probably just jealous, because NBC wasn't doing too well, and ABC's newly termed Jiggle TV was raking in the audiences like mad. It was a formula that worked, no matter what the jealous competitors said ... And so begun a trend based on TV-centered sexual gratification ..." (*flashbak.com*)

The formula, for lack of better word, really did work – at least in terms of getting viewer attention for a TV show. Of course, the series would have to good or interesting or entertaining beyond that to become a hit, none of which *Sugar Time!* could lay claim to and each of which *Charlie's Angels* and *Three's Company* pulled off.

Nonetheless, ABC was rife with T&A attempts in the mid-70s, a full Jell-O-mold of Jiggle TV, from *Wonder Woman* and *The Bionic Woman* and *The Love Boat* and *Vegas* (the hits) to *Tabitha* and *Operation Petticoat* and *Blansky's Beauties* (the misses). Between 1976 and 1978, producers couldn't spell ABC without a including at least one double-D.

TV Guide, IBT Media Newsweek Media Group, Pro Arts Inc., NBC, Sony, 20th Century Fox Television

The term "jiggle TV" or "T&A TV" came into true prominence following the premiere of *Charlie's Angels* in 1976 with Fawcett, Smith, and Jackson cracking cases in bikinis and busting baddies braless. (*fastcompany.com*)

And however much NBC may have looked down on the strategy, it wasn't immune to adopting it. *Police Woman* may have been launched in 1974 with the burgeoning feminist movement in mind, but the ground-breaking female-detective at its center was named "Pepper." And the main-title sequence, as well as several episodes that found her in undercover work, put star Angie Dickinson's own assets on clear and full display. NBC's post-*Charlie's Angels*/*Three's Company* inspirations included *Quark*, *Cliffhangers*, *Who's Watching the Kids?* (original title: *Legs*), and *Supertrain*.

CBS, too, played along, with *The Ted Knight Show*, *The American Girls*, *Flying High*, and even *Wonder Woman*, plucking the superhero show from the dustbin after ABC cancelled it in 1977. This is on top of the seasoning it oversaw of some of its other series with the likes of Loni Anderson (*WKRP in Cincinnati*), Charlene Tilton (*Dallas*), and Catherine Bach (*The Dukes of Hazzard*).

And none of this is even counting what became the poster-program of Jiggle TV as of the mid-1970s, ABC's *Battle of the Network Stars* (as well as the lower-profile CBS rip-offs, *Celebrity Challenge of the Sexes* and *Circus of the Stars*). Never before on TV has there been more cheesecake and beefcake on display in one program. Ratings, unlike the swimsuits, were huge.

The irony behind the Jiggle TV movement of the 1970s is that it arose during – or perhaps even was the result of – the application of FCC-mandated Family Viewing Hour in 1975, which relegated programming deemed as not "family friendly" to the later hours of prime-time, away from kids' eyes, and which yielded more high-concept sitcoms. Guns and sex were out; big breasts were in (and out). Nonetheless, like that FCC regulation, which lasted all of a year, the

Jiggle TV strategy eventually waned. By 1979, smarter, less-obvious sitcoms and new takes on the one-hour-drama genre were on-call.

As of the mid-1970s, though, network television learned a lesson more and more taught since the 1960s: Sex, or at least the tease and promise of it, sells. The floodgates here, too, opened to raunch and to ribald humor, along with more and more skin. T&A was becoming as elementary as ABC.

ABC / The Komack Company

The Rockford Files
1974-80 NBC
(66)

The Rockford Files is often remembered as much for who worked on it (future wunderkinds Steven Bochco, Stephen J. Cannell, and David Chase) as for being one of the decade's best dramas. That it represented one last warm breath of life for the dying private-eye genre makes its luster shine even brighter.

James Garner, the 1950s small-screen star who went on to a successful film career in the 1960s before coming back to series TV, starred as Jim Rockford, an ex-con eking out a living in Los Angeles as a private detective specializing in cold cases.

Working for his famous "two hundred bucks a day, plus expenses" and based in mobile-home that's seen better days (albeit one that's still parked right on the Pacific), Rockford invariably falls into as much trouble as he takes on with his cases. This made sense, since they tended to involve the city's most notorious and lethal mob figures, drug kingpins, femme fatales, and other ne'er-do-wells.

NBCUniversal

But it wasn't Rockford's cases that made *Rockford* stand out. It wasn't the stories -- at least not necessarily the stories. It was the story*telling*. *The Rockford Files* featured some of the best writing ever in the one-hour drama genre. Breezy, believable, relatable, grounded, even funny (the last of which the network reportedly tried to squelch), the series spun out episodes that depicted what seemed like actual people doing actual work, even if those actual people were the bad guys. In addition, the cases themselves were interesting and well-constructed by the writers; and the episodes were well cast, with non-traditional supporting regulars and with unconventional guest-stars that ranged from Isaac Hayes to Lauren Bacall.

Rockford as protagonist, especially as played by James Garner, was the perfect out-of-the-box imperfect hero for an imperfect decade -- equal parts charming and cantankerous, friendly and snarky, cooperative and resistant, accepting and rebellious. When Jim Rockford threw a punch, he showed that it hurt. It was a whole different approach to TV crime, even if the cases sometimes ended up unsolved.

> This show has appeared on many Top 50 or Top 100 lists of the best series of all time and has occasionally appeared on Top 10 lists. The reasons often cited were the quality of the writing and acting, but also because the show broke with so many conventions, such as Rockford not being a "glamourous" private investigator; not always being very successful financially; not always being on friendly terms with the police; getting arrested fairly often; not always winning fist-fights, including getting hurt or plain old beaten up... (*imdb.com*)

The Rockford Files was nominated for 17 Emmy awards during its six seasons on NBC, winning five, including two in 1978 -- one for Garner as Outstanding Lead Actor and one for the show itself as Outstanding Drama. The series both softened and rounded the hard right-angles of the private-eye show, providing a sort of missing link between its black-and-white just-the-facts early days and the everyman-genre it spawned in the 1980s with *Magnum P.I.* and *Simon & Simon*. It was by all accounts the realest and coolest crime show of the 1970s.

Fred Silverman
(67)

> As a measure of Fred Silverman's status and influence, on the day in January of 1978 when his defection [from ABC to NBC] was announced, the Wall Street stock price of ABC dropped $1.75 a share, while stock in the parent company of NBC, the Radio Corporation of America (RCA), jumped $1.25.

> -- Michael McKenna
> Real People *and the Rise of Reality Television*

Fred Silverman, the programming executive who by the end of the 1970s had run all three broadcast networks -- first at top-ranked CBS, then at second-place ABC, which under him became Number One, and then at last-place NBC, where his magic touch stalled -- defined 1970s TV.

How many other television executives of the era made the cover of *Time* between 1970 and 1979? (**Spoiler Alert**: None.)

Born in 1937, Silverman was raised in New York – and raised on TV. His Ohio State master's thesis was a study of ten years' worth of ABC programming, and the legend is that it so impressed CBS executives that he was hired there at age 25.

He eventually made his way up to head of all programming, becoming the man to help re-imagine the network as the old-fashioned 1960s gave way to the new-age 1970s. Silverman is credited with executing CBS's legendary 1971 Rural Purge, the sweeping cancellation of most all of its rural- and older-skewing series in an effort to make room for younger-skewing and more topical shows like *All in the Family, The Sonny & Cher Comedy Hour, Maude*, and *M*A*S*H**. At CBS, Silverman shook things up like a snow globe. But it worked. The network managed an important image turnaround at the start of a critical decade, while holding on to its long standing as the country's most-watched network.

Sept. 5, 1977

Time Inc.

In 1975, he was recruited by struggling ABC with the hope he could work the same kind of magic there at a network with much less to brag about. For the 1974-75 TV season, ABC had introduced 18 new series. Fifteen failed. (This was the season of famously maligned *Sonny Comedy Revue* and *Get Christie Love*.)

Its few hits when Silverman was hired were *The Six Million Dollar Man*, *The Streets of San Francisco* and *Monday Night Football*. Under Silverman, ABC became the top-rated network inside of a year, ending CBS's 20-year-reign, the result of a mixture of acumen, luck, and timing. The struggling single-camera sitcom *Happy Days*, introduced on ABC in January 1974, was converted to a multi-camera live-audience show, with the focus shifting to Henry Winkler's Arthur Fonzarelli character. It became a monster hit.

The aging variety-series format was reimagined for a younger generation with *The Donny & Marie Show*. It became a Friday-night staple. New mass-appeal down-the-middle series were ordered (*Charlie's Angels, What's Happening!!, Eight Is Enough, Three's Company, The Hardy Boys/Nancy Drew Mysteries*) that didn't so much challenge viewers as reward them with lighthearted adventure and broad comedy. And heart.

Lots and lots of heart.

New formulas were explored for age-old genres -- the family drama (*Family*), the adult sitcom (*Soap*), and the anthology (*The Love Boat*). Network equity was maximized with spin-off attempts of existing hits (*Laverne and Shirley* from *Happy Days*; *The Bionic Woman* from *The Six Million Dollar Man*, *Fish* from *Barney Miller*, *The Brady Bunch Variety Hour* from *The Brady Bunch*; *Mr. T and Tina* from *Welcome Back Kotter*). Silverman even greenlit more-noble fare like game-changers *Rich Man, Poor Man* and *Roots*.

His misses were obvious, but his hits were grand-slams. In his short reign at ABC, he created a national prime-time party. ABC became the place to be. He created events out of single airings of shows, and he built three-hour must-watch blocks of programming that rendered a TV-viewer's remote-control pointless.

Night after night, weekly wins after weekly win. That he came from a Number One network to do it all over again there at ABC made him a celebrity in his own right.

(How successful was Silverman? So successful that few remember he was behind some of the decade's quickest-to-fail and most-derided shows, among them *Holmes & Yoyo, Blanksy's Beauties, Sugar Time!, Lucan, The Redd Foxx Show, The Captain & Tennille Show*, and arguably the worst and most cynical TV series of the decade, if not in television history, *The Brady Bunch Variety Hour*. A smash-hit such as *Charlie's Angels* can mask that kind of failure.)

In 1978, Fred Silverman was lured yet again to defect from head of a winning network to take over a struggling one. NBC wanted its shot at him.

At the time, it had just one series in the Top 10 (*Little House on the Prairie*) and only four in the Top 20 -- all of which were found on either Sunday or Monday, meaning that on five nights of any given week the NBC lights were barely on. Silverman was recruited in the middle of a disastrous season that started with *The Richard Pryor Show* and came to include seven new dramas that quickly ran aground (including what were seen as close to sure-bets *The Man from Atlantis* and *Richie Brockelman, P.I.*) and the pitiful attempt to salvage scraps from the long-running and just-ended *Sanford and Son* with a new comedy spin-off called *Sanford Arms*. (Featuring neither Sanford nor son, it, too, was gone almost as soon as it arrived.)

What few series it had that could be qualified as successes of any kind were aging (*The Rockford Files*), ending (*Police Story, Police Woman*) or sinking (*James at 16, Chico & the Man*).

The 1978 NBC fall schedule that Silverman inherited offered a schedule that featured exactly one show that had been introduced the previous season – *Chips*. The new line-up: *Grandpa Goes to Washington, Dick Clark's Live Wednesday, W.E.B., The Waverly Wonders, Who's Watching the Kids?, The Eddie Capra Mysteries, Sword of Justice*. Nothing that appealed to or answered any sort of viewer calling; nothing that re-worked a genre, offered a compelling narrative, or even featured a famous name (beyond that of Joe Namath). Every single one of them was gone by Christmas. (Two of the new shows never made it past October.)

The TV industry of 1978 was a markedly different one from the one of just eight years earlier (thanks in part to Silverman himself). And Silverman found that as TV's adolescence had settled in on its way to adulthood, it had become less easy (or certainly more routine) for a new show to get attention simply by being shocking or provocative.

Tastes had already changed. The industry as a whole was changing, with network TV beginning to feel the pinch of competition from both first-run syndication and cable TV. More specific to his job at NBC, Silverman was faced with trying to take down shows on two other networks that he had helped to build. Not an easy task. He was forced into a game of imitation rather than innovation, putting less-thans into production such as *Supertrain*, *Mrs. Columbo*, and *Hello, Larry*.

NATAS

He ordered up a slew of new programming more or less ripped from the Silverman playbook: high-concept (*Sweepstakes*, *Turnabout*, *Highcliffe Manor*, *Supertrain*), spin-offs (*Little Women*, *Harris and Company*), movie rip-offs (*Brothers and Sisters*), and genre re-imaginings (*Whodunit?*, *Presenting Susan Anton*, *Cliffhangers*). Every one of them failed.

Three shows introduced as replacement series in the 1978-79 seasons did find audiences: *Diff'rent Strokes*, which would go on to last eight seasons; *Real People*, TV's first successful modern-day reality series; and *Hello, Larry*, an innocuous but also charmless single-parent sitcom that had more jokes told *about* it than in it.

But each was ridiculed, and Silverman, his celebrity-executive status crushed and his credibility assailed, was in the crosshairs himself. In a February 1979 *Saturday Night Live*, guest-host Kate Jackson appeared in a sketch that parodied her then-hit private-detective show *Charlie's Angels*. The sketch found the Angels taking on a case that reveals Fred Silverman is still secretly working for ABC, planted at NBC to sabotage its prime-time. Says Jane Curtin as angel Kris Munroe: "That explains *Hello, Larry*."

The handful of 1978-79 hits gave way to two more TV seasons at NBC for Silverman that, with the exceptions of *Diff'rent Strokes* spin-off *The Facts of Life* in 1979 and the not-insignificant launch of *Hill Street Blues* midway through the 1980-81 seasons, proved woeful for both him and the network. Some 28 new shows came and went, from *The Brady Brides* and *Harper Valley PTA* to series versions of *From Here to Eternity* and *Buck Rogers in the 25th Century*.

By 1981 NBC had ended its relationship with Silverman. The legendary executive went on to decades of success as a respected TV producer of old-fashioned drama series hits (*Matlock, Jake & the Fatman, Diagnosis: Murder*) from his own company. (**Fun Fact:** At one point in the 1990s, Silverman the producer had a series on each of the three broadcast networks that he once ran.)

If he didn't exactly change NBC the way he changed CBS and ABC, Fred Silverman certainly contributed to his legacy as an executive who changed TV. Five important things came of his NBC tenure: *Real People* and *Lifeline*, which marked the starts of the modern-day reality or non-scripted series; *Centennial* and *Shogun*, epic mini-series that upped the standards for longform programming; and *Hill Street Blues*, which re-invented both the cop show and the one-hour drama. (The number rises to six if *notorious* also counts as *important*. Silverman brought to prime-time something called *Pink Lady & Jeff*, a weekly variety-series that paired unknown American comedian Jeff Altman with two unknown non-English-speaking Japanese singers -- with whom he'd had no prior association -- and which quickly joined the ranks of TV's Worst Ideas Ever.)

At the end of the day, Fred Silverman is associated with the best of TV during its most critical decade. As observed in the *New York Times* in January 1978, when he was hired by NBC:

> At the age of 40, with more than 15 years in the industry behind him, Fred Silverman no longer qualifies as television's wunderkind. Instead, with the announcement that he is leaving ABC to become the top executive of NBC, the former CBS vice president has become television's man for all networks. Praised for achieving high ratings, damned for pandering to low tastes, lauded as an innovator, belittled as a caretaker, deified as a programming strategist but downgraded as a corporate politician, the heavy-set, rumpled but still boyish-looking Mr. Silverman possesses the capacity to unite fans and critics alike on one point: His love for television.

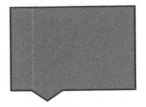

"Love means never having to hear 'I'm pregnant.'"

-- Vinnie Barbarino
Welcome Back, Kotter

Soap
1977-81 ABC
(68)

The controversy around *Soap* began before the show even aired. In the spring of 1977, months before the program's scheduled fall debut, ABC previewed the first two episodes for its affiliates, as well as for Newton Dieter, the director of the Gay Media Task Force...When word of the program's sex-saturated humor reached the press, religious groups began to agitate against the show, protesting the inclusion of the gay character as well as the romantic triangle between the middle-aged, married Jessica Tate, her twenty-something daughter, Corrine, and a male tennis pro...They deluged ABC with protest letters and, as a result, seventeen affiliates refused to air the first two episodes, forty-seven more scheduled them an hour later that the network feed, and multiple advertisers withdrew their sponsorship.

-- Elana Levine
Wallowing in Sex:
The New Sexual Culture of 1970s American Television

In the handful of years that followed her writing the controversial 1972 abortion episode of *Maude*, Susan Harris got two sitcoms she created picked up and on the air. The first, *Fay*, launched in September of 1975, starred Lee Grant in the trending role of a new divorcee re-discovering life in her 40s.

The sitcom was announced by NBC with much fanfare -- Grant had starred in SHAMPOO earlier in the year (she'd go on to win the Oscar) -- and it promised to be a funny and frank look at a liberated and single middle-aged woman. Which meant it fell prey to network skittishness at the time over adult subject matter, especially those airing in the first hour of prime-time. (Why NBC opted to schedule the series at 8pm in the first place would forever be a mystery.) Against *The Waltons*, TV's highest-rated drama, *Fay* was gone after three episodes.

Harris' second sitcom attempt, *Loves Me Loves Me Not*, showed up on CBS six months later, in April 1977. Its focus was on the relationship between a young couple. No controversy. No network skittishness. No Oscar-winning stars. But also no viewers. It lasted six episodes.

Then came Harris's third shot: *Soap*. And as shots go, this one was heard around the world.

TV Guide / ABC Sony

Early in 1977, ABC, Number One and hoping to add some sophisticated adult sitcoms to its rasher of popular youth-appeal ones (*Happy Days*, *Laverne & Shirley*, *Welcome Back Kotter*), announced that a new show called *Soap* would be part of its upcoming fall schedule.

A sitcom parody of the daytime soap-operas crowding all three networks' afternoon schedules, *Soap* would tell of the lives of two middle-aged sisters living in Connecticut – one upper-class, one middle-class – and of their extended often-warring families. Like the daytime soaps, the prime-time *Soap* promised storylines chock-a-block with all manner of vice.

The first two half-hour episodes, amounting to an hour-long pilot for the new show, were screened early for ABC executives. They made two things clear: 1) *Soap* was indeed a spoof of daytime drama; and 2) the spoof would take advantage of TV's relaxing standards by pushing the prime-time content envelope to the point of disrepair -- up to and including an effeminate dress-wearing adult gay son, a bed-hopping daughter who's having an affair with both her married mother's lover and a priest, a shell-shocked senior-citizen war veteran; and an adult son plotting to kill his mother's new husband.

That, and it offered scripted television's first-ever use of the sex-euphemism *boff*.

By June 1977, three months before the show even premiered, in what would become an infamous memo leaked to the press, ABC was directing producers to scale back on the risqué material. Among the requests were for the elimination in the scripts of the words "slut" and "Tinkerbell," as well as of all references to oral sex or any activity at all related to homosexuality. Plus, producers were to find replacement language for a scene that features a detailed description of male-to-female sexual-reassignment surgery.

(As for the sexually active Catholic priest: "Father Flotsky's stand on liberalizing the Mass will have to be treated in a balanced, inoffensive manner. By way of example, the substitution of Oreos for the traditional [Communion] wafer is unacceptable.")

Not helping: A false report circulated after the pilot had been screened, suggesting even more outrageous content. And thus begat The Summer of *Soap*. Three months of controversy and headlines in newspapers across the country -- front pages as well as the TV pages -- with religious protests and other advocacy-groups firing warning-shots about TV having once again gone too far.

ABC / Sony

But *Soap* weathered the summer storm and made it to premiere night in September 1977, albeit blacked out in some markets by still-skittish local-affiliate executives. And almost immediately it tossed aside the baggage of protests by ... being funny. And well done. And then highly viewed and critically praised. The consensus: ABC finally did have its sharp, well-written, well-cast adult sitcom.

In its own way, and in Susan Harris's innovative hands, the sitcom accused of being blasphemous and inflammatory was one of the most pro-family-values series of the 1970s: sisters Mary Tate and Jessica Campbell, each other's best friend, loved one another as much as they loved their own individual messed-up broods; and they each fought to keep their family units intact as life's troubles mounted.

Amid the din of physical farce and sight-gags – not least of which came to involve a brilliantly realized adult-son character of a ventriloquist whose dummy surfaces as the sanest member of either family -- the show also presented a deeply felt platonic love story between white matriarch Jessica Tate and her black housekeeper Benson Dubois that often resulted in the show's most emotionally realistic scenes. Father Tim Flotsky adored girlfriend Corrine Tate, and his related fall from priesthood pained him, given his faith in and love for God. Mary and Burt Campbell's marriage was proof that love and passion can be found at mid-life. And Jodie Dallas' feelings for lost boyfriend Dennis were genuine and palpable, as was football-star Dennis's own struggle to fit in to his life and to his own skin.

The Tate-and-Campbell households represented satire; the Tate-and-Campbell relationships, however, represented love.

TV Guide

Soap ended the 1977-78 TV season as a new hit for ABC, nominated for six Emmy awards, including one as Outstanding Comedy series and two for Outstanding Lead Actress. (Over the course of its four seasons it would be nominated for a total of 17 Emmys, with cast regulars Robert Guilliame, Cathryn Damon and Richard Mulligan winning one each along the way.)

Harris, an unsung TV pioneer among writers and an uncredited soldier on the frontlines of the 1970s TV revolution, wrote every one of *Soap*'s 25 episodes during its first, and in most views best, year. (Her first-season task was Herculean: Establish a premise, trigger the satire, introduce thirteen characters, and weave storylines that not only connected each but also serviced a season-long murder arc that would come to implicate five regulars, ending in a season-ending trial and conviction. All while being funny against a backdrop of social protest and corporate nervousness.)

If the series went downhill soon after, perhaps it's because lightning can flash for only so long. Still, the remaining three seasons of *Soap* continued to pull out more stops as all the while it continued to present (mostly) relatable stories that helped to usher in a modern age of emotional, character-driven, comedic storytelling.

Whatever *All in the Family* did for TV in 1971, whatever revolution it kicked off – for the industry, for the country, for the culture – *Soap* trumped it. Just as the post-*All in the Family* dust-up of *Maude*, *That Certain Summer*, *Steambath*, *Born Innocent*, and *Hot L Baltimore* from 1971 to 1975 had started to settle, resulting in a mix of viewer responses from "There's nothing left to shock us with" to "This <u>has</u> to stop," *Soap* arrived to redefine them.

It arrived on the scene in 1977 at a high-water mark, the single most revolutionary year of a revolutionary decade. Twelve months that began in January with *Roots*, ended in December with Edith Bunker questioning the existence of God, and in between featured Bill Murray joining *Saturday Night Live*, the Rev. Donald Wildmon's "Turn the Television Off" Week decency campaign, the premieres of both *Three's Company* and *Eight is Enough*, the mini-series *Jesus of Nazareth*, and *Soap*, Richard Pryor, and *James at 15*.

Aaron Spelling
(69)

One of the biggest behind-the-scene names in the history of contemporary TV actually started out in front of the camera, in its earliest days, as a journeyman actor, guest-starring on shows from *I Love Lucy* to *Gunsmoke*. The roles, like the actor, were undistinguished. So beginning in the early 1960s Aaron Spelling turned his attention to the production end of television, with a slate of series that were either short-lived but iconic (*Honey West*) or longer-lasting but routine (*Burke's Law*), with a few (*The Guns of Will Sonnett, The New People*) ranked somewhere in between.

The 1970s saw his efforts expand considerably: As the made-for-TV-movie genre began to take off, Spelling established himself as its go-to producer, responsible for 50 movies-of-the-week between 1969 and 1975. It was during this time that he also had his first two big series hits -- *The Mod Squad* (1968-73) and *The Rookies* (1972-76) -- each of which tapped into a changing TV world and the changing nature of TV, establishing Spelling as the man who seemed to have his fingers on the beating pulse of a new generation.

If the 1970s had comedy factories associated with Norman Lear, MTM Enterprises, and Garry Marshall, its drama factory was run by Aaron Spelling, working with partner Leonard Goldberg under the Spelling-Goldberg Productions banner.

As *The Rookies* launched and as *The Mod Squad* wound down -- both on ABC -- Spelling began a Sherman-esque march through prime-time, with one project after another for the network. (In the 1972-73 season alone, he made 12 TV movies.)

The first was a *Rookies* spin-off called *S.W.A.T.*, about the group of elite Los Angeles policemen who made up its Special Weapons and Tactics division. The hard-charging violent series became his most-talked-about show, if for the wrong reasons, having had the misfortune of coming along at the same time the TV industry was being assailed for its excessive violence. Slammed by both critics and advocacy groups, it was a hit for ABC, but it was also a hot potato. *S.W.A.T.* ending up cancelled in just its second season.

In the fall of 1975, Spelling-Goldberg introduced another new show that while just as trigger-happy was also grounded in a warm buddy-relationship between of a pair of bantering odd-couple-type West Coast detectives. *Starsky & Hutch*, starring David Soul and Paul-Michael Glaser, was an instant hit and would end up running four years. And then in the spring of 1976 came a rare non-crime show from the Spelling called *Family*, which brought the one-hour family drama into the 1970s and served as a marked departure from the breezy and escapist Spelling formula.

Family became an Emmy magnet and critical favorite, leading to begrudging respect for Spelling, who by this time was beginning to be disparaged by critics and competitors for what was seen as a canon of fluff. The trio made for three hits in 13 months for Spelling. And then came the show that eclipsed them all – *Charlie's Angels*.

Borne of a movie-of-the-week that aired in March 1976, and then heavily promoted that summer during ABC's Montreal Olympics, *Charlie's Angels* became Spelling's biggest hit to date. It also became one of the most popular first-year shows in TV history -- a rarity called a runaway hit, making its debut in the Top Ten and then never leaving. *Charlie's Angels* ended the season the 5th highest-rated series on TV and the number-one drama.

Equal parts loved and loathed, heralded as a series that either embodied and spoke to the feminist movement (by having three women as series leads in roles usually reserved for men) or destroyed (by having them referred to as "girls" and "angels" and judged more on how they look than what they do), *Charlie's Angels* was a prime-time phenomenon and a social statement in one. Stars Kate Jackson, Jaclyn Smith, and Farrah Fawcett-Majors became worldwide celebrities. And Aaron Spelling and his Spelling-Goldberg Productions became a global franchise. The series ran for five lucrative seasons.

Spelling followed up *Charlie's Angels* with the lighthearted escapist anthology series *The Love Boat* and *Fantasy Island*, launched months apart in the 1977-78 season, and then over the course of the following two seasons introduced the lighthearted wish-fulfillment private-eye shows *Vegas* and *Hart to Hart*.

These rolled out as more TV movies, a mini-series, short-lived other series, and several pilots did as well. (Some of the output was in conjunction with Goldberg; some was not.) Along the way there was the occasional *Family*-style attempt at projects outside the bubble-gum formula, including a short-lived but earnest 1979 drama called *Friends*, about the relationships formed among three eleven-year-olds (a white girl, a white boy, and a black boy), and the 1976 TV-movie *The Boy in the Plastic Bubble*, an Emmy-winner that became a rite-of-passage classic for teens.

For equal measure, Spelling achieved a bit of infamy as producer of the 1977 teen-prostitute movie *Little Ladies of the Night*, one of the most highly-viewed TV movies of the decade (and considered one of its most salacious, too).

Virtually everything that came from producer Aaron Spelling in the 1970s – 11 series, 70-plus movies – aired on ABC. In the 1977-78 TV season alone, his shows accounted for six of the network's 22 hours of programming. (The following season, the number grew to seven). So much of ABC's line-up was made up of Spelling productions that the network was jokingly referred to as Aaron's Broadcasting Company.

But there's little doubt that the name was integral to ABC's ratings dominance in the last half of the 1970s.

Aaron Spelling went on to launch scores of new series in the 1980s, though only one, *Dynasty*, broke through as the kind of landmark show he produced in the 1970s. Two attempts at sitcoms -- *At Ease* (1983) and *Life with Lucy* (1986) – failed badly. The latter, Lucille Ball's trumpeted return to sitcoms after 12 years, was so spectacularly bad and so quickly cancelled that it temporarily tarnished the legacies of both its star and producer. (Ball died fewer than three years later.)

But in 1989, a Spelling TV movie called *Day One*, about the creation of the atomic bomb, won him his first Emmy after 30 years as a TV producer. And he went on to win another, five years later, as producer of HBO's *And the Band Played On* (1993), based on Randy Shilts' book about the early years of the AIDS epidemic.

Spelling had a late-career renaissance in the 1990s, which saw him leaning in to still more change to the TV landscape borne of still another generational shift. As he did with *The Mod Squad* and *The Rookies* 20 years earlier, Spelling aimed for a crowd of young TV viewers looking for something new. *Beverly Hills 90210* (1990) and spin-off *Melrose Place* (1992), for the recently launched and young-viewer friendly FOX network, were the results. And they put him back on top. He followed the pair with handfuls of still-more new series for both the traditional as well as the upstart FOX and WB networks. His tally for the 1990s and 2000s – another 24 series on the air.

In 1996 Aaron Spelling was inducted into the TV Academy Hall of Fame. He died ten years later, in June 2006, at age 83, having achieved another distinction -- listed in *The Guinness Book of World Records* as the most prolific producer in TV history.

His contribution to the 1970s – series with women in lead roles, series about coming-of-age, series that redefined family drama, movies that took on social issues, in addition to those hundreds of hours of escapist hour-long shows that just entertained -- is often undervalued but can never be erased.

"It was an ordinary convention, just like any other."

-- American Legion member
July 1976

Three's Company
ABC 1977-84
(70)

Fair or not, it doesn't take much to see what got *Three's Company* on the air in 1977 and then made it a hit with viewers, as well as a scourge for self-appointed television-decency advocates: It comes 22 seconds into the sitcom's first-season opening credits, when Suzanne Somers, one of its two female stars, seen reclining face-down on a beach chaise, turns back-to-front in her black one-piece.

It wasn't the sight of the chair.

ABC / *FremantleMedia*

The silliest of shows based on the flimsiest of premises, developed over the course of two years and three pilots, somehow considered daring in the mid-1970s, *Three's Company* was about sex. Having it. Not having it. Wanting it. Wanting more of it. Looking for it. Losing it.

Talking about it. Defining it. Questioning it. Getting into endless situations that lead to misunderstandings about it. And then talking about it some more. Or, rather, not talking about it but in such a way it was obvious it was being talked about.

The comedy marked yet another American adaptation of a successful British show, here the early-70s hit called *Man About the House*. *Three's Company* re-fashioned its story to be about two beautiful 20-something women (Somers and Joyce DeWitt) who agree to share a Santa Monica apartment with a handsome single man (John Ritter) -- so long as he in turn agrees to pretend he's gay in order to appease an uptight landlord who's opposed to "hanky-panky" among his tenants.

Despite the juvenile premise if not the silly ruse, *Three's Company* did still appeal to changing times -- both with the consistent thread of its sexualized storylines and with the inclusion of even a fake gay character in a starring role. It gave homosexuality a face (of sorts) and in the process made the subject a weekly TV staple, making it less of a shocking thing than a funny thing. And then making the funny part about it the landlord who finds the concept so shocking.

But that's where the innovation ended. Week after week, episode after episode, season after season for seven seasons, *Three's Company* made sex -- of any kind -- something to giggle about. Social statements and learning lessons were for the scores of other sitcoms on the air elsewhere. The aim here was farce, predicated on the reliable TV trope of misunderstanding that it elevated to a stale art. (A telling joke from NBC's *Friends* a generation later, during a scene that finds the six friends watching a *Three's Company* rerun, leading to Chandler deadpanning: "Oh, I think this is the episode where's there's some kind of misunderstanding.")

The show was critically roasted for its juvenile humor, its T&A casting, and its over-the-top performances that bordered on camp.

"It seems telling," wrote *Washington Post* TV critic Tom Shales in a 2003 remembrance, "that on the same night that *Eight Is Enough* premiered in 1977 on ABC to give the network a bit of -- for its day – prestige, *Three's Company* premiered to earn it a slight badge a shame."

The thing to remember about *Three's Company*, though: It was also very funny. Especially in its early episodes, a credit to what turned out to be the comedic physical gifts of John Ritter, who until 1977 was best known for his occasional role as a minister on *The Waltons*. And it was a massive ratings hit, ending its brief first season in eleventh place and then zooming to third the following year.

That it aired directly after the two most popular comedies on TV -- *Happy Days* and *Laverne and Shirley* -- helped. But *Three's Company* distinguished itself as an audience favorite in its own right with Ritter's masterful pratfalls and rubbery doubletakes and its check-the-brain-at-the-door sexual farce.

The latter did put it dead center of controversy for a while, too. With its weekly barrage of innuendo -- both straight- and gay-focused -- and with its forever who's-sleeping-with-whom storylines and its barely there wardrobe for its two female leads (it covered less as the ratings grew), the sitcom drew the ire of those losing sleep at night in their ongoing campaigns for what they called TV decency, especially in the wake of the failure known as the Family Viewing Hour.

By February 1978, the *Three's Company* cast was featured on the cover of *Newsweek*, Somers' breasts front and center and barely contained by her teddy, with the cover-line screaming "Sex and TV."

Much fire and fury, though, ultimately signifying nothing. The fun went on.

Three's Company did roll on, ranked as TV's Number Two show for the next two years. It rolled past backstage dramas and past performer egos and past cast and storyline changes that by 1984 had made its premise obsolete, when it was cancelled and then immediately re-imagined that fall as *Three's a Crowd*, with Ritter's character now living, romantically

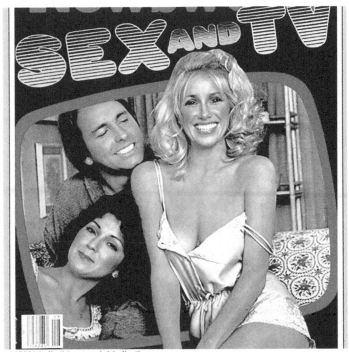

IBT Media/Newsweek Media Group

and somewhat scandalously, with a woman not his wife. Ritter was the only cast member kept on for the new series. It lasted a single season.

Three's Company was never the prestige sitcom that ABC found in the latter half of the 1970s with *Barney Miller* or *Soap* or *Taxi*. It scored just five Emmy nominations for its 174 episodes, three of which were for Ritter. But it bowed only to the Garry Marshall *Happy Days* / *Laverne & Shirley* / *Mork & Mindy* trifecta as one of the biggest comedy hits of the entire decade.

And even if pretense, it also gave TV its first gay lead, making the gay community a part of a weekly, if often cringe-worthy, conversation.

Baby steps.

"The world has never known a day quite like today."

-- Walter Cronkite, reporting on Three Mile Island
The CBS Evening News March 28 1979

CONCLUSION

At some point between Watergate and The Love Canal, between Nixon and Carter, between Vietnam and Afghanistan, between the Hurricane Creek Mine Disaster and the Riverfront Coliseum Stampede, between Martha Mitchell and Margaret Thatcher, between POWs and Americans Held Hostage, between Robert Altman and Steve Martin, between The Supremes and The Ramones, between Helen Reddy and Blondie, between Joe Namath and Pete Rose, between Burger Chef and The Happy Meal ... the 1970s happened. And TV tried to keep up.

It began on January 1 1970 when *Family Affair*'s teenaged Cissy stayed out all night after high-school graduation, and it ended on December 31 1979 with burnt-out drug-using Johnny Fever talking to God on *WKRP in Cincinnati*.

It began with three broadcast networks routinely corralling 90% of all TV watchers, and it ended with TBS, HBO, Showtime, ESPN, PBS and something new called the VCR corralling the networks in turn, cutting in to their action, upping the antes and changing the game.

It began with it roots still in the radio business that spawned it, and it ended with the branches and limbs of premium cable, pay-per-view, and first-run syndication overtaking it.

It began with the economic power connected to it still comfortably held in the executive boardroom; it ended with part of that power now ceded to the viewer's living-room.

An art form and communications medium had become big business, doing what General David Sarnoff had predicted it would do when he officially unveiled it in 1939 at the New York World's Fair -- change the world. But what was coming clear was that the change was beyond what he or anyone could have imagined.

The 1970s saw the start of more and more of those involved *in* television heeding calls to do more *with* it. Part of the first generation to be raised on it, they were also witnesses to real-life tumults that were their 1950s childhoods and their 1960s awakenings. They began to wonder, to hope, to see, how one could connect to the other. They envisioned that TV could make a difference outside of the screen.

"Most television producers are more concerned with creating profitable television programs than with creating groundbreaking television; however, some producers, either by accident or design, create television shows that become part of our cultural legacy," writes David S. Silverman in *You Can't Air That: Four Cases of Controversy and Censorship in American Television Programming.* Those *some* came from that mix.

So much change. TV had to change with it.
Maybe TV could change *for* it.
TV now for everyone; TV now about everything.

"I've never heard that anybody conducted his or her life differently after seeing an episode of *All in the Family,*" writes Norman Lear in his memoir *Even This I Get to Experience.*

> If two thousand years of Judao-Christian ethic hadn't eradicated bigotry and intolerance, I didn't think a half-hour sitcom was going to do it. Still, as my grandfather was fond of saying – and as physicists confirm – when you throw a pebble in a lake the water rises. It's far too infinitesimal a rise for our eyes to register, so all we can see is the ripple. People still say to me, "We watched Archie as a family and I'll never forget the discussions we had after the show." And so that was the ripple of *All in the Family.* Families talked.

That was also the ripple of the decade. People watched. And talked. And times changed.

On television, the form as well as the content changed. "One of the first precursors to this eventual evolution," observed Michelle Donnelly in her 2015 *scriptlab.com* essay "The Evolution of American Television Storytelling, "was *The Mary Tyler Moore Show.*"

> While following an episodic format, the show was unique in that it allowed for story arcs that saw its characters change over time and which highlighted these characters in more realistic and complex relationships. Likewise, the show *M*A*S*H* created deep character enrichment through the building of interpersonal relationships while it also provided searing social commentary. No longer just content with portraying situations and relationships predicated on laughs, these writers expanded beyond sketch comedy to develop intricate stories between complex characters.

Between the two, both the *what* and *how* of storytelling started to change; a template was starting to form that revealed a sort of a palimpsest beneath all content, both comedic and drama.

Did the 1970s affect television? Or did the televised content of prime-time in the decade change the country? The people and projects and precedents described in this book suggest that the answer is yes.

The social revolution of the 1970s, all that was in the decade, was televised. TV, it seems, served as both its conduit and facilitator.

In a 1995 speech at an industry gathering in Las Vegas, Lear said, "Television gets the rap for so many problems if only because it is so obvious, so ubiquitous. The big question is how did we get here and what are we going to do about it?"

Decades on, the question holds.

THE LISTS

PROGRAMMING OF THE DECADE

DRAMA
Family

It re-shaped what the family-drama genre was, speaking to the pain and confusion and even disappointment that sometime accompany the joy and community that is family.

COMEDY
All in the Family

A default and obvious choice but, still ... *All in the Family* changed what we watch and how we laugh, demonstrating more than any series of its time how TV's reach could extend beyond its grasp.

UNSCRIPTED
An American Family

An unprecedented documentary-series that examined the contemporary American family. Innovative, heartbreaking, funny, prescient, it became the time-capsule for a generation.

MOVIE
"Roots"

A television landmark that defined a decade and created a national conversation.

TV *Guide* / Warner Bros. / ABC / McCaffrey & McCall / Filmation / NBCUniversal / CBS / Garry Marshall

HONORABLE MENTION

Alice (1976-85 CBS)

Not a particularly great show, *Alice* nonetheless championed working women at a time when it was both necessary and important. Both it and star Linda Lavin ended up on the frontlines of the feminism movement.

Bicentennial Minutes (1974-76)

An unprecedented achievement running every night for two years, as the country counted down to its 200th birthday. It made history interesting, a minute at a time.

"Brian's Song" (November 30 1971 ABC)

The TV movie about a football player's life and death crushed a nation and made it acceptable for men to cry.

The Corner Bar (1972-73 ABC)

A summer replacement sitcom about life among the denizens of salon regulars -- *Cheers*-ish without the central romance -- did little more than feature TV's first gay barfly. But it was more than enough three years after Stonewall. The world didn't end.

Fat Albert and the Cosby Kids (1972-84 CBS)

Comedy, community, and kid-friendly Bill Cosby -- animated life-lessons from a North Philadelphia junkyard when racial tensions were high and cultural identity was important.

"Hustling" (February 22 1975 ABC)

Assistant-turned-producer Lillian Gallo was a trailblazer for women in the 1970s and proved it with an unflinching depiction of prostitution, based on Gail Sheehy's raw best-seller and written by Fay Kanin. Nominated for two Emmys.

Lifeline (1978-79 NBC)

Fred Silverman's reign as head of NBC is remembered as "ill-fated," but it did feature a groundbreaking reality series ahead of the TV curve, about the daily lives of doctors.

Garry Marshall

Norman Lear got the headlines and MTM Enterprises got the acclaim. But Garry Marshall produced the crowd-pleasers in the 1970s. With *Happy Days*, *Laverne & Shirley*, *Mork & Mindy*, and *Angie*, he had four of the five highest-rated shows of the entire 1978-79 TV season.

Schoolhouse Rock (1973-85 ABC)

Because all these years later it's still fun to say, "Conjunction Junction, what's your function?"

The Waltons (1972-81 CBS) / ***Eight Is Enough*** (1977-81 ABC)

EIE was cheesy, but it broke one-hour comedy ground. And fellow big-family hit *The Waltons* was smarter than it gets credit for, tackling issues from religious and racial intolerance to Nazism as it celebrated the written word and the human condition.

ABC / CBS / Dick Cavett / 20th Century Fox Television / Sony / NBC Broadway Video

TEN OF THE MOST MEMORABLE MOMENTS OF THE 1970S

All in the Family "Sammy's Visit" (February 12 1972 CBS)
> Guest-star Sammy Davis, Jr., visits the home of world-class bigot Archie Bunker. The episode-ending surprise kiss Davis plants on Archie's cheek becomes the longest live-audience laugh in the series 8-year run.

The Carol Burnett Show (March 29 1978 CBS)
> In the final episode of her long-running show (11 seasons), a genuinely moved Carol Burnett is surprised by guest-star and longtime idol Jimmy Stewart, who serenades her with "Ragtime Cowboy Joe."

The Dick Cavett Show The Loud Family visit (February 20 1973, ABC stations)
> Members of the Loud family go on the defensive in the wake of a public excoriation brought on by their PBS docu-series *An American Family*.

M*A*S*H* "Abyssinia Henry" (March 18 1975 CBS)
> The first three years -- some say the best three years -- of a post-modern TV classic comes to a close with the death of a beloved regular character/father figure Henry Blake (McLean Stevenson). His tearful goodbye to his camp-mates told us that life could be sweet; his death soon after told us that it can also be unfair.

Mary Tyler Moore "Chuckles Bites the Dust" (October 25 1975)
> After enduring (and criticizing) a litany of bad-taste jokes made by her colleagues about the death of station celebrity Chuckles the Clown, Mary Richards laughs herself silly -- and to tears -- at the clown's funeral.

The Odd Couple "Password" (December 1 1972 ABC)
> Felix and Oscar meet game-show host Allen Ludden when they compete as contestants on *Password,* and in the process make a ridiculous TV star out of Aristophanes.

Roots "Part I" (January 23 1977 ABC)
> The tiny newborn Kunta Kinte is held aloft by his proud father. "Behold," intones the patriarch, "the only thing greater than yourself." A world is changed.

The Sonny & Cher Show "Premiere" (February 1 1976 CBS)
> They'd come to CBS in 1971 as a flower-power couple for a young generation. Then came an ugly divorce. The bizarre post-divorce re-teaming for a variety show in which they continue to sing love songs becomes one of TV's most cringeworthy moments.

Saturday Night Live (December 13 1975 NBC)
> Chevy Chase *v.* host Richard Pryor. Dark comedy wins. No pun intended.

Taxi "Reverend Jim: A Space Odyssey" (September 25 1979 ABC)
> Six words: "What does a yellow light mean?"

THE WORST OF THE 1970S

(The What-Were-They-Thinking? Hall of Fame)

WORST HORRIBLY TITLED NONETHELESS-STILL-BAD SERIES
Me & The Chimp (1972 CBS)
Dirty Sally (1975 CBS)
Lannigan's Rabbi (1976-77 NBC)
The Snoop Sisters (1973-74 NBC)
David Cassidy: Man Undercover (1978 NBC)

WORST RIP OFF
Supertrain (1979 NBC)

WORST SPIN-OFFS
The Ropers (1979-80 ABC)
Mrs. Columbo / Kate Loves a Mystery (1979-80 NBC)

WORST ATTEMPTS AT RESCUCITATING THE VARIETY-SHOW GENRE
The Sonny Comedy Revue (1974 ABC)
Saturday Night Live with Howard Cosell (1975-76 ABC)
The Shields & Yarnell Show (1977-78 CBS)
The Captain & Tennille Show (1976-77 ABC)
The Starland Vocal Band Show (1977 CBS)

WORST TV-MOVIE(S)
The NBC *"Portrait of ..."* Collection:
Sara T.: Portrait of a Teenage Alcoholic (1975)
Dawn: Portrait of a Runaway (1976)
Billy: Portrait of a Street Kid (1977)
Sharon: Portrait of a Mistress (1977)
Katie: Portrait of a Centerfold (1978)
Portrait of a Stripper (1979)

WORST PROGRAM OF THE DECADE
(tie)

The Brady Bunch Variety Hour (1977 ABC)

Chico and the Man, season 4 (1977-78 NBC)

BECAUSE OF THIS (MOVIE) ...
THERE WAS THAT *(SERIES)*

ALL THE PRESIDENT'S MEN (1976) ...
    Kingston: Confidential (1977 NBC)
    The Andros Targets (1977 CBS)
    Lou Grant (1977-82 CBS)

AMERICAN GRAFFITI (1973) ...
    Happy Days (1974-84 ABC)
    Sons and Daughters (1974 CBS)

ANIMAL HOUSE (1978) ...
    Delta House (1979 ABC)
    Brothers and Sisters (1978 NBC)
    Co-Ed Fever (1979 CBS)

BUTCH CASSIDY AND THE SUNDANCE KID (1969) ...
    Alias Smith and Jones (1971-73 ABC)

CHINATOWN (1974) ...
    City of Angels (1975 NBC)

NETWORK (1976) ...
    W.E.B. (1978 NBC)

SATURDAY NIGHT FEVER (1977) ...
    Makin' It (1979 ABC)
    Joe & Valerie (1979 NBC)

SHAMPOO (1975) ...
    Snip (1976 NBC, cancelled before it ever aired)

STAR WARS (1977) ...
    Battlestar Gallactica (1978-80 ABC)
    Quark (1978 NBC)

BASED ON THE MOVIE

Alice (1976-85 CBS)
...based on ALICE DOESN'T LIVE
    HERE ANYMORE (1974)

Born Free (1975 NBC)
... based on same-name film (1966)

Adam's Rib (1973 ABC)
... based on same-name film (1949)

Anna and the King (1972 ABC)
...based on ANNA AND THE KING
    OF SIAM (1946)

The Bad News Bears (1979 CBS)
...based on same-name film (1976)

Bob & Carol & Ted & Alice (1973 ABC)
...based on same-name film (1969)

Barefoot in the Park (1970 ABC)
...based on same-name film (1967)

Billy Liar (1979 CBS)
...based on same-name film (1963)

The Cowboys (1974 ABC)
...based on same-name film (1972)

Delta House (ABC 1979)
... based on ANIMAL HOUSE (1978)

Flatbush (1979 CBS)
...based on THE LORDS OF
    FLATBUSH (1974)

House Calls (1979-82 CBS)
...based on same-name film (1978)

How the West Was Won (1976-78 ABC)
...based on same-name film (1962)

Little Women (1979 NBC)
...based on multiple films and 1978 mini-
    series

Logan's Run (1977-78 CBS)
...based on same-name film (1976)

Love Story (1973-74 NBC)
...based on same-name film (1970)

M*A*S*H* (1972-83 CBS)
...based on same-name film (1970)

Matt Helm (1975-76 ABC)
...based on 1960s film series

The New Land (1974 ABC)
...based on THE EMIGRANTS (1971)

The Odd Couple (1970-75 ABC)
...based on same-name film (1968)

Paper Moon (1974 ABC)
...based on same-name film (1973)

Planet of the Apes (1974 CBS)
...based on the 1960s/1970s films

Popi (1976 CBS)
...based on same-name film (1969)

Serpico (1976-77 NBC)
...based on same-name film (1973)

Shaft (1973-74 CBS)
...based on same-name film (1971)

Swiss Family Robinson (1975-76 ABC)
...based on same-name film (1960)

What's Happening!! (1976-79 ABC)
...based on COOLEY HIGH (1975)

(plus, unsold movie-adaptation pilots of the 1970s)

The African Queen (1977) ... from same-name film (1951), with Warren Oates and Mariette Hartley in for Humphrey Bogart and Katharine Hepburn

Black Bart (1975) ... from BLAZING SADDLES (1974), with Louis Gossett, Jr. in for Cleavon Little

Car Wash (1979) ... from same-name film (1976), with T.K. Carter and John Anthony Bailey in for Darrow Igus and Otis Day

Cat Ballou (1971 and 1971) ... two pilots developed from same-name film (1967), one with Lesley Ann Warren and Jack Elam and the other with Jo Ann Harris and Forrest Tucker -- in for Jane Fonda and Lee Marvin

Catch-22 (1973) ... from same-name film (1970), with Richard Dreyfuss in for Alan Arkin

Guess Who's Coming to Dinner? (1975) ... from same-name film (1967), with Eleanor Parker, Richard Dysart, Bill Overton, and Leslie Charleson in for Katharine Hepburn, Spencer Tracy, Sidney Poitier, and Katharine Houghton

The Last Detail (1975) ... from same-name film (1973), with Robert F. Lyons and Charles Robinson in for Jack Nicholson and Otis Young

Mother, Juggs, & Speed (1978) ... from sorta-same-name film* (1976), with Ray Vitte, Joanne Nail, and Joe Penney in for Bill Cosby, Raquel Welch, Harvey Keitel (*film spelling was "Jugs")

The Owl and the Pussycat (1975) ... from same-name film (1971), with Buck Henry and Bernadette Peters in for George Segal and Barbra Streisand

Pete 'N' Tillie (1974) ... from same-name film (1972), with Cloris Leachman and Carmine Caridi in for Carol Burnett and Walter Matthau

To Sir, With Love (1974) ... from same-name film (1967), with Hari Rhodes in for Sidney Poitier

The Sunshine Boys (1977) ... from same-name film (1975), with Red Buttons and Lionel Stander in for George Burns and Walter Matthau

True Grit (1978) ... from same-name film (1969), with Warren Oates in for John Wayne

What's Up, Doc? (1978) ... from same-name film (1972), with Harriet Hall and Barry Van Dyke in for Barbra Streisand and Ryan O'Neal

ZEITGEIST: SERIES INSPIRED BY 1970s INTEREST IN ...

... martial arts and eastern mysticism:
Kung Fu (1972-75 ABC)
plus, unsold pilots *Men of the Dragon* (1974), *Judge Dee* (1974), *Samurai* (1974), *The Disciple* (1974)

... ESP and paranormal:
The Sixth Sense (1972 ABC)
The Girl With Something Extra (1973-74 NBC)
plus, unsold pilot *Baffled* (1973)

... the back-to-nature/pioneer movement:
The New Land (1974 ABC)
The Life and Times of Grizzly Adams (1977-78 NBC)
Young Dan'l Boone (1977 CBS)
plus, mini-series *The Awakening Land* (1978 NBC), *The Young Pioneers* (1978 NBC)

... the occult/supernatural/sci-fi/something-is-out-there movements:
Kolchak: The Night Stalker (1974-75 ABC)
Logan's Run (1977-78 CBS)
The Fantastic Journey (1977 NBC)
Project: UFO (1978-79 NBC)
Quark (1978 NBC)
Battlestar Gallactica (1978-80 ABC)
plus, unsold pilots *Genesis II* (1973), *The Stranger* (1973), *Planet Earth* (1974) *Questor* (1974), *Strange New World* (1975) *Earthbound* (1976), *Time Travelers* (1976)
Good Against Evil (1977) and *World of Darkness* (1977 and 1978), *American 2100* (1979)
Starstruck (1979)

...the rise of Southern nationalism movement:
Carter Country (1977-78 ABC)
Dallas (1978-91 CBS)
Nashville 99 (1977 CBS)
The Dukes of Hazzard (1979-85 CBS)
plus, unsold pilot *Murder in Music City* (1979)

... the c.b./trucker/"Smokey & The Bandit" movement:
Movin' On (1974-76 NBC)
B.J. & the Bear (1979-81 NBC)
The Dukes of Hazzard (1979-85 CBS)

"GET ME THE NEXT...!"

...*Charlie's Angels* (1976-81 ABC)
Flying High (1978-79 CBS)
The American Girls (1978 CBS)
plus, unsold pilots *Cover Girls* (1977), *Ebony, Ivory and Jade* (1979)

...*Eight Is Enough* (1977-81 ABC)
Mulligan's Stew (1977 NBC)
The Fitzpatricks (1977-78 CBS)

...*Laverne & Shirley* (1976-83 ABC)
On Our Own (1977-78 CBS)

...*The Love Boat* (1977-86 ABC)
Supertrain (1979 NBC)

...*Police Story* (1973-78 NBC)
Medical Story (1975-76 NBC)

...*The Six Million Dollar Man* (1973-78 ABC)
Lucan (1976 ABC)
The Man from Atlantis (1977 NBC)
plus, unsold pilots *The Ultimate Imposter* (1977) *Exo-Man* (1977), *The Power Within* (1979)

...*Upstairs, Downstairs* (1971-76 PBS)
Beacon Hill (1975 CBS)

...*The Waltons* (1972-81 CBS)
Apple's Way (1974-75 CBS)
The Family Hovak (1974 NBC)

A DECADE OF SPIN-OFFS

from *All in the Family* (1971-79 CBS)
    Maude (1972-78 CBS)
    Good Times (1974-79 CBS)
    The Jeffersons (1975-84 CBS)
    Hanging In (1978 CBS)

from *Barney Miller* (1974-82 ABC)
    Fish (1977-78 ABC)

from *Bewitched* (1964-72 ABC)
    Tabitha (1976, 1977-78 ABC)

from *BJ & the Bear* (1979-81 NBC):
    The Misadventures of Sherriff Lobo
    (1979-80 NBC)

from *Cannon* (1971-76 CBS)
    Barnaby Jones (1973-80 CBS)

from *Columbo* (1971-78 NBC)
    Mrs. Columbo (1979-80 NBC)

from *Dallas* (1978-91 CBS)
    Knots Landing (1979-93 CBS)

from *Diff'rent Strokes* (1978-86
    NBC/ABC)
    The Facts of Life (1979-88 NBC)
    Hello, Larry (1979-80)

from *Gunsmoke* (1955-75 CBS)
    Dirty Sally (1974 CBS)

from *Happy Days* (1974-84 ABC)
    Laverne & Shirley (1976-83 ABC)
    Blansky's Beauties (1977 ABC)
    Mork & Mindy (1978-82 ABC)
    Out of the Blue (1979 ABC)

from *Mary Tyler Moore* (1970-77 CBS)
    Rhoda (1974-78 CBS)
    Phyllis (1975-77 CBS)
    Lou Grant (1977-82 CBS)

from *The Partridge Family* (1970-74
    ABC)
    Getting Together (1971-72 ABC)

from *Police Story* (1973-78 NBC)
    Police Woman (1974-78 NBC)
    Joe Forrester (1976-77 NBC)
    David Cassidy: Man Undercover
    (1978-79 NBC)

from *The Rockford Files* (1974-80 NBC)
    Richie Brockelman, Private Eye (1978
    NBC)

from *The Rookies* (1972-76 ABC)
    S.W.A.T. (1975-76 ABC)

from *Sanford and Son* (1972-76 NBC)
    Grady (1976 NBC)
    Sanford Arms (1977-78 NBC)

from *Soap* (1977-81 ABC)
    Benson (1979-86 ABC)

from *The Six Million Dollar Man* (1973-
    78 ABC)
    The Bionic Woman (1976-78
    ABC/NBC)

from *Three's Company* (1977-84 ABC)
    The Ropers (1979-80 ABC)

from *Welcome Back, Kotter* (1975-79
    ABC)
    Mr. T and Tina (1976 ABC)

(plus, a decade of revivals and reunions)

from ***The Adventures of Ozzie and Harriet*** (1952-66 ABC)
Ozzie's Girls (1972, 1973-74 syn)

from ***Father Knows Best*** (1954-60 CBS/NBC)
Father Knows Best Reunion (1977 NBC)
Father Knows Best: Home for Christmas (1977 NBC)

from ***Gilligan's Island*** (1964-67 CBS)
Rescue from Gilligan's Island (1978 NBC)
The Castaways on Gilligan's Island (1979 NBC)

from ***Make Room for Daddy/The Danny Thomas Show*** (1953-64, ABC/CBS)
Make Room for Granddaddy (1970-71 ABC)

from ***The Many Loves of Dobie Gillis*** (1959-63 CBS)
Whatever Happened to Dobie Gillis? (1977 CBS)

from ***Maverick*** (1957-62 ABC)
The New Maverick (1978 ABC)

from ***The Mod Squad*** (1968-73 ABC)
The Return of the Mod Squad (1979 ABC)

from ***Perry Mason*** (1957-66 CBS)
The New Perry Mason (1973-74 CBS)

from ***Peyton Place*** (1964-69 ABC)
Murder in Peyton Place (1977 NBC)

from ***Rowan and Martin's Laugh-In*** (1968-73 NBC)
Laugh In (1977-78 NBC)

from ***The Wild Wild West*** (1965-69 CBS)
The Wild Wild West Revisited (1979 CBS)

Tuesday
EVENING

MARCH 18, 1975

who is threatening to commit suicide in Los Angeles. Mallory: Martin Milner. Rand: Kent McCord. MacDonald: William Boyett. Woods: Fred Strothers. Guest Cast . . . . Harvey: Tom Drake. Dee Hawkins: Ronnie Troup. Grace Robertson: Sheila Bromley. Clinic Administrator: Armand Alzamora.

24 HAPPY DAYS—Comedy
Richie gives it a spin when he's offered a job as the new disc jockey on radio station WOW. Richie: Ron Howard. Howard: Tom Bosley. Marion: Marion Ross. Potsie: Anson Williams. Ralph: Donny Most. Fonzie: Henry Winkler. Joanie: Erin Moran. Marsha Beatrice: Colan. Wendy: Misty Rowe. Guest Cast . . . . . . Charlie the Prince: Warren Berlinger.

SWISS FAMILY ROBINSON —Adventure
It's Elizabeth's birthday and the children choose to sleep in a cave to allow their parents to have a "Second Honeymoon." Elizabeth: Diana Leblanc. Johann: Chris Wiggins. Ernest: Michael Duhig. Franz: Ricky O'Neil.

DEALER'S CHOICE—Game

57 AMERICA—Documentary
Alistair Cooke concludes his Emmy-winning series with a look at the pluses and minuses in American life. He visits a New Hampshire commune, discusses racial discrimination and takes viewers to Hawaii, an Island state that epitomizes the Nation's problems and promise. (Repeat) (Last show of the series; next week, a six-part documentary series about solar energy premieres at this time.)

8:30 11 M*A*S*H
Lt. Col. Henry Blake's farewell. See the Close-up below.

13 MOVIE—Crime Drama
"The Imposter," a 1975 TV-movie, follows a former Army intelligence officer, who has a talent for impersonation. His skills are put to the test after he agrees to pose as a bounty-hunter and almost gets blown up in the process. (90 min.)

Cast
Joe Tyler . . . . Paul Hecht

Continued on page A-52

M*A*S*H
8:30 11

ABYSSINIA, HENRY
Henry Blake says goodbye to Korea. It's a red-letter day for the 4077th when Henry (McLean Stevenson) gets the news that he has been discharged. Sentimental moments mix with bon-voyage hoopla as the C.O. prepares to take his leave, and Frank (Larry Linville) prepares to take command. Directed by series creator Larry Gelbart.

Supporting Cast
Hawkeye . . . . Alan Alda
Trapper . . . . Wayne Rogers
Hot Lips . . . . Loretta Swit
Radar . . . . Gary Burghoff
Klinger . . . . Jamie Farr
Father Mulcahy . . . . . . William Christopher
Kim . . . . Kimiko Hiroshige

McLean Stevenson

A-50 TV GUIDE

TV Guide

GONE TOO SOON

The Associates (1979-80 ABC)

Launched as the next big ensemble hit from the producers of *Taxi*, the show about a group of young lawyers at a tony Wall Street firm was doomed before it began by ABC's foolish decision to use it and an unnecessarily re-tooled *Mork & Mindy* (which viewers rejected, killing the show in just its second season) to take on CBS Sunday night comedy block.

Ellery Queen (1975-76 NBC)

Jim Hutton starred in the tailor-made role of New York sleuth Ellery Queen, from 1970s crime-show hit-makers Richard Levinson and William Link. It broke the fourth wall at the end of each episode to ask viewers if they knew who the murder was, but it never broke though Nielsen's wall opposite *The Six Million Dollar Man* and *Cher*.

Kolchak: The Night Stalker (1974-75 ABC)

Never quite as good as the creepy stand-alone TV movies that spawned it, *Kolchak* was a well-executed supernatural crime thriller, long before the show said to be inspired by it -- *The X-Files* -- made the genre TV-cool. But ABC couldn't find any sign of an audience on Friday nights in 1974 against established hit *Sanford and Son* and new hit *Chico and the Man*.

On the Rocks (1975-76 ABC)

On the Rocks was to be the show that, like *Barney Miller*, with which it was originally paired, brought adult-sitcom prestige to ABC. The ensemble just never caught on. Not helping: setting a sitcom inside a prison just as the Family Viewing Hour was calling attention to decency on TV.

The Paper Chase (1978-79 CBS)

It was based on a film that wasn't a huge hit; it starred a group of mostly unknown actors; and it was in an arena (law school) that didn't exactly sound like it would make for compelling TV. But *The Paper Chase* was one of the best-written and best-acted dramas of the decade. Too bad no one knew about it: CBS scheduled it against the two of the biggest hits on the air -- *Happy Days* and *Laverne & Shirley*.

The Practice (1976-77 NBC)

Not to be confused with the other sitcom on the air at the time about an irascible elderly old-school GP -- *Doc* (1975-76 CBS), from the MTM sitcom factory -- *The Practice* was a solid, down-the-middle old-fashioned sitcom enhanced by an all-star line-up of TV pros (Danny Thomas, David Spielberg, Dena Dietrich, Shelley Fabares, Mike Evans). It was funny and well-done and should have lasted longer. So, too, should have its gifted creator, Steve Gordon, who went on to be nominated for an Oscar five years later for writing the movie *Arthur* (which he also directed) and who died the following year of a heart attack at age 44.

Quinn Martin's Tales of the Unexpected (1977 NBC)

It was little more than a horror anthology -- a different spooky story each week. But in the hands of Quinn Martin, one of the most successful TV producers in history (18 series, at least one each season from 1958 to 1980), it was an entertaining and watchable drama. Sadly, it had the bad fortune of airing against first-year phenom *Charlie's Angels*.

The Tony Randall Show (1976-78 ABC/CBS)

It's probably the best show ever cancelled from the heralded writers' factory known as MTM. *The Tony Randall Show*, about the work and home lives of a Philadelphia judge, had a proven Emmy-winning lead and perfectly calibrated comedy ensemble supporting him. More critical, it had a future Who's Who of TV comedy giants behind the scenes -- including Tom Patchett, Jay Tarses, Hugh Wilson, and Garry David Goldberg as its producers and David Lloyd, Earl Pomerantz, Ken Levine and David Isaacs among its writers. It also had decent Top 30 ratings during its first season. But citing what it called "an embarrassment of riches," Number One network ABC cancelled it to make room for *Carter Country*, *A.E.H Hudson Street* and *Fish*, which all failed. (Suck it, ABC.) CBS wisely picked it up from the scrap-bin then foolishly left it to wither on a struggling Saturday night.

We'll Get By (1975 CBS)

Alan Alda cashed in on his growing clout as star of *M*A*S*H** by getting CBS to buy a new series he created called *We'll Get By*, a comedy about a middle-class New Jersey family (no doubt inspired by own family life at the time in a small northern Jersey town). It wasn't the satire that *M*A*S*H** was nor the social statement it became, but as headed by Paul Sorvino it was a funny and relatable family show.

When Things Were Rotten (1975 ABC)

A Robin Hood satire from master satirist Mel Brooks, it was worthy of a better fate due to it title alone.

THE TEN HIGHEST-RATED BROADCASTS

OF THE 1970S

1. *Roots* (part VIII)
January 30 1977
ABC
51.1 rating / 77 share

2. **GONE WITH THE WIND (part 1)**
November 7 1976
NBC
47.7 / 65

3. **GONE WITH THE WIND (part 2)**
November 8 1976
NBC
47.4 / 64

4. **Super Bowl XII** (Cowboys over Broncos)
January 15 1978
CBS
47.2 / 67

5. **Super Bowl XIII** (Steelers over Cowboys)
January 21 1979
NBC
47.1 / 74

6. *Bob Hope Vietnam Christmas Show*
January 15 1970
NBC
46.6 / 64

7. *Roots*, **part VI**
January 28 1977
ABC
45.9 /66

8. *Roots*, **part V**
January 27 1977
ABC
45.7 /71

9. *Bob Hope Vietnam Christmas Show*
January 14 1971
NBC
45.0 / 61

10. *Roots*, **part III**
January 25 1977
ABC
44.8 / 68

HIGHEST-RATED TV SERIES BY SEASON

1970-71
Marcus Welby, M.D.
ABC

1971-72
All in the Family
CBS

1972-73
All in the Family
CBS

1973-74
All in the Family
CBS

1974-75
All in the Family
CBS

1975-76
All in the Family
CBS

1976-77
Happy Days
ABC

1977-78
Laverne & Shirley
ABC

1978-79
Laverne & Shirley
ABC

1979-80
60 Minutes
CBS

"You aint nobody until you do what you want"

-- The Fonz
Happy Days

FRUITS AND VEGETABLES
(CTW/Palm Productions)

This is a non-sequitur comedy revu
"Laugh-In" or "Saturday Night Liv
features a talented group of zanie:
from the topical to the absurd and
charms and comedic abilities of th
performers.

BABY, I'M BACK
(Charles Fries Productions)

DEMOND WILSON stars in this co
likeable Ray Ellis, a man who retu
young children after temporarily "d
years. Ray's happy reunion with h
sour, however, when he learns tha
NICHOLAS) has had him legally c
can marry her boss at the Pentago
Ray's attempts to regain the love
realized his mistake. It won't be
into the apartment next door, Luz
mother-in-law, will also be there
of the way.

Two pilots from 1977 with titles that could have passed muster only in the 1970s. (The Demond Wilson one made it to air but didn't last.)

Section 8

(Edgar Scherick Productions)

CONCEPT:
This comedy series centers on the wild and wacky goings-on in a World War II Army combat fatigue ward. Maxwell Ringer (JAMES CANNING), one of the patients, is a real war hero who is convinced that if he goes back to combat once more, he's sure to get his rear end blown off. However, Maxwell is a constant source of help to the patients and wages his own war against the usual Army and medical plutocracy.

EXECUTIVE PRODUCER:
EDGAR SCHERICK
(The Silence - TV Movie; Sleuth, Law and Disorder, The Taking of Pelham One Two Three, The Stepford Wives, The Heartbreak Kid - Features)

PRODUCERS:
HARVEY BULLOCK/RAY ALLEN
(Alice)

DIRECTOR:
BILL D'ANGELO

WRITERS:
PETER BENCHLEY
(Jaws, The Deep - Novels)
PAUL ZIMMERMAN
HARVEY BULLOCK
RAY ALLEN

CAST.
Maxwell Ringer........................JAMES CANNING
Dr. Goldstein.........................DAVID SPIELBERG
Major Scabbard........................ROGER BOWEN
Nurse Wixler..........................MARYGRACE CANFIELD
D.D...................................LONI ANDERSON
Phillips..............................BILL CORT
Weaver................................WHITNEY RYDBECK
Stern.................................ELLIOT STERN
Chauncey..............................MICHAEL McMANIS
Preacher..............................RAY VITTE

PRODUCTION DATA:
Taped at KTLA in Los Angeles, November 1977.

Another title -- this was a sitcom -- that probably couldn't work today.

BIBLIOGRAHY AND SUGGESTED READING

America in the 70s
Beth L. Bailey, David R.
Farmer, eds. / University
Press of Kansas

The Columbia History of American Television
Gary R. Edgerton /Columbia University
Press

*The Complete Directory to Prime Time Network
and Cable TV Shows 1946-Present*
Tim Brooks and Earle Marsh / Ballantine
Books

*Easy Riders, Raging Bulls: How the Sex-Drugs-
and-Rock 'N' Roll Generation Saved Hollywood*
Peter Biskind / Simon & Schuster

Electronic Media Law
Roger L. Sadler / Sage Publications

*Empire: William S. Paley and the Making of
CBS*
Lewis J. Paper / St. Martin's Press

Even This I Get To Experience
Norman Lear / Penguin Press

*Genre and Television: From Cop Shows to
Cartoons in American Culture*
Jason Mittell / Routledge Press

The HBO Effect
Dean J. DeFino / Bloomsbury Academic

*The Hippest Trip in America: Soul Train and
the Evolution of Culture and Style*
Nelson George / William Morrow

*How We Got Here The 70s: The Decade That
Brought You Modern Life -- For Better or Worse*
David Frum / Perseus Books

Inside Prime Time
Todd Gitlin / Pantheon Books

*Mary and Lou and Rhoda and Ted: And All the
Brilliant Minds Who Made* The Mary Tyler
Moore Show *a Classic*
Jennifer Keishin Armstrong / Simon &
Schuster

*The Prime Time Closet: A History of Gays and
Lesbians on TV*
Stephen Trapiano /Applause Theatre &
Cinema Books

Real People *and the Rise of Reality Television*
Michael McKenna / Rowman & Littlefield

Roots: The Saga of An American Family
Alex Haley / Doubleday

*The Seventies: The Great Shift in American
Culture, Society, and Politics*
Bruce J. Schulman / Da Capo Press

*Staying Alive: The 1970s and the Last Days of
the Working Class*
Jefferson R. Cowie / The New Press

*Target: Prime Time: Advocacy Groups and the
Struggle Over Entertainment.*
Kathryn C. Montgomery / Oxford
University Press

*Tinker In Television From General Sarnoff to
General Electric*
Grant Tinker and Bud Rukeyser / Simon
& Schuster

Total Television
Alex McNeil / Penguin Books

*Unsold TV Pilots: The Almost Complete Guide
to Everything You Never Saw on TV*
Lee Goldberg / Citadel

It Seemed Like Nothing Happened: America in the 1970s
Peter N. Carroll / Rutgers University Press

Love, Peace, and Soul: Behind the Scenes of America's Favorite Dance Show Soul Train: Classic Moments
Ericka Blount Danois/ Backbeat Books

MTM Quality Television
Jane Feuer, Paul Kerr and Tise Vahimagi (Eds.) / BFI Publishing

Mad As Hell: The Making of Network *and the Fateful Vision of the Angriest Man in Movies*
Dave Itzkoff / Henry Holt and Company

Unsold Television Pilots 1955-1989
Television Series Revivals
Lee Goldberg / McFarland & Company

Wallowing in Sex: The New Sexual Culture of 1970s American Television
Elana Levine / Duke University Press

What Were They Thinking? The 100 Dumbest Events in Television History
David Hofstede / Back Stage Books

You Can't Air That: Four Cases of Controversy and Censorship in American Television Programming
David S. Silverman / Syracuse University Press

SPECIAL THANKS

abc.com

advocate.com

americansportscastersonline.com

ampas.com

associatedpress.com

avclub.com

blackworld.com

bostonherald.com

cbs.com

chicagoreader.com

chicagotribune.com

commonsensemedia.org

crazyaboutTV.com

dallasvoice.com

emmys.com

encyclopediabritannica.com

entertainmentweekly.com

espn.com

fcc.gov

fastcompany.com

flashbak.com

forwomen.org

freetobefoundation.org

historian.com

hollywoodreporter.com

huffingtonpost.com

humanitas.org

imdb.com

independent.co.uk

jta.org

kab.org

law.justia.com

losangelestimes.com

mentalfloss.com

mic.com

museum.tv

nab.org

nbc.com

newsweek.com

newyorktimes.com

nfl.com

normanlearcenter.org

ozy.com

paleycenter.org

pbs.org

peabody.org

philly.com

pitchfork.com

popdose.com

pophistorydig.com

producersguild.org

rollingstone.com

scriptlab.com

socionomist.com

televisionheaven.com

terrencemoss.blogspot.com

theatlantic.com

theguardian.com

theroot.com

time.com

tv.com

tvguide.com

tvobscurities.com

tvtechnology.com

ultimateclassicrock.com

uproxx.com

vh1.com

washingtonpost.com

wga.org

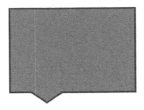

"I much fear serious trouble with the fuselage Frederick."

-- Felix Unger
The Odd Couple

Religion, Feminism, and the Family

Anne Carr
Mary Stewart Van Leeuwen
editors

93876

Westminster John Knox Press
Louisville, Kentucky

Scripture quotations, unless otherwise indicated, are from the New Revised Standard Version of the Bible, copyright © 1989 by the Division of Christian Education of the National Council of the Churches of Christ in the U.S.A., and are used by permission.

Grateful acknowledgment is made to Greenwood Publishing Group, Inc., for permission to reprint portions of chapter 17 from Toinette M. Eugene, "Sometimes I Feel Like a Motherless Child: The Call and Response for a Liberational Ethic of Care by Black Feminists," in *Who Cares? Theory, Research, and Educational Implications of the Ethic of Care*, edited by Mary M. Brabeck (Wesport, Conn.: Praeger Publishers, 1989).

Book and cover design by Jennifer K. Cox

First edition

Published by Westminster John Knox Press
Louisville, Kentucky

This book is printed on acid-free paper that meets the American National Standards Institute Z39.48 standard. ∞

96 97 98 99 00 01 02 03 04 05 — 10 9 8 7 6 5 4 3 2 1

Library of Congress Cataloging-in-Publication Data

Religion, feminism, and the family / edited by Anne Carr and Mary
   Stewart Van Leeuwen — 1st ed.
        p.   cm. — (The family, religion, and culture)
   Includes bibliographical references and index.
   ISBN 0-664-25512-4 (alk. paper)
   1. Family—Religious life—United States. 2. Jewish families—Religious life—
United States. 3. Family—United States. 4. Feminism—United States.
5. Feminism—Religious aspects—Christianity. 6. Feminism—Religious aspects—
Judaism. 7. Judaism—Doctrines. 8. Christianity—United States. 9. United
States—Religion—1960-. 10. United States—Social conditions—1980-.
I. Carr, Anne E. II. Van Leeuwen, Mary Stewart, date. III. Series.
BV4526.2.R46 1996
249'.0973—dc20   96-8818

Contents

Series Foreword

There is an important debate going on today over the present health and future well-being of families in American society. Although some people on the political right and left use this debate primarily to further partisan causes, the debate is real, and it is over genuine issues. The debate, however, is not well informed and is riddled with historical, theological, and social-scientific ignorance.

This is not unusual as political debates go. The American family debate, however, is especially uninformed and dogmatic. This is understandable, for all people have experienced a family in some way, feel themselves to be experts, and believe that they are entitled to their strong opinions.

The books in this series, The Family, Religion, and Culture, discuss these issues in ways that will place the American debate about the family on more solid ground. The series is the result of the Religion, Culture, and Family project, which was funded by a generous grant from the Division of Religion and the Lilly Endowment, Inc. and was located at the Institute for Advanced Study in The University of Chicago Divinity School. Part of the project proceeded while Don Browning, the project director, was in residence at the Center of Theological Inquiry at Princeton, New Jersey.

The series advances no single point of view on this debate and gives no one solution. The authors and editors contributing to the volumes represent both genders as well as a variety of religious and ethnic perspectives and denominational backgrounds—liberal and conservative; Protestant, Catholic, and Jewish; evangelical and main-line; and black, white, and Asian. A number of different authors and editors met annually for a seminar and discussed—often with considerable intensity—their outlines, papers, and chapters pertaining to the various books. The careful reader will notice that many of the seminar members did influence one another; but, it is safe to say, each of them in the end took their own counsel and spoke out of their own convictions.

The series is comprehensive, with studies on the family in ancient Israel and early Christianity; on economics and the family, law, feminism, and reproductive technology and the family; the family and American faith traditions; congregations and families; and two summary books—one a handbook; the other, a critical overview of the American family debate.

This book, *Religion, Feminism, and the Family*, edited by Anne Carr and Mary Stewart Van Leeuwen, demonstrates the ecumenical character of the series. It also features several male authors, breaking an informal tradition that feminism is a topic that men should not address.

The writers move in a clear direction, which is all the more powerful because it emerged in the writing process and was not previously imposed. Their chapters constitute a powerful testimony to the truth that feminism, religion, and the family are *not* incurably antagonistic to one another, a view which is contrary to the widespread popular belief. When properly defined, these traditions not only reinforce one another but are also dependent on one another for their respective fulfillments. The authors' claims, which are softly stated but stunning in impact, can be summed up as follows: first, to gain its fullest hearing, feminism must come to terms with Western religious precedents for some of its deepest institutions; second, to regain their position in postmodern societies, Christianity and Judaism must include the insights of contemporary feminism; and finally, families themselves need both a feminism that is religiously articulate and a religion that is sensitive to the needs of families.

This book promises to reshape the church's understanding of feminism, religion, and the family and goes far in stimulating a rethinking of the relationship between these traditions in both the contemporary women's movement and the wider debate over the future of American families.

Don S. Browning
Ian S. Evison

Contributors

MARVIN L. ANDERSON, Ph.D. candidate in Theology, University of Saint Michael's College, Toronto, Ontario, Canada; Adjunct faculty, Emmanuel College, Victoria University/Toronto School of Theology, Toronto, Ontario, Canada.

MARGARET LAMBERTS BENDROTH, PH.D., Johns Hopkins University, Baltimore, Maryland; Lecturer, Andover Newton Theological School, Newton Centre, Massachusetts; Author of *Fundamentalism and Gender, 1875 to the Present* (Yale University Press, 1993).

CATHERINE A. BREKUS, PH.D., Yale University, New Haven, Connecticut; Assistant Professor of the History of Christianity, The University of Chicago Divinity School, Chicago, Illinois; Author of *Let Your Women Keep Silence in the Churches: Female Preaching in America, 1740–1845* (University of North Carolina Press, forthcoming).

ANNE CARR, PH.D., The University of Chicago Divinity School, Chicago, Illinois; Professor of Theology at the University of Chicago Divinity School, Chicago, Illinois; Author of *Transforming Grace: Christian Tradition and Women's Experience* (Harper & Row, 1988) and other books and articles.

PAMELA D. COUTURE, PH.D., The University of Chicago Divinity School, Chicago, Illinois; Assistant Professor of Pastoral Care, Candler School of Theology, Emory University, Atlanta, Georgia; Publications include *Blessed Are the Poor? Women's Poverty, Family Policy, and Practical Theology* (Abingdon Press, 1991).

TOINETTE M. EUGENE, PH.D., Associate Professor of Christian Social Ethics, Garrett-Evangelical Theological Seminary/Northwestern University, Evanston, Illinois; Member, Graduate Faculty, Northwestern University, Evanston, Illinois; Author of many articles on womanist ethics.

TIKVA FRYMER-KENSKY, PH.D., Professor of Hebrew Bible, The University of Chicago Divinity School, Chicago, Illinois; Author of *In the Wake of the Goddesses* (Free Press, 1992).

IVY GEORGE, PH.D., Brandeis University, Boston, Massachusetts; Professor of Sociology, Gordon College, Wenham, Massachusetts; Native of India and active in the area of women and development, including its religious aspects; Author of articles on this subject.

CHRISTINE E. GUDORF, Professor of Religious Studies, Florida International University, Miami, Florida; Author of *Victimization: Examining Christian Complicity* (Trinity Press International, 1992) and several other articles.

ALLAN KENSKY, M.H.L., PH.D., Rabbi and Associate Dean of the Rabbinical School, Jewish Theological Seminary of America, New York, New York; Author of many articles.

JUNG HA KIM, PH.D., Professor of Sociology of Religion, Gender, and Race Relations, Georgia State University, Atlanta, Georgia; Coordinator of community educational programs, Pan Asian American Community Center, Atlanta, Georgia; Author of *Bridge-makers and Cross-bearers* (Scholars Press, forthcoming).

BONNIE J. MILLER-MCLEMORE, PH.D., The University of Chicago Divinity School, Chicago, Illinois; Associate Professor of Pastoral Theology and Counseling, Vanderbilt University Divinity School, Nashville, Tennessee; Author of *Also A Mother: Work and Family as Theological Dilemma* (Abingdon Press, 1994).

ROB PALKOVITZ, Associate Professor, Department of Individual and Family Studies, University of Delaware, Newark, Delaware; Coeditor, *Transitions to Parenthood* (Haworth Press, 1988) and author of numerous articles.

SALLY PURVIS, Pastor, United Church of Christ; formerly Assistant Professor of Ethics, Candler School of Theology, Emory University, Atlanta, Georgia; Author of *The Stained Glass Ceiling* (Westminster John Knox Press, 1995), and many articles.

WILLIAM D. ROMANOWSKI, PH.D. in American Culture Studies, Bowling Green State University, Bowling Green, Kentucky; Associate Professor of Communication Arts and Sciences, Calvin College, Grand Rapids, Michigan; Contributing author of *Dancing in the Dark: Youth, Popular Culture, and the Electronic Media* (Wm. B. Eerdmans Publishing Co., 1990).

ROSEMARY RADFORD RUETHER, PH.D., Claremont Graduate School, Claremont, California; Professor of Applied Theology, Garrett-Evangelical Theological Seminary/Northwestern University, Evanston,

Illinois; Author of *Sexism and God-Talk: Toward a Feminist Theology* (Beacon, 1983) and many articles on women and Christianity.

DOUGLAS J. SCHUURMAN, PH.D., The University of Chicago Divinity School, Chicago, Illinois; Associate Professor of Theology and Ethics, St. Olaf College, Northfield, Minnesota; Contributing author of *After Eden: Facing the Challenge of Gender Reconciliation* (Wm. B. Eerdmans Publishing Co., 1993); Author of a work on recent Protestant theology.

MARY STEWART VAN LEEUWEN, PH.D., Northwestern University, Evanston, Illinois; Professor of Psychology and Philosophy, Eastern College, St. Davids, Pennsylvania; Resident Scholar, Center for Christian Women in Leadership, Eastern College, St. Davids, Pennsylvania; Author of *Gender and Grace* (InterVarsity Press, 1990); Coeditor of *After Eden: Facing the Challenge of Gender Reconciliation* (Wm. B. Eerdmans Publishing Co., 1993).

ROBERT SWEETMAN, PH.D. in Medieval Studies, University of Toronto, Toronto, Ontario, Canada; Senior Member, History of Philosophy Department, Institute for Christian Studies, Toronto, Ontario, Canada; Author of articles on women in medieval Europe.

MERRY E. WIESNER, PH.D., University of Wisconsin-Madison, Madison, Wisconsin; Director, The Center for Women's Studies, University of Wisconsin-Milwaukee, Milwaukee, Wisconsin; Professor of History, University of Wisconsin-Milwaukee, Milwaukee, Wisconsin; Author of many articles on women in the Reformation.

Introduction

MARY STEWART VAN LEEUWEN

This volume on religion, feminism, and the family is one of a series of books sponsored by the Religion, Culture, and Family Project, which is funded by the Lilly Endowment through an interdisciplinary committee associated with The University of Chicago Divinity School. Like others in the series, it is intended to be a "crossover" book: One written by knowledgeable, front-running scholars in the area being addressed but accessible to interested laity as well as to fellow academics. Our target audience more or less reflects the diversity of contributors to the volume: liberals and conservatives among Catholics, Protestants, and Jews, both sexes, and various ethnicities. We also hope that these chapters will prove helpful to those who do not profess any formal religious affiliation but recognize the importance of religion as a social, intellectual, and moral force and wish to understand better its interaction with feminist theory and changing family relations.

Our general goals for the volume are as follows: to address the relationship of various forms of feminism to the structure and functioning of families; to examine whether there is an inherent conflict between families as defined in the past and the current goals of feminism; to explore what kind of ethic can best promote gender justice while strengthening family life and the family as a societal institution; and to explore what religiously based feminism can contribute to the resolution of the above questions. Our stance as authors and editors includes a belief that the term "religious feminism" need not be an oxymoron and a desire to be critically faithful to our respective religious traditions. That is, we wish to affirm core religious norms of justice and reconciliation by showing that feminist insights are an asset rather than a threat to the healthy development of those norms. We also wish to show that feminist theory and activism are less than

complete if they ignore insights about, and from, women who profess
allegiance to a religious worldview.

This book is divided into four sections. Because there is so little literature dealing with the variables of religion, feminism, and the family together, we begin with two chapters that "mediate the terms" of
the debate: the first dealing with religion as it relates to feminism; the
second, with feminism as it relates to the family. In the first of these
chapters, Anne Carr and Douglas Schuurman present a case study of
feminist Christianity, which they consider to be ecumenical, comprehensive in its concerns, attuned to women's experience, and committed to a model of justice that respects both gender equality and gender
difference. They then use these criteria to evaluate some feminist-
based reforms in theological anthropology, the doctrine of God
(including the issue of God-language), Christology, and Christian
ethics. In chapter 2, Mary Stewart Van Leeuwen shows how feminist
theorizing since the 1960s has moved from an oppositional to a more
nuanced view of families, and how feminism has changed the conduct
of family research and family policy debate. She also explains how and
why feminists differ regarding the normative shape of the family and
defends egalitarian, heterosexual co-parenting as a core norm but
with somewhat flexible boundaries.

Part two presents Jewish and Christian reflections on the anthropology and ethics of family life. Tikva Frymer-Kensky begins with
a survey of family relations as represented by the Hebrew Bible's
various genres (law, proverbs, narrative) and periods (the founding
of the nation, the period before the monarchy, and the period of the
Davidic court). She contends that although the Hebrew Bible shares
with other ancient Near Eastern cultures the assumption of a patriarchal family, this structure is presumed to be rooted in the Fall
and not in Creation. This structure is mitigated by the norms of justice and care for the vulnerable and by a generational hierarchy in
which mothers as well as fathers are to be honored by children. She
locates the control of women's sexuality by men in the context of
concern for the expansion and purity of Israel, and traces women's
substantial—if covert—influence over husbands and sons throughout the "ancestor tales" of Genesis. Women's vulnerability and
men's preoccupation with family lineage and honor emerge as
themes in the premonarchial period. With the consolidation of the
kingdom comes an interposition of state control over family politics, which has ambivalent results for women; nevertheless,
through all genres and periods the family remains the normative
unit of Israelite society.

Allan Kensky follows with a survey of family ethics in rabbinic Judaism, in which family life is seen as essential both to human ful-fillment and to the service of God. The destruction of the temple and the dispersion of the Jews led to the centering of religious observance in the home which, while formally remaining a generational and gen-dered hierarchy, at its best embodied ideals of mutual love and sacri-fice in the context of four basic family values: sexual purity, the rearing of children, filial respect, and household peace. The author shows how the development of rabbinic marriage-contract law helped to reduce women's vulnerability in marriage, although problems remain with the locus of divorce initiative still in the hands of men only. He finishes with a survey of challenges to the modern Jewish family, which include living with the myth of the mutually devoted, extended family in an age of increasing family fragmentation and voli-tional singleness, and dealing with Jewish feminist insistence on the fuller inclusion of women in religious and communal life.

In the third chapter of this section, Rosemary Radford Ruether pro-vides a historical review of biblical and systematic theologies of gen-der, both Catholic and Protestant. She supports neither "difference feminism," which essentializes and romanticizes the stereotypically feminine, nor an androgynous (but covertly androcentric) feminism which ignores women's unique experience. Instead, she sees human-ness for everyone as an ongoing journey into wholeness that respects yet transcends traditionally gendered qualities. Rejecting both the patriarchal family (which stifles the selfhood of other family mem-bers) and modern liberal individualism (which too easily discards the relational baby along with the patriarchal bathwater), she envisages a third way for both family and public life, in which selfhood and com-munity are mutually reinforcing goals.

In the final chapter of this section, Sally Purvis develops the theme of relational anthropology and ethics in more detail. She sees the dual love command (to love God, and one's neighbor as oneself) as the foundation for Christian ethics, and relationality (with God, with oth-ers) as an inherent—not an acquired or secondary—feature of person-hood. Against the Kantian norm of "disinterested" love spread equally to everyone, she advances a model of "extravagant" and specific love as developed in friendship and family at their best, but one which avoids the parochialism of the biological family by locating the latter within the more basic family of faith united by "a common love" for God. Such love—normed by the standards of justice, liberation, and recon-ciliation—ideally spreads beyond the household of faith to include and nurture the diverse members of God's entire human family.

Part three consists of six historical chapters on women, Christianity, and the family (the term "feminism" being something of an anachronism if applied to periods before the emergence of individual rights language). Our survey begins with Robert Sweetman's treatment of some of the lives of the women saints during late antiquity and the Middle Ages. He shows that until the late sixth century, marriage and motherhood were not considered impediments to holiness, and that even up through the end of the medieval era, women—whether virgins, wives, or widows—could effectively appeal to a godly calling in order to sidestep the constraints of arranged marriages, husbandly headship, and a life limited to domesticity. Indeed, his case studies show that women saints could symbolically turn the existing order upside down by becoming "spiritual mothers" to the very men (fathers, brothers, actual and potential husbands) who would otherwise control their lives.

In her chapter on the early Modern period, Merry Wiesner describes how these earlier sources of women's public authority—maternal and religious—were threatened by legal and economic changes that began to privatize both family life and religious belief and sever them from the developing capitalist economy. She shows that both Catholic and Protestant women resisted such changes not by appropriating the emerging political language of abstract individual rights but by appealing to past traditions, such as women's guild membership, family-based modes of production, and the authority-conferring call of God to public and maternally grounded religious roles.

Our third and fourth historical chapters focus on nineteenth-century America, before and after the Civil War. Catherine Brekus shows that by midcentury the gendered dichotomy of public and private life—with middle-class women firmly assigned to the latter—was an accepted societal norm. American feminism (a term soon to emerge in the context of liberal political ideals) challenged this dichotomy by mixing the earlier religious language of "calling" and "sacred cause" with the modern rhetoric of natural human rights. Nevertheless, most of these women are best described as biblical feminists who used mainly exegetical arguments for more egalitarian families and churches where women and men would share equal rights and responsibilities. They were also "domestic feminists" who opposed divorce, contraception, and abortion as practices that did more to encourage men's irresponsibility than women's opportunity, and who based their claim to expanded public roles less on women's similarities to men than on their differences, including their supposed moral superiority.

Margaret Lamberts Bendroth continues this analysis, focusing on the period between 1865 and 1920. She shows that appeals to religious, feminist, and familial norms remained intertwined and mutually supportive until after the turn of the century, when the face of American feminism became more secularized and less family friendly, and organized religion in turn became increasingly antifeminist and prone to romanticize the (now declining) nineteenth-century bourgeois family. She lists several reasons for these shifts, including the entry of middle-class women into the waged work force, an increasing fear that American religion was becoming feminized (with the parallel rise of a "muscular Christianity" movement among men), and the progressive transfer of childhood education from the home to the school.

William Romanowski then examines the interaction of such socioeconomic changes with twentieth-century popular culture, focusing on the output of the American film industry from the time of its emergence through to the 1990s. He shows how this form of urban, public entertainment both reflected and contributed to the emerging ethos of individualism, consumerism, and the separation of dating and courtship from family control—with mixed results for women and an ambivalent relationship to feminism.

As urban life changed in wake of the Industrial Revolution, so did rural life. In our last historical-sociological chapter, Marvin Anderson examines the "reluctant feminism" of women who are family farmers in the United States and Canada. He notes that the myth of the family farm leads people to romanticize rural life, even as they ignore the economic crisis state of family farming and the low self-esteem of men and women farmers, which results from longstanding scorn for their supposed lack of culture and the more recent anxieties about foreclosure and bankruptcy. As suicide rates among male farmers continue to climb, it is largely farm women who have taken the initiative to name the underlying problems (both psychological and structural) and become activist in dealing with them. At the same time, their daily lives are laden with paradox. On the one hand, women's farm work is usually unpaid, undervalued, and largely invisible. On the other hand, although farm women tend to reject feminism because its perceived call to female autonomy ignores the essential interdependence of farm family members, the very nature of the farm family business operation makes them "functional feminists" in the degree of skill and responsibility that they exercise.

In part four we attempt to bring culture, ethics, and religion together in a critical conversation with practical-theological implications. We begin with Pamela Couture's reflections on private and public patriarchy, both past and present. The former looks to the positive emotional ties of family life to produce a just society but at the cost of maintaining severe gender and class boundaries; the latter looks to the state to produce justice but at the cost of both devaluing and overregulating domestic life. She shows how these two choices, which go back to Aristotle and Plato respectively, are replayed in the private patriarchy of market states such as the United States, and the public patriarchy of welfare states such as Sweden. She also reveals how nineteenth-century feminists for example, Frances Willard in the United States and Ellen Key in Sweden, anticipated and tried to steer between these two unsatisfactory choices by appealing to family metaphors and values as the basis for structuring both civil society and the state—a "third way" which she defends as a still-viable ideal for today.

Bonnie Miller-McLemore continues with her chapter on the ambiguities of "having it all." She points out that both Freudian and biblical anthropology affirm the irreducibility of "love and work" as human motives. Thus women's urge to "have it all" reflects, at its best, the generically human desire to integrate self and others, work and family, self-sacrifice and self-fulfillment. Too often, however, this integration comes at the cost of women adding public responsibilities to their domestic tasks, while the reverse is rarely true for men. Alternately, elite women may purchase domestic and childcare services from others in order to avoid the burnout associated with the "double day" but see no injustice as they pass this burden on to women who have fewer economic choices than they themselves do. She draws on the work of feminist-analytic psychologists to explore the female desire to "have it all" and, at the same time, to support men's greater participation in nurturing functions. She concludes with some theological reflections on the Eve narrative—a narrative of female desire—relating it to the enduring issues of freedom, limitation, and the necessity for divine correction and redemption.

In the third chapter of this section, Christine Gudorf shares aspects of her own family narrative in order to show how parenting tasks interact with parents' own adult development, particularly as they cope with the residue of their childhood relationship to their own parents. She criticizes the received view of parenting as a "sacrificial" endeavor, instead seeing the parent-child relationship as a source of growth and enrichment for both parties. She shows how the romanticization of supposed parental sacrifice serves in several ways as an ideological cover for gender and generational power imbalances.

Moreover, she suggests, the injudicious use of parenting metaphors for God may foster passivity and ethical irresponsibility on the part of people constantly exposed to such metaphors. She advances instead a model of God-human relations rooted in images of friendship and co-creation, while retaining those aspects of the parenting metaphor that point to the steadfast permanence, or givenness, of the bond between the Creator and ourselves.

Family studies researcher Rob Palkovitz then introduces readers to the growing historical and social-scientific literature on fathering. He shows how the switch from an agrarian to an industrial economy reduced the normative function of fathers mostly to breadwinning and gender role modeling, in contrast to their previously more organic calling to be children's spiritual, moral, emotional, and behavioral guides. He agrees that a new, feminist-influenced ideology of father-hood has emerged—one that calls fathers to be deeply involved in the day-to-day care of infants as well as older children, and daughters as well as sons. But he shows that actual behavioral change lags far behind these ideals in all but a fraction of educated, financially comfortable households. He lists some forces that help to maintain this split between ideology and behavior, and finishes with a short biblical theology of parenting in which gender roles take second place to the generic call to love God and neighbor in lives of mutual affirmation.

Our closing case studies illustrate the complex blend of religious, feminist, and familial concerns in communities other than those represented by white, middle-class North America. While we had hoped in the North American context to include case studies by Spanish-American, African-American and Asian-American scholars, unforeseen complications in the process of assembling this volume have regrettably limited us to two rather than three ethnic communities. In the first of these chapters, Toinette Eugene introduces readers to the black feminist tradition known as womanism and demonstrates its close interaction with black familial and religious concerns. Fueled by the survival challenges of black communities past and present, womanism represents a unique blend of toughness and compassion, and of particularist and universalist ethical ideals. Committed to the survival and flourishing of an entire culture, womanists embed their critique of patriarchy within a critique of racism, aiming to challenge the former while at the same time empowering black men within the wider society. Religiously, womanism is seen as grounded in the Old Testament prophetic tradition and in a New Testament theology of servant-leadership as exemplified by Christ, thus making justice and love its twin ethical pillars.

Jung Ha Kim then explores the historical and contemporary shape of Asian-American families. She details the problems that result from lumping diverse Asian immigrant groups together under the rubric "Asian-American" but concedes that such groups do share common challenges rooted in their immigrant labor history, with its attendant fragmentation of families and skewed sex ratios. She examines and qualifies the myth of the "stable, cohesive Asian family" and shows how its difficulties are compounded by the longstanding American reverence for a gendered public/private dichotomy. She concludes with an appeal for the endorsement of alternative family forms as "viable and valuable survival strategies" for various groups of peoples.

Finally, sociologist Ivy George uses her native India to examine the interaction of gender, religion, and economic development. Drawing on the flexible imagery associated with two female Hindu deities, she shows that religion can either retard or support gender-equitable development. The latter possibility is illustrated by the remarkable Chipko movement, in which women have combined Hindu cosmology and ethics with a unique feminist consciousness in order to challenge the natural resource depletion of rural India. By contrast, standard androcentric models of development—mediated by patriarchal religious and cultural practices—almost always disempower women socially, economically, and in family relations.

Throughout these chapters, readers will find some recurring themes and also certain tensions—as is to be expected, given that our authors represent a range of both religious and feminist perspectives. We summarize and reflect on some of these themes and tensions in the conclusion to the volume; but, in the meantime, invite readers to dig deeply into the intervening chapters, joining us in a "critical conversation" relating three important but seldom-linked topics: religion, feminism, and the family.

PART 1

Defining the Terms

1

Religion and Feminism

A Reformist Christian Analysis

ANNE CARR
DOUGLAS J. SCHUURMAN

> Religious symbol systems focused around exclusively male images of divinity create the impression that female power can never be fully legitimate or wholly beneficent. This message need never be explicitly stated. . . . A woman completely ignorant of the myths of female evil in biblical religion nonetheless acknowledges the anomaly. . . . She may see herself as like God (created in the image of God) only by denying her own sexual identity and affirming God's transcendence of sexual identity. But she can never have the experience . . . available to every man and boy in her culture, of having her full sexual identity affirmed as being in the image and likeness of God.
>
> —Carol P. Christ

Religion and religious studies comprise a global and diverse range of human life-orientations, including beliefs and practices, and the symbols, rituals, and doctrines that express beliefs and inspire practice. In the American context, however, religion often means Judaism or Christianity. Because our own experience and expertise is in Christian belief and practice, this chapter focuses on the relations between feminism and Christianity as a central "case study" of the way a traditional religious heritage is variously perceived by feminist thinkers.

The Possibility of a Feminist Christianity

Religious feminists, while diverse in their approaches, are united in the conviction that both feminism and religion are significant for the lives of women and men. That shared concern includes both feminists who work for the reform of traditions—Jewish, Catholic, Orthodox, mainline or evangelical Protestants—and those who, having declared Judaism and Christianity irredeemably biased against women, find religious homes elsewhere.

Feminist writers within the Christian context, for all their variety, agree that sexism is a massive distortion of the historical and theological tradition, a distortion which systematically denigrates women, openly or covertly affirms women's inferiority and subordination to men, and excludes women from full participation in church and society. These writers also aim to free women from ideologies and structures that hinder their self-actualization as full human persons and their self-transcendence as fully religious persons. They all agree as well on the importance of the interpreted experience of women as a source for theological reflection, especially as such interpretation—whether secular or religious—reflects the diversity of women's experience in terms of race, class, ethnicity, or nationality.

Differences within feminist thought as it relates to Christianity reflect different perceptions of the depth of sexism within the historical tradition and in current structures and practices. At one end of the spectrum, some (e.g., Mary Daly, Judith Goldenberg, Carol Christ) argue that the intrinsic character of the major Jewish and Christian symbols is patriarchal and detrimental to women. At the other end are those (e.g., Judith Plaskow, Rosemary Radford Ruether, Elisabeth Schüssler Fiorenza, Anne Carr) who claim that sexism and patriarchy are not intrinsic to Judaism or Christianity: These traditions must be purified to allow for the full participation of women within them. In terms which are useful but perhaps also too simple, these groups have been labelled "revolutionaries" and "reformists."[1] Somewhere between the two groups are those who accept some feminist claims (e.g., women's equality in church and society), but not others (e.g., the use of inclusive language for God).[2]

Moreover, though all Christian feminists affirm the "equality" of women and men, they do not all affirm women's "sameness" with men. Positions that promote some model of "complementarity" between women and men are seen by some thinkers as disguised forms of patriarchy that only appear to exalt women by affirming their special virtues (receptivity, capacity for sacrifice, intuition, and nurturance) or their "essential motherhood" as supposedly built into the created order for marriage and family. Others are more sympathetic to the "dimorphic" views of gender advanced by secular feminists such as Carol Gilligan, Nancy Chodorow, and Sara Ruddick. These thinkers acknowledge the "different voice" of women expressed in moral reasoning and elsewhere, often grounding the causes of this "difference" in experiences related to maternal potentialities and practices, especially as these are structured by social systems that shape gender relations. They insist that social practices and institutions be restructured so that what is distinctively "feminine" will not disadvantage women. But whether one affirms the "sameness" or the "difference" ideal, the key question is: Who does the defining? So long as women have been excluded from that process, men have formed definitions that favor their own power, whether in generic definitions of "humanity" or in complementary ideals for men and women. Still other Christian feminists object to the whole enterprise of defining gender, on the ground that definitions are inadequate to express the complexity of reality and are constraints that serve the interests of those in power.

Our own point of view in this chapter is "reformist." That is, we believe that Christianity is not intrinsically sexist or patriarchal, even though these elements are present in many of its historic and contemporary configurations. We also believe that feminism, both as the movement of women (and men) for full "liberation" and as reflected in the discourse of women's studies and feminist thought, represents a significant challenge to Christian understanding. We believe that Christianity *can* be reformed through a mutually critical correlation of the central insights of feminism and Christianity. We hold, moreover, that a creative correlation of Christianity and feminist insight is not only possible but necessary for the flourishing of both women and the Christian tradition. At stake in this task is the truth embodied in both the Christian event and in the full humanity of women as persons before God.

Theoretical Perspectives and Methods of Feminist Christianity

Feminist Christians are not monolithic in their understandings of "feminism," "Christianity," or the construction of a feminist Christianity. Differences extend to strategic questions as well as to fundamental practical and theoretical issues. As secular feminists gravitate toward liberal, Marxist, Freudian, or other modes of diagnosing and ending patriarchy, so too feminist Christians are not unanimous in favoring one or another school of feminist analysis.[3] Some feminists fear that theoretical differences are deep enough to threaten the progress of the feminist movement; others have called into question the very project of classifying feminists at all.[4] But in spite of dangers of oversimplification and exclusion, we will identify some of the salient elements of feminist Christian thought. Our characterization of the perspectives, methods, and doctrines of feminist Christianity are of course tentative and exploratory, not fixed and final.

In the first place, Christian feminist theorizing begins and ends in *experience*. Two millennia of predominantly male church leadership—with men writing and canonizing scripture, formulating liturgy,

preaching, writing history, and theorizing about God and God's relations with the world—have in subtle and blatant ways neglected the
experiences and contributions of women and perpetuated women's
subordination. But feminist Christians also believe there are elements
of Christianity, past and present, that promote the liberation of women
and the reconciliation of men and women. The task is thus not only to
criticize; it is also to identify, retrieve, and develop these elements
while at the same time reconstructing Christian practice in the church,
society, and home.

Recently Christian feminists have become more aware of a class and
race bias beneath earlier understandings of "women's experience."
African-American women, Asian women, Native American women, and
impoverished women—in the United States and around the globe—
have pointed out that "women's" experience often meant white, middle-
class, educated, Western women's experience.[5] The struggles articulated
in Betty Friedan's *The Feminine Mystique*, for example, excluded and
indirectly contributed to the oppression of impoverished single mothers
whose day-to-day struggles were far removed from those of suburban
women. What might be liberative for women of privileged class and race
might be destructive for women whose experience was shaped by class
and racial oppression.[6] To signal these concerns many black and
Hispanic women, for example, identify themselves as "womanists" or
"mujeristas" rather than feminists.[7] In addition, notably absent from
much of the feminism of the 1970s was a positive revaluation of
women's maternal and domestic roles. Now a broader range of women's
experiences is included in feminist writings.[8] Tensions among various
views concerning the nature of "women's experience" can threaten the
unity and effectiveness of feminism, Christian and secular. But these
tensions have also brought about a more self-critical stance among
feminists, who realize that just as hegemonic men used the idea of
"humanity" in ways that excluded women, so too economically and
racially privileged women used the idea of "women's experience" in ways
that excluded poor women and women of color. Such tensions also
motivate efforts to explore the interlocking nature of sexism, classism,
and racism within the common project of challenging women's subordination. Although women of diverse ethnic, racial, and economic groups
experience systemic injustice in different ways, women's socially and
culturally subordinated status, and their maternal capacities and functions, provide a common ground that spans other differences. Feminist
Christianity aims to remove women's subordination and restore dignity
and value to maternal and domestic spheres and to the characteristics
which flourish in those spheres.

In the second place, feminist Christianity is *comprehensive* in its approach to faith and life in the world. The powers that contribute to the neglect, subordination, and abuse of women are seen as psychological, cultural, social, political, and spiritual. Efforts to transform the church and Christian theology are thus intimately bound up with a comprehensive transformation of all institutions. Church leadership must include women as well as men; church worship must use inclusive language for God and God's people and express the experiences of women as well as men; patriarchal patterns of thinking must be challenged in every theological field of study—biblical, historical, systematic, moral, and philosophical. Though there is debate about precisely how to revise patterns of Christian thought and practice, the impact of feminist concerns on religious institutions has been extensive.[9]

Since patriarchy permeates the family, the paid workplace, culture, and society, and since God's will for gender reconciliation and justice reaches beyond the church into the world, feminist Christians have a transformative mission in the world. Feminists of the 1960s and 1970s concentrated mostly on simple equality—women's equal access to jobs, equal pay for equal work, equal opportunity for advancement, and so forth. The feminism of the 1980s and 1990s is engaged in a more profound critique of the cultural, domestic, economic, and political systems that have hindered and devalued women. In the academy this calls for a transformation of natural, social, and humanistic disciplines.[10] In society it calls for the restructuring of institutions so that women can flourish and their concerns be respected. Feminist Christians advocate active engagement in the broader social and cultural orders to bring about transformation of institutional powers so that they serve gender justice, rather than mere equality of access to male-defined activities.

In the third place, feminist Christianity is *ecumenical* denominationally, spanning Catholic, Protestant and, recently, Orthodox Christianity. Particular concerns may vary. Catholic feminists, for example, confront the ways that hierarchical patterns of Church leadership promote sexism, whereas evangelical Protestant feminists are more concerned with patriarchal patterns in the Bible and its interpretation. But their shared commitment to the transformation of ecclesial and societal institutions creates a basis for ecumenical relations. Though feminist and antifeminist perspectives now divide Christians in ways that denominational boundaries once divided Christians, feminist Christian concerns unify members of many denominations.

Feminist Christians are also ecumenical in seeking interrelations among multiple modes of oppression, especially among sexism, heterosexism, classism, and racism.[11] But it is possible to trivialize more severe modes of oppression by grouping them all together. The oppression and struggle of an impoverished, single mother of four living in a crime-infested inner city, for example, is more severe than the subordination experienced by wealthy suburban women. As Andrea Dworkin discerns, for many black and Native American women the "first identity"—"the one which brings with it as a part of its definition death . . . the identity of primary emergency"—is that of race or class rather than gender.[12] Though analysis of gender should not be omitted in such situations, the analysis should include attention to the primary cause of harm. There is an emergent consensus that to treat one mode of systemic injustice, one must treat them all, and that in resisting patriarchy one is also committed to resist all that opposes God's *shalom*, particularly poverty, racism, and heterosexism.

There is also a growing interreligious ecumenism among feminists. Feminist Christians find conversation partners, for example, among Jews, Muslims, and Hindus. The growing interest in interreligious dialogue and the growth of feminism in many countries and cultures of the world unite religious feminists of many kinds to work against sexism while maintaining loyalties to their respective faiths. Feminists are also ecumenical in using resources from secular disciplines as they seek to analyze and dismantle patriarchy and to work for a more just and inclusive society. Christian convictions are combined with insights into the causes and symptoms of patriarchy developed by psychoanalytic, socialist, Marxist, deconstructionist, liberal, and other schools of feminist scholarship.

Fourth, feminist Christians strive to actualize a *new humanity* in which women and men develop and use their gifts for the well-being of the human and nonhuman communities of life. Minimally this calls for justice in the ecclesial and social orders, a justice which respects both equality and the relevant differences between women and men. In its fullness it calls for mutual dependence and delight between women and men as they develop their God-given potential in all relational and institutional contexts. Because gender relations are so pervasively infected by sinful cultural, social, and personal attitudes and practices, and because many are unaware of this fact, feminist Christians expose sexism and criticize it. But the goal of this criticism is the transformation of church and society toward a way of life in which women are no longer silenced and oppressed but rather recognized and celebrated, and in which women and men are reconciled as partners serving God's creative and redemptive purposes. Feminist reconstruction of the church and Christianity is one important part of this larger aim.

Feminist Christian Theology

The theoretical dimensions of feminist theology just outlined are illustrated by the following sketch of some of the major Christian symbols as interpreted from different feminist perspectives. We begin with Christian theological anthropology, since the question of the human nature, and women's place within human nature, is the first issue that feminist Christians addressed, and one which formed the substantive base for feminist transformation of other themes.

Theological Anthropology

Contemporary theology is characterized by its concern with human experience in all its variety. This concern with the pluralism of experience is apparent in the focus of political and liberation theologies on the experience of the poor under oppressive social and economic systems, and in the grounding of these theologies in the particular experiences that mark Latin American, black, or Asian situations. Christian feminist theologies examine the meaning of the gospel and Christian tradition in relation to the plural experiences of women who, in different situations, are almost universally understood as a subordinate group in church and society. Feminist theologians criticize theoretical perspectives and institutional practices that place women in secondary status; they also reformulate traditional theologies and call for new structures and practices that take the experience of women seriously.

In attempting to delineate the experience of women, feminist theologians are wary of universalizing or "essentializing" that experience, for it is surely different in different contexts. Thus Jewish feminist Judith Plaskow points out that her description of women's experience is that of white, middle-class, western women as disclosed in some contemporary novels about these women's struggle for autonomy or self-actualization. The temptation or "sin" of such women, she holds, is in their failure to acquire a strong sense of self or to assume responsibility for their lives through reasoned and free decisions. Typically male theological formulations, which describe sin as prideful self-assertion and grace as self-sacrifical love, are irrelevant to women who have sacrificed too much of their selves. Plaskow builds her discussion on an earlier, groundbreaking essay by Valerie Saiving that showed the androcentrism (male-centered character) of most western Christian theology; not only was theology written by men, it (unconsciously perhaps) privileged male experience. While such formulations may speak to men in situations of power, they fail to connect with the experience of most women, who seldom wield much power either in personal or societal relations.[13]

Christian feminist perspectives on sin and grace are complicated by the distinction between the personal and the social. There is important truth in the early feminist axiom that "the personal is political"; many personal situations are reflective of wider social and political structures which, in turn, shape the personal. The complication arises when issues of class and race are introduced; early on Rosemary Radford Ruether pointed out the "inter-structuring" of these dimensions in the lives of women, which means that black women and poor women are doubly or triply oppressed. When feminist theologians revise doctrines of sin and grace they attend to both personal attitudes and social-cultural structures. Thus Ruether's work criticizes social systems that perpetuate sexist or "sinful" patterns, and envisions others that would empower women by patterning "graceful" or inclusive relations, not only among women, men, and children but with the earth and all its creatures.

In her study of Protestant theologies of sin and grace, Plaskow suggests that a theology rooted in women's experience and friendship, as they search for autonomy and interdependent freedom, might express the experience of *joy* in the divine-human relationship. The experience of grace or the Spirit that she describes is neither "shattering" (Niebuhr) as by an authoritarian father-judge nor a quietistic "acceptance" as by an understanding mother (Tillich). It is neither subordination nor self-denying participation, but rather an experience of grace or the Spirit best expressed in "co-words"—co-creating, co-shaping, co-stewardship—or "in process" words like living, changing, loving, pushing. This suggestion is similar to those made by Dorothee Soelle about the special import of the mystical tradition for women, with its language of "fountainhead, source, spring of all goodness, living wind," "ground, love, depth, sea." These are images that describe God not as a distant other but as a loving, passionate God, seeking union, not obedience. The "great surrender" of mystical thought, in this interpretation, involves giving up the depressed and empty self that women so often experience, and giving up familiar images of God so that God might be found in love for and solidarity with others. Such an idea connects with the metaphor of friendship for the divine-human relation developed by Sallie McFague.[14]

A final issue in anthropology that has received major discussion from feminist theologians is the question of conceiving human nature as one or two. Feminists who emphasize equal rights typically argue for a single-nature anthropology, holding that women and men share common human characteristics and that a dual-nature perspective inevitably classes women as secondary, defined by their biology, with the capacity for motherhood denoted as their particular "essence."

Other feminists argue that women *are* characterized by their fundamental "difference," whether by virtue of their innate traits or their historical conditioning, and have special gifts to bring to theology, church and society. Both sides of this "sameness vs. difference" dispute have produced fruitful theological proposals.

God and God-Language

> I raise my eyes to the hills, looking for help and protection.
> Our help comes from El Shaddai, Mother of heaven and earth!
>
> She is the mighty, breasted God of the mountains.
> She will not let your feet slip as you journey along.
> She will watch and keep you with unsleeping eye.
> She who watches Her children never slumbers!
>
> El Shaddai is Your shelter and shade.
> You have nothing to fear in the brightness of the sun,
> nor in the light of the moon.
> El Shaddai will guard you from evil.
> She will preserve your soul and protect your life.
> El Shaddai will always be with you as you come and go,
> both now and forever. Amen.
>
> Psalm 121 (Paraphrased)[15]

Feminist Christians "encounter both their deepest struggle and their most profound security in the fundamental doctrine or symbol of God."[16] Imagery and language about God reach incisively into the depths of experience and into the structure of the church's communal worship. Because of this, conflicts between feminists and antifeminists are most intense around this issue.[17] Christian feminists urge that the language for God be revised to become more inclusive, expanding God-imagery to include "feminine" and "masculine" similes, metaphors, and pronouns, as well as nongendered personal and natural imagery. For reasons of historical accuracy and integrity, feminists are often willing to concede that in Bible translation the patriarchal aspects of the original text language should be retained. But they insist that the lectionary, hymnody, prayer, and preaching become inclusive. Discovering the female aspects of God and celebrating them in worship touches the lives of women and men in ways that constitute profoundly new experiences of the reality of God and God's relations with people.

One reason for resistance to masculinist God-language is that it perpetuates patriarchy. Feminist revisions aim at transforming personal consciousness and social structures so that they are inclusive and affirm women as well as men. Sallie McFague argues that the dominance of masculine imagery for God—father, king, lord, sovereign—distorts the Christian God in ways that legitimate patriarchy.[18] When this slides into an idolatrous equation of God with males, it perpetuates gross injustice against women as well as more subtle forms of women's subordination to men. To accept the gender system's view of masculinity as detached, independent, controlling, and then infer that God is masculine, is to generate and sustain dualistic understandings that promote social oppression as well as the exploitation of nature.

Another basis for revising God-language is theological. God is neither male nor female, but is the ground of both. If "masculine" means detached, self-sufficient, unrelated, controlling, then major strands of Christian tradition oppose a masculine God. The Bible itself uses female imagery for God. Yahweh is the one who says "I bore [Israel] on eagles' wings and brought [her] to myself" (Exod. 19:4); whose passion for Israel leads Yahweh to say, ". . . now I will cry out like a woman in labor, I will gasp and pant" (Isa. 42:14); who describes Israel as a people "who have been borne by me from your birth, carried from the womb" (Isa. 46:3); who says to Israel, "Can a woman forget her nursing child, or show no compassion for the child of her womb? Even these may forget, yet I will not forget you" (Isa. 49:15). Wisdom is often depicted as a female figure in the Old Testament writings. Because Christ is wisdom (*sophia*, *logos*) incarnate, some feminists refer to Christ as "Christa," highlighting the female aspects of God (see next section). Retrieving these and other female notions of God from the Bible and the tradition is important in feminist theology.

Recently feminists have reexamined trinitarian doctrine in light of feminist concerns. Two particularly thorough and insightful treatments are those of Elizabeth A. Johnson and Catherine Mowry LaCugna.[19] Unlike some feminists who reject trinitarian language because of the centrality of masculine titles and the way social subordination had been justified by appealing to the subordination of the Son to the Father, LaCugna and Johnson retrieve aspects of tradition that are both reflective of women's experience and faithful to central strands of the tradition. Here, we only briefly identify a few of the themes they develop in illuminating and historically rich ways.

One theme is that because God's being is mysterious, all our language about God is analogical. The Christian God is not a ruling monarch, but a "tripersonal mystery of love."[20] The attempt to capture God's nature in reified "names" that rigidly designate God's being fails to recognize that before the wondrous mystery of God all thought and language fall far short. A second theme is that the Trinity, properly understood, points to the primacy of relationality. LaCugna rejects Arius and Eunomius, who made God's "nonrelationality" primary, siding instead with the Cappadocians who insisted that the Son was "begotten." This means that "love for and relationship with another is primary over autonomy, ecstasis over stasis, fecundity over self-sufficiency. Thus personhood, being-in-relation-to-another, was secured as the ultimate originating principle of all reality."[21] Personhood and communion are the twin foci of trinitarian understandings of God. A third theme is that the relations of the persons of the Trinity—among the persons and between the Trinity and the world—are marked by equality and mutuality. To argue, as many have, that the subordination of the Son to the Father is the theological basis for the subordination of women to men, or of any human group to another, is to promote the Arianist view that the Son was subordinate to the Father, a view which was condemned as heresy by the early church. Genuine communion implies equality and mutuality as its necessary conditions.

These themes are merely examples of feminist revisions of language and thought about God. In addition to criticizing the dominance of masculinist God language, feminists identify and emphasize long-neglected female imagery, and they reexamine traditional theological debates and formulations in view of feminist concerns. What emerges is a vision of God as dynamic, personal, immanently present in the world and in our salvation, donative, life-giving, and a paradigm for *shalom-producing* relations of mutual care and delight.

Jesus the Christ

The mystery of Jesus as the Christ is central to Christianity and to the reinterpretations of feminist theology. "A feminist theologian *must* question whether the historical man Jesus of Nazareth can be a role model for contemporary women, since feminist psychological liberation means exactly the struggle of women to free themselves from all male internalized norms and models."[22] Early in the contemporary women's movement, feminist theologians questioned the significance of a male savior figure: "Can a male savior help women?"[23] That Jesus was a male is not negotiable. But Mary Daly pointed out the effects for women of what she called "Christolotry" in the Christian tradition, even as she noted that Jesus was a free and nonpatriarchal man, and Dorothee Soelle warned of the political consequences of "Christofascism."[24] The startling rhetoric of these critics points to the *uses* of the Christ symbol in theological anthropology, ecclesiology, and ministerial theology to support political, social, and ecclesiastical patriarchy, as well as the sexist subordination of women at every level of Christian life, including family structure. Feminist theologians maintain that such uses are in fact a perversion of the meaning of Christ.

They demonstrate that the ancient traditions never emphasized the maleness of Jesus. Instead these were concerned to highlight Jesus' full humanity, as well as his divinity, in the conviction that "what was not assumed was not redeemed." These words of the church fathers implicitly undermined their own negative appraisals of women.[25] For the affirmation of Jesus' humanity entailed the goodness of the flesh and the material realm with which women were associated in the ancient world. The same affirmation, feminist theologians hold, was implied in the various christologies articulated throughout Christian tradition, as these maintained the full humanity of Jesus. It is a distortion of the tradition simultaneously to hold, as some theologies have, that women are not only naturally inferior or subordinate, but that men are superior because they share in Jesus' maleness. Moreover, feminist theologians not only demonstrate that an authentic Christology fully includes women who are baptized members of the Christian community; they have further shown that the earliest biblical traditions, when studied from a feminist perspective, show that Jesus himself treated women as fully equal and that the earliest Christian mission included the "equal discipleship" of women and men.[26] Ecclesial patriarchy, as a development in the later parts of the New Testament and then throughout Christian tradition, is an accommodation to culture that is a perversion of the original, countercultural equality of earliest Christianity. At this juncture, it should be noted, there is concern among feminist theologians not to blame patriarchy on Judaism, both since patriarchy is more ancient than Israelite religion and because such a stance could easily lead to anti-Judaism or antisemitism.[27]

Feminist thinkers have further argued, in detailed historical studies, that Jesus is positively depicted throughout the New Testament as the female figure of Wisdom, the divine Sophia of the Hebrew Bible. The Prologue of the Fourth Gospel portrays Jesus as incarnate Sophia, suggesting the reality of the female in God.[28] A similar Sophia-Christology, Elisabeth Schüssler Fiorenza shows, pervades the early Christian missionary movement.[29] Elizabeth Johnson affirms that "from Paul, who calls Jesus the wisdom of God (1 Cor. 1:24), to John who models Jesus and his long discourses upon Sophia, wisdom christology offers the possibility of affirming the significance of Jesus Christ and of confessing his divinity in a non-androcentric framework."[30] The naming of Christ as Wisdom or Sophia is an important aspect of feminist Christology, its critical edge subverting traditional male interpretations of the significance of Jesus.

Beyond the wisdom theme, Christian feminist theologians turn to the Gospel stories of the earthly Jesus, who is portrayed as reversing and overcoming gender stereotypes. "The New Testament does not transmit a single androcentric statement or sexist story of Jesus. . . ."[31] Also of importance is the belief in the risen, transcendent, and present Christ. While the human figure of Jesus is male (just as many aspects of his earthly humanity are similarly contingent and historically conditioned), in the victory of the resurrection, the risen Christ is understood to have transcended all the particularities and limitations of earthly existence in the new life of the resurrection. This life with God is a life and energy extended by the action of the Holy Spirit into the earthly community, even now, in its "already but not yet" life of discipleship.[32]

Womanist theology, a recent African-American development, stresses the centrality of Jesus rather than Christ for black women. Womanist theologians such as Jacquelyn Grant and Kelly Brown Douglas point out that the experience, both historical and contemporary, of black women struggling under the oppressions of race and class as well as sex, leads them to formulate the meaning of risen Christ not only as black but as a black woman who has enabled their survival and is their intimate friend, co-sufferer, and Lord who knows their troubles.[33]

Feminist Christology is therefore not separate from feminist reinterpretation of salvation, or soteriology. In this work, feminist theologians stress the importance of the unity of the person and work of Jesus Christ, linking his ministry and his message of the radical inclusivity of God's love and empowerment with the doctrines of Christ's incarnation, saving death, and resurrection. Then the incarnation of Jesus as the Christ is seen "from above," not only as the birth of God among us in the lowly form of the Christmas infant but as the taking on of a fully human life. The incarnation means that Jesus took on a wholly human history that can be understood, if not in its detail or particular psychology, in the central meaning of its story and pattern "from below,"—in the historicized faith narratives that are the Gospels. These stories suggest that Jesus died because of the way he lived, because he ran afoul of the religious and political powers that were threatened by the radical inclusivity of his message, perhaps even by its nonpatriarchal character,[34] and that he was sent to his death by human beings like us. Thus, avoiding the "divine child abuse" theme,[35] feminist theologians argue that the death of Jesus is "God's plan" only in the sense that God willed for Jesus to live a truly human history. The unfolding of that history meant that Jesus' message of God's inclusive love was not accepted by those in power. God did not determine Jesus' death; human beings did.

Finally, the resurrection and saving power of Jesus is understood in some feminist theology as the vindication of one whose life was lived out in commitment and fidelity both to God and to humankind. That is, Jesus is both model and representative precisely because of the all-inclusive character of his commitment and fidelity. Jesus' death was suffered, as his life was lived, in twofold solidarity with God and with people, especially with the marginalized: the women, the outcasts, the poor, the sinful, the lost. Jesus is the Christ in a solidarity that unites all those baptized in faith, all those actively committed to him in his solidarity with God and with humankind. Jesus is Christ in the church that is his Body, the gift of the Spirit who is the bond of unity, the Spirit given through the raising of the one who was faithful in this double solidarity to the end. It is confidence in the presence of Christ's Spirit that gives Christianity its unique hope in the eschatological future, and that gives women their hope in the church of the future.[36]

Christian Ethics

Since feminist theology arises out of women's experiences of oppression, and theorizes about God, humanity, and world with a view to changing personal consciousness and the social order, this theology "by definition . . . is at the same time ethics."[37] Feminist theology is part of a worldwide movement whose goal is a transformation of the social, cultural, ecclesial, and political orderings of life so that women and men might live together in mutual respect, care, and delight. It therefore rejects ethics as a sequestered category of Christian thought, insulated from other branches of theology. Feminist Christians enter debates typically associated with Christian ethics, including issues such as war and peace, domestic abuse, reproductive technology, bioethics, pornography, and social policy. They also reconsider foundational ethical matters such as moral reasoning, moral agency, the relation of public to private life, and norms of justice and love.[38]

Feminist understandings of *agency* are shaped by their vision of God. Protestantism typically depicts the divine-human relationship as a conflict over whose will shall prevail, the divine or the human. According to Beverly Harrison, nearly all the Protestant theological ethics from 1920 until the present bear "the stigma of this envisagement of God as all-controlling agent. The watchword for the Christian life and faith . . . remains 'obedience'—the giving over of self-control to another."[39] As an alternative to this "masculinist" view of agency feminist Christians view relations between God and humanity, among human beings, and between humanity and the natural environment in nonhierarchical, mutually dependent and interactive ways. For feminists such as LaCugna and Johnson who retain a trinitarian understanding of God, this relational view of agency is grounded in the communion of the divine persons. Others establish theological bases in relational imagery for God drawn from the Bible or tradition. The corresponding view of human agency is one of "co-capacity-in-relationship,"[40] which affirms moral agency, but within the context of an interdependent community of divine and human persons whose mutuality enables effective agency in the world. This emphasis also leads feminist ethicists to heightened awareness of the relational contexts of moral problems and of the ethical reasoning which is used to examine them.[41]

Some feminists agree that descriptively there are distinctively "feminine" and "masculine" affective, intellectual, and social characteristics. Ostensibly women more than men tend to be nurturant, relational, and intuitive, and men tend to be active, independent, and rational. Debates emerge about how to identify these characteristics, and how to determine the blend of genetic, hormonal, and social factors that cause these differences. The normative question is whether there *ought* to be an androgynous ideal that combines or transcends the best "feminine" and "masculine" virtues, or a dimorphic ideal which celebrates the "feminine" virtues alongside the "masculine" ones. Even as African Americans struggle between the "integrationist" ideal of Martin Luther King, Jr. and the "separationist" one of Malcolm X, so too many strategic differences for social reform will be shaped by whether the "difference" or the "sameness" is stressed as the normative ideal for moral character in relation to gender.

Feminist Christians usually call for a single ideal that integrates the best of what is typically meant by "feminine" and "masculine." Mary Ellen Ross holds as normative "the ideal of the moral agent striving toward justice, assisting and receiving the assistance of a deity. . . ."[42] Though she acknowledges the cultural and historical importance of different "feminine" and "masculine" traits, Beverly Harrison argues that at the ontic and moral levels feminist theory "must begin by rejecting the notion that there is any *fundamental* dimorphism in human nature/being."[43] Anne Carr likewise calls for a normative ideal that values both the traditional female characteristics "especially as these relate to the concerns of home and family, and the strengths associated with traditional male traits, particularly the values of autonomy and agency that women have not been encouraged to develop. . . ."[44] Differences are relevant especially for justice, and its demand for equal treatment, which must take differences between the sexes into account in applications to cases and rules.[45] When particular biological or historical circumstances create disadvantages for individuals and groups, then fairness demands "different" treatment to enable genuine equality. To this extent, feminist Christians affirm "difference," but the normative ideal is not a "two natures" ideal. Thus the ideal applies to men as well as to women.

Feminist ethics is critical of *dualisms* of all sorts: God/world, humanity/nature, men/women, soul/body, reason/emotion, and so forth. The two sides of these binary constructions of reality are traditionally asymmetrical, for the first element in each pair hierarchically rules the latter one, keeping it controlled within its subordinate place. In its most damaging forms, this dualistic worldview despises the second element in each pole by construing it as demonic or sinful: Thus women and women's bodies are seen as sinful, unholy, polluted. In place of this dualistic worldview, feminist ethics puts a multi-faceted, interactive, interdependent set of agencies and forces. It affirms the complexity and essential goodness of creation in all its parts, thereby avoiding the "demonizing" of women.

This critique of dualism shapes much of feminist ethics, but it has particular importance in challenging the "public/private" split that functions as an ideology to keep women in their (domestic) place and to isolate victims of domestic abuse from public help they might receive. In North America it is conservatively estimated that physical abuse and sexual abuse each involve as many as one in four women.[46] Legal, political, cultural, and economic structures unite in a vicious cycle to reinforce men's control over women's bodies. "Universal in its scope while variable in its expression, patriarchy is said to have controlled women's sexuality to men's advantage through institutions as diverse as prostitution, pornography, rape, sexual harassment, battering, foot-binding, suttee, purdah, clitoridectomy, witch-burning, and reproductive technology."[47] Feminist Christian revision of the relations between "public" and "private" spheres is a response to the call for justice and care in both these domains. Feminists show how sexism co-opted the split so that it ironically and tragically serves to isolate victims of domestic abuse from outside help and keep women in their economically and socially subordinated place.

According to the "public/private" ideology, women are "naturally" fitted for the "private" spheres of marriage, family, and friendship; men are "naturally" fitted for the "public" spheres of the marketplace, academy, and politics. *Agape*, understood as self-sacrificial love, then becomes the appropriate norm for women's action and character in the private sphere; justice, understood as receiving what one rightfully deserves, becomes the ethical norm for men's action and character in the public sphere. As *agape* is inappropriate to public life, so justice is inappropriate to private life. The family is then idealized as a haven in a heartless world; public life is viewed "realistically" as a harsh, competitive zone where self-assertion rather than self-sacrifice is appropriate, though this self-assertion is limited by justice and fair play. Many twentieth-century Protestant theologians advanced this understanding of private and social life, led by Reinhold Niebuhr, who made it a part of his theological anthropology.

In feminist Christian ethics the challenge to this influential view of ethical norms and their applications to private and public life began with Valerie Saiving's 1960 essay.[48] Saiving criticized the theological anthropology underlying the emphasis on sin as self-assertion and love as self-sacrifice, arguing that while this accurately depicts men's experience it neglects and harms women, who struggle to resist self-abnegation and excessive dependence upon others and must learn to assert themselves. Twenty years later, Barbara Hilkert Andolsen expanded Saiving's analysis by showing how the public/private split exacerbates the problems of an ethic centered on agapic self-sacrifice. She holds that too often women have found that in practice "Christian self-sacrifice means the sacrifice of women for the sake of men. . . . Men have espoused an ethic which they did not practice; women have practiced it to their own detriment."[49] She shows the way this Niebuhrian view prevents Christian love from becoming a transformative social force by limiting it to "private" life. Andolsen also points to Catholic theological traditions that view agapic love as mutuality, rather than unilateral self-sacrifice, and suggests that a revised understanding of love be grounded in a doctrine of the Trinity.

By insisting on the "public" nature of "private" life, feminist Christians reject the split that many place between these domains. They also oppose gender-based role assignments that ascribe exclusively private roles to women and public ones to men. They call instead for men to become more involved in domestic activities, and for women to develop gifts and interests that can be exercised in the spheres of the marketplace, academy, law, and politics. Mary Stewart Van Leeuwen calls for mutual transformations so that more justice will be practiced in "private" spheres, and more love and care in "public" ones.[50] Self-sacrifice may be necessary as a means to mutuality and justice, but it is not the goal of Christian love. This goal is mutual care, respect, and delight—a participation in the divine life and a cooperation with God's activities in the world.

In their work to break the barriers erected by the public/private split, some feminists implicitly accepted the devaluation of domestic life perpetrated by patriarchal economic and social systems. Antifeminists accordingly accused feminists of neglecting the family and marriage, and simplistically blamed feminists for all major ills of society. But, as this volume illustrates, feminists are reevaluating marriage and family life and celebrating maternal powers and functions even as they continue to work for expanded opportunities for women outside their traditional domestic roles.[51] Feminist Christians also call on men to yield economic and social power to women, to oppose the ways in which the gender system constricts their relationships and experiences, and to participate more fully in the responsibilities of marriage and family life.

Feminist Christians call the church to be both example and agent in the process of societal transformation. By affirming and celebrating women's gifts and leadership as pastors, priests, and bishops, the church can model the mutuality and equality between women and men conferred in baptism. Inclusive language in the liturgy and hymnody of the church illumine the depths and riches of Christian speech about God and acknowledge the female in God and in ourselves. The church must serve the larger mission of God in this world. That mission is the inauguration of God's *shalom*, the blessed condition in which all relations—between God and humanity, among human beings, between humanity and creation—are marked by justice, flourishing, and delight.[52] The subordination and oppression of women as well as the patriarchal systems that reinforce them are blatant violations of God's *shalom*. The church, as harbinger of the eschatological fulfillment of God's promised *shalom*, is called to bear witness to God's redemptive mission by its example and action.[53]

This sketch of feminist Christian thought samples only a few methodological and substantive themes. The intellectual vitality of feminist Christianity is born of moral and religious passion springing from the depths of human experience. As in any vital intellectual tradition there is diversity of opinion and debate; there is self-criticism as well as prophetic critique of patriarchal institutions and theory. The diversity finds its unifying center not in one or another strategy or dogma but rather in the conviction that the patriarchal structures that harm women are part of a sinful, fallen world which God wills to redeem, and in the aspiration that feminist theology become part of God's redemptive energies which will one day renew heaven and earth and bring about *shalom* in its fullness.[54]

NOTES

1. See Introduction to *Weaving the Visions: New Patterns in Feminist Spirituality*, ed. Judith Plaskow and Carol P. Christ (San Francisco: Harper & Row, 1989), 6–7.

2. See, for example, Elizabeth Achtemeier, "Female Language for God: Should the Church Adopt It?" in *The Hermeneutical Quest*, ed. Donald G. Miller (Allison Park, Pa: Pickwick Publications, 1986), 97–114.

3. See, for example, Alison M. Jaggar, *Feminist Politics and Human Nature* (Totowa, N.J.: Rowman & Allanheld, 1983); Rosemarie Tong, *Feminist Thought: A Comprehensive Introduction* (Boulder, Colo.: Westview Press, 1989); and Kathy E. Ferguson, *The Man Question: Visions of Subjectivity in Feminist Theory* (Berkeley, Calif.: University of California Press, 1993) for introductions to theoretical differences among secular feminists. See Rosemary Radford Ruether, *Sexism and God-Talk: Toward a Feminist Theology* (Boston: Beacon Press, 1983), 214–34; and *After Eden: Facing the Challenge of Gender Reconciliation*, ed. Mary Stewart Van Leeuwen, et al. (Grand Rapids: Wm. B. Eerdmans Publishing Co., 1993), 19–69 for a thematic and historical overview of versions of feminism with special reference to Christian concerns.

4. See Tong, *Feminist Thought*, and Plaskow and Christ, eds., *Weaving the Visions*, 6–7, where the editors note a distinction drawn in their earlier volume, *Womanspirit Rising* (ed. Carol P. Christ and Judith Plaskow [San Francisco: Harper & Row, 1979]), between reformist and revolutionary Jewish and Christian feminists as dualistic, reifying, and heierarchical.

5. See Delores S. Williams, *Sisters in the Wilderness: The Challenge of Womanist God-Talk* (Maryknoll, N.Y.: Orbis Books, 1993); Jacquelyn Grant, *White Women's Christ and Black Women's Jesus: Feminist Christology and Womanist Response* (Atlanta: Scholars Press, 1989); Susan Thistlethwaite, *Sex, Race, and God: Christian Feminism in Black and White* (New York: Crossroad, 1989); Mark K. Taylor, *Remembering Esperanza: A Cultural-Political Theology For North American Praxis* (Maryknoll, N.Y.: Orbis Books, 1990); Chung Hyun Kyung, *Struggle to be the Sun Again: Introducing Asian Women's Theology* (Maryknoll, N.Y.: Orbis Books, 1990); Ada Maria Isasi-Diaz and Yolanda Tarango, *Hispanic Women's Prophetic Voice in the Church* (San Francisco: Harper & Row, 1988); and Maria Pilar Aquino, *Our Cry For Life: Feminist Theology From Latin America* (Maryknoll, N.Y.: Orbis Books, 1993).

6. The prevalence of father-absence in African-American communities leads Diane Tennis to oppose feminist proposals to remove father imagery from Christian worship, on the ground that positive father imagery in worship is needed to help inspire black males to become more caring and present as fathers (*Is God the Only Reliable Father?* [Philadelphia: Westminster Press, 1985]).

7. See Wendy Kaminer, "Feminism's Identity Crisis," *The Atlantic Monthly* 272: 4 (October 1993): 51–68; and the introduction in Judith Plaskow and Carol P. Christ's *Weaving the Visions*, esp. 3–8, as well as other chapters in this volume.

8. In addition to other chapters in this book, see Bonnie J. Miller-McLemore, *"Also A Mother": Work and Family As Theological Dilemma* (Nashville: Abingdon Press, 1994); Christine E. Gudorf, "Parenting, Mutual Love, and Sacrifice," in *Women's Consciousness, Women's Conscience: A Reader in Feminist Ethics*, ed. Barbara Hilkert Andolsen, Christine E. Gudorf, and Mary D. Pellauer (Minneapolis: Winston Press, 1985), 175–91; Pamela D. Couture, *Blessed Are the Poor? Women's Poverty, Family Policy, and Practical Theology* (Nashville: Abingdon Press, 1991); Mary Stewart Van Leeuwen, *Gender and Grace: Love, Work and Parenting in a Changing World* (Downers Grove, Ill.: InterVarsity Press, 1990); and *After Eden*, esp. 389–451, 503–33. See also Sara Ruddick, *Maternal Thinking: Toward a Politics of Peace* (New York: Ballantine Books, 1989); and Susan M. Okin, *Gender, Justice, and the Family* (New York: Basic Books, 1989).

9. These influences are seen in (1) increasing percentages of women seminary students, pastors, and church leaders, (2) inclusive language in biblical translations, liturgies, and educational settings, (3) numerous journals and a growing number of books devoted to feminist Christianity, (4) greater integration of feminist concerns by publishers of books and journals who traditionally shaped Christian teaching and scholarship, (5) women's studies and gender studies courses and concentrations in colleges and graduate schools with strong religious interests, (6) greater awareness of and organized resistance to sexual and domestic abuse. The changes in these areas over the past twenty years are astonishing.

10. See, for example, Elizabeth K. Minnich, *Transforming Knowledge* (Philadelphia: Temple University Press, 1990).

11. See note 5, above.

12. Andrea Dworkin, *Woman Hating* (New York: E. P. Dutton & Co., 1974), 24, as cited by Beverly Wildung Harrison, "Feminist Social Ethics: Social Policy and the Practice of the Churches," in *Making the Connections: Essays in Feminist Social Ethics*, ed. Carol S. Robb (Boston: Beacon Press, 1985), 89.

13. Judith Plaskow, *Sex, Sin and Grace: Women's Experience and the Theologies of Reinhold Niebuhr and Paul Tillich* (Lanham, Md.: University Press of America, 1980); and Valerie Saiving Goldstein, "The Human Situation: A Feminine View," *Journal of Religion* (April, 1960): 100–112.

14. Sallie McFague, *Metaphorical Theology: Models of God in Religious Language* (Philadelphia: Fortress Press, 1982), esp. the last chapter.

15. Marchiene Vroon Rienstra, *Swallow's Nest: A Feminine Reading of the Psalms* (Grand Rapids, Mich.: Wm. B. Eerdmans Publishing Co.; New York: Friendship Press; and Leominster, Eng.: Gracewing, 1992), 194.

16. Anne E. Carr, *Transforming Grace* (San Francisco: Harper & Row, 1988), 134.

17. See *Speaking the Christian God: The Holy Trinity and the Challenge of Feminism*, ed. Alvin F. Kimel, Jr. (Grand Rapids, Mich.: Wm. B. Eerdmans Publishing Co. and Leominster, Eng: Gracewing, 1992) for a sampling of the major challenges by Christians who are opposed to feminist revisions of God-language.

18. McFague, *Metaphorical Theology*, 147–48; idem. *Models of God: Theology for an Ecological, Nuclear Age* (Philadelphia: Fortress Press, 1987), 13. See also Ruether, *Sexism and God-Talk*, 53, and Carr, *Transforming Grace*, 134–44.

19. Elizabeth A. Johnson, *She Who Is: The Mystery of God in Feminist Theological Discourse* (New York: Crossroad, 1992); and Catherine Mowry LaCugna, *God For Us: The Trinity and Christian Life* (San Francisco: Harper Collins, 1991).

20. Johnson, *She Who Is*, 192.

21. Catherine Mowry LaCugna, "God in Communion With Us: The Trinity," in *Freeing Theology: The Essentials of Theology in Feminist Perspective*, ed. Catherine Mowry LaCugna (San Francisco: HarperCollins, 1993), 86–87.

22. Elisabeth Schüssler Fiorenza, "Toward a Feminist Biblical Hermeneutic," in *The Challenge of Liberation Theology*, ed. Brian Mahan and L. Dale Richesin (Maryknoll, N.Y.: Orbis Books, 1981), 107 (emphasis ours).

23. Ruether, *Sexism and God-Talk*, 125; see also her *To Change the World: Christology and Cultural Criticism* (New York: Crossroad, 1981).

24. Mary Daly, *Beyond God the Father* (Boston: Beacon Press, 1973), 69–81, 114–24; Dorothee Soelle, cited in Tom Driver, *Christ in a Changing World* (New York: Crossroad, 1981), 3.

25. See Patricia Wilson-Kastner, *Faith, Feminism, and the Christ* (Philadelphia: Fortress Press, 1983).

26. See Elisabeth Schüssler Fiorenza, *In Memory of Her: A Feminist Theological Reconstruction of Christian Origins* (New York: Crossroad, 1983).

27. See Ruether, *To Change the World*, 31–44, and Rabbi Phillip Segal, "Elements of Male Chauvinism in Classical Halakhah," *Judaism: A Quarterly Journal of Jewish Life and Thought* 24 (spring 1975): 226–44.

28. Adela Yarbro Collins, "New Testament Perspectives: The Gospel of John," *Journal for the Study of the Old Testament* 22:1 (1982): 47–53.

29. Fiorenza, *In Memory of Her*, 133ff.

30. Elizabeth A. Johnson, *Consider Jesus* (New York: Crossroad, 1990), 112; idem. "Redeeming the Name of Christ," in LaCugna, ed., *Freeing Theology*, 115–37; see also her *She Who Is*.

31. Elisabeth Schüssler Fiorenza, "Feminist Theology as Critical Liberation Theology," *Theological Studies* 36:4 (1975): 605–26.

32. Carr, *Transforming Grace*, 181.

33. See Jacquelyn Grant, *White Women's Christ and Black Women's Jesus: Feminist Christology and Womanist Response* (Atlanta: Scholars Press, 1989); and Kelly Brown Douglas, *The Black Christ* (Maryknoll, N.Y.: Orbis Books, 1994); idem. " 'Come to My Help, Lord, For I'm in Trouble': Womanist Jesus and the Mutual Struggle for Liberation," *Reconstructing the Christ Symbol: Essays in Feminist Christology*, ed. Maryanne Stevens (Mahwah, N.J.: Paulist Press, 1993), 54–71.

34. Bernard Cooke, "Non-Patriarchal Salvation," *Horizons* 10:1 (1983): 22–31.

35. See *Christianity, Patriarchy, and Abuse: A Feminist Critique*, eds. Joanne Carlson Brown and Carole R. Bohn (New York: Pilgrim Press, 1989).

36. Carr, *Transforming Grace*, 188.

37. Lisa Sowle Cahill, "Feminism and Christian Ethics," in *Freeing Theology*, 213.
38. See Harrison, *Making the Connections*, and *Women's Consciousness, Women's Conscience: A Reader in Feminist Ethics*, ed. Barbara Hilkert Andolsen, Christine E. Gudorf, and Mary D. Pellauer (San Francisco: Harper & Row, 1987).
39. Harrison, *Making the Connections*, 36.
40. Ibid.
41. See Lisa Sowle Cahill, "Feminism and Christian Ethics," in *Freeing Theology*, 218–20.
42. Mary Ellen Ross, "Feminism and the Problem of Moral Character," *Journal of Feminist Studies in Religion* 5:2 (fall 1989): 48.
43. Harrison, *Making the Connections*, 29.
44. Carr, *Transforming Grace*, 206.
45. See Jean Bethke Elshtain, *Public Man, Private Woman: Women in Social and Political Thought* (Princeton, N.J.: Princeton University Press, 1980); and Elizabeth H. Wolgast, *Equality and the Rights of Women* (Ithaca, N.Y.: Cornell University Press, 1980).
46. Van Leeuwen, et al., *After Eden*, 411.
47. Ibid, 393.
48. Goldstein, "The Human Situation."
49. Barbara Hilkert Andolsen, "Agape in Feminist Ethics," *Journal of Religious Ethics* 9 (spring 1981): 75.
50. See her "Private versus Public Life," and "Family Justice and Societal Nurturance," in *After Eden*, 389–451, and her *Gender and Grace*.
51. See also Anne E. Carr and Elisabeth Schüssler Fiorenza, eds. *Motherhood: Experience, Institution, Theology, Concilium* 206 (Edinburgh: T.& T. Clark, 1989).
52. Nicholas Wolterstorff, *Until Justice and Peace Embrace* (Grand Rapids, Mich.: Wm. B. Eerdmans Publishing Co., 1983), 69–70; see also Letty M. Russell, *Human Liberation in a Feminist Perspective: A Theology* (Philadelphia: Westminster Press, 1974), 106–13; Douglas J. Schuurman, *Creation, Eschaton, and Ethics: The Ethnical Significance of the Creation-Eschaton Relation in the Thought of Emil Brunner and Jürgen Moltmann* (New York: Peter Lang, 1991), 1–12, 149–74.
53. See Ruether, *Sexism and God-Talk*, 193; idem. *WomenChurch: Theology and Practice of Feminist Liturgical Communities* (San Francisco: Harper & Row, 1985); Letty M. Russell, *Church in the Round: Feminist Interpretation of the Church* (Louisville, Ky.: Westminster/John Knox Press, 1993); and Mary E. Hines, "Community For Liberation: Church," in *Freeing Theology*, 161–84.
54. Special thanks to Barbara Pitkin, St. Olaf College, for helpful suggestions on an early draft of this chapter.

2

Re-Inventing the Ties that Bind

Feminism and the Family at the
Close of the Twentieth Century

MARY STEWART VAN LEEUWEN

As we have acknowledged in the introduction to this volume, the
terms *religion, feminism,* and *family* are subject to various uses, and
as topics are rarely dealt with together. Hence our approach has been to
simplify matters by dividing the terms, offering first an overview of religion and feminism, and now of feminism and the family. I begin with a
working definition of feminism, then describe the shift in feminist theorizing (beginning in the late 1970s) from an emphasis on the negative
aspects of family life to a concern for retrieving and preserving its positive features. I then detail some ways feminist theorizing in general has
affected the conduct of family studies research and family policy debate.
Finally, I review the current feminist debate on the shape of the family
and draw some conclusions in light of that debate.

A Working
Definition of Feminism

An adequate definition of contemporary feminism should acknowledge both the individual and institutional aspects of distorted gender
relations. It should also acknowledge the dialectical tension between
"sameness" and "difference"—that is, between feminist views that stress
the common humanness of women and men while downplaying the
existence and origin of any differences, and those that prefer to do the
opposite. By these criteria, I will define a feminist as a person of either
sex who works to bring about social, economic, and political justice
between women and men in a given society. Such work is motivated by
a conviction that the devaluation of women and their activities is
wrong, and that the systematic disempowering of women in relation to
men is unjust. Feminist activity thus focuses on the situation and needs
of women, even though it may eventually benefit people of both sexes.
It assumes that women and men share a common humanity but also

that their different experiences (whatever their origin) must be taken into account.[1]

Given the development of feminist theory over the past thirty years, most feminists would probably agree with the general thrust of this definition while differing on the parts of it they might emphasize. It is less easy, however, to arrive at a working definition of *family*, for while there is now a rich literature on the diverse uses of the term feminism,[2] second-wave feminists have until recently dealt with the family largely by negation.[3] Why has this been so, and when and why did this focus begin to shift?

From Opposition to a More Nuanced Analysis of the Family

Historians often date the beginning of the second wave of American feminism from the 1963 publication of Betty Friedan's *The Feminine Mystique*, a volume that argued for women's need to enter the public sphere in order to exercise the autonomy and rationality which classic liberalism sees as the essence of true personhood.[4] From then until the late 1970s, American feminists were more concerned to expose the disadvantages to women of the culturally hegemonic, patriarchal nuclear family than they were to sift wheat from chaff in their analysis of family relations. A prominent goal was the exposure of the degree to which "normal" family life collaborated with legal, economic, religious, and cultural constraints to keep women from exercising the autonomy and opportunities for self-development accorded to men.[5]

From about 1975 on, however, there has been a steady growth of feminist scholarship *about*, rather than *against*, the family.[6] Several factors have contributed to this shift. First, however incomplete they may remain, legislative gains for women in both public and private life (for example, the Equal Employment Opportunity and the Title IX Educational Amendments Acts of 1972, the Equal Credit Opportunity Act of 1974, and the Pregnancy Disability Act of 1978) have led to a decreased sense of victimization and a cautious willingness to look for strengths as well as weaknesses in various social institutions, including the family.

A second factor has been the emergence of nonwestern feminism and African-American womanism, both of which have challenged the western, middle-class feminist assumption that the family is primarily a locus of oppression for women. For racially and economically marginalized groups, these critics argue, the family is just as often a source of cooperative resistance to forces that would fragment such groups even further.[7]

Third, there has been a growing disenchantment with liberal political theory as a fully adequate model for the reform of gender relations. Within the terms dictated by modernity, liberalism's stress on human rationality, autonomy, and individual rights provided an essential foundation for women's entry into the public spheres of the academy, marketplace, and political forum. But liberalism's failure to recognize the importance of nurturant activities, interpersonal connection, and group identity has led even some of its chief beneficiaries—middle-class professional women—to question its androcentric assumptions about what is needed for full human flourishing. Ironically, the success some women have had penetrating institutions shaped by the liberal, masculine ideals of individualism, competition, and emotional containment has contributed to their disenchantment with those ideals.[8] The flip side of this growing skepticism about life in the public realm as a panacea for women's discontent is the recognition that male success in modern public life has depended on the invisible support of wives who relieved their husbands of myriad domestic worries, large and small. Because husbands rarely reciprocate such support when their wives enter the public realm, middle-class women now face the dilemma that their working-class sisters have always had to cope with—namely, how to find enough time to do justice to the needs of family and household over and above the demands of a forty-hour waged work week.[9]

A final factor helping to shift the terms of debate about the family has been a renewed appreciation for the developmental needs of children and the (admittedly ambiguous) satisfactions of rearing them. Part of this is attributable to the no-fault divorce revolution: Custody battles have given parents a deeper awareness of the emotional bonds they share with their offspring, and research concerning the effects of divorce on children has begun to educate all adults, whether parenting or not, about the advantages to children of a stable, as well as a nurturing and economically viable, home environment.[10] Indeed, a 1988 review of the relevant literature included the following observation:

> Most feminists and conservatives would agree on a "bottom line" of childrearing—that infants and young children need constant, committed devotion from a stable cast of adults. Nor does there appear to be an irremediable polarization over how such basic children's needs are to be met. The right prefers the full-time presence of the biological mother but is not implacably opposed to at least a limited array of alternative arrangements. Some feminists are deeply opposed to the institution of full-time motherhood under conditions of patriarchy. Others . . . celebrate the possibility of the reconsecration of mothering in a domestic setting that may

or may not involve shared parenting. Some feminist theories
appear to prefer dual, heterosexual parenting; others reject or do
not require such arrangements.[11]

The above quotation suggests that feminists and conservatives may
yet be able to agree on a middle ground regarding the shape of family
life and the kind of public policies that should support it. But it also
confirms that the concept of family remains a matter of contested terrain. While less likely than they were thirty years ago to dismiss it as a
tool of patriarchal capitalism, feminist theoreticians still differ as to
whether the family can be reformed within the two-parent heterosexual
model, or whether it should be pluralized to include any adult or combination of adults committed to raising one or more children in a stable
household. I will return to a comparison of these alternatives later. To
set the context, however, it will help first to understand some ways in
which feminist theorizing has already altered the terms of family
research and, by extension, family policy debate.[12]

The Impact of Feminism on
Family Research and Family Policy Debate

Family as Both Socially Constructed
and Actively Negotiated

To begin with, feminists have pushed both scholars and public policy specialists to recognize the degree to which family forms are socially
and historically constructed. In other words, they have challenged the
assumption that the modern nuclear family, with its pattern of breadwinner husband and full-time wife and mother, is the only legitimate
family form to be aspired to in all times and places, either for biological
or social-functional reasons. Such an assumption not only ignores the
variety of successful household forms that have existed across time and
space; it also perpetuates male dominance, given the isolation and economic dependence that the modern nuclear family imposes on wives
and mothers, and given the modern legal apparatus that has long subsumed wives and children under the authority of male "heads of households."[13]

At the same time, there has been a shift in feminist theorizing away
from a pure "politics of victimization" in the analysis of family life.
Rather than simply concentrating on patterns of domination and con-
straint, feminists during the 1980s began to examine women's resistance to, and active negotiation of, the structures that confine them.[14]
This has been an important shift for two reasons. First of all, it reaffirms

the important truth that women can and do exercise self-promoting agency even within the constraints of patriarchal systems. In philosopher Rosemarie Tong's words, "Although few women have been entirely able to control the course of their own destinies, labeling most women *total* victims places an unfair burden on their shoulders. It is, in fact, to admit defeat [for the feminist cause]. For how could *total* victims ever rise up and demand equality?"[15]

Acknowledging the importance of women's agency has also taught middle-class, educated feminists to be less judgmental about the choices made by other women. For example, when Irish women in the late 1980s publicly protested the proposed liberalization of their country's divorce laws by carrying placards that read "A Woman Who Votes for Divorce Is Like a Turkey Who Votes for Christmas," feminists were less likely to perceive them as victims of false consciousness than as women who were actively protecting what they saw as the terms of a cultural bargain: men's lifelong economic support in return for women's domestic services.[16] Thus there is now a more nuanced trade-off between an analysis of the family as a force that can oppress women and a recognition of women's agency within it.

Relativizing the Family
as a Unit of Analysis

A second way feminists have altered the terms of family research and policy debate is by reversing the standard question—"What do women do for the family?"—to ask instead, "What does the family do to women?" In other words, rather than taking for granted "the family" as the basic unit of analysis, feminists have insisted on using gender—and, increasingly, generation, ethnicity, class, and sexual orientation—as analytic categories.[17]

One reason for this shift has been a desire to examine the distribution of power within the family. This has not been an easy agenda to promote, either among academics or agents of public policy, because modern industrial society has functioned according to the fiction that power is irrelevant to family life, the nuclear family being the designated "haven in a heartless world" whose "natural affectional bonds" compensate for the negative effects of individualism and competition in the wider society. But the success of feminist efforts is shown in the accumulation of books, agencies, and legislation aimed at exposing and overcoming domestic violence (physical, sexual, and psychological) and the economic vulnerability of women and children, especially in wake of divorce. In all of this, sociologist Barrie Thorne notes,

"Feminists have rescued gender, and gender relations, from the realm of the taken-for-granted and made them problematic."[18]

Feminists have found additional ways of moving "beneath and around" the family as a unit of analysis, including the examination of experiences such as kinship, intimacy, and domestic sharing that "weave ambiguously throughout the notion of 'family.'"[19] As early as 1966, Juliet Mitchell proposed that the concept of family be divided into its constituent functions of sexuality, production, reproduction, and the socialization of children, not all of which are equally central to family life in all times and places.[20] This has gradually led to an emphasis on the modern family as the invisible and undervalued locus of "social reproduction," that is, of "the activities and attitudes, behaviors and emotions, responsibilities and relationships directly involved in the maintenance of family life on a daily basis, and inter-generationally."[21] Not surprisingly, the activities of social reproduction—the preparation of food; the maintenance of shelter and clothing; the physical and emotional care of family members throughout the life cycle; the expression of sexuality—turn out to be differently organized by class, ethnicity, and historical period, with differential involvement of other institutions such as the state, the market, the church, the school system, and the community. All of this, feminists point out, renders problematic the attempt to essentialize a given family structure for all times and places.[22]

De-Gendering the Public/Private Dichotomy

Even so, in modern industrial society the activities of social reproduction have been consistently labelled the "natural" domain of women, with love as the taken-for-granted coin of the realm. As a result, almost all feminists are adamant about one issue: If the family is to be redeemed in any form which approximates its modern nuclear version, it will require a radical "degendering" of public and private life, such that the public domain ceases to be male, individualist, and strictly rights-oriented while remaining parasitic on women's invisible labor of love in the private sphere of social reproduction. Historian Stephanie Coontz believes that American society is not yet prepared for such a change, despite its grudging acceptance of women's entry into the public sphere. She points out that when commentators bemoan the collapse of family values, they usually mean the taken-for-granted *female* duties associated with the doctrine of separate spheres for men and women:

> The crisis of commitment in America is usually seen as a problem associated with *women's* changing roles, because women's family functions have historically mediated the worst effects of competition and individualism in the larger society. Most people who talk about balancing private advancement and individual rights with "nurturance, mutual support, and long-term commitment" do not envision any serious rethinking of the individualistic, antisocial tendencies in our society, nor any ways of broadening our sources of nurturance and mutual assistance. Instead, they seek ways— sometimes through repression, sometimes through reform—of rebuilding a family in which women can continue to compensate for, rather than challenge, the individualism in our larger economy and polity. . . . American individualism [continues to be built on] the subordination of women's individuality.[23]

Sociologist Judith Stacey concurs with Coonz's observation. She also finds it odd and shortsighted that conservatives blame *women* for abandoning domesticity, since there is plenty of evidence that even after entering into full-time waged employment, it is women who continue to carry most of the responsibility for child- and eldercare, and for sustaining kinship ties within families. So much is this the case that according to the research of sociologist Arlie Hochschild, wives in paid, full-time positions work the domestic equivalent of a full month of twenty-four-hour days per year more than their husbands.[24] Stacey adds that women have "amply demonstrated [their] continuing commitment to kin ties." Consequently, she concludes, "If there is a family crisis [in America], it is a male family crisis."[25]

The Recovery of Nurturing

Finally, although insisting that public life cease to take for granted women's nurturing work, most contemporary feminists do not want to dismiss nurturing out of hand. They aim rather to make its nature and ambiguities more visible, to make it an experience in which more people consistently share, and to restructure society so that the activities and values of nurturing—too long reduced to a domestic "revitalization" function that keeps competitive, capitalist society going—are the ends, and not just the servants, of public life.

Prior to the 1980s, feminists concentrated on challenging the ideology (or in Adrienne Rich's terms the "institution") of motherhood which, they argued, had too frequently functioned as an instrument of patriarchal oppression. The problem as they saw it was not the experience of motherhood *per se*, but the fact that women mothered "when, where, and how *men* want[ed] them to."[26] Hence feminist writings stressed the need for *women* to choose not only whether to become mothers but also under what circumstances. Some emphasized the right of mothers not to be swallowed up entirely by mothering, but to have equal access with men to economic, social, and cultural life in the larger society. Others challenged the virtual male monopoly of obstetrics and gynecology, the daily separation of fathers from their children (and hence the functional equation of "parenting" with "mothering"), and the lack of adequate (and adequately funded) daycare for children of working parents.[27]

But having advanced a critique of the institution of motherhood and seen some reforms start to follow, feminists in the late 1970s began to examine the actual experience of mothering more closely. It was not enough, Adrienne Rich pointed out, for certain radical feminists to dismiss mothering without envisaging its potential "in a wholly different political and emotional context."[28] What would mothering be like, she asked, in a situation where patriarchal psychoanalysts and pediatricians no longer undermined women's confidence by blaming them for whatever went wrong in their children's lives? What might mothering become in a situation where men no longer demanded sons for the wrong reasons, "as heirs, field-hands, cannon-fodder, feeders of machinery, images and extensions of themselves?"[29]

Part of the answer came in a spate of books, beginning in the early 1980s, devoted to analyzing what have come to be known as women's and/or maternal ways of thinking, interacting, and making moral choices.[30] With regard to thinking, the writers of these volumes both affirmed and expanded the agenda of the postmodern philosophy of science. That is, they rejected the artificial separation of reason from emotion and from personal and ideological commitments, and demonstrated the extent to which women, more often than men, consciously let all of these function simultaneously in their cognitive activities.[31] With regard to social interaction, they documented the extent to which women aim for cooperation and the preservation of human networks, while men more often strive to maintain hierarchies marked by interpersonal competition.[32] And with regard to morality, they rejected the mainstream (largely male) ethical assumption that adequate moral decisions are always based on abstract, universal principles, and never on particular commitments to actual people, such as one's own children, other kin, and friends.[33]

Most writers in these areas are agnostic as to the source of any differences between women's and men's cognitive, social, and moral styles. They are, after all, only *average* differences, which makes it hard for either feminists or antifeminists to essentialize them. Thus there are men whose cognitive, social, or moral style is more like the average woman's and women whose style is more like the average man's.[34] Moreover, these differences are significantly qualified by race and ethnicity, as Deborah Tannen (for example) has shown in her comparison of conversational patterns between men and women, but also among different cultural groups.[35] All of this suggests that such differences as do exist are more the result of cultural construction than of some biological or metaphysical essence distinguishing women from men.

Nevertheless, some critics remain nervous about the gradual turn from "feminist" to "feminine" ethics. By this they mean the switch in theoretical focus from the elimination of patriarchal domination and the attainment of justice for women to the search for women's unique moral voice with its focus on care, compassion, and communication.[36] At worst, they fear, this change in focus will provide an excuse for hegemonic males to reassign women to the home front, on the grounds that only they have the right mix of skills to socialize children and maintain family, kin, and community networks. Alternately, it might result in women's being drawn into a "compassion trap," whereby they are pressured to add public nurturing tasks to their already demanding domestic responsibilities. Sociologist Miriam Johnson points out that

> there is a danger for women in embracing maternal thinking if it means feeling that we must take care of everybody else in the world besides ourselves. [This] could be interpreted as calling upon women to mother not only children, but also everybody else on earth and the earth itself. Surely there is a danger here of women becoming careworn with caretaking, while men continue to be cared for. Many women feel over-burdened with caretaking already, especially poor women.[37]

Mention of this concern returns us to the question I promised to consider earlier—namely, the disputed fate of the family in contemporary feminist thought. Is motherhood to be evacuated, at least until men learn some necessary lessons in distributive gender justice? Can the heterosexual, two-parent family be reformed without such a radical interim step? Or should society begin to acknowledge and support a plurality of family forms in which children might be successfully raised? We close this chapter with a review and assessment of these alternatives.

Should Motherhood Be Evacuated?

In spite of the distinction between motherhood as institution and experience, some feminists remain unconvinced that there is a safe form of motherhood that women can embrace—that is, one that does not

make them unacceptably vulnerable and limited in the options they can
pursue. Radical lesbian feminist Jeffner Allen recommended in the early
1980s that women "evacuate" motherhood for the foreseeable future, in
order to concentrate on the power *not* to have children, rather than on
the power to produce them. Defining motherhood as "men's appropriation of women's bodies as a resource to reproduce patriarchy," Allen
proposed the moratorium period in order to develop "new modes of
thought and existence," by and for women.[38] Later in the decade
philosopher Rosemarie Tong added that

> were females also to decide not to engage in *social* mothering—that
> is, nurturing, nursing, consoling, counseling, teaching, and tend-
> ing the old and young, the sick and the disturbed, the homeless
> and the disadvantaged—then not only women's but also men's
> ways of thinking and acting would be fundamentally altered.[39]

Tong concedes that such a walk-out scenario conjures up "images of
old and young people left alone, of sick and disturbed people left suffering, of homeless and disadvantaged people left cold and hungry."
And yet, she reluctantly concludes, "I suspect that unless women stop
mothering, men will never learn how to mother."[40] Like the Athenian
and Spartan women in Aristophanes's *Lysistrata*, who contrived to deny
their husbands sexual relations until they stopped fighting with each
other, some feminists have been ready to shelve whatever biological
urges they must in order to achieve more just gender relations.

Should Family Structure
Be Pluralized?

However, such voices do not represent the majority of women—
feminist or otherwise—in the early 1990s. With the progressive de-
stigmatization of divorce and out-of-wedlock births, a growing number
of women in all social classes have opted simply to raise children outside of marriage. One study of American Census Bureau data showed
that births by never-married women aged 18 to 44 jumped from 15
percent of all births in 1982 to 24 percent in 1992. Although most of
that increase was among African-American women and women (across
all ethnic groups) who had not completed high school, single motherhood among never-married women holding professional or managerial
jobs also went from 3.1 to 8.2 percent in the same period. Moreover,
fertility rates among never-married women increased most among those
in their thirties, suggesting that some women were having children outside marriage because their jobs and education gave them the economic

security to accommodate the constraints of the biological clock without the additional risk of dealing with a husband whose views might turn out to be too traditionalist, or whose commitment too unreliable.[41]

I noted earlier, however, that a consensus seems to be emerging across the political and feminist spectrum regarding the developmental needs of children. Family disruption and re-configuration are less frequently defended as triumphs for the cause of diversity. There is a growing recognition that, other things being equal, children thrive best in economically secure households with a reliable cast of adults exercising stable authority structures and nurturant emotional bonds.[42] But the question now arises: Must moral and public policy support be given only to stable households whose "cast of adults" is composed of a heterosexual couple? What about the single father or mother who shares a household with his or her child's grandparents? What about monogamous lesbian or gay couples with adopted children, or the single lesbian mother who can count on the long-term involvement of same-sex friends?[43] In other words, does "good enough" parenting generally require only an optimal *number* of long-term, committed adults, or do children of both sexes need sustained interaction with adults of both sexes for optimal cognitive, emotional, and gender-identity development?

Those feminists who reject the principled evacuation of motherhood tend to be strong supporters of the pluralization option. "In the post-modern period," writes Judith Stacey, "a truly democratic gender and kinship order, one that does not favor male authority, heterosexuality, a particular division of labor, or a singular household or parenting arrangement [becomes] thinkable for the first time in history."[44] Psychologist Diane Ehrensaft agrees:

> It is imperative that mothering, the daily acts, concerns, and sensibilities that go into the nurturance and rearing of a child, does not become obsolete, but that society makes room for mothering to extend to any combination of adults—women and men, women and women, or men and men—who are committed to raising a child together. In other words, it is time for mothering to become a genderless affair.[45]

The Argument from Object Relations Theory

Are there feminist voices that contest this family pluralization model? Aside from those whose religious convictions support heterosexual monogamy, one group that would hesitate to endorse such a vision are those adhering to the depth-psychological approach known as object-relations theory. Since I have some sympathy for this approach, let me present its essence and empirical track record briefly.[46]

Concerned to challenge the Freudian concept of the Oedipus complex as the crossroads of gendered personality development, these feminists focus instead on the earlier period of infancy when children are highly bonded to their primary caretaker, who is usually a woman. That little girls thus have a same-sex primary love-object while little boys do not is said to become significant around the age of three, when children of both sexes acquire "gender constancy"—that is, the recognition that being male or female is a permanent state of nature. This realization is less problematic for little girls, who proceed to learn their expected gender roles simply by doing what they would do anyway—namely, copy what their mother does. But little boys are placed in something of a quandary: They are expected to disidentify with the most powerful and admired person in their small world, and instead to become like the other big person in the family whom they rarely see—namely, their father.

Feminist object-relations theorists hold that this asymmetrical pattern is at the root of both the "reproduction of mothering" *and* the "reproduction of misogyny." Little girls, strongly bonded to their mothers and not required to disidentify with them just when their gender identity is being consolidated, tend to grow up with more permeable ego-boundaries and a greater desire to stay connected with others, including children of their own. Boys, by contrast, are forced to figure out what it means to be culturally masculine in the virtual absence of a same-sex caretaker. As a result, they are apt to conclude that becoming a man means becoming as unlike *women* as possible. As they grow older, they may escalate this exercise in compensatory masculinity, distancing themselves from whatever they see as women's work, including the hands-on caretaking of their own children. And so the cycle continues through successive generations.

If this object-relations account is substantially correct, then some empirically testable hypotheses follow. First, other things being equal, misogynist attitudes and hypermasculine behavior should be greatest in families and cultures where the caretaking of young children is most assiduously avoided by men. Oppositely, low levels of misogyny and hypermasculinity—among younger and older males alike—will be likeliest in families and cultures where there is strong father involvement in childcare. Empirical research in western settings supports both the first[47] and the second[48] of these hypotheses.

Critics of this line of argument point out that in western culture father-absent families are apt to be both economically strained and socially stigmatized, factors which themselves might contribute to misogyny and hypermasculinity. Consequently we need also to look at the correlates of father absence in cultures where it is more normative and less confounded with economic deprivation. But this literature also supports both the hypotheses mentioned above, as well as another: Girls from father-absent households (perhaps concluding that male parental effort is not crucial to childrearing) tend to engage in sexual activity earlier and more indiscriminately than girls from father-present households. They also tend to form less stable pair-bonds as adults.[49]

Such research findings lead feminists with an object-relations orientation to be strong supporters of co-parenting—that is, the equal distribution of hands-on childcare between men and women.[50] However, their conclusions have not gone unchallenged by those endorsing the pluralized family model. For example, psychologist Joseph Pleck claims that the root problem is not the absence of fathers but the traditional practice of imposing rigid gender roles on boys and girls. For example, if cultural ideals about what is appropriately "masculine" were to become more flexible, boys raised only by women would not need to act hypermasculine to prove their manhood, for it would be quite acceptable for "real men" to be empathic, caring, and emotionally connected.[51]

Feminist object-relations theorists would certainly not deny that rigidly gender-stereotyped roles help to reproduce misogyny and other forms of exaggerated masculinity. However, as Myriam Miedzian points out, the anthropological, psychological, and sociological data suggest that it is precisely the *lack* of paternal involvement that produces rigid, dichotomous, and hierarchical notions of gender roles in the first place. "It may be," she writes, "that male involvement in nurturant fathering is a *condition* of more fluid sex roles and decreased [male] violence."[52] This is a statement that future research may support as the effects of pluralized family forms filter down to the next generation. However, we should note that to reduce misogyny and promote greater male involvement in childrearing, feminist object-relations analysis requires only that children of both sexes have stable, nurturant adult role models of both sexes. It does not require that these role models always or only be the child's biological parents. This leaves room for some flexibility of family forms around a core norm of egalitarian, heterosexual co-parenting. It also suggests encouragement for the recovery of mediating institutions—such as churches, cultural organizations, and community groups—which can supply auxiliary parenting for children, provided that the role models in such institutions are nurturant, empowered adults of *both* sexes.

Feminist research and debate have strongly challenged both men's patriarchal prerogatives and the immutability of gender roles within the family. In addition, "feminine" approaches to cognition, ethics, and social interaction have made the virtues and activities of nurturing more visible and shown the degree to which public life depends on them, even while taking them (and the women who mainly perform them) largely for granted.

While American society has begun to pay lip service to these lessons, there is little evidence that men in general are matching women's entry into the public, wage-earning arena by an equal commitment of their own time and energy to the tasks of social reproduction. This asymmetry of commitment to nurturing, along with escalating rates of divorce and family violence, has contributed to feminist skepticism about the potential for reform of the heterosexual, two-parent nuclear family, despite the evidence from object-relations theorists about the positive effects of involved, egalitarian co-parenting.

Religiously committed people who, by reason of their worldview, wish to make a case for the normativity of the two-parent family would be well advised to spend less time claiming the high moral ground for their position, and more time showing by example that they are committed to egalitarian gender relations between spouses, to a radical degendering of both public and private spheres of life, and to the development of institutions supportive of childrearing that promote both female achievement and male nurturance. There is, as usual, little evidence that religious believers in general are in the forefront of attempts to implement these essential reforms.

NOTES

1. Adapted from Mary Stewart Van Leeuwen, et al., *After Eden: Facing the Challenge of Gender Reconciliation* (Grand Rapids, Mich.: Wm. B. Eerdmans Publishing Co., 1993), 22–23. See also Karen Offen, "Defining Feminism: A Comparative Historical Approach," *Signs*, 14:1 (1988):119–57.
2. See Rosemarie Tong, *Feminist Thought: A Comprehensive Introduction* (Boulder, Colo.: Westview Press, 1989), and also her *Feminine and Feminist Ethics* (Belmont, Calif.: Wadsworth, 1993).
3. "First wave" American feminism is generally defined as the movement that was active from about the 1860s (when women began to extend the arguments for slave emancipation to the cause of their own enfranchisement) until 1920, when national suffrage was granted to women. After a subsequent four-decade period of relative feminist inactivity, "second wave" feminism began in the 1960s and continues to the present.
4. Betty Friedan, *The Feminine Mystique* (New York: W. W. Norton & Co., 1963). For a survey of second wave feminist activity in the United States through 1987, see Marcia Cohen, *The Sisterhood: The Inside Story of the*

Women's Movement and the Leaders Who Made It Happen (New York: Fawcett-Columbine, 1988).

5. For representative collections of essays from this period, see Leslie B. Tanner, ed., *Voices from Women's Liberation* (New York: Signet, 1970) and Vivian Gornick and Barbara K. Moran, *Woman in Sexist Society: Studies in Power and Powerlessness* (New York: Basic Books, 1971).

6. Just as the appearance of Friedan's *The Feminine Mystique* represents an arbitrary yet mythic beginning for second wave feminism, so too it is difficult to date the exact time when feminist discourse began to mix recovery themes more evenly with critical discourse on the family. An important early expression was Adrienne Rich's *Of Woman Born: Motherhood as Experience and Institution* (New York: W. W. Norton & Co., 1976). Subsequent works include *Rethinking the Family: Some Feminist Questions* ed. Barrie Thorne and Marilyn Yalom, (Boston: Northeastern University Press, 1982; revised, 1992); Nel Noddings, *Caring: A Feminist Approach to Ethics and Moral Education* (Berkeley, Calif.: University of California Press, 1984); Diane Ehrensaft, *Parenting Together: Men and Women Sharing the Care of Their Children* (Urbana, Ill.: University of Illinois Press, 1987); Sanford M. Dornbusch and Myra H. Strober, eds., *Feminism, Children, and the New Families* (New York: Guilford, 1988); Susan Moller Okin, *Justice, Gender, and the Family* (New York: Basic Books, 1989); Sara Ruddick, *Maternal Thinking: Towards a Politics of Peace* (New York: Ballantine Books, 1989); Judith Stacey, *Brave New Families: Stories of Domestic Upheaval in Late Twentieth-Century America* (New York: Basic Books, 1990); Sylvia Hewlett, *When the Bough Breaks: The Cost of Neglecting Our Children* (New York: Basic Books, 1991); and Miriam Lewin, *Lesbian Mothers: Accounts of Gender in America* (Ithaca, N.Y.: Cornell University Press, 1993).

7. For an introduction to the relevant literature, see Margaret Koch, "A Cross-Cultural Critique of Western Feminism," in Van Leeuwen et al., eds., *After Eden*, 70–113, and also Marcia Riggs, "The Logic of Interstructured Oppression: A Black Womanist Perspective," in *Redefining Sexual Ethics*, ed. Susan E. Davies and Eleanor H. Haney (Cleveland, Ohio: Pilgrim Press, 1991).

8. See, for example, Betty Friedan, *The Second Stage* (New York: Summit, 1981); Nancy Hartsock, *Money, Sex, and Power: An Essay on Domination and Community* (New York: Longman, 1983); and Kathleen B. Jones, *Compassionate Authority: Democracy and the Representation of Women* (New York: Routledge & Kegan Paul, 1993).

9. See, for example, Arlie Hochschild, *The Second Shift: Working Parents and the Revolution at Home* (New York: Viking Penguin, 1989).

10. See, for example, Lenore Weitzman, *The Divorce Revolution: The Unexpected Social and Economic Consequences for Women and Children in America* (New York: Free Press, 1985); Judith S. Wallerstein and Sandra Blakeslee, *Second Chances: Men, Women and Children in a Decade After Divorce* (New York: Ticknor & Fields, 1989) and Susan E. Krantz, "Divorce and Children," in *Feminism, Children, and the New Families*, 249–73.

11. Susan Cohen and Mary Fainsod Katzenstein, "The War Over the Family Is Not Over the Family," in *Feminism, Children, and the New Families*, 25–46 (quotation from 36–37). There are also commentators who do not appear to regard the phrase "conservative feminism" as an oxymoron. See, for example, Katherine Kersten, "What Do Women Want? A Conservative Feminist Manifesto," *Policy Review* Washington, D.C., The Heritage Foundation (spring 1991), reprinted in *Moral Issues and Christian Perspective*, 5th ed., ed. Paul T. Jersild and Dale A. Johnson (Fort Worth, Tex.: Harcourt Brace Jovanovich, 1993), 111–27.

12. The following summary draws on Barrie Thorne's "Feminism and the Family: Two Decades of Thought," in *Rethinking the Family*, 3–30.

13. See Jane Collier, Michelle Z. Rosaldo, and Sylvia Yanagisako, "Is There a Family? New Anthropological Views," in *Rethinking the Family*, 31–48.

14. See, for example, Robert W. Connell, *Gender and Power: Society, the Person, and Sexual Politics* (Stanford, Calif.: Stanford University Press, 1987); Deniz Kandiyotti, "Bargaining With Patriarchy," *Gender and Society*, 2 (1988): 274–90; Arthur Brittan, *Masculinity and Power* (New York: Basil Blackwell, 1989); and Annelies Knoppers, "A Critical Theory of Gender Relations," in *After Eden*, 225–67.

15. Tong, *Feminine and Feminist Ethics*, 62–63.

16. For the analysis of an American parallel, see Rebecca Klatch, *Women of the New Right* (Philadelphia: Temple University Press, 1987).

17. Joyce McCarl Nielsen, ed., *Feminist Research Methods: Exemplary Readings in the Social Sciences* (Boulder, Colo.: Westview Press, 1990).

18. Thorne, "Feminism and the Family," 12. See also Weitzman, *The Divorce Revolution*; Elizabeth Pleck, *Domestic Tyranny: The Making of American Social Policy against Family Violence from Colonial Times to the Present* (New York: Oxford University Press, 1987); Linda Gordon, *Heroes of Their Own Lives: The Politics and History of Family Violence* (New York: Viking Penguin, 1988); and Stephanie Coontz, *The Way We Never Were: American Families and the Nostalgia Trap* (New York: Basic Books, 1992).

19. Thorne, "Feminism and the Family," 12.

20. Juliet Mitchell, "Women: The Longest Revolution," *New Left Review*, 40 (Nov–Dec 1966): 11–37.

21. Barbara Laslett and Johanna Brenner, "Gender and Social Reproduction: Historical Perspectives," *Annual Review of Sociology* 15 (1989): 381–401.

22. See for example Stacey, *Brave New Families*; Coontz, *The Way We Never Were*; and Thorne and Yalom, eds., *Rethinking the Family*, esp. chaps. 3, 4, 13.

23. Coontz, *The Way We Never Were*, 40–41. See also Okin, *Justice, Gender, and the Family*; Jean Bethke Elshtain, *Public Man, Private Woman: Women in Social and Political Thought* (Princeton, N.J.: Princeton University Press, 1981); A. F. Robertson, *Beyond the Family: The Social Organization of Human Reproduction* (Berkeley, Calif.: University of California Press, 1991); and Van Leeuwen et al., eds., *After Eden*, chap. 12, "Private Versus Public Life: A Case for Degendering," and chap. 13, "Family Justice and Societal Nurturance: Reintegrating Public and Private Domains."

24. Hochschild, *The Second Shift*. See also Emily Abel and Margaret K. Nelson, eds., *Circles of Care: Work and Identity in Women's Lives* (Albany, N.Y.: State University of New York Press, 1990); Marjorie L. DeVault, *Feeding the Family: The Social Organization of Caring as Gendered Work* (Chicago: University of Chicago Press, 1991); Patricia Hill Collins, *Black Feminist Thought: Knowledge, Consciousness, and the Politics of Empowerment* (London: HarperCollins, 1990), esp. chaps. 3, 4, 6; and Micaela di Leonardo, "The Female World of Cards and Holidays: Women, Families, and the Work of Kinship," in *Rethinking the Family*, 246–61.

25. Stacey, *Brave New Families*, 268–69.

26. Tong, *Feminist Thought*, 160. See also Anne Carr and Elisabeth Schüssler Fiorenza, eds., *Motherhood: Experience, Institution, Theology,* theme issue of *Concilium* 206 (Edinburgh: T. & T. Clark, 1989).

27. See Mary O'Brien, *The Politics Of Reproduction* (London: Routledge & Kegan Paul, 1981), and also her *Reproducing the World: Essays in Feminist Theory* (Boulder, Colo.: Westview Press, 1989). See also Dorothy Dinnerstein, *The Mermaid and the Minotaur: Sexual Arrangements and Human Malaise* (New York: Harper & Row, 1977); Nancy Chodorow, *The Reproduction of Mothering: Psychoanalysis and the Sociology of Gender* (Berkeley, Calif.: University of California Press, 1978); and Jessica Benjamin, *The Bonds of Love: Psychoanalysis, Feminism, and the Problem of Domination* (New York: Pantheon, 1988).

28. Rich, *Of Woman Born*, 174. Rich's criticism was directed especially at Shulamith Firestone's *The Dialectic of Sex* (New York: Bantam Books, 1970), which (somewhat naively) envisaged reproductive technology as the means by which women could be freed from the burdens of pregnancy, childbirth, and patriarchy, with the eventual emergence of an androgynous culture from which the biological family would disappear as an institution.

29. Rich, *Of Woman Born*, 57.

30. For example, Carol Gilligan, *In A Different Voice: Psychological Theory and Women's Development* (Cambridge, Mass.: Harvard University Press, 1982); Joyce Treblicot, ed., *Mothering: Essays in Feminist Theory* (Totowa, N.J.: Rowman & Allanheld, 1983); Nel Noddings, *Caring: A Feminine Approach to Ethics and Moral Education* (Berkeley, Calif.: University of California Press, 1984); Barbara H. Andolsen, Christine E. Gudorf, and Mary D. Pellauer, eds., *Women's Consciousness, Women's Conscience: A Reader in Feminist Ethics* (San Francisco: Harper & Row, 1985); Mary Field Belenky, et al., *Women's Ways of Knowing: The Development of Self, Voice, and Mind* (New York: Basic Books, 1986); Sara Ruddick, *Maternal Thinking: Toward A Politics of Peace* (New York: Ballantine Books, 1989); Ann Garry and Marilyn Pearsall, eds. *Women, Knowledge and Reality: Explorations in Feminist Philosophy* (Boston: Unwin Hyman, 1989).

31. For example, Genevieve Lloyd, *The Man of Reason: "Male" and "Female" in Western Philosophy* (London: Methuen, 1984); Evelyn Fox Keller, *Reflections on Gender and Science* (New Haven, Conn.: Yale University Press, 1985); Belenky, et al., *Women's Ways of Knowing*; Sandra Harding,

The Science Question in Feminism (Ithaca, N.Y.: Cornell University Press, 1986), and also her *Whose Science, Whose Knowledge? Thinking From Women's Lives* (Ithaca, N.Y.: Cornell University Press, 1991); Jane Duran, *Toward A Feminist Epistemology* (Savage, Md.: Rowman & Littlefield, 1991).

32. For example, Gilligan, *In A Different Voice*; David Graddol and Joan Swann, *Gender Voices* (New York: Basil Blackwell, 1989); and Deborah Tannen, *You Just Don't Understand: Women and Men in Conversation* (New York, William Morrow & Co., 1990).

33. A volume that develops the significance of this ethical challenge for family life—and one that demonstrates that mainstream philosophers have begun to take it seriously—is Diana Teitjens Meyers, Kenneth Kipnis, and Cornelius F. Murphy, Jr., eds., *Kindred Matters: Rethinking the Philosophy of the Family* (Ithaca, N.Y.: Cornell University Press, 1993), esp. chaps. 1–4.

34. In fact, there is a growing tendency among writers in this tradition (e.g., Ruddick, *Maternal Thought*) to use the verb "mothering" generically—that is, to describe the activities of anyone, male *or* female, who pursues the activities involved in bonding with, caring for, and socializing children. Analogously, the verb "fathering" has been used to describe what is seen as a disturbing trend among elite women, who are now able to behave like traditional (i.e., modern) "fathers," appropriating the labor of economically disadvantaged women to do their childcare for them, and even physically to bear their children for them. See Barbara Katz Rothman, "Women as Fathers: Motherhood and Child Care Under a Modified Patriarchy," *Gender and Society*, 3 (1989): 89–104.

35. Tannen, *You Just Don't Understand*.

36. See Betty A. Sichel, "Different Strains and Strands: Feminist Contributions to Ethical Theory," *Newsletter on Feminism* 90:2 (winter 1991): 90; Susan Sherwin, *No Longer Patient: Feminist Ethics and Health Care* (Philadelphia: Temple University Press, 1992), and Tong, *Feminine and Feminist Ethics*. The tension between feminine and feminist ethics is not unique to second wave feminism, but was a regular point of debate among nineteenth-century (first wave) American feminists as well. See for example Aileen Kraditor, *The Ideas of the Woman Suffrage Movement* (New York: Columbia University Press, 1965).

37. Miriam Johnson, *Strong Mothers, Weak Wives: The Search for Gender Equality* (Berkeley, Calif.: University of California Press, 1988). See also Carole Pateman, "Equality, Difference, Subordination: The Politics of Motherhood and Women's Citizenship," in *Beyond Equality and Difference: Citizenship, Feminist Politics, and Female Subjectivity*, ed. Gisela Bock and Susan James, (New York: Routledge & Kagan Paul, 1992), 17–31.

38. Jeffner Allen, "Motherhood: The Annihilation of Women," *Mothering*, 315–30 (quotations from 317 and 326).

39. Tong, *Feminist Thought*, 89 (my emphasis).

40. Ibid., 90.

41. United States Census Bureau, "Fertility of American Women, June 1992," as summarized in Associated Press Wire Report, "More and More Women

Becoming Moms Outside Marriage," *Grand Rapids Press* (14 July 1993): A3. Some (unstated) proportion of these never-married mothers are lesbians. Indeed, Miriam Lewin, in *Lesbian Mothers*, says of the "lesbian baby boom" that began in the 1980s that "the increasing visibility of lesbians who become mothers through donor insemination or adoption constitutes the most dramatic and provocative challenge to traditional notions both of the family and of the nonprocreative nature of homosexuality" (19). However, as a lesbian nonmother herself, she fears that the trend towards lesbian motherhood is both a sign of accommodation to mainstream cultural standards for "normal" womanly activity, and a practice that may produce divisions in the lesbian community between those who consider themselves "responsible parents" and those labelled "self-centered (i.e., non-parenting) hedonists."

42. See, for example, David Popenoe, *Disturbing the Nest: Family Change and Decline in Modern Societies* (New York: Adeline deGruyter, 1988); Wallerstein and Blakeslee, *Second Chances*; Weitzman, *The Divorce Revolution*; Nicholas Zill and Charlotte Schoenborn, "Developmental, Learning, and Emotional Problems: Health of Our Nation's Children, United States, 1988," National Center for Health Statistics, DHHS Publication PHS-91-1250; and James Q. Wilson, "The Family-Values Debate," *Commentary* 95:4 (April 1993): 24–31.

43. See Lewin, *Lesbian Mothers*.

44. Stacey, *Brave New Families*, 258.

45. Ehrensaft, *Parenting Together*, xi. See also Thorne, "Feminism and the Family."

46. Dinnerstein, *The Mermaid and the Minotaur*; Chodorow, *The Reproduction of Mothering*; Benjamin, *The Bonds of Love*; Lillian Rubin, *Intimate Strangers: Men and Women Together* (New York: Harper & Row, 1983); Mary Stewart Van Leeuwen, *Gender and Grace: Love, Work and Parenting in a Changing World* (Downers Grove, Ill.: InterVarsity Press, 1990); Myriam Miedzian, *Boys Will Be Boys: Breaking the Link Between Masculinity and Violence* (New York: Doubleday, 1991); and (in part) Ehrensaft, *Parenting Together*.

47. See, for example, Jeffrey Hearn, *The Gender of Oppression: Men, Masculinity, and the Critique of Women* (Brighton, Eng.: John Spiers, 1987); Michael Lamb, ed., *The Role of the Father in Child Development* (New York: Wiley, 1981); Miedzian, *Boys Will Be Boys*; Marvin E. Wolfgang, Leonard Savitz, and Norman Johnson, eds., *The Sociology of Crime and Delinquency* (New York: Wiley, 1962). For an account by an African-American psychologist focusing specifically on the dynamics of black American male socialization, see Richard Majors and J. Mancini Billson, *Cool Pose* (New York: Lexington, 1992).

48. For example Ehrensaft, *Parenting Together*; Nancy Eisenberg, ed., *The Development of Prosocial Behavior* (New York: Academic Press, 1982); Michael E. Lamb, *Nontraditional Families* (Hillsdale, N.J.: Lawrence Erlbaum, 1982); Miedzian, *Boys Will Be Boys*; Kyle D. Pruett, *The Nurturing Father* (New York: Warner, 1987). See also the chapter in this volume by Rob Palkovitz.

49. For example, Margaret K. Bacon, Irvin L. Child and Herbert Barry, "A Cross-Cultural Study of the Correlates of Crime," *Journal of Abnormal and Social Psychology* 66:4 (April 1963): 291–300; Patricia Draper and Henry Harpending, "Father Absence and Reproductive Strategy: An Evolutionary Perspective," *Journal of Anthropological Research* 38:3 (fall 1982): 255–73; Barry S. Hewlett, *Intimate Fathers: The Nature and Context of Aka Pygmy Paternal Infant Care* (Ann Arbor, Mich.: University of Michigan Press, 1992); Beatrice B. Whiting and John W. M. Whiting, *Children of Six Cultures* (Cambridge, Mass.: Harvard University Press, 1975). It should be noted that because we cannot randomly assign babies at birth to live in various kinds of families, there can never be *conclusive* proof (at least of a scientific sort) for the thesis that certain family forms are better for children than others. The next best approximation to a causal analysis comes in the form of longitudinal studies, whereby randomly selected groups of children already living in assorted family configurations are followed from birth to maturity, with various measures of stress and adjustment taken at regular intervals. This literature, which does support the thesis that two-parent families are on average better for children at all socioeconmic levels, is summarized in Wilson, "The Family-Values Debate."

50. To say that father-absent families are "at risk" for producing misogynist, hypermasculine sons and sexually undiscriminating daughters is *not* to say that these outcomes are inevitable in every case, just as saying that certain groups of persons are genetically "at risk" for heart attacks does not mean that every person in those groups will inevitably suffer from heart attacks. Both kinds of statements are based on statistical generalizations from correlational and/or longitudinal data. However, in each case it is fair to say that eliminating risk-enhancing behaviors reduces the risk of the problems in question.

51. Joseph H. Pleck, *The Myth of Masculinity* (Cambridge, Mass.: MIT Press, 1983).

52. Miedzian, *Boys Will Be Boys*, 87–88.

PART 2

Jewish and Christian Families

3

The Family
in the Hebrew Bible

TIKVA FRYMER-KENSKY

The biblical family was a closely ordered hierarchical system in which ultimate authority resided with the father, and children were subordinate to the parents. The central narrative of the Hebrew Bible (Genesis–Kings), which relates the development of Israel from the family of Abraham to the centralized state, reflects on issues of political order, power, and control. These stories reveal the problem with "family values": The power that men have over their children can lead to abuse and chaos, and society has an obligation to create a layer above the power of the patriarch to which men will be subordinate. In the biblical view, this is a major function of the state and monarchy, which place state bureaucracies above the authority of the father. Since these state bureaucracies are all male, this development does not eliminate patriarchy. It "evens out" the condition of women, protecting them from the worst abuses but at the same time increasing their distance from the locus of political power.

The second chapter of Genesis, which details the creation of humanity, begins with a solitary Adam, the earthling. The difference between human and animal becomes apparent as God is unable to provide the earthling with a companion by creating new creatures from clay. God's answer is to split the Adam and create a pair-bond of male and female. The new male, seeing the female, instantly recognizes his mate: "this is flesh of my flesh and bone of my bones" (Gen. 2:23). The point of the story is obvious, but the narrator, wanting to make sure that the readers reach the correct conclusion, interjects a direct comment: "Therefore a man leaves his father and mother and cleaves to his wife and they become one flesh" (Gen. 2:24). The stage has been set: The family, in particular the nuclear heterosexual pair-bond, has been established as the basic unit of society.

The rest of Genesis portrays a different kind of family: an extended, patrilineal family where the patriarch might have more than one wife, and where brothers stay in close contact with each other and with their father. This disparity is less contradictory than it seems, for biblical archaeology shows that both types of family existed side by side. The Israelite villages were composed of small houses, with an estimated occupancy of 4.1–4.3 persons per house. This was the dwelling of the nuclear family, which had on average two children surviving past infancy. These houses were arranged in clusters comprising the compound of the patriarchal family, the *beyt ab*, which was the constitutive social unit of the *mishpahah*, the larger kinship community. Because of shifting family relations as people die and reach maturity, half of the population would be living in extended families at any given time.[1]

The rules and operations of the family have to be deduced from the Hebrew Bible itself, with supplementary information provided by ancient Near Eastern documents and comparative anthropology. Three types of texts within the Hebrew Bible illumine the workings of the family: biblical collections of laws, proverbs, and stories. The biblical law collection, like all the ancient Near Eastern legal collections and, to a certain extent, like all laws, defines a reality that is believed to correspond most to the society's ideas of equitable justice. Proverbs, too, represent advice given to promote certain family dynamics. It is easy to see the "ideal" character of laws and proverbs, but by contrast we tend to think of stories as "slices of life" that represent lived reality. Such a conclusion is particularly tempting because the biblical stories do not represent "ideal" people of unsullied virtue nor "ideal" families with paradigmatic interrelationships. On the contrary, biblical heroes are always flawed, and their families are troubled with all the stresses and problems of family life. Often they are even dysfunctional. But this does not mean that they are "real." On the contrary, a closer examination of biblical stories show that they are ideologically driven narratives, chosen and custom-fitted to support particular historical, political, and theological ideas. Of course, none of these genres—law, proverbs, narrative—could be accepted by readers if the families portrayed were too far from people's experience to have verisimilitude; nevertheless, we cannot speak about the "ancient Israelite family" but only about the family in the Bible.

Patriarchy and Property

Biblical law assumes a typical patriarchal household structure in which the family is both patrilineal and patrilocal, and in which legal authority is vested in the male head of household. Women left their fathers' households and authority at marriage and physically moved to their husband's domain. If the husband was still under authority of his father, then the wife would also come under that authority. When the father-in-law died, authority would pass to his sons. This patriarchal family structure is not a biblical invention; it is characteristic of all ancient societies, including those of the ancient Near East. It is both notable and important for our understanding of biblical family structure that the Bible does not justify this male dominance by derogatory statements about women. There are no generic statements about the character or abilities of women such as we find in later attempts to justify patriarchy. Instead, the Bible "explains" this dominance of the male partner by means of a story: When the first couple, Adam and Eve, ate of the tree of knowledge, they had to leave their natural habitat (the Garden of Eden) and enter the domain of real life, characterized by labor and civilization. Part of the package, God predicts, is that women will love men who will rule over them.[2] Patriarchy is the "mark of a fallen universe"[3] or, in other words, it is simply an inherent part of the real civilized world with which Israel was familiar. Israel neither invented nor actively promoted patriarchy and, as we shall see, it may have alleviated extreme abuses. On the other hand, Israel neither recognized nor tried to eradicate the inequalities of patriarchy. The Bible is not a radical social document and does not eliminate the inequities of society in the ancient world, like slavery, patriarchy, and poverty. It often takes the side of the underdog, alleviates the condition of the slaves, poor, and women, and shows a "preferential option" for the poor and disadvantaged, but it does not prescribe a major transformation of social structure in order to eliminate these evils.

The economic cornerstone of biblical patriarchy is land ownership. Control over the family property belongs to the father, and passes with his death to the sons. Women do not ordinarily inherit property. The Bible's humanitarian injunction to care for widows and orphans (Exod. 22:21; Deut. 10:18 and elsewhere) is predicated on the assumption that widows will *need* protection because they do not have economic assets. There is one exception to the rule that women do not inherit. The book of Numbers relates the story of the five daughters of Zelophehad who had died without sons. The daughters petition to inherit, arguing that their father's patrimony—and memory—should not disappear, since he had done nothing to deserve such a terrible fate. Their petition is granted with a decree that daughters would inherit whenever a man died without sons.[4] Later, a provision was added that the inheriting daughters should marry within their own clan so as to keep the land in the family.[5]

The enormous difference that the possession of land could make to a woman's life is dramatically indicated in the story of the Great Woman of Shunnem,[6] whose initiative and independence are noteworthy. She is of course wealthy, which gives her greater freedom of action than poor women have. But her independence goes deeper than that, for her independent actions vis-à-vis her husband indicate that her economic well-being does not depend on her husband's goodwill. When Elisha wants to reward her for her generosity, she answers him that she needs nothing, because "I live among my own kin," and it is Elisha's servant Gehazi who points out that she is childless, so that Elisha rewards her with a son. There are two odd facts here: Married women usually live among their husband's kin, and the Shunnemite is the only childless woman not portrayed as actively seeking children. A further peculiar fact about the Shunnemite emerges later: On Elisha's advice, she and her family have fled Israel's famine for seven years. When she comes back, she petitions the king, who gives instructions to restore her property and the accrued revenue from her farms. The land is called "hers"; not her husband's (if he is alive) or her sons'. By contrast, the kin among whom Naomi lived before going to Moab were her husband Elimelech's kin, and the land that is ultimately restored to her is clearly called "the field portion that belonged to Elimelech." The difference for the Shunnemite is not only one of wealth; the Shunnemite's dwelling among her own kin and owning her own land indicates that she may have inherited from a sonless father. The Shunnemite's notable independence certainly shows what a difference title to land could make in this ancient culture.

Family Hierarchy

In the biblical account, the husband's authority over his wife is buttressed both by his control over the family's economic assets and by custom and social expectation. There is a significant difference, nevertheless, between a husband's control over his wife and the authority of parents over children. The commandment to "honor your father and your mother"[7] establishes the primacy of generation over gender; the biblical family is a multi-tiered hierarchy in which the parental level (husband, then wife) is ranked above the children's level (older son, then younger sons, then sisters). Children may not treat their parents as their parents treat them. The laws provide the death penalty for the one who strikes or demeans his father or mother.[8] Deuteronomy provides a legal procedure for enforcing these dictums: If a father and mother bring a son before the elders and swear to his disobedience, the elders decree his fate and the community is to stone him.[9] The book of Proverbs admonishes children to heed the instructions of both father and mother, even when they are old,[10] and predicts disaster for those who do not.[11] Parents must teach their children the sacred history, reciting to them the story of the miracles that God performed for them at the Exodus from

Egypt and the dry crossing of the Red Sea.[12] They must also teach them how to behave properly, and Proverbs urges that parents reinforce their instruction with physical discipline: "If folly settles in the heart of a child, the rod of discipline will remove it."[13] Such discipline is not only permitted, it is understood to be lifesaving for the child: "Do not withhold discipline from a child; if you beat him with a rod he will not die. Beat him with a rod, and you will save him from the grave."[14]

Distasteful as this form of punishment might be to us, we should acknowledge that none of the narratives portray parents striking their children, and that Proverbs, which considers striking a necessary part of education, also admonishes against the use of excessive force.[15] We should also note that husbands are *not* given either the right or duty to admonish their wives with force. The book of Proverbs often ponders the problem of argumentative wives, declaring that the arguing of a wife is like the incessant dripping of water, and that it is better to live in the desert or on a roof than with such a wife.[16] But nowhere does it suggest that a husband apply the "rod of discipline" to his wife. By contrast, the Middle Assyrian Laws explicitly declare that a man has the right to pull out his wife's hair or mutilate her ears whenever he wants.[17] In the Bible, the wife is not the ward of her husband. She is not considered less intelligent or less mature than he; as a result, he has no obligation (or right) to "educate" her by forceful means. Despite her dependent position in the family and her subordinate position in society, the wife is considered an adult person in her own right.

There is one very large exception: men—first father, then husband—own women's sexuality. The daughter owes her father chastity; the wife (and the betrothed woman) owes her husband sexual fidelity. The difference between wife-as-person and wife-as-sexual-property shows up in the Decalogue itself. The fourth commandment, about the Sabbath, prescribes rest for "you, your son, your daughter, your manservant, your maidservant, your cattle and the stranger in your gates."[18] There is no separate statement of "your wife"; she is included (albeit invisibly) in the "you". On the other hand, the tenth commandment reads, "Do not covet your neighbor's house or your neighbor's wife. . . ."[19] The coveting involves sexual attraction, and here the wife is instantly reduced to a possession. If the wife willingly sleeps with another man, both the woman and the man she sleeps with are to be killed.[20] A husband who suspects that his wife has slept with another can accuse her and bring her to the sanctuary for the "trial of the suspected adulteress," a particularly solemn oath procedure in which the priest prepares a potion by taking a scroll on which this legislation is written and dissolving its words in a bowl of holy water combined with dust from the floor of the sanctuary. The woman drinks this potion while answering "Amen, Amen" to the priests' declaration that if she is guilty "her belly will swell and her thigh fall out" (probably a reference to a prolapsed uterus).[21] Should this not happen and, on the contrary, she should become pregnant, this would conclusively prove her innocence. Her husband, however, is not punished for false accusation. Ensuring that a wife does not get away with adultery is not only his right; it may be his obligation. He is therefore protected from any consequences of an unproved accusation, which for any other crime would entail suffering the punishment envisioned for the falsely accused.

The Narratives of Genesis

Sons

The workings of the family are presented in stories that deal with three different periods in Israel's history: the ancestor tales in Genesis, located in the remote past of the very beginnings of the nation; the tales of the book of Judges, which depict the conditions before the consolidation of the state; and the tales of the court of David, which deal with affairs of the royal family. Each of these cycles of stories has a different purpose, one which colors both the selection and the presentation of the stories.

The ancestor tales of the book of Genesis deal with the transmission of the promises of God from Abraham to Isaac and then Jacob. The transfer of power between generations is a main preoccupation of myths from the ancient Near East, particularly of the great mythological epics written in the second millennium. In Babylon, the Enuma Elish relates how Marduk became king of the gods by defeating the primordial mother of them all, subsequently acquiring all the functions and powers of the gods his fathers. In Canaan, the emphasis is on the rivalry between brothers: the Ugaritic Ba'al epic relates the battles between Ba'al, Yam, and Mot to see who would takeover the headship from the elderly El. In Genesis, the issue is, of course, not contests between gods, but humans. The Genesis stories relate the many dimensions of a single central problem: Who will inherit the father's dominant position in the family? Often this is discussed as an issue of the "birthright": Who will be considered the firstborn who, in addition to being dominant, inherits twice as much of the paternal estate as his brothers? But being "firstborn" is not a simple matter of being the first to be born. In the Genesis stories, as in the surrounding Near Eastern legal documents, the term "firstborn" refers to a designated position, not a simple biological one. The father retained the right to appoint any child as the "firstborn." This, of course, had the result of greatly intensifying sibling rivalries, and these ancestor stories relate the contests between Ishmael and Isaac, Jacob and Esau, and Joseph and his brothers on this very issue. After the consolidation of the state, the book of Deuteronomy limits the powers of the father to choose by declaring that a man cannot choose the first son of his favored wife over the son of another wife: From now on, the first born chronologically must be considered the firstborn.

It is noteworthy that the elder brother in Genesis never wins the contest, for God steps in with preference for the younger sibling. But God does not act alone or through supernatural interventions. The ancestor tales of Genesis are also stories about *mothers* and the way that they act to ensure the succession of their preferred child. The portrayal of mothers in the book of Genesis gives us a glimpse of the actual powers of women in family life, and the picture they present conforms to our picture of the many ways in which women exercise power (defined as the ability to influence events) in social systems that give *authority* (the power that accrues from hierarchically recognized status) to men.[22] The husband has the authority to make decisions, but Sarah achieves her goals by persuasion, and Rebekkah by persuasion and deception. These are the classic powers of the (officially) powerless, and the Bible portrays both woman and marginalized men as successful in their use.[23] Ultimately, these are the powers that Israel itself must have if it is to make its way in a world populated by powerful empires.

Wives

The Genesis stories also show the weaknesses of women in such patriarchal families. The matriarchs are most often portrayed in relation to their children, in keeping with the main preoccupation of Genesis, which is the birth of the nation. But Sarah, Rebekkah, and Rachel are all initially barren and do not have children until God acts: God "paid attention" to Sarah (Gen. 21:1), listened on behalf of Rebekkah (Gen. 25:21), and remembered and listened to Rachel (Gen. 30:22). So too, Leah's secondary barrenness ended when God heard Leah (Gen. 30:17). The barrenness of the matriarchs is a literary *topos* that heightens the drama of the development of Israel by showing how it almost didn't happen. It also makes two important theological points: that God controls childbirth and intervened miraculously to create Israel. The matriarch's quest for children is not unique to women, for it mirrors Israel's great desire for children. The first blessing is "be fruitful and multiply" (Gen. 1:28); the first commandment is the same (Gen. 9:1, 7), and all children are

considered "a gift from God." But this also reveals the precarious position of childless women in their families. Sarah attempts to provide
Abraham with a child by using a practice known also from the ancient
Near East, in which a barren wife provides her husband with a slave
woman who will serve as "surrogate mother".[24] A wife might do this
because she is obligated by her marriage contract, like some of the Near
Eastern documents; or because she fears that otherwise her husband
would take another wife, as is intimated by the Old Babylonian Laws of
Hammurabi; or because she, like her husband, longs for a child who will
bring joy to the family, will care for the parents in their old age, and will
provide for them after their death. To die without descendants is, in the
Bible's view, the worst of all possible fates; the threat of this is the most
powerful divine sanction, (called *karet*).[25] This is Sarah's concern, for she
declares her desire to be "built up" through her handmaiden Hagar. But
making a slave a surrogate mother carries the danger that the slave will
start thinking herself a wife and become a rival to the wife herself. The
Code of Hammurabi envision this situation, and the same thing happens
to Sarah when Hagar begins to treat her with less honor. This sets up one
of the tragic stories of the Bible, the "text of terror"[26] about the confrontation of Sarah and Hagar in Genesis 16 and 20. Sarah, knowing that
her position depends entirely on Abraham, is frightened when Hagar no
longer acts deferential toward her. Sarah then begins to "abuse" Hagar—
to treat her without the proper respect her new status as pregnant concubine demands. Hagar runs away but God tells her to return and
submit. Obeying God, she returns to Abraham and Sarah until they
finally send her away, emancipating her and her son. The story shows
the relations between women in a patriarchal family. Relative to Hagar,
Sarah has the power, but Sarah's power may be transient. Sarah feels
threatened by pregnant Hagar; she is even more threatened by mother
Hagar and her son, for both she and her infant son Isaac are totally
dependent on Abraham's goodwill.

As with any story in Genesis, there is more to it than it seems. The
biblical reader is torn between ethnic loyalty to Sarah, progenitor of the
nation, and pity for Hagar, the victimized prototype of Israel itself. Just
as Hagar is told that she must submit to abuse (Gen. 16:8), Abraham is
told that his descendants will be abused (Gen. 15:13). Like Israel, Hagar
is ultimately freed and goes out to the desert, where she suffers until God
provides her with water and then reveals his promise to her. Like
Abraham, Hagar is promised that she will give birth to a numberless
nation. A biblical audience would not have missed these allusions and
parallels, and would have felt the dilemma of the characters even more
than we do. Sarah's actions would have seemed even more problematic

to them—but also even more vital to her own survival. For despite her class advantage over Hagar, Sarah was right to feel powerless and subject to Abraham's whims. Abraham could easily dispose of her, as he did when he denied that she was his wife and allowed first Pharaoh, then Abimelech to take her away.[27] Abraham has the right to dispose of *everyone* in his family, which he does—giving Sarah to foreign kings, sending away Hagar and Ishmael, taking Isaac to be sacrificed. There is no limitation of his rights over the members of his family.

This ability to dispose of the members of his family is shared by all the heads of the Genesis households. Lot offers his two daughters to the Sodomite mob; Isaac gives Rebekkah to King Abimelech and holds the destiny of his two sons in his hands; Lot arbitrarily gives Leah rather than Rachel to Jacob; Jacob's favoritism towards Rachel and Joseph causes intense rivalry in the families precisely because of the practical effects it could have. The laws also show the father able to sell children into slavery, and pledge them for his debts. Only three factors mitigate this absolute life-and-death control. First, fathers and sons expect to stay together for the life of the father and to work together for the family's economic well-being. The hard work of agriculture makes children indispensable and encourages multigenerational family ties. Together they are the family unit, and their actions are expected to be for the good of this unit. Second, the father's power is limited by the mother. Even though she herself is vulnerable, the Genesis mother intervenes actively to influence her husband's behavior. Sarah persuades Abraham to clear the way for Isaac by sending Ishmael away; Lot's daughters get their father drunk and milk his semen so that they can get pregnant; Rebekkah tricks Isaac into giving Jacob the blessing and talks him into sending Jacob to Babylon for a wife; Rachel reaches an agreement with her sister Leah about conjugal relations with Jacob. The third factor limiting the power of the father over his subordinate family members—or at least mitigating its effects—is divine intervention. God saves Sarah by closing the wombs of Pharaoh's household and transmits the truth about Rebekkah to Abimelech in a dream; the angelic envoys rescue Lot's daughters by blinding the Sodomites; God rescues Ishmael in the desert and prevents Abraham from killing Isaac.

Daughters and Daughters-in-law

By the fourth generation, once the family of Israel is well established, God no longer intervenes in family affairs. Moreover, with the death of Rachel (and the disappearance of Leah from the story), there are no more mothers to intervene. And here the stories turn to the most vulnerable members of the patriarchal household, the daughters and daughters-in-law. Unlike sons, they were somewhat marginal to the family identity, for a daughter is expected to be given away, to change her identity at marriage (which was usually soon after puberty), and to move from being the daughter in one man's household to being the daughter(-in-law) in another man's household. Therefore the issue of control, mitigated with sons by the need for family coherence, becomes the central factor in the relations between fathers and daughters. The daughter is expected to be faithful to her father by remaining a virgin; if not, she has "whored against his house"[28] The Bible does not mention the possibility of father-daughter incest. It tells no stories about it (with the exception of the daughter-initiated milking of Lot's semen while he was unconscious), and does not even mention it explicitly in the laws that list forbidden, incestuous relationships in Leviticus 18. The prohibition of father-daughter incest is subsumed under the blanket prohibition of a man not "sleeping with his own flesh" in Leviticus 18:6. But it is not explicitly mentioned in the extensive list of tabooed women that follows, a list that includes father, mother, sister, half-sister, and granddaughter. Either Israel was in deep denial that such incest could happen, or mentioning it was felt to be an affront to the father's control of daughters. Whatever the cause, the sexual fidelity that a father owes his daughter takes the form of chastity. This biblical concern for the daughter's virginity is very similar to the patterns that have been identified elsewhere in the world, particularly noted in the regions around the Mediterranean but also found elsewhere. The honor and status of the family rests on the ability of the father to establish control and authority within the family. The virginity of the daughter is proof of this control; or rather, the loss of her virginity proves the opposite. A family's "honor" has significant economic repercussions: Since men will want to be allied with a family of high status, they will pay a high bride-price for a virgin daughter and accept a lower dowry. Conversely, if the honor of the family is damaged, the father will have to offer larger dowries and accept lower bride-prices. Even more, the daughter's brothers will suffer economically, for they will be able to afford only wives of lesser status if the honor of the family is lost.[29] This is the underlying reason (although it may not be consciously realized) that brothers are the ones who most often take the initiative to restore the family's honor by punishing (usually through murder) their offending sister and her lover.

Dinah

This set of expectations underlies the story commonly known as "the rape of Dinah" in Genesis 34. This very complex story reflects a serious discourse about national identity and boundaries, but on another level it is a saga of family "honor" and revenge. The story begins when Dinah "goes out" to see the daughters of the land. The perspective is clearly that of the home—she is out of their property and hence out of their control. This accords well with ancient Near Eastern mores, for even though women were not sequestered, they were expected to be "about" only on specific errands. The Code of Hammurabi, for example, provides that if a woman wants a divorce, she comes before the tribunal, which investigates the case. If she has been a sterling wife and her husband a profligate, she gets her divorce and dowry; if he has been a wonderful husband and she a "gadabout" (literally, a "goer-outer"), then she is thrown into the river. The situation that Dinah encounters in her travels—being seen and desired by a man—is considered in ancient Mesopotamian religious and legal texts. In one of the Dumuzi-Inanna love songs, Dumuzi meets Inanna and wishes to take her away. She, however, responds properly, asking "What should I tell my mother?" And even though he offers to teach her the lies that women tell in such situations, she refuses, and convinces him to come speak to her mother first.[30] The Sumerian legal texts also echo the expectation that a man must not sleep with a girl he meets in the street without parental approval.[31] A girl's going out certainly renders her vulnerable to whatever might befall her. From the point of view of the family, however, a girl's going out renders the entire family vulnerable; her actions determine their honor. In this story, the family worry and perspective is repeatedly emphasized by the text's continual identification of Dinah as "Jacob's daughter" and "their sister."

Traditional interpretations of this story have characterized Shechem's actions as "rape," thus clearly casting him as a villain and perhaps conditioning the reader to accept the violent reaction of the brothers.[32] But the word 'inah does not mean "rape." It is used in a variety of circumstances, such as Sarah's treatment of Hagar and the Egyptians' treatment of Israel, and means "to treat someone improperly."[33] Shechem's sleeping with Dinah without the prior consent of her parents constituted an improper act even without the use of force. Whether she consented or not is totally irrelevant from the family's point of view, because she had no right of consent. In other words, the act was statutory rape, even if not forcible. Even in our society, consensual sex with a girl below the age of consent is considered statutory rape. Dinah, who is called a "girl-child" (yaldah) in this story, would not have the right of consent even in our own times.

This story is not thus about Dinah. Neither her consent nor her reactions to the events that followed are mentioned by the narrator. The story focuses on her breach of propriety and on the attempt to restore position, honor, and status to Jacob's house. Once Jacob and his sons are gathered, Shechem, earnestly in love with Dinah, has his father offer marriage, and offers to pay any bride-price, no matter how great. Jacob might have been satisfied with this—after all, a giant bride-price from a prince would certainly counteract the loss of honor that Dinah's precipitous action had caused. But this offer is not enough for the brothers, whose own honor is at stake. They pretend to go along with the marriage, demanding only that Shechem and his people become circumcised like Israel. After they have done so, the brothers raid the city, kill its inhabitants, and kidnap their sister.[34] They discount Jacob's worries that aggression could lead to their destruction; to them, the most important factor is that their sister has been treated like a whore.

To be "treated like a whore" does not imply rape. On the contrary, the whore is one of the few women who has the right of consent—women who do not live under the control of a family structure with a male at its apex. In this she is joined only by divorcees, full widows, and possibly priestesses.[35] These are not necessarily women of liberty and power; the right of consent doesn't necessarily mean much without the economic power to say no. Nevertheless, they are autonomous; other women, however, are not.

Tamar and Judah

The same kind of fidelity-as-chastity expected from a daughter is also demanded of a widowed daughter-in-law who is awaiting a levirate marriage. The relationship between a man and his new daughter-in-law was legally the most important new bond created by the marriage, and the Hebrew terms *hatan* and *kalah*, which later are defined as "bridegroom" and "bride," mean in the Bible "father-in-law" and "daughter-in-law." The father-in-law, as the head of the new family, had the same kind of power over his daughter-in-law that he had over his daughters, and he expected the same kind of fidelity. In Genesis 38, Tamar, the daughter-in-law of Judah, is widowed before she has had children. Her father-in-law, Judah, then mates her with her dead husband's brother. This custom, called "levirate marriage," is known also from the Middle Assyrian Laws. It was designed to provide a continuance of the name and patrimony of the dead man and, additionally, to provide women with a new attachment to the family into which they have married. At the same time, it required economic self-sacrifice on the part of dead man's brother, the levir. Judah had two surviving sons: the elder could expect to inherit a double portion, or 67 percent of the paternal estate once the brothers divided it; if, however, Onan provided his dead elder brother with an heir, that child would get the 50 percent of the paternal estate that the eldest of three could expect, and Onan would be left with only 25 percent. This proved to be too great a sacrifice for Onan to make, so he violated his obligations by engaging in *coitus interruptus*. Then he too died. The reader is told clearly that God killed both Er and Onan, but Judah doesn't know this. Suspecting that Tamar is not a lucky bride, Judah doesn't want to marry her to his one surviving son, Shelah, and he sends her back to her birth home until Shelah grows up. After years pass, and it becomes obvious to Tamar that Jacob is not going to mate her with Shelah, she takes matters into her own hands, disguises herself as a prostitute, and sleeps with Judah. When she becomes pregnant, Judah is outraged. His daughter-in-law has "whored;" she has not been faithful to his house. Judah immediately sentences her to death. But Tamar has taken the precaution of holding onto Judah's seal, his "I.D.," and is thus able to prove that she has kept her sexuality for his house after all, and has only maneuvered Judah himself into being the levir. He acknowledges her righteousness, takes her back into his household, and all ends extremely happily when their child becomes the ancestor of King David.

The Book of Judges

Judah was ready to kill Tamar, and no one would have stopped him. In the classic patriarchy of Genesis, where there is no power stronger than the family, the head of the patriarchal family has such power over his children that he may even kill them with impunity, as Abraham was ready to kill Isaac. The same social system prevails in Judges, the collection of stories from the time of the settlement of the land of Canaan until the establishment of the state. As in the time of Jacob's children, God no longer intervenes to rescue family members. Moreover, in Judges there are no mothers—no one is around to mitigate the father's power. Judges concentrates on the daughters, and presents abuses rising to the horrific, overwhelming the reader with the need for someone to introduce order into a society destroyed by the powers of the patriarchs. Judges opens with a fairly benign story about daughters. Caleb vows to give his daughter Achsah to whomever conquers the town of Kiryat-sefer. This turns out to be his younger brother Othniel. When Achsah complains that she was "given away empty," Caleb gives her watered fields as her gift.[36] This represents the patriarchal system at its best: The daughter has no say in her marriage—she is a prize awarded by her father—but her relations with her father are so good that he acknowledges the justice of her complaint. The father normally received a bride-price in money and, according to custom, passed the bride-price along as a gift to the marrying couple. They could also usually expect a dowry, to which the girl normally retained some title and use, and which she could expect to take with her if she was divorced. Achsah's bride-price was a military conquest that conveyed no benefit to her, and her father, admitting this, acted to provide for his daughter.

In the story of Jephthah's daughter, we see the fate of a daughter who is not so fortunate. This story starts with the victimization of a family member. Jephthah is the son of a prostitute, living as a son in his father's house. But when his father dies, his brothers kick him out. This is a breach of what we know was Near Eastern customary law, but they, as the heads of their family, could do as they wished. Later, Jephthah has made good—he is invited back to fight for this family and then rule over them. But he is caught in the web of his own power. As patriarch, he vows to reward God for victory by sacrificing the first one to greet him if and when he comes home victorious. When this turns out to be his only daughter, he is devastated. He has no other children, and thus is cutting off his own name from Israel. But his daughter reminds him that he has no choice, that he must fulfill his vow. The reader is troubled, not only for the daughter, who is portrayed as a great heroine of faith, but for Jephthah, who is the classic biblical hero—the victim who succeeds, the outsider become leader, a prototype of the King David legend. In spite of all this, he is trapped into killing his daughter and entering into oblivion.[37] No one will punish him for killing his daughter—and no one can release him from his vow and enable him not to do so. God does not save her, and Jephtah "did to her that which he had vowed."

These issues come into sharp focus in the horrific end of the book of Judges, where abuse escalates into mass horror and the text soberly remarks that this is what happened "in those days when there was no king in Israel." The story begins with an unhappy concubine,[38] who runs away from her husband back to her father. When her husband comes after her, her father gives her back. Her wishes do not matter—she legally belongs to her husband, not her father. The men have a fine time together, and the husband, a Levite, delays his departure until too late in the day to reach home safely. Rather than spend the night in a town of aliens, he turns aside to the Israelite town of Gibeah, wrongly assuming that he will be safer there. But Gibeah repeats the story of Sodom. The Levite is given hospitality by an outsider who lives there, and the Benjaminite townspeople come demanding to "know" him. The host offers his daughter, but the Levite pushes his concubine out the door instead. Once more, there is no divine intervention; the concubine is raped all night and dies at the threshold of the host's house. The Levite is filled with outrage; when he gets home he cuts her body into pieces and sends them to rally the tribes to a war against the tribe of Benjamin, who are protecting the men of Gibeah. The Israelites rally and take battle oaths not too marry their daughters to Benjaminites and to take revenge on those who do not take part in this war.

By the time the battles are over, only six hundred men of Benjamin are left. Israel, having spent its anger, wants to repopulate Benjamin. But there are *no* women left. The death of the concubine has been dwarfed by what has happened to the women of Benjamin, who have all been killed or taken captive into families of Israel. And the outrages do not end there. The Israelites have vowed not to give their daughters to Benjamin, so they attack the town of Jabesh-Gilead (which had not joined the war), kill all the men and married women, and take the unmarried girls as brides for Benjamin. But this new outrage yields only four hundred girls, so the men of Israel arrange for men to snatch their own daughters as they dance at the next festival. Like the Sabine women, the Israelite girls are captured as brides.[39]

The Family and the State

By the end of the book of Judges, the reader has confronted the horrors of the social system and is eager for the consolidation of the state, in the person of the king, to ensure order and to protect people from abuse by their heads of household. The laws of Deuteronomy, which come from the classic period of Israel, show how the state superimposes itself over the rights of the *paterfamilias*. A man who captures a woman in war must marry her fully or set her free; he may not sell her as slave. A father cannot choose the son of a favored wife over the son of a lesser wife; unlike Jacob, whose preferential treatment of Joseph created havoc, a father must take the first one born as the firstborn; a father with a rebellious son can no longer dispose of him on his own authority—he must denounce him to the elders, who will convict him and authorize the community to stone him. Similarly, if a father discovers that a daughter has been unfaithful to him by not remaining a virgin, he cannot simply order her killed, as Judah ordered Tamar burnt; she must be convicted and then stoned. Even the father's right to marry off his daughters is to an extent controlled; in Exodus, the father can take the virgin's bride-price from a man who has already slept with his daughter and then give her to him in marriage or not, as he pleases; in Deuteronomy, he must give her to the man, who can never divorce her.[40] Of course, results of such changes are not always what was intended. Since the father and mother must decide whether to denounce the child as rebellious, they retain power over the child's life.

Since the father of the bride is the one to hold on to the marital sheet that will prove or disprove her virginity, he retains power over his daughter's life, for he can decide whether to bloody it as "proof" of her virginity. On the other hand, the rule that he must marry her off to a man who slept with her before marriage actually opens the door to a situation (such as has been documented in southern Europe) in which a couple can force the father's consent through elopement.

The interposition of state control over "family values" is a mixed blessing. In the old, premonarchic system, women and children are dependent on the moral rectitude and goodwill of the patriarch. When men act badly, women and children suffer grievously. On the other hand, when the head of household acts well, everyone prospers, and women can have considerable prestige and power in both family and village. Under the patriarchal state, the worst abuses are controlled, but in the monarchial state new layers of power are introduced between the household and state authority, so that women are further distanced from decision making. Since women are not part of the new hierarchies, which remain patriarchal, they cannot achieve as much control over events as they previously could. The ups are eliminated along with the downs.

Questions about family are raised throughout the Bible. During the monarchy, the old, uncontrolled patriarchal pattern continues in the royal family, with the predictable results of strife and rape. To some extent, such stories demonstrate that the monarchy, by not being able to control itself, could not save Israel from its ultimate destruction. And when the monarchy disappears with the exile, there is a new focus on the importance of family.[41]

The intensity of family relationships provides Israel with a way to understand the emotional ties between Israel and God. Hosea, Jeremiah, and Ezekiel portray God as husband, Israel as wife in a relationship that is intense and tempestuous and in which the husband punishes his wife to the point of abuse. In Jeremiah 31, God is father, Israel is son in a relationship full of both love and discipline, and God is father, Israel is daughter in a restoration of family harmony. In Isaiah 40—66, God is husband, Zion is wife, and Israel is both husband and children in the joyous love of the eschaton. The divine family is not the paradigm of human families; in human families children do not marry their mother; father and children may not marry the same woman; and a man may not remarry a woman he has sent away if she has married another in the meantime. But the use of family metaphors invokes the intensity of family emotions and relationships to provide the emotional content of Israel's special relationship to God.

The use of these metaphors highlights the fact that, problematic though it might be, the family unit never ceases to be the basic component of social life. It is for this reason that Malachi predicts that just before the end of days, God will send Elijah the prophet to make sure that parents are reconciled with children and children with parents.[42] Without this reconciliation, the land is doomed; with it, all is possible.

NOTES

1. These statistics, based on archaeology and comparative ethnography, come from the ground-breaking article by Lawrence Stager, "The Archaeology of the Family in Ancient Israel," *Bulletin of the American Schools of Oriental Research* (1985): 1–35.
2. For an analysis of the Garden of Eden story see Tikva Frymer-Kensky, *In the Wake of the Goddesses: Women, Culture and the Biblical Transformation of Biblical Myth* (New York: Free Press, 1992), 108–17.
3. This phrase is from Phyllis Trible, *God and the Rhetoric of Sexuality* (Philadelphia: Fortress Press, 1978).
4. Num. 27:1–11.
5. Num. 36.
6. 2 Kings 4:8–37; 8:1–6.
7. Exod. 20:12.
8. striking: Exod. 21:15; demeaning: Exod. 21:17; Lev. 20:9 and cf. Prov. 20:20.
9. Deut. 21:18–21.
10. Prov. 1:8, 4:1; 6:20; in old age: 23:20.
11. Prov. 20:20; 30:17.
12. Exod. 13:8; Deut. 26:20–25; Josh. 4:21–23.
13. Prov. 22:15.
14. Prov. 23:13–14. Similar recommendations of such discipline are found in Prov. 13:1, 19:18, 22:15, and 29:17.
15. Prov. 19:18.
16. Prov. 19:13, 14; 21:19; 25:24; 27:15–16.
17. Middle Assyrian Laws tablet A, 59.
18. Exod. 20:10.
19. Exod. 20:17.
20. Adultery must be consensual; if the woman is raped, she is not condemned as an adulteress and suffers no penalty. The test is whether she shouted for help, or was raped in a place where the shout would not have been heard (Deut. 22:24–26).
21. Num. 5:11–21. For study and discussion see Tikva Frymer-Kensky, "The Strange Case of the Suspected Sotah (Numbers V 11–21)" *Vetus Testamentum* 34 (1984):11–26.

22. For a discussion of such power, see the introduction to Jill Dubisch, ed. *Gender and Power in Rural Greece* (Princeton N.J.: Princeton University Press, 1986), 3–41.
23. For details see Frymer-Kensky, *In the Wake of the Goddesses: Women, Culture and the Biblical Transformation of Biblical Myth* (New York: Free Press, 1992), 118–43.
24. Tikva Frymer-Kensky, "Near Eastern Law and the Patriarchal Family," *Biblical Archaeologist* 44 (1981): 209–14.
25. See Tikva Frymer-Kensky, "Pollution, Purification and Purgation" in *And the Word of the Lord Shall Go Forth*, ed. Carol Meyers (Winona Lake: Eisenbrauns, 1983), 399–414; and Donald Wold, "The Kareth Penalty in P: Rationale and Causes" in *Society for Biblical Literature 1979 Seminar Papers*, ed. P. Achtemeier (Missoula, Mont.: Scholars Press, 1979) I: 1–46.
26. The term is Phyllis Trible's, in *Texts of Terror: Literary-Feminist Readings of Biblical Narratives* (Minneapolis: Augsburg Fortress, 1984). Overtures to Biblical Theology 13 (Philadelphia: Fortress Press, 1984). Her careful reading of the Hagar story is there on pages 9–35.
27. Gen. 12:10–20 and 20:1–18.
28. Deut. 22:21.
29. For the financial question, see Karen Paige and Jeffrey Paige, *The Politics of Reproductive Ritual* (Berkeley, Calif.: University of California Press, 1981); for the general situation see Julian Pitt-Rivers, *The Fate of Shechem or the Politics of Sex: Essays on the Anthropology of the Mediterranean*, (Cambridge: Cambridge University Press, 1979); and Maureen Giovanni, "Female Chastity Codes in the Circum-Mediterranean: Comparative Perspectives," in *Honor and Shame and the Unity of the Mediterranean*, ed. David Gilmore, (Washington D.C.: Special Publications, 22, American Anthropological Association, 1987).
30. Text published in Bernhardt and Kramer, TMH III 25, Eng. Trans. Thorkild Jacobsen, "The Wiles of Women," in *The Harps That Once: Sumerian Poetry in Translation* (New York: Yale University Press, 1987), 9–12.
31. See YBT I 28; see also the Middle Assyrian Laws 55 and 56.
32. Ilona Roshkow, *Upon the Dark Places: Anti-Semitism and Sexism in English Renaissance Bible Translation*, Bible and Literature Series 28 (Sheffield, Eng.: Almond Press, 1990), 97–119.
33. See Frymer-Kensky, *In the Wake of the Goddesses*, 194, 274. The verb has more recently been studied by Lyn M. Bechtel, "What if Dinah was not Raped (Gen. 34)," *Journal for the Study of the Old Testament* 62 (1994): 19–36, who points out that when 'inah follows skb ("he lay with") as it does in this story, the implication is never rape.
34. For such revenge see Julian Pitt-Rivers, *The Fate of Shechem or the Politics of Sex*; and Lucy Mair, *Marriage*, 159–76.
35. The sacred woman, the *gedesha*, is not a sacred prostitute, though she may have had free exercise of her sexuality. For discussion see Frymer-Kensky, *In the Wake of the Goddess*, 199–202 and the literature cited.
36. Judg. 1:8–15.

37. Judg. 10—12. There is much to say about the story of Jephthah's daughter, but this is not the place. See Peggy Day, "From the Child Is Born the Woman: The Story of Jephthah's Daughter" in *Gender and Difference in Ancient Israel* (Minneapolis: Fortress Press, 1989), 58–74; and Frymer-Kensky, *Victors, Virgins and Victims: Reading the Women of the Bible* (New York: Schocken Books, forthcoming), with literature cited there.

38. We know nothing about the institution of *pilegesh*, "concubine" or wife of lesser status. We can speculate that girls who could not command a full bride-price, or who came equipped with a lower dowry, might become a *pilegesh* rather than an *ishah*. We might also suggest that the essence of the difference is that the *pilegesh's* son would not become the firstborn, or chief heir, but this is guesswork.

39. Judg. 19—21.

40. The captive bride, Deut. 21:10–14; the law of the firstborn, Deut. 21:15–17; the rebellious son, Deut. 21:18–21; the nonvirgin daughters, Deut. 22:13–21; 22:39–29. For discussion, see Tikva Frymer-Kensky, "Deuteronomy," in *The Women's Bible Commentary*, ed. Carol Newsom and Sharon Ringe (London: SPCK, 1992), 52–62.

41. For this development see Claudia Camp, *Wisdom and the Feminine in the Book of Proverbs*, Bible and Literature 11, (Sheffield, Eng.: Almond Press, 1985).

42. Mal. 3:23–24.

4

The Family
in Rabbinic Judaism

ALLAN KENSKY

Rabbinic Judaism views the family as essential to human fulfillment and to service of the Divine. Family life is elevated to the rank of *mitzvah*, of religious obligation.[1] The commandment to engage in family life is derived from the call to the first humans, "Be fruitful and multiply" (Gen. 1:28). While this charge was, according to Genesis, given to both men and women, rabbinic Judaism saw the commandment to procreate as devolving particularly on men. Though one Talmudic sage, Rabbi Johanan ben Beroka, saw the commandment as obligating both males and females, the majority of the sages, for one reason or another, saw propagation as obligatory for males and voluntary for females.[2] Among the suggested reasons for this distinction is the realization that women undertake serious risks in giving birth, and they could not be obligated to place their lives in danger.[3]

A rabbinic reading of Genesis 1—2 sees marriage as part of the divine plan for the proper functioning of the world. In linking the two accounts of the creation of humanity as described in Genesis 1 and 2, the rabbis read Genesis 1:28, "and God blessed them," as referring to God's active role in sanctifying the "marriage" of Adam and Eve. "God took a cup of blessing and blessed them," comments Genesis Rabbah,[4] which sees God as serving as the officiant in the marriage of the first two humans. The rabbis see the arrival of woman in Genesis 2 as completing the work of creation. At least one source points out that Adam is called "man" only after the creation of woman—before that the first human is referred to only as *adam*, earthling.[5] True fulfillment for a man, according to this view, can occur only in marriage. The classic statement of man's "need" to marry is found in Genesis Rabbah:

> Rabbi Jacob taught: Whoever has no wife exists without good, without help, without joy, without blessing, without atonement. Without good—"It is not good for the earthling to be alone (Gen. 2:18)." Without help—"I will make a helper for him." Without

joy—as it says, "You shall rejoice, you and your household (Deut. 14:26)." Without blessing—"to set a blessing in your house (Ezek. 44:30)." Without atonement—"and he shall atone for himself and for his house (Lev. 16:11)." Rabbi Simon in the name of Rabbi Joshua ben Levi said: Also without peace, as it says, "and you are at peace and your house is at peace (1 Sam. 25:6)." Rabbi Joshua of Sikhnin in the name of Rabbi Levi said: Also without life, as it says, "Enjoy life with the woman you love (Eccl. 9:9)." Rabbi Hiyya bar Gamda said: He is also not a complete human, as it says, "and God blessed them and called their name Adam (Gen. 5:2)." And some say: He also causes the Divine image to be diminished, as it says "for God created the earthling in the Divine image (Gen. 9:6)." What does it say immediately after? "And you be fruitful and multiply (Gen. 9:7)."[6]

In other comments on marriage, the Midrash clearly gives weight to the psychological and emotional components of the marital bond and the role of marriage in supplanting earlier emotional attachments, namely the parent-child bond. In commenting on Genesis 2:24, "therefore a man leaves his father and mother and cleaves to his wife and they become one flesh," Pirke de Rabbi Eliezer writes:

From here you learn that until one marries, his love is directed towards his parents. After a man marries his love is directed to his wife, as it says, Therefore a man leaves his father and his mother and cleaves to his wife. Can a man abandon the commandment of honoring his parents? Rather, it means that his soul's love cleaves to his wife, as it says, and he shall cleave to his wife.[7]

One should note that other, more legalistically oriented voices, interpret the words "and he shall cleave to his wife" as warning against adultery and homosexuality.[8]

The religious underpinnings of marriage in the rabbinic system can be seen most clearly in the seven benedictions of marriage recited by the officiant at the marriage ceremony. The traditional Jewish wedding ceremony consists of two parts, betrothal (erusin) and marriage (nisuin). Now celebrated as one event, originally the two ceremonies were distinct, with betrothal taking place as much as a year before the marriage. Upon betrothal, the legal commitment of the couple to one another was established, but the couple continued to live apart. With nisuin, married life began. The betrothal ceremony is androcentric, with the man "taking" his bride by means of a declaration of betrothal and the presentation of a ring. In the marriage ceremony the bride and groom are addressed as a unit by the officiant, who recites seven blessings on their behalf.

These seven blessings, found in complete form in the Babylonian Talmud,[9] establish the mythic context for the marriage that is being celebrated. Not surprisingly, it is the imagery of Genesis that is first invoked in these blessings. Immediately after the blessing of thanksgiving is recited for the cup of wine, God is praised for creating the universe for his glory. The third blessing praises God for creating humanity, and the fourth praises God for creating in humanity the ability to perpetuate itself. The fifth blessing recalls Zion, mother of the people, and points to Zion's joy in seeing her children return. The sixth blessing calls on God to bring joy to the "beloved companions" as it once was brought to the first humans in Eden. The seventh, and longest, blessing expands on the themes of the earlier blessings. It proclaims God as the source for joy, companionship, and love and expresses the hope that the sound of the bride and groom will once again fill the courtyards of Judah and Jerusalem. Through these blessings, the individual man and woman celebrating their marriage are led to see their wedding as a link in the divine plan leading from Creation to Redemption. They are linked both with the universal, through allusions to the first humans, and with the particular history of Israel, through references to Zion. The blessings clearly express the divine pleasure in both the physical and emotional aspects of marital bonding, and point to love as the ideal in marriage.

The rabbinic ideal of marital love is captured in stories of rabbis and their wives who were linked by strong emotional bonds and who displayed great devotion to one another. Stories tell of self-sacrifice going in both directions. Generations of Jews have been nurtured on the story of the wife of Rabbi Akiba, who suffered years of separation from her husband so that he could study Torah in the academy.[10] Such self-sacrifice on the part of the wife is counterbalanced by rabbinic statements that praise men who love their wives as themselves and who honor and provide for their wives more than they would for themselves.[11]

The rabbinic family was clearly hierarchical. The responsibilities to support the family and educate the children rested on the husband and father. The husband and his male children above the age of thirteen were bound by the full range of public and private religious observances; women were exempted from the "positive time-bound" commandments, which included public worship. The wife had defined duties of service to her husband. Children were obligated to honor and obey parents. Despite the patriarchal nature of the family, the wife was afforded a revered place in the home. In the traditional weekly Sabbath observance, practiced in Jewish homes for centuries, the wife stood beside her husband at the Sabbath eve table as he read her the tribute to the "woman of

valor" from Proverbs 30. To this day, Orthodox Jewish literature emphasizes the separate but revered place of the woman in the Jewish home,
and is wont to point to the woman's role as "queen of the household."[12]

The rabbinic emphasis on the family as a basic religious unit was
made more urgent after the destruction of the Temple and the loss of
the people's geographic center. In the absence of the Temple, the family and home, alongside the synagogue, became the *mikdash me'at*, the
miniature sanctuary. The major rituals of Judaism were moved to the
home. The table became the altar, with blessings and prayers offered
around it. The Sabbath was ushered in and brought to a close with the
home rituals of candle lighting, *kiddush*, and *havdalah*. The Passover eve
service, once celebrated in the Temple precincts with the eating of the
paschal lamb, was moved to the home, where the elaborate Seder service and meal was now celebrated. While all these observances could be
performed alone or with a larger community, the clear ideal was to
observe them in a home, a familial setting. This process of moving the
major ritual observances of Judaism to the home was largely the work
of the Pharisees, who taught and legislated in the generations immediately following the destruction of the Temple by the Romans in 66 C.E.
The Pharisees established the family as the prime Jewish religious and
educational unit: Temples and synagogues could be destroyed, but if
the family would remain intact, Judaism would survive.

Four major "basic Jewish family values" emerge from the Talmud
and serve as the family ideal for traditional Jewish society.[13] The first,
now termed *taharat hamishpaha*, purity of the family, recognizes the
possibility of hallowing sexuality through marriage. Sexual activity is
limited to marriage. Adultery, defined as intercourse with a married
woman, is forbidden by force of biblical law. Premarital and extramarital relations with an unmarried woman are likewise forbidden, though
not with the same weight as adultery.[14] Traditional Judaism sees marital sex as being necessary not only for the propagation of the species but
for the physical and emotional health and well-being of both partners.[15]

As with other areas of life, sexual relations within marriage are
guided by religious law. Husbands are obligated to have intercourse
with their wives at regular intervals, the frequency of the relations
depending on the husband's availability as a result of his employment.[16]
Wives too were advised to be responsive to their husbands' sexual
needs. For scholars, Friday night was considered the appropriate time
for intercourse. Coming on the Sabbath, the act was seen not only as an
aspect of enjoyment of the Sabbath but as another manifestation of the
holiness of the day.[17] In their sanctioning of marital relations on the
Sabbath, the Pharisees distinguished themselves from earlier sectarians,

as well as from the later opponents of rabbinic tradition, the Karaites, who considered sexual activity on the Sabbath to be prohibited.[18]

While some medieval sources viewed sexual relations within marriage exclusively through the lens of obligation, other sources, especially those influenced by Kabbalist thinking, clearly saw marital sex as lovemaking and called on husbands to arouse their wives through romantic words and foreplay.[19] In the classic Kabbalist formulation, the sexual union of husband and wife is seen as a source for divine energy entering the universe, and symbolic of God's love for God's people.[20]

The rabbinic laws on menstruation call for husband and wife to abstain from sexual intercourse from the onset of the monthly period until the woman immerses in a *mikveh*, a ritual bath, after counting seven "clean" days from the cessation of her period. The system is clearly based on Levitical concepts of impurity, which were intensified by the rabbis. Modern thinkers, in reinterpreting these laws, have sought to move away from the language of impurity, and suggest that the separation of husbands and wives for close to two weeks out of every month serves to increase their desire for one another.[21] Increasingly, in certain circles, the separation followed by immersion has taken on meaning as a "woman's ritual" focusing on hallowing the woman's body and the sexual act.[22] In some circles the immersion is also followed by men so as to equalize the practice.

A second "basic Jewish family value" is the obligation to rear children. A man must father at least two children in order to fulfill the commandment to "be fruitful and multiply."[23] Talmudic law outlines definite responsibilities of parents to children. A father is considered obligated to circumcise his son, to redeem him, to teach him Torah, to marry him off, and to teach him a trade. Some sages added the requirement to teach him to swim.[24] While this rabbinic formulation is directed to sons, Jewish tradition clearly saw parental responsibilities as including both boys and girls. Fathers are obligated to support their daughters to adulthood.[25] They are responsible to marry and dower them.[26] They are charged with guiding all their children in God's ways.[27] While the obligations of parents to their children are framed in terms of concrete acts, some authorities see a clear obligation to "love" one's children.[28] Letters found in the Cairo Genizah describe with great tenderness the love of parents to children.[29]

The third traditional Jewish family value is *kibud av va'em*, filial responsibility. The child has obligations to honor and respect his parents as long as they live, and after death. The child was considered responsible for his parents' welfare in their old age, and was called on to honor them through mourning and commemorative observances after death. The rabbis often placed the commandment to honor one's parents on the same level as the commandment to honor God.[30] A person had, according to the rabbis, three creators: father, mother, and God.[31]

More than one commentator has pointed out that the Torah does not command the child to love his or her parents.[32] The biblical "honor" and "fear/respect/awe" (Hebrew, *mora*) are given concrete application by the rabbis. One respects one's parents by not contradicting their words or sitting in their place. One honors one's parents by attending to their needs, and by leading them in and out.[33] According to the Talmud, one should remain silent in the face of embarrassment wrought by a parent. If a parent should take one's wallet and throw it into the sea in one's presence, one should accept the abuse silently.[34] Obedience to parents is, however, not unconditional. Commenting on the verse, "Each man shall revere his mother and his father, and you shall observe my Sabbaths (Lev. 19:3)," the rabbis pointed out that reverence for God's Sabbath (and other commandments) supersedes the commandment to obey one's parents.[35] Similarly a person may exercise an independent choice regarding marriage, as that too involves fulfilling God's commandment.[36]

The fourth value of family life is *shalom bayit*, peace in the home. It flows from the words of the seventh marriage blessing, "love and unity, peace and companionship." The rabbis saw peace in the home as a major goal of marriage, and encouraged a spirit of compromise to attain it. Even compromise on religious matters was deemed acceptable if it served to bring husband and wife together.[37] When commenting on the judicial procedure of the suspected adulteress of Numbers 5, the rabbis pointed out that God allowed the divine name to be erased in the preparation of the potion because of the importance of bringing peace to husband and wife.[38] The rabbis commented that God lied when telling Abraham that the reason that Sarah laughed when learning that she would have a child was that she, rather than Abraham, was old. God lied, according to the rabbis, to maintain peace in the home of Abraham and Sarah.[39]

Jewish Law and the Family

The patriarchal nature of the Jewish family as described by rabbinic Judaism is seen most clearly in the traditional *halakhah* that governs marriage, divorce, and inheritance. In all these areas rabbinic Judaism delineates status along gender lines. The rabbinic conception of woman is totally different from its conception of man. Man is the "conqueror," the one who goes out to the world, who earns an income.[40] Woman, in the rabbinic view, is more vulnerable. She does not take initiative in relations between the sexes; she is not a public person; she needs to be protected by her husband and by society.[41] It is this view of woman which underlies the *halakhah* of marriage, divorce, and inheritance.

In the traditional marriage, it is the man who "takes" a woman to be his wife. The groom pronounces the declaration of betrothal as he places a ring on the right index finger of his bride; the bride accepts the ring but offers no verbal response. Similarly, it is the husband who authorizes the writing of a *get*, a writ of divorce, to his wife. The traditional *ketubah*, or marriage contract, records for the most part the groom's acceptance of obligations towards his bride; the bride's acceptance is described through the brief response, "and she consented and became his wife." The passivity of the woman in these changes of status reflects the rabbis' view that women are the objects of the rituals. Needless to say, this view of women is a source of considerable discomfort for many contemporary Jewish women.

Dating as far back as the fifth century B.C.E., the *ketubah*, or marriage contract, was further developed by the rabbis as a statement of the obligations of the husband to his wife and as a guarantee of a basic financial settlement for the wife in the case of divorce or widowhood. Under the *ketubah*, the groom obligated himself to a bridal gift and to restoring the value of his bride's dowry in the case of death or the dissolution of marriage. In the case of a virgin, these amounts totalled four hundred Tyrian *zuzim*, a significant sum that would have served as a serious deterrent to divorce.[42] (At various points in time, the value of the four hundred *zuzim* was translated into the prevailing currency.) Included in the *ketubah* were three principal areas of obligation to one's wife: food, clothing, and sexual relations.[43] The rabbis also obligated the husband to redeem his wife if she fell into captivity and to provide for her medical needs should she become ill.[44]

The rabbis recognized the right of the wife to retain her own earnings. If she did so, however, her husband was not to be considered obligated to provide for her food.[45] A longstanding dispute revolved around who was to pay for the housekeeper.[46] While the woman could provide other arrangements for household chores, she remained obligated to perform the more intimate task of washing her husband. A woman's right to lead an independent social existence was recognized. A wife had to be free to visit friends and family, the sick, and the mourners. Maimonides warned that a wife was never to feel as a prisoner in her own home.[47] Jewish law recognized that husbands and wives could arrive at new understandings of their relationship. In regard to all domestic relations between husband and wife, any agreement mutually accepted by both parties was valid and binding, provided it did not violate biblical law or the public good.[48]

While the text of the *ketubah* became fairly standardized in the Middle Ages, earlier *ketubot* exhibited considerable variation. The size of the dowry varied widely until it became a set amount in Ashkenazic communities in the twelfth century. Recent studies of specimens of *ketubot* found in the Cairo Genizah and written according to traditions prevailing in Palestine during the rabbinic period indicate that these *ketubot* contained a clause acknowledging the wife's right to divorce her husband.[49] A wide-ranging study by S. D. Goitein of *ketubot* in the Islamic world as found in the Cairo Genizah points to the *ketubah*'s function in addressing numerous marital concerns. In some marriage contracts, for example, the wife's right to work outside the home was guaranteed. In others, her husband specifically promised not to take another wife or a maidservant without his wife's explicit permission. The insertion of this clause was a major protection against polygamy in the Sephardic and Oriental Jewish communities.[50]

The rabbinic view of marriage saw wives as obligated to honor their husbands. The Talmud clearly outlined a number of household tasks that a wife was obligated to provide for her husband. These included grinding flour, baking, washing, cooking, knitting, nursing, making her husband's bed, mixing his drinks, and washing his face, hands, and feet.[51] This list of chores led some medieval commentators to describe the wife as a servant. An extreme position saw this subservient role as a fulfillment of God's curse to Eve, "and he shall rule you" (Gen. 3:16).[52] While Maimonides granted husbands the right to discipline their wives, including "with the stick," in this regard Maimonides has gone beyond Talmudic precedent and is not followed by later authorities.[53] From Talmudic times on, wife-beating has been considered improper and unacceptable behavior towards one's wife. Post-Talmudic authorities have ruled that the husband should be ordered to cease this practice, and if he continues to beat his wife, he should be compelled to divorce her and pay her the *ketubah*.[54]

Regarding polygamy, while the Talmud did not forbid its practice, it was a rarity in rabbinic times.[55] As we have seen, in Sephardic countries it was held in check by means of a clause in the *ketubah*. In Northern Europe, it was virtually eliminated by the *herem*, the ban, of the Court of Rabbi Gershom of Mayence (eleventh century). Rabbi Gershom's ban, most probably originally intended for the Jewish communities in the Rhineland, was soon accepted throughout Northern Europe and became the standard practice among Ashkenazic Jews. Due to its association with Rabbi Gershom ("The Luminary of the Exile"), the ban was considered to be of such force that it could override earlier, even biblical, law—such as the law of levirate marriage requiring a man to marry his brother's widow when his brother has left no children.[56] The ban remains in effect today. Some authorities speak of its expiring after a millennium, though most of the earlier sources do not speak of such a limitation.[57]

The nature of Jewish religious divorce has occasioned problems for women faced with husbands who refuse to cooperate in the issuing of a divorce. According to *halakhah*, Jewish divorce originates with the husband. While originally the husband could present his wife with a divorce without her consent, Rabbi Gershom of Mayence, in another communal decree, required the wife's consent for a divorce.[58] According to Jewish law, a wife can petition a court to compel a husband to write a divorce in a number of designated instances, including lack of support and his restricting her freedom.[59] Nonetheless, the husband must authorize the writing of the *get*. In earlier times, when Jewish communities exercised sanctions against their members, the threat of communal sanction must have served as sufficient pressure for recalcitrant husbands to relent and write divorces for their wives. In more recent times, when the power of local Jewish communities has weakened, such communal pressures have become largely ineffective. For this reason, over the past century rabbis have spent considerable time pondering legal remedies to the question of the *agunah*, the anchored woman, unable to remarry because of her husband's refusal to grant her a *get*. The remedies proposed have included conditional marriage, prenuptial agreements, a clause in the *ketubah* obligating the parties to the decisions of a rabbinic court, annulment of the marriage, and appeal to the civil courts.[60] None of these potential remedies have gained universal acceptance, and some, such as the prenuptial agreement and clause in the marriage contract, have had only limited success when applied.[61] The problem of the *agunot* remains. Although found recently in ancient Palestinian *ketubot*, allowing the wife to initiate a divorce has not been seriously considered as a remedy to date.

The third area in which the patriarchal nature of the Jewish family as described by rabbinic Judaism is evident is in the area of property and inheritance. While a married woman's right to own property was traditionally upheld, in effect a woman lost control over such property upon marriage. The husband was granted the right of *usufruct* for benefit of the household, though he could sell such property only with his wife's consent. Clearly, the husband still held the upper hand over this property.[62] Similarly, inheritance was transferred through the sons. While a father might give a gift to any of his children during his lifetime, after death his sons were his heirs. His daughter inherited only in the absence of sons. A man's wife could not be his heir.

This does not mean, however, that a wife has no portion in her husband's estate according to Jewish law. A wife's claim on her husband's estate through her *ketubah* takes the force of a lien against the estate and must be paid before the heirs receive any of their inheritance. A widow is entitled to receive from her husband's estate the type of support she was accustomed to during the years of her marriage. Similarly, a man's daughters are entitled to be supported from the estate and to receive dowry from the estate. In actuality, the portion alloted to the widow and daughters of the deceased may exceed the portion inherited by the sons.[63]

An egalitarian view of man and woman inevitably leads to a questioning of the rabbinic law on marriage, divorce, and inheritance. Contemporary liberal Jews have taken steps to change the ground rules in the first of these areas, that of marriage. The past three decades have seen the proliferation of *ketubot*, many of which incorporate egalitarian ideas. Some of these *ketubot* add sections that express the couple's commitment to support one another and create a home together, while retaining the traditional statements of obligation of husband to wife. Others have eliminated these obligations altogether.[64] Many couples now are married in double ring ceremonies. In some, the bride as well as the groom says, "You are consecrated to me by this ring in accordance with the law of Moses and Israel." The modifications in the wedding ceremony, occurring as they do under the individual wedding canopy and arrived at through negotiations between the officiating rabbi and the couple who are married, do not threaten the legal foundations of the community. In the area of divorce, where the ramifications for the community are greater, change is much slower.

Changes in the law often lag behind changes in reality. If rabbinic family law contains elements that seem anachronistic, it is undoubtedly because it does not reflect the egalitarian—or largely egalitarian—family pattern that is the norm in liberal Jewish families today. Given the fairly rapid empowerment of women in virtually all wings of the Jewish community today, it appears likely that the next decades will witness an increasing reevaluation of the status of women in Jewish family law. The prime question, of course, is the malleability of *halakhah* in these areas. A further question is the degree to which minor adjustments of the *halakhah* will be considered acceptable. Finding the *halakhic* means to compel recalcitrant husbands to provide divorces for their wives may relieve the problem of the *agunot*, but it will not address the inequality of a woman's inability to issue a divorce. One suspects that the call will increase for a fundamental reworking of the *halakhic* frameworks of marriage. As communal norms shift, one can hope that there will be a new "rabbinic will," which will be followed by a new "*halakhic* way."[65]

Myths and Realities

Recent studies on the Jewish family in history have pointed to diversity as well as continuity in the family down to modern times. Change, as much as stability, marked the Jewish family. Through this long period, however, the emphasis on marriage was a constant. In medieval Europe, this led to adolescent marriage, arranged by the parents for their children. According to the historian Jacob Katz, this was done largely to prevent violations of the sexual codes.[66] These early marriages went against the clear advice of the Talmud, and the medieval French Tosafists therefore felt called on to justify the practice. The practice of arranged marriages, with bride and groom not meeting one another until their wedding day, clearly contradicted the Talmudic insistence that a couple could enter marriage only by the free consent of both parties. The medieval authorities explained, therefore, that even though the bride and groom did not know each other before marriage, their entry into the marriage was with consent. Similarly, the rabbis of the day confronted the reality of financial considerations, which assumed prime importance in arranging marriages and appeared to contravene Talmudic warnings against marrying for money. As the medieval rabbis saw it, the Talmud was warning against marrying *solely* for material reasons.[67]

The rabbinic statements on marriage and family life often contrasted with actual life in those families most intimately connected with the world of the Talmud, namely rabbinic and scholarly families. For many men in these families, the Torah and its study were the most important outlets for passion and devotion. The Talmud itself relates stories of rabbis who absented themselves from their families for long periods of time in order to study in the academies.[68] Studies of rabbinic families in Poland and Lithuania at the dawn of the modern era document severe disruptions in such families, caused by the rabbis' need to find employment in distant cities or to devote enormous amounts of time to their studies. In such cases it was largely the wife, though also at times the children, who assumed the economic support of the household.[69]

It was the entry into the modern world, with its new emphasis on individualism, that saw the shift from adolescent to adult marriage and from arranged marriage to marriage by choice. In Western Europe this occurred by the early nineteenth century; in Eastern Europe it occurred later. Arranged marriage for one's adolescent children remained the norm in Eastern Europe until the last decades of the nineteenth century.[70] The *maskilim*, the Enlightenment thinkers of Eastern Europe, railed against this practice and spoke of the pain in such marriages: They were spent largely in the orbit of the young bride's family, where the son-in-law, supported by his in-laws so that he could continue his Talmudic studies, was not always appreciated.[71]

The late nineteenth century saw the emergence of the bourgeois family among Central and Western European Jews, alongside the close-knit family of the Eastern European *shtetls*, or small villages, and the extended family of the North African and Middle Eastern Jews. It is to a great extent the folk memory of life in such family settings that provides contemporary Jews with their conceptions of traditional Jewish family life. In particular, the group recollections (or imagining) of communal celebration of life cycle events and holy days in the *shtetl* have entered into the mythic consciousness of contemporary Jews. Life in the *shtetl* is also remembered for the intensity of affective life in the family, characterized by extreme devotion on the part of the parents, especially the mother, and the expectation that children would grow up to lead exemplary lives as Jews and as *mentschen* ("human beings"), thereby bringing their parents joy and *nakhes*.[72] In particular, Jewish society expressed the expectation that the child would grow up "to the wedding canopy and to a life of good deeds,"[73] thereby perpetuating the life of the Jewish people. These attributes of the *shtetl* family, which made for both solidarity and tension, have continued to mold Jews to the present, more than a century after the mass immigration from Eastern Europe began.

The Contemporary Jewish Family

The great upheavals in Jewish life of the past century have had a significant impact on the Jewish family. Vast waves of immigration have affected all major Jewish communities. The century has seen the mass immigration of East European Jewish immigrants to the United States and their successful adaptation to and integration into American life. Russian Jewry was largely secularized under the sway of Soviet Communism. The traditional East European centers of Jewish life were decimated, their survivors scattering over six continents. The State of Israel grew, absorbing many diaspora communities, and in the process it brought many traditional Jewish cultures into rapid contact with the modern world.

Contemporary Jewry lives in the shadow of the myth of the traditional Jewish family. The myth of the extended *shtetl* family with its warmth and solidarity is frequently invoked as an ideal to which contemporary families should aspire. Often the burden of the myth weighs heavily on Jews whose family lives in no way match up with that idealized image.[74] Sociologists writing about Jewish life as late as the 1970s lauded the continuity in Jewish family life and saw the solidarity of the Jewish family as one of the major factors making for the successful

adaptation of Jews to American life.[75] To be sure, significant changes
occurred in the family as American Jews adapted to the surrounding
culture. The nuclear family became the norm, replacing the extended
family of the *shtetl*. The "child-centered" family replaced the earlier
patriarchal model.[76] But the family itself appeared to be solid. More
recent writings have pointed to assimilatory trends affecting the shape
and character of American Jewish families. Clearly, by the 1980s the
Jewish community had become deeply concerned about the future of
the American Jewish family, as studies pointed to the increasing number of singles, divorced men and women, gay and lesbian couples, and
the great number of Jews married to non-Jews.[77] The National Jewish
Population Survey of 1990, the first wide-ranging demographic study
of American Jewry in two decades, documented this shift away from the
conventional family. The traditional family, comprising parents and
children living under one roof, totalled approximately one-third of all
identified Jewish households. Significantly, an enumeration of types of
households in which American Jews resided indicated that the single-
person household was the most prevalent household type, comprising
some 20 percent of all Jewish households. Over ten percent of
American Jews resided in such households, which consisted of the
never-married and the widowed and divorced without children,
including many of the elderly.[78]

The National Jewish Population Survey sent shock waves through
the organized Jewish community, largely because of the decline in
Jewish identification and affiliation that it documented. The connections between the solidity of the Jewish family and Jewish continuity
had been indicated by a major study by Steven M. Cohen in 1982,
which documented lesser rates of affiliation and participation in Jewish
ritual life by those living in alternative households.[79] He suggested that
Jewish organizations, which were traditionally family-oriented, expand
their vision in order to engage in serious efforts of outreach directed to
those living in alternative households. In the absence of such programs
of outreach, Cohen expressed the hope that those living alternative
lifestyles would themselves develop their own Jewish subcultures.[80]

A different response to the changing demographic situation has
come from those communal leaders who have sounded the call for an
increased emphasis on programs of "family life education" in synagogues and religious schools.[81] The aim of such programs is to bring
whole families into the synagogue for celebratory and educational
events, whose goal is both to increase the Jewish identification with the
family and its solidarity as a unit. The programs seek to avoid the pitfalls of many other Jewish educational efforts, which have been aimed

exclusively at children and which therefore fail to address the low level of Jewish cultural knowledge present in the children's parents.

The Feminist Challenge

The impact of the feminist revolution on American Jewish life and on the Jewish family has been dramatic. In a period of less than three decades, feminism has brought about a full-scale reexamination of many assumptions of Jewish life that affect the place of the Jewish woman in the home, synagogue, and workplace. Energies released by the feminist awakening have inspired a burst of creativity in liturgy and ritual and are helping to reshape the contours of American Judaism as it approaches the twenty-first century.

The feminist challenge to Judaism has taken several distinct forms. A major thrust has been towards the full inclusion of women in religious and communal life.[82] Beyond that, feminist thinkers have challenged the patriarchal assumptions of biblical and rabbinic religion. Feminist theologians have questioned the very bases of a religion developed largely by men and centering on a God described primarily through male lenses and addressed through male imagery and gender-based language.[83] The shock waves emanating from the feminist challenge have heavily impacted the liberal movements in Judaism, and have been felt in segments of Orthodoxy as well.

The past quarter century has seen large numbers of American Jewish women entering the workforce, in proportions exceeding that of other religious groups.[84] This has led to a broad redefining of the role of the woman in the home. In the setting of the individual home and family, new patterns of division of labor have emerged, with men increasingly taking part in childrearing functions and in household tasks.[85] Feminists have challenged the Jewish community to develop a system of childcare that would allow women to pursue careers while continuing to raise children.[86]

Jewish feminists have felt acutely the tension between the pulls of self-fulfillment and Jewish communal expectations regarding family life. While Jewish tradition affirmed the right of women not to bear children,[87] most Jewish women, educated in schools and from families that warned against granting Hitler "posthumous victories," have felt called on to raise families. Feminists have, however, sought to remove the onus for Jewish continuity from the Jewish woman. Some have pointed to the irony that a demographic alarm is being sounded precisely at the time that Jewish women are beginning to find self-fulfillment outside the home.[88] Others have suggested that the role of the family in Jewish survival itself has been exaggerated—the community is no less responsible for the welfare of the family than is the family for the welfare of the community.[89]

The pull towards self-actualization that underlies much of feminist aspiration has led many Jewish women to alternative lifestyles. A significant number of women are single by choice. Some single women have chosen to become parents as unattached mothers. Large numbers of women have opted out of failed marriages. Many Jewish women have intermarried. Lesbian couples are no longer a rarity. Not surprisingly, given the strong pro-nuclear family leanings of the Jewish community, women leading alternative lifestyles have often felt called on to explain their choices to the community.[90] Some have argued that Jewish continuity can be expressed in means other than giving birth and raising children; others have suggested that the community, rather than the family, should be seen as the fundamental unit of Jewish life.[91] Virtually all express respect for those women engaged in marriage and childrearing, while seeking to broaden the community's vision to include support of alternative lifestyles. Nonetheless, traditionalists have attacked these alternatives to the nuclear family, arguing that the contemporary American focus on self-fulfillment runs counter to the traditional Jewish values of service to God and community.[92]

Jewish feminists have seriously challenged the place of women in traditional Jewish law. The theoretical challenge has been directed at the woman as the "other"—as the one acted on by men and seen largely in relation to men. As the "other," the Jewish woman was traditionally excluded from the public domain, including the ritual life of the community.[93] The strong feminist push for equality in the last two decades has led to the almost total inclusion of women in public religious life and leadership in Reform, Reconstructionist, and Conservative Judaism (though a segment of the Conservative movement remains opposed to equal participation by women). A broad consensus among Jewish women, including Orthodox women, has emerged regarding the inequity of traditional divorce laws, which have left many women unable to remarry because their husbands have refused to grant them a get.[94] The various remedies suggested have either not been fully implemented, or when implemented have not eliminated the problem. The situation regarding divorce continues to highlight the patriarchal nature of the family in Jewish law, an issue yet to be resolved by the halakhic system.

Under the influence of feminism, other assumptions regarding the Jewish family have been reexamined. The existence of domestic violence and abuse in Jewish families has been recognized and a profile of the Jewish battered wife developed. Unwilling to believe that a Jewish husband would engage in wife-beating without reason, the victim more often than not considers herself responsible. When she can no longer take the punishment and seeks communal support, incredulous family members and rabbis refuse to believe her.[95] Social workers have pointed to the danger in rabbis' invoking *shalom bayit* (the value of domestic tranquility) as a reason to keep marriages intact in this and other instances of marital distress. Invoking this concept can serve to condemn a woman to a painful, destructive marriage.[96]

The past two decades have seen major innovations in Jewish religious expression, brought about by the inclusion of women in the public religious life of the community. New rituals and prayers addressing the major stages in the lives of women have been created and accepted. Alongside the traditional low-key naming ceremony for girls, rituals of *Simhat Bat* (rejoicing for the daughter) and *Brit Banot* (covenant for daughters) have been developed.[97] The Bat Mitzvah ceremony, first introduced by Mordecai Kaplan for his daughter Judith in 1922, is observed not only by Reform, Reconstructionist, and Conservative Jews, but increasingly in modern Orthodox congregations, which allow the celebration, generally including the demonstration of competence in Torah study by the celebrant though without a liturgical role. In all modern Jewish movements girls have been granted access to traditional study. In Reform, Reconstructionist, and Conservative Judaism this extends to the rabbinate and cantorate. In modern Orthodoxy, this now extends to include Talmudic study in the level of the *yeshivah*, the Talmudic academy, though not as leading to rabbinic ordination. Voices within modern Orthodoxy, however, have begun to argue in favor of the ordination of women rabbis.[98]

Beyond those points in the life cycle traditionally marked by ritual, new prayers and rituals have been created by Jewish women for menarche, for pregnancy and childbirth, for menopause, and for other events in the life stages of women.[99] By "sanctifying" the particular change or transition a woman is experiencing and enabling her to benefit from the community's wisdom at crucial turning points in her life, these rituals can serve to enhance the place of the woman in the family. At the same time, the creators of these rituals are well advised to be careful not to invalidate those women who cannot or do not wish to participate in these events or rituals.

It is not surprising that the discussions of "Jewish continuity" inevitably turn to the state of the Jewish family. For centuries the family sustained Judaism. Not only are the Sabbaths and holy days celebrated primarily in the family, but the life cycle events of circumcision, naming, Bar and Bat Mitzvah, and marriage, which have become important occasions for the celebration and renewal of Jewish identity, are in effect family rituals. As families celebrate their own continuity in these events, they are also celebrating the continuity of Jewish life. As traditional family life decreases, so does active involvement in Jewish communal life.

As we have seen, family life is basic to the rabbinic conception of Judaism. A Judaism that sheds its emphasis on the family would be a highly altered form of the faith. On the other hand, a failure to expand the definition of the family to include the large numbers of Jews who live alone or in "alternative families" would cause the Jewish community to be cut off from many of its own children, with all the implications that step would have for the continuity of Judaism. The Jewish community's devotion to its children is too fundamental to allow it to turn its back on those who lead unconventional Jewish lives. If past history is any indication of the future, we can expect the Jewish people to adapt and respond to the many challenges posed by the changing faces of Jewish families at the cusp of the twenty-first century.

NOTES

1. Arnold Jacob Wolf, "Toward a Theology of Family," *Journal of Religion and Health* 6 (1967): 281.
2. *Babylonian Talmud Yebamot* 65b. Hereafter Babylonian Talmud is abbreviated as *bt*.
3. Tikva Frymer-Kensky, "Woman Jews," in *Women's and Men's Liberation: Testimonies of Spirit*, ed. Leonard Grob, Riffat Hassan, and Haim Gordon (New York: Greenwood Press, 1991), 35. Judith Hauptman suggests that women were not considered obligated to procreate because sexual initiative was in the hands of the male. She also suggests that one rabbinic text, the Tosefta, saw women as obligated to procreate. See Judith Hauptman, "Maternal Dissent: Women and Procreation in the Mishna," *Tikkun* 6 (Nov.–Dec. 1991): 81–82, 94–95.
4. *Genesis Rabbah* 8:13.
5. Pirke de Rabbi Eliezer, chap. 12. (For English, see Gerald Freiedlander, trans. [New York: Hermon Press, 1965], 88).
6. *Genesis Rabbah* 17:2, commenting on Gen. 2:18.
7. Pirke de Rabbi Eliezer, chap. 32. (Friedlander translation, 234).
8. *bt. Sanhedrin* 58a.
9. *bt. Ketubot* 8a.
10. *bt. Ketubot* 62b–63a.
11. *bt. Yebamot* 62b.
12. Eliyahu Kitov, *The Jew and His Home* (New York: Shengold Publishers, 1963), 70.
13. Benjamin Schlesinger, *The Jewish Family* (Toronto: University of Toronto Press, 1971), 6–7; Leon S. Lang, "Jewish Values in Family Relationship," *Conservative Judaism* 1 (June 1945): 9–18.

14. Moshe Meiselman, *Jewish Woman in Jewish Law* (New York: Ktav Publishing House, 1978), 124.

15. David Feldman, *Birth Control in Jewish Law* (New York: New York University Press, 1968), 70.

16. *bt. Ketubot* 61b; Maimonides, *Mishneh Torah*, Hilkhot Ishut 14:1–2.

17. David Biale, *Eros and the Jews* (New York: Basic Books, 1992), 54; Feldman, *Birth Control in Jewish Law*, 100–102.

18. S. D. Goitein, *A Mediterranean Society: The Jewish Communities of the Arab World as Portrayed in the Cairo Geniza, Vol. III: The Family* (Berkeley, Calif.: University of California Press, 1978): 168–69.

19. Meiselman, *Jewish Woman in Jewish Law*, 120.

20. Moshe Idel, "Sexual Metaphors and Praxis in the Kabbalah," in *The Jewish Family: Metaphor and Memory*, ed. David Kraemer (New York: Oxford University Press, 1989), 201–205.

21. See Norman Lamm, *A Hedge of Roses* (New York: Philipp Feldheim, 1972), 63; Meiselman, *Jewish Woman in Jewish Law*, 27.

22. See Rachel Adler, "*Tuman* and *Tahara*: Ends and Beginnings," in *The Jewish Woman*, ed. Elizabeth Koltun (New York: Schocken Books, 1976), 63–69.

23. The prevalent view among the sages was that the commandment was fulfilled upon the birth of a child of each sex. See *Mishnah Tevamot* 6:6.

24. *bt. Kiddushin* 29a.

25. *bt. Ketubot* 49a–49b.

26. *bt. Kiddushin* 30b; Louis Epstein, *The Jewish Marriage Contract* (New York: Jewish Theological Seminary of America, 1927), 189.

27. Gerald Blidstein, *Honor Thy Father and Mother: Filial Responsibility in Jewish Law and Ethics* (New York: Ktav Publishing House, 1975), 122.

28. Ibid., 57–58; Shoshana Matzner-Bekerman, *The Jewish Child: Halakhic Perspectives* (New York: Ktav Publishing House, 1984), 13–14. See also Yishak ben Eliakim, *Sefer Lev tov* (Poznan: np, 1620), 54b and Israel ibn al-Nakawa, *Menorat ha'maor*, ed. H. G. Enelow (New York: Bloch Publishers, 1931), IV, 144, quoted in Gershon David Hundert, "Jewish Children and Childhood in Early Modern East Central Europe," in *The Jewish Family: Metaphor and Memory*, 82–83.

29. Goitein, *Mediterranean Society*, 225–29.

30. Blidstein, *Honor Thy Father and Mother*, 4–8.

31. *bt. Niddah* 31a; *bt. Kiddushin* 30b.

32. Blidstein, *Honor Thy Father and Mother*, 55–56.

33. *bt. Kiddushin* 31a.

34. *bt. Kiddushin* 32a.

35. Blidstein, *Honor Thy Father and Mother*, 80–81.

36. Ibid., 88.

37. Kitov, *The Jew and His Home*, 41.

38. *Derekh Eretz Zuta* 11:9.

39. Ibid., 11:6.

40. *bt. Yebamot* 65b.

41. Meiselman, *Jewish Woman in Jewish Law*, 11–14.

42. Epstein, *The Jewish Marriage Contract*, 196.

43. Ibid., 149.

44. Ibid., 162, 164.

45. *bt. Ketubot* 58b.

46. Meiselman, *Jewish Woman in Jewish Law*, 82.

47. Maimonides, *Mishneh Torah*, Hilkhot Ishut 13:11.

48. Epstein, *The Jewish Marriage Contract*, 269.

49. Mordechai A. Friedman, *Jewish Marriage in Palestine: A Cairo Genizah Study* (New York: Jewish Theological Seminary of America, 1980), 18.

50. Goitein, *A Mediterranean Society*, 147; Epstein, *The Jewish Marriage Contract*, 272.

51. *bt. Ketubot* 59b, 61a.

52. See commentary of Nahmanides and Ibn Ezra on Gen. 3:16.

53. Maimonides, *Mishneh Torah*, Hilkhot Ishut 21:10; See Goitein, *A Mediterranean Society*, 185.

54. Epstein, *The Jewish Marriage Contract*, 219.

55. Louis Epstein, *Marriage Laws in the Bible and Talmud* (Cambridge, Mass.: Harvard University Press, 1942), 20.

56. Louis Finkelstein, *Jewish Self-Government in the Middle Ages* (New York: Jewish Theological Seminary of America, 1924), 27.

57. Finkelstein, *Jewish Self-Government*, 29.

58. Ibid., 24.

59. Meiselman, *Jewish Woman in Jewish Law*, 100.

60. Ibid., 103–10.

61. Ibid., 110–15.

62. Epstein, *The Jewish Marriage Contract*, 113.

63. Meiselman, *Jewish Woman in Jewish Law*, 94.

64. See Daniel Leifer, "On Writing New Ketubot," in *The Jewish Woman: New Perspectives*, ed. Elizabeth Koltun (New York: Shocken Books, 1976), 50–61.

65. Blu Greenberg, *On Women and Judaism: A View from Tradition* (Philadelphia: Jewish Publication Society of America, 1981), 44.

66. Jacob Katz, "Marriage and Family Life at the end of the Middle Ages (Hebrew)," *Zion* (1944): 22–23.

67. Katz, "Marriage and Family Life," 24.

68. *bt. Ketubot* 62b–63a.

69. Immanuel Etkes, "Marriage and Torah Study Among the *Lomdim* in Lithuania in the Nineteenth Century," in *The Jewish Family: Metaphor and Memory*, 153–73.

70. David Biale, "Childhood, Marriage and the Family in the Eastern European Jewish Enlightenment," in *The Jewish Family: Myths and Reality*, ed. Paula Hyman (New York: Holmes and Meier, 1986), 48.

71. Biale, "Childhood, Marriage and the Family," 49–57.

72. Mark Zborowski and Elizabeth Herzog, *Life is with People: The Culture of the Shtetl* (New York: International Universities Press, 1952), 330–60.

73. Included in the text of the traditional blessings recited at circumcision, naming, Bar and Bat Mitzvah.

74. See Paula Hyman, ed. *The Jewish Family: Myths and Reality*, 3–4; Paula Hyman, "The Modern Jewish Family: Image and Reality," in *The Jewish Family: Metaphor and Memory*, 179–80.

75. See Jack Balswick, "Are American Jewish Families Closely Knit?" in *The Jewish Family*, 15–24; Gerald S. Berman, "The Adaptable American Jewish Family: An Inconsistency in Theory," *Jewish Journal of Sociology* 18 (1976): 9–12; Gerhard Lenski, *The Religious Factor: A Sociological Study of Religious Impact on Politics, Economics and Family Life* (New York: Anchor Books, 1963), 219.

76. Nahum Glatzer, "The Jewish Family and Humanistic Values," *Journal of Jewish Communal Service* 36 (summer 1960): 269–73.

77. Steven M. Cohen, "The American Jewish Family Today," *American Jewish Year Book 1982* (New York: American Jewish Committee and Jewish Publication Society of America, 1981), 139–44.

78. Barry Kosmin, et al., *Highlights of the CJF National Jewish Population Survey* (New York: Council of Jewish Federations, 1991), 32–33.

79. Cohen, "The American Jewish Family Today," 148–53.

80. Ibid., 154.

81. See Samuel Heilman, *The Jewish Family Today: An Overview* (New York: Memorial Foundation of Jewish Culture, 1984), 47.

82. See Anne Lapidus Lerner, " 'Who Hast Not Made Me a Man': The Movement for Equal Rights for Women in American Jewry," *American Jewish Year Book 1977* (New York: American Jewish Committee and Jewish Publication Society of America, 1976), 3–38.

83. For an early formulation of this question, see the introduction to *On Being a Jewish Feminist: A Reader*, ed. Susannah Heschel (New York: Schocken Books, 1983), xxxii. For a thorough discussion of the issue see Judith Plaskow, *Standing Again at Sinai: Judaism From a Feminist Perspective* (New York: Harper & Row, 1990). For a discussion of gender and God-language see Tikva Frymer-Kensky, "On Feminine God-Talk," *The Reconstructionist* 59:1 (spring 1994): 48–55.

84. Sylvia Barack Fishman, "The Impact of Feminism on American Jewish Life," *American Jewish Year Book 1989* (New York: American Jewish Committee and Jewish Publication Society of America, 1989), 25.

85. See Sylvia Barack Fishman, *A Breath of Life: Feminism in the American Jewish Community* (New York: Free Press, 1993), 85–87; Allan Kensky, "The Dual Career Family: One Man's View," *Sh'ma* 20:395 (May 1990): 113–14.

86. See Anne Roiphe, "The Jewish Family: A Feminist Perspective," *Tikkun* I:2 (1986): 74–75; Ruth F. Brin, "Jewish Working Mothers: The Need for Pro-Family Policies," *The Reconstructionist* 52:4 (Jan.–Feb. 1987): 15–18.

87. See Tosefta Yebamot chap. 8 and Maimonides, *Mishneh Torah*, (Laws of Forbidden Relations chap. 21, no. 26), which state that a woman is not obligated to marry. Other authorities require a woman to marry to remove suspicion of misconduct. On a woman's status vis à vis the obligation to procreate, see Feldman, *Birth Control in Jewish Law*, 53–56.

88. Shirley Frank, "The Population Panic: Why Jewish Leaders Want Jewish Women to be Fruitful and Multiply," *Lilith* 1:4 (fall/winter 1977–78): 13–17.

89. See Susan Weidman Schneider, *Jewish and Female: Choices and Changes in our Lives Today* (New York: Simon & Schuster, 1984), 258–60; Paula Hyman, "The Jewish Family: Looking for a Usable Past," in *On Being a Jewish Feminist: A Reader*, 19–26.

90. See Laura Geller and Elizabeth Koltun, "Single and Jewish: Toward a New Definition of Completeness," in *The Jewish Woman: New Perspectives*, 43–49; Ruth Mason, "Single by Choice," in *Jewish Marital Status*, ed. Carol Diament (Northvale, N.J.: Jason Aronson, 1989), 42–46; Vicki Lindner, "Saying No to Motherhood," *Jewish Marital Status*, 283–90; Sheila Peltz Weinberg, "The Jewish Single-Parent Family," *Response* 14:4 (spring 1985): 77–84; Evelyn Torton Beck, ed., *Nice Jewish Girls: A Lesbian Anthology* (New York: Persephone Press, 1984); Christie Balka and Andy Rose, eds., *Twice Blessed: On Being Lesbian, Gay and Jewish* (Boston: Beacon Press, 1989).

91. See Martha A. Ackelsberg, "Families and the Jewish Community: A Feminist Perspective," *Response* 14 (spring 1985): 5–19; Martha A. Ackelsberg, "Jewish Family Ethics in a Post-halakhic Age," in *Imagining the Jewish Future: Essays and Responses*, ed. David A. Teutsch (New York: State University of New York Press, 1992), 149–64.

92. See Sylvia Barack Fishman, *A Breath of Life: Feminism in the American Jewish Community*, 245–46; See the introduction to Heschel, *On Being a Jewish Feminist*, xviii.

93. See Rachel Adler, "The Jew Who Wasn't There: *Halakhah* and the Jewish Woman," in Heschel, *On Being a Jewish Feminist*, 12–18; Paula Hyman, "The Other Half: Women in the Jewish Tradition," in *The Jewish Woman: New Perspectives*, 139–48; Judith Plaskow, *Standing Again at Sinai*. Judith Hauptman, in "Women's Liberation in the Talmudic Period," *Conservative Judaism* 26:4 (summer 1972): 22–28, points to the movement of the Talmudic sages to equalize the treatment of women in comparison with earlier practice.

94. See Blu Greenberg, "Jewish Divorce Law: If We Must Part, Let's Part as Equals," in *Jewish Marital Status*, 177–87.

95. Mimi Scarf, "Marriages Made in Heaven? Battered Jewish Wives," in Heschel, *On Being a Jewish Feminist*, 51–64.

96. Faith Solela, "Family Violence: Silence Isn't Golden Anymore," *Response* 14 (spring 1985): 101–106.

97. Daniel Leifer and Myra Leifer, "On the Birth of a Daughter," in E. Koltun, *The Jewish Woman: New Perspectives*, 21–30; see Sharon Strassfeld and Michael Strassfeld, eds., *The Second Jewish Catalog* (Philadelphia: Jewish Publication Society of America, 1976), 30–37; Debra Orenstein, ed. *Lifecycles: Jewish Women on Life Passages and Personal Milestones*, vol. 1, (Woodstock, N.Y.: Jewish Lights Publishing, 1994).

98. Blu Greenberg, "Will There Be Orthodox Women Rabbis?" *Judaism* 33 (winter 1984): 22–33.

99. See Orenstein, ed. *Lifecycles* 1; See Susan Grossman, "Finding Comfort after Miscarriage," in *Daughters of the King: Women and the Synagogue*, ed. Susan Grossman and Rivkah Haut (Philadelphia: Jewish Publication Society of America, 1992), 284–89; Tikva Frymer-Kensky, "A Ritual for Affirming and Accepting Pregnancy," idem., 290–96.

5

Christian Understandings of Human Nature and Gender

ROSEMARY RADFORD RUETHER

Christian anthropology in its classical theological development manifests profound ambiguities toward women. On the one hand, the Pauline credo that in Christ there is neither male nor female (Gal. 3:28) seems to dissolve all differences of gender and to put women on an equal footing with men in the redeemed humanity. If women were defined as inferior and subordinate in the classical societies of the Hebrew and Greco-Roman worlds, Paul's claim seems to leave us with two possible interpretations: Either this subordination was always sinful and contradicts God's intention in creation, or the subjugation of women came about as God's punishment for sin, but has now been removed by redemption, restoring and renewing women's original equality with man.

Both of these options have been affirmed in Christian history, the latter in classical tradition and the former in modern liberal theology. A third option, that the patriarchal God of creation and the egalitarian God of redemption are different deities, was ruled out by the Christian rejection of the Marcionite split of the God of creation from the God of redemption. Key to Christian thought is the affirmation that there is one God who is both creator and redeemer. The God of Genesis and the God who is the Father of Jesus Christ is one and the same. Jesus, the Christ, the redeeming Messiah, is the Logos through which the world was created in the beginning (cf. Heb. 1:1–5; Col. 1:15–20).

This affirmation of women's equal share in redemption in Christ, however, has been contradicted by an insistence that women cannot exercise representative authority in either society or in the church. This insistence on women's continued subordination in Christian society and church order finds expression in the claim that women, by their very nature, cannot "image Christ" and that the male is, by nature, the "head" of the female, mandated by God to exercise domination over her in the family, church, and society.[1]

This insistence on women's continued subordination has been justified by varied combinations of two assertions: that woman is innately inferior in the very nature of things, and/or that woman has been placed under male subjugation as punishment for (her) sin. We might summarize this view in the following double-bind formula: Women are naturally subordinate, but also naturally insubordinate, and have been put under male domination both to reaffirm their subordinate nature and to punish them for their sinful rebellion against it.

But how does this claim of original subordination and its reaffirmation in Christian society square with the Pauline claim that in Christ there is "neither male nor female"? The various forms of Christian theological anthropology of gender are more or less conscious efforts to reconcile this contradiction between equality in Christ and continued subordination in Christianity. This is attempted through various interpretations of the relationship of the status of women in the original Creation, in the Fall, and in redemption.

In this chapter I will explore the various options for combining these relationships systematically, and in their historical development, in classical and modern Christian views. I will then explore a possible reinterpretation of this tradition from a contemporary feminist perspective.

Gender and Creation

Are women created in the image of God? Are women fully and equally "human"? These are the key questions for exploring views of women's status in the original Creation. Modern Christian theologies, even conservative ones, affirm that women are equally "in the image of God." But they often imply a difference in how women and men image God that justifies subordination. In this view, "image of God" is reflected in the heterosexual couple, who together in relationship make the complete "image." This assumes that neither women nor men are complete in themselves. It also inserts a complementarity into the concept of "image of God" that makes male leadership over the woman and a female auxiliary relation to the man internal to the "image of God as relationship."

This modern strategy for including women in the image of God by affirming difference in relationship departs from the classical Christian tradition of the church fathers. Here there were two options for viewing women's relation to the image of God. In the Eastern tradition the image of God was identified with the soul, seen as spiritual and asexual. Women and men in their spiritual natures have equally redeemable souls. In the original Creation there was no subordination but also no gender, sex, or reproduction. Gendered bodies arose as a result of the Fall, which resulted in both sin and death and the necessity of sex and reproduction.[2]

The Latin tradition represented by Augustine, on the other hand, claimed that subordination was intrinsic to the original Creation in a way that sin and death were not. In this tradition, the image of God refers to the soul in both its rational nature and its representation of God's domination over nature. Both men and women were created with rational souls, but only men possess this capacity for dominion, while women represent nature or the body that is under dominion. Therefore, for Augustine, women in their femaleness lack the image of God and are related to God's image only by being included under male headship.[3]

For Augustine, God's image in "man" is thus androcentric and corporate. Its essence is the quality of rationality as sovereign power to be exercised by the individual male over his own bodily passions and by the male as corporate head of creation over women and the rest of nature. Augustine's view reflects the patriarchal legal tradition of the male head of family as corporate individual.

These differences among the Greek, Latin, and modern views raise key questions about the relation of the image of God to gender. How is the soul, spirit, or mind seen as related to sex and the gendered body? Is mind, spirit, or soul sexually neutral, possessed by men and women equally, separate from the sexed body? Or are humans a union of body and soul-mind, such that sexual distinctions also make for differences in women and men's "ways of thinking"? In modern feminist thought this question is extended by the distinction between sex and gender— sex referring to biological differences while gender is seen as socially constructed.[4]

The differences between Greek and Latin views of *imago dei* and gender also point to different understandings of the meaning of the "image of God" as a quality of humanness. Is God's image in humans a shared essence between God and humans or a shared role? The author of Genesis 1:27 intended the latter meaning; that is, humans are like God—not ontologically, but through sharing or representing God in God's dominion over the (rest of) creation. Although this role as God's representative in dominion is given to Adam (the "Human") generically, the priestly author undoubtedly assumed that it was exercised in practice by the patriarchal male.[5]

As Phyllis Bird has shown in her careful exegesis of this passage, the "image of God" given to Adam corporately is not identified with, but distinguished from, sexual differences that the humans share with animals but not with God. Thus "image of God" cannot be identified literally with male or female biological sex. But since dominion is exercised only by patriarchal males, not by women or slaves, it is patriarchal males who exercise the role of "image" as corporate individuals on behalf of the whole community.

With the incorporation of Greek soul-body dualism into Christian thought, Christians also came to think of the "image of God" as an ontological "likeness" between God and humans, located in the immortal soul and seen as participating in the eternal spiritual being of God. The body is seen as the vehicle of both sin and death, while the soul is the "part" of humans that they share with the divine. The soul is seen as a self-subsistent being originally without mortal body. The soul is put into a mortal body as a "testing place," or as a fall into sin, but the soul must discard the body in order to return to its pure state.

The soul, although without body originally, was also seen as innately rational, and thus linked with masculinity. The ruling-class male is thus the normative human, while women and slaves come about through a failure of the soul to control the body and its reincarnation in "lower" states.[6] Although Greek Christianity rejected reincarnation, its division of an asexual spiritual soul from a gendered body reflects this Platonic anthropology. Augustine synthesizes elements of both the Platonic essentialist and the Hebrew functional views of the image of God. The image of God is normatively male as rational soul exercising dominion over women, body and nature.

Thus far we have noted that Greek Christians identified the image of God with the asexual soul possessed by both men and women, while Augustine assumed a corporate concept of the image as dominion, which women do not possess but are possessed by. Both traditions, however, tend to think of "femaleness" as a quality of soul as well as body, linked to sense emotions and lack of willpower as psychic qualities of the body. Thus women are also seen as lacking equality of mind, as having a deficient rationality and hence an inferior soul.[7]

The ascetic tradition suggested, however, that when women are converted, particularly those who repudiate sex for celibacy, this inferiority of soul is overcome, and they are given "manly and virile" souls.[8] Whether this new virility of soul in Christian virgins is a new dispensation of God or a restoration of a quality women originally possessed but lost in the Fall is unclear. Some radical ascetics claimed that the Christian virgin wins autonomy through her transformation into spiritual "virility." But most church fathers, East and West, backed away from this implication to suggest rather that the redeemed woman would express her redemption by redoubled self-abnegation and subjugation to males, particularly to her spiritual "heads" in the church.

Gender and Sin

Christian anthropology is unclear about whether or not women were equal in God's original creation and shared equally in the "image of God." The Greek ascetic traditions hint of an original equality of soul, and hence a shared "image of God," but this is contradicted by views of woman as innately inferior by reason of her bodily and psychic "femaleness" and her location in an "order" of creation under a headship that the patriarchal male exercises as corporate representative of God's dominion.

But all classical traditions agree in stressing woman's priority in sin, and its consequence being female subjugation. For the egalitarian tradition this means that woman lost her original equality and fell into this subjugation. For the tradition that sees woman as always having been subordinate, her subordination in the Fall is redoubled both as punishment and as a means of expiating her primary fault. Women are punished through painful childbearing and subjugation to their husbands, as the Genesis text suggests, though voluntary submission to this punishment is also women's means of salvation.

Thus Christianity reads both gender difference and female scapegoating into its view of sin and the Fall. The silencing of woman in church, her marginalization from any public leadership roles, her repressed and servile status—these are both her nature and her punishment for rebellion. Men are thus justified in redoubling this repression in order to punish any signs of further rebellion in women. Woman's unprotesting acceptance even of unjust repression is her way to salvation through suffering, a suffering that she deserves and yet can use to expiate her sin. On a more contemporary note, this is the theology of the "battered woman" syndrome.[9]

Sin is also connected with women in the Christian tradition through the Platonic linking of femaleness, body, sex, mortality, and evil. The body is seen as the source of appetites that draw the immortal soul down into sin and death and cause it to forget its original "pure" nature. Sex is seen as the extreme expression of the sin and death-prone tendencies of the body. The linking of femaleness with this view of sex and body means women are seen as being by nature more sin-prone than men. To shun women is to shun sin. To repress women is to repress both her proneness to sin and her capacity to "tempt" men into sin.

A third option lurks in the Genesis 3 narrative: Women's subjugation to males is neither a re-ratification of her original subordination nor a punishment for the sin of insubordination, but is itself sinful. The original parity of woman and man of paradise has been lost by the emergence of relations of domination and subjugation. Sin reigns in human relations through this unjust, distorted relationship. But this option will be developed only in modern feminist theologies.[10]

Gender and Redemption

Here we return to the basic Pauline assertion that "In Christ there is neither male nor female." In the Christian tradition this has meant that women are equally saved by Christ, are equally included in the redemption won by Christ, to be baptized equally with males. It also has meant that women, although not equal in rationality or power, are nonetheless equally capable of holiness. Since it is holiness, not power or learning, that "ranks" in heaven, women are as likely to have high rank in heaven as men.[11]

Yet this equality in Christ, in baptism, and in capacity for holiness, has been related to women's status in the church and society in various ways. For most of classical tradition women were normatively to exercise their holiness differently from men. Although humility is appropriate for both holy men and holy women, it is also seen as normative for women *as women*. Thus, voluntary acceptance of subjugation is both a woman's place in "nature" and her path to holiness as expiation of sin.

Radical ascetics suggested that the redeemed woman overcame her subjugation to man particularly as a celibate, and hence attained a new "virility" and independence. This idea was read differently, however, by male and female ascetics. When female ascetics asserted it as independent control of their own religious communities, it was generally opposed by male church leaders.[12]

Only in modern feminist theologies has there emerged the possibility of another option for reading gender relations in terms of the drama of creation, sin, and redemption. If original equality is our true nature, and domination-subjugation the expression of sin, then the restoration and development of egalitarian relations is both the means and the expression of redemption.

This affirmation of equality as original-redeemed gender relations raises the underlying question, however, of how gender is related to "humanness." Do we assume a gender-neutral or gender-inclusive (androgynous) definition of humanness shared equally by men and women? Can we then speak of redemption in terms of both men and women becoming "fully human" and affirming a parity in which the "full humanness" of each affirms that of the other? Or is it impossible to extricate the concept of generic humanness from its androcentric history, in which the male is the norm of humanness and the female is deficient in relation to this norm?

Do women need to claim a new definition of "good femaleness" that will be different from androcentric normative humanness? Is there sufficiently greater difference than similarity between human males and human females that we cannot construct a concept of a common "species ideal" to which men and women can and should aspire "equally"? Do we need different ideals for male and female "humanness," and if so, can we avoid a hierarchical valuation of these different norms, in which neither the male norm nor the female norm is valued as superior? These questions plague modern Western anthropology and prevent feminist thought from reaching consensus about what is meant by "equality" of women and men.[13]

Classical and Modern Christian Anthropologies

In this section I will summarize briefly the typologies and development of classical and modern Christian anthropologies that bring us to this contemporary impasse in feminist thought. Classical Christian anthropology (in its Western development) is characterized by a dominant patriarchal tradition that asserts some combination of woman's subjugation in nature and in the Fall with her continued subjugation in Christian society and the church. This continued subjugation in the order of redemption expresses both woman's nature and her punishment for sin, while affirming her ultimate redeemability and equality in "heaven" through voluntary acceptance of humility while on earth.

This view found its classical definition in Augustine's thought. As we have seen, Augustine believed that the subjugation of woman to man is intrinsic to the original created order. Man alone possesses the "image of God" in himself, and women are included in this image only under male headship as part of the corporate extension of the dominion given to "man" over "nature." This does not mean, however, that Augustine thought that women were innately inferior in soul. Rather their role is different, and they obey God by obeying the man as their "head."

Augustine never completely extricated himself from the Manichaean-Platonic tendency to see the body—and especially sexuality—as the main seat of sin and its plunge into death. His focus on lust as the cause and expression of sin, however, centers on male, not female, sexuality. Sin originates in disobedience, the rejection of God's command, but Augustine is not willing to give woman primary credit for the Fall. Although she may have initiated the disobedience, it could only become the Fall of Man when the male, as head, complied.[14]

Sin, for Augustine, is expressed particularly in the disordering of the male's rational control over his own bodily lusts, epitomized in the erection of the penis, which is "out of control" of the male's rational will. Sin, moreover, is transmitted from generation to generation through the male concupiscence that accompanies the sexual act in its fallen state.[15]

Augustine's exploration of the human tendency to sin focuses on male sins: sexual lust in its "use" of women, and the lust for career advancement through knowledge and power. The ego-drives of the self are central to Augustine's view of sin, based on his critical examination of his own development. Redemption can only come as a gratuitous gift of God that breaks this egoistic will to power and creates a will able to submit to God's will.

Although Augustine assumes that redemption, for men, is to be expressed particularly in rejection of sex and hence of relations with women, the problem is still primarily the breaking of male lust and ego-ism, not the idea that women are innately more sinful. It is impossible to say what Augustine thinks of female nature independently of men, for he has no view of women independent of men: His anthropology is thoroughly androcentric. One might surmise, however, from his remarks about his mother, Monica, that although he assumes women are naturally subordinate to men and are acceptable to God by accep-tance of that subordination (even when unjustly excessive), he also assumes that women are more naturally able to submit to subjugation and so are less prone to egoistic pride.[16]

Does this mean that women are less deeply "fallen" than men and more readily accept a salvation based on submission to God's will? If so, then Augustine unconsciously assumes that women are more naturally "Christian" than men. His relation to his Catholic mother, who hounds him to submit to the Church, deeply shapes both his concept of the church as "Mother" and his description of God's relation to him. Despite his male language for God, Augustine's God, who chose him from birth and hounds him until he submits his will to "Him," is remarkably like his mother.

Augustinian anthropology was reworked by Thomas Aquinas in the thirteenth century through the incorporation of Aristotelian philoso-phy. Aquinas incorporated Aristotle's view of the female as innately inferior in mind, will, and body and hence lacking complete human-ness. Her subjugation is thus the expression of her inferiority and inca-pacity for self-rule. Thus in Aquinas the idea that women are subordinate in the original order of creation is read through the assumption of female inferiority in nature in a way that was absent in

Augustine.[17] This leads to the further assertion that Christ had to be male to possess full or "perfect" humanness, and thus only the male can represent Christ as priest. This is the anthropology that lies behind the contemporary papal assertions that women cannot "image" Christ.

During the Reformation Luther and Calvin expressed variants on the classical anthropological tradition. Luther leaned toward the ascetic tradition that women were originally men's equals in soul as well as partners in paradise, but their primacy in sin caused them to lose this original partnership. Now women's subordination stands as expression of their punishment for sin.[18] Calvin, by contrast, came closer to Augustine's view. Woman's subordination to man is an expression of a divinely given order of creation, but implies no innate inferiority by nature. As sinners elected by God's grace, women and men stand on equal footing; however, woman is to express her election through voluntary submission to her rightful place as man's subordinate and "helpmeet."

In the twentieth century, theologian Karl Barth elaborated the classical Calvinist position that the divinely mandated "order of creation" dictates a relation of leader and follower between man and woman. "Man is A and woman is B" is Barth's famous way of expressing this relationship of male priority and female auxiliary status. However, this implies no innate inferiority of spiritual nature before God. Both are equally sinners, equally elected by God's sovereign grace, but both are to express their redeemed lives through voluntary acceptance of their "place" in God's order.[19]

Barth also develops the modern Protestant emphasis on the "image of God" as "being in relationship." Maleness and femaleness are read into the idea of "image of God" to suggest that the heterosexual couple is together the normative expression of the image of God as I-thou relationship. Barth's anthropology of gender assumes, however, that this normative "being in relationship" as male and female will be construed as a complementarity of masculine primacy and female auxiliarity, not as a mutuality of two "equal" partners.[20]

Side by side with this dominant patriarchal anthropology exists a minority tradition found in some of the mystical and millennialist lines of Christian thought. This minority tradition is rooted in an early Christian notion that men and women were spiritually equal as androgynous beings in an original paradise, but fell into separate genders and into sexuality and death through sin. In redemption both sexuality and mortality are overcome and the androgynous nature of humanity is restored. Redemption is linked to celibacy and restoration of spiritual wholeness. Women, through redemption, are freed from the curse of Eve—painful childbearing and subjugation to the male. They become whole, regain their "virile and manly" natures, and are able to co-lead in the church as teachers and prophets.[21]

Elements of this theology of "original and redeemed spiritual equality" are found in both ascetic mystical theology, particularly among woman mystics, and in millennialist movements in the Medieval and Reformation eras, particularly those led by women. It is beyond the limits of this chapter to explore the variants of this pattern in detail. As one example, I will describe its nineteenth-century development in the English-American mystical-millennialist sect, the Shakers, a group that had a significant influence on mainstream American theological anthropologies.

The Shakers, founded by Ann Lee in England in the late eighteenth century, migrated to the United States and rapidly expanded until the 1840s, when they entered a closed-in "spiritualist" stage and gradually declined in numbers. Their Scripture and theology were elaborated by male leaders after Lee's death. In Shaker theology God is androgynous, a complementarity of male and female elements. Humans are in God's image in the joint relationship of male and female as father and mother.

According to Shaker theology, in the original paradise humans were spiritually whole. Sin caused the fall into sexuality and death. Redemption restores spiritual wholeness, and is expressed in the celibate community of men and women who have transcended sexual relations and who anticipate the Millennial Order where there is "no more marrying or giving in marriage." The male Christ represents the male aspect of God, but salvation is incomplete until the female aspect of God is revealed in Ann Lee, the Wisdom or Mother-aspect of God.

The Millennial Church expressed this wholeness as male and female through a parallel leadership of elders and elderesses who governed the male and female sides of the community. Although this pattern sounds egalitarian, it also assumed a concept of distinct male and female roles that meant that men administered the whole community while women did the housework for the whole group and were subordinate to male governance. Only at the end of the nineteenth century, when women became the great majority of members, did Shaker women take over roles of external governance. It was then that some Shakers, like Anna White, interpreted Shaker theology to include a genuine equality of gender.[22]

Nineteenth-century American thought saw a shift in the ideology of gender. The classical division between patriarchal and millennial traditions was transmuted into a new division between liberal monist and romantic binary anthropologies.

Liberal monism asserts that there is one universal generic human "nature" shared equally by all humans. This human nature is characterized by rationality and moral conscience. Human rights and equality before the law are identified with the possession of these generic human qualities. Since all humans have these qualities, all have the same human rights and are to be considered equal before the law. Liberalism identified this equality with an original nature that all humans have by virtue of "creation." Inequality of legal rights or social hierarchy is not based on a divinely created "order of nature," but on a human disordering of nature that imposes unjust differences of rights. The liberal revolution thus involves both a restoration of original nature and a redemptive new era in which governments are created based on "natural equality."[23]

Liberal feminists sought to claim this same equality before the law for women. But they were frustrated by the unstated androcentrism of the liberal definition of "human nature." Normative humanness was identified with male public roles from which women had been historically excluded. In the liberal constitutions of the eighteenth and nineteenth centuries women and other subordinate people were excluded from the "rights of man," because the rights belonging to all men "by nature" continued to be seen as rights to be exercised exclusively by white, propertied males. The patriarchal male continued to be seen as a corporate self, acting for both himself and those "under him"; i.e., dependent women, children, and servants.

Through a series of social revolutions and reforms such as abolition, universal manhood suffrage, and women's suffrage, the rights of "man" were eventually extended to all adults (provided they were neither imprisoned nor mentally incompetent). This resulted in a more thoroughgoing individualism that partly broke down the idea of the family head as corporate personality. But women continue to be disadvantaged in a scheme of equality based on public roles and jobs, which ignore the private sphere and women's roles and work in it. Thus women in liberal systems are both overworked and defeated in their quest for equality, since they are expected simultaneously to fill the "same" roles as men in public employment while also doing the lion's share of the domestic work in the home that was traditionally associated with women.

By contrast, romantic binary anthropologies affirm the distinct roles of women in the family, and the distinct "feminine" psychic qualities associated with it that are ignored by androcentric, liberal monism. Men and women are defined as "complementary"; that is, as having a supplementary relation of distinct and opposite psychic qualities. Men are masculine; that is, rational, aggressive, and autonomous. Women are feminine; that is, intuitive, passive, and auxiliary. Only together are these distinct halves brought together in an ideal whole. Romantic anthropology often sees feminine qualities as morally superior, linked to love and altruism. Male aggression and egoism thus need to be refined and "uplifted" by female altruism.

This binary understanding of male and female as masculine and feminine lends itself to several distinct social ideals. In conservative romanticism, male and female differences are linked with public and private spheres respectively. Women are to stay out of the public sphere and uplift the male by their devoted mothering at home. Victorian women reformers shifted this view by insisting that women must crusade *into* the male public sphere and uplift it through social reform that would make the public sphere more "homelike." But there were also separatist feminists who exaggerated the implied moral superiority of women by suggesting that women should shun men altogether, creating an autonomous female world based on superior female qualities.[24]

Feminist anthropology today is divided between the dual heritages of liberal monism and romantic dualism as just described. It is still seeking some satisfactory synthesis in order to affirm that women are simultaneously "equal" to men yet "different" in ways that are often tacitly assumed to be morally superior to "masculine" tendencies.

Beyond Androgyny:
Toward a Feminist Anthropology

A feminist anthropology must transcend both androcentric monism, which identifies generic humanness with what historically have been male qualities demonstrated in public life, and the romantic binary split between "masculine" men and "feminine" women. We need to start by asserting that the qualities labeled masculine and feminine in patriarchal culture, that is, rationality and autonomy versus intuition and altruism, are potential capacities of both men and women. Only when we bring together all the qualities that have been split into these binary gender stereotypes do we get a glimpse of what "whole" human beings might be.

It is not enough, however, to paste these qualities together in their traditional forms into an "androgynous" union of masculine and feminine, for their binary splitting also expresses a distorted relationship of men as dominant and women as subordinate—hence reflecting a distortion of the appropriate relating of these qualities. We need a synthesis in which rationality and intuition, autonomy and relationality each transform the other.

We also need to recognize that men and women, through a combination of biological development and socialization, make this journey into wholeness from different starting points. Thus they gradually come to wholeness and mutuality by helping each other to develop those aspects of the self that gender stereotypes have tended to repress. Women need to help men develop more relationality, and men need to help women develop more independence. While women have traditionally been seen as providing something of the first for men, men have seldom called themselves to provide the second on behalf of women.

What does this understanding of humanness as a journey into wholeness beyond gender stereotypes mean for our understanding of the theological concepts of "image of God," sin, fallenness, and redemption? I believe it means that our understanding of the image of God cannot be based on gender stereotypes, not even an androgynous sum of both masculine and feminine aspects. Further, it cannot be based on a concept of domination over subjugated peoples, on a false concept of "nature," or on a splitting apart of mind and body. The whole creation must be seen as the "bodying forth" of the Word and Wisdom of God, which are sacramentally present in all beings.

If God is thought of as being present in creation by bringing forth all things in life-giving interrelations and by a constant process of renewing such relations, then humans are most expressive of God's presence when they manifest this creative and healing process. Sin is what breaks this creating and healing process, resulting in distorted relationships of domination and exploitation that aggrandize one side of a relationship by inferiorizing and impoverishing the other side. Sexism and all forms of exploitative domination, then, are not expressive of the image of God, but are forms of sin. Salvation is the process of conversion from distorted relationships and the regrounding of selves in healing relationality.

How then can we think about human gender as related to the "image of God"? First we must affirm that God, not being a mammal of any kind, does not literally have sex or gender. God is neither male nor female, yet is present in and through all relatedness, including that of gender. In so far as we use gender images metaphorically for God, we must do so in a way that clearly reveals them as metaphorical, not literal. Our metaphors must include both male and female in a complex transformative synthesis that points us beyond stereotypes toward wholeness. This wholeness, furthermore, is not a known ideal, but goes ahead of us into an incompleted future, just as redemption itself is still incomplete.

Moreover, "image of God" cannot be identified with dominion. In addition, dominion can be reinterpreted as "stewardship" only with the cautionary proviso that we recognize our call to care for all of creation as a corrective to the very recent emergence of humans as the dominant species and our destructive use of such dominance. We do not "possess" the earth, but are to be converted to a caring for the earth that sustains rather than destroys.

Finally, we need to ask how individuation and family or community are connected in our anthropology of gender. Patriarchal anthropology was based on the assumption that the (free, ruling-class) male was not just an individual, but a corporate person who exercised "headship" over a "body" of persons: women, children, and servants. Women were credited with legal autonomy only when this concept of the family as the base of rights was replaced with an individualism in which each adult was considered to be autonomous. This liberal individualism thus abstracted men and women from their social context as isolated "atoms," each motivated by its own self-interest.

In contrast, a feminist anthropology needs to restore an understanding of men and women as embedded in and responsible for the corporate life of the family, but not in such a way as to cause the personhood of women to disappear once more into the corporate representation of the male "head of family." Rather, we need to think of men and women as both relational *and* individuated in an interactive process. The marriage relationship thus becomes a mutual covenant for interdependence *and* individuation of *both* partners. Childraising is a cooperative process of both parents, male and female, who are capable of such mutuality in interdependence and individuation as persons in their own right.

Feminist anthropology must thus reject both the patriarchal family, where only the patriarch is fully a person, and liberal individualism, where all are assumed to be autonomous persons but isolated from relationships, in order to envision new families in a new society where individuation and community can be interrelated.

NOTES

1. The first argument is more typical of Roman Catholics; that is, *The Declaration on the Question of the Admission of Women to the Ministerial Priesthood*, Vatican City, 15 October 1976, sec. 1–5. The second is more typical of Evangelical Protestants; see Donald Grey Barnhouse, "Document 11: 'The Wife with Two Heads'," cited by Letha Scanzoni and Susan Seta, "Women in Evangelical, Holiness and Pentecostal Tradition," in *Women and Religion in America: Volume 3, 1900–1968*, ed. Rosemary Keller and Rosemary Radford Ruether (New York: Harper & Row, 1986), 261–62; also Letha Scanzoni, "The Great Chain of Being and the Chain of Command" in *Women's Spirit Bonding*, ed. Janet Kalven and Mary I. Buckeley (New York: Pilgrim Press, 1984), 41–55.

2. For example, Gregory of Nyssa, *De Opif. Hom.* 16.
3. Augustine, *De Trinitate*, 7.7.10; see Kari Borresen, *Subordination and Equivalence: The Nature and Role of Woman in Augustine and Thomas Aquinas* (Washington, D.C.: University Press of America, 1981), 15–34.
4. See Mary Field Belenky, et al., *Women's Ways of Knowing* (New York: Basic Books, 1986); also Ann Snitow, Christine Stansell, and Sharon Thompson, *The Powers of Desire: The Politics of Sexuality* (New York: Monthly Review Press, 1983). The person credited with the distinction between sex and gender is Gayle Rubin, in "The Traffic in Women: Notes on the 'Political Economy' of Sex," in *Toward an Anthropology of Women*, ed. Rayna R. Reiter (New York: Monthly Review Press, 1975), 157–210.
5. Phyllis Bird, "Male and Female He Created Them: Gen. 1:27b in the Context of the Priestly Account of Creation," *Harvard Theological Review* 74:2 (1981): 129–59, and her development of this essay in *Image of God and Gender Models*, ed. Kari Borresen (Oslo: Solum Forlag, 1992), 11–34.
6. Plato, *Timaeus*, 23.
7. Rosemary Radford Ruether, "Misogynism and Virginal Feminism in the Fathers of the Church," in *Religion and Sexism: Images of Women in the Jewish and Christian Traditions*, ed. Rosemary Radford Ruether (New York: Simon & Schuster, 1974), 150–73.
8. Kari Borresen, "Becoming Male: A Gnostic and Early Christian Metaphor," in *Image of God*, 172–87.
9. Christian women who are trying to break away from battering relations often attest to the importance of this theology in their past acceptance of battering; see chapters in *Christianity, Patriarchy and Abuse: A Feminist Critique*, ed. Joanne C. Brown and Carole R. Bohn (New York: Pilgrim Press, 1989).
10. Rosemary Radford Ruether, *Sexism and God-Talk: Toward a Feminist Theology* (Boston, Mass.: Beacon Press, 1983), 159–92.
11. See Eleanor McLaughlin, "Women, Power and Holiness in Medieval Christianity," in *Women of Spirit: Female Leadership in the Jewish and Christian Traditions*, ed. Rosemary Radford Ruether and Eleanor McLaughlin (New York: Simon & Schuster, 1979), 99–130.
12. The history of Catholic nuns as a struggle for self-government against the clerical hierarchy, based on the implied theology of celibacy as giving women independent personhood, is yet to be written, but it is implied in many accounts. See, for example, Mary Ewens, "Women in the Convent," in *American Catholic Women*, ed. Karen Kennelly (New York: Macmillan Publishers, 1989), 17–47; and Madonna Kolbenschlag, *Authority, Community and Conflict* (Kansas City, Mo.: Sheed & Ward, 1986).
13. Lynda M. Glennon, *Women and Dualism: A Sociology of Knowledge* (New York: Longman & Green, 1979).
14. Augustine, *The City of God* 14, 11.
15. Augustine, "De Nuptiis and Concupiscentia," *Corpus Scriptorum Ecclesiasticorum Latinorum*, ed. Caroli F. Urba and Josephi Zycha (Prague and Vindobonae: F. Tempsky, 1902) 42:210–319.
16. For Augustine's remarks on his mother in the *Confessions*, see Conf. III, 11, 19–20; 12, 21; V, 8, 15; VI, 1, 1; IX, 8, 17; 9, 22.

17. Thomas Aquinas, *Summa Theologica*, pt. 1, q. 92; see also Borresen, *Subordination and Equivalence*, 141–78.
18. Martin Luther, *Lectures on Genesis*, Gen. 2:18, 3:16, in *Luther's Works*, vol. 1, ed. Jaroslav Pelikan, (St. Louis: Concordia Publishing House, 1958), 115, 202–203.
19. Karl Barth, *Church Dogmatics*, vol. 3, sec. 4 (Edinburgh: T. & T. Clark, 1975), 158–72.
20. Rosemary Radford Ruether, "Imago Dei, Christian Tradition and Feminist Hermeneutics" in Borresen, *Image of God and Gender Models*, 271–74.
21. For Gnostic anthropology, see Borresen, *Image of God and Gender Models* and also Rosemary Radford Ruether, "Women in Utopian Movements," in *Women and Religion in America: Volume 1, The Nineteenth Century* (New York: Harper & Row, 1981), 47–48.
22. For Shaker theology, see Marjorie Procter-Smith, " 'In the Line of the Female': Shakerism and Feminism," in *Women's Leadership in Marginal Religions*, ed. Catherine Wessinger (Chicago: University of Illinois Press, 1993), 23–40. For Shaker church order and its historical development, see Karen Nickless and Pamela Nickless, "Sexual Equality and Economic Authority: The Shaker Experience, 1784–1900," in *Women in Spiritual and Communitarian Societies*, ed. Wendy Chmielewski, et al. (Syracuse, N.Y.: Syracuse University Press, 1993), 119–32.
23. For a classical statement of liberal egalitarianism, see "Condorcet's Pleas for the Citizenship of Women," *The Fortnightly Review* 13:42 (June 1870, trans. from his speech of 3 July 1790), 719–20; see Ruether, *Sexism and God-talk*, 102–104.
24. Ruether, *Sexism and God-talk*, 104–109.

6

A Common Love

Christian Feminist Ethics
and the Family

SALLY PURVIS

A s a Christian feminist ethicist I was at first startled by a request to
write about the family. I want to begin these reflections, then, by
introducing some problems for a Christian feminist ethicist in working
with the topic.[1]

First, Christian feminist literature by and large does not address "the
family" *per se*. Issues tend to be identified in more focused ways, as in
the literature on motherhood, gender relations, reproductive issues,
and so on. Or the issues are broader and deal with contextual questions
of power relationships, economic factors and systems, sexual orientation, friendship, etc.[2] Family relations have received normative attention in contemporary Christian ethics from ethicists such as James
Gustafson, Gilbert Meilander, and Stanley Hauerwas, but their treatments do not take into account feminist perspectives in any direct way[3]
Conversely, Christian feminist ethics does not ordinarily deal with the
family.

In fact, the family sometimes seems to be the conceptual property of
those who see feminists as the enemy of Christianity, and "family values" has become a slogan for such groups as the Christian Coalition.
The phrase functions as a euphemism for a complex normative agenda
embraced by the Coalition and other conservative Christian groups,
including but not limited to their homophobic stance.[4] Part of the reason that the family sometimes seems incompatable with feminism,
then, is that the phrase *the family* as it is commonly used trades on the
assumption that there is one model, one normative shape for families.
In fact, much of the traditional Christian teaching about the family
tends to support that assumption: The Christian family is a constellation of related persons whose core is one or more heterosexual married
couples, and there exists a nest of satellite assumptions and values and
norms that have to do with roles and relationships appropriate to various persons within that constellation. The family so understood has

been one conceptual and institutional fortress of patriarchy, sexism, and heterosexism.

With so many of the traditional assumptions and teachings regarding human sexuality and gender relations being challenged by Christian feminist ethicists, it is tempting to say that the family is not a fertile place for our work. It could be argued that we should simply jettison the term with its concomitant assumptions, and talk instead about right relationships in all settings and roles where they are found. Feminist ethics, however, is concerned with the realities of women's lives, whatever official fictions may be told about those lives. It continues to be the case that the family is central to the lives, loves, work, and concern of many, many women, though perhaps not in the way the traditional literature would suggest. Therefore it is appropriate that we reclaim the territory from a feminist normative position.

I propose, then, to offer some thoughts regarding the family from a Christian feminist perspective. I will begin by stipulating the dual love command, "You shall love God with all your heart and with all your soul and with all your mind, and your neighbor as yourself," as the foundation for a constructive Christian feminist ethic.[5] With that foundation, the basic building blocks of my approach are the Christian feminist insight that persons are constitutively relational, and the Christian communal values of diversity and inclusivity. Some comments about those choices are in order. From the beginning of the recent wave of Christian feminist literature, feminists have rejected an anthropology that would characterize persons as fundamentally separate individuals whose maturity is developed through, and rests on, greater and greater degrees of separation and self-reliance. Rather, feminist anthropology (or "gynepology") always insists on the deeply, formatively relational character of persons whose lives are interdependent in ways that are sometimes obvious and sometimes very subtle.[6] Feminist anthropology does not deny or denigrate individuality but affirms that individuality is itself constituted by its relationships, which for Christians includes the God-relationship. I will couple this insight regarding the constitutively relational character of human persons with the Christian values of diversity and inclusivity in our communities. I will claim the strand of the Christian tradition that understands membership in Christian community as radically independent of status in the wider society, and in some sense, at least, as subversive of "the divisions among us." This approach will offer a way to begin to develop new understandings of families that include the traditional understandings but that expose theological roots that support other types of clusters of persons as well.

I analyze the issue and choose the constructive concepts as one who has been shaped by and continues to confess a place on the liberal edge of "old line" Protestantism in North America. I am a white, middle-aged, privileged member of the United Church of Christ who taught in a mostly Methodist seminary in Atlanta, Georgia. These factors, as well as the particularities of my life experience, are my lenses. I trust that they will be transparent enough to provide some focus for these issues.

Some Notes on Christian Love

Anyone who posits the dual love command as foundational for Christian ethics has to wrestle, at least to some degree, with the question of the character of the love we are to hold and share. In fact, Christian love, *agape*, has a central place in the work of Christian ethicists both traditional and feminist. In his volume *Agape: An Ethical Analysis*, Gene Outka provides an overview of some of the key treatments of *agape* in the Christian tradition as well as offering his own constructive interpretation of the term.[7] In the traditional interpretation and use of *agape*, both the qualities of self-sacrifice and of disinterestedness were thought to be constitutive. In one of the earliest feminist theological challenges to the tradition, Valerie Saiving deconstructed Reinhold Niebuhr's characterization of sin as "pride," and showed the (white) male bias of his analysis. In that context, she also argued persuasively that the conceptualization of *agape* as necessarily self-sacrificial is "normative and redemptive precisely insofar as it answers to man's deepest need. If human nature and the human situation are not as described by [Niebuhr], then the assertion that self-giving love is the law of man's being is irrelevant and may even be wrong."[8] Thus her critique of Niebuhr's interpretation of *agape* as essentially self-sacrificial love emanates from her general critique of his Christian anthropology and doctrine of sin, a critique rooted in the perspective of "female experience." Both the content and the analytical method of Saiving's article have become classics in Christian feminist work and are richly suggestive for further developments by others.[9]

Christine Gudorf has criticized a conception of *agape* as essentially self-sacrificial from a different perspective—her experience in parenting "medically handicapped children."[10] She argues that while persons observing her behavior might want to describe it as self-sacrificial, her experiences—or complex set of experiences—suggest that mutuality is a better way to characterize the interactions of the persons involved. She is not primarily engaged in self-sacrifice, but rather in mutual development and transformation that involves all of the participants.[11]

Valerie Saiving and Christine Gudorf both rebut, from women's experience, the traditional characterization of *agape* as *essentially* self-sacrificial. Self-sacrifice may be a temporary or tangential feature of what is involved when we love each other as Christians, but from the perspective of women, at least, and probably other socially disadvanged groups as well, mutual relationship is closer to the heart of the experience.

The second aspect of traditional definitions of *agape* that has received challenges from Christian feminists is that of disinterestedness. It has been thought that "special relations" constitute a problem for *agape* in that *agape* is equal regard for all, thus special relations, like those of mother-child, friend-friend, and so on mean more regard for some than for others. One traditional solution to the "problem" is to prohibit "special relations"; the monastic tradition in Roman Catholicism and celibacy in general have represented attempts to address this "problem."

It is the case that special relations constitute a "problem" for *agape* if *agape* is thought to be disinterested love.[12] Special relations are intensely interested, even passionate. Some Christian feminists have argued that the "problem" is not the presence of intense love but rather our suspicion of passion, which leads us to confine it so narrowly. The problem shifts, then, from that of renouncing passion in human relationships in favor of general disinterested regard on the one hand to that of a concern for the challenge of the inclusivity of passion itself on the other. If we expand our understanding of the energy and deep interestedness of passion, then the work of Christian *agape* is to make that passion more broadly available and more widely felt. The task is not to curb passion, but to nourish it and channel it.

Carter Heyward's work, though not strictly in conversation with the agapic tradition, provides rich and diverse arguments for impassioned engagement on the part of Christians. Her most direct argument in that regard is her discussion in *Our Passion for Justice*, but all of her writing offers both a plea and an invitation to employ the affective self in all activity for both normative and epistemological reasons.[13]

I developed a somewhat different argument against characterizing *agape* as disinterested love by offering "mother-love" as a model for *agape* in light of an exegesis of Luke's story of the good Samaritan.[14] This and other scriptural texts do not render an account of *agape* as disinterested but rather as extravagant outpourings of concern that are surprising only because they occur in relations with strangers as well as friends and family. Like mother-love, Lukan *agape* is intensely involved, other-regarding, and unconditional, and in his account inclusive.[15] Again, the "problem" is not that we sometimes manage to love our children with this love, and perhaps other persons in our lives as well, but that we do not manage to love very many in such a way.

What does this discussion have to do with the family? In traditional interpretations of *agape*, the family has been part of the problem of special relations. That is, if Christian love is to be self-sacrificial and disinterested, then the special interests and loves and even obligations that a family entails are a threat to the Christian ideal.[16] There is a conflict on both the theoretical and experiential levels between agapic love (general, disinterested, self-sacrificial) on the one hand, and love of family (specific, passionate, perhaps even self-fulfilling) on the other.

With a feminist understanding of *agape* as mutual, passionate, deeply interested, and unconditional, the "problem of the family" shifts. The challenge is not the renunciation of affect and intensity but rather the development of wider and wider circles of intense, passionate love. The traditional family, then, is rendered problematic not because of its "special relations" but only insofar as the family is defined as a unit of separation or division over against other relationships.

Christian love, *agape*, remains at the center of our normative analysis, but it is a very different model from that which the tradition has offered us. Christians are understood, as all persons are understood, to be deeply relational and constituted by the relationships in their lives, including the relationship with God. Love is the flow of that relationality when it is right relation: mutual, passionate, caring, and offered as widely as possible.[17]

The Family in
Christian Community

Just as *agape* is central to any Christian normative reflection, so such reflection must take place in terms of Christian community. Just as persons are radically relational, so Christian ethics is radically communal. I will make some general comments regarding the nature of the family and then place those observations within a Christian communal context.

I believe it is true to say that in all cultures through time "the family" constitutes some sort of biological relationship. The ordering of those relationships and facts about them vary widely, but biological connection is a part of what we mean when we speak generally about the family.

But the family is also a sociological reality, often a complex one. Contemporary family systems theory addresses some of the sociological complexity within family units, however defined. Likewise, sociological theory addresses the family as a social institution, affecting and affected by other social institutions in which it is located. The feminist slogan

"the personal is the political" captures some of the permeability of the
boundaries between the family and those wider social forces that shape
it and which it in turn helps to shape.[18] Arguments about the institution
of the family, about what does and does not count as family, about the
advantages and sometimes disadvantages of being a family with regard
to social services, and so forth, all suggest the fact and the complexity of
the sociological reality of the family in our culture(s).[19]

What happens when we put the family as biological unit and the
family as sociological unit in the context of Christian community? The
record indicates that from the earliest times, both the biological reality
and the sociological reality of the family were relativized by the theological reality of the family. Jesus' claim that those who do God's will
were his mother and brothers and sisters (Mark 3:35; Matt. 12:50; Luke
8:21) is an explicit redefinition of "Christian family" in theological
terms. The extensive use of familial language to refer to persons who
were related only through Christian community and not through biological or sociological family units as well as Paul's explicit relativizing
of family relations in the context of the coming *parousia* (1 Cor. 7), are
other manifestations of the theological relativization of both the biological and sociological aspects of the Christian family. It is not the case, of
course, that Christian community and the Christian family were hostile
to or intentionally destructive of biological and sociological families.
Jesus' relationship with his mother is a prominent feature of our foundational narratives. The sons of Zebedee and the siblings Mary, Martha,
and Lazarus, among others, are comfortably incorporated into Christian community. Paul's letters teach us that sometimes whole Roman
households, with their own complex mix of biological and sociological
ties, were converted to this new movement, and "house churches" play
a prominent role in his accounts. It is the case, however, that the
Christian community itself is the normative context for assessing their
value. If and when biological and/or sociological units threaten the
community unit, the community takes normative precedence (e.g.,
words attributed to Jesus regarding the fundamental definition of his
family noted above; Paul's advice in 1 Corinthians regarding "interfaith"
marriages; and most significantly, the appropriation of familial language to characterize Christian relationships themselves).

It is probably stating the obvious to note that this theological relativization of biological and sociological families was both a function
of and an incorporation of the understanding that all love and all relationships are set within the context of love for God. When the God-
relation is put in the center of life, whether individual or communal,
and when that relationship is valued foundationally, then a certain tele-

ology of loving begins to emerge, and all relationships are ordered in service of the central one. The measure, then, of the structure and the function of all human relationships becomes the degree to which they enhance and expand the God-relation for all persons. All other relationships—biological, sociological, or affective—are in service of a community that exists for the purpose of enabling and enhancing persons' relationship to the God known through Jesus Christ.

These norms, of course, function more as critical principles than as concrete realities, now and in the past. There is great danger in conflating the institution(s) of church, or communal claims to be God-centered, with a vision of Christian community that has at its heart the God-relation. Groups such as the Branch Davidians remind us of the possibility of relativizing the family in pernicious ways. The community as God-centered, however, is both the goal and the judge for all groups that call themselves Christian, and therefore the community as God-centered can be said to have concrete normative power even if it is not fully embodied, now or ever, by any actual community.

Christian community that has the God-relation at its core is a community formed around a common love, not a common enemy. Unlike most groups with which we are familiar, groups whose self-definition is over against something or someone else, Christian community exists in common attraction to a common love. Furthermore, this love is *all* that the members of the community are required to hold in common. The common love constitutes both the heart and the boundaries of community life, and in principle, therefore, is open to everyone without regard for other sorts of social connections or divisions that may exist.

All love, then—all relationships, including all family groups—are to be valued according to their relation to the common love. Insofar as a family enhances the God-relation of its members and the community, it is to be judged good. Insofar as it harms that relationship, it may be rearranged or abandoned in light of the deeper love for God, thus human relationships that enhance that love become the family.

We can see in the New Testament, and even more dramatically in the later history of the development of Christianity as a world religion, that the sociological reality of family—and to a lesser extent its biological reality, with its hierarchical structures and its economic and political import—became a growing concern for Christian normative teachings. I do not wish to ignore that history. Nor do I mean to deny the economic and political ramifications of rethinking the reality of family in theological terms. I am simply exposing and reclaiming an early—and I think normatively central—insight regarding the Christian family: Its fundamental reality is theological, and whatever else it may be it is to be formed by, and measured by, its fruitfulness for the common love of all Christian life.

Relationality, Diversity, and Inclusivity

"Whoever does the will of God is my brother and sister and mother" (Mark 3:35). These words, attributed to Jesus and clearly part of the self-conscious memory of early Christian groups, can serve as a kind of summary for the normative definition of the family toward which the section above has moved us. Without mounting an extensive exegetical defense, it is clear, I think, that doing "the will of God" is a fair characterization of the demands of *agape*. Christian love is never simply a question of attitude or affect; doing the will of God is never simply a matter of behavior somehow disconnected from character or motive. In direct contrast to, if not in conflict with, claims of those connected to him as biological and sociological family, Jesus, at least in the view of those who remembered him, offers a definition of the family that is theological and that takes priority over every other definition we can put forth.

Furthermore, this is not an isolated theme restricted to one passage in Mark (and its synoptic parallels). The question about who counts as family receives a reply that is consonant with Jesus' response to the question about who counts as neighbor. Both responses break out from common social definitions and understandings and emphasize the radical inclusivity and potential diversity of Christian community. *Family* is defined in terms of a common God-relation. *Neighbor* is defined in terms of the deeds of love. Relations among Christians are to be ordered by and determined only by a common love. No group or person is in principle ineligible for inclusion; the only commonality is love for God in Christ.

If we shape our question a bit differently in light of the argument above, we can inquire about who it is that is to be the beloved for a Christian. The answer, in principle, is "everyone." At the least, the answer would have to include "everyone with whom we come in contact."

Issues regarding the obligating scope of *agape* have occupied Christian theological ethicists throughout the tradition. Augustine, in fact, offers a helpful analysis as he wrestles with questions regarding what limits on the duty to love a Christian can rightfully acknowledge. Without accepting his questionable duality of the earthly and heavenly realms, it is instructive to note that Augustine readily acknowledges the proximal limits of persons. He understands neighbor-love, or *agape*, primarily to consist of the honoring and nurturing of the neighbor's relation to God. He also understands, however, that there are limits on the degree to which this is possible, and on the number of persons it is possible for anyone to assist in this way. Thus he articulates the second part of the love command as "the observance of two rules: first, to do no harm to anyone, and second, to help everyone whenever possible."[20] To use contemporary language, the principle of nonmaleficence is universally applicable without qualification. The principle of beneficence is subject to the limits of the mortality of the human person including the constraints of time, energy, opportunity, and so forth.

For Augustine, natural human limitations given in creation are not a problem for the understanding and implementation of the command to love our neighbor, since it is precisely to such limited creatures that the command was given. His treatment of the issue combines the theological rigor of the centrality of love of God with the exceptionless universality of the obligation of nonmaleficence, and a relaxed and common sense acceptance of human limitations.

Our world is dramatically different from Augustine's, so we must modify his helpful exposition of the proximal limits to *agape* in light of both the fact of and our awareness of implications of our actions, affections, and relationships for persons far beyond those with whom we actually come in contact. In light of the relational nature of human persons and the inclusivity and diversity, at least in principle, of the Christian family, we also need to add some remarks about how the social structures and policies within which we live have affected not only the theological but also the biological and sociological realities of families. It is clear at this point in our discussion that Christian concern for the family is informed by a concern for all persons based on our conviction that all persons are created by and beloved of God, and that all persons are essentially constituted by the centrality of their relationship to God. *Agape* has no boundaries in principle; the actual boundaries that Augustine articulated are themselves compromised by the fluidity of the boundaries between the personal and the political, in theory and in fact. Thus, any appeal to the well-being of the biological or sociological family at the expense of any person or group is, from a Christian point of view, an inversion of the priorities of Christian values. From the Christian perspective I have expressed, justice is the necessary context for normative claims about and evaluations of the Christian family, where justice is understood to be the instantiation of the theological reality of the common love at the heart of all Christian relationships, including the family.[21]

Justice is the norm of right relations both within and outside of biological and sociological family units. Justice within the biological and sociological family unit would include a respect for diversity and the agapic obligation to nurture each person in his or her particularity. Intra-family relationships would be characterized by the features of *agape* that were discussed above: mutuality, passionate concern, intense caring. Justice outside the family, too, would invite intense caring, passionate concern, mutuality, commitments to the betterment of persons' lives—with no limits in principle. The inclusivity of the Christian understanding of family means that the norm of right relation is always both theological and universal. There are no persons or groups who in principle are outside the scope of "our passion for justice," our commitment to the well-being of all. The stringent universality of the principle of nonmaleficence that Augustine's analysis recommends thus means that, in our world, we must take account of the effects of our behavior and our lives on persons whom we may never personally meet but who are affected by our choices.

Justice is the necessary context for Christian normative claims about and evaluations of the family. Justice in the family condemns the inequities and abuse that are so common within the biological and sociological units that are designated as families. It is also true that justice, as the social instantiation of the right relations required by our common love, must be the norm and guide for relationships within our Christian communities, the Christian families that are not necessarily family units in the ordinary sense.[22]

If the Christian community is a foundational context for our ethical reflection on the family, then we cannot assume that unjust church structures can support just biological/sociological family structures. We cannot ignore the inequalities, oppression, and even abuse that are all too frequent in our churches as we attempt to analyze and reform other social units. "The divisions among us" do move through the doors and walls of our churches; our common love is not necessarily the functional center of our communal lives. Without that center, the family will not thrive.

The Christian Family and a Common Love

When we set our reflections about the family within the theological context that I have outlined here, it becomes clear that family is an entity existing beyond biological definitions, while still encompassing them. What we mean first by family is Christian community, formed, shaped, and sustained by a common love of God. That was and is the context within which we understand and practice all human relationships. The

biological family is not less valuable when viewed in this way, bu̲
accountable both to and for the norms of justice that are required by the
common love of God.[23] The sociological family as an economic and
political unit likewise continues to exist and function, but the economic
and political boundaries are understood to be more permeable than is
sometimes acknowledged. Our relationships, behaviors, and choices
about earning, saving, and spending—as well as our political choices—
have implications far beyond the narrow scope of our daily lives, and
those implications must become part of our daily choices.

If we understand all Christian life to be centered in and ordered
around a common love of God, then there are in principle no limits to
the scope of our family. Although the theological insights are specifically Christian, our common love of God means that our agapic concern and commitment is not confined to those who call themselves
Christian. If we understand *agape* to be intense, caring, passionate,
other-directed, and respectful of the specificity of the beloved, then we
can envision the normative flow of our individual and communal lives
as ever-widening circles of *agape*. If we take seriously the centrality of
relationality as a feature of the human person and the centrality of community in our self-understanding and normative reflection, then our
moral reflections on the Christian family move us far beyond any biological or sociological units that might obtain in a given society and into
a consideration of the family as including all those whom God loves.
The "special relations" in our lives, the relationships in which we care
most deeply and love most strongly, do not encompass the range of our
obligation to love but rather serve as guides and models for the movement outward into concern for all human beings.

Struggles for the Future

This Christian feminist ethical discussion of the family has led us
through and beyond the assumptions about the family that would
understand it only or primarily in terms of biological and sociological
units centered around a heterosexual union. The family, including
appropriate concern for families from a Christian theological ethical
perspective, is understood to be the human family, including all those
whom God loves. Insofar as we understand the goodness or health of
families in relation to the presence of a wage-earning male, or in relation to any particular social form, we have lost our normative center. A
Christian theological ethical understanding of the family encompasses
and goes beyond all social arrangements of persons. The relevant questions have to do not with who is or is not a member but rather with how

the members, whoever they are, are relating to one another and to the contexts of their lives. Our attention, then, shifts from familial constellations to concern for community, in whatever form, that exists in and around a common love of God.

Families, of whatever size and shape, must constitute places and spaces in which the common love of God is nurtured. In our world that means they must be communities of liberation and reconciliation, in that order.[24] As Rebecca Chopp has so eloquently argued, our communities must be vehicles for emancipation and transformation.[25] They must be vehicles for widening the circles of relationships formed around a common love.

We will not find good answers unless we ask good questions. I have challenged the sort of questions Christians commonly ask about the family and offered a different perspective and a different set of questions by which we should proceed. There are few answers here, because answers about how to love require the intersection of theory and concrete situations. We cannot always know in advance what love will require of us, but we can know that love's demands must shape our lives.

Insofar as the Christian family is defined as a biological and/or sociological reality apart from its theological center, it is an inadequate mechanism through which to consider its own problems. We must place it in the context of the relationality, inclusivity, and diversity of a community shaped around a common love. Only then can we accurately define its problems and begin to live toward solutions.

NOTES

1. Several chapters in this volume address in detail some of the problems I raise here. I will merely acknowledge them and will leave their fuller development to my colleagues.
2. The prominent exception to this point is in the field of feminist sociology. See, for example, Kristine M. Baber and Katherine R. Allen, *Women and Families: Feminist Reconstructions* (New York: Guilford Press, 1992); and Judith Stacy, *Brave New Families: Stories of Domestic Upheaval in Late Twentieth-Century America* (San Francisco: Basic Books, 1991). Both of these volumes have helpful bibliographic information.
3. See the second volume of James Gustafson's *Ethics From A Theocentric Perspective* (Chicago: University of Chicago Press, 1984); Gilbert Meilander's *The Limits of Love: Some Theological Explorations* (University Park, Pa.: The Pennsylvania State University Press, 1987); and Stanley Hauerwas's *A Community of Character: Toward a Constructive Christian*

Social Ethics (Notre Dame, Ind.: University of Notre Dame Press). My point in listing these references is to note the widespread assumptions regarding the nature of the family that these authors share with the very conservative Christian groups, even though they may share very little else.

4. For example, the information number for the American Family Association of Florida is 1-800-GAY-LAWS.

5. I am stipulating the foundational nature of the dual love command for a Christian ethic rather than presenting an argument for it. That argument would itself require at least a chapter, but my choice here is sufficiently traditional that I shall proceed with the constructive project itself.

6. For a full and careful statement of a feminist anthropology, see Margaret Farley, "A Feminist Version of Respect for Persons," *The Journal of Feminist Studies in Religion*, 9:1, 2 (spring/fall, 1993): 183–98.

7. Gene Outka, *Agape: An Ethical Analysis* (New Haven, Conn.: Yale University Press, 1972).

8. Valerie Saiving Goldstein, "The Human Situation: A Feminine View," *Journal of Religion* 40 (April 1960): 100–112.

9. One of the fullest of those developments was Judith Plaskow's published dissertation, *Sex, Sin, and Grace: Women's Experience and the Theologies of Reinhold Niebuhr and Paul Tillich* (New York: University Press of America, 1980).

10. Christine Gudorf, "Parenting, Mutual Love, and Sacrifice," in *Women's Consciousness, Women's Conscience*, ed. Barbara Hilkert Andolsen, Christine E. Gudorf, and Mary D. Pellauer (Minneapolis: Winston Press, 1985), 175–91. In that chapter, she uses the phrase "medically handicapped children," 176ff.

11. See Gudorf's chapter in this volume.

12. For a defense of "special relations" in the context of a Christian ethic from a nonfeminist perspective, see Stephen Post, "Love and the Order of Beneficence," *Soundings: An Interdisciplinary Journal* 75:4, (winter 1992): 499–516.

13. Carter Heyward, *Our Passion for Justice: Images of Power, Sexuality and Liberation* (New York: Pilgrim Press, 1984).

14. Sally B. Purvis, "Mothers, Neighbors and Strangers: Another Look at Agape," *Journal of Feminist Studies in Religion* 7:1, (spring 1991): 19–34.

15. As I argue more fully in my article (see n. 14, above), mother-love is only one aspect of the activities of mothering, and most of us do not manage in any sustained way the full embodiment of these qualities. They are, however, the essential features of mother-love when we are loving as we wish to do. The danger of using this model is that of idealizing mothering to the detriment of mothers. Its strength lies in its suggestive power with regard to *agape*.

16. There are suggestions of this even in Paul, of course. See his discussion of marriage in 1 Corinthians 7.

17. Many feminists, myself included, would characterize "right relation" as justice. I do not have the space in this chapter, however, to develop that claim with the fullness and specificity it deserves, so I simply note it here.

18. In conversation, Barbara Wheeler, President of Auburn Theological Seminary, used the phrase "culture soup." I find that a very helpful image.
19. I put the "s" in parentheses because I am less convinced than Barbara Wheeler that there is a *common* cultural soup.
20. Augustine, *City of God*, XIX, 14. See also *On Christian Doctrine* I, 28–29.
21. I am aware, of course, of the complex conversation in traditional theological ethics regarding the relationship between love and justice. Given the feminist critique and revision of traditional definitions of *agape*, however, and given the principles of inclusivity and diversity that emerge from considerations about the scope of *agape*, the possible conflict between love and justice is recast if not eliminated.
22. I am being intentionally vague about the specifics of the behaviors and attitudes entailed by this commitment to justice. A careful articulation of the normative structures for Christian community, and Christian life in general, is a project all its own. What I am attempting to do here is to lay out the theological/ethical logic that would undergird the specification of norms.
23. For a similar point see Clarice J. Martin, "The *Haustafeln* (Household Codes) in African American Biblical Interpretation: 'Free Slaves' and 'Subordinate Women,'" in *Stony the Road We Trod: African American Biblical Interpretation*, ed. Cain Hope Felder (Minneapolis: Fortress Press, 1991), 206–31, esp. 212.
24. Delores Williams, among other womanist writers, argues for the importance of kinship ties in the African-American community. The same importance holds for other groups as well. My argument is not an attempt to subsume or undermine the importance of kinship relations. Rather, I am insisting on the relativization and necessary normative scrutiny of any of their forms. See Williams's discussion in *Sisters in the Wilderness: The Challenge of Womanist God-Talk* (Maryknoll, N.Y.: Orbis Books, 1993).
25. Rebecca S. Chopp, *The Power to Speak: Feminism, Language, and God* (New York: Crossroad, 1989).

PART 3

The Background
for the Present Context

7

Christianity, Women, and the Medieval Family

ROBERT SWEETMAN

The present study addresses the impact of Christianity on the roles and status of women within late antique and medieval Christian families. It examines the possibility that Christianity could have affected the roles and status of women in families similarly across a millennium and a half of European history. It identifies a body of primary literature that suggests such continuity and describes the pattern that emerges.

A short study such as this cannot claim to survey all possible familial and religious configurations that affected Christian women in late antiquity and medieval times. Instead, by the use of representative examples or synecdoche, it illustrates a dynamic present in the lives of many Christian women and their families throughout late antiquity and the Middle Ages. This dynamic does not exhaust what can be said about the effect of Christianity on premodern women and their families. Although it represents a particularly resilient effect which perdured across the changing social and religious makeup of Europe in late antiquity and medieval times, there are other stories that could be told. I chose to tell this particular story because it allows for a relatively detailed examination of women whose lives were richly imagined in a format—namely, the lives of saints—that provided medieval writers, readers, and listeners an occasion for exploring the intersection of Christianity, women, and families.

The present study, then, examines the lives of Christian women saints, at least as those lives are captured (or not) within hagiographical vitae. This choice of source is not, of course, without its problems. Nevertheless, hagiographical sources recommend themselves in important ways. Vitae were biographies written by members of a community of faith to record the pattern of sanctity deemed present within the life of the vita's subject.[1] Hagiographical subjects were chosen because they were seen by one or more communities to provide unsullied examples of God's presence and favor. Thus they provided an opportunity to imagine the limits of human promise and possibility, to imagine how Christian communities might be if only their members were better habituated, if only more thickly graced. The motifs common to the vitae of women who lived centuries apart and in different cultural milieus mark out a continuity of imaginative project, namely, the effect which medieval religion (purified of all worldly attachment) had on the social structures and relationships of "this world." This represents a fruitful vantage point for examining the intersection of Christianity, women, and family, at least as it was imagined in the course of the first 1500 years of the common era.

We begin with the emergence in early Christianity of a distinctive nexus of themes surrounding the place of saintly women within families. There follows an examination of two vitae of the later Middle Ages that point to the enduring currency of this nexus in the medieval centuries. The focus of attention is on unmarried women in their struggles with parental authority, and on married women and their dealings with husbands and children.

The dynamic that emerges can be summarized briefly. Religious seriousness, imagined as heroic commitment to the virginal state or its near equivalents, gave to some women a spiritual license and power which engendered social agency. In other words, these women were seen as effectively resisting constituted authority within their families. This agency, however, came at considerable cost. When married women were identified as graced with sanctity, their relations with spouses and children were imagined to be troubling distractions. Indeed, family remained a source of tension and unease for married women saints until family members recognized that sanctity dissolved the normal social and biological ties of a saintly woman's body to the will of husband and children. True heart's ease in the families of married women saints could only be imagined within new patterns of religious filiation—in other words, within purely spiritual bonds of companionship and dependency. Thus early and medieval Christianity subordinated social and biological ties to spiritual ones. As a result, it tended to resignify the family structures it encountered with reference to analogous, even competing, structures of religious familiarity.

Early Christian Background and Representative Lives of Saints

It is not surprising that one effect of medieval Christianity was the relativization of socially and biologically defined family structures. One finds already in the New Testament a variety of statements that seem to subordinate familial and other social bonds in favor of new patterns of association centered on the community of faith.[2] Early on, the subversive force of these statements seemed to be confirmed by the demographic weight and exemplary courage of women martyrs, and by the egalitarian ethos among Christian prisoners awaiting their gruesome ends. Indeed, the giddy liminality of the martyrs' circle worked its way deep into the Christian imagination from the third century onward, taking on a charge strong enough to call ancient ways of being into question.

Until the year 200 C.E. Christian communities of the Roman world, like their Jewish counterparts, were in effect constituted by networks of households, each under the direction of an elder (usually male) head.[3] These household heads, in turn, constituted the pool from which a community's clergy and leadership were drawn. The households themselves were patriarchal, adhering to the values and practices of the wider world around them; family structures within the Christian community differed little from other antique communities.[4] This does not mean, however, that early Christians assumed Christianity had no impact on women's place in the family. Christian communities of the year 200 C.E. were still heavily peopled by those who had chosen to bind themselves to the community, often at personal cost. Faith among such people often had a corrosive effect on their personal experience of family, an effect capable of setting a daughter against her father in the most excruciating and agonizing ways. In times of persecution and martyrdom, such faith-filled resistance to a paterfamilias was associated in Christian memory with the passion of women martyrs. Their *passiones* allow us our first glimpse of how a pure and heroic Christian faith was imagined to empower a woman of this early Christian world.[5]

The *Passion of Sts. Perpetua and Felicitas*, for example, tells of a group of Christian catechumens arrested at Carthage in March of 203 C.E.[6] It is a particularly apt source, in large part drawn from the prison diary of one of its protagonists, the woman Vibia Perpetua. She is introduced to the reader as one "well-born, liberally educated, honorably married, having father and mother, and two brothers, one like herself a catechumen, and an infant son at the breast."[7]

The *Passion* takes care to indicate that Perpetua comes from a middle-class Carthaginian family. It is equally clear that her family has close ties to the Christian community in Carthage. She and one of her brothers are named Christian catechumens. Moreover, Perpetua views her father's resistance to her assumption of Christian identity as an oddity in her family circle: "He *alone* of all my kindred would not have joy in my suffering."[8]

It is difficult to imagine a well-born Roman household in which the paterfamilias would be so singularly at odds with the religious predilections of his household. Perhaps one can best see him as a Christian "fellow traveler" who chooses to respond to persecution by withdrawing from dangerous religious associations. Whatever the case, he appears in the *Passion* on three occasions, each time in an attempt to undermine his daughter's Christian resolve. Consequently, whatever his past association with Christians, he assumes in the context of his daughter's last days a non-Christian role. Indeed, Perpetua does not shrink from calling his voice demonic.[9] His confrontations with Perpetua over her Christian faith drive a wedge deep into the operative structure of the Roman family.

It is not that the father's titular status as paterfamilias is called into question; this is not a systemic critique of patriarchal privilege. Indeed, one sees on occasion a Roman father's characteristic use of anger and violence in the exercise of his will. Perpetua reports that at one point her father "threw himself upon me as though to pluck out my eyes."[10] On two subsequent occasions he uses his power vis-à-vis Perpetua's baby in an effort to unsettle his daughter. "Look upon your son," Perpetua recalls him saying, "who cannot live after you are gone." The statement is terse and enigmatic, but it is hard to forget that a paterfamilias held the right to decide which infants born into the household were to live and which were to be "exposed."[11] Later, at Perpetua's examination before the city magistrates, her father tries again: carrying her baby in his arms, he calls out, "Have pity on your son." Then, after Perpetua's sentencing, when she is once again in prison and has sent to him for her son, he refuses to deliver the child to her.[12]

Thus a martyr's faith is seen as capable of upsetting the concord of a Roman family. A daughter rebels against the authority of her paterfamilias. Moreover, she does so with an invincible faith-given power. Her father's appeals, even his allusion to rights vis-à-vis his daughter's child, take on the ritualized form of a client's postulation. Perpetua describes the scene as follows: "So spoke my father in his love for me, kissing my hands, and casting himself at my feet; and with tears called me by the name *not of daughter but of lady*."[13] Perpetua has become in this tableau the family *patrona*, a woman able to grant or withhold at will. Her hands are to be kissed in supplication, for the fate of the household lies in those same hands.

The most dramatic indication of Perpetua's transformation into familial *patrona* is in regard to her brother Dinocrates. Shortly after her father's refusal to hand over her son, Perpetua begins to think of her brother who died horribly when he was seven. She is granted a vision in which he appears to her. She sees him in a dark place, hot and thirsty, pale and squalid, marked still by the sores of his illness. She begins to pray fervently for him. Some time later he appears to her in the same "place." Now, however, he is "clean in body, well clothed and refreshed." His sores have healed and "he came forward being glad to play as children will." Perpetua has no doubts about what this all means. "Then I knew that he had been released from punishment."[14] This is a patron of note, harbinger of saint-patrons of later centuries whose power to give and take would so play upon medieval hopes and fears.[15]

If Perpetua's authority is a striking feature of her *Passion*, so too is her unabashed treatment of maternal duties and their physical repercussions. Throughout her incarceration she is wracked with anxiety over her baby, for he is still being breastfed. Soon after her arrest she arranges to have her baby brought to her in her cell to suckle. She commends him to mother and brother but remains anxious about his welfare until she "obtained leave for my baby to remain in prison with me."[16] Her anxiety is doubtless as much tied to physiological as to psychological discomfort. This becomes clear later after her father refuses her further access to her son. Providentially, her son no longer needs her milk. Moreover, this time her breasts do not become engorged. Indeed, "God willed . . . that I might not be tortured by anxiety for the baby and pain in my breasts."[17] There is here an acceptance of the physical facts of motherhood, of the goodness of such carnal occupation, which contrasts with later sensibilities. Physical motherhood is not treated as an impediment to Perpetua's sanctity. Nor is it placed in subordination to the spiritual motherhood she comes to exercise vis à-vis Dinocrates. Her climactic entrance into the circus on the threshold of her martyrdom and triumph seems a fitting opportunity for the *Passion's* author to underline again her maternal condition. When she was led nude into the circus, "the people were horrified, beholding . . . a woman fresh from childbirth, milk dripping from her breasts."[18]

Her biological father, too, receives empathetic treatment. Perpetua clearly has a spiritual father, Saturnus, who guides her in vision and in death.[19] Nevertheless, her physical father is spoken of with respect and affection even when his claims of power and authority are called into question. Perpetua consistently identifies his motivation as love and affection. Indeed, she grieves for the sorrow he must suffer in his old age.[20] Thus in the *Passion of Sts. Perpetua and Felicitas* there is an unproblematic comfort to ordinary bodily life, even of a woman's body, which is seen as a legitimate site of a woman saint's sanctity.

The *Passion* was taken up and studied subsequent to its "publication" and affected subsequent passion accounts.[21] Nevertheless, it too was subject to external influence, and was gradually reworked in response to new and potent sensibilities arising in the early Christian churches of the third and later centuries.

As already noted, in the first two centuries Christian communities functioned, in effect, as networks of households, in which the heads of the member households made up the community's "natural" leadership. In the third century, however, the structure of leadership in Christian communities leaned in new directions. Christian clergy increasingly developed a sense of identity directed, in part, over and against the Christian laity. Increasingly the great divide that protected this identity was a person's active involvement in sexual relations. Consequently, in Peter Brown's ironic description, "married men trembled on the brink of being demoted to the position of women: their physiological involvement in sex made them ineligible for roles of leadership in the community. Some women, however, edged closer to the clergy: continence or widowhood set them free from the disqualifications associated with sexual activity."[22]

This brief description already indicates that sex became in the course of the third century a primary metaphor for the fearful and deadly power of "the world." By contrast, virginity became a primary, if vulnerable, metaphor of Christian triumph over "worldly power." The more weak and vulnerable the virginal body, the greater its metaphoric triumph. This sensibility, too, came to be associated with the story of Christian heroism. It was a sensibility exquisitely conformed to one of the most richly affective genres within letters of antiquity, the romance.[23] The Christian writer had merely to substitute "the virginal state" for "true love." Christian "romances," or apocryphal acts, began to circulate in the third century. Perhaps none of these acts had more influence than the *Acts of Paul and Thecla*. In its portrayal of Thecla we see a new imaginative layer added to Christian understanding of the effect of true religion upon women and their place within family life.

Thecla, like Perpetua, is introduced in terms of her familial status and prospects. She is "a virgin"; "her mother is Theoclia"; she is "betrothed to a man named Thamyris."[24] These short phrases tell the reader of late antiquity all that is needed to call to mind a young heroine. She is an unmarried daughter of a leading Iconian family who has been promised to the son of another leading family. All is as it should be; hence her subservient demeanor and response to any circumstance is also assured.

In this story, however, our heroine encounters and is transformed by Christian faith upon hearing the voice and message of the apostle Paul. Moreover, Paul's message of faith is deeply imbued with the radical sensibilities of Syrian Christianity. It is a faith that takes as its principal instrument the slender frame of the virginal body.[25] Consequently, Thecla's own virginal body becomes at once a site of struggle and a weapon capable of slicing open the great corporeal mass of worldly social order.

Her mother is keenly aware of this threat. She summons Thamyris and brings him up to speed. Her summons is dripping with import, for we learn that Thamyris views the summons as an invitation to proceed to the nuptials—in other words, to the possession of his bride's body. He is allowed to enter Thecla's chamber. There, he addresses her as his bride, his new possession: "Thecla, my bride, what is happening to you? What disease has brought you to this present confusion? Turn back to your Thamyris, and be ashamed!"[26] He is rebuffed by an invincible silence.

Thamyris responds to this affront with an aristocrat's telltale moderation. He neither breaks off his engagement nor arranges Paul's assassination. Rather, he assumes that Thecla has been addled by words of sorcery and that, consequently, Paul is a dangerous sorcerer. He proceeds to raise a hue and cry and has Paul brought before the Roman proconsul. The result of the proconsul's examination should be predictable. Paul will be shown the gates of the city as an undesirable alien, Thecla will be disenchanted, and life will resume its normal course. Thecla, however, has assumed the faith of Christ. The omission implicit in her earlier silence becomes a sin of commission once Paul has been arrested. She bribes the jailer and enters Paul's chamber. The parallel with Thamyris's earlier entrance is deliberate. Her entrance of Paul's cell is a spiritual "nuptial" whereby she is united with Paul, and through Paul with Christ. This sexual double entendre is brought to a climax, so to speak, when Paul is summoned to his hearing and Thecla proceeds to roll her body around in the place where Paul has been sitting.[27]

Thecla too is brought before the civil magistrate. Her case, however, is different from Paul's. She is no alien but rather an Iconian citizen, bound by its laws. "Why do you not marry Thamyris," the proconsul demands, "in accordance with Iconian law?" Thecla resumes her silence. The wisdom of the world, however, breaks into her silence in the person of her own mother: "Burn the outlaw! Burn the miscreant bride in the theatre so that all women who would learn from him [Paul] may be filled with anxious fear!"[28] Faith, concentrated in Thecla's virginal purity, has set her against mother and fiancé, and outside the very law of her community. To fleshly eyes, her body must be annihilated, that is, burned.

The impure flames of this world, however, cannot devour the purity of heaven. Thecla survives the pyre, becoming an alien to her natal world, and so is allowed to leave Iconium in search of Paul, her spiritual mate. Together they travel the open road to Antioch. When they arrive, Thecla's physical vulnerability becomes even more extreme. She is espied by Alexander, a high noble of the city, who falls immediately in love. He assumes she is bound in some social or biological way to Paul (that she is his to give), and offers to buy her. Paul and Thecla's spiritual union cannot, however, be expressed in such pedestrian terms, even to ensure her protection. Thus Paul denies any connection at all. As a result, Alexander feels free to assault her then and there, and attempts to possess her body. Thecla resists, proclaiming loudly that she is his social equal—that in fact he is attempting to force a dedicated virgin (his religious equal, as he is a priest). At the same time she grabs him, tearing his cloak and knocking off his laurel crown (sign of his priestly office in the cult of the emperor). She succeeds in transforming this man of power into an object of ridicule. For her efforts, she is brought before the civil magistrate and condemned to animal combat at games which Alexander himself is to sponsor. Again her inviolate body is at issue: This time it is to be dismembered.[29]

Her jailer is a kindhearted imperial relative, Tympana, who treats her as a surrogate for the daughter she has lost. A strong bond develops. Still, over Tympana's loud protests, Thecla is led nude into the circus, her offending body exposed for all to see. Her physical vulnerability, however, only emphasizes her triumph. Lions lie docile before her and defend her from a bear's attack. Hungry seals are frightened away from her by a cloud of fire. As a public humiliation and execution the games are a great disappointment—Thecla is in control. When she sees the aquarium with the seals she cries out, "Now it is time for me to wash," and dives in, baptizing herself in the process.[30] In the end, the games are cut short and Thecla is released.

The entire spectacle serves to convert Tympana, transforming her into a spiritual mother for Thecla, one whose solicitude contrasts heavily with the harsh insensitivity of Thecla's physical mother. Indeed, together Paul and Tympana serve to replace Thamyris and Theoclia. They provide for Thecla an alternative set of filiations in terms of which she can locate herself. But that is not the end of the matter. This is no modest North African tale. It is not good enough that the worldly order make room for the spiritual. The victory of the Spirit must be complete. Thus Thecla travels to Iconium where she finds Thamyris dead but her mother still alive. Thecla speaks to her mother the words of salvation and in so doing reconfigures their relationship. She becomes Theoclia's spiritual mother, through whose bodily presence Theoclia is reborn. Only in this spiritual transumption of Thecla's fleshly family is the triumph of the new order complete.

Like the *Passion of Sts. Perpetua and Felicitas*, the *Acts of Paul and Thecla* describes the subversive effect faith works on a saintly woman's place within the well-born Roman family. In the *Acts*, however, the site of conflict has been shifted somewhat. Here the struggle centers around a young woman's body and her efforts to keep its virginity intact. Virginity becomes a virtual *sine qua non* for the empowerment of subsequent saintly women. In the process, there is lost that serene acceptance of a woman's ordinary bodily life in families that we noted in Perpetua's *Passion*. Henceforth, all matters pertaining to reproduction will be imagined to be problematic, a distasteful hindrance to women's expressions of sanctity. Indeed, Perpetua's *Passion* itself was reworked to conform to the new taste for virginity so graphically displayed in the Thecla legend.[31]

Early Medieval Interlude

The tight world of third-century Roman provincial elites, whether in North Africa or Syria, slowly fades away in subsequent centuries. In the Frankish, Gothic, and Anglo-Saxon lands of western Europe, Roman order comes to jostle alongside different "Germanic" or "barbarian" ways. Urbanity and deliberative habits, that is, Romanity, are forced to share center stage with "desert" cunning and strength. The age-old exploitation of slave and client is supplemented by theft and countertheft among the rich and powerful.[32] The exact texture of familial culture also encompasses Germanic as well as Roman norms and institutions.[33] Aristocratic families become increasingly constituted by unstable kindred groupings which use daughters as pawns in a vast game of shifting marriage alliances, the ultimate purpose of which is to forge a connection with the royal family in order to receive royal offices (such as countships) or royal influence in the election of bishops or abbots.

Consequently, we see the narrative hues of early medieval saints' vitae change, registering the salient features of the new social landscape. For example, women saints among the Merovingian Franks (ca. 500–751) are often abducted (*raptae*) at a tender age to be raised in the household of their abductor and prospective groom, victims of the endemic thievery that passes for social, economic, and political competition among the powerful families of Merovingian and Carolingian *Francia* (ca. 500–ca. 950). Social agency is still tied to spiritual power, which is housed, as it were, in the wholesome purity of a virgin's body. But the early medieval church provides new supports for the virgin life that were unnecessary for Perpetua and unavailable to Thecla. The virginal life and its near equivalents come to be institutionalized by the late sixth century. All over *Francia* monasteries are established for women whose vows of continence have been made publicly before, and recognized officially by, the local bishop.[34]

Despite these shifting themes an early medieval saintly woman's dilemmas change little from those of her sisters in Christ of antiquity. This resistance to change is hardly surprising, for whether a woman be subject to Roman *patrocinium* or Germanic *mundium*, the brute fact remains that her body is not her own. It belongs to others to be disposed of as they will: The social, economic, and political order depend upon that fact. Thus, religious purity, whether literal virginity or its near equivalent, continues to act subversively. Its recognition continues to infuse women saints with power sufficient to resist the socially legitimate physical claims of male authorities (or their surrogates). But that same religious purity severely restricts a woman's expression of sanctity within the family circle. Her relations with parents and husbands are marked by conflict until such time as the woman saint is released, in effect, from her familial obligations.

Saintly Women and Family Life in the Later Middle Ages

There are many more changes to the social landscape during the tenth and eleventh centuries. The fluid kinship structures and partible inheritance patterns of barbarian Europe begin to change dramatically in the eleventh century with the introduction among aristocratic families of the principle of primogeniture and the centralization of family wealth upon a core set of holdings.[35] In general, this leads to a diminution in the role that a daughter's marriage is expected to play in securing family honor and wealth. Daughters' marriages are still used to create or confirm connections with other noble families. More often than not, however, women marry men of lower station and means— men whose loyalty to the head of the family is deemed advantageous, or whose long service calls for a fitting reward. Thus, in the new world of the twelfth century, an aristocratic woman's body is still not her own, though it is now worth less on the marriage market. Aristocratic family structures may have changed, but only in ways that buttress their patriarchal bias.

The first of our saints of the later Middle Ages, Christine of Markyate (ca. 1096–ca. 1166), is born of a noble family in Huntingdon, which lies in the rolling lands north of London, lands then dominated by the bishop of Lincoln and the monks of St. Alban's. Her father's name is Autti, her mother's Beatrix. She herself is baptized Theodora and comes only later to choose the name Christine for herself (*sibi Christianam accepit*).[36] Her family is an Anglo-Saxon family with close ties to other remnants of the Anglo-Saxon elite who are struggling to maintain something of their wealth and privilege in the Norman England created by King William I in the wake of the Battle of Hastings in 1066.[37]

Christine appears to be an only child, an heiress whose deft marriage is crucial to the family's survival. But early on Christine assumes a spiritual father, Sueno of Huntingdon, who fills her with stories of the difficulties and glories of the virginal life. His stories find a willing ear. In an episode patterned on the ritual of enserfment, Christine approaches an altar, votive penny in hand. She prays, "O Lord God . . . receive my oblation through the hands of Thy priest. For to Thee, as a surrender of myself, I offer this penny. Grant me, I beseech Thee, purity and inviolable virginity whereby Thou mayest renew in me the image of Thy Son. . . ."[38]

Her intent is not easily realized. Her trials begin when the archbishop of York visits the family manse, casts lustful eyes upon Christine's body, and attempts her seduction. Here is another spiritual father, but one who acts as the fleshly tempter. The archbishop maneuvers her into his rooms while her parents are busy with their cups elsewhere. Christine's situation is extremely delicate: "To consent was out of the question: but openly resist she dared not because if she openly resisted him, she would certainly be overcome by force."[39] She escapes by a clever ruse.

Christine has made a dangerous enemy who determines to be avenged. Since her bodily purity causes her to offend, she must be deprived "of her virginity, either by himself or by someone else." The archbishop convinces a wealthy nobleman, Burthred, to sue for her hand. Christine's parents agree to the match and find some way of pressuring her into accepting espousal. She flatly refuses, however, to proceed to the nuptials.[40]

Her position and prospects are not good. Parents and betrothed combine, with sanctioned authority, to claim her body. Her resistance is viewed as willfulness to be worn down as quickly as possible. When Christine's resolve remains firm, her parents opt for rape. They let Burthred into her chamber, hoping that "if he found the maiden asleep, he might suddenly take her by surprise and overcome her."[41] Their hope is in vain. Christine negotiates with her addled would-be groom, offering him the prospect of a "spiritual marriage." In her words, "that your friends may not reproach you with being rejected by me, I will go home with you: let us live together there for some time, ostensibly as husband and wife but in reality living chastely in the sight of the Lord . . . making a promise that in three or four years' time we will receive the religious habit and offer ourselves to some monastery which providence shall appoint."[42]

Burthred is tempted but is later shamed into renewing his assaults on Christine's body. Somehow she manages to escape every attempted rape. The hagiographer ascribes her good fortune to the protection of her true spouse, Christ.[43] Spiritual nuptials have already taken place, making a mockery of Burthred's earnest lunges.

Her familial opponents do succeed in driving a temporary wedge between Christine and her spiritual father, Sueno of Huntingdon. For a brief period, she is stripped of all human attachments. Christine is crushed by the loss, and yet finds in her solitude a deeper level of agency, one by which she repudiates the name given her at baptism to assume a name of her own fashioning.[44]

Thus, despite being alone in ways that our other saints never were, Christine assumes an invincible will which she wields to the destruction of her family order. Having become increasingly desperate, her father appeals to the prior of St. Mary's, Huntingdon to mediate the dispute. His plea is a succinct summation of the wisdom of Christine's world: "Yet no matter how she was led into it, if she resists our authority and rejects it, we shall be the laughing-stock of our neighbours. . . . Wherefore, I beseech you, plead with her to have pity on us: let her marry in the Lord and take away our reproach. Why must she depart from family tradition? Why should she bring this dishonor on her parents?"[45]

The prior does as he is bidden. He reminds Christine of her spiritual duties as daughter and as espoused. Moreover, he teaches her of the way of salvation that comes to a woman via motherhood. Christine treats the prior's speech as a juridical entity, that is, a mediator's reca-pitulation of the plaintiff's case. She in turn reponds as advocate for the defense. She first denies that espousal has taken place. She has been forced into agreeing to it; there has been no mutual consent and hence no sacrament. Second, there exists an impediment to her and Burthred's espousal. She has previously taken a vow of virginity before Christ, and spiritual vows have greater force than other types, including marriage vows. In light of her vow before Christ, there is also no failure to honor her father and mother, for to obey Christ by honoring the vow made before him cannot contradict the spirit of Christ's command to honor one's parents. As for the saving way of motherhood, Christine is dismissive: "Certainly virgins are saved more easily."

When the prior suggests that she is rejecting Burthred only in hopes of gaining a richer spouse, Christine offers to undergo an ordeal to prove her integrity.[46] At last the prior admits defeat and so refers the dispute on to the local ordinary, the bishop of Lincoln. Unexpectedly, the bishop sides with Christine. Her father's response contains a dis-tant echo of Perpetua's father's despair: "Well, we have peace today, you are even *made mistress over me*. . . . So come and go as I do, and live your own life as you please. But don't expect any comfort or help from me."[47]

The dispute, as it turns out, is far from over. Sueno of Huntingdon (who is back on Christine's side) uses the bishop's decision to broker an agreement with Burthred. Burthred declares himself "prepared to release her before God and you, and I will make provision for her out of my own pocket: so that if she wishes to enter a monastery, she can be admitted by the community without hindrance."[48] In other words, he releases funds (presumably a portion, if not all, of her dowry) by which she will be able to pay her entrance fee into a house of nuns.

This is no solution for Christine's parents. They lose both Christine's dowry and control of Christine. They also lose the potential earnings of her marriage connections and their claim on Burthred and his family. Consequently, they bribe the bishop of Lincoln into reversing his decision (another spiritual father gone bad). He remands Christine into her parents' custody.

Her father loses control and threatens to grant her her desire by turning her out nude and penniless to follow Christ.[49] Her mother, however, remains better focused. At issue is control of Christine's body. Since her power comes from its virginal purity, her body must be fouled. Consequently, Beatrix "swore that she would not care who deflowered her daughter, provided that some way of deflowering her could be found." She commissions love potions from "old crones" and a Jewess. She has Christine beaten and brought all lacerated and disheveled to banquets to be derided and leered at by the revellers.[50] Christine's trials drag on endlessly.

In the end, Christine, through the indefatigable efforts of Sueno of Huntingdon, gains the patronage of sufficiently powerful ecclesiastics to flee her parents once and for all. She takes refuge in the forest, first in the company of the recluse Aedwina and later in a cell attached to the hermitage of Roger of Markyate. Here she remains until Burthred renounces his marital rights and her virginity receives episcopal consecration.[51]

Christine has defeated and in fact destroyed her natal family. She settles into a new spiritual family, assuming occupation of the hermitage proper upon Roger of Markyate's retirement. But she must yet contend with the desires of the cleric who administers her pastoral care, and so the pattern of juxtaposing good and bad spiritual fathers remains constant.

What emerges from this reading of Christine's life is, if you will, "the old, old story." Serious religious attachment dissolves the ordinary bonds that hold a woman bound in body to a parent's or husband's will. With the help of spiritual fathers she resists her physical father; with the help of her spiritual spouse she resists her physical spouse. We witness, however, a significant upping of the ante in Christine's *Vita*. Spiritual fathers are not always trustworthy. Even the spiritual family can impede a woman's progress in sanctity, for it can function much like a physical family. In the end, Christine has only her faith in Christ and Christ's consequent protection. Indeed, she is alone in ways unimaginable to Perpetua or even Thecla. She is a solitary, a participant in the hermetical movement that swept through Europe in the eleventh and twelfth centuries, driving men to settle alone in the forest and women to wall themselves up in cells adjacent to monastery oratories, hermit's chapels, or rural parish churches. Christine too is one of those religious who (to speak the idiom of the day) engages the devil in single combat.[52]

For our last saint we turn away from the perils of Norman England to the burgeoning towns of late twelfth and early thirteenth-century Hainault (a medieval lordship straddling the border between modern-day French-speaking Belgium and northern France), to the town of Huy and the life of Juette (1158–1228), daughter of a patrician burgher of means—a wife, widow, and mother. We first meet her as a girl of thirteen, newly marriageable. Her parents are under pressure from friends and associates to find her a match from a crowd of eager suitors. Once again, one presumes that she is an only child and heiress to the family wealth. But Juette is deeply afraid. Unlike Christine of Markyate, it is not an attachment to virginity per se that motivates her fear. Rather, she considers "the law of marriage to be a heavy yoke." She fears "the heavy burdens of the womb, the dangers of childbirth, the upbringing of children, the fickle fortunes of men, the care of family members and the administration of a household." Above all, she fears the spiritual wear and tear of "that great labor of quotidian responsibility." She begs her parents to allow her "to remain without a man."[53]

Juette, however, is neither Christine nor Thecla. She bows before the cumulative weight of parental and social expectation and takes a husband at enormous personal cost. She soon finds that she hates married life even more than she had feared. Her anger and despair focus narrowly upon payment of the conjugal debt. She comes "to despise each and every coupling."[54] She is overcome by a profound ennui and begins to hope for her husband's death. She later repents of these feelings, learning slowly over time to view them as sins of great magnitude.[55]

After five years of marriage, Juette's husband, indeed, "goes the way of all flesh," but not before Juette has given birth to three children, two of whom survive. Juette becomes a widow, still young at eighteen, rich, fair, an heiress to great wealth, and demonstrably fertile. Clearly here is a "purchase" of worth in the local marriage market. Her father (presumably a widower by this time) urges her to remarry.[56] He actually speaks of the dangers of life and the need to ensure the family line, but the hagiographer takes care to mention that he is also being swayed by the counsel of his social peers (perhaps because their sons might profit from such a match). Juette flatly refuses.[57]

Her father reacts to resistance by arranging for spiritual mediation by Ranulph, Bishop of Liège (1167–1191), whom Juette's father serves as financial officer or "cellarer."[58] One thinks of Christine of Markyate's father and his appeal to the prior of St. Mary's, Huntingdon. Bishop Ranulph summons Juette to his court and, once she is overawed by the presence of so many dignitaries, takes her aside to speak in soft, persuasive tones in favor of remarriage. But Juette, like Christine before her, rebuts each of the bishop's arguments. She prefers to be a widow. In addition, she has taken a vow of continence before Christ which she would keep for the rest of her life.[59]

The bishop is convinced of her rectitude and henceforth acts as her advocate, defending her against all objections and commanding her father to desist from applying pressure on her.[60] It appears that Ranulph's leverage is powerful enough to have his way, for from this time Juette's struggles with her father no longer concern the disposal of her body. Rather, they clash over the welfare of her two young sons.

All that we have been considering is familiar enough. Juette may be a married saint. Still, virginity and later its near equivalent, the widow's continence, act as conditions *sine qua non* of her progress in sanctity. To the degree that parent and husband claim the right to dispose of her body, to that degree she resists, successfully so upon becoming a widow (with the aid of a powerful ecclesiastical personage).

What makes Juette's *Vita* significant in the present context is the subsequent focus of her struggles. Juette's *Vita*, like Perpetua's *Passion*, highlights her status as mother, but does so out of the "Theclan" tradition of locating sanctity in sexual continence and outside of the social and biological family. After Juette's acquisition of the bishop of Liège's patronage, the focus of her *Vita* shifts to the delicate balance she attempts to maintain between her responsibilities as a mother and her religious vocation.

For five years after her husband's death Juette remains at home "taking care of the household and her sons whom she raised with all possible zeal in the complete fear of the Lord."[61] When her older son reaches the age of seven (*infantiae limites*) he is sent off to school, that is, to the "study of letters" in preparation for a life in sacred orders. Her younger son, however, she keeps with her.[62]

The balancing of maternal obligation and religious impulse is often difficult. Juette's generosity toward the poor, for example, is so profligate that her father, who is likely her children's legal guardian, intervenes, "fearing that the children were being disinherited by their mother's alienation of family wealth." He eventually even removes the boys from her care for a time in an effort "to lessen her control of matters and to prevent her from selling their birthright without his knowledge. . . ." In the end he returns them to their mother, for she misses and loves them tenderly.[63] Her impasse seems especially poignant in this vignette.

If Juette's religious heroism at times threatens her maternal responsibilities, her role as provider also threatens her religious progress. For example, she seeks her father's advice on fiscal matters and so invests money with a local businessman, unaware that in so doing she is made guilty of the sin of usury.[64] When she discovers her error, she is wracked with remorse. Still, her hagiographer feels compelled to offer a long theological gloss on the event, explaining how it can be that a saint is vulnerable to this kind of sin.[65]

An encounter with her late husband's relative marks another instance of her delicate predicament. He ingratiates himself to her by speaking with her "as if to help her with her and her son's domestic affairs; he posed as if he loved them, as if he were, indeed, their next of kin."[66] In the event, he becomes Juette's right-hand man (velut manum dexteram ejus), until he is barred access to her home. What is clear from all three episodes is that, in the hagiographer's eyes, family obligations continue to open Juette to the deadly power of "the world" and so impede her progress in sanctity. She feels increasingly frustrated: "She came to long for a place of solitude where she could redeem the time remaining to her in this life."[67]

At the age of twenty-three, Juette decides on a bold move. Against the wishes of father and friends she arranges for the needs of children and household and moves to a leper colony on the edge of town. Her move causes shock waves within her social circle: "All the townsfolk marvelled that a youthful woman of fine station as to life, wealth and age (according to the world's reckoning), should reject worldly glory, by desiring such misery, a misery heavier than all miseries, i.e., to serve and live among lepers."[68]

We do not know just how her children are to be provided for; such provision fades against the backdrop of Juette's insatiable religious need. Significantly, however, her move to the leper colony does nothing to diminish her maternal routines. Rather, there she busies herself preparing food, washing the lepers and their bedclothes, and so on. Her identification with them becomes so strong that she washes herself in their bath water and wishes she could become one of them.[69] Such spiritual maternity soon issues forth in children of the spirit. Men and women leave Huy to gather round Juette in the leper colony, forming a religious community which Juette instructs in the rules of their new familiarity. This is not yet fully religious life, however, in the sense of life lived in the context of public vows and in accordance with a Rule.

The climax of Juette's religious vocation is achieved when she moves to a fully religious station—when she is enclosed as a recluse within a cell attached to the leper colony's chapel.[70] Juette, like Christine, moves beyond the comforts of a spiritual family to become a religious solitary, an anchoress who engages the devil in single combat. She is enabled to make this final move by a sudden change in her ties to family members. Shortly before the account of her enclosure we are told that her father undergoes a religious conversion. He joins a nearby house of regular canons, that is, a community of clerics following the Rule of St. Augustine.[71] He becomes dissatisfied when he realizes that he receives honor among his confreres because of his former worldly prominence. After consulting with Juette, he arranges for episcopal permission to move to a hermit's cell, which, like Juette's, is built into the side of the leprosarium's chapel. He becomes, in effect, Juette's spiritual son. In the end, under Juette's guidance he moves again to join the Cistercian monastery of Villers-en-Brabant where he lives out the remainder of his life.[72] Juette's oldest son also joins a Cistercian community at his mother's behest, the Cistercian monas-tery of Orval, located in present-day Luxembourg.[73] Juette feels that their inclusion within new spiritual families fulfills her maternal obligations toward them, leaving only the youngest son "in the world." Juette now has the space needed to move toward a greater spiritual isolation.

Juette's relationship with her youngest son proves more difficult to stabilize. He has taken up with bad company and assumed a prodigal and worldly mode of life. Indeed, Juette's subsequent exchanges with this son recall a number of canonical "prodigal son" narratives simulta-neously. The boy's dissolute life and ultimate conversion reenact biblical stories of prodigal sons.[74] Juette's persistent, tearful prayers and admo-nitions recapitulate the tenacious concern of St. Monica, St. Augustine of Hippo's careworn mother.[75] Twice Juette summons her recalcitrant son to her cell to receive her motherly correction. The first time he seems to capitulate, departing "as an unhappy Cain from the face of the Lord."[76] When he quickly resumes his secular ways, he is made to appear before her again and banished to another ecclesiastical province. He acquiesces and goes into exile, where he is visited with a terrible presentiment of damnation. He converts and returns immediately to inform his mother, who responds as a latter-day Simeon. In the end, this son too joins a Cistercian monastery (Trois-Fountaines) at his mother's request.[77]

A final peace descends upon Juette's family, as well it might, since it has, strictly speaking, ceased to exist. Physical and spiritual deaths have broken the social and biological bonds constituting it. Henceforth, each surviving family member lives in the grip of a new religious familiarity.

But floating, as it were, above these new religious filiations is the spiritual maternity of Juette, moving each to their appointed ends. Indeed, Juette has become a mighty materfamilias, guiding and directing a sprawling spiritual family of which her father and sons form but a small part. She acts out her maternal care from the huge height afforded by her hermetical solitude, counseling her "children" to embrace the soteriological security present within the reformed Benedictine monasticism of the Cistercian Order.

Christine of Markyate and Juette of Huy bring our examination of the intersection of Christianity, women, and family into the thirteenth century. But the dynamic we have been following perdures for centuries. It is at work whenever medieval women assume a religious seriousness, for such seriousness demands that they take control of their own bodies and of their proper disposal.

One cannot read the stories of Perpetua and Thecla, Christine, and Juette without acknowledging the extent of their victimization. Indeed, their stories are a small part of the long story of women and their suffering under various patriarchal family systems operative during late antique and medieval centuries. On the other hand, it is equally hard to read their stories without acknowledging their resourcefulness in resisting whatever and whomever within their familial and social contexts they experienced as impeding them. Clearly these are women capable of grasping and wielding power.

The present study, however, is designed neither to lament the ways in which medieval women were hurt and their agency denied, nor to celebrate the ways in which some of them found means of exercising agency in spite of dire constraints. Saints' vitae simply do not allow the transparent access to their women subjects that such projects would demand. Rather, as noted above, saints' vitae allow one to see how medieval societies imagined the effect of a purified Christianity (crystallized in the saint's sanctity) on the place of women in the family structures of an ambiguous, fallen world. What our vitae suggest is that this imagined effect was surprisingly stable and continuous. Sanctity was seen to dissolve the family structures it encountered, giving to women power to act in their own right, to construct patterns of familiarity for themselves in accordance with their own determination of spiritual vocation. Christianity, then, was consistently imagined in the Middle

Ages as relativizing social and biological definitions of family and their implicit structures in favor of competing, spiritual filiations.

This leads us to a final observation, one which speaks directly to the current debate among North American Christians concerning the family. Any attempt to say that Christianity contains within itself, as part of its very nature, an implicit family structure that is defined only in social-biological terms cannot appeal to the actual history of Christianity for support. For the first millennium-and-a-half after Christ, Christians, both male and female, consistently imagined the intersection of Christianity and family structure in different and far less determinate ways.

NOTES

1. I am particularly indebted in my own attempts to define the saint's *vita* by Thomas J. Heffernan, *Sacred Biography: Saints and Their Biographers in the Middle Ages* (Oxford: Oxford University Press, 1988), 1–32; and the classic study of Hippolyte Delehaye, *The Legends of the Saints* (Notre Dame, Ind.: University of Notre Dame Press, 1961).
2. See Peter Brown, *The Body and Society: Men, Women, and Sexual Renunciation in Early Christianity* (New York: Columbia University Press, 1988), 33–64.
3. For the Roman church of the first two centuries, see Brown, *The Body and Society*, 65–73.
4. Ibid., 5–32.
5. Herbert Musurillo has compiled and translated several *passiones* including the *Passion of Sts. Perpetua and Felicitas* (henceforth cited as *Passio Perpetuae*, paragraph number and page number), in *The Acts of the Christian Martyrs* (Oxford: Clarendon Press, 1972).
6. See Herbert Musurillo's introduction to the *Passio Perpetuae* in *The Acts of the Christian Martyrs*, xxvi–xxvii.
7. *Passio Perpetuae*, 2.108.
8. Ibid., 5.112 (emphasis added).
9. Ibid., 3.108.
10. Ibid., 3.108.
11. Ibid., 5.112. For the rights of a paterfamilias over the survival of infants born to his household, see John Boswell, *The Kindness of Strangers: The Abandonment of Children in Western Europe from Late Antiquity to the Renaissance* (New York: Vintage Books, 1990), 53–94.
12. *Passio Perpetuae*, 6.114.
13. Ibid., 5.112 (emphasis added).
14. Ibid., 7–8.114–16.
15. See, in this regard, Peter Brown, *The Cult of the Saints: Its Rise and Function in Latin Christianity*, The Haskell Lectures in History of Religions, New Series 2 (Chicago: University of Chicago Press, 1981).
16. *Passio Perpetuae*, 3.110.

17. Ibid., 6.114.
18. Ibid., 20.128.
19. Ibid., 4.110–12, 21.128–30.
20. Ibid., 9.116.
21. Robin Lane Fox, *Pagans and Christians* (New York: Alfred A. Knopf, 1986), 440.
22. Brown, *The Body and Society*, 146; see also Jo Ann McNamara, *A New Song: Celibate Women in the First Three Christian Centuries* (New York: Harrington Press, 1985).
23. Brown, *The Body and Society*, 155–56.
24. An English translation of the *Acts of Paul and Thecla* (henceforth cited as *Acta Theclae*, paragraph and page number of the edition being used) is available in William Wright, *Apocryphal Acts of the Apostles* (New York: Georg Olms Verlag, 1990), 116–45. Because that text limits itself to the Syriac text, I have chosen to use and retranslate the German edition of Edgar Hennecke, *Neutestamentliche Apokryphen in Deutscher Übersetzung*, ed. Wilhelm Schneemelcher (Tübingen: J. C. B. Mohr, 1964), 2.243–251. The present citation is *Acta Theclae*, 7.244.
25. For a succinct portrayal of radical Syrian Christianity, see Brown, *The Body and Society*, 83–102.
26. *Acta Theclae*, 10.245.
27. Ibid., 20.246.
28. Ibid., 20.246.
29. Ibid., 26–27.248.
30. Ibid., 33–34.249.
31. Peter Dronke, *Women Writers of the Middle Ages* (Cambridge: Cambridge University Press, 1984), 282.
32. For a general introduction to the period, see Patrick J. Geary, *Before France and Germany: The Creation and Transformation of the Merovingian World* (New York: Oxford University Press, 1988).
33. Suzanne Fonay Wemple, *Women in Frankish Society: Marriage and the Cloister 500–900* (Philadelphia: University of Pennsylvania Press, 1981); and Jo Ann McNamara and Suzanne Fonay Wemple, "The Power of Women Through the Family in Medieval Europe, 500–1100," in *Women and Power in the Middle Ages*, ed. Mary Erler and Maryanne Kowaleski (Athens, Ga.: University of Georgia Press, 1983), 83–101.
34. Wemple, *Women in Frankish Society*, passim.
35. For this change in aristocratic marriage practice and its French origins, see Georges Duby, *The Knight, the Lady, and the Priest: The Making of Modern Marriage in Medieval France*, trans. Barbara Brey (New York: Pantheon Books, 1983).
36. *The Life of Christine of Markyate: A Twelfth-Century Recluse*, ed. and trans. C. H. Talbot (Oxford: Clarendon Press, 1959), (henceforth *Vita Christianae*, paragraph and page number). The passage referred to here is *Vita Christianae*, 1.34.
37. For a brief evocation of the English situation under the early Norman kings, see David C. Douglas, *The Norman Fate 1100–1154* (Berkeley, Calif.:

University of California Press, 1976), 1–30. For the situation of Christine's family see the editor's prologue to *Vita Christianae*, 10–13.

38. *Vita Christianae*, 4.40.
39. Ibid., 5.42.
40. Ibid., 6–7.42–44.
41. Ibid., 10.50.
42. Ibid., 10.50.
43. Ibid., 12.54.
44. Ibid., 13.54–56.
45. Ibid., 15.58.
46. Ibid., 15–16.58–62.
47. Ibid., 19.64–66, emphasis added.
48. Ibid., 21.68–70.
49. Ibid., 22–23.70–72.
50. Ibid., 23.72. The "old crones" and the Jewess are introduced in 23.74.
51. Ibid., 28–43.80–114.
52. For a general introduction to the religious awakening of the eleventh and twelfth centuries that pays special attention to the hermetical movement, see Henrietta Leyser, *Hermits and the New Monasticism: A Study of Religious Communities in Western Europe, 1000–1150* (New York: St. Martin's Press, 1984).
53. Hugh of Floreffe, *Vita Juettae sive Juttae, viduae reclusae, Hii in Belgio*, in *Acta Sanctorum* (*Januarii, 2*), ed. G. Henschen (Paris: Victor Palmé, 1863), 145–69 (henceforth *Vita Juettae*, chapter, paragraph, and page numbers). The passages being cited here are *Vita Juettae*, 1–2.147. The following analysis of this *Vita* owes a debt to Jennifer Carpenter, Ph.D. candidate at the Center for Medieval Studies of the University of Toronto, especially the chapter of her thesis entitled "Juette of Huy, Recluse and Mother (1158–1228): Children and Mothering in the Saintly Life."
54. *Vita Juettae*, 2.10.146.
55. Ibid., 15.46–47.154.
56. Ibid., 5–6.13–15.147–48.
57. Ibid., 6.15.148.
58. Ibid., 6.15.148.
59. Ibid., 6.16.148.
60. Ibid., 6.16.148.
61. Ibid., 9.26.150.
62. Ibid., 5.13.147–48.
63. Ibid., 9.25.150.
64. Ibid., 9.26.150.
65. Ibid., 9.27–32.150–52.
66. Ibid., 8.20.149.
67. Ibid., 9.32.152.
68. Ibid., 10.34.152.
69. Ibid., 10.34–35.152.
70. Ibid., 14.42.153.
71. Ibid., 13.39.153.

72. Ibid., 13.40–41.153.
73. Ibid., 14.42.153.
74. Ibid., 19.53.156.
75. Ibid., 19.54.156. Augustine's account of his mother's tears is to be found in *Confessiones* 3.12.21.
76. *Vita Juettae*, 19.55.156.
77. Ibid., 20.57–59.156–57.

8

The Early Modern Period

Religion, the Family,
and Women's Public Roles

MERRY E. WIESNER

When the editors of this volume asked me to write a chapter exploring "religion, feminism, and the family" in early modern Europe, I at first thought I had heard wrong, for as the editors themselves have pointed out, these three topics are rarely considered together. Moreover, although scholars use the word "feminist" to describe women and men living before the French Revolution who recognized and deplored ideas and institutions that hindered women, they usually do so only with great reservations and long explanations.[1] The word "feminist" was not used by early modern women, and it often implies concepts of individual rights that only emerged in western society with the American and French Revolutions.

The more I thought about it, however, the more I realized I had already been linking these three topics in lectures I'd presented or papers I'd written. I was simply defining "feminism" in a slightly different way than it is used by contemporary feminists or by those of the first wave of feminism in the nineteenth century. For women living in early modern Europe, roughly between 1500 and 1750, being a feminist meant asserting that women had a public role, that they had public authority. In this they were not unlike their feminist sisters in the nineteenth and twentieth centuries, but their justifications for this emphasis were somewhat different. For early modern women, the source of their public authority was not an abstract notion of human rights, but their position within a family or their duty to God, or a combination of both. Such women offer an interesting parallel to the domestic feminists of the Victorian period because both groups often used the same types of justifications for their actions—their responsibilities as mothers and as Christians.

The parallel is not exact, for there are also significant differences between the two groups. First, no one in the early modern period believed women to be more moral or virtuous than men; on the contrary, women were widely regarded as more lascivious, devious, and deceitful. Thus early modern women never argued that their involvement in public affairs would "sweep the country's kitchen clean," end corruption and vice, or bring a higher standard of morality to political life the way nineteenth-century women did.

Second, and more important, the early modern period was one of transition, when the idea began that the family was part of a private realm and that religion could be a matter of private conscience. Women thus responded to actual legal and political changes, not to an inherited tradition. They were trying to retain a public role, not re-create one, as their nineteenth century granddaughters would. Therefore many of their arguments looked backwards, since they saw themselves upholding traditions rather than challenging them. They accepted the generally held belief that the golden age was in the past, in the same way that nineteenth-century women's rights advocates accepted the notion of progress and a golden age in the future. Thus to explore "religion, feminism, and the family" in this period we need to investigate how women used what they viewed as traditional ideas about the family and religion to argue for what many of their male and female contemporaries saw as highly untraditional—a public role for women.

The Family

Feminist scholarship over the last twenty years has paid great attention to the dichotomy between public and private, and to the ways in which the boundaries between what is considered "public" and what is considered "private" have changed over time. Most historians now see contemporary western ideas of "public" and "private" as originating in the early modern period with the development of a new ideal of intimate family life among the urban middle classes. Many bourgeois women accepted this ideal and began to develop a new domestic culture centered on the nuclear family.

There were other women, however, who objected to the increasing domestication of the family. By their words, and more often by their actions, they fought this trend and asserted that their role and function within the family gave them the right—or indeed the duty—to be involved in other public issues. To understand the basis for their arguments, and to see what specific changes women were objecting to, we need first to examine both the continuation and limitation of the public functions of the early modern family. These functions were highly class specific, so I will make some distinctions between the experience of noble, bourgeois, and lower-class women, although some factors are common to all of them. My discussion will largely be limited to the cities, both because more sources are available for urban women and because this is where the ideal of the privatized family began.

Noble families retained a great many public functions during the early modern period. Europe was still an aristocracy in many ways, and noblewomen's experience continued to be determined more by their class than by their gender. Female rulers governed their territories and made decisions in matters of religion, social welfare, and economic policy as well as politics. This never changed in Europe, as historians of Victoria's reign well know, but for the first time in the early modern period individuals began to question the appropriateness of a woman ruler. Ideas about women's inferiority and natural subjection led to increasingly shrill and strident complaints about female monarchs: John Knox's *First Blast of the Trumpet Against the Monstrous Regiment of Women*, written in 1558 to protest the reigns of Mary of Guise as regent in Scotland and of Mary Tudor in England, is only one of a long series. These ideas were not only expressed by the intellectual elite but also occasionally by ordinary men—and women—through public protest or pamphlets, as the work of Carole Levin on the reigns of Mary and Elizabeth Tudor has shown.[2] Though there were no successful revolts against female rulers simply because of their gender, there was a gradual change from viewing female rulership as equal to that of male to viewing it as simply a necessary expedient.

For noblewomen who were not rulers, ideas about female inferiority combined with actual political and military changes to restrict their public role significantly. With the growth of centralized states, rulers increasingly relied on professional armies and bureaucracies, reducing the power of the nobility. Noblemen might make up for this loss of inherited power by military training or a university education and thereby still play an important political role. This was not possible for noblewomen, who were, of course, excluded from the universities and humanist academies and no longer given military training. As Margaret Cavendish, the Duchess of Newcastle, wrote in 1656: "All heroic actions, public employments, powerful governments, and eloquent pleadings are denied our sex in this age."[3]

This is not to say, however, that noblewomen lost their public role completely, particularly when compared to women of other classes. Rural aristocratic and gentry women still managed estates, handed out relief to the poor, tended the sick and elderly, and supported education, activities which may not be considered "public" if that word is taken to mean the realm of institutionalized power only, but which were certainly public—that is, reaching beyond the household—in their effects.

Such activities continued into the nineteenth century, and, as Jessica Gerard has pointed out, were extremely important in establishing relations of deference and paternalism between classes. Indeed, they were perhaps more important than the more formal power relationships between noble and gentry men and their lower-class tenants.[4]

Bourgeois families also retained a great many public functions during the early modern period. Some of these were economic: Many bourgeois families were still centers of production, with female members playing a shrinking, though still important, role in the production and sales of goods; all of them were economic units for tax purposes, as taxes were assessed by household.

This recognition of the household as the smallest unit of society was not simply economic, but also political. In political theory—at least until Thomas Hobbes—the household, not the individual, was the smallest component of society. During the early modern period, the political functions of the household were more rather than less stressed, as governments became increasingly concerned about public order, discipline, and morality. Governments—whether monarchies, principalities, or free cities—viewed the household as the smallest unit of social control, with the head of household responsible for the behavior of all dependent members, including nonrelated servants.

In addition to this, the family was held responsible for educating children, for giving them both a usable trade and sound moral guidance. For Protestant families, this included religious instruction, since Protestant theorists from Luther to the English and American Puritans emphasized the role of the family in the health and stability of a Christian community.[5] After the Council of Trent (1545–1563) the Catholic church attempted to build up the power of the priest, but it still viewed domestic religious activities, at least prayer and fasting, as very important.[6]

Along with these practical public functions, families linked persons to the larger public arena in the realm of ideas as well. For bourgeois as well as nobles, the family remained the source of one's identity. One gained or lost honor and reputation as one's family did, and conversely, brought honor or shame to the family by one's own actions. Though men had more opportunities for determining the fortunes of their family, a woman's actions might affect the political careers and community standing of the male members of her family. For example, Willibald Pirckheimer, the prominent Nuremberg humanist, was held somewhat suspect as the city became Lutheran not only because he was rather weak and vacillating in his acceptance of the Reformation, but also because his sister Charitas, the abbess of the St. Clara convent in the city, inspired her nuns in their adamant refusal to disband or convert.[7]

For an unmarried woman, the status of her birth family might allow or even require her to carry out functions that were certainly regarded as public. In Catholic areas, her family's status and reputation might enable her to become the abbess at a prominent convent, thus making her the head of a very large household. Though this was not an option for Protestant unmarried women, they often served as the heads of charitable endowments or as hospital directors with financial and administrative functions.[8] They were not required to have any relevant professional training but assumed such positions because of their family connections and their own reputation for competence; the two were regarded, of course, as intimately related. (Women were not, as I noted before, given such positions because they were regarded as more charitable and virtuous than men; that ideology developed later, and was used to *exclude* middle-class women from hospital positions.) In addition, the careers of upwardly mobile sons might depend on their sisters remaining unmarried and carrying on the family business, in order to support them while they attended a university.[9]

Though the actions of an unmarried woman were thus rarely seen as totally private, a woman's public role increased when she married and assumed authority over children and servants, and increased further when she became a widow.[10] The husband was seen as the head of the household, this smallest yet extremely important public institution, but the wife was not excluded or exempt from most of its public functions. Though he was ultimately held responsible for her actions, she was responsible for the actions of her children and servants, and mothers could be hauled in for questioning if their children were not under control. The public nature of a mother's function was recognized in theory as well as practice. William Gouge, the Puritan writer, was not alone in his opinion that the role of a mother "may be accounted a public work."[11]

Married women also had a family function independent of their husbands, for at least in northern Europe, their connections with their birth families continued after they were married. Christiane Klapisch has discovered that in Florence, Italy, women's birth families and also their names and individual identities were forgotten or ignored in both official and private family records.[12] This was decidedly not the case in northern Europe, where women continued to assist their male and female siblings in a variety of ways long after their marriages. Women's continued attachment to their birth families often meant that they, rather than their brothers, were the ones who took care of elderly parents or younger orphaned siblings.

Bourgeois women thus continued to play numerous public roles during the early modern period, but new restrictions and limitations were also being imposed. Ideas of female inferiority which called into question the rule of a queen also called into question the legal role of a middle-class housewife. Middle-class women were increasingly forbidden from appearing in court on their own behalf and were ordered to get lawyers to argue for them. Widows in many parts of Europe were required to have guardians, which limited their ability to control their family's future wealth and prosperity. Unmarried women could no longer control their own property but were given court-appointed guardians who might be totally unrelated to them.[13]

These legal changes, generally justified as protecting weak and inexperienced women, were actually related to larger economic and ideological trends. As guilds were threatened by the rise of capitalist production and changing patterns of trade, they responded by tightening up membership requirements, limiting the number of masters, and shortening the time a widow was allowed to keep operating a shop after the death of her husband. Widows were also limited in the number of journeymen and apprentices they could hire and were never given a voice in guild leadership. In their attempt to retain as many workplaces as possible, journeymen pushed for a total exclusion of all women from guild shops, even including the master's wife. Poorer masters and journeymen were often hired by wealthier masters—their work thereby proletarianized—as crafts gradually changed from guild-based to protoindustrial organization.[14]

The wives of such wealthier masters and other entrepreneurs gradually retreated from, or never assumed, an active role in the family business. It is among this class that a new family ideology developed that required women not to work out in public or as part of the market economy. For some occupations, such as officials, physicians, and scientists, this ideology combined with increasing requirements for a formal education to prevent wives from sharing in their husband's work as they often had before the sixteenth century.[15] Such occupations opened up new ways for middle-class men to gain prestige, status, and wealth during the early modern period. However, the prestige of an occupation was directly related to how fully women were excluded, so that as occupations such as apothecaries attempted to become more respectable and professional, they followed this pattern and immediately excluded women, even wives of male apothecaries. Thus middle-class women whose work identity and family identity had been linked in the medieval economy—"the wife of a gatekeeper" was an occupational as well as a marital label—lost their identification with the world of work.

Lower-class women could not quit working, but the practical and ideological exclusion of women from many types of labor meant that they were often limited to marginal employment. They were specifically

excluded from guild or professional positions, and many changed occupations frequently, moving into and out of paid employment when
their family situations changed. Even those who did stay in the same
occupation most of their lives were still listed as simply "doing" that
occupation rather than "being" it, for instance, Joan "who makes
clothes" rather than Joan "the seamstress."[16] Thus lower-class women,
who certainly worked, gradually lost the authority that came from
being identified with an occupation. Midwives were the one exception
to this among honorable occupations. Their occupation, not their family's status, was the reason for their continued public role as witnesses
in illegitimacy and infanticide cases, examiners in cases of fornication,
and distributors of public welfare.[17]

Thus, although middle- and lower-class households retained many
of their public functions during the early modern period, gradually
more and more of these functions were viewed as properly performed
by a male head of household only. Female heads of household continued to be taxed, but attempts were also made to encourage widows and
unmarried women to move in with their sons or brothers, so that the
female-headed household could be regarded as simply transitory.[18] We
should note that this was during the time when ideas of individual citizenship were emerging in some parts of Europe, with rights based
partly on one's position as head of household. Because the male head of
household was increasingly the norm, women's claims to rights of citizenship were very ambiguous.[19] (The ambiguity continues, of course,
right up through the U.S. Constitution.)

Restrictions on women's public role and the accompanying domestication of the family thus resulted from a wide variety of changes going
on in the early modern period. Women's objections to these trends took
a correspondingly wide variety of forms.

One mild way in which women opposed the privatization of the family was by continuing to define their "family" in the broadest possible
terms. Women tended to include a much wider range of kin in their wills
than men did, paying close attention to who received each of their
worldly possessions and less to their primary heirs.[20] They also frequently identified themselves as members of two families, their birth and
marital, and worked to improve the fortunes of both. For example,
Argula von Grumbach, a German noblewoman and vigorous supporter
of the Reformation, called herself not only "von Grumbach," her husband's title, but also "von Stauffen," her father's.[21] German, Dutch, and
English bourgeois and gentry women often used both their birth and
marital family names when signing letters or making out wills, and
women who married more than once used three or four names to identify

themselves, or chose the one with the highest rank or status.[22] Early modern husbands tried to prevent their wives from remarrying after their deaths so that they would continue an allegiance with the first husband's family, but this seems to have been successful only in Florence.[23]

Women also artificially extended their kin groups through godparenting, thus creating neighborhood-wide or village-wide networks of family-like relationships.[24] Their contact with a broader group of actual and honorary kin frequently gave women the role of matchmaker in their children's marriages, an informal public role that may have given them more power within their own families. (In this instance women's public role led to greater family authority, as well as vice versa, a good example of the dialectic between public and private.)

Widows were particularly adamant defenders of their public legal and economic rights, refusing to name guardians and appearing in court on their own behalf.[25] They often argued that their mothers and grandmothers had always represented themselves and that these new restrictions were insulting and demeaning. Their arguments often included a listing of other family members—both male and female— who had proved themselves capable.

Masters' widows used various means to get around restrictions against their continuing to run a shop, often arguing that tradition was on their side. As occupations professionalized or entrance requirements were expanded, women affected by these changes showed intimate knowledge of the new regulations, particularly the clauses that exempted current practitioners of the trade from the new restrictions. Brigitta Mueller, a stocking knitter in the south German town of Memmingen, argued that she had as much right to sell her stockings as her brother did, for both of them had learned from their father, though his had been a formal apprenticeship while hers had not. The brother, who had tried to stop her from making stockings, was doing their family's reputation a disservice, according to Mueller, and was motivated only by jealousy.[26] Jeane Giunta, a book publisher in Lyon, France, was similarly motivated, commenting in a 1579 dedication that she was "devoted to the typographical art, lest the honor that her father and Florentine ancestors won thereby be lost."[27]

Middle-class women thus used family honor as one reason for retaining the right to work. Both they and lower-class women also used their obligations to support their families as another justification. For example, Brigitta Mueller first mentioned that her husband was unemployed, and in a later appeal noted that she was now widowed with young children to support.[28] This may have been done primarily to evoke sympathy or to threaten authorities with the specter of more public welfare charges, but it was a successful tactic that kept women working in the public arena. Though most of these were extremely poor women struggling to keep their families from starving, in some cases the women concerned were able to continue on in highly skilled trades and make a decent living working independently. We have been trained to view family needs and women's individual self-development as "at odds," as indeed they have been throughout much of modern history for white middle-class women. But family responsibilities can be a spur, as well as a block, to public activities.[29] As Natalie Davis commented in a slightly different context, "embeddedness did not preclude self-discovery, but rather prompted it."[30]

Women's embeddedness in their families also led them to another sort of public activity—namely, writing. Women wrote about their husband's activities and lives, or wrote and published wedding and funeral orations for family members, generally their fathers or mothers.[31] Women's writing was more often spurred by their feelings of responsibility to their children, which female authors generally noted in the introductions to their works. Anna von Schleebusch, a German noblewoman, extended this to include her duty as a grandmother, comparing herself to Jacob who blessed not only his own children but his son Joseph's children.[32]

Female rulers sometimes interpreted their maternal responsibilities even more broadly, to include the task of mothering their subjects. Queen Elizabeth I's rhetoric along these lines has been noted by many scholars, but we can find it in lesser-known female rulers as well.[33] Elisabeth of Braunschweig and Emilie-Juliana of Schwarzburg-Rudolstadt both wrote advice books for their subjects, in Emilie's words "out of our sovereign motherly heart and hand for the strengthening edification of our subjects [Lands-*kinder* in German]."[34] Her book consists of prayers and hymns written especially for families, to help them through difficult times such as the death of children. It includes special prayers for midwives and pregnant women, prayers which ask God to provide physical strength and wisdom, and to make the delivery quick and uncomplicated. This was very different from similar prayer books written by pastors, which typically tell women to leave everything passively up to God and to remember that their labor pains are divinely ordained.[35]

Religion

As a number of the examples noted above make clear, women often combined family and religious responsibilities when justifying their writing or acting in the public sphere. There were also some who viewed religion alone as a strong enough justification, who argued that

divine inspiration had forced them to write or act. Argula von Grumbach wrote to the University of Ingolstadt protesting the University's
treatment of a young teacher accused of Lutheran leanings: "I am not
unfamiliar with the words of Paul that women should be silent in
church, but, when no man will or can speak, I am driven by the word
of the Lord when he said, "He who confesses me on earth, him will I
confess, and he who denies me, him will I deny."[36] She describes herself as a mother bear defending her young, not from starvation or a
wanton life, but from incorrect theological doctrine, and goes on to say
that her role as a Christian woman—she does not say mother here but
woman—required that she speak out when she felt injustices were
being done. She uses Matthew 10:11–14 in her argument, noting that
cities, towns, and households are all held equally responsible for their
"worthiness" before God; thus the borders of concern and activity for
the pious housewife were at least the town walls, if not beyond. She is
thus basing her right to speak out on religious issues on her responsibility as a member of a larger household (and thus a part of one public
institution) and not simply on her concern for her own children.

This sentiment—that a woman's duty as a member of a Christian
household extended well into the public realm—comes out even more
strongly in Katherina Zell, the wife of a Protestant pastor in Strasbourg
who in fact had no children. She wrote an open letter to women suffering because their husbands had been banished for religious reasons
and, shortly before she herself died, gave the funeral sermon for a
woman accused of heretical leanings. Her actions indicate that she felt
herself clearly capable and even required to carry out the same sorts of
duties that her husband did, and she writes that she wants to be judged
"not according to the standards of a woman, but according to the standards of one whom God has filled with the Holy Spirit."[37]

Catholic as well as Protestant women used religion as a justification
for public action. Many in the sixteenth century were nuns or other
female religious who protested the forced closing of their convents by
Protestant political authorities. Some did this in quiet ways, such as the
Irish and English nuns who fled to continental religious houses rather
than returning to their families, but others engaged in much more public demonstrations of their loyalty to Catholicism. In some German convents, nuns stuffed wool or wax in their ears rather than listen to
Protestant sermons and sang hymns when townspeople gathered around
the convent walls to shout insults and throw rotten food. Abbesses wrote
to their political and religious superiors protesting their treatment, particularly when efforts to close convents involved the destruction of
buildings rather than simply economic pressure. They used the power of

their families to exert political pressure as well, and in some cases their protests were successful. In parts of central Germany, for example, Protestant authorities just gave up trying to convert the convents, and simply let them die out slowly by forbidding the taking in of new novices, or else gave up completely and let them exist as Catholic islands in Protestant lands. Though nuns protesting the Reformation do not quite fit our own model for feminists, they were, as well as defending their faith, defending the rights of at least some women to make their own religious choices and to live in an all-female community.[38]

The most dramatic examples of women using religion to argue for a public role in early modern Europe were provided by the English Civil War in the mid-seventeenth century. Though most Puritan writers and preachers did not break with Anglicans or continental Protestants on the need for wifely obedience or women's secondary status, certain aspects of Puritan theology and practice prepared women for a more active role. All believers, male and female, were to engage in spiritual introspection, and in particular to focus on their experience of conversion. This experience was an indication that one was among the elect, and in more established Puritan communities such as those of New England it became a requirement for membership in a congregation. A particularly dramatic conversion could give one a certain amount of power, especially if it resulted in the healing of an illness or a continuing experience of divine revelation. Women's conversion narratives are often very personal and physical, yet they discuss female spiritual development publicly in a very new way.[39]

Puritans also regarded prayer as an active force that could influence state affairs. Puritan women (and men) privately and publicly prayed for certain political changes, and were firmly convinced that prayer aided one's family, community, and political allies. For Puritans, who had rejected the efficacy of exorcism, group prayer was the most powerful weapon in cases of possession, and many tracts report on the efficacy of such prayers against that worst of enemies, Satan.

Women's prayers and conversion narratives often grew into more extended prophecies in seventeenth-century England, some of which were described by people as hostile to the women or the message, and some of which were published by the women themselves. Female prophets were occasionally criticized for speaking out publicly on political and religious matters, but they had Old Testament and classical precedents for what they were doing, and they were usually viewed in the way they viewed themselves—as mouthpieces of God, or as, in the words of some, "impregnated with the Holy Spirit."[40] Women who went beyond prophecy to actual preaching also emphasized the strength of their calling, but this was not enough in the eyes of most observers to justify such a clear break with the deutero-Pauline injunction forbidding women to teach. It is difficult to know how common female preaching actually was during the English Civil War decades, for most reports of it come from extremely hostile observers who were in turn criticized for making up some of their accounts. Women tended to preach spontaneously at informal or clandestine meetings, where their listeners never thought to record the content of their sermons, so it is unclear how much sustained influence they exerted.

Women clearly did have an impact on the spread of more radical religious ideas through two other activities: organizing what were known as "gathered" churches in their own homes, and publishing pamphlets. Puritan women had often organized prayer meetings and conventicles in their houses during the early part of the seventeenth century, and after the Restoration in 1660 (which restored the Anglican Church as the official religion of England at the same time it restored the monarchy) they continued to open their homes to Baptists, Presbyterians, Quakers, and other groups.[41] Post-Restoration commentators belittled such groups by pointing out the large number of women they attracted, though again we have few objective records with which to judge the actual gender balance. Political and religious pamphlets authored by women appeared most frequently during the two decades (1641–1660) when censorship was not rigorously enforced, as part of a more general explosion of pamphlet literature by a wide range of authors. Though most female authors deprecated their own abilities and described themselves as "instruments of God's power," they clearly intended their works to be read by men and felt no limits as to subject matter, delving into complex theological and doctrinal matters and directly challenging the actions of the King or Parliament.

A sense of urgency pervades most of these women's pamphlets, an urgency that occasionally led women to more overtly political actions. Several times during the English Civil War decades, women petitioned Parliament directly; in 1649 hundreds of women petitioned for the release of the Leveller leader John Lilburne and in 1659, seven thousand Quaker women signed a petition to Parliament for the abolition of tithes, a type of religious tax. The language of the Leveller women clearly indicates that they felt a right to operate as political actors: "We cannot but wonder and grieve that we should appear so despicable in your eyes as to be thought unworthy to Petition or represent our Grievances to this Honourable House. Have we not an equal interest with the men of the Nation, in those liberties and securities contained in the Petition of Right, and other good Laws of the Land?"[42]

Such actions came to an abrupt end with the Restoration, and most of the radical groups in which women had participated died out. The most important exception to this were the Quakers, who had been the most supportive of women's independent religious actions throughout the decades of the English Civil War. George Fox, the founder of the Quakers, did not advocate women's social or political equality, but he did support women's preaching and separate women's meetings charged with caring for the poor, ill, prisoners, and children. Quakers taught that the spirit of God did not differentiate between men and women, and they advocated qualities for all believers similar to those that most Protestants stressed primarily for women: humility, self-denial, piety, devotion, modesty. These were not to make one weak in the face of persecution, however, and Quakers were the most viciously persecuted of all the radical groups, perhaps because they were the most adamant in proclaiming their beliefs. Quaker women preached throughout England and the English colonies in the New World, and were active as missionaries also in Ireland and continental Europe well into the eighteenth century. They were whipped and imprisoned for preaching, for refusing to pay tithes or take oaths, or for holding meetings in their houses; no special treatment was accorded women for age, illness, pregnancy, or the presence of young children. Quaker women also published a large number of pamphlets, most of them apocalyptic prophecies or "encouragements" for co-believers, and they wrote spiritual autobiographies, which are one of the few primary sources we have from the seventeenth century written by middle- or lower-class women.[43] Margaret Fell Fox, who eventually married George Fox after years of organizing, preaching, visiting prisoners, and being imprisoned herself for her Quaker beliefs, published Women's Speaking Justified in 1669, which argued that Paul's prohibition of women's preaching had been meant only for the "busie-bodies and tattlers" of Corinth, and which provided a host of biblical examples of women who publicly taught others.[44] Fell did not argue for women's equality in secular matters; for Quakers spiritual matters were more important in any case. The women's meetings that she organized gave many women the opportunity to speak in public and to engage in philanthropic activities for persons outside of their own families. Though Quakers as a group became increasingly apolitical in the eighteenth century, social action by Quaker women continued; many of the leaders of the abolitionist and women's rights movements in nineteenth-century America were Quaker women.

Of all the women I have been discussing, Margaret Fell Fox probably comes closest to the contemporary definition of a feminist, articulating a position in favor of women's increased public role and greater parity (though not equality) with men. We may wish to go a bit further, however, and use Adrienne Rich's phrase, "feminist in action," to describe all of the women I have been discussing.[45] All of them viewed themselves as worthy and important family members and as Christians accountable for their own salvation, with responsibilities both to their families and to a larger community because of their families or their duty to God. It may seem somewhat odd to describe this self-concept as "feminist," but it is important to keep in mind that the idea of a "self" apart from "family" or "community of Christians" was relatively rare in the early modern period, and would have been even rarer for women who were denied access to the learning that taught about "self-fashioning."[46] Politics and culture were becoming more separate from the family (more "public" as we would define it), and more secularized, a trend that was definitely gender-related, since the virtues associated with political power—reason, good judgment, strength of will—were increasingly seen as secular, individual, and male, while female virtues—piety, charity, humility— were regarded as both Christian and domestic. Until the eighteenth century, however, no one would have viewed Christian virtues as private; they were just as essential to a ruler or citizen as secular virtues.

It may seem that as women were more and more excluded from existing sources of public authority—official positions, guild membership, professional education—or not included in new sources of public authority such as voting citizenship, they desperately clung to the only ones they still had—the family and religion—though the importance of these spheres was clearly shrinking. This view misinterprets early modern society, however, and expects women to have had incredible foresight. Early modern women viewed the family and religion as the strongest possible sources of public authority because they always had been, for men as well as women. Indeed, they may have had more foresight than we give them credit for, since it would take another four centuries or more before the idea of "the self," the autonomous individual endowed with certain rights, would be extended to women and would allow them some of the public authority that some early modern women gained through their families or their churches.

NOTES

1. See, for example, the introductions of three recent books: Hilda Smith, *Reason's Disciples: Seventeenth-Century English Feminists* (Urbana, Ill.: University of Illinois Press, 1982); Moira Ferguson, *First Feminists: British*

Women Writers, 1578–1799 (Bloomington, Ind.: Indiana University Press, 1985); Constance Jordan, *Renaissance Feminism: Literary Texts and Political Models* (Ithaca, N.Y.: Cornell University Press, 1990).

2. Carole Levin, *The Heart and Stomach of a King: Elizabeth I and the Politics of Sex and Power* (Philadelphia: University of Pennsylvania Press, 1994).

3. *Nature's Pictures*, (London, 1656), quoted in *The Female Spectator: English Women Writers Before 1800*, ed. Mary R. Mahl and Helene Koon (Bloomington, Ind.: Indiana University Press, 1977), 141.

4. Jessica Gerard, "Lady Bountiful: Women of the Landed Classes and Rural Philanthropy," *Victorian Studies* 30:2 (1987): 183–210.

5. Margo Todd, "Humanists, Puritans, and the Spiritualized Household," *Church History* 49 (1980): 18–34.

6. R. Po-Chia Hsia, *Society and Religion in Münster, 1535–1618* (New Haven, Conn.: Yale University Press, 1984), 68.

7. Franz Binder, *Charitas Pirckheimer: Aebtissen von St. Clara zu Nürnberg* (Freiburg: Herder'sche Verlagshandlung, 1878); Harold J. Grimm, *Lazarus Spengler, A Lay Leader of the Reformation* (Columbus, Ohio: Ohio State University Press, 1978), 26.

8. Merry E. Wiesner, *Working Women in Renaissance Germany* (New Brunswick, N.J.: Rutgers University Press, 1986), 37–49, 77–78.

9. Mary Prior, "Women and the Urban Economy, Oxford 1500–1800," in *Women in English Society 1500–1800* (London: Methuen, 1985), 98.

10. Louise Mirrer, ed., *Upon My Husband's Death: Widows in the Literature and Histories of Medieval Europe* (Ann Arbor, Mich.: University of Michigan Press, 1992); Barbara J. Todd, "The Remarrying Widow: A Stereotype Reconsidered," in *Women in English Society*, 68; Barbara Diefendorf, "Widowhood and Remarriage in Sixteenth Century Paris," *Journal of Family History* 7 (winter 1982): 387, 393.

11. William Gouge, *Of Domesticall Duties* (London, 1622), 18.

12. Christiane Klapisch Zuber, *Women, Family, and Ritual in Renaissance Italy* (Chicago: University of Chicago Press, 1985), 285.

13. Merry E. Wiesner, *Women and Gender in Early Modern Europe* (Cambridge: Cambridge University Press, 1993), 30–35.

14. Wiesner, *Working Women*, 149–85 and Merry E. Wiesner, "Guilds, Male Bonding and Women's Work in Early Modern Germany," *Gender and History* 1 (1989): 125–37.

15. Wiesner, *Working Women*, 49–55, 79; Londa Schiebinger, *The Mind Has No Sex? Women and the Origins of Modern Science* (Cambridge, Mass.: Harvard University Press, 1989), 61–63; Heide Wunder, *"Er ist die Sonn,' sie ist der Mond": Frauen in der Frühen Neuzeit* (Munich: C. H. Beck, 1992), 119–39.

16. Michael Roberts, "'Words they are Women, Deeds they are Men': Images of Work and Gender in Early Modern England," in *Women and Work in Preindustrial England*, ed. Lindsay Charles and Lorna Duffin (London: Croom Helm, 1985), 139.

17. Wiesner, *Women and Gender*, 64–70; Merry E. Wiesner, "The Midwives of South Germany and the Public/Private Dichotomy," in *The Art of*

Midwifery: Early Modern Midwives in Europe, ed. Hilary Marland (London: Routledge & Kegan Paul, 1993), 77–95.

18. Zuber, *Women, Family, and Ritual*, 34–35.

19. Lyndal Roper, "'The Common Man,' 'the Common Good,' 'Common Women': Reflections on Gender and Meaning in the Reformation German Commune," *Social History* 12 (1987): 1–21; Christine Fauré, *Democracy Without Women: Feminism and the Rise of Liberal Individualism in France* (Bloomington, Ind.: Indiana University Press, 1991).

20. Sherrin Marshall Wyntges, "Survivors and Status: Widowhood and Family in the Early Modern Netherlands," *Journal of Family History* 7 (winter 1982): 400–403; Nuremberg Staatsarchiv, Nürnberger Testamenten, Rep. 78 (Old nr. 92), Testamentenbücher 1–6.

21. "Wie ain Christliche Fraw des Adels . . . Sendtbrieffe die Hohenschul zu Ingolstadt" (1523), in *Historien der heyligen Ausserwolten Gottes Zeugen, Bekennern und Martyrern*, ed. Ludwig Rabus (n.p., 1557).

22. Joel T. Rosenthal, "Aristocratic Widows in 15th-Century England," in *Women and the Structure of Society: Selected Research from the 5th Berkshire Conference on the History of Women*, ed. Barbara J. Harris and Joann K. McNamara (Durham, N.C.: Duke University Press, 1984), 45; Nuremberg Staatsarchiv, Nürnberger Testamenten, Rep. 78 (Old nr. 92).

23. Zuber, *Women, Family and Ritual*, 130; Todd, "Remarrying Widow," 73.

24. John Bossy, "Blood and Baptism: Kinship, Community and Christianity in Western Europe from the 14th to the 17th Centuries," in *Sanctity and Secularity: The Church and the World*, ed. Derek Baker, Studies in Church History 10 (Oxford: Basil Blackwell Publisher, 1973), 129–43.

25. Wiesner, *Working Women*, 25, 31; Wyntges, "Survivors," 398.

26. Memmingen, City Archives (Stadtarchiv), Zünfte, 441(3).

27. Natalie Zemon Davis, "Women in the Crafts in 16th-century Lyon," in *Women and Work in Preindustrial Europe*, ed. Barbara Hanawalt (Bloomington, Ind.: Indiana University Press, 1986), 185.

28. Memmingen, City Archives (Stadtarchiv), Zünfte, 441(3).

29. Janet Sharistanian comments that this is also true in the nineteenth century: "Conclusion: Historical Study and the Public/Private Model," in *Gender, Ideology and Action: Perspective on Women's Public Lives*, Contributions in Women's Studies 67 (New York: Greenwood Press, 1986), 232–33. *At Odds* is the title of Carl Degler's book (Oxford: Oxford University Press, 1980).

30. Natalie Davis, "Boundaries and the Sense of Self in 16th-century France," in *Reconstructing Individualism: Autonomy, Individuality and the Self in Western Thought*, ed. Thomas C. Heller, Morton Sosna, and David E. Wellbury (Stanford, Calif.: Stanford University Press, 1986), 63. Nancy Chodorow, in the same volume ("Toward Relational Individualism: The Mediation of Self Through Psychoanalysis," 197–207) points out that the object-relations model in post-Freudian psychoanalysis also stresses that the self must always be viewed in its relation to others, that setting autonomy and relatedness in opposition to each other sets up a false dichotomy. This object-relations perspective thus appears to be returning to an idea that was common sense in the early modern period.)

31. Davis, "Boundaries", 57; Henry Huth, *Prefaces, Dedications, Epistles Selected From Early English Books 1540–1701* (printed for private circulation, 1874), 368; C. F. Paullini, *Hoch und wohlgelahrtes Teutsches Frauenzimmer*, 2d ed. (Frankfurt and Leipzig: Johann Michael Funcke, 1712), 43–84.

32. Anna Elisabeth von Schleebusch, foreword to *Anmuthiger Seel-erquickender Würtz-garten oder auserlesenes Gebet-Buch . . .* (Leipzig, 1702).

33. See Levin, *Heart and Stomach.*

34. Emilie Juliana von Schwarzburg-Rudolstadt, title page to *Geistliches Weiber-Aqua-Vit . . .* (Rudolstadt, 1683).

35. Johann Hugo, *Trostlicher und kurtzer bericht/wes sich alle Gottsforchtige schwangere Ehefrauwen/vor und in kindnoten zu trosten haben*, (Frankfurt, 1563).

36. Rabus, *Historien.*

37. Roland Bainton, *Women of the Reformation in Germany and Italy* (Boston: Beacon Press, 1971), 55–76.

38. Merry E. Wiesner, "Ideology Meets the Empire: Reformed Convents and the Reformation," in *Germania Illustrata: Essays Presented to Gerald Strauss*, ed. Andrew Fix and Susan Karant-Nunn (Kirksville, Mo.: Sixteenth Century Essays and Studies, 1992), 181–96.

39. Barbara Ritter Dailey, "The Visitation of Sarah Wight: Holy Carnival and the Revolution of the Saints in Civil War London," *Church History* 55 (1986): 438–55.

40. Phyllis Mack, *Visionary Women: Ecstatic Prophecy in Seventeenth-Century England* (Berkeley, Calif.: University of California Press, 1992).

41. Keith Thomas, "Women and the Civil War Sects," *Past and Present* 13 (1958): 42–62; Dorothy Ludlow, "Shaking Patriarchy's Foundations: Sectarian Women in England, 1641–1700," in *Triumph Over Silence: Women in Protestant History*, ed. Richard L. Greaves (Westport, Conn.: Greenwood Press, 1985), 93–123.

42. Quoted in Smith, *Reason's Disciples*, 55.

43. Catherine La Courreye Blecki, "Alice Hayes and Mary Penington: Personal Identity within the Tradition of Quaker Spiritual Autobiography," *Quaker History* 65 (1976): 19–31; Phyllis Mack, "Feminine Behavior and Radical Action: Franciscans, Quakers, and the Followers of Gandhi," *Signs* 11 (1986): 457–77; Phyllis Mack, "Teaching about Gender and Spirituality in Early English Quakerism," *Women's Studies* 19 (1991): 223–38.

44. Reprinted in Ferguson, *First Feminists.*

45. "Compulsory Heterosexuality and Lesbian Existence," *Signs* 5:4 (summer 1980): 652.

46. The phrase is Stephen Greenblatt's in *Renaissance Self-Fashioning: From More to Shakespeare* (Chicago: University of Chicago Press, 1980).

9

Restoring the Divine Order to the World

Religion and the Family in the Antebellum Woman's Rights Movement

CATHERINE A. BREKUS

In the summer of 1848, in the town of Seneca Falls, New York, a small group of female reformers—Lucretia Mott, Martha C. Wright, Elizabeth Cady Stanton, and Mary Ann McClintock—decided to call a convention to air their grievances against women's lack of equality in the family, church, and state. Searching for the right words to express their sense of injustice, they turned to one of the most revered documents in American civic culture: the Declaration of Independence. In an echo of the celebrated words of Thomas Jefferson, they wrote: "We hold these truths to be self-evident: that all men and women are created equal; that they are endowed by their Creator with certain inalienable rights; that among these are life, liberty, and the pursuit of happiness." As they sat in McClintock's parlor around her mahogany table (which today stands in the Smithsonian Institution), they listed eighteen examples of men's "tyranny" over women, including their refusal to allow women to vote, attend college, or work in male occupations. Within the family, they complained, married women were not allowed to own property, and even more belittling, they were "compelled to promise obedience" to their husbands, who were free to "deprive [them] of [their] liberty, and to administer chastisement." Even the church, the institution that was supposed to affirm women's full humanity and dignity, perpetuated their subordination. Not only had man excluded woman from "any public participation in the affairs of the Church," but he had "usurped the prerogative of Jehovah himself, claiming it as his right to assign for her a sphere of action, when that belongs to her conscience and to her God."[1]

Mott, Stanton, and the one hundred other men and women who signed the "Declaration of Sentiments" at the first woman's rights convention in Seneca Falls were radical for their day. To conservative clergymen, who were shocked by their criticisms of the family and church, they seemed to be atheists. Instead of softening their language to woo public opinion, these women asserted bluntly that they had "too long rested satisfied in the circumscribed limits which corrupt customs and a perverted application of the Scriptures" had marked out for them.[2] Despite their radical rhetoric, however, most of these women were middle-class, liberal Protestants who found inspiration for their cause in the well-thumbed pages of their Bibles. Their first convention was held in a Wesleyan chapel, and throughout the 1840s and 1850s, they frequently held their meetings within the sacred spaces of churches.

Most early women's rights activists were biblical feminists who were deeply committed to strengthening both the family and the church. At a time when the family was widely perceived to be in "decline," they were portrayed as dangerous, anti-Christian radicals who wanted to undermine the authority of fathers and husbands. In reality, however, most of these women were devout Protestants who shared their culture's idealization of marriage and motherhood. In their speeches and published writings, they portrayed themselves as Christian reformers who had embarked on a divinely inspired crusade: to improve and strengthen the relationships between husbands and wives, parents and children. With the Bible as their guide, they hoped to create new, more egalitarian families and churches where men and women would share equal rights and responsibilities. In the words of Elizabeth Oakes Smith, they wanted to "restore the divine order to the world."[3]

The "Sacred Cause" of Female Equality

Until recently, most historians have ignored the religious dimensions of the early woman's rights movement. For example, one of the most cited overviews of the suffrage movement—Eleanor Flexner's *Century of Struggle: The Woman's Rights Movement in the United States*—virtually ignores the religious beliefs of many antebellum feminists. Similarly, in her classic study of *Feminism and Suffrage*, Ellen DuBois claims that women were unable to form their own independent political movement until they moved beyond the pieties of their religious faith.[4]

Why have these historians devoted so little attention to the religious roots of the woman's rights movement? In part, they seem to have projected contemporary attitudes and assumptions onto the women whose lives they have studied. By the early years of the twentieth century, the women's movement had largely severed is ties to Christianity,[5] and many feminists viewed established religion as one of the most formidable obstacles to female equality.

Yet even more important, these historians have been influenced by their reading of Elizabeth Cady Stanton, one of the foremost leaders of the movement and its most outspoken critic of institutional Christianity. Although in her early career Stanton defended the Bible, affirming that "the best of Books is ever on the side of freedom," by the late 1860s she had begun to describe the church in bitter terms as a "police institution."[6] In the opening pages of *The Woman's Bible*, a feminist critique of the scriptures, she complained:

> The Bible teaches that woman brought sin and death into the world, that she precipitated the fall of the race, that she was arraigned before the judgement seat of Heaven, tried, condemned and sentenced. Marriage for her was to be a condition of bondage, maternity a period of suffering and anguish, and in silence and subjection, she was to play the role of a dependent on man's bounty for all her material wants, and for all the information she might desire on the vital questions of the hour, she was commanded to ask her husband at home.[7]

In one devastating paragraph, Stanton exposed the Bible as a pillar of male supremacy, tainting its claim to divine inspiration. In her opinion, women would never be able to achieve full political, legal, or social equality within the framework of traditional Christianity.

Stanton's anticlericalism influenced her interpretation of the woman's rights struggle in her monumental, multivolume *History of Woman Suffrage*, the source most frequently used by historians interested in the early movement. Because of its extensive reports of local and national conventions, historians have been tempted to read it uncritically as a transparent mirror of past events. However, *The History of Woman Suffrage*, like all histories, does not merely document the past but interprets and explains it. Stanton was more secular than other women in the movement, and she wanted future readers to share her point of view.[8] Of course, there were several other feminist leaders who shared her distrust of religious institutions. Ernestine Rose, for example, a Jewish immigrant, caused controversy whenever she spoke at women's rights conventions because of her unapologetic atheism.[9] Yet even though women such as Stanton and Rose have dominated contemporary scholarship, they were not representative of rank and file members. Indeed, when Stanton's *Woman's Bible* was published in 1896, her colleagues in the National Woman Suffrage Association took pains to distance themselves from her views, voting tersely that they had "no official connection with the so-called 'Woman's Bible' or any theological publication."[10]

A careful reading of Stanton's *History of Woman Suffrage*, combined with woman's rights tracts, newspapers, and convention reports, reveals that the early woman's rights movement was deeply influenced by the tenets of liberal and evangelical Protestantism.[11] Most antebellum feminists belonged to dissenting religious groups such as the Hicksite Quakers, Congregational and Progressive Friends, Wesleyan Methodists, Christian Unionists, and the Liberal Free Churches.[12] Although they phrased many of their arguments in the Jeffersonian language of natural rights, claiming that they were entitled to equality by "the laws of nature and of nature's God," they also declared that they had been specially "anointed," "sanctified," and "baptized" by a personal savior who had called them to fight for a "sacred cause": the divinely ordained equality of women.[13] Cleverly, these women adjusted their language to suit their audience. In official petitions, they appealed to their constitutional rights as human beings, but in speeches to other women, they used a distinctively religious rhetoric.[14] For example, at the Syracuse National Convention in 1852, Elizabeth Oakes Smith reflected,

> it does seem to me that we should each and all feel as if anointed, sanctified, set apart as to a great mission. It seems to me that we who struggle to restore the divine order to the world, should feel as if under the very eye of the Eternal Searcher of all hearts, who will reject any sacrifice other than a pure offering.[15]

Similarly, in 1856 Frances D. Gage exulted that "thousands are becoming ready to be baptized into a new faith, a broader and holier recognition of the rights of humanity."[16]

Instead of discarding the Bible, many of these early feminists tried to transform it into a defense of their equality to men.[17] Historically, Christianity and feminism have often been linked; for centuries, women have been inspired by Paul's words, "there is neither Jew nor Greek, there is neither bond or free, there is neither male nor female, for ye are all one in Christ Jesus."[18] Echoing this language, Antoinette Brown Blackwell argued that the Bible sanctioned female preaching as well as female equality. At an 1852 convention she resolved that, "the Bible recognizes the rights, duties, and privileges of woman as a public teacher, as every way equal with those of man; that it enjoins upon her no subjection that is not enjoined upon him; and that it truly and practically recognizes neither male nor female in Christ Jesus."[19] A year later, in 1853, she became the first woman to be ordained in the Congregational Church.

Like other woman's rights activists, Blackwell reinterpreted scripture through a feminist lens, picking out egalitarian passages that she could use as ammunition against her opponents. The feminist arsenal included Genesis 1:26–27 ("God created man in his image, in the image of God created he him; male and female created he them"), which was interpreted as evidence of the simultaneous creation of the sexes; Joel 2:28 ("your sons and your daughters shall prophesy"), which was used to defend women's religious leadership; and the scattered accounts of biblical "prophetesses" and heroines such as Deborah and Anna. "Real" religion, these women claimed, recognized the mutual dependence and equality of the sexes. "We had all got our notions too much from the clergy, instead of the Bible," Lucretia Mott complained. "The Bible . . . had none of the prohibitions in regard to women."[20]

In the battle over which biblical texts represented authentic Christianity, no text caused feminists more trouble than the Pauline injunction, "Let your women keep silence in the churches." Sarah Grimké, an abolitionist as well as feminist, questioned whether the King James Version was an accurate translation of the Bible. If the Bible appeared to sanction either slavery or women's subordination, perhaps its true meaning had been obscured. In her *Letters on the Equality of the Sexes*, she declared, "King James's translators certainly were not inspired. I therefore claim the original as my standard, *believing that to have been inspired. . . .*"[21] Other women, such as Lucretia Mott, claimed that Paul's command had pertained only to the women of Corinth, not women in general. More radically, a few women augured Germany's Higher Critics by reading the Bible as poetry or metaphor instead of literal truth. According to Hannah Tracy Cutler, the spirit of the Bible was more important than the letter. In a speech delivered in 1854, she expressed her frustration that the Bible was used to defend "tyranny and oppression"—namely, slavery and women's "subjection." Her solution was to "proclaim the beautiful spirit breathed through all its commands and precepts, instead of dwelling so much on isolated texts that have no application to our day and generation."[22] Stephen S. Foster, a Garrisonian abolitionist as well as a feminist, was more blunt. "I love the Bible because it contains so many truths," he proclaimed, "but I was never educated to love the errors of the Bible."[23]

Because they questioned the inerrancy of the Bible, feminists were accused of being "unsexed women, who make a scoff of religion . . . and blaspheme God."[24] Not surprisingly, many of their most outspoken critics were conservative clergymen. In 1851, for example, at the first woman's rights convention held in Indiana, a Methodist minister chided his listeners, "the Bible had placed the *final appeal* in all disputes in man; that if women refused obedience, God gave man the right to use force."[25] Similarily, in 1854 the Reverend Henry Grew—father of Mary Grew, a well-known woman's rights activist—disrupted a woman's rights convention by quoting "numerous texts to show that it was clearly the will of God that man should be superior in power and authority to woman; and asserted that no lesson is more plainly and frequently taught in the Bible, than woman's subjection."[26] According to these men, Christianity and feminism were fundamentally opposed, representing two visions of womanhood that could never be reconciled without destroying the church and the family.

Feminism and the "Decline" of the Family

Nineteenth-century critics of the woman's rights movement seem to have been particularly concerned about its possible impact on the sanctity of the family. Historically, debates over the proper role of the family and debates over the ethical teachings of religion have often been connected; the family has been regarded as a miniature church, a model of God's relationship to God's human children. Across the centuries, conservative Christian theologians have claimed that obedience to God as "father" requires submission to earthly fathers as well. To nineteenth-century clergymen, the woman's rights movement seemed to pose a distinct threat to the "traditional," father-headed family of Victorian America. For example, in 1848, at one of the earliest conventions, a minister lamented the "deplorable" consequences that would follow equality in marriage. According to him, the unity of husband and wife would be threatened by disputes over matters as diverse as politics and the education of children.[27] For many clergymen, "the unity and oneness of the married pair" was more important than whether women could own property or vote.[28]

The mid-nineteenth century was a time of profound anxiety about the integrity of the family. Contrary to popular myth, the nineteenth century was not a "golden age" for parents and children; our current concerns about the decline of the family stretch back to the 1800s. As historian John Demos explains, "for at least a century now the American family in particular has been seen as beleaguered, endangered, and possibly on the verge of extinction. The sense of crisis is hardly new; with some allowance for periodic ebb and flow, it seems an inescapable undercurrent of our modern life and consciousness."[29]

By the middle of the nineteenth century, the family was no longer the fundamental economic, political, educational, and religious unit of society.[30] In the wake of the American Revolution, a new ethic of republican individualism undermined patriarchal authority. Not only did sons and daughters exercise greater control over whom they would marry, but new inheritance laws gave widows and daughters greater power over property.[31] Generally speaking (and all generalizations admit of exceptions), the authoritarian family of colonial America was replaced by a "modern" family where intimate, emotional ties were prized over strict parental discipline.[32]

These ideological changes were accompanied by demographic and economic changes that had far-reaching implications. Most striking, the average family size grew smaller as men and women began to exert greater control over their fertility. Before 1800, the average family contained seven or eight children, but by the mid-nineteenth century, that number had decreased to five or six.[33] This demographic revolution was linked to changing economic structures. In a market rather than an agrarian economy, children were no longer perceived as economic assets. During the colonial era, men, women, and children had all contributed to the family economy; together, they produced goods for household consumption. By the end of the eighteenth century, however, the family had begun to lose many of its economic functions as paid employment moved outside the home. In working-class families, economic necessity often forced women to find jobs in mills or factories, but in middle-class families, men's and women's "spheres" were increasingly separated.[34] Indeed, even though women of all classes continued to toil for long hours in household manufacturing—spinning thread, stitching clothing, brewing beer, and churning butter—their labor at home did not generate wages and so was not recognized as "work." At the same time that American culture celebrated the self-made man, women's labor had become invisible.

As many historians have argued, the ideology of domesticity arose in response to the dramatic economic dislocations caused by the market revolution. Beginning in the late eighteenth and early nineteenth centuries, women were expected to raise children at home while men battled for financial security in the marketplace. In contrast to the colonial period, when childrearing pamphlets had been addressed to men because they were expected to be more rational and responsible, Victorian Americans exalted motherhood. Mothers, not fathers, were now supposed to take primary responsibility for raising virtuous children. For example, in a typical article entitled, "For What is a Mother Responsible," *The Parent's Magazine* answered,

> She is responsible for the principles which her children entertain in early life. For her it is to say whether those who go forth from the fireside shall be imbued with sentiments of virtue, truth, honor, honesty, temperance, industry, economy, benevolence, and morality;—or those of a contrary character—vice, fraud, drunkenness, idleness, extravagance, and covetousness.[35]

In the nineteenth century, mothers would become accustomed to earning the sole praise, but also the sole blame, for the choices made by their children.

For middle-class women, the ideology of separate spheres repre-sented both a gain and a loss. On the one hand, countless sermons and tracts written by men of every religious persuasion praised women for being morally superior. For example, one South Carolinian exulted, "Hail woman! . . . hail [thou] bright benignant star! a star, which shoots forth to all mankind, the most lovely, the most resplendent virtues."[36] Yet even though women were celebrated for their "natural" piety and morality, they still lacked concrete political and legal equality: They could not vote, own property, make contracts, or sue. For the first time in American history, large numbers of women were taught to read and write, but they were educated to become good mothers, not to partici-pate in the intellectual, "masculine" world of politics and law.

The separation of work and home was also a mixed blessing for fathers, who became less involved in the daily lives of their children. In 1842, the Reverend John S. C. Abbott warned:

> Paternal neglect is at the present time one of the most abundant sources of domestic sorrow. The father, in almost every walk of life, eager in the pursuit of business, toils early and late, and finds no time to fulfill those duties to his children which, faithfully ful-filled, would secure to him the richest share of temporal and spir-itual blessings.[37]

Abbott lamented the transformation, but his words of warning did little to stem the tide. Many men may have wanted to spend more time with their children, but to be successful breadwinners they had to spend long hours away from home. Most troubling, the exaltation of feminin-ity meant that maleness (in the words of historian John Demos) "seemed to carry a certain odor of contamination." First and foremost, the family was now perceived as a shelter from the corruption of the outside, "masculine" world.[38] This was a dramatic reversal of the earlier (and equally unrealistic) exaltation of male rationality and responsibil-ity over women's supposed irrationality and lack of self-control.

In this cultural climate, many religious men and women feared that the woman's rights movement would destroy the already beleaguered family. Horace Bushnell, the liberal clergyman best known for his theology of "Christian nurture," decried woman's suffrage as a "reform against nature." He predicted that if women could vote, many would leave their husbands, filing for divorce in unprecedented numbers. In his dystopian vision of the future, rebellious wives would assert their independence by voting against their husbands, stirring up "feeling[s] of hurt." "Such contrary vote need not do any fatal harm," he admitted, "and yet there is a loosening touch in it."[39] Weary husbands would return home each night "not to cease and rest, but to be dinned with the echo, or perhaps bold counter-echo of his own harsh battle. The kitchen dins the parlor, and one end of the table dins the other. Upstairs, down-stairs, in the lady's chamber—every where the same harsh gong is ringing, from year to year."[40] Worst of all, "femininity" itself would disappear, leaving in its wake a new race of aggressive, masculine women with "sharp" looks and "wiry and shrill" voices.[41]

To twentieth-century ears, Bushnell's fears sound overwrought, but his vision of "masculine" women tapped into the deepest fears of many of his readers. Throughout history, gender (like race) has been a primary means of establishing self-identity, and the specter of independent, ballot-wielding women challenged basic nineteenth-century assumptions about the differences between "masculinity" and "femininity." Rather than reexamining the categories they had created to understand sexual difference, many preferred to dismiss woman's rights activists as deviants or crackpots. *The New York Herald*, for example, assured its readers that these women were "entirely devoid of personal attractions. They are generally thin maiden ladies, or women who have been disappointed in their endeavors to appropriate the breeches and the rights of their unlucky lords."[42] Another newspaper described them as "mannish women, like hens that crow."[43]

Women as well as men claimed that female equality would undermine the family. Rather than embracing the goals of the early feminist movement, Sarah Worthington King Peter, a Catholic convert, believed that women should be given greater educational and employment opportunities but not complete political equality.[44] Similarly, Catharine Beecher, one of the most prominent reformers of the nineteenth century, did not argue that women were *naturally* inferior, but she urged them to accept their subordination for the good of society. Disturbed by the sectional, racial, and class tensions that were threatening to splinter American culture, she hoped that sex could serve as the primary social division. In her ideal world, sexual hierarchy would help reduce the inherent conflicts of a democratic society. As she explained, women "are made subordinate in station, only where a regard to their best interests demands it, while, as if in compensation for this, by custom and courtesy, they are always treated as superiors."[45] In a culture where women were raised to be selfless, women such as Peter and Beecher believed that social and familial stability took precedence over women's "natural" rights.

The Feminist Vision of the Family

In response to their critics, feminists claimed that they wanted to strengthen and protect the family, not destroy it.[46] Indeed, most woman's rights advocates shared popular concerns about the "decline" of the family. Idealizing the home, feminists at the Albany Convention in 1854 passed a resolution affirming that "the family, by men as well as women, should be held more sacred than all other institutions."[47] Like many of their critics, they were troubled by the dramatic social and economic changes that were reshaping everyday life, but they differed in their solution to the nation's ills. In contrast to Catharine Beecher, who wanted to shore up patriarchal authority by making men's and women's responsibilities even more distinct, feminists wanted to break down the rigid, artificial divisions that had been created between the sexes.

In order to win greater support, woman's rights activists claimed that their reforms would benefit men as well as women. As Ernestine Rose explained, "Man forgets that woman can not be degraded without its reacting on himself."[48] Inviting men as well as women to participate in the movement, they denounced "antagonism between the sexes" as detrimental to their larger goals. For example, an advertisement for a woman's rights convention held in 1850 urged men and women not to "take hostile attitudes toward each other," but to "harmonize in opinion and co-operate in effort, for the reason that they must unite in the ultimate achievement of the desired reformation."[49] What these women promised was nothing less than egalitarian, fulfilling marriages based on mutual respect. Marriage was not simply a "domestic" or "social union," Hannah Tracy Cutler explained, but "a complete and perfect union, conferring equal rights on both parties."[50] With utopian zeal, Paulina Wright Davis declared that "True marriage is a union of soul with soul, a blending of two in one, without mastership or helpless dependence."[51]

To achieve their goal of "mutual dependence," early feminists concentrated not only on suffrage, but on a host of reforms aimed at promoting women's legal and social equality. Legally, most supported the passage of married women's property acts, which would allow women to keep their own inheritances and wages.[52] Even more radically, they suggested that women's subordination within the family made it possible for men to subject them to physical and psychological abuse. At a convention in 1853, an outraged Lucy Stone testified, "I know a wife who has not set foot outside of her husband's house for three years, because her husband forbids her doing so when he is present, and locks her up when he is absent." This woman was "gray with sorrow and despair," yet she had no legal recourse "because the law makes her husband her master, and there is no proof that he beats or bruises her; there is nothing in his treatment of her that the law does not allow."[53] In the feminists' vision of the ideal family, women would no longer be helpless to challenge the authority of their husbands and fathers but would be protected by the full force of the legal system.

In many ways, antebellum feminists sound startlingly modern; they were pioneers in the struggle against domestic abuse and legal exploitation. But in comparison to twentieth-century feminists, they were moderate and even conservative in their attitudes toward women and the family. Most were white, middle class, and heterosexual, and they found it difficult to envision a plurality of women or a plurality of families. The *woman's* rights movement would not be transformed into the *women's* movement until the twentieth century.

Most antebellum feminists were too cautious to propose a sweeping reorganization of family life. First, with the prominent exception of Elizabeth Cady Stanton, most firmly opposed divorce.[54] Even though Antoinette Brown Blackwell believed that women should be able to seek legal separation for "personal and family protection," she still claimed that "even such separation can not invalidate any real marriage obligation." No matter what crimes her husband had committed, "she is never to forget that in the sight of God and her own soul, she is his wife, and that she owes to him the wife's loyalty; that to work for his redemption is her highest social obligation."[55] Moreover, almost all antebellum feminists objected to contraception. Hoping to impose a single standard of sexual morality on both women and men, they advocated "voluntary motherhood" through abstinence.[56] Most important, few questioned women's "natural" domesticity. Even Antoinette Brown Blackwell— abolitionist, feminist, and minister—asserted that women should not "enter in earnest upon the great work of life outside of its home and relations" until their children were grown.[57]

Paradoxically, many of these women based their claim to equality on their *difference* from men rather than their similarity.[58] There were two strands of feminist thinking in antebellum America: Some women stressed their common humanity with men, while others celebrated their special qualities as women.[59] In some ways, the assertion of female uniqueness seems to have been politically calculated. While their opponents argued that their differences from men made them subordinate, feminists countered that it was exactly *because* they were different that they deserved equality. Yet many of these women seem to have genuinely believed in the essential differences between the sexes. In a letter to the woman's rights periodical *The Una*, Hannah Tracy Cutler insisted that women did not want to be like "stern" and "cold" men, whom she envisioned as corrupt and contaminated.

> The objector meets us with the oft repeated cry, "would you unsex woman and render her the same selfish being that you find man, when immersed in the strife and chicanery attendant upon politi-

cal relations?" Once and for all, let the answer be an emphatic NO!! But since, because men here have had no appropriate balance, all this evil has occurred, we feel that the moral harmony of the world demands woman's interest and influence. We ask to use it, not that we may become like men in our moral natures, but because that we are *unlike* them; and hence harmony demands the counterbalancing influence of our softer sympathies, our more gentle natures, to balance the stern, cold, calculating spirit of the other sex.[60]

Cutler, like many other nineteenth-century women, had internalized the language of the cult of domesticity.

Yet despite their Victorian sensibilities, the feminists' vision of marriage as an equal, mutual partnership undermined the very concept of separate spheres. Indeed, a few women seem to have recognized that their reforms would change the basic social organization of the home. In 1878, Antoinette Brown Blackwell reversed her earlier thinking by calling for "a general reconstruction in the division of labor. Let no women give all their duties to household duties, but require nearly all women, and men also, since they belong to the household, to bear some share of the common household burdens."[61] Later in the century, more radical voices would wonder why women were forced to "choose" between motherhood and service to the world.[62]

To Victorian men and women, questioning the sexual division of labor was nothing short of revolutionary. In the 1840s and 1850s, newspapers ran columns with titles such as "Insurrection Among the Women," and "The Reign of the Petticoats." After a convention in Albany, a writer for the *Mechanic's Advocate* described woman's rights activists as "women out of their latitude." Their proposed reforms would "set the world by its ears," he complained.

> To be practically carried out, the males must change their position in society to the same extent in an opposite direction, in order to enable them to discharge an equal share of the domestic duties which now appertain to females, and which must be neglected, to a great extent, if women are allowed to exercise all the "rights" that are claimed by these Convention-holders. Society would have to be radically remodelled in order to accommodate itself to so great a change in the most vital part of the compact of the social relations of life. . . .[63]

This writer did not believe that such a future was possible, but his words proved prophetic. Feminism, it soon became clear, would require a fundamental transformation of family, church, and society.

Historically, the equality of women and the institution of the family have often been at odds. In the words of Carl Degler, "the historic

family has depended for its existence and character on women's subordination."[64] Antebellum woman's rights activists wanted to shatter that
dependence; they believed that they should not have to choose between
their commitment to equality and their responsibilities to their husbands and children. Fusing their religious beliefs with political zeal,
they dedicated themselves to transforming every institution—church,
state, and family—according to a new ethic of sexual equality. Little did
they know how much resistance they would face in their struggle to
"restore the divine order to the world." Today, more than a century
later, we are still struggling to achieve their vision.

NOTES

All biblical quotes cited in this chapter have been taken from the King James
Version.
1. Elizabeth Cady Stanton, Susan B. Anthony, and Matilda Joslyn Gage,
   History of Woman Suffrage, vol. 1, 1848–1861 (1881; reprint, New York:
   Arno Press, 1969), 70–71. Hereafter cited as *HWS*.
2. *HWS*, 1, 72.
3. Ibid., 523.
4. Eleanor Flexner, *Century of Struggle: The Woman's Rights Movement in the
   United States*, rev. ed. (Cambridge, Mass.: Harvard University Press, 1975);
   Ellen Carol DuBois, *Feminism and Suffrage: The Emergence of an Independent
   Women's Movement in America 1848–1869* (Ithaca, N.Y.: Cornell University
   Press, 1978), 33. For a critique of DuBois, see Elizabeth Clark, "Religion,
   Rights and Difference: The Origins of American Feminism, 1848–1860,"
   Institute for Legal Studies *Working Papers* 2:2 (February 1987).
5. See Nancy F. Cott, *The Grounding of Modern Feminism* (New Haven, Conn.:
   Yale University Press, 1987), 36.
6. Elizabeth Cady Stanton, *Address of Mrs. Elizabeth Cady Stanton, Delivered at
   Seneca Falls and Rochester, New York, July 19 and August 2d, 1848* (New
   York: Robert J. Johnston, 1870), 3; and Elizabeth Cady Stanton, "Religion
   for Women and Children," *The Index*, 11 March 1886, Container 3,
   Elizabeth Cady Stanton Papers, Library of Congress, quoted in Mary
   Pellauer, *Toward a Tradition of Feminist Theology: The Religious Social
   Thought of Elizabeth Cady Stanton, Susan B. Anthony, and Anna Howard Shaw*
   (Brooklyn: Carlson Publishing, 1991), 21.
7. Elizabeth Cady Stanton, *The Woman's Bible*, 7. For a discussion of
   Stanton's religious beliefs, see Pellauer, *Toward a Tradition of Feminist
   Theology*, 15–152, and Kathi Lynn Kern, "*The Woman's Bible*: Gender,
   Religion, and Ideology in the Work of Elizabeth Cady Stanton, 1854–1902"
   (Ph.D. diss., University of Pennsylvania, 1991).
8. For an excellent discussion of this point, see Nancy Gale Isenberg,
   " 'Coequality of the Sexes': The Feminist Discourse of the Antebellum

Woman's Rights Movement in America" (Ph.D. diss., University of Wisconsin-Madison, 1990), 1–45.

9. For a biographical sketch of Rose, see *HWS*, 1, 95–100.

10. Susan B. Anthony and Ida Husted Harper, *History of Woman Suffrage*, vol. 4, 1883–1900 (1902; reprint New York: Arno Press, 1969), 263–64.

11. For scholarship that emphasizes the importance of religion to early American feminism, see Clark, "Religion, Rights and Difference"; Donna A. Behnke, *Religious Issues in Nineteenth-Century Feminism* (Troy, N.Y.: Whit-ston Publishing Company, 1982); and Isenberg, " 'Coequality of the Sexes.' "

12. Isenberg discusses all these groups in chap. 4 of "Coequality of the Sexes." On Quaker leaders of the feminist movement, see Margaret Hope Bacon, *Mothers of Feminism: The Story of Quaker Women in America* (San Francisco: Harper San Francisco, 1986); and Nancy A. Hewitt, "Feminist Friends: Agrarian Quakers and the Emergence of Woman's Rights in America," *Feminist Studies* 12 (spring 1986): 27–50.

13. *HWS*, 1, 383.

14. Clark, "Religion, Rights, and Difference," 28–29.

15. *HWS*, 1, 523.

16. Ibid., 656. Abby Kelley, a Quaker who gained recognition as a leader of both the feminist and abolitionist movements, often claimed that God had "called" her to become a reformer. See Dorothy Sterling, *Ahead of Her Time: Abby Kelley and the Politics of Antislavery* (New York: W. W. Norton & Co., 1991), 60–81.

17. See Behnke, *Religious Issues in Nineteenth-Century Feminism*, 115–39.

18. For an excellent overview of the connection between feminism and Christianity, see Gerda Lerner, *The Creation of Feminist Consciousness: From the Middle Ages to Eighteen-seventy* (New York: Oxford University Press, 1993).

19. *HWS*, 1, 535–36.

20. *Proceedings of the Woman's Rights Conventions, Held at Seneca Falls and Rochester, New York, July and August, 1848* (1870; reprint, New York: Arno Press, 1969), 5.

21. Sarah M. Grimké, *Letters on the Equality of the Sexes and the Condition of Woman* (1838; reprint. New York: Burt Franklin, 1970), 4 (Grimké's emphasis).

22. *HWS*, 1, 380.

23. Ibid., 143.

24. *The Albany State Register*, quoted in *HWS*, 1, 608.

25. *HWS*, 1, 310.

26. Ibid., 380.

27. *Proceedings of the Woman's Rights Conventions*, 13.

28. *HWS*, 1, 80.

29. John Demos, *Past, Present, and Personal: The Family and the Life Course in American History* (New York: Oxford University Press, 1986), 26. See also Steven Mintz and Susan Kellogg, *Domestic Revolutions: A Social History of American Family Life* (New York: Free Press, 1988), xiv–xv. A good

introduction to American family history is Michael Gordon, ed., *The American Family in Social-Historical Perspective*, 3d ed. (New York: St. Martin's Press, 1983).

30. Mintz and Kellogg, *Domestic Revolutions*, xiv–xv.

31. Gordon Wood, *The Radicalism of the American Revolution* (New York: Alfred A. Knopf, 1992), 145–68, 183–85; Jay Fliegelman, *Prodigals and Pilgrims: The American Revolution Against Patriarchal Authority, 1750–1800* (New York: Cambridge University Press, 1982); Ellen K. Rothman, *Hands and Hearts: A History of Courtship in America* (New York: Basic Books, 1984), 26–30; and Marylynn Salmon, *Women and the Law of Property in Early America* (Chapel Hill, N.C.: University of North Carolina Press, 1986).

32. On the characteristics of the "modern American family," see Carl N. Degler, *At Odds: Woman and the Family in America from the Revolution to the Present* (Oxford: Oxford University Press, 1980), 8–9. See also Jan Lewis, *The Pursuit of Happiness: Family and Values in Jefferson's Virginia* (Cambridge: Cambridge University Press, 1983), and Mary Ryan, *Cradle of the Middle Class: The Family in Oneida County, New York, 1790–1865* (New York: Cambridge University Press, 1981).

33. Mintz and Kellogg, *Domestic Revolutions*, 51; Degler, *At Odds*, 178–209; and Robert V. Wells, "Family History and Demographic Transition," *Journal of Social History* 9 (fall 1975): 1–19.

34. See Nancy Cott, *The Bonds of Womanhood: "Woman's Sphere" in New England, 1780–1835* (New Haven, Conn.: Yale University Press, 1977).

35. "For What Is A Mother Responsible?" *The Parent's Magazine* 1:10 (June 1841): 221.

36. Myer Moses, "An Apostrophe to Women" (1806), reprinted in *The American Jewish Woman: A Documentary History*, ed. Jacob R. Marcus (New York: Ktav Publishing House, 1981), 65. See also John Todd, *Woman's Rights* (Boston: Lee and Shepherd, 1867).

37. John S. C. Abbott, "Paternal Neglect," *The Parent's Magazine, and Young People's Friend*, 2:7 (March 1842): 148. See also "A Word to Fathers," *Mrs. Whittelsey's Magazine for Mothers* 1:2 (February 1860): 51–53; Demos, *Past, Present, and Personal*, 49–50; and Joe L. Dubbert, *A Man's Place: Masculinity in Transition* (Englewood Cliffs, N.J.: Prentice-Hall, 1979), 20–22.

38. Demos, "The Changing Faces of Fatherhood," in *Past, Present, and Personal*, 55.

39. Horace Bushnell, *Woman's Suffrage; The Reform Against Nature* (New York: Charles Scribner & Co., 1869), 155.

40. Ibid., 62.

41. Ibid., 135.

42. Editorial in *The New York Herald*, 7 September 1853, reprinted in *HWS*, 1, 556.

43. *HWS*, 1, 853.

44. See James J. Kenneally, *The History of American Catholic Women* (New York: Crossroad, 1990), 63–64.

45. Catharine Beecher, *Treatise on Domestic Economy* (New York: Harper & Brothers, 1847), reprinted in *Root of Bitterness: Documents on the Social History of American Women*, ed. Nancy F. Cott (Boston: Northeastern University Press, 1986), 173. For an excellent discussion of Beecher's ideology of domesticity, see Kathryn Kish Sklar, *Catharine Beecher: A Study in American Domesticity* (New Haven, Conn.: Yale University Press, 1973).

46. On feminists' view of the family, see Carolyn Johnston, *Sexual Power: Feminism and the Family in America* (Tuscaloosa, Ala.: The University of Alabama Press, 1992), especially chap. 5. William O'Neill claims that the later feminist movement eventually failed because it focused too much on suffrage and ignored women's subordination within the family. See William L. O'Neill, *Feminism in America: A History*, 2d rev. ed. (New Brunswick, N.J.: Transaction Publishers, 1989).

47. *HWS*, 1, 593. On Victorian attitudes toward the home, see Colleen McDannell, *The Christian Home in Victorian America, 1840–1900* (Bloomington, Ind.: Indiana University Press, 1986).

48. *HWS*, 1, 239.

49. Ibid., 221. See also Gail Hamilton [Mary Dodge], *Woman's Wrongs: A Counter-Irritant* (Boston: Ticknor & Fields, 1868), 75.

50. *HWS*, 1, 164.

51. Ibid., 535–36. Many of these women were speaking from their own personal experiences as wives and mothers. See Blanche Glassman Hersh, " 'A Partnership of Equals': Feminist Marriages in 19th-Century America," in *The American Man*, ed. Elizabeth H. Pleck and Joseph H. Pleck (Englewood Cliffs, N.J.: Prentice-Hall, 1980), 187–88.

52. *HWS*, 1, 254–55. See also C. I. H. Nichols, "The Responsibilities of Woman," *Woman's Rights Tracts*, no. 5 (n.p., 1854), 5.

53. *HWS*, 1, 576. See also Sarah Grimké, *Letters*, 85.

54. See the speech Stanton delivered at the Tenth National Women's Rights Convention in New York in 1860, reprinted in Paulina Wright Davis, *A History of the National Woman's Rights Movement, for Twenty Years . . . From 1850 to 1870* (New York: Journeymen Printers' Co-operative Association, 1871), 60–83.

55. *HWS*, 1, 723–25. On attitudes toward divorce in nineteenth-century America, see Glenda Riley, *Divorce: An American Tradition* (New York: Oxford University Press, 1991), 71–78.

56. On the social purity movement, see John D'Emilio and Estelle B. Freedman, *Intimate Matters: A History of Sexuality in America* (New York: Harper & Row, 1988), 150–56; Johnston, *Sexual Power*, 58–61; and Linda Gordon, *Woman's Body, Woman's Right: A Social History of Birth Control in America* (New York: Penguin Books, 1977), 95–115.

57. *HWS*, 1, 728.

58. Clark, "Religion, Rights, and Difference," 11–13.

59. See Cott, *Bonds of Womanhood*, 200–204.

60. *The Una*, 1:1 (1 February 1853): 14. See also Thomas Wentworth Higginson, "Woman and Her Wishes. An Essay," *Woman's Rights Tracts*, no. 4 (n.p., 1854), 25.

61. *The Woman's Journal* (8 November 1873), quoted in Johnston, *Sexual Power*, 38.
62. See Charlotte Perkins Gilman, *Women and Economics* (1898), ed. Carl N. Degler (New York: Harper & Row, 1966), xxviii.
63. Reprinted in *HWS*, 1, 803.
64. Degler, *At Odds*, vi.

10

Religion, Feminism, and the American Family: 1865–1920

MARGARET LAMBERTS BENDROTH

In late nineteenth-century American society, women's rights and evangelical religion joined forces within the sacred confines of the middle-class home. Suffragists and temperance advocates marched together under the banner of Home Protection, recasting the soft contours of woman's sphere in biting and vivid coloration. As feminist May Wright Sewall declared in 1881, "It is because of our *business* as wives, mothers, and home-makers that we demand political freedom. The highest success of the home cannot be wrought without it."[1]

But was the alliance really successful? The suffrage movement won its constitutional amendment in 1920, but after that it virtually disbanded, without addressing the economic and social discrimination that the majority of American women still faced. It would take another half century before the Equal Rights Amendment, first introduced in 1923, even became a political possibility.

The matter of success evokes other questions as well. Some early feminist scholars have suggested, for example, that feminists lost their critical edge by adopting the essentially conformist agenda of middle-class housewives. Others countered that feminism introduced a subtle critique of the Victorian family, which was easily the most influential presence in the lives of nineteenth-century women. What social, economic, and cultural forces created the late nineteenth-century historical moment in which feminists cast their lot with the traditional Victorian family? And what then accounts for the so-called failure of feminism after 1920? These are by no means simple questions, and they are, of course, deeply relevant to the current debate over the future of feminism and of the family.

Feminist scholarship, as the first half of this chapter will illustrate, has evolved considerably in its assessment of post–Civil War feminism, often into sharply opposing viewpoints. Moreover, each round of the controversy has recast it along broader lines. At this point in time, retelling the story of feminism, religion, and the family after 1865 involves far more than a simple chronicle of the suffrage reform. Rather, the plot unfolds as a complicated interplay between evangelical Protestant zeal, Victorian domesticity, and the rising political aspirations of middle-class women. Our definitions of what was "feminist" a century ago have widened considerably, and the narrative has become considerably richer for it.

The configuration of feminism as a movement often in opposition to family and religious loyalties began only in the early twentieth century. The reasons for this shift, which I will discuss in the second half of this article, are complex. To state the argument briefly, by the 1920s, the ethic of social duty that underlaid the rigid structure of middle-class Victorian families gave way to a consumerist ethic of individual self-realization. The splintering of evangelical Protestant culture into fundamentalist, liberal, and noncombatant camps also fractured its traditionally feminine power base. As I shall argue, the decline of feminism after 1920 involved far more than the moral consequence of the suffrage movement's capitulation to middle-class domesticity; this decline is in a sense a metaphor for the transition of American society from its settled Victorian categories into the flux and change of the twentieth century.

Of course, it is not entirely fair to judge a movement's success by its historical fortunes. Post–Civil War feminism offers few simple moral lessons for present-day debates on women and the family. It is a powerful reminder, however, that over the long history of American feminism, religious and familial concerns have been intrinsic to the movement's self-understanding and, for that reason alone, these concerns are not likely to disappear.

Modern Feminists and the Post–Civil War Legacy

Feminist scholars of the late 1960s and 1970s were generally critical of the post–Civil War suffrage movement. In their view it accomplished little, except to win the vote through an ill-fated, pragmatic compromise with middle-class domesticity. The movement failed, they argued, because it did not emancipate women from the family. In his influential history of American feminism, *Everyone Was Brave* (1969), William O'Neill portrayed nineteenth-century feminism as a "ruthlessly self-centered" movement that "prevented women from coming to grips with the conditions that made their emancipation necessary, that is, with the domestic system itself." The collapse of feminist reform after 1920,

O'Neill believed, grew from its unwillingness to confront Victorian patriarchy within its main stronghold: the traditional family.[2]

Early feminist scholars criticized turn-of-the-century feminists for refusing to look beyond their middle-class households and ignoring the political and economic roots of women's subordination. Without such a critical edge the post–Civil War movement easily succumbed to political expediency. As feminist historian Gerda Lerner argued in 1970, the suffragists' pragmatic insistence on the ballot as a "cure-all for the ills of society" blinded them to the economic injustices that their domestic ideology imposed on their African-American and poorer sisters. "By the turn of the century," Lerner concluded bluntly, "feminist leadership . . . was nativist, racist, and generally indifferent to the needs of working-class women."[3]

None of these conclusions was beyond dispute, however. Less willing to view the family as an instrument of social control, Daniel Scott Smith described a feminist revolution of sorts within the family itself. Smith coined the term "domestic feminism" to describe the new control Victorian women were taking over their fertility and, presumably, over male sexuality. "If the average woman in the last century failed to perceive her situation through the modern feminist insight," Smith argued, "this did not mean she was not increasing her autonomy, exercising more power, or even achieving happiness within the domestic sphere." Women's rising control within their own households thus explained the close ties between political feminism and the home; put simply, motherhood provided unique access to social power.[4]

But relocating feminist consciousness meant redefining it. Mirroring the individualist feminist agenda of the 1970s, O'Neill's and Lerner's model, echoed by Aileen Kraditor, equated feminine liberation with personal autonomy; by contrast, Smith's model, which reflected the communitarian ethic of feminists in the late 1970s and 1980s, emphasized women's ability to create and define community within their own domestic sphere. This new interpretation also shifted historical attention away from elites—that is, the leaders of the suffrage movement—and highlighted changes in the lives of so-called "anonymous Americans," women who neither desired nor hoped to achieve autonomy from their families.

Linking Arms:
Feminists, Domesticity, and
Evangelical Protestantism

In this light, other domestically oriented women's movements, once dismissed as narrowly conservative, took on a brighter feminist hue.

Ruth Bordin's study of the Woman's Christian Temperance Union (WCTU), for example, found feminist ideals at the heart of its Home Protection campaign against saloons, a notoriously male enclave in nineteenth-century culture. "Many women had always seen the drunken husband as a threat to the home, no matter whose husband he was, and in whose home," Bordin wrote. In linking the domestic ideal of Home Protection to the necessity of women's suffrage, the WCTU made "conscious political use of the doctrine of domesticity to move women into public life."[5]

Although this brand of domestic feminism did not fundamentally challenge the social necessity of the traditional family, it did invest motherhood with theoretically unlimited power. "It is not enough that women should be home-makers," WCTU president Frances Willard insisted, "but they must make the world itself, a larger home."[6] Such rhetoric stretched the traditional boundaries of women's sphere almost beyond recognition. In the name of "woman's mission," "Gospel Temperance," and "Home Protection," nineteenth-century women picketed saloons, marched for suffrage, and demanded ordination rights in the churches.

The WCTU thrust thousands of conservative, churchgoing women into public advocacy for prohibition and, ultimately, political enfranchisement. Willard's emphasis on suffrage as a means of Home Protection endowed the cause of women's rights with a mantle of moral superiority that all but wilted its religious opposition. "To demand the vote is . . . no monstrous piece of unregulated female ambition," she argued; "it is the only way we can reassert . . . the rightful influences which we exercised in the home."[7]

This new and wider perspective also prompted a reevaluation of the complicated relationship between feminists and evangelical Protestantism. Early accounts of the movement often highlighted the epic clashes between anticlerical feminist leaders and the Protestant establishment. During the late nineteenth century, the well-publicized careers of "free love" advocates like Frances Wright, Victoria Woodhull, and her sister Tennie C. Claflin titillated a public eager to associate women's rights with feminist homewrecking. As if this were not enough, Elizabeth Cady Stanton continued to roil the Christian public with her unorthodox theology and unconcealed distaste for organized religion. Her publication of the two-volume *Woman's Bible* in 1895 and 1896 forced an open disavowal by her more orthodox sisters.[8]

And indeed, the suffrage movement did tap a range of social anxieties. In 1870 a Presbyterian writer excoriated the unmistakable "tendency toward licentiousness" among women's rights advocates. If not stopped, he warned, they would "convert the community into some-thing far worse than the polygamy of Salt Lake City; it will rather resem-ble the Sandwich Islands before the Gospel, where the caprice of each individual was the only law of marriage."[9] As the century progressed, fears escalated that in their zeal for equal rights women would abandon the home as well. "Woman's work in the home . . . is of fundamental importance and dignity and influence," fumed a Southern Presbyterian clergyman. "To remove her, is to remove the foundations; the founda-tions not merely of the home, but the foundations of society, of the state and of the church. . . . To remove her, means total ruin, total chaos."[10]

Indeed, one stream within the suffrage movement, led by Elizabeth Cady Stanton, would have counted that a positive outcome.[11] Firmly convinced (from her own experience) that the traditional family was inherently unjust to women, she advocated "no-fault" divorce and egal-itarian roles. "We shall have the family, the greater conservator of national strength and morals," she argued, only "after the present idea of man's headship is repudiated and woman set free."[12]

But Stanton's view was only part of the story. Within a broader per-spective, late nineteenth-century feminism looks decidedly less secular. One important strain in the narrative of women's rights in the post–Civil War period, largely dismissed by early scholarship on political feminism, is a deepening alliance with evangelical Protestantism.

On the surface, the religion of the Gilded Age, like the politics of the era, seemed cynically consumed by wealth and bureaucracy; however, at the layperson's level evangelical Protestantism was expanding vigor-ously. Here the personal initiatives and growing organizational strength of women proved crucial. The late nineteenth and early twentieth cen-turies marked, in many ways, the high point of women's power within the churches. The post–Civil War decades brought forth wide-ranging activities of women in missionary and temperance organizations, and a concerted campaign to win the pulpit.[13]

The feminist impulse behind such activity, and its broad and useful appeal to women, emerges clearly in the growing organizational power of black Baptist women in the late nineteenth century. As Evelyn Brooks Higginbotham has argued, the rising sense of religious preroga-tive among white northern Baptist women enabled them to transcend many of their own racial prejudices, and to forge an "unlikely sister-hood" with black women in the South. Black women themselves adapted the idea of "woman's mission" to serve an even larger purpose. As Higginbotham states, separate organizational work "gave to black women an individual and group pride that resisted ideologies and insti-tutions upholding gender subordination. The movement gave them the

collective strength and determination to continue their struggle for the
rights of blacks and the rights of women."[14]

The highly publicized clashes between feminists and Christians in the
late nineteenth century often obscured the suffrage movement's growing
alliance with the evangelical churches. The controversy over the
Woman's Bible, for example, emerged against a background of increasing
public acceptance for a feminist reading of the scriptures. Because
proslavery Southerners had mounted carefully literal defenses of slavery
from selected biblical texts, thoughtful Protestants now knew the pitfalls
of overeager proof texting. Likewise, temperance advocates, faced with
Paul's advice to Timothy to "take a little wine for your stomach's sake,"
had to develop scriptural arguments that took the entire thrust of biblical ethics into account. Adopting a similar hermeneutic, advocates for
women's right to speak in the churches, and by extension their right to
a political voice, grew in numbers in the late nineteenth century.[15]

Aided by its alliance with the temperance movement, suffrage won
increasing support among the churches. A 1916 debater's handbook,
reporting on an informal survey of clergymen, Sunday school superin-
tendents, and editors in suffrage states, found overwhelming support.
Of the 624 answers received, 516 were positive, affirming that "equal
suffrage has made women more intelligent companions for their hus-
bands and better able to instruct their children."[16] The National
American Woman's Suffrage Association's (NAWSA) Committee on
Church Work, established in 1902, also reported steady gains in
Protestant backing. At NAWSA's national convention of 1905, held in
Portland, Oregon, female preachers blanketed the city. Anna Howard
Shaw, Charlotte Perkins Gilman, Antoinette Brown Blackwell, and a
host of others, both ordained and non-ordained, filled local pulpits.
Standing in for the venerable Baptist pulpiteer, J. Whitcomb Brougher,
Susan B. Anthony nearly brought down the house. According to a
report from a local paper, the enthusiasm ran so high that "when she
appeared on the rostrum the applause was as vigorous as though it had
not been Sunday and the place a church. There was not room in the big
Temple for another person to squeeze past the doors."[17]

This feminist linking of arms with Protestant churches was far more
than cynical ploy for mainstream support; it was a shrewd, and largely
successful, attempt to maximize a real source of feminine power.
Suffragist leaders repeatedly emphasized that women's moral role in the
churches entitled them to greater social freedom. And they warned that
if the churches chose to ignore their primary constituency, they would
ultimately suffer for it. "It needs neither figures nor argument to establish that church attendance and church worship are in a condition of

decline," Mary Craigie, chair of the Committee on Church Work, warned in 1911. "The church is not appreciating the resources that are left lying dormant, when two-thirds of its membership—the women—are left powerless to carry on the moral and social reform work, because, as a disenfranchised class having no political status, they are not counted as a potential force."[18]

Following the temperance movement's lead, suffragists pressed their case by re-visioning the home as a positive moral force, far more than a place of passive nurturing. In doing so they convinced a generation of middle-class women that they could, and must, manage a dual commitment to home and society. Arguing that concern for the family has consistently formed the heart of the American feminist agenda, Carolyn Johnston states that "these women, who have been most often accused of being antifamily, are precisely the ones who have been profamily."[19]

The Alliance Reconfigured:
Religion, Feminism, and the Family
in the Early Twentieth Century

By the 1920s, however, the home, womanhood, and the religious idealism that had once made them inseparable had lost considerable moral force and social power. In the early twentieth century, sentimental Victorian notions gave way to more pragmatic, utilitarian attitudes toward gender differences and toward the home as a social institution. Both, in effect, became less religious and more secular.

The importance of this shift is hard to underestimate, especially as it relates to modern feminist self-understanding. More than just a simple foil to women's liberation, the nineteenth-century middle-class home was a complicated mix of religious idealism and economic necessity.[20] Neither completely private nor fully public, it was, in Victorian eyes, the stable core of a morally healthy society. "Our homes make us," Methodist educator John Heyl Vincent wrote in 1887, for they provide "the directions . . . which determine the immortal destiny."[21]

The nineteenth-century home had an almost sacramental quality. Victorian Protestants and Catholics met daily for family devotions and filled their homes with religious artwork, prie-dieux, and elaborate family Bibles, constant reminders for both children and adults of the moral meaning of family life. As Colleen McDannell has observed, "Domestic religion, in its uniquely religious and generally cultural forms, bound together what was truly meaningful in Victorian society."[22]

By the 1920s, Protestant leaders were voicing alarm at the erosion of this tradition. In 1924 Charles Clayton Morrison and Herbert Willett, introducing a family devotional, lamented that "one of the regrettable features of modern life is the neglect of private prayer and the family altar. Like that altar which Elijah found at Carmel, it is broken down and abandoned."[23] It is not difficult to trace the reasons why: The decline of Protestant hegemony as well as the new mobility of parents and children, and the increasing demands of work and leisure, made the old-style practices hard to rationalize, and harder to maintain.

Yet concern over declining family piety reflected something much deeper than simple Protestant nostalgia. From a utilitarian perspective, social scientists warned that the home was losing its economic purpose. No longer the center of material production, education of the young, or care of the sick, "the home is maintained more as a comfort and a luxury than as a necessity," as one sociologist wrote in 1909. "The cost becomes more burdensome in proportion to the service rendered, and the temptation to 'break up housekeeping' increases. It is cheaper to board."[24] The economic ties that once bound women to the home also appeared to be weakening. Social acceptance for the employment of middle-class women expanded significantly in the late nineteenth and early twentieth centuries.[25] Although genuine opportunities for economic independence were far too few, younger women still found more options than their grandmothers for remunerative work in what would be called "pink-collar" occupations. The growing twentieth-century service economy promised a measure of economic freedom for the women stenographers, department store clerks, and social workers it enlisted.[26]

A new generation of feminist theorists, led by Charlotte Perkins Gilman, saw this trend as an opportunity. In her influential book, *Woman and Economics* (1898), Gilman argued that the time was ripe for liberating women from the tedium of housekeeping. She advocated a revolutionary scheme of cooperative housekeeping in which centralized childcare and city-wide kitchens would unburden women from their traditional role.[27] Financial independence would free them from the "legalized prostitution" of modern marriage and enable women to enter the world not as privileged representatives of their sex but simply as persons. Asking no favors because of her sex, the "new woman" would insist on equality.

But in her journey she would encounter some unusual allies; men too were growing weary of their secondary role in the home and church. Late nineteenth-century feminists exalted women's moral power at the expense of males; they often argued their case for greater influence in the churches and in moral reform by depicting men as feeble compromisers, willing slaves to the god of mammon. As some historians have recently argued, the new popularity of contact sports, adventure novels, and "muscular Christianity" at the turn of the century reflected a rising masculine frustration over this "feminization" of middle-class culture.[28] Thus, according to Peter Filene, "feminism aroused such furious debate less because of what men thought about women than because of what men were thinking about themselves. . . . [At] the turn of the century they were finding it acutely difficult to 'be a man.' "[29]

To be sure, feminist claims to a monopoly on virtue did not stand well against reason and common sense. "In the very charge of inferiority launched against men by the women, they [feminists] present the strongest indictment of their own sex," antisuffragist Annie Nathan Meyer wrote in 1904. "These men, who are so weak, so corrupt, so far below the standards of the women—had they no mothers?"[30]

But in fact, twentieth-century social, intellectual, and economic changes were also demythologizing Victorian motherhood. Increasing access to public education, as well as the gathering power of the popular entertainment industry, emerged as tough competitors for the mother's power of "moral suasion" over her children.

At the same time, twentieth-century mothers found new allies among professional social scientists. "Scientific motherhood," mediated through the advice of pediatric specialists and home economists, promised to make women's work swift, clean, and efficient. As a new source of moral authority, the experts issued empirically validated rules of hygiene, feeding schedules, and methods of discipline, arguing that maternal instinct alone was hardly capable of producing independent, well-rounded children.[31]

In this sense, the Progressive era demystified motherhood and shortened its moral reach. "The birth of the 'professional mother,' " as Barbara Ehrenreich and Deirdre English have argued, "was shadowed, from the start, by the simultaneous birth of another kind of professional—one who would make it *his* specialty to tell the mothers what to do."[32] Whatever power and confidence women gained by their alliance with social scientists and reformers they lost in the moral arena. For as specialists constantly warned, a wise mother encouraged her children toward greater independence; she imposed her moral will on them only to their detriment.

Twentieth century science also began to demystify femininity. In the field of experimental psychology and anthropology, young scholars such as Helen Thompson Woolley, Elsie Clews Parsons, and Jessie Taft chipped away at the biological determinism that located women's inferiority in their evolutionary past. Such views, however, set them at odds with their academic colleagues—and with mainstream feminists—for, as Rosalind Rosenberg points out, "to challenge the belief in a biologically unique female personality was to challenge the ideological underpinnings of the whole suffrage movement."[33]

On the eve of the 1920s a new feminism emerged, challenging the Victorian assumptions that linked women's social freedom with their domestic role. A rising generation of feminists, led by Gilman and sexual radicals like Margaret Sanger and Emma Goldman, reopened the question of women's place in American society, declaring that the traditional family was incompatible with the social and sexual liberation of women.

The new feminist movement, originating within Greenwich Village's avant-garde intellectual community, experimented with companionate marriage and sexual freedom. Two couples who advocated "open marriage" were Neith Boyce and Hutchins Hapgood, and Susan Glaspell and George Cram Cook. These four shared household chores and childrearing, and collaborated in reform and literary activities. Emma Goldman, an anarchist socialist who campaigned for free love and birth control, denounced marriage as legalized prostitution and scorned women's suffrage as a hopelessly halfway measure.[34]

The new feminism not only repudiated Victorian maternalism, but it had little use for evangelical Protestantism. In her searching critique of Western Christianity, *His Religion and Hers* (1923), Charlotte Perkins Gilman contrasted its masculine, death-obsessed rigidity with the practical, life-affirming tenets of feminine religion. In fact, most feminist radicals were indifferent or hostile to mainstream organized religion, although some ventured into New Thought and theosophy.[35] It seemed no longer necessary, or perhaps truly possible, to be both a Christian and a feminist.

In the Protestant churches, old-style feminist idealism declined accordingly. After 1920, as Virginia Brereton writes, mainline churchwomen walked a difficult tightrope as "subordinated insiders," always careful to exercise leadership in a deferential, ladylike manner. Separate women's organizations, formed in the 1870s and 1880s, declined in popularity or were absorbed forcibly into male-dominated denominational bureaucracies.[36]

Fundamentalists went further, openly repudiating feminism as yet another modern example of Eve's refusal to accept her subordination. "Twenty-five years ago," William Bell Riley wrote in 1929, "I became a woman suffragist and as opportunities have risen, I have advocated the vote as a woman's right. Today I seriously doubt whether I have had either reason or revelation to back up my opinions upon the subject. . . . When eternity breaks, presiding over public assemblies in stunning gowns, making eloquent speeches, playing the part even of a

Washington picket in the interests of suffrage, will look mighty small, if the whole of it has resulted in the husband's spiritual demoralization, and in spiritual death to the neglected souls of the children."[37]

By 1920, the relationship of feminism, religion, and the family had largely settled into its present-day configuration. Feminism had begun to steer an independent course from its earlier dependence on domesticity and evangelical religion. The church and the home loomed as obstacles rather than allies to women's liberation, and conversely, the Christian churches dismissed feminism with degrees of open loathing or vague hostility. Small wonder that once the Nineteenth Amendment passed, domestic feminism soon disappeared from view. It had spent its moral capital decades earlier.

As modern feminists reconsider the relationship between women and the family, however, post–Civil War feminism is bound to take on new significance. It is, of course, no longer possible to dismiss it as a middle-class evasion of reform; for in some fashion, turn-of-the-century feminists, like those today, were grappling with gender inequality in its most intimate and complicated form—within the middle-class family. Though the issues that rallied these women, suffrage and temperance, hardly seem the stuff of contemporary radical politics, they directly challenged the dependent role of women within the home, and through this means generously expanded the boundaries of the movement for women's rights.

NOTES

1. May Wright Sewall, "Domestic Legislation," *National Citizen and Ballot Box* 6 (September 1881): 1.
2. William O'Neill, *Everyone Was Brave: A History of Feminism in America*, 5th ed. (New York: Quadrangle Books, 1974), 352. See also Aileen Kraditor, *The Ideas of the Woman Suffrage Movement, 1890–1920* (New York, Anchor Books, 1971).
3. Gerda Lerner, *The Majority Finds Its Past: Placing Women in History* (New York: Oxford University Press, 1979), 34. The quotation is from an article that first appeared in 1970.
4. Daniel Scott Smith, "Family Limitation, Sexual Control, and Domestic Feminism in Victorian America," in *Clio's Consciousness Raised: New Perspectives on the History of Women*, ed. Mary S. Hartman and Lois Banner (New York: Harper & Row, 1974), 124.

   Arguing from a different perspective, Ellen DuBois, whose history of the suffrage movement resurrected its radical legacy, argued that the very demand for public citizenship weakened the grip of the traditional family on nineteenth-century women. As DuBois wrote in 1974, "the significance of the woman suffrage movement rested precisely on the fact that it bypassed women's oppression within the family, or private sphere, and demanded instead her admission to citizenship, and through it admission to the public arena." DuBois, "The Radicalism of the Woman Suffrage Movement: Notes Toward the Reconstruction of Nineteenth-Century Feminism," *Feminist Studies* 3 (fall 1975): 63. See also Ellen DuBois, *Feminism and Suffrage: The Emergence of an Independent Women's Movement in America, 1848–1869* (Ithaca, N.Y.: Cornell University Press, 1978).

5. Ruth Bordin, *Women and Temperance: The Quest for Power and Liberty, 1873–1900* (New Brunswick, N.J.: Rutgers University Press, 1990), 58. Compare with Jill Conway, "Women Reformers and American Culture," *Journal of Social History* 5 (winter 1971–72): 164–77.

6. Frances Willard, *Annual Address of Miss Frances E. Willard, President, Before the 19th Annual W.C.T.U. Convention* (Chicago: Women's Temperance Publishing Association, 1892), 28–29.

7. Ibid.

8. On the "Woman's Bible" controversy see James H. Smylie, "The 'Woman's Bible' and the Spiritual Crisis," *Soundings* 59 (fall 1976): 305–28. On religious beliefs of nineteenth-century feminists, see Donna A. Behnke, *Religious Issues in Nineteenth-Century Feminism* (Troy, N.Y.: Whitson Publishing Co., 1982). In religious issues Stanton's strongest ally was Matilda Joslyn Gage. See her *Woman, Church, and State* (Chicago: Charles H. Kerr, 1893; reprint, Watertown, Mass.: Persephone Press, 1980).

9. "Women's Rights and Marriage," *New York Observer*, 10 November 1870, 358.

10. P. D. Stephenson, "The Woman Question," *Presbyterian Quarterly* 13 (1899): 721.

11. In 1869 the movement split into two factions: The American Woman's Suffrage Association (AWSA), led by Lucy Stone and Henry and Alice Stone Blackwell, pushed for a suffrage amendment, while the National Woman's Suffrage Association (NWSA), led by Susan B. Anthony and Elizabeth Cady Stanton, advocated a broader range of social transformation. But by 1890, when the two groups merged into the National American Woman's Suffrage Association, rising social acceptance for their cause muted old differences.

12. Stanton's article on "Home Life" (1875) is quoted in Carolyn Johnston, *Sexual Power: Feminism and the Family in America* (Tuscaloosa, Ala.: University of Alabama Press, 1992), 40. On Stanton's marriage see Elisabeth Griffith, "Elizabeth Cady Stanton on Marriage and Divorce: Feminist Theory and Domestic Experience," in *Woman's Being, Woman's Place: Female Identity and Vocation in American History*, ed. Mary Kelley (Boston: G. K. Hall, 1979), 233–51.

13. See, for example, Lucille Sider Dayton and Donald Dayton, "Your Daughters Shall Prophesy: Feminism in the Holiness Movement," *Methodist History* 14 (January 1976): 67–92; Virginia Lieson Brereton and Christa Ressmeyer Klein, "American Women in Ministry: A History of Protestant Beginning Points," in *Women in American Religion*, ed. Janet

Wilson James (Philadelphia: University of Pennsylvania Press, 1980), 171–90. On women's foreign missionary organizations, see Patricia Hill, *The World Their Household: The American Women's Movement and Cultural Transformation, 1870–1920*, (Ann Arbor, Mich.: University of Michigan Press, 1985).

14. Evelyn Brooks Higginbotham, *Righteous Discontent: The Women's Movement in the Black Baptist Church, 1880–1920* (Cambridge, Mass.: Harvard University Press, 1993), 18.

15. See, for example, Frances Willard, *Woman in the Pulpit* (Chicago, 1889; reprint, Washington, D.C.: Zenger Publishing Co., 1978); Donald Dayton, introduction to *Holiness Tracts Defending the Ministry of Women* (New York: Garland Publishing, 1985); Margaret Lamberts Bendroth, *Fundamentalism and Gender, 1875 to the Present* (New Haven, Conn.: Yale University Press, 1993), chap. 2.

16. Edith M. Phelps, *Selected Articles on Woman Suffrage* (New York: H. W. Wilson Co., 1916), 103.

17. *History of Woman Suffrage*, vol. 5, ed. Ida Husted Harper (New York: Arno Press and the *New York Times*, 1969, reprint), 140.

18. Ibid., 325.

19. Carolyn Johnston, *Sexual Power: Feminism and the Family in America*, ix.

20. See, for example, Colleen McDannell, *The Christian Home in Victorian America, 1840–1900* (Bloomington, Ind.: Indiana University Press, 1986).

21. John Heyl Vincent, *The Home Book for Very Little People, Their Brothers and Sisters, Their Mothers and Teachers* (New York: Phillips & Hunt, 1887), 5, 4.

22. McDannell, *Christian Home*, 151.

23. Charles Clayton Morrison and Herbert Willlett, foreword to *The Daily Altar: An Aid to Private Devotion and Family Worship* (Chicago: Christian Century Press, 1924).

24. James P. Lichtenberger, *Divorce: A Study in Social Causation* (New York: Columbia University, 1909), 103, 165.

25. Alice Kessler-Harris, "Independence and Virtue in the Lives of Wage-Earning Women in the United States, 1870–1930," in *Women in Culture and Politics: A Century of Change*, ed. Judith Friedander et al. (Bloomington, Ind.: Indiana University Press, 1986), 3–17.

26. Sheila Rothman, *Woman's Proper Place: A History of Changing Ideals and Practices, 1870 to the Present* (New York: Basic Books, 1978), 13–60; Rosalind Rosenberg, *Divided Lives: American Women in the Twentieth Century* (New York: Hill & Wang, 1992), 25–35.

27. See Dolores Hayden, *The Grand Domestic Revolution: A History of Feminist Designs for American Homes, Neighborhoods, and Cities* (Cambridge, Mass.: MIT Press, 1981). Feminist visions overlapped rising scientific interest in the field of "home economics." See, for example, Georgie Boynton Child, "The New Housekeeping Movement," *Independent*, 9 May 1912, 1000–1004.

28. See, for example, Ann Douglas, *The Feminization of American Culture* (New York: Alfred A. Knopf, 1977); John Higham, "The Reorientation of American Culture in the 1890s," in *Writing American History*, ed. John Higham

(Bloomington, Ind.: Indiana University Press, 1970); Mark C. Carnes and Clyde Griffen, eds., *Meanings for Manhood: Constructions of Masculinity in Victorian America* (Chicago: University of Chicago Press, 1990).

29. Peter Filene, *Him/Her Self: Sex Roles in Modern America* (New York: Mentor Books, 1976), 69.

30. Annie Nathan Meyer, "Woman's Assumption of Sex Superiority," *North American Review* 178 (1904): 106–107.

31. Rothman, *Woman's Proper Place*, 97–132.

32. Barbara Ehrenreich and Deirdre English, *For Her Own Good: 150 Years of the Experts' Advice to Women* (New York: Anchor Books, 1978), 196, 210.

33. Rosalind Rosenberg, "In Search of Woman's Nature, 1850–1920," *Feminist Studies* 3 (fall 1975): 152. See also Rosalind Rosenberg, *Beyond Separate Spheres: The Intellectual Roots of Modern Feminism* (New Haven, Conn.: Yale University Press, 1982).

34. Johnston, *Sexual Power*, 79–91.

35. Rosemary Radford Ruether, "Radical Victorians: The Quest for an Alternative Culture," in *Women and Religion in America, vol. 3: 1900–1968* (New York: Harper & Row, 1986), 1–47.

36. Virginia Lieson Brereton, "United and Slighted: Women as Subordinated Insiders," in *Between the Times: The Travail of the Protestant Establishment in America, 1900–1960*, ed. William R. Hutchison (Cambridge: Cambridge University Press, 1990), 143–67.

   In one revealing episode, in which a committee of 15, appointed by the northern Presbyterian church in 1928, debated the philosophy of separate women's organizations, the women defended their gender-segregated work, and the men argued for equality. Robert Speer summed up the prevailing view with the declaration that "Any statement of difference of function which rests on sex is not according to the facts. . . . The only differences inside Christianity are differences of ability and capacity. There is no application of sex differentiation to those members of the body of Christ." ("Conference of the General Convention with 15 Representative Women at the Fourth Presbyterian Church, Chicago, Ill., November 22, 1928" [Philadelphia: Presbyterian Historical Society, 327]).

37. William Bell Riley, "The Ideal Family," *Northwestern Pilot* 10 (October 1929): 10. See also Bendroth, *Fundamentalism and Gender*.

11

"Take Your Girlie to the Movies"

Dating and Entertainment in Twentieth-Century America

WILLIAM D. ROMANOWSKI

"Take your girlie to the movies if you can't make love at home" was a popular song in 1919. Like other songs from New York's Tin Pan Alley, it was written to capitalize on a current fad or fashion, in this instance, a changing trend in courtship practices. There is little in the song that strikes us as new or particularly interesting today; for a long time now movies have been a very popular place to go on dates. But the song refers to a relatively new convention in the early twentieth century—the practice of couples going *out* of the home together on a *date*. For urban couples, going to a movie theater was not only an escape from parents and troublesome siblings, but the ideal place to be alone and to learn, and even practice, lovemaking. "Find a cozy corner where it's nice and dark," the lyric goes. "Take your hint from Douglas Fairbanks and have love scenes of your own."[1] The song also reveals much about gender relationships and courtship roles in the early twentieth century. A young man took a woman out of her home into the public world; he also paid for the night's entertainment. As the diminutive term "girlie" suggests, the power belonged to the man.

Shaped by both the limitations and opportunities of urban industrial life, dating emerged around the turn of the century, eventually replacing the practice of "calling" as the new system of courtship in America. The conventions of dating centered around public entertainment, giving the entertainment industry a remarkable niche in society. American cities were fast becoming places of both work and entertainment. Dance halls, amusement parks, restaurants, movies, and vaudeville theaters became public places where young people could meet and spend time with members of the opposite sex. During the 1920s, for example, general spending on amusement and recreation increased by 300 percent. Average weekly movie attendance more than doubled, sales of tickets leaping from $40 million in 1922 to $90 million by the end of the decade. That figure dropped in the early years of the

Depression to $60 million in 1932, but continued to climb thereafter, peaking at $90 million in the years during and immediately after World War II.[2]

Most of the entertainment audience was composed of young people, and especially women in their formative years, a period coinciding with the courtship years. As a provider of social amusements the entertainment industry became a powerful transmitter of culture and a means of social criticism, having significant consequences for the role of traditional institutions in the process of courtship. Capitalizing on the extraordinary appeal of love and romance among moviegoers, the Hollywood cinema both reflected and influenced conventions of dating, sexual mores, and accepted behavior for men and women alike.

The appearance and dynamics of this social arrangement are the focus of this chapter. Several motifs are woven together and loosely arranged historically in three sections, each covering a period of about thirty years. The first part treats the emergence and evolution of dating as the new system of courtship in the twentieth century. I discuss the implications of dating and the new sexuality as a rejection of Victorian ideology and a correlate of women's movement into the public sphere, including both they waged workplace and world of entertainment. The importance of the latter, though generally overlooked, should not be underestimated. As Kathy Peiss observes in her study of working women's culture in New York around the turn of the century, places of amusement were "social spaces in which gender relations were 'played out,' where notions of sexuality, courtship, male power, female dependency, and autonomy were expressed and legitimated." Further, she writes, "Leisure activities may affirm the cultural patterns embedded in other institutions, but they may also offer an arena for the articulation of different values and behaviors."[3] The world of entertainment, and especially its prominent role in courtship, is critical to our understanding of gender and American family life throughout the twentieth century. Having established the role of entertainment in dating, I turn in the second section to social changes that occurred between the Depression and the 1960s. I give more attention to the Hollywood cinema and especially to the shift in audience from middle-class families to youth. The final section focuses on trends in contemporary cinema related to gender. Throughout this chapter, I highlight specific moments in the history of the Hollywood cinema to show that the movies, while serving an important role in dating, also reflected filmmakers' perceptions about ideals and trends, anxieties and preoccupations in American life. These are reflected in portrayals of women, courtship and marriage, gender roles, and family.[4]

Courting in the Twentieth Century

The powerful forces of modernism transformed American life around the turn of this century. Vast population growth fueled by millions of immigrants, rapid industrialization and urbanization, the emergence of national transportation and communication systems, as well as the development of national cultural media—magazines, radio, and movies—all these created new opportunities and limitations that profoundly altered ideas and conventions of courtship in America. In response to the conditions and cultural patterns in urban industrial centers, dating emerged as the new system of courtship.

By the late nineteenth century, the middle-class family was divided into separate, gender-based spheres. Men were thought to be more rational and aggressive, traits deemed appropriate for their role as economic provider working in the "public" sphere. Women, on the other hand, were believed to be the "weaker" sex by nature, in need of male protection and relegated to the "domestic" sphere. They were trained for a life of service in the home (sewing, cooking, childrearing), and were entreated to suppress their public aspirations and their sexuality. In this nineteenth-century Victorian social model, women were supposed to be models of love and kindness, purity and morality; the family was regarded as a haven from the corruption of the outside world.

These gender roles were the foundation of courtship in Victorian America. During the nineteenth century a young man had to secure an invitation to "call" on a young woman at her home. They might spend an evening sitting on the front porch sipping lemonade, singing songs around the parlor piano, or attending a community event. The young woman and her mother determined the acceptability of suitors, the length of the visit, proper topics of conversation and the amount of chaperonage. There was a small-town, rural orientation to the calling system that kept courtship securely within the bounds of the Victorian home and family.

For the urban working class around the turn of the century, however, the front porch and parlor piano were relics of the past. One writer in 1914 observed of Manhattan's West Side that "The girls' homes are not very advantageous places for entertainment and fun. They are too cramped and often too forlorn."[5] While many ethnic families tried to preserve the customs and conventions of the calling system, more and more young women "fled the squalor, drabness, and crowdedness of their homes to seek amusement and intimacy elsewhere," according to Beth L. Bailey. "And a 'good time' increasingly became identified with public places and commercial amusements."[6] Especially for the young, the city's amusements also represented and confirmed their integration into modern urban life, for as Peiss writes, public entertainment became "the embodiment of American urban culture, particularly its individualism, ideology of consumption, and affirmation of dating and courtship outside parental control."[7] While dating originated among the urban working class, it became a middle-class practice in the early years of the twentieth century. Between 1890 and the mid-1920s, going out on a "date" almost completely replaced the chaperoned visit. The watchful eye of the local neighborhood and community was replaced by the anonymity of public space, where young people met casually and had the freedom to explore intimacy and sexuality.

In essence, the reform movements of the first quarter of the twentieth century tried to reimpose the nineteenth-century Victorian model of the family on the urban-industrial world. Reform efforts were designed to protect the family, on the assumption that it would serve as a humanizing element against the fierce competition and exploitation unleashed by industrial capitalism. The effects of industrialism had mostly released the middle-class home from productive labor, shifting its emphasis to the education and socialization of children. The woman's primary social duty was to her home. She was to support and inspire her husband for economic success in the external world, and nurture their children in middle-class Protestant values and behaviors.

A contrasting trend emerged, however, as women entered the labor force in unprecedented numbers in the first decade of this century, if only for the financial survival of their families. Between 1900 and 1910, the proportion of all women who worked outside the home rose from 20.4 percent to 25.2 percent, remaining nearly constant until the Second World War when the size of the female labor force increased by over 50 percent. The demographic profile also changed during this period. Prior to 1900, the average female employee was single and under twenty-five and thought of waged work as a temporary situation until marriage. After 1900, however, the median age of the woman worker rose to over thirty, and the number of married women employed outside the home increased significantly. While in 1900 only 5.6 percent of married women worked outside the home, the number jumped to 10.7 percent by 1920, and rose from 11.7 percent in 1930 to 15.2 percent in 1940. The proportion of married women who did waged work increased to over 24 percent by the end of World War II.[8]

This trend changed the boundaries between the spheres and the sexes, creating what Peiss called a "heterosocial culture." Wage-earning women now had at least some money and greater social freedom. They went to restaurants, amusement parks, dance halls, vaudeville theaters, and nickelodeons (though attendance still largely entailed a financial dependence on men and a rebellion against parents). This was a clear invasion of the public "male" domain, namely the world of amusement previously reserved for men and forbidden, at least to unchaperoned, "respectable" women. Behind much of the reformist activity at the time was a fear that "immigrant amusements" were subverting the Victorian ethos by expanding beyond urban vice districts. Working women from all classes were patronizing entertainment establishments that had previously been the province of "charity girls" and prostitutes. In their campaign to prevent the degeneration of women's morals, reformers connected the new freedom in women's fashion, the use of cosmetics (also associated with prostitutes), and more liberal sexual mores with the popularity of the city's amusements.

The working woman's desire for amusement was "a reaction against the discipline, drudgery, and exploitative conditions of labor," Peiss explains. "A woman could forget the rattling machinery or irritating customers in the nervous energy and freedom of [dances like] the grizzly bear and turkey trot, or escape the rigors of the workplace altogether by finding a husband in the city's night spots."[9] The percentage of women in the audience for commercial amusements increased steadily throughout the first quarter of this century. The new dance crazes emphasizing sensuality were fueled primarily by young women of all classes, according to surveys conducted at the time. One observer said the new dances created "a social mixture such as was never before dreamed of in this country—a hodge-podge of people in which respectable young married and unmarried women, and even debutantes, dance, not only under the same roof, but in the same room with women of the town."[10] Women represented one-third of the vaudeville audience in New York in 1910 and, according to recreation surveys, women and children together comprised almost 50 percent of the vaudeville audience in the major cities. It was estimated that the percentage of women among the moviegoing audience increased from 40 percent in 1910 to 60 percent in 1920; *Moving Picture World* put the figure at 83 percent in 1927.[11] According to Peiss, for single women the movies became "convenient places for meeting men, courting, and enjoying an inexpensive evening's entertainment."[12] Moreover, as a novel form of entertainment, the movies were "not intimately linked to male culture and could be incorporated into the social world of married women," Peiss writes. In working-class districts, nickelodeons were a part of the neighborhood, safe public gathering places that "married women could incorporate into their own culture of kinship, neighborhood, and church ties."[13] Married women could safely leave their children at the nickel theaters. Single women could usually afford the price of a ticket and did not have to depend on men to treat them. Consequently, the flirtatious mingling and sexual risks of the dance halls and amusement parks were reduced, lessening the danger of a woman losing her reputation at the movies.

The accessibility of the movies made the cultural commentary provided by this new form of entertainment all the more compelling to women. But the new images of women, while they may have repudiated the Victorian ethos, were still situated in the context of patriarchal institutions. "Movie-makers delighted in the young woman capable of navigating her way through urban territory and sexual pitfalls, and who found pleasure in men's company and commercial amusements, not reformers' schemes and feminist utopias," Peiss notes. "Linking personal freedom with the culture of consumption and heterosociality, these films undercut feminist demands, not simply through direct criticism and humor, but by refashioning the socially appropriate behavior and norms that governed gender relations."[14] Likewise, Elizabeth Ewen argues that for immigrants early films served as a bridge between their traditional culture and the new urban society. But in aiding the transition to a modern consumer culture, movies helped create new cultural ideals and images that remained oppressive for women. "As women moved from the constricted family-dominated culture to the more individualized values of modern urban society," writes Ewen, "the form and content of domination changed, but new authorities replaced the old. In the name of freedom from tradition, they trapped women in fresh forms of sexual objectification and bound them to the consumerized and sexualized household."[15] This discussion highlights the complex relation between Hollywood production and cultural meaning, as well as the difficulty of interpreting audience receptivity. Threatened by demands for censorship, filmmakers catered to the urban ethos while making movies that would not offend middle-class sensibilities. It is hard to determine how audiences responded to these images and how those responses may have differed by gender and age, for example. I will return to these issues in the final section of this chapter, dealing with images of women in the contemporary cinema.

The transformation of American life and courtship also affected the role of traditional nurturing institutions in young people's lives. Nontraditional institutions, like the peer group and the movies, now had greater influence on the young, displacing family and local community. Young women and men could meet at work or at places of public entertainment, making dating more a matter of choice between individuals, rather than a family affair based on class and ethnicity as in the calling system. The practice of dating broke down distinctions between Victorian and immigrant cultures, and also between the classes and the sexes. The mother's responsibility to screen suitors and supervise the visit was all but eliminated. Modern urban life expanded possibilities for middle-class youth, but primarily young men, that had begun during the previous century, giving them greater choice of occupation, place of residence, companions, and spouse.[16] Middle- and upper middle-class parents could still exert some control over the pool of potential marriage partners by their choice of neighborhood, church, school, and later college or university. But the rising age of marriage made courtship even more a matter of individual choice and increasingly one based on passion and the romantic ideal—a dominant motif in Hollywood films (especially romantic comedies) of the 1930s and 1940s.

The removal of courtship from the home and local community to the public world completely reversed Victorian patterns, shifting the power in courtship from women to men. The initiative belonged to the man now, who invited a woman to go "out" on a date, into the public "male" world. That the man paid for the date only increased his control, for as Bailey points out, "what men were buying in the dating system was not just female companionship, not just entertainment—but power."[17] Not surprisingly, in the culture of industrial capitalism, dating began to be understood in terms of economic analogies, as a system of exchange.

Working culture reinforced this ideology. Working women's earnings were below the "living wage"; what they did make was quickly consumed by room, board, and clothing. With little discretionary income to spend on recreation, women became dependent on men's "treats." Peiss writes that young women offered "sexual favors in varying degrees" in return for the drinks men bought them at the saloons and dance halls. Even though this usually amounted to "only flirtatious companionship," women were still "capitalizing on their attractiveness and personality," behaving according to cultural patterns that commodified women's sexuality. Likewise, at the amusement parks, Nasaw notes, "single working women, unable to afford a day's vacation on their meager wages, looked for men who could treat them—and not ask too much in return."[18] This mentality not only informed conventions of urban dating but was also reflected—then as now—in the popular culture of the time. A popular song of the twenties described a young man pleading with his fiancée, "Gimme a little kiss, will ya huh?" In the final verse, the woman suggests that he give her a mink coat, a bracelet, diamond ring, or a car: "I'll even take a Rolls and you can add a chauffeur man / But don't you give me a little Ford, will ya huh? Or I'll give it right back to you."[19] A woman (and especially her sexuality) became a commodity that a man purchased, her value based on her virtue.

Contrary to popular belief, there was not a dramatic increase in premarital sexual intercourse during this time. Middle-class college youth began redefining sexual relationships in the 1920s, inaugurating trends that later spread to other social and age groups. That all sex outside marriage was taboo became an outdated assumption. Rejecting the Victorian standard of purity that divided women into categories of good and bad, respectable lady and whore, young men and women negotiated new boundaries for acceptable erotic behavior, guided by their childhood training and peer group pressure. Petting was permitted and became commonly accepted behavior; intercourse did not (with the exception of engaged couples). There was now greater possibility for intimacy, fuller affectionate relations, and sexual exploration within certain prescribed limits. But these attitudes and practices also opened the door to seduction games as peer group definitions of social status based on personality, popularity, and sexual attractiveness replaced those provided by parents and family.[20]

But a residual nineteenth-century Victorian ideology still lingered; the double standard, though in altered form, remained. Illicit sexual behavior was a far greater offense for women than men; virginity was still valued in a bride. The responsibility for controlling sexual activity (and by extension, social morality) was vested in women, who by "nature," according to the Victorian model, were the embodiment of moral purity and better able to control their sexual urges.[21] Further, it was reasoned that they had to flee fornication or jeopardize their virtue, synonymous with their worth in the marriage market. Even worse, they could become pregnant. Consequently, women were urged to control themselves, especially their sensual desires, a key factor in adolescent development. Should there be a sexual misadventure (i.e., pregnancy), the woman was to blame for not drawing the line and resisting the sexual advances of the man, who was by "nature" unable (or simply unwilling) to control his libido. It is not hard to see how this ethical and sexual double standard wreaked havoc on gender relations. A young bride was expected to simply reverse years of social and psychological training, release her inhibitions on the night of her wedding, and engage a man as an equal sex partner in marriage for the rest of her life. These roles and gender stereotypes continued to fuel sexual fantasies, adding to the confusion about sex and gender. The popular media capitalized on their almost mythological appeal, using them to sell everything from lingerie to car wax.

Changes in courtship and gender roles coincided with and were precipitated by the concept of adolescence, first introduced as a distinct stage of life by G. Stanley Hall near the turn of the century. Joseph F. Kett described this romanticized, transitional time between childhood and adulthood as "the period after puberty during which a young person is institutionally segregated from casual contacts with a broad range of adults."[22] Adolescents thus were defined in part by their sexuality. Sex and youth became synonymous in the popular media and imagination, represented by female cultural icons: the "flapper" in the 1920s, the Playboy "bunny" in the 1950s, the "free love" hippie in the 1960s. The adolescent years, between the onset of puberty and marriageable age (the threshold of adulthood), became the courtship years. Much energy and activity in the youth culture centered on dating—clothing, cosmetics, parties, sexual exploration, and entertainment—made affordable by part-time jobs that greatly increased the discretionary income of "teenagers" in the 1950s.

By altering generational, gender, and institutional relationships, the practice of dating amplified both the presence and the role of entertainment in American life, especially for young people going through the courtship years. The movies were more than a source of pleasure and enjoyment while out on a date. They also helped young people understand contemporary life, and particularly the nature of romance and courtship, gender, and marriage. "Before the movies, the art of love played almost no part in the culture's public curriculum," film historian Robert Sklar notes. "In movies, however, it became the major course of study."[23] Movies, most notably the domestic dramas of Cecil B. DeMille and Erich Von Stroheim, exploited sexual themes and served to heighten sexual awareness, while also emphasizing physical attractiveness. In this way, the cinema legitimized subjects formerly considered taboo.

The proprietors of middle-class culture recognized this. They were also painfully aware that they had little control over the output of film companies, which were largely owned by first- and second-generation Jews. Religious, social, and cultural antagonisms were veiled in the controversy over the movies, which centered on protecting the young and the family from the intrusion and corruption of the public world. Social reformers blamed the movies for changes in the behavior of youth, and especially for more liberal attitudes about sex. One sociologist writing in the 1920s argued that "more of the young people who were town children sixteen years ago or less are sex-wise, sex-excited, and sex-absorbed than of any generation of which we have knowledge. Thanks to their premature exposure to stimulating films, their sex instincts were stirred into life years sooner than used to be the case with boys and girls from good homes, and as a result in many the 'love chase' has come to be the master interest in life."[24] The well-known Payne Studies, conducted between 1929 and 1932, revealed just how much young people learned about dating and sexual behavior from the movies. The author of one of the studies concluded that the movies were "a gigantic educational system with an instruction possibly more successful than the present text-book variety."[25]

Religious groups also perceived entertainment as a serious threat to religious and family life. Through the late nineteenth century, the church had almost universally condemned "amusements" on the grounds that these activities bred immorality, impiety, and sloth. Around 1900, however, all but the most conservative religious groups relented on their complete condemnation of entertainment; the churchgoing middle class contributed to the general boom in entertainment that took place at that time. Conservative groups, however, remained wary. Describing a typical scene at a storefront movie theater in 1918, one writer in a conservative religious publication wrote: "In our large cities you can see the baby in the carriages on the street, and mother inside to have her mind bewitched with worldly folly; and perhaps no dinner or supper ready when the husbands come home from work."[26] Such commentary revealed the underlying fear that movies represented a challenge to established gender roles and expectations within the family structure.

Romance and the Movies

The cinema developed as a place for romance and sexual expression not only in the social space of the theater but also in the thematic content and imagery of the movies projected on the screen. Hollywood filmmakers were aware that they were often entertaining couples out on dates, so romance became a prominent feature of films. Heterosexual relations were treated in one-third of the comedies produced between 1898 and 1910. In their seminal study of the classical Hollywood cinema, Bordwell, Staiger, and Thompson determined that romance was the main or secondary storyline in ninety-five percent of Hollywood's output between 1915 and 1960, and the principal one in eighty-five percent. "Screenplay manuals stress love as the theme with greatest human appeal," Bordwell said. "Character traits are often assigned along gender lines, giving male and female characters those qualities deemed 'appropriate' to their roles in romance. To win the love of a man or woman becomes the goal of many characters in classical films."[27] Film theorist Robin Wood showed how the classic Hollywood cinema reaffirmed an implicit ideology in the development of the genres during the Studio Era (1928–1950). Heterosexual marriage and family in a male-dominated society served to validate the belief in capitalism and the work ethic, as well as assumptions about gender distinctions. The ideal male figure emerged as "the virile adventurer, the potent untrammeled man of action," Wood explained, and the ideal female as "wife and mother, perfect companion, the endlessly dependable mainstay of hearth and home."[28] The Hollywood mythology was perhaps most appealing in its idealization of romance and marriage, which ultimately reaffirmed established gender roles, especially regarding sex and work.

Hollywood films of the Studio Era emphasized romantic love as the source of personal fulfillment and the basis for marriage. Marriage was shown as the conclusion of the search for love and romance, sparked by an initial attraction usually between opposites in personality (a solid comedic device with at least some anchor in reality). In the screwball comedies, "women, however beautiful, were always zany, unpredictable, irresponsible and in need of an authoritative man who would bring them under control," popular culture historian Richard Maltby writes. "Almost always this man advertised his responsibility as a middle-class virtue, and in the movies, as elsewhere in the late 1930s, there was a celebration of the culture of the middle classes as being more truly American than any other."[29] Movie stars became romantic ideals themselves, their physical beauty and emotions enhanced by the close-up, their love consummated by the kiss. Sixty out of one hundred randomly sampled films from the Studio Era ended in this manner.[30] As film critic Molly Haskell showed, however, there was no connection between the fairy-tale romance, culminating in the long-awaited climactic kiss, and the veracity of married life—passion and sex, children, sacrifice, and psychological adjustments. A series of misadventures concluding with "THE END," followed by the final fade-out, left the realities of romance and marriage—summed up in "and they lived happily ever after"—to the imagination of the audience.[31]

These idyllic Hollywood portrayals of romance stood in contrast to the realities of the Depression. The years of economic hardship and high unemployment had a direct impact on dating, marriage, and family. Financial insecurity made men less confident in their role as breadwinner. As a result, the marriage rate dropped 13.5 percent in the early thirties, while the average age of marriage rose dramatically during the decade, with more men postponing marriage and family.[32] These trends were accompanied by a strong reaction against women, and especially married women, doing waged work during the national disaster. According to the prevailing mythology, women belonged in their traditional roles of wife, mother, and homemaker to preserve the moral and social cohesion of American society during the national crisis; what jobs were available during the Depression should be reserved for men.

Legislation, labor, the media, and popular opinion all worked together to discourage women, especially married women, from taking jobs.[33]

Ironically, while women were being urged to stay at home, the prohibition against nudity and indecent exposure in the Motion Picture Production Code of 1930 moved women out of the bedroom and into the workplace in films of the thirties and forties. Katherine Hepburn as an attorney in *Adam's Rib* (1949) and Rosalind Russell as the driven news reporter in Howard Hawks's *His Girl Friday* (1940) are prime illustrations. Casting women in such roles, however, did not prevent them from reaffirming the predominant ideals about romance, relationships, and gender roles. While smart, ambitious women worked in these films, they were expected to "give up everything" for love. In contrast, the man's career was at least as important as the woman of his desire. To have it otherwise "would go against the grain of prevailing notions about the female sex," Haskell said. "A movie heroine could act on the same power and career drives as a man only if, at the climax, they took second place to the sacred love of a man. Otherwise she forfeited her right to that love." Movies of the thirties and early forties, like Frank Capra's *It Happened One Night* (1934) and Howard Hawks's *Bringing Up Baby* (1938), may have questioned gender roles, but these films were "rooted in the security of the sexual and social framework at large," Haskell argued.[34] However, while these portrayals tried to affirm certain "traditional" gender roles, they were "largely mythic," ignoring real social and intellectual trends.

While still trying to appeal to the general family market in order to attract the largest possible audience, Hollywood changed its strategy during the 1930s. Film studios began courting the male audience to increase the proportion of men among moviegoers. Men were featured prominently in the film genres established during the Studio Era, with women relegated to secondary, stereotypical roles—the schoolmarm or chorus girl/prostitute in the classic western, for example. Marked by the institution of the Production Code between 1933 and 1934, this trend stood in sharp contrast to the 1920s and early 1930s when women dominated screen images during what Haskell referred to as "one of the truly 'liberated' periods of cinema" insofar as women's roles were concerned.[35]

By the 1940s, systematic audience studies showed that the most frequent moviegoers were the young and educated from the middle and upper-middle classes, with little difference between men and women. Postwar surveys revealed much of the same regarding gender patterns and film attendance, but the force of the young was unmistakable. Seventy-two percent of the weekly audience was under thirty with over half under the age of twenty; this group constituted only fifty percent of the total population. Further, it was clear that moviegoing was a group activity; groups of two or more people represented eighty-one percent of weekly admissions. The fact that single people accounted for over half of all admissions, while representing only 27 percent of the total population, is solid evidence (though hardly surprising) of the popularity of moviegoing for dates and social activities.[36] In this cultural climate, the postwar baby boomers, who had grown up with television as a "third parent," intensified the role of movies and other entertainment media in the youth culture.

Beginning in the postwar years, the idea of adolescence became a social reality for the majority of teenagers, including the working and lower classes. By the 1960s, ninety-five percent of fourteen- to seventeen-year-olds were in high school, with over half continuing their education in college. As a social construction, however, adolescence took the form of an age-segregated youth culture, which is in many ways a leisure-oriented microcosm of adult life. Existing largely in isolation and distinction from the adult world, adolescents spend most of their time with their peers. They have more leisure time and discretionary income than adults, making them a prime demographic audience for entertainment; their separation from adults also makes them more susceptible to manipulation by the media. Young people are also relieved, to a great extent, from the responsibilities and decision making required of adults, allowing them to postpone making significant life decisions, from vocational choice to marriage partner. Increasingly throughout this century dating became disassociated from marriage and family, reflecting instead social status, competition, and popularity within the youth culture.[37]

This is perhaps best illustrated by the idea of "going steady," which became popular after World War II when, for the first time, women outnumbered men in the United States. Going steady offered greater security amid more intense competition and held out the promise of "popularity, social acceptance, and emotional security" for young people during the tumult of adolescence.[38] Prior to the war, going steady meant something like getting engaged does today, when a couple announces their intentions of moving toward marriage. Beginning in the 1950s, however, going steady might have little to do with getting married. Actually, few couples intended it as such but instead acted as if they were married while they went steady. The young couple exchanged signifying tokens (usually rings) and agreed not to date anyone else. In many respects, couples who went steady were living together; they talked regularly on the telephone, saw each other several evenings a week, and it was expected that they would become more sexually intimate. An effect of adolescence, Bailey points out, was that "the emphasis in courtship shifted to the social and recreational process of dating, but without giving up the romantic and sexual explorations that had characterized the final stage of courtship in the previous century."[39] Going steady became the adolescent version of young children playing house: marriage without responsibility or commitment. But that left only leisure activities and sex as the focus of relationships. Not surprisingly, these became the center of courtship and youth culture. Consequently, the most popular dating partners (and therefore marriage partners) were those young people who were physically attractive and socially outgoing, even though these qualities did not necessarily translate into making one a responsible, committed, and loving spouse.

The practice of going steady coincided with the tremendous social and cultural changes that occurred after World War II. "Masculinity" and "femininity" were thrown into a crisis in the postwar world as the "separate spheres" no longer adequately defined gender roles and conventional behavior appropriate to them. The resulting confusion over male and female identities was intensified by the increased presence of the popular media, especially in the youth culture. "Traditional" ideas about gender were resurrected to resolve the crisis between the sexes; to be masculine was to be dominant and aggressive, to be feminine was to be passive and submissive (perhaps symbolized best by the Playboy "bunny"). The conventions of going steady reified these gender roles and affirmed within the youth culture the retreat into domesticity that followed the societal crises of the Depression and World War II. Though antithetical to the real situation during the war, these ideas and practices gave some sense (however apparent) of stability to gender roles and courtship in the postwar period. As Bailey explains it, the reestablishment of "traditional" gender roles after World War II

> expressed fundamental fears about the amount of power women were gaining in society. The etiquette of gender sought to draw a line between "public" lives (where barriers between men and women were breaking down in the worlds of work and education) and "private" relationships. Although the "public" and the "private" were ultimately inseparable, the etiquette of gender served as a barrier against new definitions and behaviors. It was a cushion against change.[40]

An unprecedented number of women began working for wages by contributing to the war effort, a situation that had a dramatic effect on American social life, especially regarding gender roles and expectations. After the Allied victory, however, women were expected to forsake their careers and return to previously established roles in the home as mothers and housewives. The intense gendering of the spheres in the 1950s, which was reflected in the media, precipitated a shift in attitude. As one marketing report revealed, the young bride in the 1950s sought "as a conscious goal that which in many cases her grandmother saw as a blind fate and her mother as slavery: to belong to a man, to have a home and children of her own, to chose among all possible careers the career of wife-mother-homemaker."[41] This was accompanied by a sharp decrease in the average age of marriage in the postwar years (from 26.7 for men and 23.3 for women in 1939 to 22.6 for men and 20.4 for women in 1951). In addition, many who had postponed marriage during the Depression and war years were now getting married, contributing to a postwar marriage explosion with ninety-five percent of all Americans of marriageable age "tying the knot." These same factors combined with an increase in the number of children couples were having to fuel the skyrocketing birthrates that produced the baby boom.[42] The parents of the baby boomers poured into the newly developed suburbs, a Leave-It-To-Beaverland where "Father Knows Best."

By the early 1960s, however, many suburban housewives whose lives by all appearances were the epitome of contentment and happiness, suffered from dissatisfaction, a lack of personal identity and fulfillment, and a sense of desperation. Betty Friedan identified this "problem that has no name" in *The Feminine Mystique*, a 1963 book that historians mark as the beginning of the "second wave" of feminism. Friedan argued persuasively that the occupation housewife-mother had been reified in American culture as the ultimate fulfillment for women. It made "certain concrete, finite, domestic aspects of feminine existence—as it was lived by women whose lives were confined, by necessity, to cooking, cleaning, washing, bearing children—into a religion, a pattern by which all women must now live or deny their femininity," she explained. Previously "women envied men, women tried to be like men, instead of accepting their own nature, which can find fulfillment only in sexual passivity, male domination, and nurturing maternal love." The nature of femininity remained obscure, the consequence of being considered inferior to the nature of man and undervalued historically. The feminine mystique offered a new image for American women, proposing that "the highest value and the only commitment for women is the fulfillment of their own femininity."[43]

But in the postwar period, the only means of such fulfillment was through the occupation of housewife-mother, since women were restricted or even excluded from the waged workplace. In the absence of "larger goals and purposes for American women," Friedan explained, sex was exaggerated "beyond the limits of possibility" to fill the vacuum in women's lives. Throughout the 1950s, the number of references to sex in the American media more than doubled, as sociological studies, magazines, advertising, television, and films "pander[ed] to the voracious female appetite for sex phantasy," Friedan said. "It is not an exaggeration to say that several generations of able American women have been successfully reduced to sex creatures, sex-seekers."[44] The availability of an oral contraceptive at once gave women more control over their bodies than ever before, but also made it more difficult for them to refuse sex. The "pill" also changed men's attitudes toward women, who were expected to be more willing and available for sex. In effect, then, women were ultimately exploited by the sexual revolution.

During the 1960s, women enrolled in and graduated from college and entered the professional workplace in unprecedented numbers. But in the popular media, the political agenda of the women's movement and its real achievements were overshadowed by the sexual revolution; feminism was associated mainly with liberated sexuality. The sexual frontier emerged as a dominant theme in movies with metaphors of sexual revolution replacing those of economic exchange in representations of romance and relationships. Easier birth control and loosening of societal restraints resulted in a separation of sexuality from marriage and a celebration of single life. Cinematic portrayals of relationships between men and women increasingly centered on sex; going to bed largely replaced the kiss as the fulfillment of both character and audience fantasies. Men were paramount. Provocative and romantic portrayals of women were replaced with women as simply sex objects, stereotyped either as submissive Playboy bunnies or, in rejection of the double standard, nymphets. "With the substitution of violence and sexuality (a poor second) for romance," Haskell writes, "there was less need for exciting and interesting women; any bouncing nymphet whose curves looked good in catsup would do."[45] Films like *Lolita* (1962), *Barbarella* (1968), and the host of James Bond portrayals (recall Pussy Galore in *Goldfinger* [1964]) celebrated the sexual power of the new American woman. Women's roles fell prey to virgin/whore stereotypes: Julie Andrews as a governess in *Mary Poppins* (1964) and *The Sound of Music* (1965); Jane Fonda as a prostitute in *Walk on the Wild Side* (1962) and *Klute* (1971).

The cultural preoccupation with and exploitation of the sexuality of the American woman coincided with a metamorphosis in the film industry. One effect of the dramatic social change in the postwar period was to diminish the proportion of moviegoers over thirty, while expanding the percentage of frequent movie attenders among youth. Leisure opportunities for young people increased dramatically, as did their discretionary income. Between 1944 and 1958 weekly income for teenagers (derived from allowance and part-time employment) leaped from $2.50 to about $10.00. The number of cars in use doubled between 1940 and 1955, and again between 1950 and 1965, giving young people greater freedom and unchaperoned transportation. The emergence of a car culture was accompanied by the rapid expansion of the drive-in movie theater, a teenage haven that became a cultural icon of the period. It was estimated that as much as 75 percent of the drive-in audience was under age twenty-five.[46] The number of drive-ins increased from 480 in 1948 to a peak 4,000 in 1958, during which time an equal number of regular indoor theaters were forced to close. Drive-ins became an important aspect of the dating ritual, as a *Variety* reference to them as "passion pits with pix" indicates. In 1965 it was estimated that teenagers spent $1.5 billion on entertainment and accounted for 53 percent of all movie tickets sold.[47] The film industry was slow to respond to the postwar changes, continuing to produce family-oriented pictures despite a devastating absence of that audience at the box office. Eventually the production of youth-oriented pictures became a dominant trend in the cinema, having an impact on both the content and marketing of movies.

During the early 1960s, independent filmmakers like those at American International Pictures (AIP) began specializing in youth-oriented movies, tailoring their product to the underage twenty-five population. Though resembling the films of the Studio Era, films now portrayed teenagers and not adults winning the affections of the men and women of their dreams. These low-budget pictures reaped relatively high profits and inaugurated many of today's teen genres, with beach and surfing films, horror, teenage comedy and, later in the sixties, countercultural films.[48] From their research into the drive-in crowd, AIP executives developed a marketing strategy to capture the adolescent market. Two assumptions were gender-based: A girl will watch any movie a boy will watch, but the reverse did not necessarily hold. Consequently, AIP producers aimed their films at the nineteen-year-old male in order to capture the greatest audience in the youth market.[49] This scheme was blatant in the beach party films, for example, with their cast of bikini-clad young women gyrating and jiggling to the beat of rock 'n' roll. The commercial success of AIP was not lost on the major film studios, which began courting the postwar baby boomers in the late 1960s.

The Gendering of the Box Office

Beginning in the 1960s, then, films for the youth audience were made to appeal to the dreams and desires of young men. There were at

least two significant events in the late 1970s and early 1980s that reinforced the male adolescent formula. First, the blockbuster success of
Jaws (1975), the *Star Wars* trilogy (1977, 1980, 1983), and *Raiders of
the Lost Ark* (1981) drew Hollywood's attention to the new youth audience, the post-baby boom cohort. The unprecedented success of these
and other films was attributed to young males under twenty-five, "who
bring along dates or groups of friends, and consider repeat viewings as
a kind of pubescent badge of honor," the *Los Angeles Times* reported.[50]
Hollywood courted the eighties' youth culture with a series of "teen-
pics" treating adolescent issues. Most, like *Porky's* (1982) for example,
simply exploited (often with great financial success) the adolescent
market by appealing to male hormonal drives. There were notable
exceptions, however. In contrast to most of the films about the youth
culture conceived from a male perspective, director Amy Heckerling's
Fast Times at Ridgemont High (1982) showed the pain and disillusion-
ment of a young girl trying to establish her identity and experience real
intimacy through imprudent sex. The John Hughes trilogy starring
Molly Ringwald—*Sixteen Candles* (1984), *The Breakfast Club* (1985),
and *Pretty in Pink* (1986)—was provocative in its exploration of adolescent emotions and concerns regarding sex, dating, peer relationships,
and social class. *Say Anything* (1989) and *Pump Up the Volume* (1990)
were notable for insightful treatments of generational conflict and the
vulnerability of adolescence; the former concluded with a gender role-
reversal, a young man following his brilliant high school sweetheart off
to graduate school.

The second important event was the advent of MTV (music television) in 1981. Males between the ages of 12–25, who were also the primary market for both recordings and movies, represented the largest
portion of MTV's audience. MTV revolutionized the entertainment
industry and inspired a wave of films with rock soundtracks aimed at
the under twenty-five demographic: *Flashdance* (1983) was followed by
Footloose (1984), *Top Gun* (1986), and *Dirty Dancing* (1987). The MTV
video world is one of intense passion, sexual energy, and excitement.
Despite the specter of AIDS and other socially transmitted diseases (and
public service warnings on MTV), spontaneous and casual relationships
very quickly, and often impulsively, become sexual in three-minute
videos. In such a setting, the myth that women are nymphomaniacs
does not appear strange or abnormal. To the contrary, these videos
function, as Roland Barthes observed of myth in general, to make that
myth seem completely natural.[51] Music videos have taken to an extreme
the images of women fabricated in the 1960s. Men are virile sexual
aggressors but emotionally detached from women who are, like subhu-

mans, exploited as sexual conquests in the mating game. Women are inordinately depicted as constantly fantasizing about sex and even rape but socially conditioned to resist their own desires and male advances. Ironically, these outrageous images are used to legitimate "traditional" patterns of dating and gender roles. Men are empowered as pursuers; women are depicted as having only one ambition, finding fulfillment as sexual playthings for men (symbolized by Madonna's "Boy Toy" belt).

Until recently, then, most films were aimed at young men, based on the assumption that male audiences drove mega-hits. The spate of action-adventure movies in recent years—*Die Hard, RoboCop, Lethal Weapon, Terminator, Total Recall*, and their sequels—shows that not much has changed. Mainstream Hollywood did not, however, ignore the continued social discourse on gender and family. After all, romance was a staple of Hollywood productions. But the Studio Era model of romance declined throughout the 1960s, culminating in the male "buddy" films in the following decade. When romance was the central theme, women were positioned in "traditional" gender roles as in *Grease* (1978) and *An Officer and a Gentleman* (1982). The patriarchal family was resurrected in the 1970s and early 1980s as a haven from the threatening outside world. *Kramer vs. Kramer* (1979) blamed the discontented woman for the breakdown of the family; commitment to patriarchal familial bonds was obligatory in *Terms of Endearment* (1983). As always, there were a number of crosscurrents in the cinema. Independent women also began to make their way back into movies in the late 1970s: Faye Dunaway as the television executive in *Network* (1976), Jane Fonda as a reporter in *The China Syndrome*, and Sally Field as a union-organizing textile worker in *Norma Rae* (both 1979). There were also a number of "feminist" films in the late 1970s including *An Unmarried Woman* (1978) and *Private Benjamin* (1980). These pictures reflected the advances made by professional working women and also paved the way for new images of women in the late 1980s and 1990s.[52]

Industry observers noted that the box office success of several films during this period was driven by female attendance. Surveys showed, for example, that the audience for *Rain Man* (1988), starring Dustin Hoffman and Tom Cruise, was 55 percent female and 45 percent male (even though executives would have liked these figures reversed). Women composed 61 percent of the initial audience for *Three Men and a Baby* (1987) and 69 percent for *Cocktail* (1988), also starring Cruise. Film executives speculated that the increase in female attendance was due in part to the location of theaters in shopping malls which, according to one producer, "has made young girls and older women feel as if they can safely go to the movies without a date or husband."[53] Whatever the reason, the increase did not go unnoticed by Hollywood decision-makers who courted, however modestly, the female audience with films like *Beaches* (1988) and *Steel Magnolias* (1989). The more recent *Sleepless in Seattle* (1993) was a self-reflective romantic comedy that took a page from the script of the 1957 tearjerker, *An Affair to Remember*, a film Tom Hanks's character jokingly labeled a "chick's movie."

Since the advent of motion pictures, portrayals of the relation between men and women have dominated the screen, often with paradoxical images: the mixture of sex and violence when James Cagney smashed a grapefruit in Mae Clark's face in *The Public Enemy* (1931), the distrust and uncertainty between Fred MacMurray and Barbara Stanwyck in *Double Indemnity* (1944), the equality of Katherine Hepburn and Spencer Tracy in *Adam's Rib* (1949), the lack of agency of women in James Bond movies. Contemporary cinematic treatments of gender relations and the family have sparked tremendous controversy while also achieving notable box office success. There is much hostile disagreement over their meaning, audience receptivity, and social effects, even among feminist critics. *Indecent Proposal* (1993) and *Basic Instinct* (1992), as examples, were both lauded as feminist statements portraying women in control of their bodies, and condemned for depicting women as chattel or sadomasochistic killers.[54] I do not propose to resolve the discussion, but merely to make an observation about the relation between Hollywood production and cultural meaning.

The myriad images of women in recent films indicate not only a preoccupation with the struggle over the underlying assumptions about sexuality and the need for both personal and institutional change, but also the difficulty of dealing with these changes in the mass cultural discourse. The necessity of attracting a large audience in order to be financially profitable has created a conservative tendency in the Hollywood cinema. Popularity, which translates into box office revenues, is largely dependent on a film's ability to capture the cultural expectations of a wide and diverse public. This is all the more difficult when there is a lack of social consensus. Consequently, Hollywood has always relied on audience familiarity with popular mythology, heroes, stereotypes, rituals, and established genres and story formulas as an effective (and efficient) means of communicating with a mass audience. The prevailing notions on any subject rule the day insofar as they ensure (as much as is possible) the financial success of a film. Still, any tear in the social fabric that garners public attention is acceptable fare for filmmakers, especially when the controversy promises long lines at the cineplex. A strain in the dominant paradigm, however, usually receives treatment within the larger context of the established value system, thereby enhancing the persuasive power and meaning of these films while also increasing their popular appeal.

Portrayals of women in the contemporary cinema reveal the major film studios' long-held conviction that men account for mega–box office hits; it is also no secret that the majority and most powerful decision makers in the industry are men. Most films display a male point of view and are symbolic representations of a patriarchal society. Independent women inordinately appear on the screen as projections of men's desires, fears, and anxieties, from the Cinderella prostitute in *Pretty Woman* (1990) to the psychotic working woman in *Fatal Attraction* (1987). The movement of women away from full-time domesticity and their advances in the public realm constitute a challenge to this system of cultural representation. But treatment of changing gender roles and relations, in mainstream Hollywood movies at least, has occurred within the conventions of traditional moviemaking and patterns of communication with a mass audience.

In assorted ways recent films have blurred the boundaries of historically conceived gender roles and relations either by criticizing them, reversing them, or investing women with power (albeit sexual) over men. For example, *A League of Their Own* (1991) showed women carving a niche in the male domain of sports during World War II. Films like *Silence of the Lambs*, *Sleeping With the Enemy*, and *Mortal Thoughts* (all 1991) portrayed women trapped in a psychotic male-dominated world. Other films cast women in roles traditionally reserved for men: Geena Davis and Susan Sarandon as the gunslinging "buddies" on the lam in *Thelma and Louise* (1991), or the action-adventure hero(ine) played by Linda Hamilton in *Terminator 2: Judgement Day* (1991), or Sigourney Weaver in the *Alien* series (1979, 1986, 1992). The controversial box office hit of 1992, *Basic Instinct*, was a throwback to the film noir pictures in its empowering of the female character. In the now famous interrogation scene, Catherine (Sharon Stone) turned the tables on the male detectives using the alluring power of her sexuality; in love affairs, she was completely disengaged and emotionally detached from her partners, a characteristic normally attributed to men. These and other films have had an effect on Hollywood's output and found a niche, however dubious, in the changing cultural landscape.

By no means a feminist revolution in the cinema (some critics in fact consider them lost ground), portrayals of women in film today offer disparate and enigmatic, and yet distinguishing and significant, cinematic metaphors. Their meaning and ultimate cultural impact is obfuscated by filmmakers' use of traditional, male-oriented Hollywood conventions to deal with profound changes in gender roles and relationships. Like the filmic tendencies discussed earlier, these movies do represent struggles and trends in American life. Recent polls show that a majority of American women support feminist ideals (though they do not necessarily identify themselves as feminists). Currently, the majority of American women (66.9 percent) work for wages; the number of married women with children working outside the home rose 65 percent from 10.2 million in 1970 to 16.8 million in 1990. More flexible hours and work schedules have led to an increase in the time fathers spend doing childcare. The percentage of single-parent households run by women leaped from 30.9 percent in 1969 to 46.2 percent in 1985; the percentage of single fathers raising children on their own increased from 10 to 15 percent between 1980 and 1991. The social issues and psychological complexity of women "having it all," that is, career and family, are constant fare in popular magazines and talk shows; the idea of fatherhood is being redefined.[55] Despite creative shortcomings, the profit-driven film industry keeps entertaining people while providing an important forum for sharing cultural ideals and exploring the issues and concerns surrounding courtship and marriage, gender roles, and family. But portrayals of alternative gender roles that keep pace with social realities, and more significantly, the beliefs, values, and practices associated with them, have only begun to enter the mass cultural discourse provided by film and the entertainment industry at large.

NOTES

1. Edgar Leslie, Bert Kalmar, and Pete Wendling, "Take Your Girlie to the Movies," *Come Josephine in My Flying Machine: Inventions and Topics in Popular Song 1910–1929*, New World Records NW 233. This song was also part of a publicity campaign to boost movie attendance during a slump following World War I.
2. Geoffrey Perrett, *America in the Twenties: A History* (New York: Simon & Schuster, 1982), 224; David A. Cook, *A History of Narrative Film*, 2d ed. (New York: W. W. Norton & Co.), 298.
3. Kathy Peiss, *Cheap Amusements: Working Women and Leisure in Turn-of-the-Century New York* (Philadelphia: Temple University Press, 1986), 4.
4. Two histories treating women and film were published in the early 1970s: Marjorie Rosen's *Popcorn Venus: Women, Movies and the American Dream* (New York: Coward, McCann & Geoghegan, 1973), and Molly Haskell's *From Reverence to Rape: The Treatment of Women in the Movies*, 2d ed. (Chicago: University of Chicago Press, 1974, 1987). At the same time, feminist film critics began using gender as a category for criticism, an effect of the second wave of American feminism begun the previous decade. They have focused on a number of key issues that include images of women in film and female roles in specific genres; concerns about film

realism, female spectatorship, and the possibility of a countercinema; and analysis of the very nature of cinematic production as it affects gender portrayals and audience reception. For overviews of feminist film criticism see *Sexual Stratagems: The World of Women and Film* (New York: Horizon Press, 1979) and *Issues in Feminist Film Criticism* (Bloomington, Ind.: Indiana University Press, 1990), both volumes edited by Patricia Erens.

5. Quoted in David Nasaw, *Going Out: The Rise and Fall of Public Amusements* (New York: Basic Books, 1993), 110.
6. Beth L. Bailey, *From Front Porch to Back Seat: Courtship in Twentieth-Century America* (Baltimore: Johns Hopkins University Press, 1988), 18.
7. Peiss, *Cheap Amusements*, 6.
8. William H. Chafe, *The American Woman: Her Changing Social, Economic, and Political Roles, 1920–1970* (New York: Oxford University Press, 1972), 55–56, 135, and 144–45.
9. Peiss, *Cheap Amusements*, 45.
10. Quoted in Nasaw, *Going Out*, 105. The silent "serial queens" brought wage-earning women to the screen as heroines in weekly features with titles like *The Perils of Pauline* (1912–1914) and *The Hazards of Helen* (1912–1915). While still resembling her Victorian predecessor, however, "this modern female opened up an unprecedented possibility for love and marriage," film historian Lary May said. "Not only does her freedom bring her in contact with a wider range of available males, but the very fact that she attracts them with sexual allure raises the chance for an ensuing union based on something other than gentility" (Lary May, *Screening Out the Past: The Birth of Mass Culture and the Motion Picture Industry* [New York: Oxford University Press, 1980], 108).
11. Peiss, *Cheap Amusements*, 148; Nasaw, *Going Out*, 27, 233.
12. Peiss, *Cheap Amusements*, 151.
13. Ibid., 149–50.
14. Ibid., 158.
15. Elizabeth Ewen, "City Lights: Immigrant Women and the Rise of the Movies," *Signs: Journal of Women in Culture and Society* 5:3 (spring 1980): S65.
16. See John Demos, *Past, Present, and Personal: The Family and The Life Course in American History* (New York: Oxford University Press, 1986), 102.
17. Bailey, *From Front Porch*, 23.
18. Peiss, *Cheap Amusements*, 109; Nasaw, *Going Out*, 90.
19. Roy Turk, Jack Smith, and Maceo Pinkard, "Give Me A Little Kiss, Will Ya Huh?" *Yes Sir, That's My Baby: The Golden Years of Tin Pan Alley 1920–1921*, New World Records NW 279.
20. For a fuller discussion of sexual mores during the 1920s see Paula S. Fass, *The Damned and the Beautiful: American Youth in the 1920s* (New York: Oxford University Press, 1977).
21. Carl N. Degler argued that "the so-called Victorian conception of women's sexuality was more that of an ideology seeking to be established than the prevalent view or practice of even middle-class women" ("What Ought To Be and What Was: Women's Sexuality in the Nineteenth Century," *American Historical Review* 79:5 [December 1974]: 1467–90).

22. Joseph F. Kett, *Rites of Passage: Adolescence in America, 1790 to the Present* (New York: Basic Books, 1977), 36.
23. Robert Sklar, *Movie-Made America: A Cultural History of American Movies* (New York: Vintage Books, 1976), 137.
24. Quoted in Sklar, *Movie-Made America*, 137–38.
25. Henry James Forman, *Our Movie Made Children* (New York: Macmillan Co., 1933), 64–65.
26. "The Effect of the 'Movies' Upon the Minds of Men and Women, Boys and Girls," *The Banner*, 28 March 1918, 224.
27. Peiss, *Cheap Amusements*, 154; David Bordwell, "The Classical Hollywood Style, 1917–60," in *The Classical Hollywood Cinema: Film Style & Mode of Production to 1960*, ed. David Bordwell, Janet Staiger, and Kristin Thompson (New York: Columbia University Press, 1985), 16.
28. Robin Wood, "Ideology, Genre, Auteur," in *Film Theory and Criticism: Introductory Readings*, 4th ed., ed. Gerald Mast, Marshall Cohen, and Leo Braudy (New York: Oxford University Press, 1992), 477.
29. Richard Maltby, ed., *Passing Parade: A History of Popular Culture in the Twentieth Century* (New York: Oxford University Press, 1989), 112. The film noir heroines offered a contrasting image to the women in the screwball comedies. Instead of winning the heroine as a romantic partner, the protagonist finds that she obstructs his quest or holds him in her power. Sexually alluring but potentially dangerous, film noir heroines expressed "the inability of the American nation to deal with the freedoms that wartime had offered its women" (128).
30. See Virginia Wright Wexman, *Creating The Couple: Love, Marriage, and Hollywood Performance* (Princeton, N.J.: Princeton University Press, 1993), 19; David Bordwell, *Narration in the Fiction Film* (Madison, Wis.: University of Wisconsin Press, 1985), 159.
31. Haskell, *Reverence to Rape*, 2–4.
32. Bailey, *From Front Porch*, 42, 120.
33. The actual level of women working outside the home remained relatively constant, although the proportion of women employed in the professions dropped during the thirties from 14.2 to 12.3 percent (See Chafe, *The American Woman*, 59).
34. Haskell, *Reverence to Rape*, 4, 129–332. Though often debated, the meaning of cinematic portrayals and audience receptivity is something of interest here. On their return trip to Middletown in 1935, the Lynds observed that unemployment shook the confidence of men accustomed to the "traditional" role as financial provider for the family. They noted that even though gender roles remained fixed, the Middletown man may have "felt new inadequacies as a husband and lover in these days when grand passions are paraded nightly before Middletown in the movies" (Robert S. and Helen M. Lynd, *Middletown in Transition* [New York: Harcourt, Brace & Co., 1937], 177–78).
    Conversely, Haskell thought the effect of these films on women was simply to confirm "traditional" gender roles. "After all," she said, "most women were housewives and they didn't want to be made to feel that there

was a whole world of possibilities they had forsaken through marriage or inertia; rather, they wanted confirmation of the choice they had made" (See Haskell, *Reverence to Rape*, 151).

35. Haskell, *Reverence to Rape*, 91. Sklar noted that the effort to boost male attendance coincided with a trend toward increased sex and violence in film, the assumption being that such films had greater appeal to men than women and children (Sklar, *Movie-Made America*, 178).

36. Sklar, *Movie-Made America*, 269–71; Garth Jowett, *Film: The Democratic Art* (Boston: Focal Press, 1976), 375–76.

37. See the chapter on "The Economy of Dating" in Bailey, *From Front Porch*, 25–56.

38. "Going Steady . . . a national problem," *Ladies Home Journal* (July 1949): 44.

39. Bailey, *From Front Porch*, 10.

40. Ibid., 117–18.

41. Quoted in Betty Friedan, *The Feminine Mystique* (New York: Dell Publishing Co., 1963), 210.

42. Bailey, *From Front Porch*, 42. See the chapter titled "The Procreation Ethic" in Landon Y. Jones, *Great Expectations: America and the Baby Boom Generation* (New York: Ballantine Books, 1980), 20–39. For a discussion of the American family see Stephanie Coontz, *The Way We Never Were: American Families and the Nostalgia Trap* (New York: Basic Books, 1992); Rodney Clapp, *Families at the Crossroads: Beyond Traditional and Modern Options* (Downers Grove, Ill.: InterVarsity Press, 1993).

43. Friedan, *Feminine Mystique*, 37–38.

44. Ibid., 250. See the chapter titled "The Sex Seekers" for the full discussion.

45. Haskell, *Reverence to Rape*, 323–24.

46. "Z as in Zzz, or Zowie," *Newsweek*, 5 May 1967, 61.

47. For a discussion of the postwar youth culture and entertainment see "Risky Business: Youth and the Entertainment Industry," in Quentin J. Schultze et al., *Dancing in the Dark: Youth, Popular Culture and the Electronic Media* (Grand Rapids, Mich.: Wm. B. Eerdmans Publishing Co., 1991), 76–110. See also "Today's Teenagers," *Time*, 29 January 1965, 57; Jones, *Great Expectations*, 84–85.

48. For a fuller treatment of film and the youth market see "Looking at Teen Films: History, Market, and Meaning," in Schultze et al., *Dancing in the Dark*, 211–49; R. Serge Denisoff and William D. Romanowski, *Risky Business: Rock in Film* (New Brunswick, N.J.: Transaction Publishers, 1991).

49. See Alan Levy, "Peekaboo Sex, or How to Fill a Drive-in," *Life*, 16 July 1965, 82.

50. Nina J. Easton, "What's Driving 'Rain Man'? Women," *Los Angeles Times*, 10 February 1989, Home Edition, Calendar, pt. 6, p. 1.

51. See Roland Barthes, *Mythologies*, trans. Annette Lavers (New York: Hill & Wang, 1972). For a discussion of music video see the articles published in *Journal of Communication*, 36:1 (winter 1986); Sally Stockbridge, "Rock Video: Pleasure and Resistance," in *Television and Women's Culture: The Politics of the Popular*, ed. Mary Ellen Brown (Newbury Park, Calif.: Sage Publications, 1990), 102–13; Sut Jhally, "Dreamworlds: Desire/Sex/Power

in Rock Video," videocassette (Amherst, Mass.: University of Massachusetts, Dept. of Communications, 1990).

52. For a fuller treatment see the chapter titled "The Politics of Sexuality" in Michael Ryan and Douglas Kellner, *Camera Politica: The Politics and Ideology of Contemporary Hollywood Film* (Bloomington, Ind.: Indiana University Press, 1988; Midland Book Edition, 1990), 136–67.

53. The initial audience for *Working Girl* was 54 percent female; 56 percent for *Big*, and 54 percent for *Crocodile Dundee II*. See Easton, "What's Driving 'Rain Man'?" 1.

54. See Bernard Weinraub, "Women's Roles in Films Draw Women's Fire," *New York Times*, 2 June 1992, sec. B, pp. 1, 6; Richard Grenier, "Killer Bimbos," *Commentary* (September 1991), 50–52; Marilyn Stasio, "Let's Face It. We all Love a Good Sex Scene," *New Woman*, November 1993, 88–92. See also Susan Faludi, *Backlash: The Undeclared War Against American Women* (New York: Anchor Books, 1991); Marilyn French, *The War Against Women* (New York: Ballantine Books, 1992). Of note, even the 1993 re-release of the Disney classic *Snow White and the Seven Dwarfs* drew harsh criticism of the princess's dependence on a man for her survival and the fulfillment of her dreams—a sharp contrast to the film's reception when it first ran in theaters in 1938. See Susan D. Hass, "Heigh-Ho? Oh No!" *Grand Rapids Press*, 18 July 1993, sec. G, p. 8. The heroine in *Beauty and the Beast* showed perhaps that Disney creators were aware of changes in popular attitudes.

55. See Jerry Adler, "Kids Growing Up Scared," *Newsweek*, 10 January 1994, 44; *After Eden: Facing the Challenge of Gender Reconciliation*, ed. Mary Stewart Van Leeuwen, (Grand Rapids, Mich.: Wm. B. Eerdmans Publishing Co., 1993), 504, 512; "More Dads Baby Sit while Moms Work, Study Says," *Grand Rapids Press*, 22 September 1993. Jean Seligmann et al., "It's Not Like Mr. Mom," *Newsweek*, 14 December 1992, 70–73. See also Nancy R. Gibbs, "Bringing Up Father," *Time*, 28 June 1993, 53–61; Michele Ingrassia et al., "Daughters of Murphy Brown," *Newsweek*, 2 August 1993, 58–59; Barbara Dafoe Whitehead, "Dan Quayle Was Right," *Atlantic Monthly* (April 1993): 47–84.

12

Reluctant Feminists

Rural Women and the Myth of the Farm Family

MARVIN L. ANDERSON

The typical caricature of rural women in the United States and Canada lends itself to bucolic images of farmers' wives with either a politically conservative or apolitical outlook—hardly suggestive of anything to do with feminism. Granted, for some rural women, feminism is almost a dirty word. Though I am reluctant to call rural women in general, or even women farm activists, "feminists," I would contend that many rural women are, indeed, "reluctant feminists"—that is, "functional feminists"—in light of the values by which they live and think. But rural women have often felt snubbed by feminists as inferior and unsophisticated, compared to urban and well-educated women. For this reason, rural women may be justified in their reluctance to identify themselves in any way with the cause célèbre of the professional white middle-class women whom they would consider feminists.

Furthermore, many rural women who actually farm would never consider themselves farmers as such. Meanwhile, other rural women are now questioning the assumption that the "true" farmer in the traditional farm family is the husband and father.[1] Though many of these women belong to traditional rural women's groups in their local church and community, they are also members of farm activist lobbies and support groups throughout Canada and the United States that stand outside the mainstream farm organizations dominated by male farmers. Their presence and voice thus challenge the patriarchal authority and paternalism of well-established farm organizations in speaking on behalf of farm women and families, while not fully acknowledging women's integral role in farming and decision making. Ironically, farming is one of the few occupations in which rural women have not had to fight to share the work. Yet the word "farmer" is still generally seen as synonymous with the male gender.[2] Any mention of farmers seldom renders images of women hard at work during planting season or driving trucks at harvest time. Women do farm, but by and large in society's eyes, they only farm by association with their husbands or fathers. This perception of farm women holds true in small towns and farming communities as much as it does in cities. Only rarely are women referred to, or even identified as, farmers. Women on the farm are usually called housewives or farmwives, but rarely are they called farmers.[3]

In recent years, younger rural women have made it especially clear that they resent being perceived as mere appendages of their husbands. They want to be recognized as persons in their own right and not seen as standing in the shadow of their husbands, fathers, or sons.[4] Like the farm family itself, rural women are frequently depicted in terms of stereotypes and sentimental images that efface women's active contribution to farming. From popular Canadian and American women's magazines and farm journals, to the advertising world and the food and beverage industry, the mass media not only perpetuates clichéd images of rural women in general, but also obscures the stressful conditions and financial anxiety among most contemporary farm families. For this reason, it is impossible to understand the actual situation of rural women, and farm women in particular, without contextualizing them within the celebrated icon of the North American farm family.

No icon or myth, however, lends itself to strictly empirical analysis, and the farm family is no exception. For many people myth refers only to a fabrication or misconception of something, fictitous in nature. Myth can, however, become an ideological tool in the service of overtly political or propagandist purposes. This usage of myth can suggest a fabrication or falsehood but with a significant difference: When myth functions as ideology, it presumes the deliberate and politically expedient function of justifying the self-interests of a particular group in power. An ideology represents a body of thought resulting from the universalization of a partial and narrow social point of view. Thus, as Marx described it, ideology "defends," "justifies," "legitimizes," and "speaks for" a particular social group.[5] It does not just reflect some arbitrary and personal predilections, blindspots, or ignorance, but rather a systematic and pervasive bias. Since it is systematically biased, an ideology gives license to "distort," "conceal," "disguise," "mystify," or deliberately "misunderstand" its subject matter.[6]

Therefore, when a myth functions ideologically, it is explicitly used to control people. When a myth becomes ingrained into popular consciousness, it is often considered "common sense." It retains its appeal precisely because most people never realize they have been manipulated in the first place.[7] Myths thus serve an extremely useful function for those who benefit from them, and for those who want to make sure others think the way they do. Their strength and persuasive power lie in their ostensibly factual and historical presentation of social reality; their power to control people lies in their illusionary aspects and semblance of truth.[8]

The myth of the family farm may well outlive the actual institution of the family farm itself, if current projected trends on the decline of the family farm continue. In light of its well-documented demise, how could one account for the unanimous public support for "saving the family farm," were the family farm not a sacred institution? Leaving aside the popularity of Willie Nelson and his fellow musicians, it is obvious that the successful fundraising of repeated Farm Aid concerts comes from a widespread consensus that we need to protect this "way of life." The public rally in defense of the family farm in the midst of its decline illustrates the ideological usage of myth described above.

The frequent invocation of "the family farm" actually becomes *religious* in its fervor and dogmatism, and in turn becomes yet another political catchword as vague and emotionally charged as democracy and Christianity.[9] Yet many of the government farm policymakers and agricultural experts who have lamented the impending demise of family farming have, simultaneously, colluded in its destruction in the name of progress. Herein lies the inherent contradiction of the ideological myth of the family farm. According to this myth, family farms dominate agricultural production in almost all sections of the United States, and in most of Canada's populated areas. As Ingolf Vogeler argues in his exposé of this myth, the assumption that family farms are the norm in U.S. agriculture has been consistently used to disguise the actual trends towards large-scale farming and agribusiness.[10] Despite the ever-increasing size and volume production of farm operations, and the accelerated integration of the farm sector within national and transnational corporate economies, the ideological myth of the family farm persists because it is supported by several other myths.

If we examine this cluster of supporting myths, we can begin to ascertain why the contradictory nature of family farming continues to be obscured, not to mention the central role of women in the family farm operation. The fallacious assumptions underlying the economic and ideological myths of the family farm have been adequately discussed elsewhere, as have the historical roots of the present farm crisis.[11] The myth of the small family farm, however, has occupied a longstanding and powerful place in the cultural history and national ethos of the United States and Canada. From its ideological inception as the agrarian model most likely to foster Jeffersonian democracy, to its practical adoption as the Christian communitarian ethic of numerous sectarian and mainstream religious communities across North America, the small farm family has been imbued with a mythological character as diverse as the religious groups in which it is found.

To speak of myth in reference to the farm *family*—as opposed to the family farm—provides a more nuanced appraisal of rural women and families than prevailing caricatures of farmers permit. Using myth as an analytic framework enables us to respect the narrative and archetypal patterns among families whose primary livelihood has, until recently, been derived from working the land on which their survival depends. Only myth, therefore, can make sense of both the "natural" and financial catastrophes which have historically hovered over the heads of farm women and their spouses, from the unexpected loss of a crop by a sudden hailstorm to the ultimate and devastating tragedy of losing the family farm itself to bankruptcy.

The mythic forces behind the first settlement of the North American frontier by European immigrants were competing Christian communitarian visions of the New Jerusalem.[12] For some, the New World held similar promise of a New Eden, following a pilgrim "exodus" from the indentured servitude and oppression of their native lands. With few exceptions, the rural women who headed those immigrant families and pioneer households were at least nominally, if not devoutly, religious. Furthermore, Christian lay women and women's missionary societies were primarily responsible for the growth and maintenance of rural churches and congregational life, as well as for the administration of schools and other community activities. Because of the patriarchal bias towards male clergy in the respective histories of these religious and ethnic communities, the formidable leadership role of lay women in most fledgling Christian denominations is only now being recognized.[13]

The contradictory nature of the myth of the family farm can, first of all, be traced to its mythic origins among those ancestral ethnic families who homesteaded the frontier territories spanning continental North America. In the words of rural anthropologist Harland Padfield, perhaps the oldest cultural contradiction in the United States is embodied in two ideal images of the *pilgrim* and *pioneer* community where citizens were both private investors *and* communal Christians.[14] Padfield has aptly described the operative myth for those first generations of mostly European immigrant settlers whose progeny would immortalize the family farm as the "backbone of the nation." Furthermore, he notes the irony in the remarkable "transformation of hordes of would-be agrarian capitalists into a regimented industrial labor force" and, eventually, a consumer society, with no visible change in the ordinary (North) American's perception of reality. "The compelling effects of the agrarian past exist to this day [in] the nostalgia for the childhood farm, the rural school, and the rural community of yesteryear as if nothing had changed and, worse still, as if the social contradictions in the rise of the rural community had not been there from the beginning." This phenomenon is more than a cliche—"It is a fundamental illusion of [North] American culture: the persistent celebration of rural life in the midst of its destruction."[15]

The Historical
Exodus from the Farm

The enduring fascination with the family farm draws its lifeblood from a lingering nostalgia and sentimentality about past rural life. One reliable indicator of this phenomenon is the popularity of novels about farm life. Only a few were written in the nineteenth century when the United States was largely rural. Most date roughly from 1920 through 1945, coinciding with the unprecedented rural-urban migration in the U.S. and Canada. The audience for such books was mostly made up of nonfarmers, who were sentimental about a passing way of life.[16] Meanwhile, for ex-farmers' reminiscing about childhood memories of "the farm" or "the country school," the distance in years and miles is gladly traversed for the *emotional* gratification it offers in reliving the past. For many people, the sentimental return home for a family or country school reunion provides an opportunity to rejoin the world one has left behind; for others, the self-indulgence in nostalgia provides a retreat into a static and secure past. Still others are content to ignore what they left behind: While one former school chum longs to re-enter the past, another spurns it. This latter middle-western attitude is described by the Wisconsin writer Glenway Wescott as "a state of mind of people born where they do not like to live."[17] Both attitudes symbolize *escape* from farming and the hard life associated with it.

Wendell Berry, the well-known poet and farmer from Kentucky, comments that one hears over and over again about the specialists and experts of agriculture who are introduced as "old farm boys" who have since gone on (as is invariably implied) to better things.[18] But unlike university professors or agricultural consultants, farmers—that is, working family farmers—"do not have tenure, business hours, free weekends, paid vacations, sabbaticals, and retirement funds; they do not have professional status" of any sort. Moreover, Berry continues, the likely career direction of agricultural professionals is typically not toward farming or toward association with farmers. Rather, it aspires "upward" through the hierarchy of a university, a farm bureau, or an agribusiness corporation. They do not, like Cincinnatus, the Roman patriot of the fifth century B.C.E., leave the plow to serve their people and return to the plow. They leave the plow for good.[19] For their present-day rural counterparts, the old moral taboo is reversed; if farm boys or farm girls do not actively seek higher education or a professional livelihood, they are implicitly condemned to a lesser life by staying on the farm. Thus, they are guilty of that equally loathsome *modern* offense: not advancing yourself beyond your family of origin.

The "old farm boy" attitude toward the undesirability of farming exemplifies the first corollary myth of the farming family—"the myth of the dumb farmer." This myth simply presumes the undesirability of farming, and hence the inferior intelligence of those who pursue it. One often hears this among farmers themselves, when they self-consciously compare themselves to those people who have done better: "If I was that smart, I wouldn't be farming!" Although disguised as humor, this sentiment underlines the extent to which many farm families have unwittingly consented to this myth. The projected lack of intelligence among farmers is subsequently tied to their inability to get out of farming, and presumably to make more money elsewhere. The prospect of higher-paying jobs has undoubtedly been one of the drawing cards for the millions of farmers and small town residents who have moved to the city throughout this century.

In the 1920s, the internationally renowned novelist Willa Cather noted this myth among farm women and men in her newfound home of Nebraska: "All the farmers' sons and daughters seem to want to get into the professions where they think they may find a soft place. 'I'm sure not going to work the way the old man did,' seems to be the slogan of today. Soon only the Swedes and Germans will be left to uphold the prosperity of the country."[20] But even hard-working Swedes and Germans were not immune to the myth of the dumb farmer. Cather was disturbed by the increasing self-contempt she noticed among the second and third generations of immigrant farm families in Nebraska. They were ashamed of their pioneer parents and their calloused, weather-beaten hands, the babushkas over their heads, their hesitating and broken English—if they could speak any English at all.[21] Through her own literary work, Cather may have been consciously trying to repudiate the "character assassination" imputed by the myth of the dumb farmer. In a retrospective on the publication of *O Pioneers!* in 1912, Cather wrote that until that time "the Swede [farmer] had never appeared on the printed page in this country except in broadly humorous sketches; and the humour was based on two peculiarities: his physical strength, and his inability to pronounce the letter 'j.'"[22] But in fact, the frontier that Cather evoked so poignantly in her writing had been settled in the 1880s by cultured first-generation Bohemian, Russian, German, French, Swedish, and Norwegian immigrants, as well as by families from New England and Cather's native Virginia.[23] Most of them belonged to the same generations of pilgrim Christians and agrarian entrepreneurs described above.

This actual history offers a stark contrast to the common image of a cultural wasteland of "dumb hicks" and "clodhoppers" exploited by comedians and television sitcoms like *Green Acres* and *The Beverly Hillbillies*. The clichéd image of the farmer—typically white and male, attired in overalls with a piece of straw dangling from his mouth—is also front and center of the comical sketches in one of the longest running country music shows on television, *Hee Haw*. The commercial success of *The Beverly Hillbillies* and *Green Acres* may be due in part to the astute comedic packaging of the age-old country versus city antagonism, intrinsic to the myth of the dumb farmer. On the one hand, moral virtue and innocence are abstractly projected as universal traits of villagers and "country folk," especially over against the evil and corrupt city. On the other hand, a predominant urban bias indulges in routine jokes about the backwardness of our "country cousins." The romantic elevation of country life seems to go hand in hand with the denigration of rural people. Therefore it should come as no surprise that rural women and men are frequently self-deprecating; they can never quite measure up to the *civilized* standards of conversation, etiquette, and lifestyle identified with the city. No one describes this internalized sense of inferiority among rural people more bluntly than Pat Keyser, a woman farmer who lives and farms near Landen, Saskatchewan: "There has always been this idea that we have to be more like city people. You know, there's always that quote: 'Oh, that's such a farmer thing to do' or 'Don't act like such a farmer.' It's a real putdown. So we all want to be sophisticated and 'dine' at seven-thirty in the evening. We're really trying to be more like city people. . . ."[24]

Rural women and men, like everyone else, raise their children to attain the ritual confirmation of personal worth that comes with an education. The notion that everyone is born incompetent and remains stupid until they receive a formal education is one that writer Ivan Illich has coined the "doctrine of original stupidity," analogous to the theological doctrine of "original sin."[25] The widespread belief in the presumed incompetence of uneducated, or less formally educated, people thus reinforces the internalized psychology of personal inadequacy mediated by the myth of the dumb farmer. Similar to most working-class families, parents of farm families have learned to rationalize their hard-working lives of sacrifice as a way of ensuring their children's material and professional "salvation" through a proper education. This in turn ensures them a ticket to the "better life" in the city. If higher education is thus believed to be the primary means for "getting ahead," or "getting out," where does that leave the millions of rural women who do not, or simply cannot, attain the elusive goal of upward mobility through a formal education? In most cases, it leaves them resigned to making every sacrifice necessary to secure the educational opportunities for their own children.[26] When combined with the other sacrifices expected of mothers, especially in traditional rural communities, it is easy to see why many rural women have readily lived their life through and for their children—with no room of their own.

The Mythical Survival of the Farm Family

The unprecedented "exodus" of rural women and men from the traditional family farm has gone largely unreported. Underlying this indifference is the common assumption that the country exists for the city, and thus has no intrinsic value in itself. By providing "natural resources" as well as a ready pool of unemployed laborers, rural families and their communities have been readily exploited for the *raw material* they provide for urban and suburban centers. Indeed, without proximity to a city, any kind of rural community—be it a small town, village, or hamlet—risks geographical and cultural oblivion, or so we tend to think. Because the primary meaning of "rural" is determined by its juxtaposition to a suburban or urban area, the implication is that rural *culture*, as such, simply does not exist.

We have already seen how rural women and men are expected to fit the expedient caricatures and stereotypes seen in reruns of *Hee Haw* and *The Beverly Hillbillies*. Hollywood's humorous sketches of farmers serve to trivialize the real exigencies and stresses of farm families, thus negating the tragic elements of rural life. Farm and peasant families have never been credited with the resourcefulness and economic versatility that have enabled them to survive despite overwhelming odds. Their repertoire of "vernacular skills"[27] for survival is constantly being tested by both the market and natural forces impinging on their livelihood. In fact, the precarious historical survival of peasant and farm families has included all the risks and hazards of agriculture to be expected at one time or another—bad seasons, storms, droughts, floods, pests, badly eroded soil, animal and plant diseases, crop failures, not to mention natural catastrophes like plagues and fires, or the trampling and pillaging of crops during wars.[28] For millennia, millions of peasant and farm families have had to contend with these variables in order to survive, and the situation is no different for the majority of the world's population today.

Though the historical and economic conditions of survival for peasants throughout the world obviously represent a different context than that of contemporary Canadian and American farm families, the fate of both peasant and farm families is generally subject to arbitary and powerful state policies that presume their *expendability*.[29] Generations of North American farm families have experienced the systemic exploitation and expropriation of their farmland, their crops and produce, their labor and that of their children. Farm women, in particular, have frequently been most vocal in protesting the capitalist exploitation of farm families. Billie Johnson, who farms with her husband in one of the poorest counties in Kentucky, says the problem for the farmer is that "the other fellow sets the prices of produce and machinery. We *exist*, that's all the farmer ever does" (emphasis mine).[30] But the exploitation of farmers does not stop there. Susan Glover, a dairy farmer from Grey County in Ontario, laments the consumer-driven expropriation of farmers *and* their farmland as idyllic scenery.[31] Glover satirizes the feverish opportunism of real estate agents in promising "fast-track downtowners" a pastoral respite from the stresses of metropolitan life in Toronto and other cities. After recounting the seasonal demands of summer haying time, the daily regimen of milking, feeding, and other chores on a dairy farm, as well as business and family responsibilities, she notes her cynical reaction in coming across a recent *Chatelaine* magazine's promotion of "Chic Country Retreats" as an escape to the country. The rustic showcasing of bargain-priced farmland properties is yet another example of the myth-driven expropriation of the farm family. Thus, Glover sardonically concludes that "rural existence is of no value until given the imprimatur or endorsement of the vacationing middle class."[32]

As the farm family becomes more valuable as an object of urban consumption and rural nostalgia, its mythic character becomes even more pronounced. A classic example of this mythical appropriation of the beleaguered farm family is found in the story "Going Under," in the November 1985 issue of *Life* magazine. The story centered around one farm family's valiant fight to save their farm near Verdigre, Nebraska, a small farming town of Czech descendents boasting a population of six hundred. The editorial for this issue indicated that the plight of the American farmer had been of interest to *Life* for over a year, but qualified their Johnny-come-lately coverage with the statement that because a subject "is deserving or even urgent doesn't mean *Life* can quickly set out to do it." Moreover, in a self-congratulatory note, the editorial says

Life is "a photo-driven magazine, and we must always find the compelling visual narrative that will dramatize a theme."[33] The bankruptcy of Roger and Carolyn Vech's farm is subsequently dramatized by *Life* with a "photo-driven" countdown of camera shots, climaxing with the auction barn sale of the last remaining cattle. This "compelling" sequence of photos takes the reader—*qua* spectator—through this farm family's intimate experience of anguish and grief. *Life*'s voyeuristic coverage of the Vech family losing their farm thus meets their editorial and commercial requirement for sensational media fare for mass (i.e., urban) consumption. Meanwhile, we learn nothing of the meaning of this traumatic event for the Vech family itself, in particular, the shame and self-recrimination that most farm families experience in front of their friends and neighbors, so dramatically ritualized in the public humiliation of a farm auction.[34]

The Myth of the Independent Male Farmer

The most dominant myth surrounding the farm family is found in the idealization of the independent and self-sufficient yeoman male farmer. According to the founding mythology of the American revolution, the yeoman farmer was industrious and self-reliant, and he wanted to be free of despotic restraints on his agricultural productivity. Once free, he could voice his own opinions and express them accordingly in political action.[35] Both Thomas Jefferson and his political adversary, John Adams, apotheosized the farmer to the status of a civic demigod, and the first president of the republic, George Washington, followed suit.[36] But Jefferson's dream of a truly egalitarian society of independent farmers never materialized to the degree he wished, or, for that matter, to the degree commonly believed.[37] "Despite its place in the nation's value system," according to rural sociologist Charles Geisler, "widespread private ownership was a myth by 1880."[38] Yet the resilient image of the small family farmer has retained its mythological hold on the American political imagination.[39] The well-known economist Thorstein Veblen, the son of a Wisconsin farmer, recognized the power of this myth among the farmers of his own generation in perpetuating their denial of their eroding political and economic clout. Writing in 1923, Veblen sounded dubious praise for "the independent farmers" who, as a group, succumbed to "the timeworn make-believe that they still are individually self-sufficient masterless men . . . each for himself."[40] With tongue in cheek, he commended this indefatigable spirit among farmers that has obviously "achieved many admirable results, even though the results have not all been to the gain of the farmers."[41]

In wake of the imminent collapse of the market economy in 1929 and the subsequent Depression of the "dirty thirties," the specters of foreclosure and bankruptcy loomed over many farm families. As foreclosures led to absentee ownership, the ensuing mood of resignation and defeatism among liquidated farmers was psychologically devastating.[42] Although rents proved less onerous than taxes and interest, the loss of ownership and title to land incurred an indelible loss for the proud, self-sufficient yeoman farmer—the forfeiture of one's pride and self-respect. Despite the intermittent successes of some farmers' political alliances and organizations, a collective strategy of fighting those "massive business interests" gave way to a *modus operandi* of individual farmers resorting to makeshift strategies for survival.[43] As studies of attitudes among young people of the 1930s Depression have shown, people found it easier to blame themselves than the economic system for their jobless plight, even though employment opportunities were scarce.[44] Though many farmers blamed both local bankers and Eastern bankers for their financial ruin, many of them turned on themselves instead.

The farmers' loss of control over local resources and any prospect of economic self-sufficiency coincided with the cultural disenfranchisement of the once-noble family farm—the mythic "backbone of the nation." The tragic result for the Middle West was a colonial status in both a commercial and psychological sense. The whole region, like other depressed rural areas since the Great Depression, suffered from "a malignant and destructive inferiority complex."[45] The words of economist and political scientist Alvin S. Johnson, in 1935, sum up the humiliating fate of the mythic independent male farmer who chooses to absolve the capitalist market system of its role in *his* failure: "Prosperity may return, but no conceivable prosperity will restore the failed bank nor vest title to the farm in the foreclosed farmer. . . . The depression casualty continues vocal for a time, but eventually his voice, too, is stilled or ignored. One can't listen forever to a man who has failed."[46]

As independent as family farmers like to think they are, their overwhelming dependence on the arbitrary gratuitousness of government programs and subsidies, which favor large producers over small and medium-size family farmers, renders them politically ineffectual and impotent. Their vulnerabilty to the volatility of international commodities markets and the General Agreement on Tariffs and Trade (GATT), as well as the discriminatory policies and floating interest rates of lending institutions, leaves them further dependent on factors beyond their control. Although traditionally farmers have abhorred the thought of being in debt or paying excessive interest, the current realities have forced farmers into unprecedented indebtedness.[47] As University of Wisconsin farm records specialist Bob Luening has pointed out, "There is a growing tendency for farmers to be perpetually in debt" for the entire length of their farming lives.[48] With respect to the vagaries of the market, the economist John Kenneth Galbraith maintains that "in the modern economy the individual farmer has no influence or control over the supply and price of what he produces. The individual farmer is one among thousands and tens of thousands responding to a market price and situation on which not even the production decisions of the largest individual operator have any appreciable effect."[49]

Despite all the evidence to the contrary, the persistent belief in rugged individualism has somehow become "the philosophic corner-stone of rural culture. . . ."[50] This individualism consequently leads to a refusal to admit the need for cooperative political action, because such an admission would suggest individual weakness or failure on behalf of the farmer. The mood of helplessness and denial continues among farm families until a crisis erupts. The symptoms of the crisis of denial are seen in the increasing incidence of domestic violence and suicide, which are obvious despite inadequacies of documentation and individual efforts to conceal them.[51]

The myth of the lone, embattled farmer almost always suggests a white, male, "rugged individualist." This myth exaggerates the power of the farmer to somehow rise above all the insurmountable odds against him and still *succeed*. Furthermore, the myth of the small independent male farmer has been deliberately appropriated by agribusiness for its own ideological purposes, as evident by the celebrity status heaped upon the modern, "progessive" farmer touted by the industrial agribusiness model. According to Marty Strange,

> "It is these farmers who get admiring stories written about them in the farm magazines, who win awards from small-town chambers of commerce (because they do a lot of business on Main Street), and who are considered top managers by agricultural experts. Their farms are on university tours and field days, [and] seed companies want them to be their local dealers (for which they get their own seed much cheaper than the neighbors they sell to). . . ."[52]

Their prominence and status in the farm community, not to mention their considerable property (even if not paid for), demonstrate their economic worth, and most of all their political power.

The weight of community sanction and praise in farm communities is now with those farmers turned successful entrepreneurs. While all types of success are given public recognition in rural communities, failure is invariably treated with silence and shame.[53] "The possibility of failure," in the words of Richard Sennett and Jonathan Cobb, "is the most uncomfortable phenomenon in [North] American life. There is no room for failure in our schemes of respect, unless the failure is found to result from some cataclysmic event like the Great Depression."[54] Yet, as we have seen, even the Great Depression and the longstanding drought of the "Dust Bowl" years were not enough to dispel the unshaken belief in the mythic self-sufficiency personified by the ennobled male farmer. The myth of the individual yeoman farmer derives its staying power from both its archetypal and ideological adaptation of the heroic motif of traditional myth. Herein lies the shadow side of the stoic masculine image of the rugged individualism that Schwab calls "the philosophic cornerstone of rural culture." Of all the possible failures, none seems to render a more definitive public verdict of being "less than a man," or less able to carry out the responsibilities of a father and husband, than the financial failure that comes with either bankruptcy or foreclosure. For most farmers and farming communities, such failure is tantamount to the "unpardonable sin."

Probably the most dramatic and telling symptom of the disintegration of once well-established farm communities is the alarming increase of suicide among farmers. The actual number of rural suicides is vastly underreported, with deaths often attributed to farm-related accidents by family members, local doctors, and county medical examiners.[55] The state of Iowa, where forty percent of its farmers were projected to lose their farms in 1986, had the highest divorce rate in the United States and one of the highest suicide rates in the following year.[56] In 1987, the number of suicides in Iowa climbed to 398, the highest number since the Depression.[57] In Ontario, 34.8 percent of the farmers who died between 1979 and 1982 were suicides.[58] Whether the act of suicide, primarily among male farmers, is thought to be the most inconspicuous way to acknowledge personal defeat, or the most honorable rite of self-absolution by a shamed father and husband, this much is clear: The financial failure of a family farm is morally equivalent to failing the farm family. The recurring self-incrimination among insolvent and bankrupt farmers only perpetuates the public shame they feel for not only letting down their immediate family members and children but the whole of their extended family. Bonnie Williams, a professor of social work at the University of Iowa, describes her own farm family: "The farm is part of the family. My great-aunt and -uncle had our farm originally; my father has lived there since the day he was born. If he lost that farm, he'd feel as if he were failing the whole family. It would say that not only was his life meaningless, but that the lives of the preceding generation were meaningless too."[59]

According to the farm journalist Osha Gray Davidson, the recent upsurge in suicides among farmers reflects the extent to which farmers have generally subscribed to the myth of the fiercely independent farmer, making them into competitors, not cooperators as they once were. Farmers who go down, go down alone.[60] As Henk deWit describes it after voluntarily liquidating his hog farm operation in southwestern Ontario in 1987: "You don't go to other farmers because you feel they are out there waiting to grab your land—like vultures."[61] This same masculine myth of independence has also made it practically impossible for farmers—especially men—to admit to having problems and asking for help. Joanne Dvorak, a mental health professional in Cedar Rapids, Iowa, who has worked with farmers for several years, says farm men "just don't want to talk about their problems openly."[62] Patty and Larry Thomann, who owned a medium-size Iowa farm until they were forced to sell out in 1985, epitomize how this pent-up sense of privacy among farm couples escalates to the point of denial. "We were artists at not letting anyone know that we had problems," says Larry. "You not only don't let your friends and family know what you're feeling," Patty adds, "but you deny it to yourself. You have to keep telling yourself that it's going to be all right, even when you know it's not, because otherwise you're sitting on a time bomb. You have to deny it just to survive."[63]

The Invisible Work
of Rural Women

We would not know the extent of the stress on contemporary farm families were it not for the investigative research and numerous surveys conducted by farm women's organizations on the impact of the farm crisis on their immediate families. In particular, recent documentation and research by rural women's groups has pinpointed the psychological and emotional effects on farm families of the systemic crisis in modern agriculture. Similar evidence of stress on rural women and their families is found in other North American natural resource industries reeling from economic downturns, such as logging, fishing, oil, and mining. Besides the vagaries of commodities market prices, the rising cost of production, and the unpredictable climatic variables during seeding time and harvest, there are other factors that add stress to the lives of farm women. These include economic pressures unlike those faced by previous generations: daily decision making, high seasonal workloads, increasing paperwork, potential family conflict, and the routine demands of off-farm activities. The symptoms of this stress are expressed physically as fatigue, irritability, insomnia, marital problems, indigestion, depression, headaches, anger, frustration, hostility, and indecision.[64] Many parents also feel guilty because their children have to work long hours without pay on the farm.

Stress is particularly high for women in farm families partly because women are traditionally expected to be the family mediators. Although women have not been seen as part of the formal decision-making team, they are still presumed responsible for satisfying all the emotional needs of the family, especially in time of crisis.[65] For this reason, it is not surprising that farm women are usually the first ones to recognize the denial of strong and uncomfortable feelings among *their men*, that is, their husbands, sons, brothers, as well as male friends, neighbors, and so on. Consequently, they are usually the ones who call for assistance when their husbands refuse to seek help on their own.[66]

The public stance taken by some farm women on the farm crisis and related issues has not always endeared them to their friends, neighbors, or parish communities. By speaking out on matters considered private and "best kept secret," rural women have often trespassed the patriarchal boundaries of propriety designated for women in small towns and rural communities. To be in financial trouble spells failure and shame to most farmers, particularly men; consequently, women farmers have had to take on the task simply of naming what is being consciously denied by many of their own family members. Furthermore, by publicizing the psychological and social problems exacerbated by the farm crisis, farm women activist groups have taken the traditional woman's role one bold step further by politicizing what is deemed personal and "nobody else's business."

The act of acknowledging that there *is* a rural crisis, and the concomitant resolve to do something about it, are still unthinkable for many people in farming communities. Some rural women have done more than risk incurring the wrath of their family members, spouses, neighbors, and friends by talking about the negative effects of financial stress. They have been ridiculed or scapegoated as troublemakers and, in some cases, ostracized by their own communities for "rocking the boat"—which Carol Bly correctly calls "the greatest anathema in small-town life."[67] Many farm women have experienced either outright hostility or at least suspicion for voicing their concerns using a feminist analysis, or for using language thought to be derived from feminism. This puts them between the proverbial "rock and a hard place," with little room to maneuver given the general ambivalence in most rural communities to feminist ideas and principles.

The constant stress of financial pressures on farm women, requiring many of them to work off the farm, combined with professional aspirations among both younger and older farm women, have forced many farm women to reexamine their identity as women. It has also created new tensions between them and their mothers and their mothers' generation, for whom "working outside the home" was taboo, and was thought to reflect badly on one's husband. For that older generation, any adult female involvement or participation in an activity perceived to be *outside* of those traditional role expectations of women as primarily mothers and housewives, or their complement of volunteering at church or in a civic group, has until recently "raised eyebrows." Therefore, the actions and motivations of some independently minded older women, or of younger generations of rural women—many of whom are well-educated and professional in outlook—will be suspect in light of older generational attitudes and traditional rural mores regarding the proper place of women.

Despite the traditionalist makeup of gender roles within farm families, the very demands of the "family business" nature of farming have, ironically, forced many rural women to transcend—if not "transgress"—the normative gender role constraints for urban as well as rural women. Although some women would adamantly deny any formal association with "feminists," many rural women do, in fact, live out a practical expression of feminism on terms quite different from urban and suburban women. Generally speaking, rural women do not labor under the same ideology of a gendered split between unpaid domestic work and paid work in the public sector as women who live in metropolitan areas tend to. They are, however, subject to the kind of economic and social exploitation that can accompany their nonstipendiary contribution to family-run farm operations. Family farmers are price-squeezed by the oligopolistic actions of industrial agribusiness, which simultaneously supplies agricultural inputs and buys farm outputs. Thus family farmers are perpetually at the mercy of market forces beyond their control and benefit.[68] In order to survive they must reduce their costs. If labor costs are the only productive factor over which they have control, gratuitous or "free" family labor must be exploited. As we have seen above, the sentimental belief in farming as a cherished "way of life" internalized by most farm families helps persuade farm men and women alike to accept their contradictory roles without complaint.[69] Outwardly, male farmers deal with the market economy as any other group would, urban or rural, but within the family they depend on unpaid family members for farm labor. Because most farm wives and children do not receive formal wages as such, their economic contributions are hidden; thus, economically speaking, they only appear viable in a private relation to a male wage earner.[70]

Besides the "free" family labor that farm women are expected to provide, many farm women carry a triple workload, having also to work off the farm to supplement the cash flow on a financially strapped farm operation. In her provincial government-funded study, "Women in Rural Life . . . The Changing Scene," based on forty-eight hearings held in twenty-four different locations across Ontario in 1984, author Molly McGhee found that estimates of the amount of time spent on childrearing and homemaking, farm work, and off-farm employment varied from 80 to 101 hours weekly.[71] By comparison, using a time budget from the May 1975 *Farm Wife News*, Elise Boulding calculated that American farm women put in a 41-hour week on farm tasks and a 58-hour week on domestic tasks, culminating in a 99-hour week.[72] On record, the overall contribution of North American farm women's labor to the maintenance of their households, families, and farm operations has been obfuscated to the point of relegating women to the status of "invisible farmers."[73] The frustration for many younger farm women is not only that their indispensable role in the efficient operation of the farm is overlooked, but that their hard work in the home is taken for granted as their mothers' was. The household work and raising of children, done almost exclusively by rural women, is not only taken for granted; it is hardly recognized.[74] If the work of farm women is to be recognized as legitimate, however, farm women must take the initiative in changing their self-image and reaffirming the inherent value and dignity of their work. Otherwise, as Suzanne Dion discovered in her 1981 study of Quebec farm women, farm women will tend to underestimate the extent of their real contribution and, at the same time, fail to see themselves as actual producers: "Some women operate machinery, some tend to the cows, some act as receptionists, secretaries, accountants, researchers, labor relations officers, personnel managers, sanitary technicians, mechanics, truck-drivers, salespeople, public relations officers, planners, buyers, and so on. *They call this 'helping out, running errands, answering the phone.'* "[75]

To the extent that the "invisible" work of rural women is thought to be incidental to the household and farm economy, women's work is taken for granted and denied both legitimate productivity and long-term security. In addition to their manual "labor of love" in reproducing the farm family, farm women have been central to successful production on the farm. They have always been willing to perform the labor of men, whatever that might involve.[76] They have voluntarily increased their own work hours to take the place of hired men during harvest and during family and farm crises. Furthermore, they have

given up the household labor of their older daughters if the husband
needed them in the fields. They have even allowed their children to be
worked harder and longer than they knew was good for them, while
making sure the work was bearable. Moreover, feminist historian Joan
M. Jensen attributes the reputation of the family farm's durability to the
versatility and flexibility of family labor, which made the family farm
more productive than large commercial farms in the nineteenth and
early twentieth century.[77] Whenever possible, farm women also developed strategies of mutuality with men. They readily and astutely
applied this principle to church and civic activities as well as to politics.
For this reason, they were among the first women to gain access to
national organizations such as the Grange, to political organizations
such as the Farmers' Alliances, and to parties such as the Populists and
Socialists. Because rural women were able to incorporate these strategies of mutuality and cooperation within their communities and
churches, rural men in the United States were the first to consistently
grant political power to women by extending suffrage to them.[78]

Granted, rural women have always had to negotiate the often strict
limitations imposed on them by the patriarchal social mores and gender
boundaries inherent in the families, religious congregations, and local
communities to which they belonged. However, the cooperation and
interdependence required of women and men in farming communities
makes *any* thought of trying to wrest power away from men, or even live
without them, seem absurd to most rural women. To the extent that
feminism has been unjustifiably stereotyped as "men-hating," or associated with strident angry women who refuse deference to any man, feminism is perceived only as a threat to the status quo of farm communities,
not to mention to the patriarchal institutions of family households and
rural church congregations. It is no wonder that misogynistic forces and
groups intent on preserving a strictly traditionalist role for women have
capitalized on the ambivalence or, in some cases, overt hostility that
many rural men and women feel towards feminism and those women
who "go out of their way" to identify themselves as feminists. This kind
of antifeminism goes hand in hand with judging and isolating "strong"
women suspected of challenging the conventional way of doing things in
rural communities and small towns.

While many farm men live in fear of losing their farm and "not making it," their spouses and other farm women seldom contemplate suicide; they're too busy thinking of new and different *cash crops* in order
to "make do" in today's volatile economy.[79] In faithfulness to their husbands and their families, and to the farm communities in which they
live, contemporary farm women have refused to accept the verdict that

their financially-strapped husbands are simply "bad managers."[80] They have, by that simple act of loyalty, defied the political scapegoating of farm families by the "orthodoxy" of farm experts, bank managers, lenders, and agricultural policymakers representing agribusiness. Working in traditional networks of church and community groups, the ongoing support farm women have always provided each other has been the basis of a distinctly rural feminism that has enabled women and their families to survive.[81]

Yet rural women have, for practical reasons, always maintained their farm families by subordinating their own interests to those of the farm family.[82] As Jensen has observed, farm women have typically made the practical concessions deemed absolutely necessary for the survival of the farm families that they headed. For example, the only "inheritance" that poor and often landless black farm women bequeathed to their children was a practical repertoire of rural survival skills. These were "handed down" through family and kinship networks, as well as through neighbors and elders in one's church and local community.[83] Millions of women of color headed farm families of sharecroppers, tenant farmers, and migrant laborers in the southern United States, many of whom joined the ranks of displaced farm families in the mass migration to the cities. For them, the hardships and sacrifices endured by rural women have only been exacerbated by pervasive and systemic racism. For these rural women, and for the rural women whom we have discussed in this chapter, the mastery of such skills has been critical in assuring the survival of farm families regardless of their class status or proprietary relationship to farmland. Rural women have always known how to reduce levels of family consumption when necessary. They have also increased their absorption of stress, developed mental flexibility, and "made do" with what scant resources they have had. They have asked only for the success of the farm family in reproducing itself, of passing the farm on to the next generation.[84]

Analogous to the "divided loyalties" many feminists feel when caught between allegiance to their own tribe, party, or kinship group, and their solidarity with women at large, many rural women are "reluctant" feminists because of their stronger commitment to their own immediate and extended families. Their identity as women, like many women in traditional societies, is too readily fused with the familial and communal ties that bind them, for good or ill. To forego those domestic commitments and familial obligations in favor of a more abstract, individualist, and gender-specific solidarity with all women feels like a betrayal of their families, friends, and neighbors. As Jensen points out, farm women have undoubtedly resented some of the sacrifices demanded of them, but they were still expected by family and community to hide that resentment.[85]

Times have changed, however, and some rural women are no longer content to accept the same kind of sacrifices they *think* their mothers' and grandmothers' generations did. Yet they continue to make sacrifices of their own for the sake of their spouses, children, and extended farm families. Like their pioneer and pilgrim ancestors, they make them when necessary to ensure the future of their own farm family. The inherent genius of rural feminism is no more premised on ideological gender politics than it is conferred by formal schooling or academic certification. It lies, rather, in rural women's shrewd capacity for making a room *for* one's children and family in the midst of scarcity and economic hardship. The enduring myth of the farm family is thus witness to the sheer resiliency and resourcefulness of rural women and their families.

NOTES

1. Lois L. Ross, *Harvest of Opportunity: New Horizons for Farm Women* (Saskatoon, Sask.: Western Producer Prairie Books, 1990), 1. See Ella Haley's chapter, "Getting Our Act Together: The Ontario Farm Women's Movement," in *Women and Social Change: Feminist Activism in Canada*, ed. Jeri Dawn Wine and Janice L. Ristock (Toronto: James Lorimer & Co., 1991), 169–83.
2. Lois L. Ross, *Prairie Lives: The Changing Face of Farming* (Toronto: Between the Lines, 1985), 40.
3. Ibid.
4. Molly McGhee, *Women in Rural Life: The Changing Scene* (Ontario Ministry of Agriculture and Food, 1984), 27; see also Gisele Ireland, *The Farmer Takes A Wife: A Study by Concerned Farm Women* (Chesley, Ont., 1983), 4.
5. Bhikhu Parekh, *Marx's Theory of Ideology* (Baltimore: Johns Hopkins University Press, 1982), 29–30.
6. Ibid., 30.
7. Ingolf Vogeler, *The Myth of the Family Farm: Agribusiness Dominance of U.S. Agriculture* (Boulder, Colo.: Westview Press, 1981), 6.
8. Ibid.
9. Wendell Berry, *Home Economics* (San Francisco: North Point Press, 1987), 162.
10. Vogeler, *The Myth of the Family Farm*, 6.
11. See Osha Gray Davidson, *Broken Heartland: The Rise of America's Rural Ghetto* (New York: Anchor Books, 1990), and Marty Strange, *Family Farming: A New Economic Vision* (Lincoln, Nebr.: University of Nebraska Press; San Francisco: Institute for Food and Development Policy, 1988).
12. See Benjamin G. Smillie, *Visions of The New Jerusalem: Religious Settlement on the Prairies* (Edmonton, Alta.: NeWest Press, 1983), and Paul A. Olson,

"Scandinavians: The Search for Zion," in *Broken Hoops and Plains People. A Catalogue of Ethnic Resources in the Humanities: Nebraska and Thereabouts* (Lincoln, Nebr.: Nebraska Curriculum Development Center, 1976), 237–90.

13. See Rosemary Radford Ruether and Rosemary Skinner Keller, *Women and Religion in America. Volume 1: The Nineteenth Century* (San Francisco: Harper & Row, 1981). On a personal note, I would like to cite two exemplary rural laywomen from my own farm family in Nebraska: Nina Cook and Maria Sophia Lanquist. Nina Cook, my maternal great-aunt, was an active member of her local United Methodist Church. She is fondly remembered to this day for her work as a nurse and librarian in the small farming community of Cozad, Nebraska. Maria Sophia Lanquist, my paternal great-grandmother, attended a Swedish Mission county church. In addition to being a mother and wife in her own farm family and working alongside her husband as most rural women do, Maria Sophia was a trusted midwife to neighbor farm women in the small farming community of Loomis, Nebraska. I wish to dedicate this chapter to their memory—in light of the enduring witness of their Christian faith and the integrity of their service to their neighbors and community.

14. Harland Padfield, "The Expendable Rural Community and the Denial of Powerlessness," in *The Dying Community* ed. Art Gallaher, Jr. and Harland Padfield (Albuquerque: University of New Mexico Press, 1980), 159.

15. Ibid. For a convincing account of this same phenomenon in the Canadian context, see R. Alex Sim, *Land and Community: Crisis in Canada's Countryside* (Guelph, Ont.: University of Guelph, 1988).

16. James R. Shortridge, *The Middle West: Its Meaning in American Culture* (Lawrence, Kans.: University Press of Kansas, 1989), 71.

17. Ibid., 69.

18. Berry, *Home Economics*, 171.

19. Ibid. Similarly, if we could draw an analogy from the list of grave sins compiled by Pseudo-Cypriot in the seventh century C.E., one of the worst transgressions lies in the desire and ambition of peasants to rise above their humble station in medieval society. Jacques Le Goff, *Time, Work, & Culture in the Middle Ages*, trans. Arthur Goldhammer (Chicago: University of Chicago Press, 1980), 91.

20. Mildred R. Bennett, *The World of Willa Cather* (Lincoln, Nebr.: University of Nebraska Press, 1961), 148.

21. Ibid.

22. Willa Cather, *On Writing: Critical Studies on Writing as an Art* (Lincoln, Nebr.: University of Nebraska Press, 1988), 94–95.

23. Bennett, *The World of Willa Cather*, xii–xiii.

24. Ross, *Prairie Lives*, 54.

25. Ivan Illich, *Toward a History of Needs* (New York: Pantheon Books, 1977), 75–76.

26. See Richard Sennett and Jonathan Cobb, *The Hidden Injuries of Class* (New York: W. W. Norton & Co., 1972), particularly 119–50.

27. For a fuller explanation of "vernacular values" and skills, see Ivan Illich, *Shadow Work* (Boston: Marion Boyars, 1981), particularly 27–51, and Ivan Illich, *Gender* (New York: Pantheon Books, 1982), 68 n. 51.

28. John Berger, *Pig Earth* (New York: Pantheon Books, 1979), 199; Marvin L. Anderson, "At the Mercy of the Marketplace: A Recollection of the Historical Struggle Against Starvation," unpublished paper, 1982.

29. See Richard L. Rubenstein, *The Age of Triage: Fear and Hope in an Overcrowded World* (Boston: Beacon Press, 1983).

30. Carolyn E. Sachs, *The Invisible Farmers: Women in Agricultural Production* (Totowa, N.J.: Rowman and Allanheld, 1983), 101.

31. Susan Glover, "Chicken Coops and Country Chic," *This Magazine* (October 1987): 20.

32. Ibid.

33. "Going Under," *Life* (November 1985): 145–50; Marvin L. Anderson, "'Going, Going, Gone': Selling the Family Farm," *Our Times* (March 1986): 26.

34. Anderson, "'Going, Going, Gone,'" 26.

35. Strange, *Family Farming*, 240.

36. Ibid., 240–41.

37. Davidson, *Broken Heartland*, 23.

38. Ibid., 24.

39. The particular appeal of the small family farmer within the Canadian political tradition is comparable to the American experience, but in a completely different historical context that warrants further examination than provided here. See, for example, Gregory Baum, *Catholics and Canadian Socialism: Political Thought in the Thirties and Forties* (Toronto: James Lorimer & Co., 1980).

40. Thorstein Veblen, *The Portable Veblen*, ed. Max Lerner (New York: Viking Press, 1948), 398.

41. Ibid.

42. Shortridge, *The Middle West*, 63.

43. Padfield, "The Expendable Rural Community," 170.

44. Robert H. Hartman, ed., *Poverty and Economic Justice: A Philosophical Approach* (Ramsey, N.J.: Paulist Press, 1984), 173.

45. Shortridge, *The Middle West*, 63.

46. Ibid.

47. Davidson, *Broken Heartland*, 53.

48. Vogeler, *The Myth of the Family Farm*, 118.

49. Jim Schwab, *Raising Less Corn and More Hell: Midwestern Farmers Speak Out* (Chicago: University of Illinois Press, 1988), 9.

50. Ibid., 18.

51. Ibid.

52. Strange, *Family Farming*, 39.

53. Arthur J. Vidich and Joseph Bensman, *Small Town in Mass Society: Class, Power, and Religion in a Rural Community* (Princeton, N.J.: Princeton University Press, 1958), 46.

54. Sennett and Cobb, *The Hidden Injuries of Class*, 183.

55. Davidson, *Broken Heartland*, 94.
56. Terry Pugh, ed., *Fighting the Farm Crisis* (Saskatoon, Sask.: Fifth House, 1987), 33.
57. Davidson, *Broken Heartland*, 94.
58. Pugh, *Fighting the Farm Crisis*, 33.
59. Davidson, *Broken Heartland*, 95.
60. Ibid., 96.
61. Rudy Platiel, "Group Aims to Aid Farm Families," (Toronto) *Globe & Mail*, 16 June 1987.
62. Davidson, *Broken Heartland*, 96.
63. Ibid.
64. McGhee, *Women in Rural Life*, 29.
65. Canadian Advisory Council on the Status of Women, *Growing Strong: Women in Agriculture* (Ottawa, Ont.: Canadian Advisory Council on the Status of Women, 1987), 191.
66. Joan M. Jensen, *Promise to the Land: Essays on Rural Women* (Albuquerque: University of New Mexico Press, 1991), 232.
67. Carol Bly, *Letters From the Country* (New York: Harper & Row, 1981), 52.
68. Vogeler, *The Myth of the Family Farm*, 291.
69. Ibid.
70. Ibid.
71. McGhee, *Women in Rural Life*, 12.
72. Rachel Ann Rosenfeld, *Farm Women: Work, Farm, and Family in the United States* (Chapel Hill, N.C.: University of North Carolina Press, 1985), 52.
73. See Sachs, *The Invisible Farmers*.
74. Marvin L. Anderson, "Rural Women: 'A Woman's Work is Never Done (Recognized)'" *Our Times*, (October 1984): 40–41.
75. Canadian Advisory Council, *Growing Strong*, 53.
76. Jensen, *Promise to the Land*, 238.
77. Ibid.
78. Ibid., 237–38.
79. See Ross, *Harvest of Opportunity*.
80. Jensen, *Promise to the Land*, 232.
81. Ibid., 259.
82. Ibid., 238.
83. Ibid., 235; see also Alice Walker, *In Search of Our Mothers' Gardens: Womanist Prose* (New York: Harcourt Brace Jovanovich, 1983); and Wendell Berry, *The Hidden Wound* (San Francisco: North Point Press, 1989).
84. Jensen, *Promise to the Land*, 238.
85. Ibid., 301.

PART 4

Current Issues

13

Rethinking
Private and Public
Patriarchy

PAMELA D. COUTURE

Private patriarchy, public patriarchy, or an alternative? By challenging the idea that a man is head of the family, on one hand, and that public life has more value than domesticity and that private life must be carefully regulated, on the other, women activists of the late nineteenth century helped shape the emerging welfare/market state into a genuine alternative to private and public patriarchy. Women such as Frances Willard and Ellen Key, writing at the end of the nineteenth century, envisioned ways to move toward a nonpatriarchal social order, but their political and religious hopes have only been partially realized. Their egalitarian vision can inform our debate about the role of markets and the welfare state today providing, among other things, a check against the tendency simply to extol matriarchy as a remedy for patriarchy.

Patriarchy and the Family

What is patriarchy? For the purposes of this study, patriarchy is a social system through which, as a group, men receive more power and privileges than women on the basis of gender, and in which traditionally male activities are valued more highly than traditionally female activities. These conditions are perpetuated through the norms and assumptions of economics, law, custom, by threats or acts of physical and sexual coercion, and by restrictions placed on both women and men who try to live differently from the rules of patriarchy. One cannot simply assume, however, that individual men are powerful and individual women are not; rather, in addition to individual differences, men and women occupy a range of places that are modified by other group characteristics, including race and sexual orientation. People who hold the assumptions of a patriarchal worldview do not necessarily believe the dominant system to be unjust; rather, they—

and the culture and institutions they shape and that shape them—aim to create their own version of justice. When individuals perpetuate patriarchy, they may be blind to the ways some persons are left inordinately vulnerable under its tenets, or they may dismiss that vulnerability as unimportant.

Patriarchy in the family has been transformed as democratic values have influenced American family life. Two hundred years ago Americans assumed that a woman's legal, economic, and political status should be collapsed with that of her father or her husband; but now women have independent legal and political identities. American political and legal culture also accepted that husbands could physically chastise their wives, but now such behavior is condemned as battering.[1] Americans cited biblical passages to demonstrate that husbands had a right to sexual intercourse on demand, but increasingly Americans have come to believe that even sex within marriage requires consent or else qualifies as rape. Men still have the physical and economic power with which to dominate women, but changes in legal, political, and social structures have altered the power balance so that women in families are now legally, politically, economically, and socially visible. Although some men still behave as if they have a right to dominate women through physical and economic threats, law and custom are less on their side than ever before.

Even so, gender relations in most families are far from egalitarian. Under a temperate patriarchy, the imbalance between men and women frequently involves a conflict between employment and domesticity. In temperate patriarchal families, men are still the family "head." Men may treat women kindly and share their income with the whole family; women may have more time at home with children and provide a support system for the needs of the whole family; and women and men may like it that way, enjoying female domesticity in return for male economic support. But times of crisis show how vulnerable these women and men really are.

If women must become self-supporting, they have earned less money, taken advantage of fewer opportunities for job advancement and personal enrichment, done more of the housework and childcare and been more emotionally responsible for other members of the household than men. When men want to participate fully in domesticity, they discover that socialization is more powerful than they think. Their ideals create new expectations, while old emotions remain.

Peers may not appreciate the obstacles their married friends and colleagues face when they share both employment and domesticity. Moreover, social institutions are usually not organized to accommodate egalitarian coupling. Government, church, business, and school officials often assume that their employee has a spouse who is free to tend the home front. Although some employers have voluntarily experimented with some family-friendly benefits, they have also fought attempts by government to standardize such benefits. Both strict and temperate patriarchy make their presence felt, even when married partners desire an egalitarian relationship. (For a similar analysis see Bonnie J. Miller-McLemore, *Also a Mother: Work and Family as Theological Dilemma* [Nashville: Abingdon Press, 1994], 71–75.)

While the pressures of employment and family may be intense for couples in various kinds of coparenting families, they can be excruciating for parents who are functioning as single parents. Genuinely single parents, parenting with little or no economic or emotional support from a partner, must provide for all of the family's domestic and economic needs. They usually seek aid from a variety of sources: family, friends, community organizations, government. When single parents turn to government for help, either because they cannot find jobs or because of the high stress of combining employment and childrearing, public help comes with a price: regulation and stigma.

Coparenting gay and lesbian couples face obstacles that overlap with those of heterosexuals, and in addition live in a society that applies constant pressure on them to end their relationship. It is routinely assumed that they are not committed parents and that their children will be confused, rather than nurtured, by their parenting partnership. To add to this stigma, they may be unable to get the employment benefits available to heterosexual couples and single parents.

In the tradeoffs of life, when men and women are forced to compromise their ideals in order to gain partial satisfaction, they tend to revert to private or public patriarchy. How did the market/welfare state attempt to help people overcome some of these obstacles, and how does it succeed or fail in doing so? To answer this question it is helpful to distinguish between private and public patriarchy.

Private and Public Patriarchy
in the Modern Welfare State

Private patriarchy pins its hope for a just society on the family or household; public patriarchy looks toward the organization of society. Each model tries to protect something that people value by ignoring or dismissing a particular kind of vulnerability. Aristotle and Plato reveal the deep structure of private and public patriarchy.[2]

Aristotle uses private patriarchy to protect a positive model of egalitarian intimate relations. *Philia* is characterized by deep affection, mutuality, and independence, usually between two social equals. It breeds human virtues, such as courage, generosity, or justice. Affection binds *philoi*, or intimate partners, together. Loving each other for the other's own sake preserves the independence of the other; yet their mutual concern for one another allows them to mutually give and receive friendship from the other. Children develop the capacity for such relationships through the family and public education; adults reexperience and strengthen their abilities for intimate, caring relationships in the family and in the polis.

Persons seeking an egalitarian society might well value Aristotle's kind of intimacy while bristling at the conditions he sets for such intimacy. Such intimacy can be regularly expected only between men of equal status. He admits that women, slaves, and craftsmen have the potential for intimacy but that their place in society does not allow it. Aristotle does not try to imagine social arrangements in which all people might participate in the good of intimacy.

Instead, from Aristotle we can learn how society accepts some persons' inordinate vulnerability through cultural beliefs that perpetuate existing social arrangements. Observing his own society, he claims that economic necessity binds superiors and subordinates to one another. Subordinates require the financial support of superiors, and their menial labor frees their superiors for intimacy among equals. In return, the superiors are morally bound to care for the subordinates. But he fails to recognize that his system leaves subordinates vulnerable: If the superior party fails to carry out his moral responsibility to care for the inferior party, the inferior party remains economically dependent on the superior and suffers the consequences. Aristotle's profound model of intimacy may be interpersonally egalitarian for some, but it leaves subordinates vulnerable to emotional and material deprivation.

Plato imagines that society might be restructured to reduce the vulnerability of intimacy, at least for the ruling class. He claims that men and women are equally capable of governing. Toward this end he proposes that men and women should have equal cultural, educational, and financial privileges. Both genders are obligated to provide society's leadership. For the sake of the best society, the governors must seek the wisdom and justice and must bear gifted children who can carry on this task.

Yet Plato's plan constitutes what I am calling public patriarchy, in which domestic activities are both devalued and regulated. Because ruling men and women must guard against anything which could create self-interest, they must renounce domesticity, whether in the realm of personal relationships or private property. To keep particular attachments from developing, men and women of the ruling class may not have exclusive sexual relations; their children must be reared in common; their material needs are to be met by public financial support.

In Plato's public patriarchy, women are integrated into the public domain of men, but men and women both abandon the domestic domain. The life of men is the life worth living; private life, the only real sphere of power and creativity for most ancient and some modern women, is carefully regulated. In this model, however, Plato agrees with Aristotle that people who are consumed with menial work cannot flourish. He protects the time and energies of the most capable persons through public support. His governing class is still dependent on subordinate classes of persons to do the necessary work of society; not all persons have access to the conditions that allow the best human flourishing.

The enduring conflicts, resolved in different ways by private and public patriarchy, are these: Personal attachments within the family can facilitate the flourishing of children and adults; such attachments may generalize into concern for the common good of society but may also lead to injustice, including extreme vulnerability and inordinate self-interest. Equalizing economic and familial conditions through public support may reduce the need for self-protection, making time and energy available for the common good; but equalization may also devalue domesticity and affection and increase the regulation of private life.

In the course of Christian history these conflicts have generated various social and institutional compromises. Early monasticism, for example, institutionalized the Platonic concern over personal attachment, equalized material support, provided care for unwanted children, and replaced the family with a communal structure aimed at contemplation and service to others. A widespread medieval practice, celibate marriage, encouraged married couples who had already borne children to separate for a life of contemplation and service in religious orders. Other Christian theologians, such as Thomas Aquinas, thought highly of familial affection and incorporated Aristotle's family model into his synthesis. The Reformation created smaller, nuclear families and reintroduced community support for the poor.

The history of monasticism demonstrates that public patriarchy offers women educational and cultural advantages and spheres of influence within public life, even though their institutions are often under the general direction of men and their domestic life is carefully regulated. The history of families shows that under some versions of private patriarchy women are able to carve out their own domestic spheres of influence, even though their public life has been limited.

The market/welfare state represents a twentieth-century variation on these themes. In industrial market/welfare states some public governmental support within a market economy equalizes some living conditions for families. In countries such as Sweden, equalization through public support for families is quite extensive; in others, such as the United States, equalization through public support is comparatively minimal. Other industrialized nations lie between these two extremes.

Private Families and
Public Families: Variations within
the Market/Welfare State

The relationship between the family and the market/welfare state varies among industrialized countries. Private families in the United States are shaped more by the morality of the market; public families of Sweden may be more influenced by the morality of government support.

Individuals in private families, such as those in the United States, are more vulnerable to market pressures. As these pressures build, commitments to family and community are increasingly eroded by the influence of economic norms, in which maximizing one's own self-interest is the highest good.[3] Alan Wolfe argues that civil society, or voluntary community organizations, once buffered families against market intrusion; in addition, when families divided labor between the bread-winning father/homemaker mother, the traditional family structure offered a compartmentalized "haven" from the market rationality. With the decline of civil society, however, private families became extremely vulnerable to the intrusion of market morality—as exhibited, Wolfe claims, by increased numbers of employed women, the decline of the economic security offered by marriage, and the lack of serious emotional responsibility on the part of older generations for younger generations. By implication, civil society protects families from the instrumental morality of the market if it also maintains the conditions of private patriarchy in the family. When civil society is removed as a buffer between families and markets, then market morality produces a more cruel patriarchy with which the family must contend.

In Sweden, by contrast, Wolfe discerns an emerging "public family." Families in Sweden have relied heavily on government both to provide support for families and to create the moral philosophy rationalizing such support. The moral philosophy of the "People's Home" sought to promote "equality, consideration, cooperation, and helpfulness." It was institutionalized in forms such as transfer payments to equalize family income and day-care programs that supported women's paid employment. Society's reliance on government for moral suasion, Wolfe theorizes, shifted the burden of caring from the family to the state. Women still do the caring, but as paid employees of the welfare state: "Socializing the young and caring for the sick, viewed traditionally as women's work, are still women's work, but now they are carried out for a government wage rather than within a family setting."[4]

The distinctions above are somewhat overdrawn; certainly, private families in the United States rely on institutionalized care and public families in Sweden are influenced by market conditions. Yet the parallels between private and public families and the deep structure of Aristotelian and Platonic forms of patriarchy are striking. The private family values interpersonal intimacy even when that can be secured only through familial hierarchy and unequal conditions between families. In this model, striving toward equality within the family or among families creates disequilibrium. The public family values social equality for families and individuals even when that equality moves women into the public world to perform domestic tasks. In the United States the public patriarchy of forced regulation has been most evident among families on "welfare," or poor-support; in Sweden the private patriarchy of social and gender inequality reemerges with increasing interest in privatization. Plato's concern—that private families create inordinate self-interest that lessens their concern for the common good—seems accurate, based on the U.S. experience; but Wolfe's analysis suggests that Swedish experience echoes Aristotle's concern—that the Platonic attempt to eliminate self-interest through social regulation may reduce the conditions for intimacy.

In the early stages of the development of the market/welfare state, the religious and political discourse of women such as Frances Willard, of the United States, and Ellen Key, of Sweden, tried to transform the conditions of private and public patriarchy. To what extent is their vision helpful in reconstructing our own?

Women's Political and Religious Discourse and the Origins of the Market/Welfare State

As an alternative to public and private patriarchy, women of the late nineteenth-century woman movement imagined a society in which the deep metaphors of the family would become the basis for society and even the state. (Women's activism of the nineteenth century was called the "woman movement." The designation "feminism" arose around 1910. "Feminism" and "the women's movement" refer to later twentieth-century social movements that were concerned with analogous, but different, issues. The historical designations are retained for clarity and historical accuracy.) Family metaphors for the ideals of humanity and society proliferated in images such as "mother-heartedness" and "social housekeeping" in the United States, "mother state" in France, and "social motherliness" in Sweden. The influence of the international woman movement is evident when we compare its metaphors to the Swedish idea of society and state as the "People's Home." Popularized in the 1930s by Per Albin Hanssen, the second (male) Social Democratic prime minister in Sweden, the "classic formulation" of the "People's Home" stresses "solidarity and equality of consideration":

> The basis of the home is togetherness and common feeling. The good home does not recognize anyone as privileged or misfavored; it knows no special favorites and no stepchildren. There no one looks down upon anyone else, there no one tries to gain advantage at another's expense, and the stronger do not suppress and plunder the weaker. In the good home equality, consideration, cooperation, and helpfulness prevail. Applied to the great people's and citizens' home this would mean the breaking down of all the social and economic barriers that now divide citizens into privileged and misfavored, into rulers and dependents, into rich and poor, the glutted and the destitute, the plunderers and the plundered.[5]

Images of home and motherhood dominated the work of both the American organizer of the Woman's Christian Temperance Union (WCTU), Frances Willard (1839–1898), and the Swedish professor of Western Civilization, Ellen Key (1849–1926), although their emphasis in the development of these metaphors was different. Willard used the metaphor of motherheartedness to describe temperance and social purity, even though she eventually stressed the themes of poverty and social support; Key used social motherliness to describe the possibility of familial and public support, even though eugenics figured into her work.

An American
Cultural Spokeswoman:
Frances Willard

Willard envisioned the day when now-cruel society would become the hospitable mother, ready to welcome her children:

Some day every child that is born will find not only that its coming has been prepared for by its mother but by that greater mother now so severe but then so reasonable and kind—Society.[6]

A loving society, whose ethic was the Golden Rule, mirrored loving homes, whose foundation was the egalitarian marriage and reciprocal bonds between parent and child. Willard's idea of egalitarian marriage was not the traditional Christian "subordination and equivalence,"[7] in which men and women were understood to be hierarchically ordered in society but spiritually equal. She had in mind a spiritual and social equality in the concrete, in which men actively cared for children and the home, parents were deeply bonded to children of both genders, and wives and husbands had equal access to education, politics, culture, church, and productive work.[8]

Willard did not assume that all women had to marry and bear children; rather, she argued for the full economic independence and social worth of single women. Patriarchy, however, had to be eradicated for such homes and society to become universal.

The abuse of alcohol, mainly by men but sometimes by women, provided the lens through which Willard discerned the reach of patriarchy. Patriarchy exerted its power on many levels—in the poverty of the homes of men who spent their earnings on alcohol, in the violence of drunken men toward women and children at home, in the saloons that seduced men from their homes, in houses of prostitution in which men exploited girls, in the vested economic interests of the alcohol producers and their influence with the United States government.

Willard's concern for social purity, with which the WCTU was so popularly associated, concentrated mainly on the elimination of alcohol and prostitution. Fundamentally, the campaign for social purity was a means toward home protection; it was not primarily a moralistic campaign, in which adherence to certain rules made a person sanctified. Rather, Willard tried to address the exploitation of women on institutional, familial, and personal levels through the so-called "do everything" policy. Politically, Willard pressured the government to accept prohibition and to resist the institutionalization of prostitution; she and her followers disrupted saloons and red light districts. She understood all of the actions as those which would help to construct and maintain loving relationships in the home and society.

Willard also understood sexual purity as a method women used to resist men's control of their bodies. In so doing, she stood in a long line of Christian women who have used celibacy as a means of self-determination. For these women, sexual and economic asceticism held the private patriarchy of the family and the public patriarchy of institutions at a distance. Sexual asceticism created a wider space within which women were freer to develop their spirituality and education. The earlier familial metaphor of the convent, at times replacing rather than extending the biological family, created an institutional sisterhood of which one hears echoes in the familial metaphors of the WCTU. Sexual asceticism was later repudiated as repressive by early twentieth-century feminists on both sides of the ocean.

Although temperance and social purity were Willard's leading themes, her developing understanding of poverty, the anesthetic effects of alcohol, and the economic desperation that brought some women to prostitution, eventually led her into Christian socialism. In 1895 Willard told the WCTU delegates: "Nothing short of wilful ignorance can account for the continued ignoring of poverty as perhaps the chief procuring cause of the brutal drinking habits with which whole areas of the population are distempered throughout the English-speaking world."[9] Similarly, she empathized with women who either were driven to prostitution to support themselves or found themselves pregnant out of wedlock.[10]

In her developing understanding of poverty, Willard, like other reformers such as Jane Addams, seems caught between the contradictory understandings of human nature that were operative in her culture. The Christian anthropology that Willard received from her Wesleyan tradition taught that as children of God, made in the image of God, the poor deserved the care of the more privileged. For Willard, as for Wesley, providing for a stranger, Christian or non-Christian, was doing for Christ himself.[11]

In the late nineteenth century, however, capitalists such as Andrew Carnegie, under the influence of Social Darwinism, reintroduced an anthropology that relied on the notions of the worthy and unworthy poor, notions inherent in the United States since colonial times. True to Christian tradition, Carnegie believed that "he who dies rich dies disgraced."[12] The wealthy were to care for the poor not by a system of handouts that would encourage begging, but by funding public education, libraries, and parks, which would help the poor catch up with more economically successful people. Willard incorporated some of the insights of "scientific philanthropy" into her international addresses but with a decided socialist twist.[13] Admitting that Christian charity could exacerbate the problem of poverty, Willard argued that the issue of poverty, as it resulted in alcoholism and prostitution, had to be addressed at a foundational, preventive level. She adopted the language of socialism as "collective ownership of the means of production," and concluded that, "In every Christian there is a socialist, and in every socialist a Christian."[14]

While Willard developed an institutional analysis of the alcohol trade and prostitution, she failed to understand the patriarchal constraints on African Americans in the United States, particularly the institutional force behind lynching.[15] As a result, her work is tainted by the same racism as that which haunts the late nineteenth-century woman movement generally. The international context of her work offers little help in confronting the poverty and violence perpetuated by racism. Although WCTU women identified deeply with women of color who were oppressed *as women*, they accepted and even exploited the racial fears of the larger society which promoted Anglo-American imperialism, both military and missionary. For example, world missionaries promoted temperance and sexual abstinence among the American and British military by pointing out that alcohol and prostitution resulted in biracial children who were ostracized by the cultures of both of their parents.[16]

Willard envisioned a flourishing human community in which "Christ reigns in our hearts," a time of "the increase of common joy." When she addressed the Third Biennial Convention of the World's Woman's Christian Temperance Union she summarized her vision:

> "Joy is the grace we say to God"; it is the outcome of balanced faculties, and an environment that presses its good gifts equally upon all. Anything short of this shows that sweet-bells are jangled; the ardent, endless aspiration of the human spirit is for nothing less than joy. It is the chief charm of intoxicating liquors, that they seem to bring this for a season, and of impurity that it is joy's deadliest counterfeit. But what if universal man should find, as a result of the combined work of countless light-bringers through the uncounted ages, that we can only "take joy home" into a brain as normal as that of the bird in yonder tree-top or the swan upon the smiling lake below? What if he should find that only by bringing the very best the world contains to everybody else can he ever really come to the best himself? What if man should grow so great as to desire the equal comradeship of the gentle partner of his gladness and his grief? What if they should go hand in hand through all the fields of education, art, society, and government? What if there should be some day no rich, educated and titled, no poor, ignorant and debased? The common joy, then, is what we seek and help to work out in the best ways we can.[17]

Most of Willard's main themes are alluded to in this summary. The reign of Christ in the mother-hearts of humankind would result in sobriety and health, the enjoyment of the outdoors, the work of men and women alike for a living wage, and the equal partnership of men and women at home and in social institutions such as church, schools, government, and culture.

A Scandinavian
Cultural Spokeswoman:
Ellen Key

Ellen Key and Frances Willard mutually informed each other but disagreed at important points. Key admired Willard as "one of the world's 'great women agitators' who 'set thousands of women into action . . . against intemperance.'" One of Key's major works, *The Century of the Child*, was used by the WCTU to promote an alcohol-free environment for children. Key, too, was deeply troubled over the destruction of the home. Key was thus partly rooted in the nineteenth-century woman movement and the international ideology of motherhood.[18]

Like Willard, Key blamed capitalism for the destruction of home life. In the transition from an agrarian to an industrial society, capitalism had drawn women away from their homes and into factories. Even though factory work allowed women to be economically independent from men, which Key supported, such work only traded one bondage for another—the bondage of industrial conditions that drained women's energy for the home and destroyed women's biological capacity to mother. She criticized those women of the woman movement who saw only economic liberation and not oppression in those conditions. When portions of the woman movement opposed protective legislation for women and children, Key argued that they addressed only the concerns of middle-class women. Key's position paralleled that of European-born socialist women in the United States, whose differences from U.S.-born socialist women have been documented.[19]

Key thought, however, that forces in addition to capitalism were destroying the home. The repressive conditions of marriage, religion, and education also destroyed the spirit of home life, she argued. Her work on love and marriage resonated not with the nineteenth-century woman movement but with the concerns that became prominent in the feminist movement after 1910.[20]

Marriage, Key thought, had to be united with love. Love, not legal or ecclesiastical sanction, made marriage thrive. Key pointed out that the same kinds of arguments Martin Luther once made against clerical celibacy could now be made against marriage: Many legally married people were consigned, unhappily, to a lifestyle against their will; others, not legally married, by virtue of the quality of their relationship, were faithful in the eyes of God. While criticizing Luther's utilitarian view of sex, Key also recognized that the turn-of-the-century free-thinkers had Luther to thank for the religious valuing of human sexuality. Like Luther, she probed theology and religious experience while rejecting traditional ecclesiology.

Key's understanding of human nature and society was consistent not only with her critical reading of Luther and other theologians but also with the Darwinist concepts of evolution that captivated the turn-of-the-century minds. Key's religious and scientific interests became evident when, in describing the depths of the human soul, she understood herself to have reunited the biological and the spiritual. The individual soul, she believed, flourished best in a nourishing environment, and in turn would transform the society in which it lived. This mutuality would give rise to what we would now call "generativity," or creativity for the sake of the next generation. In the twentieth century, children's spirits would live if children were born to parents who deeply loved one another and if children were educated in a way that respected children's individual differences and encouraged their religious imagination.[21] Key movingly described the transformations of the marriage, home life and parenting, education, religion, the woman movement, and the state that she believed were necessary to bring about such an environment for children's flourishing.

While Luther is clearly an important influence in Key's background, so is Søren Kierkegaard. In *The Century of the Child*, Key argued that children "have a right to choose their parents." By this she meant that every child has a right to be born to parents with the highest ethical relationship: "The ethically decisive factor [in a marriage] is the way [partners] live together."[22] In family life, the ethical and the aesthetic are deeply joined with one another. Children are nurtured by parents with a vibrant relationship, but they are dulled by parents whose relationship is either dead or discordant. Great love is found when, in the freedom of the soul to search for its mate, the individuality of two souls share themselves with one another and care equally for the happiness of the other. She describes egalitarian marriage:

> Someday society will look upon the arrangements of the love relation as the private affair of responsible individuals. . . . People are beginning to see that perfect fidelity is only to be obtained by perfect freedom; that complete exchange of individuality can only take place in perfect freedom; that complete excellence can only come into being in perfect freedom. Each must cease to try to force and bend the emotions, opinions, habits, and inclinations of the other towards him- or herself. Each must regard the continuance of the feeling of the other as a happiness, not a right. Each must

regard the possible cessation of this feeling as a pain, not as an injustice. Only in this way can there arise between the two souls such pure, full, freedom that both can move.[23]

Such excellence in love makes a home a work of art, the mother "one of those artists of home life who through the blitheness, the goodness, and joyousness of her character, makes the rhythm of everyday life a chance, and holidays into festivals."[24] Similarly, "Every modern woman wants to be loved not *en male* but *en artiste*. Only a man whom she feels to possess an artist's joy in her, and who shows this joy in discreet and delicate contact with her soul as with her body, can retain the love of the modern woman."[25] The desire to be loved in this way, as a passionately sought but equal partner, was for Key at the core of the women's movement. But the purpose of such a love was not just the fulfillment of individuals' desires, although that is one result; rather, such love is profoundly generative.

The freedom to love, in full biological and spiritual expression, could be found not only in adult partnership but in motherhood. Key supported the right of women not to mother, for every individual was the final arbiter of his or her path in the world. Key believed, however, that motherhood was such an expression of the unity of women's body and soul that most women want to mother. Mothering reaches beyond itself. The child is not the narcissistic expression of the fulfillment of the mother but is an end in itself. At the same time, mothering contributes so much to society that mothers who mother well fulfill a social obligation. For these reasons, Key felt that all good mothers had the right to mother, regardless of marital status; mothers who would pass undesirable traits to their offspring should be expected to refrain from reproducing.

Key believed in the importance of women's sexual and economic freedom; equally, she believed that mothers should not work outside the home during childrearing years. Key noted that many families in industrializing society required two incomes to survive, that single mothers lived in stigma and economic scarcity, and that women's economic independence was vital to the kind of partnership she envisioned. Yet she was convinced that the woman movement was making a mistake by developing an ideal of women working outside the home while children's education and home care was left to professionals. She did not support those socialists who wanted to collectivize, and thereby trivialize, the functions of the home, including education. Even though Key's values in education were consistent with the educators who became influential after the turn of the century, Key believed that children's individuality would best flourish through home schooling.

Key said little about fathering, reflecting a set of social conditions in which fathers participated little in domesticity. She did claim that "it is very important that this state of affairs be changed."[26] Unlike Willard, Key never seemed to entertain the idea that fathers' equal participation in domesticity could allow mothers' equal participation in work and culture. Instead, she reconciled her concerns for women's sexual and economic independence, women's equal contribution to society, and women's role in raising children by proposing for state-supported motherhood through children's allowances, mothers' allowances, and so on. Key's proposals formed the basis of the family policy components of the Scandanavian welfare state.

Key and Willard use similar rhetoric to establish women's right to public support. For example, both compare soldiering and mothering as civic contributions. As the soldier risks his life on the battlefield, so the mother risks her life in childbirth. According to Theda Skocpol, the original social legislation in the United States that benefited Civil War veterans was justified by the soldier's risk on behalf of society, and this analogy helped to launch benefits for mothers and children. Even as benefits for veterans grew into disfavor as "too costly," legislation such as the Sheppard-Towner Act launched health education and social benefits for some mothers and children.

Both Willard and Key were professional educators and stressed the importance of women's education for private and public purposes. In the United States women had established their first political identity through education for Republican Motherhood, or educating sons for the Republic in the privacy of their homes. Key is similarly concerned that mothers be equipped to educate their children. In the late nineteenth and early twentieth centuries women put their education to public use as they educated one another, re-created and expressed their political identities, and transformed both U.S. and Swedish society. Some women argued for public benefits for mothers within the family, using the ideology of married women's separate sphere in the home. Others created "public mothering" as employment. In the private sector, women were employed in home economics, psychology, education, and social work; in the emerging welfare state women provided the work force that put maternalist social policies into action.

Finally, both Willard and Key were deeply spiritual women who were motivated by significant religious beliefs. Each took to task a powerful patriarchal religious hierarchy. Willard's Christian faith not only motivated her secular politics but challenged her to open church doors to women's leadership. Key's religious faith led her to leave a church she saw as hypocritical in order to follow the ethics of the world's great religions and to find a spirituality of the soul.

The ideology of motherhood and the homelike society, with its convergence of politics and religion in the push for equal rights, Christian socialism, evangelical Protestantism, and family metaphors for society, was more than women's social agenda—it became women's civil religion. This civil religion had different, and at times conflicting, expressions. In the late nineteenth and early twentieth centuries in Sweden and the United States, however, women substantially outnumbered the men. When women couldn't assume that they would marry, what ideal of womanly activity could they develop for their lives? A new ideal for womanhood, social as well as biological mothering, called for a homelike society that reflected that ideal.

The Institutionalization
of the Ideology of Motherhood

The ideology of motherhood helped to transform the practical political and religious institutions in which women lived. The proponents of state support of motherhood within a developing market economy hoped to reduce the inordinate vulnerability of women and children. State support could help to free women from brutality in the family and dehumanization in industry, so that men and women, whether married or single, could create gender-equal families, could engage in fulfilling, paid, caring work, and could access the achievements and benefits of education and culture. As the women's movements participated in re-creating society, however, their ideals, goals, and achievements revealed underlying currents of gender and race relations that crossed over their religious and political goals. These currents suggest some of the reasons why the women's ideal of a homelike society became compromised in its institutionalization.

The Crosscurrents of Gender

In the United States the ideology of motherhood was spread by a politically attuned network of clubs and associations that was built largely by evangelical Protestant women.[27] Initially, the ideology of motherhood was institutionalized in settlement houses and projects which gave birth to the profession of social work. Reformers discovered, however, that government was partially complicit with those who profited from vice and that the problems of poverty were complex. They concluded that the charity of settlement projects alone did not have the power adequately to address the problems of poverty and vice in families and communities—government had to be involved.

Men in labor and government in the United States emphasized "paternalist" policies, or protective regulation, policies and benefits designed by men for working men. Protective legislation for working men threatened to restrict the "right of contract" between business and male workers and was limited in the United States. The most successful paternalist policy was built on the concept of the family wage. Proponents of the family wage assumed that women could be taken care of through their male breadwinners. Paternalist policy did not protect women without male breadwinners. Women fought for "maternalist" policy, or supports for mothers and children desired by, created by, and lobbied for by women on the basis of what benefits mothers needed in order to care for children.[28]

Analogously, maternalist policies in Sweden had intertwined religious and political origins. Waves of immigration between Sweden and the United States, popular folk movements such as the free church movement, temperance, and trade union activities, and religious enthusiasm turned secular provided fertile ground for the work of a thinker such as Ellen Key. Activists from evangelical organizations, temperance organizations, and the labor movement frequently overlapped—in fact, between 1911 and 1920, 84 percent or more of the Social Democratic members of the Riksdag were organized teetotalers.[29]

Sweden, also, would not have had its maternalist policies without the women's wing of the Social Democratic Party. When the agenda of the Social Democratic Party was almost set, women persisted in bringing family policy to the attention of its male leadership. Women's groups within the Social Democrats focused on the place "where the conflict between women's double burdens of care and breadwinning was most obvious—the issue of unmarried mothers."[30] Some women argued for "marriages of conscience" in order to circumvent women's being placed in men's legal guardianship at marriage. As early as 1910, Jan Groendahl noted that widows with small children were treated better than unmarried mothers and their children—"the children of the latter were often forcibly separated from their mothers. . . ." Women argued that mothers, rather than the "foster care industry," should care for their children. Motherhood outside of marriage was made viable in two ways: "making fathers assume their responsibilities, and promoting state intervention." Women argued that support for women as mothers should not carry the stigma of poor support but was as necessary as unemployment compensation. The theme of care and support for mothers and children recurs in Social Democratic politics of the 1900s until, in the 1970s, maternalist policies became gender-neutral family policies, specifically designed to involve fathers equally in domesticity.[31]

In Sweden, maternalist policy seems to have expanded where it could ride the coattails of paternalist policy for working-class men. Conversely, in the United States, "the failure during the Progressive Era of most proposals for workingmen's social benefits was a permanently defining moment in United States politics. . . . Along with other important factors, it ensured that the United States would never become a working-class oriented social democracy and blocked the development of a European-style welfare state."[32] Increasingly, maternalist policies became defined as poor-support.[33]

The Crosscurrents of Class and Race

People in the United States have sought to distinguish between worthy and unworthy poor women since colonial times, and often the distinction has been made on the basis of racial stereotypes. In her early work, Willard criticized women who bore children by drunkard husbands, and she characterized southern blacks as "multiplying like rabbits" and "dependent on the grog shop."[34] Even as maternalist policies developed, women and children in the United States who received public financial care carried the stigma of people who can't contribute to society or compete on their own behalf.

Swedish Social Democratic women wanted to address exactly this problem of conflating the meaning of poor support and public support. In particular, they wanted to resolve a social conflict that was put onto the backs of individual women. In the early twentieth century,

> there was a current of opinion condemning women as morally responsible for infant deaths. . . . The almost insurmountable difficulties many mothers faced in supporting and looking after their children were ignored. Mothers were at once seen as responsible and dependent: they were given the responsibility for the welfare of their children, while being economically and legally dependent and unfairly treated in a way that made it difficult to bear that responsibility. . . . To be at once powerless and held responsible for what one has no power over is most assuredly a common social mechanism for repression.[35]

In other words, the Social Democratic women wanted to use maternalist policy to solve a moral problem: inordinate vulnerability of unmarried mothers and their children. They wanted the values of the "People's Home" to extend to women and children, even when they were not being cared for by a man in their private homes. In the "People's Home," the values that government itself embraced should create a kind public family regardless of whether the family at home was benevolent.

Ironically, once poor support and public support were differentiated, the subtext of race relations worked on behalf of maternalist policy. In Sweden, maternalist policy became population policy under the leadership of the Myrdals in the 1930s. As Sweden made the transition from an agrarian to an industrial society, Swedish population declined. Demographers began to predict that Asians and Africans migrating to Sweden could make Swedes ethnically extinct within three hundred years. Proponents of pronatalist policies were able to use the Swedish people's racial fears to firmly institute maternalist policy as pronatalist "population policy."

Beyond Public and Private Patriarchy: A Homelike Society for Today

How does the political and religious, or civil religious, discourse of women in the past help us learn how to move beyond public and private patriarchy toward egalitarian families and society?

Most persons of our culture value intimacy within family life. Unlike Aristotle, they expect to find intimacy primarily with spouses and partners, and then among friends of either gender; like Aristotle, they find that equality enhances the possibility of intimacy. Intimacy is closely associated with what the nineteenth-century women would have called the values of the home. With intimates we hope that we can practice generosity, mutuality, care, and growth. We can delight in one another, be helpful to one another, and be accountable to one another—what Aristotle calls "living well together"—without being unnecessarily vulnerable. When we approximate justice in our home relationships, we provide an environment in which the more tender qualities of love can flourish.

Where some people seek love and intimacy, they find physical, emotional, and economic vulnerability. Families are still threatened by domestic violence, alcoholism and drug abuse, abandonment, lack of support after an out-of-wedlock pregnancy, poverty, and overwork. Families still struggle with stigmas based on stereotypes related to race and family structure. These problems are not traceable to any one source; rather, every aspect of society—the individual, the family, the church, corporations, the government—participates in them and must share the responsibility for resolving them.[36]

These problems persist even in a society in which women have achieved some of what Willard and Key wanted. Women today have legal, economic, and political independence. Women occupy an increasing number of leadership positions throughout society. Most women consider themselves no less sexual beings than men. Most women attend to their own spiritual and psychological growth, as do men. Women and men enter marital relationships by choice, rather than responding to economic and familial pressures. Women have created a wider range of life paths for themselves, and men are becoming more involved in domesticity. All of this has happened in a century when the federal government intentionally built a middle class out of the working class while giving some support to people at all levels of society. Most people agree that welfare programs in the United States need to be overhauled. Beyond that, some people argue for a strictly laissez-faire, not market/welfare, economy. In doing so, they want to deny the moral idea of governmental support—the idea that, on behalf of all citizens, the government to which we all contribute and which touches all of our lives should determine a level of minimum subsistence and distribute basic support. By doing away with the moral concept of welfare, that is, by denying that politics is an appropriate means of promoting the common good, we eliminate the socially connective metaphor of our government. Ironically, when conservative politicians, whose constituency is often evangelical, want to eliminate the concept of government "welfare," they are debunking the political and religious vision of evangelical women of a century ago.

We may be getting ready to cede the welfare state almost totally to market control. If we do so, we will have agreed that the untempered market should be the moral arbiter of our era. We may think we are agreeing to a new division between the private and the public, one in which the family and civil society, not government and economic institutions, is responsible for conveying caring values. If we listen to women's political and religious discourse, however, we must consider the possibility that government and the market are so capable of overwhelming the family and civil society that each must be held accountable to caring values. Reading Alan Wolfe, one senses that in the United States market values have had the power to shape not only families but also civil society.[37] Elsewhere, Richard Hester and I have documented exactly this process in what would seem to be one of the most altruistic of institutions, pastoral care and counseling.[38] If market values have already overwhelmed the family and civil society in the

United States, we may be witnessing the market's moral conquest against a stronghold whose dry bones have survived even when families and civil society have succumbed: the maternalist policies of the federal government.

If we lose the meaning of a homelike society or social motherliness, we abandon a vision of society that was so important to our foremothers that they spent their life energy for it. We forget the passion with which generations of women fought for their right to determine the paths and conditions of their lives without suffering society's stigma. We forget the conflict between production and reproduction: The fact that women and men cannot be two places at once, simultaneously earning a living while supervising children. We forget that the opportunities of family and home are intricately connected to the society in which families live. The unbridled market philosopher would again force women to resolve this conflict as individuals, without assuring that they can receive help from their families, civil society, workplaces, and government.

What would a homelike society mean in our time? Women's traditions have long held that the home is the moral school for society, and vice versa.[39] A century ago, as capitalism consolidated, our foremothers thought that the values of the home, including but moving beyond intimacy to social compassion, should push/resist the values of big business and the market. Not only civil society but also government and economic institutions would inevitably convey moral values—the only question was which set of values these structures should transmit. Ideally, government, civil society, and families need to be reclaimed as our common ways of caring for one another. Economic decisions need to be accountable to standards of human decency.

In a home, good parenting supports the self-determination of the most vulnerable dependents, whether they are young children or aging parents, while maintaining and valuing interdependence. In a homelike society, the metaphor of parenting needs to be recreated. The metaphors of mother and father need to be redeemed from their associations with patriarchalism and matriarchalism—or trading the parents' resources for control over their children's lives. Rather, parenting at its best liberates the dependents for both freedom and social responsibility. Children and parents together participate in determining the kind of support dependents and parents need to achieve their goals.

Most people recognize that homes are less than ideal. In a homelike society today, we would not want to romanticize individual families or reward only those who appear to be most successful, but to provide support for families to create good alternatives where problems exist.

Women and men could deal with the problems of family life by imagining many paths for their family. Through government we would provide some public support for these paths, recognizing that almost all of us in the middle class have benefited from our common pot through middle-class building programs such as social security, mortgage programs, public broadcasting, support for utilities, libraries, and roads. For some women and children, public assistance has also meant "welfare"—Aid for Families with Dependent Children (AFDC), Women, Infants, and Children (WIC), school nutrition programs, Head Start, and Medicaid.

Economic institutions and government could begin by reducing the pressure on intact, two-parent families so that as many as possible can survive. The market philosopher, as abetted by certain politicians, seems to think that reducing working hours to European standards (four weeks' vacation, longer lunch hours, shops closed in the evenings) would begin a slippery slope toward the "laziness" of people on public assistance. Yet others concerned with family life and children say that Americans work so much that we have too little time to raise children.[40] In a homelike society, we would rebalance time for love and employment. A flexible workplace would become the norm. If couples want to share domesticity, they each need a reduced workload. If one spouse cares for the home full time, he or she needs safeguards against losses of skills and benefits in case of a spouse's death or divorce. If single parents are to parent adequately and be employed, they need flexible work arrangements similar to those needed by an egalitarian couple. Binuclear and single-parent families would benefit even more than two-parent families by these innovations. A flexible workplace would go a long way toward reducing the effects of the market on families. Even so, civil society and government would provide important structural restraints against the power of the economy on families' vulnerabilities.

A homelike society would recognize that women's (and men's and children's) work has broader meaning than its market value. Women enter the labor force simultaneously acquiescing to and resisting the market in an effort to care for themselves and their families. Many women work longer than an eight-hour day at menial labor because they must contribute to the support of a family while also raising it. In that situation, a woman is pressured by market values with neither civil society or government providing an adequate buffer. At the same time, a woman's paid labor may also help her resist market values, even when her labor is determined by markets. Employment allows a woman to imagine many different paths for herself. She can choose among husbands or even choose whether or not to marry because she can provide her own support. She can contribute materially to her children's support, providing opportunities for them that she thinks important. Employment in desirable work is for the common woman what independent control over an inheritance is for the wealthy woman: Employment gives her an independent voice when conflicts arise between herself, husband or partners, and others. Desirable work contributes to desirable love, and vice versa. Both build a sense of psychological and social authority for a woman and allow a woman to enter, enjoy, and contribute to society and culture.

In a homelike society we would rethink the relationship between biological and social parenting and the home. Our biology—our embodiedness—has been too often construed either as determinative or as unimportant. Our bodies help to shape our worldview and our particular desires for love and work; but in order to work and love, we employ but also transcend our bodies.

A homelike society recognizes that the link between biological parents and children is important but not absolute. Many biological parents are the primary support for children. Their home is a social gathering place, a "family room" where extended family gather, where parents entertain their children's friends and children are enriched by friends of their parents. Social others come and go. But many biological parents are separated from their children, whether families are intact or binuclear. In good circumstances, children have the advantage of multiple homes. The binuclear family may introduce the issue of multiple homes into the child's life in the way that marriage and in-laws previously did. Sometimes, biological parents abandon their children. Multiple homes may exist, but children may not have access to them. Adult gays and lesbians, for example, have often created their own "homes" and "families" when their biological families have rejected them. When homes are destructive, a homelike society may need to provide social homes (adoptive homes, foster homes). If we examine biological families carefully, however, we find that they are not strictly biological: Most of us tend to create adoptive homes and family-type friends, or families of choice, while desiring positive connections—emotional or otherwise—with our biological families.

This homelike society, acknowledging that biology is both important and not absolute, would recognize the commonalities and particularities of races. African-American churches have kept the concepts of a homelike society alive in the traditions of "church mothers," or women who are respected as wise, and "play families," or family-like friends.[41] In womanist writings, the word "mother" has social and biological connotations. Ironically, the white, middle-class woman movement which feared and rejected concerns particular to women of color declined in strength, while people of color fought for an agenda with which many of the woman movement would have sympathized. The concept of homelike society owes a debt for the failures of its past, and this time would need to highlight the constructive contributions of the homes of people of color.

A homelike society recognizes the religious motivations of our generativity. Social motherliness includes what we would now more abstractly call generativity in work and love.[42] Generativity is the offering of our life to the society and the world we leave for the next generation of and beyond our biological kin. When commentators think of women's work and love only as market values infiltrating the family, or in terms of women's search for "individual self-fulfillment," they ignore the way work and love contribute to society. When we accept this interpretation, we are backed into a corner; we begin to believe others' definitions of our motives. Key and Willard remind us that whether or not women claim themselves as Christian, they often fight for desirable love and work from religious motivations—our vocation in love and work is our thanks to God for the gifts God has given us.

The proposals for a homelike society that I have offered here are only intended to be partial, based on a critical dialogue with women of a previous generation. This dialogue reminds us that a homelike society will be matriarchal or patriarchal if it is not genuinely democratic—a home to which many voices give shape.

NOTES

1. Linda Kerber, *Women of the Republic: Intellect and Ideology in Revolutionary America* (New York: W. W. Norton & Company, 1980), 119–20.
2. The ideas presented in this section are argued in more detail in Pamela D. Couture, *Blessed Are the Poor? Women's Poverty, Family Policy, and Practical Theology* (Nashville: Abingdon Press, 1991), 73–83.
3. Alan Wolfe, *Whose Keeper? Social Science and Moral Obligation* (Berkeley, Calif.: University of California Press, 1989), 57.
4. Ibid., 141.
5. Tim Tilton, "The Role of Ideology in Social Democratic Politics," in *Creating Social Democracy: A Century of the Social Democratic Labor Party in Sweden*, ed. Klaus Misgeld, Karl Molin, and Klas Amark (University Park, Pa.: Pennsylvania State University Press, 1992), 411–12.
6. Frances Willard, *Address Before the Biennial Convention of the World's Woman's Christian Temperance Union, and the Twentieth Annual Convention of the National Woman's Temperance Union* (Chicago: Woman's Temperance Publishing Association, October 16–21, 1893), 39.
7. Kari Borreson, *Subordination and Equivalence* (Washington, D.C.: University Press of America, 1981).

8. Frances Willard, *Glimpses of Fifty Years: The Autobiography of An American Woman* (New York: M. W. Hazen Co., 1889), 609–13.

9. Frances Willard, *Address, Third Biennial Convention* (London: White Ribbon Company, June 19–23, 1895), 6.

10. Ibid., 22.

11. Willard, *Address Before the Biennial Convention*, 53.

12. Peter Dobkin Hall, "The History of Religious Philanthropy in America," in *Faith and Philanthropology in America: Exploring the Role of Religion in America's Voluntary Sector* (San Francisco: Jossey-Bass, 1990), 42.

13. Willard, *Address, Third Biennial Convention*, 51–52.

14. Willard, *Address Before the Biennial Convention*, 52, 54.

15. Emilie M. Townes, *Womanist Justice, Womanist Hope* (Atlanta: Scholars Press, 1993); Emilie M. Townes, "Because God Gave Her Vision: The Religious Impulse of Ida B. Wells-Barnett," in *Spirituality and Social Responsibility*, ed. Rosemary Skinner Keller (Nashville: Abingdon Press, 1993).

16. Ian Tyrrell, *Woman's World, Woman's Empire: The Woman's Christian Temperance Union in International Perspective, 1880–1930* (Chapel Hill, N.C.: University of North Carolina Press, 1991), 196.

17. Willard, *Address, Third Biennial Convention*, 3.

18. Ian Tyrrell, *Woman's World, Woman's Empire*, 129–30; see also Couture, *Blessed Are the Poor?*, 153–54.

19. Mari Jo Buhle, *Women and American Socialism 1870–1920* (Urbana, Ill.: University of Illinois Press, 1981).

20. Nancy F. Cott, *The Grounding of Modern Feminism* (New Haven, Conn.: Yale University Press, 1978).

21. Ellen Key, *The Century of the Child* (New York: G. P. Putnam's Sons, 1909).

22. Ibid., 6.

23. Ibid., 35.

24. Ibid., 176.

25. Ellen Key, *Love and Marriage* (New York: G. P. Putnam's Sons, 1911), 84.

26. Ellen Key, *The Renaissance of Motherhood* (New York: G. P. Putnam's Sons, 1914), 135.

27. Theda Skocpol, *Protecting Soldiers and Mothers: The Political Origins of Social Policy in the United States* (Cambridge, Mass.: Belknap Press, 1992), 318.

28. Ibid., 315–17.

29. Allan Carlson, *The Swedish Experiment in Family Politics: The Myrdals and the Interwar Population Crisis* (New Brunswick, N.J.: Transaction Publishers, 1990) 3–11; Goran Thierborn, "A Unique Chapter in the History of Democracy," in *Creating Social Democracy*, 12–15.

30. Ann Sofie Ohlander, "The Invisible Child? The Struggle Over Social Democratic Family Policy," in *Creating Social Democracy*, 219.

31. Ibid., 219–20.

32. Skocpol, *Protecting Soldiers and Mothers*, 533.

33. Ohlander, "The Invisible Child?" 222.

34. Townes, *Womanist Justice, Womanist Hope*.

35. Ohlander, "The Invisible Child?" 214.

36. Couture, *Blessed Are the Poor?* 166–73.

37. Wolfe, *Whose Keeper?*

38. Pamela D. Couture and Richard Hester, "The Future of Pastoral Care and Counseling and the God of the Market," in *Pastoral Care and Social Conflict: Essays in Honor of Charles V. Gerkin*, ed. Pamela D. Couture and Rodney J. Hunter (Nashville: Abingdon Press, 1995).

39. For a contemporary version of this argument see Susan Moller Okin, *Justice, Gender, and the Family* (New York: Basic Books, 1989).

40. Richard Louv, *Childhood's Future* (New York: Doubleday, 1990).

41. Couture, *Blessed Are the Poor?* 152–53.

42. For a theological treatment of work and love see Bonnie J. Miller-McLemore, *Also A Mother: Work and Family as Theological Dilemma* (Nashville: Abingdon Press, 1994).

14

Family and Work

Can Anyone "Have It All"?

BONNIE J. MILLER-McLEMORE

> So when the woman saw that the tree was good for food, and that
> it was a delight to the eyes, and that the tree was to be desired to
> make one wise, she took of its fruit and ate; and she also gave some
> to her husband, who was with her, and he ate.
>
> —Gen. 3:6–7

When at the end of a sabbatical leave from teaching, I began this chapter with its assigned title, "Love and Work: Can Anyone 'Have It All'?" I experienced another wrinkle in my so-called desire to "have it all." At the congregation I attend with my husband and three sons, I had agreed to direct the Sunday School and teach a younger children's class as well as orchestrate the Christmas program. I had also agreed to lead a Junior Great Books group and to serve as art volunteer in my oldest son's second grade class. And, while any one of these activities alone would have sufficed, I was organizing parties and projects as room mother for my middle son's preschool. Unwittingly, I had become caught up in what one journalist calls the latest trend in education: parents-in-the-classroom and hence, "school-sponsored guilt trips." Besides full-time waged employment, cooking, cleaning, folding laundry, packing lunches, doing home repairs, "Supermom must now start teaching on the side"![1]

Why did I do this? Did I want to "have it all"? I volunteered for extra responsibilities partly because of my sabbatical. Perhaps I was paying my dues to my children, the school, and the church, in the intricate community network upheld mostly by "nonworking" women: dues for actually having forged a book out of the minutiae of such problems, *Also A Mother: Work and Family as Theological Dilemma*. It was almost as if I had to compensate for defying a claim I had quoted at the beginning of the book's preface, " 'A woman . . . either has children or writes books.' "[2] But I also wanted to participate in my children's lives. So I tricked myself into believing that I had enough time and energy, a common strategy for mothers who want to "have it all." Not surprisingly, I did not finish this chapter by the projected deadline.

While this variation on the theme of "having it all" is self-imposed and trivial in the overall scheme of life, I have come to recognize such daily, unrelenting personal conflicts as symptomatic of much broader patterns of work and family in our society. Distortions in these patterns must be better understood and challenged, and this chapter is one attempt to do so. Not only has the extra time taken to finish this chapter given me time with my family, it has deepened my reflections and sharpened my thesis: The more I think about the hackneyed cliché of "having it all," the more convinced I become about its ambiguous, deceptive, and even dangerous meanings, as well as the redemptive desire for human wholeness at its core.

The phrase "having it all" has acquired an assortment of moral connotations. On the one hand, aspirations to "have it all" assert that women have a right to have more than traditionally allotted them. When uttered with an increasingly negative and punishing tone, the implication of the phrase is that women want to "possess it all"—they want to have more than they should want or have. On the other hand, rather than acquiring, possessing, or having anything, women themselves often experience "having it all" as a "giving away" of themselves instead. Women continue to give and lose themselves to multiple competing demands. Under such circumstances, it would be more appropriate to talk about "doing it all."

Finally, "having it all" represents something other than inordinate desire. Embedded in the phrase is a positive, foundational claim that debunks work and family, self-love and love of others, self-fulfillment and self-sacrifice as false alternatives. Far from a distortion, the endeavor to "have it all" dares to suggest that women, like men, are created to love *and* to work. Central to the thesis of this chapter, the original ideals of shared responsibility for family and justice in the workplace merit retrieval as the kernels of truth behind the distortions and ambiguities of the phrase. My use of the phrase in this chapter varies between these three meanings, and is best determined by the context.

On the cover of *Also a Mother*, there is a reproduction of a painting entitled "Out of Reach, Daughters of Eve." In the book, I focus on the first phrase, "Out of Reach," but I do not explicitly discuss the second intriguing phrase, "Daughters of Eve." Although it may not seem so at first glance, women's identification with Eve and Eve's inordinate desire is intricately related to the issue of "having it all." Thus, after discussing some of the historical and cultural innuendos of the phrase itself, I will revisit the symbol of Eve, arguing for fresh psychological readings of maternal desire and fresh theological interpretations of Eve, desire, freedom, finitude, and redemption as important resources in tackling the dilemmas illustrated above.

One final comment before launching the discussion: Despite the mutuality of our marital partnership, my husband Mark will seldom, if ever, get asked to be "room *mother*" or "picture *lady*." Some schools try for "room parents" and "art volunteers," but the problem is not just linguistic. It concerns an entire way of constructing reality. Imagine a man writing an article about whether anyone can really have it all. People commonly assume that combining work and family poses few overt conflicts for men. In this sense, the dilemma itself represents an internalized, genderized oppression for many women. Until recently, "having it all" has been defined as a woman's dilemma. But as my comments will imply, this is a limited interpretation. Solutions to the dilemma of combining family and work necessarily involve men. A growing number of men today sense the loss in their lives that results when they leave relationships and family work to women. Thus, while my focus is primarily women, the issues for men are interrelated, every bit as complex, and deserve comparable treatment. (See the chapter in this volume by Rob Palkovitz.)

What Do Women Want?

The question of "having it all" arose as a peculiarly European-American, middle-class women's dilemma in the mid-twentieth century. The first women who thought about "having it all" were fighting powerful demons—a post–World War II North American mind-set that idealized the breadwinner husband, his homemaker wife, and the increasingly isolated suburban, nuclear household with its fascinating gadgets and fast foods. Behind this stood the nineteenth-century Victorian ideal of motherly domesticity, now firmly reentrenched after the period of World War II, during which many wives and mothers had worked in the defense industries. These images were bolstered by religious ideals of moral piety, sexual purity, and wifely submission, and were built on unspoken assumptions about class and ethnicity.

Although people acted as if everyone had always formed families in this way, these gender roles reflected twentieth-century Western ideals, and remained unattainable for most working-class and minority families. When the women's movement of the 1960s challenged the 1950s image of happiness and demanded something women had never had before—parity with men in the marketplace and in the household—

they were accused of unreasonably wanting to "have it all." Moreover, in seeking equal pay and shared family responsibilities, they neither anticipated the resulting emotional and social roadblocks nor understood how their challenge to sexism was blind to racist and classist superstructures that helped preserve structures of inequality.

Prior to the Industrial Revolution, European-American women did not "have it all," but some women seemed to have more than many women have today. Women have always held major responsibilities for family life, but in preindustrial times these responsibilities came with certain public claims. Women possessed indispensable skills, particularly as midwives and respected healers of the family and community. They produced clothes; they planted, pickled, and preserved food; they manufactured medicines, soap, and candles. Their participation in society, while under the rule of men, assumed an authority of its own, essential to the survival and well-being of the community. Women had vital work to do and contributions to make, however much this was directed by the edicts of men.

For many European-American women in the nineteenth century the Industrial Revolution displaced this authority and created what Barbara Ehrenreich and Deirdre English call the "Woman Question" or the "'woman problem.'"[3] The market economy shattered the previous unity of work and home and established a new world of work for men. Except for family farms and small family businesses, and for many people of color and the lower class, a line taut with moral tension arose between the public realm of waged work and the private realm of home. As women's productive activities were engulfed by the factory system, they lost a sphere of significant influence. Relegated to the increasingly restrictive domain of the home, many women lost their last few threads of connection to public life, and many men grew distant from family life. Without their former roles in the community's survival, women found themselves dependent on men for status, economic security, community, food, clothing, and recreation, and bound anew to the trivialities of daily home life. Hence the "women question"—What would become of women in the modern world?—became a gripping public issue in the late nineteenth and early twentieth centuries. Even then, it was a question implicitly asked about women from a certain class and ethnic group. Most minority and working-class women (and children) were too busy working long hours in factories and in domestic service at highly exploitative wages; hence they faced different problems of personal and community survival.

As the twentieth century closes, the question of "having it all" is simply one more variation on the European-American woman question with which the century began. Second-wave feminists—representing the period from approximately 1966—revolted against confinement and marched for equal opportunity. The ensuing rearrangement in domestic and economic life affected women's roles and identity as much as the Industrial Revolution did men's when it moved their work out of the home. Women have entered the work force at a rate of over a million women per year for the last decade, more than doubling the number of employed women since 1950. The number of married women in employed positions is more than five times what it was in 1940. In 1950 the Bureau of Labor did not even keep statistics on how many women with children under the age of one worked outside the home; today half of such women do. Overall, two-thirds of all mothers are now in the labor force.

Do these mothers "have it all"? Unfortunately, in many regards the phrase "having it all" is a romanticized, distorted, and even oppressive concept. Women have not come close to "having it all" if that means equity with men in the workplace and family. Women on average still make only about 70 cents for every dollar earned by men. Most have entered lower-paying occupations (clerical, sales, service, factory). Few have given up major domestic responsibilities, and many have added to their household chores. The statistically fastest growing family category in the United States is not the dual-career family for which the phrase "having it all" was primarily coined. This family type is far surpassed statistically by female-headed households of unwed or divorced mothers. Yet primarily white, married women with careers (as distinct from jobs) continue to receive an undue share of attention and acclaim for integrating family life and work. Glorified titles like "supermom" and "superwoman" are bestowed on them, while noncareer working women and single mothers are often blamed for the circumstances they must endure.[4] Typically, single mothers are not seen as "having it all" because they do not "have" a man. But in terms of managing households and holding down jobs, they are almost always trying to "do it all," often on low or poverty-level incomes.

When "having it all" really means "doing it all," it is a dubious honor at best. In many ways, the idea of "having it all" was doomed before it began. It arose within an economic and social system that viewed child-rearing, homemaking, and community life as "non-work," and which naively viewed market labor as almost completely independent of the labors of family and community. The dilemmas of work and family simply reveal the distortions in these views. Childrearing, housework, and community service are hard—and socially essential—work. Most women have always worked, many from the crack of dawn until long after sunset. They have provided enormous productive, reproductive, and maintenance labor, often with little or no compensation. In a word, they have controlled neither the extent nor the fruits of their labor. At the same time, the market economy has persisted in assuming that labor-power resides in lone individuals, neither hindered nor helped by personal relationships, marriage, or family commitments.[5] Yet, for most men, ability to put in a forty- to eighty-hour work week or to move across the country for a job promotion is heavily dependent on the clandestine labors of a "wife" who sustains home and community.

In trying to sustain work and family, middle-class women have finally glimpsed problems that working-class women and single mothers have always known and endured: What Arlie Hochschild popularized as the "second shift." In one study, working women "averaged three hours a day on housework while men averaged 17 minutes; women spent fifty minutes a day of time exclusively with their children; men spent twelve minutes." Based on studies on time use done in the 1960s and 1970s, Hochschild estimates that over a year women worked an "extra month of twenty-four-hour days."[6] In time-use studies done beyond the United States, the distortions are even more apparent. A 1980 United Nations report indicated that women worldwide perform two-thirds of the world's labor, receive ten percent of the pay, and own one percent of the property.

Many women do not face the dilemmas of "having it all," as they are extolled by the media and popular culture. Working-class women have had no choice but to manage reproductive and productive labors side by side, simply in order to survive. Besides gender discrimination, Asian-American, African-American, American Indian, and Hispanic mothers face racial and economic discrimination, which affects the ability of women and men alike to find satisfying, well-paid work. Men often receive less education, toil at manual labor, and face threats of homicide, substance abuse, crime, and incarceration. As a result, mothers have often had to be independent centers of strength, essential for the survival of the group and seldom confined to the private domain. Conflicts of family and home are interwoven with the problems of racism, and with dilemmas raised when the educational accomplishments and the employment rate for women are higher than that for men, or when the support system of extended family begins to break down, or when children are trapped by pervasive poverty.[7]

The pattern of working beyond the call of duty to secure the survival of children and family, as well as caring for white children, persists today.[8] The anguish of those striving to "have it all" does not make much sense and even seems elitist and uncaring to those robbed of the chance to establish safe, strong homes, or to those fighting to prepare their children for survival in a hostile and discriminatory environment.[9] The question of whether anyone can "have it all," therefore, has not been a pressing question for most women of color, poor women, lesbian women, and women in other countries. Their questions are more rightfully questions of having *anything at all*—questions of personal validation, of survival as a people and a community, and of securing a way where there is no way.

For different reasons, many upper-class women have also not encountered the plight of "having it all" experienced by the middle-class. Upper-class mothers who have desired creative, professional work and even those who do not seek paid work have often simply bought from those in lower economic brackets—housekeepers, live-in nannies, gardeners, caterers, decorators, and contractors—the home services needed to sustain family life. While money does not solve all of their internal and practical issues, it has helped many well-positioned women to avoid at least some of them. In so doing, such women perpetuate the illusion that reproductive labor requires no labor. And they approximate an ideal of "having it all" that actually depends on the labors of less well-situated women. Women's "liberation" in this vein simply shifts the weight of domestic chores "from one group of exploited women—mothers—to another group—the babysitter, housekeeper, cleaning woman, day-care staff, teacher."[10]

Hence, the dreamboat of "having it all" not only crashes up against the market distortions of human labor; it also cannot ignore the troubled waters of class and race across which it has so blithely sailed. Since many women who "want it all" have enjoyed the privileges of white society, they simply have not expected any resistance to their desires for equality. "Having it all" is a myth in a cultural and economic system that, as Rosemary Radford Ruether observes, "insists that women are equal, while at the same time structuring its economic and social life to make women economically dependent or marginal, as well as the primary parents."[11] And, I would add, in a racist society in which the gap between the "haves" and the "have nots" continues to grow (with women becoming an increasing percentage of the "have nots"), the ideal of "having it all" simply perpetuates a destructive ethos. As long as the workplace still expects the waged worker to have a wife or servant(s), as long as men remain no more willing to pick up the broom than their fathers were, as long as an underclass of women take care of the homes and children of those in the upper classes, we must contend with what Hochschild calls a "stalled revolution."[12]

How then might the "stalled revolution" be reinvigorated? Can any-one—woman or man, black or white—really sustain a fulfilling family and work life? Many current books on work and family advocate similar solutions. Ruether's list of needed changes in her essay on "Politics and the Family" is a good example, although she waxes slightly romantic about the possibilities of social reconstruction:

> Working mothers not only need good inexpensive day care, they need a restructured social order that locates home, school, nursery and work in some more coherent relationship to each other. They need a society that is rebuilding the organic supports around these realities of daily life, instead of asking the working man and woman to hold together this fragmented life through some monumental effort of self-extensions. Most of all, women need a society that promotes support for women and children by making it possible for fathers to be equal participants in the rearing of children and the building of homes.[13]

Obviously, these kinds of changes will depend on political decisions, economic policies, and social legislation which support children, parents, and a variety of current family forms. Proposals for "family-friendly" workplaces, increased tax exemptions for children, heightened paternal responsibility, and so forth, are critical.

Such solutions, however, must not sidestep cultural, moral, and theological considerations that are equally important. In *Also a Mother*, I argue that behind the middle-class struggle over "having it all" lies a fundamental religious question about the nature of the generative life. To challenge a society that has divided the burdens and rewards of family and work along gender and other lines, we must challenge psychological, biblical, and theological traditions that have been used to uphold these divisions. Something more than a revision of household roles and the construction of a family-friendly work environment is required for mutuality in contemporary families. Complex psychological, moral, and theological shifts are necessary.

Maternal Desire and Contemporary Psychology

One of my favorite cartoons features Freud reclining on his notorious couch pondering his famous question, "What does woman want?" Behind him, Mrs. Freud pushes a broom, looking somewhat perturbed. Pictured in the balloon of her own thoughts is Freud himself—sweeping! But Freud's own response missed the point. He proposed instead his own peculiar rendition of the biblical edict, "your desire shall be for your husband" (Gen. 3:16b). In his analysis, women's fulfillment lies in receiving from males what they lack by nature—a penis. Women who pursue their own creative desires, rather than experiencing them vicariously through fathers, husbands, or sons, simply have a "masculinity complex," an unnatural, unhealthy refusal to accept their castrated state. Fortunate women attain "normal femininity," a passive acceptance of biological fate and even masochistic, narcissistic resignation to a secondary role as dependents and spectators of male activity.[14]

Obviously, this view fails to deal with the realities of technology, industrialization, and democratization which have challenged the prized position of the penis and the sexual division of labor that was central to preindustrial and agrarian societies. In claiming scientific evidence for his theories about penis envy, however, Freud transformed a classic religious, symbolic depiction of female need and inferiority into an ontological fact. His theory captured the modern imagination for decades, and it has taken the work of women psychologists to begin to undermine its determinative power and to understand female desire.

This understanding has not come about easily. Analyst Karen Horney in fact suffered the neglect of academic and public attention precisely because she questioned orthodox psychoanalytic theory and Freud's view of female desire. While she acknowledges the existence of penis envy, she sees it as envy of social, not ontological or natural, superiority. Moreover, male attribution of penis envy to women is "not only a consequence of their fear of women; it is also a projection of their underlying envy" of the female capacity to bear children.[15]

Long before it became popular to do so, Horney tried to understand the pathology of wanting to "have it all" in women like herself—white, middle-class, and predominantly heterosexual women. She explored the contradictions of the "feminine type" of the 1920s, caught between the desire to please fathers and husbands and the desire to pursue her own ambitions:

> Women were permitted to pursue education but expected to become mothers. They were encouraged to be sexually emancipated but supposed to limit sexual desire to monogamous marriage combined with asexual motherhood. They were told that they could have careers but were expected to defer to men at work and at home. They were enticed by ambition but taught to find salvation in love.[16]

Horney's therapeutic goal—the "female hero"—directly opposes these stereotypical contradictions of "masculine civilization" with its presumed male superiority and female inferiority. The female hero assumes self-responsibility in claiming that she herself is worthy of care and that the world is her domain. Free of compliance to external demands and the resulting, culturally imposed neuroses, she experiences the power of her ordinary real self. Unfortunately, as needed as it was at the time, Horney's work did little to alter the bias against women at the heart of modern psychotherapeutic practice and culture.

More recent feminist psychologists have pushed their way into the therapeutic mainstream. They provide new resources for understanding female and maternal desire that help shed light on the European-American quandary of "having it all." In *Understanding Women*, feminist therapists Louise Eichenbaum and Susie Orbach construct a powerful psychoanalytical depiction of the demise of desire in female development. Many women (particularly European-American women—a distinction that neither Horney nor these authors make) inherit from their mothers a forceful interdiction against recognizing and enacting their desires, sexual and otherwise.

Drawing on the British Object Relations School, especially the work of Fairbairn, Winnicott, and Guntrip, Eichenbaum and Orbach's basic thesis is that the mother, having learned from her mother that her own desires are secondary to meeting the desires of others, systematically and often unwittingly teaches her daughter that "there is something wrong with her [and] her desires, something that needs to be kept at bay."[17] In so doing, the mother herself provides her daughter's first lesson in emotional deprivation and leaves her with a residual, repressed hunger for nurturance.

Their argument is based on years of therapy at the Women's Therapy Centre in New York, in which their women clients hesitantly reveal a part of themselves that is "needy and uncared for, undeserving, inadequate, and inarticulate."[18] On the one hand, women talk about their needs with contempt, humiliation, and shame. On the other hand, when inner needs are evoked, women are often flooded with anger, disappointment, depression, and feelings of rejection and isolation. For many women, it is less a question of struggling with distorted, deviant desires than identifying for themselves what they want at all.

Eichenbaum and Orbach identify three steps in a process that ensures the lost awareness of desire: (1) the mother identifies with her daughter because of their shared gender; (2) the mother projects onto the daughter her negative, fearful feelings about her own desires and aspirations; (3) the mother unconsciously acts toward her infant daughter as she acts internally toward the little-girl part of herself—with repugnance, fear, and disdain. On another level, the mother consciously knows that she must prepare the girl to live in a society that

expects girls and women to defer to others—to follow their lead, anticipate their needs, and articulate her own needs only in relation to theirs.

On a deeper level, this process leaves a woman with profound feelings of neediness. The infant daughter's fresh expression of her desires
unconsciously reawakens lost parts of the mother that feel needy and
want nurture, response, and encouragement. This reawakening leaves
the mother subconsciously aware of her own deprivation—resentful,
disapproving, and "annoyed with the child for displaying her needs and
for not controlling them as she herself does."[19] A daughter's expression
of needs and wants causes a restlessness and discomfort in the mother
that the same expression on the part of a son does not.

The mother conveys and the daughter learns a double message:
Don't be too emotionally dependent; don't be too independent. Don't
expect others to meet your needs; don't expect to find avenues to meet
your needs yourself. Consciously, the mother pushes the daughter to
look to a man for emotional involvement. Unconsciously, she conveys
the message that she must not expect a man to meet her needs or really
understand them. On the one hand, a woman feels afraid of her emotional needs and dependencies. At the same time, she feels fearful and
guilty about her aspirations for an independence and power that would
allow her to meet her own needs. Female desire therefore is effectively
confused, debunked, repressed, and nearly obliterated. The mandate to
curb one's desires, to split off needs, and not to expect response to
them, becomes endemic to the psyche of many females. And the
"daughter, as she learns to hide her needy little-girl part, becomes
extremely sensitive to neediness in others."[20] Such daughters, one
might assume, make good, sensitive mothers.

Or do they? Not really, contends psychoanalyst Jessica Benjamin,
another feminist object-relations theorist and clinician. In fact, because
mothers continue to hide their desires from others and from themselves, the complex system of domination and submission between
women and men is perpetuated. Her book, *The Bonds of Love*, investigates both the inner and social workings of domination. Is domination
inevitable? Or is a relationship in which "both participants are subjects—both empowered and mutually respectful" possible?[21]

Benjamin's case for the latter is based most centrally on reclaiming
female, maternal desire and what she calls a lost "subjectivity." She follows some of the same lines of thought as Eichenbaum and Orbach but
goes further in developing a constructive, normative social agenda. She
not only analyzes the demise of female desire; she makes mutuality her
normative center and follows this ideal into society at large to challenge
its gender inequities in spite of its stated commitment to equality. In

this agenda, she is less concerned with the child's and the daughter's development and more focused on the mother's—an unusual stance for any therapeutic theory thus far.

Benjamin traces the structure of domination and the demise of mutuality back to the tension between dependence and independence in infant life. The ideal balance between the human need for self-assertion (or the desire to be recognized) and the need to recognize the other all too easily collapses into the familiar polarities of destructive rulership and self-annihilating sacrifice. When reinforced by gendered differences in parenting styles—the exciting, assertive "father of liberation" versus the holding, nurturing "mother of dependency"—the child quickly associates masculinity and femininity with these two different postures. Thus the tension between dependence and independence that actually lies *within* the person gets recast as a conflict *between* women and men.

While this is a highly technical analysis, the important point is this: According to Benjamin, domination will end and mutuality begin when the "other makes a difference."[22] In a word, mothers must claim their subjectivity. Balancing the recognition of the child's needs with the assertion of the mother's needs—thus far "scarcely put forward as an ideal"—is exactly what is required. In other words, in order for the child to receive the recognition that the child seeks, the mother must have an "independent center . . . outside her child."[23]

> Only a mother who feels entitled to be a person in her own right can be seen as such by her child, and only such a mother can . . . permit full differentiation. This fact has been remarkably elusive. It seems intolerable to the narcissism of adults and children alike that the limits a mother sets should not merely be an occasional dose of medicine corresponding to the child's needs, but might actually proceed from the mother's assertion of her own separate selfhood.[24]

Just as it is necessary to put the ideal of maternal pursuit of desire and selfhood forward, it is equally essential according to Benjamin to restore the missing father as a nurturer, as someone with whom sons and daughters can identify, and as a person who models respect for the mother's subjectivity. Fathers and mothers must both become models of separation *and* attachment for their children. These changes, Benjamin claims, would realign the process of development, mitigate the hazardous polarization of gender roles, and in particular avoid the creation of destructive systems of domination.

It is hard to believe that Benjamin could take up the problem of domination without even mentioning racial and ethnic domination (her chapter on "Master and Slave" is simply a case-study analysis of Pauline Réage's *Story of O*) or without a sense that the familial relationships she describes are primarily based on European-American experiences. She is also oblivious to some of the practical impossibilities of her recommendations in the actual lives of mothers and children, to the limits of her attempted social analysis, and to the complex ethical and religious assumptions and implications of her work. Mutuality is not only an emotional construct that refers to emotional attunement; it is also an ethical and religious concept that requires both self-giving love and social justice. Without an analysis of human evil, vulnerability, and fallibility in the realization of these ideals, and without an analysis of other forms of domination, Benjamin's optimistic visions for eliminating domination are naive, and at times almost eschatological.

Nonetheless, while Eichenbaum and Orbach help us understand the psychic and social destruction of female desire, Benjamin justifies the importance of maternal desire to "have it all" in the best sense of the phrase. Her analysis captures the dangers of parental inequality and provides a much-needed developmental theory for genuine mutuality—showing both how it has been thwarted in distorted gender relations between mother and father and how it might evolve in a changed psychological and social context. She makes a strong psychological case that parents must be equal; each parent must sustain the tension between "sexual cross-identification" and provide an example of integration rather than complementarity.[25]

In this context, the cultural shame directed toward those women who dare to "want it all" (prodded along by media headlines such as "'90s Choices: Balanced Life Preferred to 'Supersuccess' ") is particularly cruel.[26] It plays facilely and harshly on the heartstrings of young women who are already prone to sacrificing internal inclinations about themselves, their abilities, their loves, and their desires to social and marital conventions. Daughters quickly learn to blame themselves for the failure to balance work and family, and to pull back from wanting so much when, in actuality, they want so little and the problems are far from theirs alone.

Re-imagining Eve:
A Theological Task

For women, desire of one's own has had a long history of being covertly yet strictly forbidden. Over the centuries of Christian interpretation, Eve has stood for wrong and misdirected desire. Ecclesiastical and theological traditions have upheld and solidified this tradition by interpreting agapic love as unconditional self-sacrifice. Many women have taken these interpretations of love and of Eve's culpability to heart. In a penitent, compensatory, and committed manner, they give of themselves willingly, relentlessly, and sometimes fiendishly.

Elaine Pagels observes that the archaic creation narrative wields such "an extraordinary influence upon western culture" that she herself is "surprised to discover how complex and extensive its effect has been."[27] For generations, creation stories have shaped human hopes for procreation, work, marriage, and human striving. While I do not attempt the sort of exegesis better performed by biblical scholars, I do want to suggest some alternative ways of thinking about Eve as important to tackling the conundrums of "having it all."

How culpable is Eve? Does she want to "have it all?" The narrative in Genesis 3 is driven by two powerful, interrelated energies with Eve at their center: healthy, vital human desire and misguided, distorted desire. On the one hand, Augustine's classic reading of the narrative of the "Fall" has been used throughout Christian history to blame women for evil and suffering and to condemn sexual desire as unnatural, contrary to divine will, and the result of human sin. On the other hand, the distinction between misdirected and properly directed desire on which he based an entire theology is both important and helpful. Although Augustine gave women a subsidiary, less favored role within his theology, his acknowledgment of the power and the place of desire in religious life was psychologically and theologically insightful.

In the second creation account in Genesis 2—3, human desire itself is part of the goodness of creation, even if what humans desire and how they pursue their desires leads to ill and evil results. In this context, the act of the woman in taking and eating and offering the fruit of the tree to her husband is understandable. It is hard to see how the woman's response could have been otherwise. It is not the nature of her desire that is wrong, it is the degree and extent of it.

That Eve becomes carried away in her desire to "have it all" becomes clear in the three-part movement of the clause that describes the rationale behind her decision. She saw (1) "that the tree *was* good for food" and (2) "that it *was* a delight to the eye" (Gen. 3:6, emphasis added). Both are appropriate observations. They capture the appeal that fosters healthy desire. It is in the last clause that a deeper note of ambiguity creeps in and the moral scale tips. She wants the fruit for yet another purpose. Finally, the woman saw "that the tree was to be desired to make one wise"—or, as the serpent has implied, to make one "like God." She knows she is wise; she wants to be wiser still, like God, omnipotent and complete. And "she took of its fruit and ate."

Lurking in her thoughts is a dissatisfaction with divine creation. She is not what she might be or could be; she suspects she could be otherwise, made better or wiser somehow. In the goodness of the human capacity "to desire" lies the penchant not just to desire, but to doubt, worry, covet, crave, envy, and forever increase what is desired. Desire for the rich goodness of created life gives way to a disregard for divinely ordered limits on creation and a drive for invincibility.

Rather than being the temptress, the source of evil and suffering, or the point of weakness, here the woman is "quintessentially human." "To be the curious one, the seeker of knowledge, the tester of limits," observes biblical scholar Susan Niditch, is to be "quintessentially human—to evidence traits of many of the culture-bringing heroes and heroines of Genesis." On this score, the woman assumes the role of central protagonist in the narrative, deliberating along the fault lines of sensual, intellectual desire. She is, in Niditch's words, "no easy prey for a seducing demon," but a "conscious actor choosing knowledge" and bringing in culture.[28] Yet desire carries the passionate human beyond the reasonable limits of human need and order as divinely created.

Why this exegesis? In this moment of Eve's deliberation, we see an intersection of relevant theological themes ignored in most treatments of "having it all"—freedom, limitation, and the necessity for divine correction and redemption. Humans are created with a divine mandate to "be fruitful and multiply, and fill the earth and subdue it" (Gen. 1:28). They are created to eat and to enjoy the delights of creation, to till the garden, to cleave to one another without restraint or fleshly shame. Yet in the midst of the garden of possibilities there are limits. These are not always obvious; they are sometimes arbitrary and even inherently tempting. In the narrative of Genesis 2, for example, Yahweh gives little explanation as to why the fruit of one tree rather than another must not be eaten.

The failure to recognize human limits is part of human sinfulness. And the failure to divide the responsibilities of creation and procreation justly among women and men is a consequence of this. When such limits are transgressed, the naturally given impulses for work and love become perverted, painful, beleaguered, and destructive. Inevitably, but not irredeemably, women who aspire in a positive sense to "have it all" go one step too far: Their acquisitiveness turns being into having, sharing into owning, growing into getting. For many women and men, today's danger is not the struggle to choose "generativity (procreativity, productivity, creativity) over self-absorption and stagnation," as identified by life-cycle theorist Erik Erikson.[29] The prime crisis and task of contemporary adulthood in the United States is more often "generativity versus fragmentation"—that is, excessive self-extension, and exhaustion. In contrast to the problems of self-indulgence that Erikson postulates, the problem is self-loss and the inability to establish just and appropriate limits to human desire. A prominent challenge and temptation of the adult stage of the life cycle is the lure of over-scheduling, over-commitment, and over-extension. A consistent, sometimes boastful, complaint seems to cut across gender, class, race, and age: not having enough time, being so terribly busy.

Just as North American society has denied death, the penchant to "have it all" refuses to acknowledge finitude. In adulthood one must focus one's generativity on a limited number of areas. Freedom to choose, to decide—in Latin *decidere*—means "to cut off." The perennial temptation is to refuse to relinquish what cannot be, to step beyond creation's boundaries, to seek more than can be humanly cared for—to want to become "like God" by "having it all." In this sense, no one can or should "have it all." "Having it all" is at heart a theologically misleading modern premise. The economics of buying and having, in Dorothee Soelle's interpretation, have inappropriately replaced "religion as 'the ultimate concern'."[30] As a result, relationships are undermined, work is subverted, and desire is deadened.

Yet "Daughters of Eve" who have desired too much have also glimpsed the new heaven and the new earth. They have recognized that work versus family, creation versus procreation, self-love versus love of others, self-fulfillment versus self-sacrifice are sets of "false alternatives." In Adrienne Rich's experience, the choice has

> seemed to be between "love"—womanly, maternal love, altruistic love—a love defined and ruled by the weight of an entire culture; and egotism—a force directed by men into creation, achievement, ambition, often at the expense of others, but justifiably so.[31]

In these terms, "Daughters of Eve" refuse to choose. In seeking ways in which "the energy of creation and the energy of relation can be united" (as they have seldom been in the history of masculine civilization) they reach for what may be the unreachable, but redemptive, possibilities of human livelihood.[32]

Work and love are the essence and goal of human creation and Creation itself. All humans were created for good work and good love. Good work means "fruitful, enjoyable, rewarding work" not based on the commodification of the marketplace but on attaining full personhood, relating to others, nature, and the world.[33] Good love preserves the subjectivity of the other and the human potential for mutuality. It expresses the human project of liberation—its wholeness in solidarity with others—with erotic, bodily love a symbol of the call to communion, and children a God-given blessing. Humans are gifted with freedom, with worth and value as human beings created to work and to love. Human failure to work and to love thus leads to the question of the nature of human salvation. To hope for the elimination of the "false alternative" is to hope for the "not yet," the coming of the kingdom in this world. Thus, in a way, even misplaced desire to "have it all" is attuned to the goodness of God.

In this sense, then, the desire to "have it all" is not wrong or evil in and of itself. The phrase has nipped at women's heels for decades, doggedly accusing "high-demand" women of wanting too much. "Daughters of Eve" have accordingly felt reprimanded, guilty, and shamed, like Eve, for their apparently inordinate desires. Economic and social structures have further made it seem that the possibility of some women "having it all" depends on the exploitation of other women to keep house, raise children, and service the elderly. Yet, while "having it all" is a cliché bogged down in racist, classist, sexist, and materialistic waters, the ideals of human worth, freedom, and fulfillment from which it sprung remain revolutionary.

A corrected interpretation of "having it all" must restore appropriate responsibility to men, local community institutions, the workplace, government, and public policymakers. Moreover, a corrected interpretation must grasp the nature of human desire in the best sense of God's intention, and will depend on God's intervening grace to guide and correct human distortions in work and families. "Daughters of Eve" have discerned a hope at the heart of God's grace that blesses love and work as endeavors to be celebrated, shared, and safeguarded as part of human creation and redemption for both men and women. Women should not be blamed for their unrealistic expectations or their failure to work it all out, nor seen as fools or guilty of wanting too much when their problems are quite relative to a particular moment in history that has forced both a false separation between paid work and family care, and an unnatural divorce between work and love, which belong together. "Daughters of Eve" and their supporting men discern and practice a truth about human fulfillment that has religious and moral roots: They have made democratic, egalitarian relationships of justice and mutuality in the family and in the workplace a priority.

NOTES

1. Barbara Brotman, "And While You're at it, Get Started on the Pyramid," *Chicago Tribune*, 5 April 1994.
2. Bonnie J. Miller-McLemore, *Also a Mother: Work and Family as Theological Dilemma* (Nashville: Abingdon Press, 1994), 13.

3. Barbara Ehrenreich and Deirdre English, *For Her Own Good: 150 Years of the Experts' Advice to Women* (New York: Doubleday, 1978), 3.

4. Rosanna Hertz, *More Equal Than Others: Women and Men in Dual-Career Marriages* (Berkeley, Calif.: University of California Press, 1986), 4–5.

5. Ulrich Beck, *Risk Society: Towards a New Modernity*, trans. Mark Ritter (London: Sage Publications, 1992), 103–50.

6. Arlie Hochschild with Anne Machung, *The Second Shift: Working Parents and the Revolution at Home* (New York: Viking Penguin, 1989), 3–4.

7. Audrey B. Chapman, "Male-Female Relations: How the Past Affects the Present," in *Black Families*, 2d ed., ed. Harriet P. McAdoo (Beverly Hills, Calif.: Sage Publications, 1988), 190–200; Marian Wright Edelman, "An Advocacy Agenda for Black Families and Children," in *Black Families*, 286–95; Donald Matthews, "The Black Child as Social Problem," *Journal of Religious Thought* (summer 1988): 70–78.

8. Evelyn Nakano Glenn, "From Servitude to Service Work: Historical Continuities in the Racial Division of Paid Reproductive Labor," *Signs* 18:1 (autumn 1992): 1–43.

9. Marie Ferguson Peters, "Parenting in Black Families with Young Children: A Historical Perspective," in *Black Families*, 236–38.

10. Bonnie J. Miller-McLemore, "Let the Children Come," *Second Opinion* 17:1 (July 1991): 12.

11. Rosemary Radford Ruether, "Church and Family IV: Recapturing a Lost Issue," *New Blackfriars* (April 1984): 178.

12. Hochschild, *Second Shift*, 12.

13. Rosemary Radford Ruether, "Politics and the Family: Recapturing a Lost Issue," *Christianity and Crisis*, 29 September 1980, 266.

14. Sigmund Freud, "Female Sexuality," in *Sexuality and the Psychology of Love*, ed. Philip Rieff (New York: Collier Books, 1963), 200–201.

15. Marcia Westkott, *The Feminist Legacy of Karen Horney* (New Haven, Conn.: Yale University Press, 1986), 54.

16. Ibid., 50–51.

17. Louise Eichenbaum and Susie Orbach, *Understanding Women: A Feminist Psychoanalytic Approach* (New York: Basic Books, 1983), 43–44.

18. Ibid., 40.

19. Ibid., 43–44.

20. Ibid., 140.

21. Jessica Benjamin, *The Bonds of Love: Psychoanalysis, Feminism, and the Problem of Domination* (New York: Pantheon Books, 1988), 8.

22. Ibid., 68.

23. Ibid., 24.

24. Ibid., 82.

25. Ibid., 114.

26. Gail Scmoller, "'90s Choices: Balanced Life Preferred to 'Supersuccess,'" *Chicago Tribune*, Sunday, 8 September 1991, sec. 6.

27. Elaine Pagels, *Adam, Eve, and the Serpent* (New York: Random House, 1988), xix.

28. Susan Niditch, "Genesis," in *The Women's Bible Commentary*, ed. Carol A. Newsom and Sharon H. Ringe (Louisville, Ky.: Westminster/John Knox Press, 1992), 13–14. See also Phyllis Trible, "Eve and Adam: Genesis 2—3 Reread," in *Womanspirit Rising: A Feminist Reader in Religion*, ed. Carol P. Christ and Judith Plaskow (New York: Harper & Row, 1979), 79; Adrien Janis Bledstein, "The Genesis of Humans: The Garden of Eden Revisited," *Judaism* 26:2 (spring 1977): 187–200.

29. Erik H. Erikson, *The Life Cycle Completed: A Review* (New York: W. W. Norton & Co., 1982), 67; and his *Childhood and Society*, 2d ed. (New York: W. W. Norton & Co., 1950, 1963), 267.

30. Dorothee Soelle with Shirley A. Cloyes, *To Work and To Love: A Theology of Creation* (Philadelphia: Fortress Press, 1984), 118.

31. Adrienne Rich, *On Lies, Secrets, and Silence: Selected Prose 1966–1978* (New York: W. W. Norton & Co., 1979), 46–47.

32. Ibid., 43.

33. Soelle, *To Work and To Love*, 76.

15

Sacrificial and
Parental Spiritualities

CHRISTINE E. GUDORF

A little over ten years ago, I published an essay called "Parenting, Mutual Love and Sacrifice" in which I objected to the common understanding of both Christian love in general, and parental love in particular, as self-sacrificial.[1] The framework of the essay was autobiographical; it focused on the insights gleaned from parenting three sons, two of whom were medically handicapped children of Hispanic and African-American background adopted by a couple of Northern European descent. I argued that my abnormal parenting situation served to illuminate more universal issues in parenting, which was, I insisted, a relationship based in the pursuit of mutuality, and not an essentially self-sacrificial exercise as so often portrayed.

The intervening years have not radically altered the direction of my thinking. But I have learned as much from the second decade of parenting as from the first, both deepening the lessons of the first decade, and learning completely new lessons. Moreover, in the process of publishing that earlier essay a major problem in publicly theologizing from one's life became clear: One's life is never just one's own life but involves the lives of others. My sons at the time of publication were sixteen, ten, and seven—certainly old enough to have a say in deciding how much of their story should be public. Soon after publication of the essay I worked out a process with my sons: I would publish nothing that mentioned them without first submitting it to them. They had full editorial power, including outright veto. My sons are now 27, 22 and 19, and while I am sure our agreement has caused me to censor quite a bit before I even submitted it to them, they have never vetoed any piece, and have seldom demanded changes. (They reason that few of their friends are likely to read the books and journals to which I contribute!) The issue of protecting their privacy seems to loom larger with me as they grow older, and why that should be has been an important question in my personal reflection. Was my greater disregard for younger

children's privacy rights because children only acquire rights to privacy
as they near adulthood? Or because younger children do not care so
much about privacy? Or because they were not likely to accuse me of
violating their privacy until they were older? I am not sure; I am
uncomfortable probing this behavior of mine.

In addition to the issue of my children's privacy, three areas for
reflection have arisen from my husband's and my parenting experience
over the last decade. The first concerns the complex interaction
between parenting one's children and the stages of one's own adult
development, especially the relationship between parenting and the
adult need/desire to resolve leftover tensions with one's own parents.
The second concerns the way sacrificial notions of parenthood function
as an ideological cover for patriarchy. The third involves the implications of sacrificial parenthood for understanding the God/human relationship. I will deal with each of these in turn.

Parenting and
Stages of Adulthood

There are a variety of ways of categorizing stages in adult life; many
contemporary schemas divide male and female adulthood separately.[2]
Some categorizations focus more on stages as marked by occupation:
education, career steps, and retirement for men, or work, pregnancy,
childcare/housework, work, and retirement for women. Other categorizations focus more on internal preoccupations, as in identity formation, competency issues, aging, loss of one's parents, and preparation for
death. Different schemas are useful for different angles of investigation.

Over the last decade my husband Frank and I have noticed the
tremendous impact of adult development issues on our parenting.
Married very young (at age nineteen), we were very conscious of fleeing
what we saw as well-meaning and conscientious but overly controlling
parents. Although childless until twenty-five, we then began with both
an adopted five-year-old and a new baby. Because we had left our families early and then put great geographical distance between us and
them, it was not until the second decade of our parenting that either of
us began to deal with the nitty-gritty issues left over in us from our own
families of origin. On the home front we were dealing with emotional
pyrotechnics from our oldest son, then in his mid-teens, over what
were to him issues of "freedom" but which seemed to us issues of
"responsibility." Of chief importance to us was his safety; at this time we
had been periodically fighting for years with him over his insistence
that "being normal" was important enough to justify major risks (e.g.,

contact sports) to his solitary and dying kidney. Most of the tensions between us embodied typical parent/teen issues (use of the car, evening curfew, attendance at events with alcohol, grades, an earring) but were placed within a context dominated by his precarious health.

About the same time two events occurred that made us independently begin to grapple with the parental relationships about which we both felt such ambivalence. Frank's father became seriously ill, never fully recovered, and died a few years later. For myself, having achieved my relatively modest career goals, I began a mid-life crisis that involved returning to unfinished identity issues connected to my own parents.[3] It is not important here to rehearse the steps in our dealing with these parental issues. Most middle-aged adults have similar stories, for in mid-life virtually all of us are forced to look back and grapple with our feelings about the parenting extended to us. If we are fortunate we are able to forgive our parents whatever injuries we felt they dealt us as children, and to establish with them different, more peerlike relationships to replace the earlier ones based on their power and our dependence. If we are very lucky we can complete this process before we have to deal with increasing dependence and the death of our parents. If we were *not* fortunate in our parents, dealing with them in middle age will involve abandoning any remaining hopes we have that they will both repent of the serious injuries they inflicted and love us as we desire.[4]

My husband and I recognized that finally dealing with longstanding ambivalent feelings toward our own parents had a dramatic impact on our own parenting. For one thing, dealing with our own parents made so many elements in our own parenting clearer. We became aware that we were in a power struggle with our oldest son, and that in some strange way we were continuing our own adolescent struggle for freedom and power over our lives by attempting to curtail our son's struggle for control over his life. We were, in effect, validating the earlier efforts of our parents to control us. It became much clearer to us why interaction with our oldest quickly became so irrational and explosive. On his part, our son's threatening medical situation made him desperate to assert some control over his own life. As we dealt with our parental relationships we began to understand not only why Frank had threatened to kick our son Victor out of the house forever when he came home with a pierced ear, but also why Victor had had the ear pierced when he really didn't even like pierced ears, and why he wore the earring only until the opposition ceased at home.

In wake of the new clarity regarding our own parents, our parenting looked very different. We began to see that the emotional fireworks had emanated from us (especially me) as well as from our oldest. We had never come to terms with his precarious health, and had convinced our-selves that our attempts to control his activities were protecting him. We also began to understand that his way of dealing with his emotional scars about being abandoned and adopted was to act out a resistence aimed at pushing us to our limits in order to test our commitment to him. As we came to establish more adult relationships with our parents, we came to see how juvenile some of our behavior with our oldest had been.

Our second son, who is six years younger than the first, had a very different experience with us. While the first son was more like us in temperament, challenging us with an in-your-face kind of defiance, the second son was less confrontational—a much more successful strategy with us. In some ways they were the two sons of the gospel parable—the older son always said no, waited until we were throughly provoked, then grumbled as he did what was asked, while the second son always agreed, and then often "forgot" to do what was asked.

But the biggest difference in our parenting these two was that we developed a much broader perspective for decision making, and we changed parenting paradigms. Where earlier we had insisted on stick ing strictly to the issue at hand (the specific permission desired, or the particular infraction of the rules), now we were more likely to include in our reflection our overall relationship with our son and his develop-mental progress, and were also more likely to engage in dialogue with him about his feelings and desires. With the greater dialogue came a feeling that we knew him better, knew his strengths and weaknesses, and were able to loosen up on a variety of issues that were not problems for this particular child. With the first child, by contrast, we made our judgments on the basis of much more abstract generalizations about, for example, what seemed a "reasonable" curfew for a seventeen-year-old, based on our stereotype of seventeen-year-old males.

To our children, of course, the explanation is either that we "mellowed out" (as the second son insists) or that we "gave up" (as the oldest son sees it). There is no doubt that we were fairer with the second son than with the first; the second son got credit for his strengths, and the first son didn't. For example, the second son is really a good driver (much better than I) and was encouraged to take on many of the family driving tasks. This, of course, gave him more or less permanent access to a car, which we had denied his brother. The oldest son was much more extroverted and confiding; the second son was more reserved. We knew the friends of our oldest son, saw them often at our home, usually knew where he could be found, and were often treated to accounts of his outings. Our second son, being much more reserved, kept his friends and all information about his activities from us, and tended to interpret any interest in his activities as interference. Nevertheless, we gave the second son much greater freedom than the first, since he arrived in his mid-teens about the time we recognized and began reversing the controlling character of our earlier parenting.

We have only recently come to see that our oldest interprets our shift of parenting paradigms as a lack of resolution on our part; moreover, he retains the traditional paradigm of parenthood as control of children. He has convinced himself that our earlier efforts at controlling him were motivated by benevolence alone, and is, to our dismay, poised to parent his own children in the same way.

One other impact that resolving our relationships with our parents had on our own parenting concerned the kind of pressure we put on our children to excel. Once we no longer felt the need to earn the parental respect and love we desired but had never felt assured of, we were able to be much more accepting of who our children were and what they wanted for themselves. We ceased to see them as extensions of ourselves who must participate in our search to prove our own worth. For example, we had put great academic pressure on both older sons. For the oldest son we claimed it was for his own good; since his health would restrict his choice of careers, he needed to do well in school. Ironically, it was not until we entirely ceased applying academic pressure that the first son returned to college and graduated, after having flunked out in his freshman year. In the same way, ending the pressure on the second son to achieve in school freed him to complete high school (which for a time had looked doubtful) and then to begin to achieve in college in a way that he never had in high school.

When I get together with my eight younger siblings to talk about our childhoods, a similar pattern emerges. My parents' initial parenting was rooted both in stereotypes about children and in their own unresolved childhood relationships with their parents. For them the second stage of parenting was explosive; it peaked when they were dealing with five daughters aged 16–22, four sons aged 11–14, a cross-country career move, and a medical crisis. It culminated in all five daughters permanently leaving home at the ages of 16–19. The third stage began after all the daughters were gone. My brothers experienced great freedom—some would even say neglect. They felt a lack of parental interest; "they just got tired of parenting" was the common interpretation. Yet by their mid-twenties my brothers had developed a relationship with our father based on shared respect for the construction skills he had taught them and for their work in his construction projects during their high school and college vacations. Parental pride in my brothers' academic achievement and later career success added to this foundation.

Such shifts in parenting occur not only with minor children. After the death of my father-in-law, my mother-in-law's way of interacting with her five adult (35+) children radically altered. My father-in-law had been dying for five years; her deep mourning after his death was relatively brief. Within six months she was ensconced in a group of twenty widows whose busy social calendar revolved around quilting for charity, attending church services, taking communion to nursing homes, playing cards, and eating out. No one recognized this new social butterfly who was never home, and who now joked (!) about how long it had been since she cleaned her house. But the most dramatic changes were that she seemed happier than anyone had ever known her, and she no longer manipulated her children through tears, silent sulks, or incessant harangues. This new behavior was celebrated by her children at the same time that it prompted in them both uneasy feelings of being unloved and uncomfortable questions as to what postponed the change until she was over seventy. But there is general consensus that she treated her adult children as adults only after she felt free to leave home and socialize as she wanted.

It would be overly simplistic to conclude that people should wait and have children later in life, when issues from their own childhood may be better resolved. This would help some but not all of us; our parenting responds to the particular stage of adult growth that we are in, whatever that may be, and people enter these different stages at a variety of ages. Moreover adults never reach a stage at which all developmental tasks are completed; all the stages of adult development can potentially support or interfere with effective parenting. What is important is recognizing the stage of development we are in, and understanding how it affects our relationship with our children.

Sacrificial Parenthood as a Mask for Patriarchy

Our culture seems to socialize us to see our parenting as sacrificial. How often do we hear parents speak of "how much I have done for that child?" It is true that parenthood in the postmodern age is more materially demanding. Children became expenses rather than economic assets as families shifted from agricultural to urban settings, and the degree of expense has continued to rise ever since. For families who must factor into the cost of childrearing four or more years of college education and expensive medical and dental care in addition to the ordinary expenses of food, clothing, and shelter, there is little doubt that parenthood involves at least some economic sacrifice. On the other hand, the presence of sacrifice within a relationship does not make that relationship sacrificial unless there is no return for that sacrifice. In my earlier essay alluded to above, I elaborated many of the ways in which parenthood gifts us, thus making parenting an exercise in mutuality, not sacrifice.[5] It is not necessary to repeat those arguments. The fact is that in an era when parenthood requires significant economic sacrifice, the involuntary infertility of fifteen percent of couples is socially perceived as a source of tremendous suffering.[6] Why would people desire so strongly an inherently sacrificial relationship? Because it is *not* essentially sacrificial. Parenthood is potentially enriching, life-enhancing, and joyous despite the real sacrificial elements within it.

How and why does the perception of parenthood as predominantly sacrificial persist? In the first place, this portrayal of parenthood as sacrificial serves as ideological support for patriarchy. Sacrificial understandings of parenthood are a part of the romanticization of the family in modern western life. This romanticization of the family serves to disguise the location and use of power in the family by pedestalizing women and children as innocent and good and therefore in need of protection by husbands/fathers.[7] The assumption that parental power is used in the interests of children serves to undermine attacks on parental (especially paternal) monopolization of power, and disguises the extent to which parental power is used in the interests of parents rather than children. If we accept the patriarchal defense that parental power protects children, then there is no need to investigate either the possibility that the power bestowed on men in the family is an obstacle to the development of subjectivity in women and children, or the possibility that women's subordination to men encourages women to sublimate their desire for autonomy in the more socially acceptable domination of children. This romanticization of parenthood as sacrificial therefore obscures the real interests of both children and parents vis à vis power.

Second, a principal function of the romanticization of parenthood as sacrificial has been to mask the extent of parental abuse of children. Investigation of the incidence of physical and sexual abuse of children in the last decade has uncovered a situation that is simply incomprehensible to the general public due to its understanding of parents as "naturally" acting in sacrificial ways in the interests of their children. In the United States we have learned that more than one in four girls and more than one in seven boys is sexually abused.[8] Four and a half percent of girls are sexually abused by their fathers.[9] Physical nonsexual abuse of children is even more widespread: In 1983, of the 1,117,500 cases of substantiated maltreatment of children about one in seven was sexual; six out of seven were cases of physical abuse.[10] Over a million runaway children flee physical abuse in their homes every year. Thousands of children are shot, beaten or starved to death by their parents every year in the United States. Other countries offer similarly appalling examples. In many Latin American (and some other) nations the press has been full of stories of systematic extermination of street children by the police, army, and vigilante gangs.[11] While some of these children are orphans, most are either abandoned (often as young as five or six) or are runaways fleeing from abuse and/or neglect by either parents or orphanage officials. Various human rights groups have recognized street children as major victims of human rights abuses.[12]

While there undoubtedly are and will continue to be examples of children falsely charging parents with abuse for a variety of reasons,[13] many attempts to dismiss abuse claims against parents are based in the refusal to surrender romantic, sacrificial understandings of parenting, and not in any critical reading of the evidence.[14] Such refusals are understandable and normal. Sacrificial notions of parenthood place parents above suspicion of mistreatment—both from their children and from others, including teachers, doctors, social workers, and neighbors. Most parents want their behavior toward their children to be above suspicion, just as most adults concur with their parents' explanations of parent-child interaction during their youth, rather than propose a distinct interpretation.[15] Many adults largely retain society's idealist approach to parents out of an unwillingness to acknowledge the suffering inflicted on them by their own parents in childhood. To acknowledge their childhood suffering would demolish the pedestal on which they have placed their parents and destroy the fictitious childhood they have laboriously constructed for themselves. Nevertheless, this romanticization of parents as sacrificial is not in the interest of either children or children-become-parents, because the denial of suffering inflicted in childhood does not eliminate the wounds. The process of conscience development requires not only the internalization of the parental injunctions within the superego of the child but also the maturation of the superego away from its primitive, destructive stage and toward a mature superego—one that gives way to the developed ego through openness to rationality and forgiveness of self and others.[16] Since the maturation of the superego develops in tandem with the child's ongoing reactions to the parents, the superimposition of a romanticized, unrealistic account of the parent-child relationship will impair the maturation of the superego/conscience.

Romantic interpretations of parenthood can also affect how parents grapple with the real temptations to misuse power over children to gratify personal desires. This process can have either positive or negative outcomes. Romantic interpretations of parenthood may blind parents to the self-interested nature of their own actions vis à vis their children, or they may provide social reinforcement of parents' conscientious reluctance to misuse children. In our own case, a heavy romanticization was pushed on us constantly, since so many people thought our adoption of handicapped children placed us in the category of saints who were above temptation of any kind. The fact that we were not the biological parents that society presumes to be "naturally" sacrificial pushed us to suspect our own motives on occasion. But the fact that we were so often forced to be advocates for the children with various medical, educational, and social work bureaucracies helped us even more to see how vulnerable the children were, how easily abused, how dependent upon us for protection. Knowing this, we constantly interrogated ourselves about our motives and our interests. When we contemplated decisions about risky surgeries for our adopted children, or whether to maintain the youngest on Ritalin, or send the oldest to boarding school, we asked ourselves: Would this option primarily serve him or us? What does he want for himself? Would we make the same choice for our biological son were the circumstances similar? Would we have wanted our own parents to make this decision for us?

A third way that sacrificial notions of parenthood maintain patriarchy is through the implicit—sometimes explicit—demand that children owe gratitude to their parents for having them. The basic form that this gratitude is expected to take is obedience to parents. But obedience to parents can mean anything from eating one's vegetables to structuring one's adolescent and adult life to suit one's parents. Alice Miller and others point out that far more people than commonly recognized are in thrall to their parents' emotional needs, living their adult lives not in response to their own feelings and needs which have been suppressed or never developed, but rather in response to the feelings and needs of their parents.[17]

Romanticization of parenthood, like romanticization of patriarchal marriage, poverty, and earlier forms of victimization such as slavery, serves to justify relationships in which one partner has power, while the other is rewarded with social approval for accepting lack of power. Submissive wives, the humble poor, docile slaves, and obedient, grateful children are rewarded for their lack of power with praise for their goodness or innocence, with affection or minor privilege, and are promised their ultimate reward in the next life.

For children, one critical problem with such a model of parent/child interaction is that it prevents children from ever reaching equality with parents, which is a central task of the emerging adult. This problem is not surprising, since patriarchy is inherently hierarchical, not egalitarian, and therefore does not aim at creating a society of peers, but rather a permanently graded society. It is not commonly recognized that the patriarchal model of parenthood that is romanticized as sacrificial is also problematic for parental development, in that a central moral task of parenthood is coming to recognize and interact with the separate identity and interests of the child. This recognition of the child as separate and self-directed is for most parents a basic part of their own adult maturation. Frequently individual decisions to parent, as well as the social approval given to parenting, are based in an understanding of the child as an extension of the parent. The child is viewed as a thing that satisfies the desires of the parent for immortality, for achievement, for companionship, for power and control, for affection, for stimulation or amusement, at the same time that the existence of a child soothes the parent's fear of death and loneliness. Gratitude and obedience to parents, of course, guarantee to the parent that these desires will be satisfied through continued control of the child. But the parent's task of reaching maturity requires that the parent separate his/her own person from that of the child so that the child can become her/his own person. Thus the parent must begin to deal with fear of death and loneliness, with desire for power, achievement, and affection, even for stimulation and amusement, without reference to the child. This coming to terms with who one is and what one wants is a constituent element of mature adulthood. The goal of Freudian psychoanalysis is this "semi-autonomy,"[18] this freedom from being determined by one's relations or desires.

In most people the motivations behind parenting patterns include both satisfying their own desires and securing the goods they wish for their children. In our own case, we wanted our children to succeed in school not only because their achievement reflected on us and because we wanted to have educational achievement in common with them, but also because educational achievement would probably give them better financial security and social status. At some point we were forced to ask whose interests were primary for us, and it became clear that the primary interests were ours. Moreover, we came to see that while our sons had not chosen to share our vocational paths, they had accepted some of our basic commitments: the oldest son completed a sociology degree and works with troubled adolescents in foster care, and the middle son's major seems aimed at a career in environmental protection.

In the last few years we have come to think that much of our pain and suffering in parenting should not be interpreted primarily in terms of self-sacrifice for the sake of our children. Though we have experienced

pain and suffering in our parenting, the pain and suffering has primarily
emerged from the later stages of our own process of individuation, from
the development of our own self-directed identities. In many ways our
children's actions during this process were only defensive. But our society is a long way from understanding that self-sacrificial interpretations
of parenting can be a form of blaming child-victims for the pain parents
endure in attempting to illegitimately annex children to the parental self.

God the Parent:
Masking/Denying Human Individuation

If the interpretation of parenthood as sacrificial masks the patriarchal
nature of the parent-child relationship and sets up conditions for
parental abuse of children to flourish, then we could expect that imag-
ing God as parent would legitimate destructive patterns of religious
control of persons. Rosemary Radford Ruether has stated very succinctly the problems with images of God as parent:

> But the parent model for the divine has negative resonance as well.
> It suggests a kind of permanent parent-child relationship to God.
> God becomes a neurotic parent who does not want us to grow up.
> To become autonomous and responsible for our own lives is the
> gravest sin against God. Patriarchal theology uses the parent image
> for God to prolong spiritual infantilism as virtue and to make
> autonomy and assertion of free will a sin.[19]

There is little doubt that the Father God of the Judeo-Christian tradition has often been depicted in just this way.[20] This God is jealous of
human beings and determined to have no rivals. Thus on seeing the
tower at Babel: "the Lord said: 'Behold, they are one people, and they
have all one language; and this is only the beginning of what they will
do; and nothing that they propose to do will now be impossible for
them. Come let us go down, and there confuse their language, that they
may not understand one another's speech." (Gen. 11:6–7) The image
here is of a God fearful of sharing creativity with human creatures,
determined to maintain a monopoly on creativity and initiative. In the
same way the author of Exodus depicts the God who gives the commandments as ferociously jealous and insecure: "You shall not make for
yourself a graven image, or any likeness of anything that is in heaven
above or that is in the earth beneath, or that is in the water under the
earth; you shall not bow down to them or serve them; for I, the Lord
your God, am a jealous God, visiting the iniquity of the fathers upon the
children to the third and the fourth generation of those who hate me,

but showing steadfast love to thousands of those who love me and keep my commandments." (Exod. 20:4–6)

As a great many twentieth-century theologians have noted without making any noticeable impact on the Christian masses, viewing the God/human relationship in terms of (parent/child) control and dependency has been challenged again and again in the process commonly called secularization. Gustavo Gutiérrez writes:

> Secularization is, above all, the result of a transformation of the self-understanding of man. From a cosmological vision, man moves to an anthropological vision, due especially to scientific developments. Man perceives himself as a creative subject. Moreover, man becomes aware—as we have noted above—that he is an agent of history, responsible for his own destiny. His mind discovers not only the laws of nature, but also penetrates those of society, history and psychology. This new self-understanding of man necessarily brings in its wake a different way of conceiving his relationship with God. . . . This is Bonhoeffer's world come of age, *mundig*, the source of his anguished question, "How can we speak about God in this adult world?"[21]

In a similar way Sallie McFague considers the God/human relationship as a parent/child pair, as a pair of lovers, and as a pair of friends, and decides that the friendship model is the most adult:

> Children are obviously dependent upon parents, and even the beloved is dependent upon being beloved by the lover, but friends are mutually interdependent in a way characteristic of adults. Part of what we mean by becoming adult is being ready to take on responsibilities, being able to share in the work of the world rather than being sustained by others. Becoming adult need not mean, although it has often in our society meant, becoming independent in the sense of becoming a solitary individual. On the contrary, in an ecological, evolutionary context, becoming adult must mean the movement from dependent status to interdependence: the recognition that mature perception and activity in our world demand interrelating not only with other human beings but also with other forms of being, both nonhuman and divine. It is above all our willingness to grow up and take responsibility for the world that the model of friend underscores. . . . The right name for those involved in this ongoing sustaining, trustworthy, committed work for the world is neither parents nor lovers but friends.[22]

Theologians such as Bonhoeffer, Gutiérrez, Ruether, and McFague share a sense of urgency. They are unwilling to accept traditional images of God as both jealous of human power, control, and initiative, and demanding human passivity in the face of divine leadership. Their unwillingness to accept a divine monopoly on initiative and creativity is rooted not only in an understanding of the threats facing our cosmos— for example, the unjust suffering of millions in the developing world, the unjust suffering wrought upon the millions of anonymous victims of German National Socialism, and the assorted threats that nuclear power, population pressures, and technological development pose to the environment of the earth. These threats have been and continue to be real. But these theologians' urgency also reflects their conviction that humans are capable of turning back the threat. Not all humans share this self-understanding; if more people did, then the image of God as a parent to infantile humans would not be nearly so popular. In fact, Gutiérrez, Bonhoeffer, Ruether, and McFague (and many others) all focus on the need for humankind to move beyond religious demands for human passivity and religious claims for God's monopolization of power and responsibility for the world.

Yet if human society were truly to commit itself to the task and responsibility of being co-creators with God in the continuation of creation, it would not be necessary to abandon the parent-child image of the God/human relationship. In my own family, I am 45, and two of my grandparents are still alive. My children who are now young adults thus have parents who have parent(s) who have parent(s). In the developed world where average lifespans approach 80, the majority of parents have adult, not minor, children. McFague's assumption that "children are obviously dependent upon parents" thus misses the point that our western Christian societies have not only imaged God as Father and humans as children, but have also imaged humans as dependent minors, and not as adult children.

One of the most valuable personal discoveries in the postmodern world is that we do not need to abandon our parents in order to escape dependency. Given sufficient social support, we can work out more egalitarian relationships with parents without using distance and silence to break the intimate but unequal and dependent ties of childhood. Given the same support from church and society, we will not need to abandon God as Parent in order to be responsible adults, and we can cease relying upon a model of divine Fatherhood that justifies parent/child domination. We must find new ways to share power between parents and children, new ways to encourage parents both to recognize their children as peers in the making and to yield increasing degrees of power and responsibility to them.

The deepest of our relationships are always multifaceted, and they can never be captured in a single image. Jews and Muslims base their prohibition against depictions of the divine One on this wisdom. In the same way, there is no one verbal expression of any human/human relationship that is capable of capturing the God/human relationship, even the model of friendship that McFague proposes. For while good friends do share many of the positive qualities we know are possible in the God/human relationship, the parent/child model of the God/human relationship retains one aspect that provides a special kind of security for us: its givenness. The God as Parent model evokes in us our experience as both children and parents. As children, most of us learn that we are inextricably bound to those who created and/or nurtured us and outlined for us the possibilities and limits of our being. As parents, most of us learn that we are also inextricably bound to those who are the fruits of our own creativity and/or nurture, because in creating and/or supporting their growth we became who we are. While the voluntariness of the God as Friend model may have great appeal for the liberal modern person struggling for freedom from social and familial constraints, many postmoderns live in a world of isolation and disconnection that no longer furnishes many signs supporting either hope or community. Postmoderns may need to depend more on the givenness of the bond between the Creator and the created, the troubled bond with the biblical Parent God who has punished and rewarded, threatened and promised—but never abandoned—unfaithful children.

NOTES

1. That autobiographical essay, "Parenting, Mutual Love and Sacrifice," was published in *Women's Consciousness, Women's Conscience: A Reader in Feminist Ethics*, ed. Barbara H. Andolsen, Christine E. Gudorf, and Mary D. Pellauer (Minneapolis: Winston/Seabury, 1985).

2. Erik Erikson's "Eight Stages of Man," in *Childhood and Society* (New York: W. W. Norton & Co., 1950) was one of the most influential. One successor was R. L. Gould, "The Phases of Adult Life: A Study in Developmental Psychology," *American Journal of Psychiatry* 129 (1972): 5, 521–31. Researchers began to separate the sexes about this time: D. J. Levinson et al., "The Psychosocial Development of Men in Early Adulthood and the Mid-Life Transition," *Life History Research in Psychotherapy*, vol. 3 (Minneapolis: University of Minnesota Press, 1974); G. E. Vaillant and C. C. McArthur, "Natural History of Male Psychologic Health: I. The Adult Life Cycle from 18–50," *Seminars in Psychiatry* 4 (1972): 4415–27; Esther Sales, "Women's Adult Development," in *Women and Sex Roles: A Social Psychological Perspective*, ed. Irene Frieze et al. (New York: W. W. Norton & Co., 1978), 157–90.

3. Perhaps most relevant here is the treatment of parental relations as obstacles to marital intimacy in Charles A. Gallagher et al., *Embodied in Love: Sacramental Spirituality of Sexual Intimacy* (New York: Crossroad, 1986), 65, 69–85.

4. That is, if our parents did us serious injury, as in the case of physical, sexual, or emotional abuse, and if our parents never admit their wrongdoing or ask our forgiveness, it would be a terrible mistake to forgive them. Alice Miller deals with this situation at some length in "The Liberating Experience of Painful Truth," in *Breaking Down the Wall of Silence: The Liberating Experience of Facing Painful Truth* (New York: Meridian Books, 1993), chap. 9.

5. Gudorf, "Parenting," 176–79.

6. Maura Ryan, "Particular Sorrows, Common Challenges: Access to Specialized Fertility Treatment in the Context of the Common Good" (The Annual Meeting of the Society of Christian Ethics, Chicago, 8 January 1994), 187–207.

7. I have developed this argument further in "Ending the Romanticization of Victims," in *Victimization: Examining Christian Complicity* (Philadelphia: Trinity Press International, 1992).

8. David Finkelhor et al., "Sexual Abuse in a National Sample of Adult Men and Women: Prevalence, Characteristics and Risk Factors," *Child Abuse and Neglect* 14 (1990): 19–28.

9. Diana E. H. Russell, *The Secret Trauma: Incest In The Lives of Girls and Women* (New York: Basic Books, 1986), 10.

10. Mary Pellauer, "Moral Callousness and Moral Sensitivity," in *Women's Consciousness*, 39.

11. Gilberto Dimenstein, *Brazil: War on Children* (London: Latin American Bureau, 1991); House Select Committee on Hunger, *Street Children: A Global Disgrace* (Washington, D.C.: Government Printing Office, 1992); Pamela Mercer, "In the Street Urchins' Dark Haunt, No Ray of Hope," *New York Times*, 6 August 1993, Sec. A, p. 4; "When Death Squads Meet Street Children," *The Economist*, 31 July 1993, 39; Sarah Bayliss, "Cold Comforts," *New York Times Educational Supplement*, 4 December 1992, S1; Paul Jeffrey, "Targetted For Death: Brazil's Street Children," *Christian Century*, 20 January 1993, 52; Kudzai Macombe, "Desperate and On The Street," *World Press Review*, November 1992, 26.

12. "On The Street of Broken Dreams," *U.N. Chronicle* 26:3 (September 1989): 49; and Lourdes Balanon, "Street Children: Strategies for Action," *Child Welfare* 68:2 (March/April 1989): 159.

13. See, for example, the widely reported 1994 court case of the Menendez brothers of Los Angeles, who shot their parents to death as they watched television; as defense they claimed the father had sexually abused the younger son for years, and had physically and emotionally abused both. Since the parents at the time of their death were worth a few million dollars, the controversy centered on whether the sons invented or exaggerated abuse to disguise their interest in securing the parents' money.

14. See, for example, Douglas J. Besharov, "The Extent of Child Abuse Is Exaggerated," in *Child Abuse: Opposing Viewpoints*, ed. Katie D. Koster (San Diego: Greenhaven, 1994), 17–24. This is an excerpt from Besharov's book *Recognizing Child Abuse: A Guide For the Concerned* (New York: Free Press, 1990).

15. In this regard, it is important to recognize how much power parents have in shaping children's interpretation of their experience. Alice Miller cites a 1989 survey in *Paris Match* in which 78 percent of French high school students who reported being beaten as children stated that the beatings they received as children were necessary and just (Miller, *Breaking Down the Walls of Silence*, 55).

16. Guyton B. Hammond, *Conscience and Its Recovery: From the Frankfurt School to Feminism* (Charlottesville, Va.: University of Virginia Press, 1993), 32–33, 107–108, and esp. 112–116.

17. Alice Miller, *The Drama of the Gifted Child* (New York: Basic Books, 1981) and *Breaking Down the Walls*. Sheila Redmond makes this point about the effect of sexual abuse on victims in "Christian 'Virtues' and Recovery From Sexual Abuse," in *Christianity, Patriarchy and Abuse: A Feminist Critique*, ed. Joanne C. Brown and Carole R. Bohn (New York: Pilgrim Press, 1989), 72–73. In the same volume J. C. Brown and Rebecca Parker, as well as Beverly Harrison and Carter Heyward, represent the Christian theological tradition on suffering as centered on deadening individuals' awareness of their suffering, and causing them to revalue their pain as positive because it is redemptive. Here the church is the parent whose needs and feelings are felt by the child in place of her/his own (J. C. Brown and R. Parker, "For God So Loved the World?" and B. Harrison and C. Heyward, "Pain and Pleasure: Avoiding the Confusions of Christian Tradition in Feminist Theory").

18. Ernest Wallwork, *Psychoanalysis and Ethics* (Hartford, Conn.: Yale University Press, 1992), 52, 73–74.

19. Rosemary Radford Ruether, *Sexism and God-Talk: Toward a Feminist Theology* (Boston: Beacon Press, 1983), 69.

20. See chap. 7 of my *Body, Sex, and Pleasure: Reconstructing Christian Sexual Ethics* (Cleveland, Ohio: Pilgrim Press, 1994), which includes an expanded treatment of this topic.

21. Gustavo Gutiérrez, *A Theology of Liberation* (Maryknoll, N.Y.: Orbis Books, 1973) 67. The reference to Bonhoeffer is to Dietrich Bonhoeffer, *Letters and Papers From Prison*, ed. Eberhard Bethge, trans. Reginald H. Fuller (London: SCM Press, 1953).

22. Sally McFague, *Models of God: Theology For an Ecological, Nuclear Age* (Philadelphia: Fortress Press, 1987), 165.

16

The "Recovery"
of Fatherhood?

ROB PALKOVITZ

The past two decades have been characterized by a rapidly expanding focus on fathers and fatherhood in both the social sciences and popular culture. This attention is marked by an increase in articles and books addressing fathers' roles, father involvement in childrearing, and the effects on children of various patterns of paternal involvement and father absence.[1] Interestingly, starkly contrasting views of fatherhood are presented. One perspective suggests that we are witnessing a "recovery" of fatherhood,[2] a return to patterns of father involvement prevalent in colonial America when fathers were recognized as having primary responsibility for children's welfare.[3] Both professional and popular media portray a "new breed" of men who have increased commitment to fathering roles, while at the same time being successful as providers and participants in their communities.[4] Yet these images come at a time when demographic data show that American men are less likely to be fathers, and more likely to have fewer children, spend less time in households with children, and to experience less "leisure time" than in the past fifty years.[5] Divorce, mother-headed households, and defaults on court-ordered alimony and child support payments are at or near all-time highs.[6] These indicators suggest that fatherhood is anything but recovering and that "family decline" is the stronger trend: witness the increase in single-parent families, father absence, and reported abuse cases. How can these starkly contrasting views of fatherhood be reconciled? Is there a balanced view of fatherhood between the extremes?

To what extent can fatherhood legitimately be said to be in "recovery"? Recovery from what, and toward what end? By reviewing historical documentation concerning family forms, paternal roles, and levels of father involvement in family matters and childrearing, and by comparing historical data with contemporary patterns of father involvement, this chapter will (1) address whether there is truly a movement toward "the recovery of fatherhood" and (2) consider factors that facilitate and hinder men's enactment of paternal roles.

A "General" Word of Caution
When Discussing "Fathers"

The great anthropologist, Ralph Linton, wrote, "In some ways each man is like all other men; in some ways, each man is like some other men; and in some ways, each man is like no other men."[7] The professional literature concerning fatherhood, whether historical accounts or contemporary reports, cover all three levels of Linton's observation: Some make general statements about fathers as though all fathers conform to the description as prescription, some focus on particular subgroups (e.g., fathers in dual-wage families, primary caregiving fathers, adoptive fathers) or styles of fathering (e.g., traditional, androgynous) to highlight the common characteristics within groups or to make comparisons across groups; and some of the literature is made up of individual case histories. It is essential that we recognize that in some ways we can discuss generic "fathers" because all fathers share some universal characteristics; but in some ways, any literature we review about "fathers" minimizes consideration of individual variations. When considering subgroups of fathers, we need to keep in mind that men within the same general classification (e.g., fathers of teen sons) will have unique histories, developmental trajectories, interaction styles, and involvement levels. Descriptions of different styles or types of fathers are "ideal types" in the Weberian sense:

> They are not ideal in the normative sense, however; neither are they accurate descriptions of reality. As a heuristic device, ideal types represent logical exaggerations of reality; as such they serve as a basis for comparison and potential measurement of concrete trends. The polar types of "traditional" and "androgynous" father serve as a point of reference for the empirical assessment of the social reality: the "typical" father.[8]

Before proceeding with this chapter it is essential to recognize that each of Linton's levels of analysis is appropriate for different purposes. While it is a goal of this chapter to summarize historical trends in fatherhood and to focus on similarities and differences between various groups of fathers, we must recognize that any generalized statements are precarious at best, and wrong at worst, when applied to the individual level. Lewis and O'Brien emphasize that the variations between individual fathers can themselves be considerable. Such a finding emerges within relatively homogenous communities irrespective of whether mothers . . . fathers . . . or children . . . are the source of data collection. It is also evident in cross-cultural comparisons. . . . The very heterogeneity of fathering roles . . . invalidates general statements about "the father."[9]

We need to recognize further that historical shifts are taking place, both at societal and individual (developmental) levels. Thus any transition from one pattern of fathering to another may be incomplete. While we tend to describe fathering styles as fixed, they are, in reality, varied and fluid.[10] Further, movement or development through diverse styles of fathering may be more the rule than the exception.[11] The paternal style manifested at any given point of data collection or analysis depends on the context, on the individual father's assessments of requirements and resources, and on the relative importance individual fathers assign to the various roles they enact (e.g., breadwinning, sex-role modeling, moral guidance, nurturance) toward their children.[12] Given these cautions, we can proceed with a review of the literature.

The History of Father Involvement and Fatherhood Roles

In comparison to the literature on mothering or parenting in general, there is a relative sparseness of literature on fathering. While recent contributions have begun to correct this, researchers' opinions vary as to whether there is a sufficiently solid basis for delineating the degree of change in American fathering roles across time. Ralph LaRossa is cautious concerning our abilities to assess historical changes in fatherhood: "Only a few scholars have systematically conceptualized the changing father hypothesis, and no one to date has marshalled the historical evidence needed to adequately test the hypothesis."[13]

Other scholars assert that there is sufficient evidence to address the degree of change in paternal roles and participation. According to Charlie L. Lewis and Margaret O'Brien, "a brief examination of the literature shows, first, that there has been a stream of papers on fathers over the past fifty years which repeatedly claim that little has been written on the topic."[14]

Most would agree, however, that this endeavor is not without peril. John Demos summarizes the complexities of describing changes in fatherhood across historical periods by stating that a

vast gulf of change separates early American fathers from their counterparts today. The differences embrace underlying goals and values; prescribed methods and styles of practice; the shape and quality of personal interaction; and the larger configuration of domestic life.[15]

To present a completely accurate picture of changes in American fatherhood it is necessary to include a discussion of predominant cultural, ideological, political, and economic forces affecting fatherhood at each point of comparison. While such a task is clearly beyond the scope of this brief analysis, several excellent reviews have been written, and when read together present a relatively comprehensive and convergent picture of the various forces that have shaped fatherhood in America from the colonial period to the present.[16]

Karl Zinsmeister asserts that "as we move into the beginnings of higher civilization we find that most of the more successful human peoples involved fathers with their children in ways that far exceeded mere protection and food sharing."[17] As we shall see, this pattern was true of colonial America as well.

Fatherhood in Colonial America

Puritan men were the authors of the first handbooks of advice on childrearing and served as the primary instructors of their children. Colonial fatherhood "involved a remarkable amount of daily care, companionship [and] concern."[18] Responsibility centered on moral teaching;[19] however, discipline, training children for their life's work, provision of material needs, control of family property, and veto power in matters of courtship and marriage were also fundamental to the father's role as well.[20] Fathers also fulfilled major functions as models, psychologists, companions, and caregivers,[21] especially with older children:

> There is no question that colonial mothers, as their counterparts today, provided most of the caretaking that infants and young children received. But fathers were nonetheless thought to have far greater responsibility for, and influence on, their children. Prescriptions for parents were addressed almost entirely to fathers: the responsibilities of mothers were rarely mentioned.[22]

Demos recognizes that descriptions such as the above give little room for individual variance in performance or role enactment over time. However, he asserts that

> almost everywhere fatherhood displayed the same active, integrated orientation. And in this, there was little apparent change through the several generations of our "colonial period."[23]

The Industrial Age Father

Perhaps the most consistent finding is that since the time of the Industrial Revolution, fathers have increasingly invested time and energies in employment away from the home setting.[24] Rotundo has chronicled changes in American society and roles during the nineteenth century. He summarizes the shift in family responsibilities:

> At the same time that the traditional ideas of patriarchy fell into decline, a new notion of womanhood emerged: a belief that women were inherently moral, more spiritual, and more tender than men. . . . Despite the decline of patriarchy and the expanded importance of mothers within the nineteenth-century family, middle-class fathers still had a significant role to play. More than ever before, the man was *the* provider in the family. That, in turn, reinforced his role as "head of the household."[25]

For the first time in American history, mothers were now viewed to be the primary parent. Culture-wide reforms in sex-role stereotypes led to redefinitions of appropriate roles for men and women in regard to work and family life:

> Certain key elements of premodern fatherhood dwindled and disappeared (father as teacher, father as moral overseer, father as companion), while others were profoundly transformed (father as counselor, father as model). . . . Although fatherhood on these terms was hardly insubstantial, it diverged in obvious and important ways from the earlier pattern. For one thing, it became part-time . . . for another, it opened some distance from the everyday workings of the household . . . preeminently for one reason. Beginning in the first decades of the nineteenth century, and increasingly thereafter, men were drawn out of their families toward income producing work.[26]

During the Industrial Age the most profound transformation in fathers' roles was an increased emphasis on father as breadwinner or provider.

> Of course, fathers had always been involved in the provision of goods and services to their families; but before the nineteenth century such activity was embedded in a larger matrix of domestic sharing. With modernization, it became "differentiated" as the chief, if not the exclusive, province of adult men. Now, for the first time, the central activity of fatherhood was sited outside one's immediate household. Now being fully a father meant being separated from one's children for a considerable part of each working day.[27]

Rotundo suggests that the separation of the father's work from the home took him outside of the "emotional currents" of the home, diminished his ability to develop deep intimacy with his children, and undermined the traditional authority of fathers.[28]

Fatherhood in
Twentieth-Century America

Nevertheless, the image of *father as provider* was stronger at the turn of the twentieth century than ever before, conferring on individual fathers special status, respect, deference, and familial love.[29] In the predominant conception of the good provider role, a man's chief responsibility was his waged work, reducing the family to subordinate significance.[30] In fact, Jessie Bernard asserts that in the twentieth century "success in the good provider role came to define masculinity itself."[31] Two world wars and an economic depression had additional societal and international impact on the conduct of fatherhood:

> The Depression attacked, and sometimes shattered, fathers in their central role as providers; but the role itself survived until the return of better times, and flourished thereafter. The wars separated millions of fathers from their families for months or years at a stretch, but the ensuing peacetimes brought a renewal (even a reinforcement) of traditional arrangements. . . . Still this is not to say that fatherhood is wholly uninfluenced by larger currents of change. And two changes, recently begun and still in progress, deserve special notice here. The first is the entry of women—most strikingly, of married women with small children—into the working world outside the home. The second is the growing incidence of divorce and thus of single parenthood (even, in a small proportion of cases, of single *father*hood).[32]

Anthony Rotundo agrees with this assessment, noting that the economic boom following World War II restored fathers to their positions as providers and "heads of households."[33] He further notes that in the revival of modern fatherhood the opposing trends of father absence and father involvement gained renewed momentum.[34]

Joseph Pleck chronicles yet another phase in the social history of fatherhood in the twentieth century, noting that from the end of the Second World War to the mid-1970s, although breadwinning and moral guardianship continued to be important, primary emphasis was centered on fathers as sex-role models, particularly for their sons.[35] Around the mid-1970s there emerged a view of fathers as active, nurturant, caretaking parents.[36]

Contemporary Fatherhood

Although very much in transition, the good provider role is still dominant in contemporary men's views of fatherhood, and the bipolar trends of father absence and involvement are continuing.[37] Restructuring of the social base and the new ideal of what a man should be has laid the basis for a "new" style of fatherhood variously labeled "involved fatherhood," "highly participant" fatherhood, "androgynous fatherhood," or "new fatherhood."[38] This style of fatherhood appears to be especially concentrated among the well-educated and families of the middle class and above. It has emerged within the past decade and a half, and has only begun to take hold. As such, a full description of this style of fatherhood is not possible, yet

> this emerging form of fatherhood can at least be outlined. As part of the evolving style, a good father is an active participant in the details of day-to-day child care. He involves himself in a more intimate and expressive way with his children, and he plays a larger part in the socialization process that his male forebears had long since abandoned to their wives. In short, the new style of parenting blurs the distinctions between fatherhood and motherhood. . . . Within this style, a good father avoids sex-typing his children and makes as little distinction as possible between sons and daughters. . . . Androgynous Fatherhood, then, involves a substantial recasting of American manhood, womanhood, and family life. It demands new emotional styles; it entails different notions of male and female; and it requires men to surrender substantial authority to their wives in return for a greater measure of involvement with their children.[39]

Despite prior precautions against generalizing about fathers, it can still be said that alongside the much heralded androgynous father[40] or the "new father" of the 1990s, "father as breadwinner" and "father as sex-role model" remain significant competitors for subscribers among fathers. Still,

> the critique of the distant bread-winning father is intensifying further. A new image, summed up in the term "the new father," is clearly on the rise in print and broadcast media. This new father differs from older images of involved fatherhood in several key respects: he is present at the birth; he is involved with his children as infants, not just when they are older; he participates in the actual day-to-day work of child care and not just play; he is involved with his daughters as much as his sons.[41]

Yet for all of the attention that the popular and professional media have focused on the "new father," many wonder about the extent to which this man actually exists. Michael Lamb asserts that "rhetorical exchanges concerning the new fatherhood abound; unfortunately, rhetoric continues to outpace serious analysis."[42] Ralph LaRossa suggests that the idea that fathers have radically changed qualifies as a folk belief.[43] Specifically, attempts to empirically chronicle involvement patterns of contemporary fathers in comparison to mothers show wide and significant gaps between men's and women's contributions to childrearing.[44]

> The discrepancy between the actual pace of change in men and the profusion of profathering imagery has led some to dismiss the image of the new, involved father as only media "hype." While this element clearly exists, it is also important to recognize that the new father is not *all* hype. This image, like the dominant images of earlier periods, is ultimately rooted in structural forces and structural change. Wives *are* more often employed, and do less in the family when they are; men *are* spending more time in the family, both absolutely and relative to women (husbands' proportion of the total housework and child care rose from 20% to 30% between 1965 and 1981 . . .). If the distant father-breadwinner has a social structural base, so too does the new father.[45]

Culture/Conduct Distinctions

LaRossa distinguishes between the imagery of fatherhood and the actual performance of paternal roles by use of the terms "culture of fatherhood" and "conduct of fatherhood," respectively.[46] Specifically, this distinction can account for the differences in rates of change between the ideological shifts (culture) and the behavior (conduct) of fatherhood.

> The institution of fatherhood includes two related but still distinct elements. There is the *culture of fatherhood* (specifically the shared norms, values, and beliefs surrounding men's parenting), and there is the *conduct of fatherhood* (what fathers do, their parental behaviors).[47]

While this refinement in our conceptualization of fatherhood has allowed theoretical and analytical power absent before LaRossa's contribution, it has not laid to rest the ongoing debate about the reality of the supposed change that has taken place in American fatherhood. If anything, these concepts have added the ammunition of clearer conceptual analysis to the debate.

> Has fatherhood changed in the wake of the social and economic changes that have taken place in America since the turn of the

century? Although the evidence is scant, it would appear that the answer to this question is both yes and no. Yes, fatherhood has changed if one looks at the culture of fatherhood—the ideologies surrounding men's parenting. No, fatherhood has not changed (at least significantly), if one looks at the conduct of fatherhood—how fathers behave vis-à-vis their children.[48]

Because the idealized image of fatherhood prescribes higher levels and greater ranges of involvement than are realized in actuality, the resulting dissonance can result in intense feelings of ambivalence, frustration, and guilt in both fathers and mothers. If the predominant culture of fatherhood is prescribing higher levels of participation than are being realized, what factors can explain the chasm between the culture and the conduct of fatherhood?

Barriers to Involved Fatherhood

One class of factors contributing to the discrepancy between the culture and the conduct of fatherhood can be described as barriers to involved fatherhood. While particular barriers, either alone or in combination, neither excuse nor explain observed levels of paternal involvement (or lack thereof) in any given case, it is important to recognize that barriers exist at societal, familial, and individual levels. The range and extensiveness of operating barriers will vary from individual to individual.

Parenting Preparation, Experience, and Fear of Failure

Fathers' fear of failure may be due to perceptions of low skill or caretaking incompetence that can inhibit involvement.[49] This can result in a vicious cycle: Because of the marginalization of modern fathers, the less they are physically present, and the less informed and competent they become.[50]

Sex-Role Socialization

The traditional male sex-role has required men to be strong, independent, competitive, emotionally restrained, and achievement-oriented.[51] These characteristics are diametrically opposed to many aspects of involved parenting. As such, it is not surprising that there is a negative correlation between male sex-role orientations and nurturant fathering.[52] Further, violation of male sex-roles by fathers can lead to anxiety and the loss of support from male peers.[53] For all of these reasons, males who score high on measures of androgyny are often found to be more highly involved as fathers than masculine-scoring males.[54]

Role Strain and Family/Work Tensions

Multiple role strain or role overload may inhibit greater paternal involvement as well.[55] Even men who are capable of maintaining professional productivity while demonstrating devotion to families tend to be perceived by colleagues and supervisors as less committed to their careers.[56] Further double binds exist in attempting to balance provider and family roles. Career pursuit can result in feelings of emptiness and alienation, but also can yield financial rewards for the family. Abdication of the role of sole or primary provider can yield relief, shame, or both.[57] The continued existence of gender-biased wage discrimination also works against those men who desire to reduce work commitments.[58]

The Timing of Fatherhood

The timing of transitions to fatherhood frequently corresponds with a point in the life cycle when the establishment of work security demands maximum commitment of time and energy.[59] In terms of the age at which fathering begins, when compared to "early" and "on time" fathers, "late" fathers are more likely to be classified as highly involved in childrearing and to have positive paternal affect.[60]

Mothers as "Gatekeepers"

A number of researchers have indicated that mothers serve as "gatekeepers" in regulating the overall amount of paternal involvement.[61] When fathers are not as involved as mothers desire them to be, family adjustments and well-being are substantially lower than those families with a good match between desired and perceived levels of paternal involvement:

> Increased paternal involvement seemed likely to have desirable
> consequences when it was valued by mothers, whereas the failure
> of fathers to be more involved only had adverse consequences
> when it was desired by the women concerned.[62]

Negative Interpersonal Experiences

Some studies of highly participant fathers have found that more involved men tend to have a greater degree of conflict with their children than less involved fathers.[63] Greater paternal involvement can be related to higher degrees of interspousal conflict as well.[64]

Cost/Benefits Analyses

If one engages in a cost/benefits analysis of involved fathering, it is clear that there are significant contributors to the positive and negative columns on the balance sheet. In the words of Lamb, Pleck, and Levine:

> Increased paternal involvement promises both advantages and disadvantages to fathers themselves. Among the costs are the likelihood of diminished earnings and career prospects as well as retarded promotion, marital friction, dissatisfaction with the boring tedium of day-to-day parenthood, and social isolation from disapproving friends, relatives, and colleagues. Among the advantages or benefits are the potential for personal fulfillment through closer, richer relationships to one's children, along with the opportunity to witness and influence their development more thoroughly. As in the case of mothers, the relative evaluation of the costs and benefits must depend on the individual's values and aspirations as well as on both economic and social circumstances.[65]

Based on considerations such as the above, Lamb, Pleck, and Levine conclude that "the fact that increased paternal involvement may have both beneficial and detrimental consequences for mothers and fathers precludes us from concluding that changes in paternal involvement would necessarily be *either* "good" or "bad" in themselves."[66]

Because of the simultaneous existence of both costs and benefits, barriers and encouragements toward involved fatherhood, it is necessary to look at principles that transcend personal and temporal implications. To date, few scholars have considered the contributions that a biblical perspective on fatherhood can make to contemporary discussions of family role enactments and equity.

Biblical Insights into Fathering

While there are many legitimate interpretations of a biblical "position" on parental roles, are there some widely accepted principles in scripture that can encourage and challenge the current generation of families? While the terms father, "fathers," "father's," "fathered," and "fatherless" appear in scripture in excess of 1,200 times, most references are in genealogical records, or are references to "the God of our fathers" or to God the Father. Few passages are directly addressed to fathers who may be in search of a "biblical job description." In a similar manner, scripture does not directly address masculinity or femininity. The strategy many Christians use to develop prescriptions for appropriate behavior in other realms ("What did Jesus do?") is not directly applicable to the consideration of paternal roles. Similarly, when attempting to construct a Christ-centered model of masculinity in family roles, we are limited because Jesus was not a husband and the details of his "business life" are not covered prior to his entry into public ministry. Given these limitations, are there some scriptural truths and principles that can be applied to fathering? I believe so.

Scripture does make it clear that it is expected and assumed that fathers know how to give good things to their children,[67] to discipline their children,[68] and to avoid exasperating and embittering their children in the training process.[69] In numerous passages in the Old Testament it is clear that paternal modeling is important in the transmission of religious values.[70] Taken together, these principles imply a significant level of fathers' direct involvement with children.

It is important to recognize the historical significance of paternalism as the route to inheritance and status. However, even in light of cultural fluctuations across time and place, there are some overriding principles that appear to transcend these. It appears that God takes special interest in and has an extra measure of compassion, protection, and provision for the fatherless.[71] This is so much the case that there is blessing associated with righteous treatment of the fatherless[72] and judgment associated with not providing for, or for taking advantage of, the fatherless.[73]

Although coming under recent criticism because it is central to traditional role definitions, fatherhood in the Bible, is associated with provision.[74] It is also associated with protection and training.[75] It should be noted that although given primary attention in traditional role enactments, none of these paternal functions preclude nor supersede more "nurturant" ways of being involved in childrearing.

In regard to role sharing with wives, we should note that as husbands, men are instructed to (sacrificially) love their wives as Christ loved the church,[76] and all are commanded to consider others as more important than themselves.[77] Regardless of the variety of doctrinal positions on "headship," it does not require major leaps in logic to assume that any family "leadership" (by males or females) would come under the servant-leader guidelines with warnings against lording it over others.[78] Fathers are no less responsible to lay down their lives (time, career, desires, etc.) for their children and wives than to do so for their "friends."[79]

Although the relative silence of scripture on issues of fatherhood and masculinity/femininity leaves much room for interpretation, one could reflect on the reasons that the scriptures are so silent concerning the specifics of gender and paternal roles. Independent of historical fluctuations in culture and gender roles, it could be argued that if persons committed to scripture are following the more central biblical principles (seeking God with all their minds, souls, and strength; seeking first the kingdom of God; doing unto others as they would have done unto themselves; doing nothing out of selfish ambition or vain conceit and considering not only their own interests, but also the interests of others; loving their neighbors as themselves; loving one another as Christ loved them[80]; etc.) then the details of masculinity/femininity and the working out of a parenting role would not need much alignment. Simply stated, if we took seriously the "greatest commandments,"[81] that is, if we were committed in our relationship to God and to others, the details of parenting and masculinity/femininity would fall into place. Perhaps the details are not more fully prescribed because they should grow out of a commitment to living in relationship to God and to family members rather than out of adherence to an external rule hierarchy. Perhaps if we really put others ahead of ourselves and treated one another as we wished to be treated, there would be a lot less focus on "equity," "whose turn" it is to perform a particular task, or the overall division of labor. Commitment to Christian principles based on biblical literacy would require less focus on gender and role dichotomies and greater emphasis on living out kingdom principles in a manner that affirms the value of others, be they wives, husbands, men, women, or children.

I recognize that this may be criticized as being a simplistic or utopian view but only in statement. It is no easy task to creatively work out lives of reciprocal agency while negotiating role enactments in a manner that does not victimize others. As Christians are transformed into Christ's image, I believe they are more capable of the mature Christian love that would be a secure foundation for living in such a manner.

How "New" is the "New Father"?

Traces of the "new father" have been around for years. Popular parenting magazines have portrayed fathers as both instrumental and expressive (therefore, androgynous) for at least a century.[82] Although fluctuations have occurred in aspects of fathering roles that have been emphasized in turn at different times, virtually all elements of today's "new" father have been present to some extent in both the culture and the conduct of fatherhood since early in our colonial period. What we have witnessed is a realignment of the different aspects of paternal roles and an extension of the ideal of active fathering, beginning with the transition to parenthood. These adjustments have been equally realized neither in all segments of society nor in all aspects of fatherhood:

Fatherhood is different today than it was in prior times, but for the most part, the changes that have occurred are centered in the culture rather than the conduct of fatherhood. Whatever changes have taken place in the behavior of fathers, on the basis of what we know now, seem to be minimal at best. Also, the behavioral changes have largely occurred within a single group—the middle class.[83]

Thus, although the culture of fatherhood appears to be undergoing relatively significant shifts in terms of portrayals of desired levels and ranges of father involvement, the actual conduct of fatherhood is lagging behind. This lag is realized at societal, subgroup, and individual levels. While there are many reasons that could be cited for the lag, one that few scholars have considered is the self-centered focus prevalent in our culture today. As long as men and women focus on the costs and benefits of different patterns of parental involvement, the possibility of living in a truly giving manner is limited. The following quotes illustrate the prevalence and limitations of such perspectives:

First, "new" fatherhood—whether it is being promulgated in the 1930s or the 1990s—is likely to be embraced, if it is to be embraced at all, by the consumers of the parenting culture. Right now, those consumers overwhelmingly are women. Second, and more importantly, reading a tract on "new" fatherhood is not likely to change one's behavior if other, more immediate concerns, like employment, loom large in one's mind.[84]

Even within the upper-middle class where Androgynous Fatherhood has taken hold, there are probably far more men who still practice the traditional style of fathering than the newer style that blurs the differences between the two parents. In fact, one can safely guess that there are more *women* who *advocate* Androgynous Fatherhood than there are *men* who *practice* it. Many men lack the emotional skills necessary to be deeply and expressively involved with their children, and others have been too thoroughly ingrained with "male" values of ambition and achievement to devote much time to daily child care. Here, as with many other current trends in fatherhood, the future depends on men's ideas of masculinity.[85]

Clearly, fathers can do better. And there is some indication that they may have begun moving, marginally, in that direction. The famous Middletown studies showed that 10 percent of all fathers were reported by mothers to spend no time with their children in 1924, compared to 2 percent in 1976, while the proportion spending more than 1 hour a day had increased. Time-diary studies of domestic work done by men (including but not limited to child care) showed no change from the 1960s to 1970s but an 18 percent increase from the 70s to the 80s (a far bigger increase than achieved by men in Canada, Denmark, Holland, Japan, Norway or the U.K.). The increases did not even come close to counterbalancing drastic drop-offs by women, however.[86]

In looking at individual cases, societies, or even species where fathers have demonstrated relatively high levels of involvement in the rearing of their offspring, Zinsmeister notes some interesting similarities among involved fathers:

> What are the possibly forgotten means by which men have been won into cooperative domesticity in the past? Studies of paternal involvement in humans and nonhuman primates show remarkable agreement in centering male decisions to participate in family life and childrearing around just a few preconditions: One is monogamy. Indeed, one of the very few places that extensive paternal care exists is among the small number of monogamous primates. A related precondition is certainty of birth—studies show men take care of their children if they're sure they are the father, and recognized as such. A final factor is female encouragement for paternal care. The keys, apparently, are the ancient ones: enduring marriage and sexual restraint. In other words, faithful legal families.[87]

More is needed, however. Even in families meeting the above conditions, women generally take primary responsibility for childrearing while men assume secondary roles, best described as "assistant parent" roles.[88] Often women's *stated* desire for greater parenting involvement by their husbands is not matched by the encouragement and relinquishment of parenting primacy needed to accomplish this goal.

In my view, we are not likely to see major shifts in the conduct of fatherhood until we see broad-based changes in our underlying culture. In this context, I think that we need much more than a restructuring of what is prescribed as paternal roles, so I am referring to more than an adjustment to the culture of fatherhood. That has already occurred, but with little impact in regard to changing fathers' behavior. True change will require more radical and far-reaching transformations in our thinking—and beyond, to what lies at the center of our being. I believe that change of a truly significant magnitude occurs only when individual men and women come to an understanding of who they are before God, and in relating to God (not through laws and commandments, but out of genuine desire for fellowship) find all other relationships transformed. As this occurs, people no longer need to focus on equity, whose turn it is, and so on, because by God's grace they are able to walk a truly other-centered, loving life. Simply put: Technology, laborsaving devices, flex time, supportive workplaces, and good counseling or family services will not entirely solve injustices in family role divisions. The solution to contemporary social dilemmas is at least 2,000 years old.

NOTES

1. See Michael E. Lamb, "Introduction: The Emergent American Father," in *The Father's Role: Cross Cultural Perspectives*, ed. Michael E. Lamb (Hillsdale, N.J.: Lawrence Erlbaum Press, 1987), 3–25; Ronald L. Pitzer and Julie E. Hessler, "What Do We Know About Fathers?" in *Working With Fathers: Methods and Perspectives*, ed. Minnesota Fathering Alliance (Stillwater, Minn.: Nu Ink Unlimited, 1992), 1–46; E. Anthony Rotundo, "American Fatherhood: A Historical Perspective," *American Behavioral Psychologist* 29:1 (September/October 1985): 7–25. For an alternative view (that interest in fatherhood has not grown, rather fluctuated) see Maxine P. Atkinson and Stephen P. Blackwelder, "Fathering in the 20th Century," *Journal of Marriage and the Family* 55:4 (November 1993): 975–86.
2. The use of the term "recovery" in this chapter is to be understood in the context that some scholars and popular writers assert that fatherhood is making a "comeback"; i.e., after a period of time when fathers spent considerable time and effort outside of the home, contemporary fathers are investing greater time and energy in child-centered activities. As such, fatherhood could be viewed to be recovering toward patterns of high involvement and participation characteristic of the historic past.
3. See John Demos, "The Changing Faces of Fatherhood: A New Exploration of American Family History," in *Father and Child: Developmental and Clinical Perspectives*, ed. Stanley H. Cath, Alan R. Gurwitt, and John M. Ross (Boston: Little, Brown & Co., 1982), 425–45; Joseph H. Pleck, "American Fathering in Historical Perspective," in *Changing Men: New Directions in Research on Men and Masculinity*, ed. Michael S. Kimmel (Newbury Park, Calif.: Sage Publications, 1987), 83–97; and Rotundo, "American Fatherhood".
4. Lamb, "The Emergent American Father." "Despite waves of optimism driving contemporary accounts, the evidence for the existence of such a man is much less convincing." (Charlie L. Lewis and Margaret O'Brien, "Constraints on Fathers: Research, Theory and Clinical Practice," in *Reassessing Fatherhood: New Observations on Fathers and the Modern Family*, ed. Charlie L. Lewis and Margaret O'Brien [London: Sage Publications, 1987], 1). "Many authors have assumed that men are becoming more involved in family life. . . . Yet such contentions are hard to justify. To begin with, there are two reasons why comparisons of paternal involvement over time might give rise to problems of interpretation. First, it may be that respondents today are under greater pressure to appear to be more involved than those a few years ago. . . . Second, we have to understand

the nature of paternal involvement within the context of other social and technological changes. . . . Thus it is especially hard to measure alterations in paternal involvement without considering the increases in maternal employment and changes in family size and structure. . . . Moreover, there are many methodological difficulties in measuring couples' division of labor in childcare and housework" (Lewis and O'Brien, "Constraints on Fathers," 2–3).

5. W. Brad Johnson, "Father Uninvolvement: Impact, Etiology and Potential Solutions," *Journal of Psychology and Christianity* 12:4 (1992): 301–11.

6. Barbara D. Whitehead, "Dan Quayle was Right," *The Atlantic* (April 1993): 47–66; Karl Zinsmeister, "The Nature of Fatherhood," an Institute for American Values Working Paper for the Symposium on Fatherhood in America (publication W. P. 11, 1991).

7. As quoted in David Guttman, "The Father and the Masculine Life Cycle," Institute for American Values Working Paper for the Symposium on Fatherhood in America (publication no. 13, 1991), 1.

8. Jarmila Horna and Eugen Lupri, "Fathers' Participation in Work, Family Life and Leisure: A Canadian Experience," in Lewis and O'Brien, *Reassessing Fatherhood*, 55.

9. Lewis and O'Brien, "Constraints on Fathers," 6.

10. Horna and Lupri, "Fathers' Participation in Work," 71.

11. Rob Palkovitz, "The Effects of Parenting on Men's Development," unpublished data, research grant funded by the University of Delaware General University Research Program (April–September, 1993).

12. Lamb, "The Emergent American Father"; Rob Palkovitz, "Parenting as a Generator of Adult Development: Conceptual Issues and Implications" (paper presented at the Theory Construction and Research Methodology Workshop, National Council on Family Relations, Orlando, Fla., November 1992).

13. Ralph LaRossa, "Fatherhood and Social Change," *Family Relations* 37 (October 1988): 451. See also Demos, "Changing Fatherhood"; Shirley M. H. Hanson and Frederick W. Bozett, *Dimensions of Fatherhood* (Newbury Park, Calif.: Sage Publications, 1987); Lamb, "The Emergent American Father"; Charlie L. Lewis, *Becoming a Father* (Milton Keynes, Eng.: Open University Press, 1986); Lewis and O'Brien, *Reassessing Fatherhood*; Pleck, "American Fathering"; Rotundo, "American Fatherhood."

14. Lewis and O'Brien, "Constraints on Fathers," 3.

15. Demos, "Changing Fatherhood," 426.

16. Interested readers are encouraged to pursue a more complete presentation than can be provided here by reading Demos, "Changing Fatherhood"; Pleck, "American Fathering"; Rotundo, "American Fatherhood"; Margaret Marsh, "Suburban Men and Masculine Domesticity, 1870–1915," in *Meanings for Manhood: Constructions of Masculinity in Victorian America*, ed. M. C. Carnes and C. Griffen (Chicago: University of Chicago Press, 1990), 111–27; and C. Degler, *At Odds: Women and the Family in America, from the Revolution to the Present* (New York: Oxford University Press, 1980).

17. Zinsmeister, "Nature of Fatherhood," 3.

18. Ibid., 4.
19. Lamb, "The Emergent American Father"; Pleck, "American Fathering."
20. Rotundo, "American Fatherhood."
21. Demos, "Changing Fatherhood."
22. Pleck, "American Fathering," 84.
23. Demos, "Changing Fatherhood," 431.
24. Jessie Bernard, "The Good Provider Role: Its Rise and Fall," *American Psychologist* 36:1, (1981): 1–12; Demos, "Changing Fatherhood"; Pleck, "American Fathering"; Rotundo, "American Fatherhood."
25. Ibid., 10–11, (emphasis in original).
26. Demos, "Changing Fatherhood," 433.
27. Ibid., 434.
28. Rotundo, "American Fatherhood," 12.
29. Demos, "Changing Fatherhood," 443.
30. John H. Scanzoni, *Sex Roles, Life Styles and Childrearing: Changing Patterns in Marriage and the Family* (New York: Free Press, 1975), 38.
31. Bernard, "Provider," 4.
32. Demos, "Changing Fatherhood," 444.
33. Rotundo, "American Fatherhood," 15.
34. Ibid.
35. Lamb, "The Emergent American Father," 5; Pleck, "American Fathering."
36. Lamb, "The Emergent American Father," 6.
37. Horna and Lupri, "Father's Participation."
38. Lamb, "The Emergent American Father"; Lewis and O'Brien, *Reassessing Fatherhood*; Glen F. Palm and Rob Palkovitz, "The Challenge of Working with New Fathers: Implications for Support Providers," in *Transitions to Parenthood*, ed. Rob Palkovitz and Marvin B. Sussman (New York: Haworth Press, 1988), 357–76; Pleck, "American Fathering"; Rotundo, "American Fatherhood"; Graeme Russell, *The Changing Role of Fathers?* (Queensland, Australia: University of Queensland Press, 1983).
39. Rotundo, "American Fatherhood," 17.
40. Ibid.
41. Pleck, "American Fathering," 93.
42. Lamb, "The Emergent American Father," 3.
43. LaRossa, "Fatherhood," 454.
44. Michael E. Lamb, Joseph H. Pleck, and James A. Levine, "Effects of Increased Paternal Involvement on Fathers and Mothers," in Lewis and O'Brien, *Reassessing Fatherhood*, 109–25.
45. Pleck, "American Fathering," 94.
46. Ibid.; Ralph LaRossa and Donald C. Reitzes, "Continuity and Change in Middle Class Fatherhood: The Culture-Conduct Distinction," *Journal of Marriage and the Family* 55:2 (May 1993): 455–68.
47. LaRossa, "Fatherhood," 451 (emphasis in original).
48. Ibid.
49. W. Brad Johnson, "Father Uninvolvement: Impact, Etiology, and Potential Solutions," *Journal of Christianity and Psychology* 12:4 (1993): 305.

50. Zinsmeister, "Nature of Fatherhood," 6.
51. Ronald F. Levant, "Toward the Reconstruction of Masculinity," *Journal of Family Psychology* 5:3–4 (March/June 1992): 379–402.
52. Michael E. Lamb, "The Father's Role in the Facilitation of Infant Mental Health," *Infant Mental Health Journal* 1 (1980): 140–49; Ronald F. Levant, "Psychological Services Designed for Men: A Psychoeducational Approach," *Psychotherapy* 27 (1990): 309–15; L. B. Silverstein, "Transforming the Debate About Child Care and Maternal Employment," *American Psychologist* 46 (1991): 1025–32; Johnson, "Father Uninvolvement."
53. L. B. Feldman, "Fathers and Fathering," in *Men in Therapy*, ed. R. L. Meth and R. S. Pasick (New York: Guilford, 1990).
54. Rob Palkovitz, "Parental Attitudes and Fathers' Interactions with their Five-Month-Old Infants," *Developmental Psychology* 20 (1984): 1054–60.
55. Johnson, "Father Uninvolvement."
56. Lamb, Pleck, and Levine, "Increased Involvement."
57. Bernard, "Provider."
58. Rob Palkovitz, "Consistency and Stability in the Family Microsystem Environment," in *Annual Advances in Applied Developmental Psychology, Volume II*, ed. Donald L. Peters and Susan Kontos (New York: Ablex, 1987), 40–67.
59. Theresa M. Cooney et al., "Timing of Fatherhood: Is 'On-time' Optimal?" *Journal of Marriage and the Family* 55:1 (1993): 205–15; J. Veroff and S. Field, *Marriage and Work in America* (New York: Van Nostrand Rinehold Co., 1970).
60. Cooney et al., "Timing of Fatherhood."
61. For further discussion of this topic refer to Palkovitz, "Parental Attitudes," idem, "Consistency."
62. Lamb, Pleck, and Levine, "Increased Involvement," 113.
63. Graeme Russell, "Shared-Caregiving Marriages: An Australian Study," in *Nontraditional Families: Parenting and Child Development*, ed. Michael E. Lamb (Hillsdale, N.J.: Lawrence Erlbaum, 1982); Norma Radin and A. Sagi, "Childrearing Fathers in Intact Families in Israel and the U.S.A.," *Merrill Palmer Quarterly* 28 (1983): 111–36.
64. Lamb, Pleck, and Levine, "Increased Involvement"; LaRossa, "Fatherhood."
65. Lamb, Pleck, and Levine, "Increased Involvement," 121–22.
66. Ibid., 123 (emphasis in original).
67. See Matt. 7:9–11; Luke 11:11–13.
68. The term discipline is *not* equivalent to punish, as it is frequently misused today. Discipline comes from the same root word as "disciple." To disciple someone implies that a good and faithful teacher is training them. Clearly, discipling entails many methods of instruction: modeling, explaining, giving of responsibilities commensurate with rights and abilities, and exposition of written materials, among others. Punishment is a much more narrow and much less effective means of instruction. See Deut. 8:5; Prov. 3:12, 13:24, 15:5, 19:18, 22:6, 22:15, 23:13, 29:17; Eph. 6:4; 1 Thess. 2:11–12; Heb. 12:7–11.
69. See Eph. 6:4; Col. 3:21.

70. See 1 and 2 Kings, where statements are made concerning the extent to which sons followed in their fathers' ways or deviated from them. While all factors affecting children's modeling of behavior are not delineated, clearly, modeling is an important factor.

71. See Deut. 10:18, 24:17; Ps. 10:14, 68:5.

72. See Deut. 24:19.

73. See Deut. 27:19; Zech. 7:10.

74. Jessie Bernard points out that God the Father is the first provider through creation. See also Matt. 7:9–11; Luke 11:11–13; 1 Tim. 5:8; Titus 3:14.

75. See Prov. 22:6; Heb. 12:7–11.

76. Eph. 5:25.

77. Phil. 2:3–4.

78. Matt. 20:25–27; Mark 10:42–44.

79. See John 15:13.

80. See Deut. 6:5; Matt. 6:33, 7:12; Phil. 2:3–4; Matt. 12:31; 1 John 13:34.

81. Mark 12:28–31.

82. Atkinson and Blackwater, "Fathering in the 20th Century."

83. LaRossa, "Fatherhood," 456.

84. LaRossa and Reitzes, "The Culture-Conduct Connection," 466.

85. Rotundo, "American Fatherhood," 20.

86. Zinsmeister, "Nature of Fatherhood," 25.

87. Ibid., 31.

88. Palm and Palkovitz, "Challenge," 363.

17

"Lifting As We Climb"

Womanist Theorizing about Religion and the Family

TOINETTE M. EUGENE

> We are asserting that what has happened in the black family affects what happens in the black church. The church in the black tradition has been an extended family; while the family, in many instances, has been, in fact, a "domestic church." Church and family together have nurtured our suffering race and preserved us through all the ordeals of our history.
>
> —J. Deotis Roberts, *Roots of a Black Future*[1]

What has happened to the black family, which has been euphemistically understood as a "domestic church?" Within the black church, which has been understood as a "homebase and safe harbor" laced with moral and religious value systems, what is happening to the sanctity of motherhood and to the revered place of the woman as wife, mother, daughter, sister? What is precipitously and precariously occurring to contemporary images of the African-American woman in urban as well as rural American reality? For African-American women, women's realities in general cannot be analyzed in isolation from their context. One anonymous woman has put it this way: "I dread to see my children grow. I know not their fate. Where the white boy has every opportunity and protection, mine will have few opportunities and no protection. It does not matter how good or wise my children may be, they are colored."[2]

Womanhood occurs in specific historical situations framed by interlocking structures of race, class, gender: for example, where the sons and daughters of white mothers have "every opportunity and protection" and the black daughters and sons "know not their fate."

Racial domination and economic exploitation profoundly shape the womanist context, not only for African-American women and women of color in the United States, but for all women.[3] Moreover, distinctive womanist moral values, even within the context of predominantly patriarchal cultural and religious-denominational environments, have profoundly shaped the context of religion and society for African-American women and other women of color. These moral values, depicted by the praxis catch phrase, "Lifting as We Climb," have carried womanists out of the pits of racist hell, through the patriarchal aisles of the still and yet prophetic if limited black church, and beyond the corridors and classist environments of the black communities even into the broader avenues of pluralistic American culture.

Black women have developed these values for themselves, and have offered them as options to the black community as well as to the members of a broader, dominant society. They cannot be understood or adequately explained apart from the historical context in which black women have found themselves as moral and ethical agents. Moreover, the moral values that black women have provided as a legacy to the black community, as well as to the feminist movement in American society, suggest a distinctive religious consciousness and discernible womanist religious traditions that have been irrepressible in redeeming and transforming an entire human environment.

The central theses of this chapter, which traces the specific moral values of black feminism to their root within black religious traditions, are also theses derived in part from the highest expressions of moral and faith development as described particularly in the theoretical research of Carol Gilligan and James Fowler.[4]

By drawing on this psychological research and by reviewing black religious history, this chapter asserts that public activism and private endurance are paradigmatic black women's value indicators in both the black religious traditions and in womanist communities. Social activism, self-sacrifice, and other similar value indicators may be verified in the lives of Mary McLeod Bethune and Nannie Helen Burroughs, to name but two exemplary models. However, these value measures and these valuable models represent more than unusual courage and strength; they also represent realistic responses to economic deprivation and political and social inequality. Black women have been forced to perform labor and to take risks that few white women have been called on to do, either in the name of religious traditions or in behalf of the survival of their race.

Black women, however, are not special specimens of womanhood; rather, they are women of color who have been given less protected and more burdensome positions in society. As Michelle Wallace has so poignantly pointed out, this has resulted in the "myth of the superwoman," which is not a description of black women but, rather, a measure of the difference between what is regularly expected of white women and what is essentially required of black women.[5] Womanists continue to lift as they climb.

It is obvious that black women have experienced the oppressive structures of racism, class bias, and male supremacy in both religion and society in this country. What is not always so obvious to a dominant white worldview, and even to feminist theological understandings, is that African-American culture and religion have generated alternative interrelated notions of womanhood that contradict those of mainstream American economics, sociology, and theology.[6] These alternative experiences, visions, and images of womanhood have been forged out of the furnace of a moral value system endemic to the black church, which is also undeniably the "domestic church" or home base for liberating revolutionary praxis. This chapter will explore aspects of the moral consciousness and value system that guide black women in their ongoing struggle for survival. It will do so through a commentary on black religious traditions that black women share. Within this commentary some reflections will also be made regarding black women's perspectives on feminism as a white women's movement, and on feminist theologies.

Black Women and
Moral Values During Slavery

Historically, the domestic black church has been the fiery furnace through which systematic faith affirmations and liberating principles for biblical interpretation have been developed by black people. Within this "invisible institution," hidden from the observation of slave masters, black women and black men developed an extensive moral value system and religious life of their own. In the language of moral development theorist Carol Gilligan, they established and operated out of a web or network of relationships and intimacy with others in community. The moral values of care, compassion, and cooperation with other black and oppressed persons served as criteria for decisions and actions intended to lay hold of the good, the true, and the beautiful.

The biblical interpretations of the antebellum black church provided black people with webs of relationships centering on the God of justice and of liberation, and these made slaves incontestably discontent with their servile condition. In the case of black women, whose bodies and spirits were wantonly violated by the immoral sexual advances of white masters, the moral value system of black people in this period encouraged slave women to overcome the sources of their oppression in order to maintain and sustain their fragile nexus with God and community as valued and trusted friends.[7] Paula Giddings, in her text *When and Where I Enter: The Impact of Black Women on Race and Sex in America*, reports on the moral resistance black slave women offered:

So, by the early eighteenth century an incredible social, legal, racial structure was put in place. Women were firmly stratified in the roles that Plato envisioned. Blacks were chattel, White men could impregnate a Black woman with impunity, and she alone could give birth to a slave. Blacks constituted a permanent labor force and metaphor that were perpetuated through the Black woman's womb. And all of this was done within the context of the Church, the operating laws of capitalism, and the psychological needs of White males. Subsequent history would be a variation on the same theme.

In its infancy slavery was particularly harsh. Physical abuse, dismemberment, and torture were common. . . . Partly as a result, in the eighteenth century, slave masters did not underestimate the will of their slaves to rebel, even their female slaves. Black women proved especially adept at poisoning their masters, a skill undoubtedly imported from Africa. Incendiarism was another favorite method; it required neither brute physical strength nor direct confrontation. But Black women used every means available to resist slavery—as men did—and if caught, they were punished just as harshly.[8]

In the midst of this dehumanizing slave environment, black families, and thus the "domestic" church, survived. They overcame the slaveholders' attempts to reduce them to so many subhuman labor units, managing to create an ongoing system of family arrangements and kin networks. Domestic life became critically important, for it was the only place where slaves had any equality and autonomy as human beings in relation to one another.[9]

Regarding domestic life and labor, Angela Davis in *Women, Race, and Class* has observed a paradox of great significance for black women and men:

The salient theme emerging from domestic life in the slave quarters is one of sexual equality. The labor that slaves performed for their own sake and not for the aggrandizement of their masters was carried out on terms of equality. Within the confines of their family and community life, therefore, Black people managed to accomplish a magnificent feat. They transformed that negative equality which emanated from the equal oppression they suffered as slaves into a positive quality: the egalitarianism characterizing their social relations.[10]

Harriet Tubman and countless others provided egalitarian images of slave women as strong, self-reliant, proud of their roots and of their ability to survive, and convinced of their right to a place in society through the liberation of all black people. Equally oppressed as laborers, equal to their men in the domestic sphere, they were also equal in their moral resistance to slavery, participating in work stoppages and revolts, fleeing north, and helping others to flee.

The ability of black people to cope in a hostile society has endured into the twentieth century. Studies of black women in urban church situations show that the means by which black families survived slavery still enable black women and their families to survive today.

Within this historical framework of past and present hostility black women have always perceived networks of relationality in the liberation struggle differently from white women. Domesticity has never been seen as entirely oppressive but rather as a vehicle for building family life under slavery. Male/female relationships have always been more egalitarian. There has usually been less emphasis on women's work as different from and inferior to men's. And finally, slaves and freed persons, both male and female, have consistently rebelled against the sexual oppression of black women as well as the emasculation of black men. It is easy to understand why many black people today see the white feminist movement as an attempt to divide black people. Contemporary womanists caution against espousing more "radical" white feminist positions because they dismiss as irrelevant black men, black children, and black families. Consequently, a primary moral value for black people is articulated in this overarching and enduring womanist position: Solidarity among all black people is essential for survival.

A dramatic statement of black women's unique attitude toward solidarity with black men is found in the 1977 statement of the Combahee River Collective, a black lesbian feminist group from Boston:

> Although we are feminists and lesbians we feel solidarity with progressive Black men and do not advocate the fractionalization that white women who are separatists demand. Our situation as Black people necessitates that we have solidarity around the fact of race. . . . We struggle together with Black men against racism, while we also struggle with Black men about sexism.[11]

These black lesbian feminists explicitly rejected a feminist separatism that equates all oppression with sexual oppression, and which fails fully to acknowledge that black women *and men* are victims of shared racial oppression. Feminist separatism is not a viable political philosophy for most black women. Ethicist Barbara Hilkert Andolsen, in her remarkable assessment of racism and American feminism, *Daughters of Jefferson, Daughters of Bootblacks*, issues a strong caveat to white women who want to understand the black feminist experience:

> Those of us who are white feminists need to be careful that we do not articulate limited strategies for dealing with sexism as if they were the only legitimate feminist strategies. White feminist separatist theories or strategies that ignore the strong bond forged between many black women and men in a shared struggle against racism do not speak to all women's experience.[12]

White feminists have a responsibility to understand the perspectives of women of color on their own issues, to analyze how racist social structures may alter the impact of white feminist proposals, and to support black women in their own self-defined struggle for liberation. Womanists are creating their own analyses of sexism and of the interconnections between racism and sexism. White feminist theologians who wish to contribute to an inclusive feminist theology that respects and reflects the diversity of women's experience need to learn from the experiences, moral values, and feminist theology articulated by black women.

There is ample material for reflection in the records of black women's distinctive theological consciousness during slavery. For example, the biblical-exegetical abilities of Maria Stewart, coupled with her philosophical assumptions (that would later be known as modernist thinking), gave black women in 1832 a freer rein to express and act on ideas that liberated them from the oppression of both sexism and racism.[13] For Stewart, simple logic demanded that in light of women's past roles, "God at this eventful period should raise up your females to strive . . . both in public and private, to assist those who are endeavoring to stop the strong current of prejudice that flows so profusely against us at present."[14] Maria Stewart was sure enough of her moral values to admonish others not to doubt the validity of black women's mission: "No longer ridicule their efforts," she counseled, "It will be counted as sin."[15]

At a woman's rights convention in Akron, Ohio in 1851, several of the most celebrated examples of early womanist theology were rendered by the legendary abolitionist and mystic, Sojourner Truth, in her famous "Ain't I a Woman" speech. From the very beginning of the conference, the white women were overwhelmed by the jeering ridicule of men who had come to disrupt the meeting. Their most effective antagonist was a clergyman who used both the maleness of Jesus and the helplessness of the women to counter their feminist arguments. Sojourner squelched the heckler by correcting his theology first, noting that Jesus came from "God and a woman—man had nothing to do with Him."[16] Secondly, she asserted that women were not inherently weak and helpless.

Raising herself to her full height of six feet, flexing a muscled arm, and bellowing with a voice one observer likened to the apocalyptic thunders, Truth informed the audience that she could outwork, outeat, and outlast any man. Then she challenged: "Ain't I a Woman?"[17] She spoke of women's strength and moral abilities to set things aright: "If the first woman God ever made was strong enough to turn the world upside down all alone, these women together ought to be able to turn it back, and get it right side up again. And now they are asking to do it, the men better let them."[18] The moral values asserted by black women who give credence to the black Judeo-Christian tradition consistently honor reconciliation as highly as liberation. The praxis of "lifting as we climb" continues as a historically documentable theme.

The accumulated experiences and expressions of black women during slavery were nuanced by their differing webs of relationship within the institutional and patriarchal black church and its biblical interpretations of the salvific power of God. These women toiled under the lash for their masters, worked for and protected their families, fought against slavery and were beaten and raped; but, unsubdued, they passed on to their nominally free female descendants a rich legacy of their own moral value system. It was a legacy of hard work decidedly different from the WASP work ethic; it was a legacy of perseverance and self reliance, a legacy of tenacity, resistance, and insistence on sexual equality—in short, a legacy of love spelling out standards for a new womanhood.[19]

Feminist Moral Values
and Black Religious Traditions

The institution of chattel slavery in America was destroyed by the most momentous national event of the nineteenth century, the Civil War. Emancipation removed the legal and political status of slavery from approximately four million black people in the United States, which meant that, in principle, these blacks owned their persons and their labor for the first time. Unfortunately for the vast majority of African Americans, the traditional practices of racial and gender subordination continued to bring them incredible suffering after that war.

The black woman began her life of freedom with no vote, no protection, and no equity of any sort. Black women, young and old, were basically on their own. The pattern of exploiting the black woman as laborer and breeder was only shaken by the Civil War; by no means was it destroyed. Throughout the late nineteenth and early twentieth centuries, black women were strongly restricted to the most unskilled, poorly paid, menial work. Virtually no black woman held a job beyond that of a domestic servant or field hand. Keeping house, farming, and bearing and rearing children continued to dominate all aspects of the black woman's life. The systematic oppression and routinized exclusion of black females from other areas of employment served to confirm the continuing, servile status of black women. As Jeanne Noble describes it, "While freedom brought new opportunities for black men, for most women it augmented old problems."[20] After emancipation, racism and male supremacy continued to intersect with patriarchal and capitalist structures in definitive ways.

The religious consciousness of the black freedwoman in the latter nineteenth century focused on "uplifting the black community." The black female was taught that her education was meant not only to uplift her but also to prepare her for a life of service in the overall community. There was a general attitude, says Noble, that "Negro women should be trained to teach in order to uplift the masses."[21] This attitude provided an additional impetus for black women such as Nannie Helen Burroughs, Charlotte Hawkins Brown, and Mary McLeod Bethune to found schools. Although the curricula of these schools included academic subjects, there were large doses of industrial arts courses, particularly homemaking, and an environment that enforced codes of morality and thrift. Biblical faith, grounded in the prophetic tradition, helped black women devise strategies and tactics to make black people less susceptible to the indignities and proscriptions of an oppressive white social order.

Understanding the prophetic tradition of the Bible and of the black church has empowered black women to fashion a set of moral values on their own terms. It has helped them to master, radicalize, and sometimes destroy the pervasive negative orientations imposed by the larger society. It has also helped them to articulate possibilities for decisions and action that address forthrightly the circumstances that shape black life.

In light of black women's biblical faith grounded in the prophetic tradition, many black women have been inspired by the Bethune and Burroughs models to regard highly a diaconal model of black feminist theology, which is extremely consistent with their experience and identity. Without necessarily rejecting white feminist models of theology that focus principally or only on mutuality and equality as *sine qua nons* of liberation, the choice made by many black feminists is for a theology of servant-leadership as espoused by Christ. This biblical model of feminist liberation theology is principally focused on solidarity with those who suffer or are marginalized in any way. A much deeper examination, integration, and expression of this black feminist perspective and alternative to "mainstream" models of feminist liberation theology is needed.[22]

Rosemary Radford Ruether has been in the forefront of white feminist theologians who have insisted that confronting racism must be a
high priority. She has produced particularly illuminating analyses of the
interconnections between racism and sexism.[23] When discussing the
future of feminist theology in the academic world, Ruether acknowledges that she speaks from a "white Western Christian context." She
calls for an inclusive feminist theology that must emerge out of "a network of solidarity" existing among many feminist communities
"engaged in the critique of patriarchalism in distinct cultural and religious contexts," rather than "one dominant form of feminism that
claims to speak for the whole of womankind."[24]

During the mass migration of southern blacks to the North
(1910–1925) tens of thousands of black women and men left home,
seeking social democracy and economic opportunity. During this
colossal movement of black people, the black church continued to
serve as the focal point and center for maintaining the moral value system and the network of relationships that sustained community life.

Not surprisingly, this accelerated movement of blacks out of the
South impinged on the black woman's reality in very definite ways.
Black women migrated North in greater numbers than black men.
Economic necessity required most black women who immigrated to the
urban centers to find work immediately. In order to survive and to provide for their families, black women once again found only drudge
work available to them.

The interaction of race and sex in the labor market exacted a heavy
toll on the black woman, making all aspects of migration a problem of
paramount religious significance. Her experience as a wife and a
mother, responsible for transmitting the moral values, culture, and customs of the black community to her children, served as a decisive factor in determining how the Bible was read and understood by her.
Simultaneously, while the black woman was trying to organize family
life according to black traditional values, the white male-dominated
industrial society required that she serve as a catalyst in their labor transition process. Her own culture shock and adaptation difficulties had to
be repressed because she was responsible for making a home in
crowded, substandard housing, finding inner-city schools that provided literacy training for her children, and earning enough income to
cover the most elementary needs of her family.

The moral and religious value system of the domestic black church
served as a sustaining force and as an interpretive grid to guide migrant
black women in facing life squarely, and in acknowledging its raw
coarseness. The white elitist attributes of passive gentleness and an

enervated delicacy, considered particularly appropriate to womanhood, proved nonfunctional in the pragmatic survival of black women. Cultivating conventional amenities was not a luxury afforded them. Instead, black women were aware that their very lives depended on their being able to comprehend the various forces in the larger world; to hold in check the nightmare figures of terror; to fight for basic freedoms against the sadistic law enforcement agencies; to resist the temptation to capitulate to the demands of the *status quo*; to find meaning in the most despotic circumstances; and to create something where nothing existed before. The expression of a moral value system for black women meant and required a "sheroic" self-sacrifice and self-giving that could never allow for shyness, silence, softness, or diffidence as a response indicating subservience.

From the period of black urban migration through World Wars I and II black women, rooted in the strong moral values and prophetic tradition of the domestic black church, became religious crusaders for justice. Mary McLeod Bethune and her associates recorded and talked about the grimness of struggle among the least visible people in the society. Bethune was adamant about the unheralded achievements of black women, always encouraging them to "go to the front and take our rightful place; fight our battles and claim our victories."[25] She believed in black women's "possibilities," moral values, and their place on this earth. "Next to God," she once said, "we are indebted to women, first for life itself, and then for making it worth having."[26] In response to a hostile environment, deteriorating conditions, and the enduring humiliation of social ostracism experienced by black people especially during these war years, Bethune and company exposed the most serious and unyielding problem of the twentieth century—the single most determining factor of black existence in America—the question of color. In their strategic attacks against the ideological supremacy of racist practices and values, Bethune and her colleagues appealed to the religious traditions of black people that began in their invisible church during slavery.

From the period of urbanization during World War II to the present, women of color still find that their situation is a struggle to survive collectively and individually against the harsh historical realities and pervasive adversities of today's world. Federal government programs, civil rights movements, and voter-education programs have all had a positive impact on the black woman's situation, but they have not been able to offset the negative effects of inequities that are tied to the historical and ideological hegemony of racism, sexism, and class privilege.[27]

Precisely because of this reality and overwhelmingly oppressive national ideology, Rosemary Radford Ruether warns white feminists to give explicit attention to the ways in which they are involved in race and class privilege. If they do not, she says, they risk social encapsulation:

> Any women's movement which is only concerned about sexism and not other forms of oppression, must remain a woman's movement of the white upper class, for it is only this group of women whose only problem is the problem of being women, since in every other way, they belong to the ruling class.[28]

Moreover, both black and white feminist groups that do not give explicit attention to the need for yoking racism and sexism will find that they can easily be manipulated by dominant males, who often appeal to unexamined class and race interests to achieve economic exploitation of all women. Work and dialogue between feminists of color and white feminists in this essential area is, in some sense, just beginning. Meanwhile, black women and their families continue to be enslaved to hunger, disease, and the highest rate of black unemployment since the Depression years. Advances in education, housing, healthcare, and other necessities are deteriorating faster now than ever before.

Both in informal day-to-day life and in the formal organizations and institutions of society, black women are still the victims of aggravated inequities rooted in the tridimensional reality of race/class/gender oppression. It is in this context that the moral values of black women and the emergence of womanist consciousness, shaped by black biblical and religious traditions, must continue to make a decisive difference in a debilitated and nearly dysfunctional human environment.

Womanist Relationships, Moral Values, and Biblical Traditions

Because of this totally demoralizing reality, and because of the religious traditions from which most black women have come, the Bible has been the highest source of authority in developing and delivering a black moral praxis and a moral theology that is usable in all circumstances. By selectively utilizing the pages of revered Old Testament books, black women have learned how to refute the stereotypes that have depicted black people as ignorant minstrels or vindictive militants. Remembering and retelling the Jesus stories of the New Testament has helped black women to deal with the overwhelming difficulties of overworked and widowed mothers, of underworked and anxious fathers, of sexually exploited and anguished daughters, of prodigal sons, and of dead or dying brothers whose networks of relationality are rooted deeply in the black community. Womanist consciousness and moral values grow out of and expand on liberationist, black biblical experience and hermeneutics.

Black feminist consciousness may be more accurately identified as black womanist consciousness, to use Alice Walker's concept and definition. In the introduction to *In Search of Our Mothers' Gardens*, Walker proposes several descriptions of the term "womanist," indicating that the word refers primarily to a black feminist and is derived from the older term "womanish," referring to outrageous, audacious, courageous, or willful behavior.[29] To be a faithful womanist, then, is to operate out of this system of black moral value indicators that flow from biblical understandings based on justice and love. It is to express in word and deed an alternative ontology or way of living in the world that is endemic to many black women. It is precisely the womanist religious responses of endurance, resistance, and resiliency offered in the face of all attempts at personal and institutional domination that may provide a renewed theological legacy of liberation for everyone concerned.

In exploring the implications contained in Walker's richly descriptive prose, it is possible to make some concluding reflections on black moral values and on the contribution of black women's life experiences as they interface with white feminist liberation theologies.

Womanist responses and black moral values gleaned from the domestic black church are meant to be alternative standards of womanhood contradictory to those of mainstream American society. Womanist images and black moral values are meant to be paradigmatic of an authentic Christian community of the oppressed, one which embraces not only the story of the Resurrection but acts as a referent for the redemptive tribulations through which Jesus as Suffering Servant has come. Womanist moral values are expressed through radical healing and empowering actions in company with those who are considered the very least in the reign of God.

Walker adds that a womanist is "committed to the survival and wholeness of entire people, male *and* female." She is "not a separatist . . . [and is] traditionally capable."[30] The practical implications of such meanings for interaction and dialogue between black women's moral values and the diverse tenets of white feminist ethics are obvious and challenging. Womanist moral values can redeem the black community from naiveté regarding the nature and function of liberation, as well as deliver them from the simplistic, black pseudoexpression of providence that "de Lawd will provide." Nonetheless, a womanist religious tradition does subscribe to the black folk wisdom that God can make a way out of no way for those, like Zora Neale Huston and others, who simply refuse to resign from the human race.

Womanist moral values of "appreciation for the struggle, a love of the folk, and a love of self—*regardless*"[31] offer to black people as well as to others a continual and open means of interaction between those who claim diverse womanist and feminist identities and experiences. Such values are relevant to all who have a significant agenda for more authentic theologies of liberation. "Lifting as We Climb" remains the watchword and the praxis project for womanist theorizing and strategizing about religion and the family.

NOTES

1. J. Deotis Roberts, *Roots of a Black Future: Family and Church* (Philadelphia: Westminster Press, 1980), 108.
2. An anonymous African-American mother in 1904, reported in Gerda Lerner, *Black Women in White America* (New York: Pantheon Books, 1972), 158.
3. In this chapter, I use the terms "womanist," African-American women, black women, and women of color somewhat interchangeably. Grounded in the experiences of groups who have been the targets of racism, the term "womanist" sometimes implies more solidarity of black women with black men involved in struggles against racism. In contrast, the term "women of color" emerges from a womanist background where racial ethnic women committed to feminist struggle aimed to distinguish their history and issues from those of middle-class, white women. Neither term captures the complexity of African-American, Native-American, Asian-American, and Hispanic women's experiences.
4. Carol Gilligan, *In a Different Voice: Psychological Theory and Women's Development* (Cambridge, Mass.: Harvard University Press, 1982) and James W. Fowler, *Stages of Faith: The Psychology of Human Development and the Quest for Meaning* (San Francisco: Harper & Row, 1981).
5. Michelle Wallace, *Black Macho and the Myth of the Superwoman* (New York: Dial Press, 1979).
6. Toinette M. Eugene, "Black Women Contribute Strong Alternate Images," *National Catholic Reporter*, 13 April 1984, 4.
7. Carol Gilligan as described in James W. Fowler, *Becoming Adult, Becoming Christian* (San Francisco: Harper & Row, 1984), 39–40.
8. Paula Giddings, *When and Where I Enter: The Impact of Black Women on Race and Sex in America* (Toronto: Bantam Books, 1984), 39.
9. Herbert Gutman, *The Black Family in Slavery and Freedom, 1750–1925* (New York: Pantheon Books, 1976), 356–57.
10. Angela Y. Davis, *Women, Race, and Class* (New York: Random House, 1981), 18.
11. Combahee River Collective, "A Black Feminist Statement," in *This Bridge Called My Back: Writings by Radical Women of Color*, ed. Cherrie Moraga and Gloria Anzaldua (Watertown, Mass.: Persephone Press, 1981), 213.

12. Barbara Hilkert Andolsen, *Daughters of Jefferson, Daughters of Bootblacks: Racism and American Feminism* (Macon, Ga.: Mercer University Press, 1986), 98.
13. Giddings, *When and Where I Enter*, 52.
14. Bert James Lowenberg and Ruth Bogin, eds., *Black Women in Nineteenth Century American Life: Their Words, Their Thoughts, Their Feelings* (University Park, Pa.: Pennsylvania State University Press, 1976), 149.
15. Ibid.
16. Ibid., 236.
17. Ibid., 235.
18. Ibid., 236.
19. Davis, *Women, Race, and Class*, 29.
20. Jeanne L. Noble, *Beautiful, Also, are the Souls of My Black Sisters: A History of the Black Women in America* (New York: Prentice Hall Press, 1978), 63.
21. Jeanne L. Noble, as discussed in Paula Giddings, *When and Where I Enter*, 101.
22. Eugene, "Black Women Contribute," 4.
23. Rosemary Radford Ruether has written about racism many times. Two of her more detailed treatments of the topic are "Between the Sons of Whites and the Sons of Blackness: Racism and Sexism in America," in *New Women/New Earth: Sexist Ideologies and Human Liberation* (New York: Seabury Press, 1975), 115–33; and "Crisis in Sex and Race: Black Theology vs. Feminist Theology," *Christianity and Crisis* 34 (15 April 1985): 67–73.
24. Rosemary Radford Ruether, "Feminist Theology: On Becoming the Tradition," *Christianity and Crisis* 45 (4 March 1985): 58.
25. Elaine M. Smith, "Mary McLeod Bethune and the National Youth Administration," in *Clio Was a Woman: Studies in the History of American Women*, ed. Mabel E. Deutrich and Virginia C. Purdy (Washington, D.C.: Howard University Press, 1980), 152.
26. Ibid.
27. Davis, *Women, Race, and Class*, 231–32.
28. Ruether, *New Women/New Earth*, 116.
29. Alice Walker, *In Search of Our Mother's Gardens: Womanist Prose* (San Diego: Harcourt Brace Jovanovich, 1983), xi–xiii.
30. Ibid., xi.
31. Ibid.

18

A Voice
from "the Borderlands"

Asian-American Women and their Families

JUNG HA KIM

An Asian-American Community Center with whose work I am familiar is increasingly receiving inquiries from relatively well off, professional women asking for Asian live-in nannies to take care of their children and do light housekeeping. One inquiry in particular comes to mind as an emblematic narrative where gender, class, race-ethnicity,[1] and religion intersect as important social constructs and variables, and present unsettling implications regarding the diverse experiences of Asian-American families in the United States.

One afternoon, a woman called from her home office to place an ad for a live-in nanny for her three-year-old son. She explained that presently there was a nanny working in the house, but "it's just that this black girl is so rude and ungrateful." Hearing about how "you people" are "culturally nurturing to babies," she wanted to replace the present nanny with "an Asian girl." The age of the Asian girl did not really matter much, but she preferred to hire either "a young girl, say around high school age" or "an elderly Asian grandmother-type." She also added that since Koreans are "religious," she would "allow the girl to attend her Korean church on Sundays," thereby granting a whole day off from work, "unless we [she and her husband] need to go out for various functions [on Sundays]."

This narrative might be understood as just another example of the deadly trio of venerable "isms" in the United States—racism, sexism, and classism—experienced by women of color. Yet it demands a different discourse in a new language to address the conspicuously silenced experiences of Asian-American women themselves. Are Asian-American "girls" ever allowed to age? Do social categories such as "Asians" and "Asian Americans" represent a monolithic unit of "you people"? Are Asian-American women "naturally," "innately," and "culturally" more nurturing than others? Is there an undeniable comeback of Asian-American women's domestic labor force experiences since the

1960s? To what extent do Asian-American women replace or compete against other women of color for underemployed job opportunities in the so-called domestic domain? Does a narrative such as this one represent a glimpse of the initial employment map of immigrants and undocumented women in our multicultural society as it undergoes restructuring of the labor force? Are all Korean Americans "religious," and affiliated with their own "ethnic" religious organizations? What happens to their own families when society gives lip service to the "stability" and "coherence" of Asian-American families and yet commodifies the caregiving and homemaking skills of Asian-American women in order to draw them into work outside their family context?

In this chapter, I attempt to provide an overview of the interacting features of Asian-American families, religions, and feminism from a Korean-American woman's perspective, paying particular attention to the foregoing questions. The chapter begins with a brief discussion of terminology, a redefinition of Asian Americans, and an assessment of socio-historical locations of Asian-American families in the United States. Then, by focusing on experiences of Asian-American women at the center of the study, I argue that they are caught up in a complex web of "both/and" expectations in their everyday life. On the one hand, Asian-American women are expected to function as the "glue"[2] that keeps their families together and preserves racial-ethnic traditions and cultures. At the same time, however, Asian-American women serve as vital "breadwinners" for their family's survival. The paradox is that their underemployment and service-intensive labor participation, while fulfilling the latter expectation, excludes them from the privilege of being the central figures in their own "domestic" realm. Unlike the few privileged Euro-American women who are full-time homemakers, Asian-American women, along with other women of color and working and poor people across racial-ethnic lines, historically have experienced the "double shift."[3] Since racial-ethnic men have been unable to earn a family wage, women's paid labor outside their home has been vital to family survival. Furthermore, their labor-intensive paid work is characterized by long working hours, low pay, limited job advancement, low prestige and (especially for immigrant women) relative isolation from the larger society. Indeed, I will argue that any feminist understanding of the family that does not incorporate criticism of the two separate spheres is not inclusive of Asian-American families' experiences. Any family that requires women to be victimized as "sacrificial lambs" for the sake of a stable and cohesive family cannot be called an ideal American family. And any Christian (or other religious) articulation of the family that does not regard the family experiences of slaves, gentiles,

and outcasts as equally sacred to that of freeborns—perhaps more so—
is not worthy of Asian-American "solemn assembly."[4]

Constructing "Asian Americans"

The racial-ethnic category of "Asian American" is a socially constructed product, "made in the U.S.A." In spite of diversity in nationality, language, history, culture, religion, and socioeconomic background,
immigrants from the Asian continent and their descendants have been
categorized and treated as a single entity in the United States. As an
attempt to correct homogenization of various groups originating in Asia,
social scientists and ethnic studies scholars are increasingly using more
specific categories instead of "Asian Americans." These terms include
"Pacific Islander Americans"[5]; "East Asian Americans" as distinct from
"Southeast Asian Americans"[6]; and "Southeast Asian Americans" as distinct from "Central and West Asian Americans."[7]

The 1980 U.S. census counted approximately thirty ethnic groups
within the Asian population and 60 subgroups of the Pacific Islander
population. The "Asian-American" population (including Pacific Islander
Americans) was 1.4 million in the 1970 census, 3.5 million in 1980, and
7.3 million by 1990.[8] Asian Americans are known as the fastest-growing
population and the third largest "minority" group in the United States.[9]
With the passage of the 1965 Immigration Acts, the foreign-born population grew steadily; nearly 50 percent of the Asian-American population
was said to be foreign-born by 1985. This is an important demographic
characteristic with implications for studying Asian Americans' struggles,
communities, cultures, and especially families.

It should be noted that people from China, Japan, Korea, the
Philippines, and Vietnam represent more than 80 percent of the total
population of Asian Americans living in the United States. Thus, when
the generic term "Asian Americans" is used in this chapter, I am referring mostly to hyphenated Americans of these five ethnic groups—
Chinese, Japanese, Korean, Filipino/a and Vietnamese—who consider
the United States as their home base.

Socio-Historical Locations
of Asian-American Families

Immigration histories of people traveling from the continent of Asia to
the United States portray a century-long struggle of people to transplant
themselves in their new "homeland." One venerable factor that has
shaped the United States is the basic law of supply and demand in a cap-

italist society. Asian sojourners and Asian Americans[10] alike were treated as units of cheap labor throughout the history of the United States of America. Until quite recently, no recognition of their family ties and no sense of empathy for their "mutilated"[11] family patterns can be found in the U.S. immigration acts,[12] labor codes,[13] civic laws,[14] or in socio-cultural representations.[15] Men from China from the mid-nineteenth century and from Japan by the end of the century provided cheap labor for establishing the foundation of the American West as miners, farmers, domestic servants, and unskilled workers building the transcontinental railroads. Most of the first wave of Asian male laborers were permanent sojourners who were prohibited from becoming naturalized citizens. The highly skewed sex ratio of men to women among Chinese- and Japanese-Americans by the turn of the century—27 to 1 and 13 to 1 respectively[16]—testifies to both legal and social sanctions against Asian-American family formation, especially before the advent of a small wave of "picture brides" and imported prostitutes,[17] who were allowed into the United States after 1910. Antimiscegenation laws prohibiting inter-racial marriages, along with the capitalist obsession to allocate cheap labor units for building the American Empire, played an important role in the production of dysfunctional Asian-American families.

The economic boom in the 1960s attracted a massive number of immigrants from the so-called third world to meet the demand of cheaper labor.[18] Among the predominantly post-1965 immigrants of Asian origin (and also from Africa and Latin America), the reversed sex ratio of men and women is noticeable. That is, women tend to predom-inate among the post-1965 immigrant population, whereas men pre-dominated in most earlier immigrations across continents. The reasons for this feminization of recent[19] immigration waves may vary; but the fact that U.S. foreign policy sets a direct blueprint for when and how one may enter into the United States, and with which status, cannot be overlooked, especially when studying the experiences of Asian-American women. One undeniable factor that contributes to the femi-nization of post-1965 immigrants from Asia is the invisible yet continuous influx of Asian wives and Amerasian children of U.S. ser-vicemen who were or are stationed in various Asian countries.[20] More recently, "a systematic importation of Asian 'mail-order brides' through advertisements in newspapers and magazines"[21] has become a socially condoned "underground" business network. Another reason for women outnumbering men in the most recent wave of Asian immigra-tion is the fundamental change since the mid-1960s from a heavy industrial market economy to a service-intensive economy, which demands female workers for a "feminized" job market.[22] Put otherwise, the U.S. presence as a colonial power in the Philippines, an imperialist power and military presence in Korea, and the aftermath of the war in Vietnam guaranteed abundant sources of labor for the bottom of the capitalist strata. Given the century-long perpetuation of a highly skewed sex ratio in Asian-American communities, it is not surprising that only since 1980 has the Asian-American sex ratio been balanced.

In sum, all five ethnic groups of Asian Americans living in the United States share rather "peculiar" characteristics in terms of their experiences as hyphenated Americans and as members of their own families: (1) the social worth of Asian Americans judged predominantly as laborers, not as members of their own families; (2) the highly skewed sex ratio; and (3) the "mutilated"[23] or the "split-household"[24] family pattern. Hence, locating Asian American families in the context of U.S. history delineates severely altered and rather "deviant" family experiences, far from the ideal, if exaggerated, American family as represented by "Ozzie and Harriet."[25] Both the rapidly changing U.S. foreign policy in the post–cold war era and the increasing feminization of the U.S. labor market have been taking a steep toll on Asian-American families, and Asian-American women in particular.

The Stable and Cohesive Asian-American Families

It is rather ironic, therefore, that Asian-American families are put on a pedestal as a rediscovered "model," and another "success" story among American families. In the development of the "model minority" scheme, at least two recent political events seem to have played instrumental roles: the rhetorical battle over "family values" during the 1992 presidential campaign and beyond and the Clinton administration's nomination of Zoe Baird for attorney general. Both events clearly highlighted family experiences as demarcated by socioeconomic class, race-ethnicity and gender. Marilyn Quayle stated, for instance, that "most women do not wish to be liberated from their essential natures as women. Most of us love being mothers or wives, which gives our lives a richness that few men and women get from professional accomplishments alone."[26] These remarks were dangerously reminiscent of the supposedly secret Moynihan report of 1964, which simultaneously portrayed an ideal American family and accused the so-called "matriarchal" African-American families of serious deficit. Among Moynihan's claims were that "ours is a society which presumes male leadership in private and public affairs" and that "the white family has achieved a high degree of stability and is maintaining that stability."[27]

Furthermore, more recent public uproar around Zoe Baird's case demonstrated that some women who want and can afford to be liberated from their "essential natures as women" experience their liberation in the "public" realm at the expense of women of color. The labor of women of color becomes an indispensable bridge[28] between the private and the public domain for some privileged women. Mainly through these two recent political events, critical questions about family life in general and the search for the ideal American family in particular have focused public attention and male-stream mass media on seemingly stable Asian-American families.

The scenario of stable and strong Asian-American families entails an intriguing combination of demographic data and quasi-religious vigor in the truthfulness of its claims. For instance, the low divorce rate among Asian Americans is now promoted as evidence of stable families; well-disciplined children who are obedient and quiet in schools are now prized as the pride of families, emphasizing the "centrality of children"[29] in Asian-American households; and close, reciprocal interdependence reflected in intergenerational relationships are credited to clearly defined family roles based on filial piety and obedience, both deeply "Confucian" aspects of Asian-American families. These indices of the apparent stability and coherence of Asian-American families, however, do not come without high costs, which are paid by Asian-American women in particular.

Asian-American Women at the Crossroads: Family, Feminism, and Religion

The conceptualization of Asian-American women as family members is a contested terrain that juxtaposes at least three distinct ways of determining "what is acceptably female in their cultures"[30]: "Asian" ways, "American" (i.e., Western) ways, and "Asian-American" ways. By turning to largely cultural analyses[31] for understanding Asian-American women's experiences within the context of their own families, I am recognizing the fluid and dynamic notion of gendered actions[32] across cultures, the seemingly contradictory and inconsistent survival strategies that Asian-American women utilize in their everyday lives, and the importance of nonmaterialistic culture, such as the role of religion, for pre- and pro-scribing "what is acceptably female."

As in East Asian and Southeast Asian societies, North American societies construct the family by assigning deeply gendered and highly "eth-class"-conscious[33] role expectations to both women and men. In general, women are assigned the primary responsibility for bearing and rearing children and maintaining "a haven in the heartless world"[34]; men provide economic means for their families and protect them from the harsh world. The culturally ascribed status of women as nurturing wives and mothers, and that of men as breadwinners and protective husbands and fathers rests on the ideological assumption of two separate spheres—the private and the public—on the one hand, and the politics of meaning based on patri-kyriarchy[35] on the other hand. "The continuous emphasis on the family as a universal private retreat and as an emotional haven" is not only "misguided in light of historical experiences"[36] of the American family, but offensive to Asian-American families (and other families of color) whose family survival requires at least two full-time wage earners. Men's domination is prevalent in the United States, but to assume that all men benefit equally from patriarchy is to deny the social reality of unequal access to social resources. To put it differently, both the cult of two separate spheres and the patri-kyriarchal meaning system systematically disempower Asian-American families and other families of color. Prior to discussing further theoretical aspects of Asian-American families, however, I will turn to concrete stories of Asian-American women as they struggle to survive and wrestle to name themselves. Numerous stories reveal the intersection of gender, race-ethnicity, class, and religion; but given the limits of space, I will discuss only two stories from the "borderlands" that effectively challenge the thesis of the "strong" and "cohesive" Asian-American families in the United States.

A nameless immigrant woman from China—who was referred to as Mrs. Chen throughout the whole court proceedings—was murdered by her husband Dong Lu Chen in New York on September 7, 1987. Dong Lu Chen struck his wife eight times with a hammer, because she was having an affair. After considering arguments from the defense, the judge acquitted Chen of second-degree murder charges and convicted him of second-degree manslaughter; Chen was assigned no jail term, and only five years of probation.[37] At the bench trial, the expert witness for the defense argued that "Mr. Chen was under extreme emotional stress aggravated by his isolation from family and community. In China, marriages are sacred, and husbands are expected to become extremely angry on hearing of their wives' infidelity. Ordinarily, however, friends and family exert a moderating influence on husbands, and violence is avoided. Isolated from friends and community in the new setting . . . Mr. Chen had no one to keep him from translating his anger into violence."[38] The court decided that since "Chen took all his Chinese culture with him to the United States except the community which would moderate his behavior,"[39] he was not fully responsible for murdering his wife.

Needless to say, the case of Mrs. Chen sent a disheartening message: The U.S. justice system will not protect Asian-American women. The dialectic between "cultural defense"[40] and "cultural bias" is colored by the pervasive racism in the United States and administered according to a double standard in the court rooms. For the sake of preserving the family, the life of an Asian-American woman was literally sacrificed, and racist and sexist practices of the U.S. legal system protected a powerless, uprooted, and forever foreign Asian-American man. To borrow a critical reflection from a churched Korean-American woman in her mid-40s on hearing the news, "We are not meant to be protected by anyone. When we were in the native land, the law protected men's rights. And when we are in America [i.e., the U.S.], the law protects White Americans first, then men second."

Another story comes from a 1.5 generation[41] Korean-American woman whose past nine years of marriage have been an ongoing history of both physical and mental abuse by her husband. Devastated by continuous battering and devaluation at home, she grew determined to end her victimization and began to seek both professional help and support groups. This decision alone is a courageous one in the context of Korean [i.e., Asian] culture, where problems in the family are considered to be personal matters that are to be avoided in most public discourse. Marital and familial problems tend to remain within families. This unbroken silence leads to the problem of underreporting[42] of both physical and psychological abuse against women in Asian-American communities, and fosters the image of harmonious and violence-free Asian-American families in the male-stream mass media. A recent study on battered Korean-American women in Chicago, however, reported the overwhelming extent of wife abuse in Korean immigrant households. Of the 150 respondents whose length of U.S. residency was 10 years or less, 60 percent reported being battered.[43] Furthermore, the traditional Korean culture places blame on the wife if there is wife abuse at home. "Abuse is seen as a reaction to an unhappy home life. The assumption is that if a man is unhappy enough to hit his wife, she deserves it. Hence, blame and shame are yet other impediments to articulating the problem."[44]

Contrary to the common practice among Asian-Americans, this abused Korean-American woman decided to share her struggle with people outside her family. Among these, at least three sources of "help" clearly rendered her experiences as being at the "borderlands": a lawyer, a feminist support group, and a Christian minister. She was told the following by a predominantly Korean-speaking male lawyer:

> Simple wife battering is rather common. . . . She needs to under-
> stand her husband's battering as a symptom of his unsatisfactory
> and frustrating life in the U.S., rather than as a sign of lack of love
> towards her. . . . She is selfish to even consider a divorce because
> she has two young children who completely depend on loving
> mother's care. . . . If she still pursues to divorce her husband, she
> will lose custody of her children regardless of what the American
> law says, because she is a Korean.

Both explicit and implicit in his messages was that for a Korean-
American wife and mother, divorce is not only unthinkable, but an un-
Korean way to manage marital and familial problems. She is reminded
of her racial-ethnic identity, wherein her foremost loyalty is taken for
granted and wherein consideration of herself as an autonomous social
agent worthy of personal happiness is selfish and un-Korean.

In need of more understanding and sympathetic support, the woman
went to a locally based feminist consciousness raising/support group,
an action that is often perceived as a threat or a sign of disloyalty to the
Asian-American community at large. The consequences of Asian-
American women's affiliation with the feminist movement are thought
to include: "weakening of the male ego, dilution of effort and resources
in Asian-American communities, destruction of working relationships
between Asian men and women, setbacks for the Asian-American
cause, co-optation into the larger society, and eventual loss of ethnic
identity for Asian Americans as a whole."[45] The Korean-American
woman was confronted by questioning and curious white feminists at
their meeting. They asked questions such as "Where do you come
from?" and "Are most Asian men so inhumane and egotistical?" When
she insisted that her family was also a source of comfort, she was told
that she needed to combat the "false consciousness" that made her identify with her husband as another immigrant like herself. In this instance
the woman experienced a profound clash of two clearly demarcated
understandings of herself—one as an independent, self-contained
entity and the other as an interdependent person, attentive to others.[46]

Disillusioned by these experiences, this woman finally sought spiritual solace from a Korean-American Christian minister. The minister
told her that suffering from domestic violence provided her with a good
opportunity to contemplate and to identify with how much Christ suffered on the cross. By bearing the cross for the whole family, she was
actually working out her own salvation and would be rewarded hun-
dreds-fold in the life to come after her death. "Endure and be faithful
unto death" was the key message that was preached to her. What happens to her abusive husband in the life to come? The minister appar-

ently cited to her Romans 3:5—"But if our wickedness serves to show the justice of God, what shall we say?"—and told her that "where sin is, grace may abound as well" (cf. Rom. 6:1).

"I feel more confused and heavy with guilt," she contended. Instead of being uplifted and empowered by the process of seeking outside help, she was re-victimized on several accounts. She was variously told that women's physical abuse is caused by their men's unsatisfactory life circumstances in the United States; that the centrality of children and stability of Asian-American families require women's unconditional endurance of pain and faithfulness unto death; that the rhetoric of sisterhood can be actualized only by women who consider themselves to be individuals apart from their own racial-ethnic communities. More-over, the patri-kyriarchal religion of Christianity legitimizes and encourages woman's silent suffering as a noble spiritual calling. In short, ensuring the stability of the family and attending to familial needs comes before pursuing her interests and happiness as an Asian-American woman.

These two stories of Asian-American women challenge the constructed ideals of cohesive and stable Asian-American families. On the economic front, the ideological construction of the family based on the two separate spheres systematically disempowers Asian Americans at large and Asian-American women in particular, because it is rooted in the politics of skin color and ignores other ethnic survival strategies, such as networks of "fictive kin"[47] and various nonnuclear family formations. Clearly demarcated spheres also contribute to low self-esteem for Asian Americans. Asian-American men's feelings of inadequacy for not being able to provide for their families are interconnected with women's feelings of guilt for not being able to stay home to take care the family; and both are interconnected with their children's feelings of confusion and displacement resulting from the discrepancy between the male-stream mass media's representation of ideal parents and their real parents, who often practice role-reversal at home. It is thus telling that while most Asian-American mothers who work outside the home perceive their employment as not separate from, but integral to, being able to provide both emotionally and financially for their children, their young children often point to their mothers' absence from home during after-school hours as an important (negative) factor in their seeking alternative nurturing experiences outside the family. Hence, a feminist understanding of the family as a social institution must criticize the cult of two separate spheres if it is truly committed to advocating equality for all, equality not only across gender lines, but also across the lines of race-ethnicity and class. Combating racism is, then, "fundamentally a feminist issue because it is so inter-connected with sexist oppression."[48]

Furthermore, since equality has different meanings for different people, any attempt to universalize and/or monopolize the portrayal cf liberated people needs to be critically reassessed. To promote the much-accepted notion of family pluralism (and more broadly, cultural pluralism) in a society such as ours, many alternative forms of the family need to be recognized as both viable and valuable survival strategies for many different people.

NOTES

The metaphor of "the borderlands" was explored in *Borderlands: La Frontera*, ed. Gloria Anzaldua, (San Francisco: Spinsters, 1987).

1. The term, "race ethnic" (without a hyphen) was coined by Maxine Baca Zinn, and it refers to social categories often labeled as "races." But each race group is also bound by ethnicity. Hence, "the concept of racial ethnic underscores the social construction of race and ethnicity for people of color in the United States" (Maxine Baca Zinn, "Family, Feminism and Race in America," in *The Social Construction of Gender*, ed. Judith Lorber and Susan A. Farrell [Newbury Park, Calif.: Sage Publications, 1991], 131).

2. George F. Sanchez, in "Go After the Women: Americanization and the Mexican Immigrant Woman, 1915–1929," talks about how Chicanas are also seen as the cultural "glue." "Go After the Women," in *Unequal Sisters: A Multicultural Reader in U.S. Women's History*, ed. Ellen Carol DuBois and Vicki L. Ruiz (New York: Routledge & Kegan Paul, 1990).

3. The term "double shift" is derived from Arlie Hochschild's coining of the "second shift." See Arlie Hochschild with Anne Machung, *The Second Shift: Working Parents and the Revolution At Home* (New York: Viking Penguin, 1989).

4. The term "solemn assembly" is borrowed from Peter Berger.

5. Harry H. L. Kitano, *Race Relations*, 4th ed. (Englewood Cliffs, N.J.: Prentice-Hall, 1991).

6. Ron Takaki, *Strangers From a Different Shore* (Boston: Little, Brown & Co., 1989). See also Taylor, *Minority Families in the United States*.

7. Vincent N. Parrillo, *Strangers to These Shores: Race and Ethnic Relations in the United States*, 4th ed. (New York: Macmillan Publishing Co., 1994).

8. U.S. Bureau of the Census, 1970, 1980, and 1990.

9. The term "minority" is used with quotation marks in order to denote a particular ideological formation of the term. Its common usage in the social sciences and humanities has very little—if anything—to do with the concept of numbers but rather with power relationships. An in-depth analysis of historical and political usage of "minority" is articulated by Barton Meyers, "Minority Group: An Ideological Formulation," *Social Problems* 32:1 (October 1984): 1–15. See also Kitano, *Race Relations*.

10. The term "Asian sojourners" refers to people from Asia who were born outside the U.S. and emigrated for various reasons but intend to return to

their homeland in Asia; whereas "Asian Americans" are those of Asian descent born in the U.S., or those who immigrated to make the U.S. their home base.

11. Kitano, *Race Relations*.
12. Sucheng Chan, *Asian Americans: An Interpretive History* (Boston, Mass.: Twayne Publishers, 1991). See also Takaki, *Strangers*.
13. Lucie Cheng and Edna Bonacich, *Labor Immigration Under Capitalism: Asian Immigrant Workers in the United States Before World War II* (Berkeley, Calif.: University of California Press, 1984); Alexander Saxton, *The Indispensable Enemy: Labor and the Anti-Chinese Movement* (Berkeley, Calif.: University of California Press, 1971).
14. Edna Bonacich, "A Theory of Middleman Minorities," *American Sociology Review* 38 (1973):583–94; Ellie McGrath, "Confucian Work Ethic," *Time,* March 28, 198, 52; Ben Tong, "The Ghetto of the Mind: Notes on the Historical Psychology of Chinese in America," *Amerasia Journal* 1:3 (1971):1–31.
15. Philip E. Vernon, *The Abilities and Achievements of Orientals in North America* (New York: Academic Press, 1982); Judy Yung, "The Social Awakening of Chinese American Women as Reputed in Chung Sai Yat Po, 1900–1911," in DuBois and Ruiz, *Unequal Sisters*.
16. Judy Yung's documentation of the sex ratio among Chinese during the nineteenth century illustrates more vividly male and female imbalance: 19 to 1 in 1860, 13 to 1 in 1870, 21 to 1 in 1880, 27 to 1 in 1890. Judy Yung, "The Social Awakening of Chinese American Women."
17. "Approximately 85% of Chinese women [living in] San Francisco were prostitutes in 1860 and 71% in 1870" (Yung, "Social Awakenings," 195–96).
18. Regardless of the public discourse on the attempt to overcome racist traits within the immigration laws by including equal quotas from all over the world, it is not an accident that the post-1965 immigrants are mostly from Asia, Africa, and Latin America, whereas earlier immigrants were over whelmingly European.
19. Social scientists tend to call immigrants and refugees from the Philippines, Korea, and Vietnam "recent" immigrants. The presence of Filipinos as "nationals" of a U.S. colony and that of Koreans as laborers and self-imposed political exiles during the Japanese occupation existed from the early twentieth century. In 1970—only after the Philippines' national independence from the U.S. and the full implementation of the 1965 Immigration Acts in 1968—did the U.S. census use the ethnic categories of "Filipino/a" and "Korean."
20. The category of unrestricted status as family members of U.S. citizens includes Asian wives of U.S. servicemen and their children, and war orphans who have been adopted by predominantly non-Asian American families in the United States.
21. Esther Ngan-Ling Chow, "The Development of Feminist Consciousness Among Asian American Women," in *The Social Construction of Gender*, ed. Judith Lorber and Susan A. Farrell (Newbury Park, Calif.: Sage Publications, 1991).

22. Saska Sassen, *The Mobility of Labor and Capital* (Cambridge: Cambridge University Press, 1988).

23. Kitano, *Race Relations*.

24. Evelyn Nakano Glenn, and Stacy G. H. Yap, "Chinese American Families," *Minority Families in the United States*, ed. Ronald L. Taylor (Englewood Cliffs, N.J.: Prentice-Hall, 1994).

25. A rather detailed description and critique of the "Ozzie and Harriet" type of American family is articulated by Wade Clark Roof in *A Generation of Seekers* (New York: HarperCollins, 1993), esp. from p. 227.

26. *Washington Post*, 20 August 1992.

27. Cited in Jewell Handy Gresham, "The Politics of Family in America," *The Nation* (July 1989): 24–31.

28. There is an anthology of writings by women of color titled *This Bridge Called My Back: Writings by Radical Women of Color* (ed. Cherrie Morragua and Gloria Anzaldua [New York: Kitchen Table: Women of Color Press, 1981]), which describes multilayered struggles of survival by women of color.

29. Delores S. Williams, *Sisters in the Wilderness: The Challenge of Womanist God-Talk* (Maryknoll, N.Y.: Orbis Books, 1993).

30. Williams, *Sisters in the Wilderness*.

31. In "Culture in Action: Symbol and Strategies," Ann Swidler challenges the conventional understanding of "culture's causal role in shaping action. . . . Culture influences action not by providing the ultimate values toward which action is oriented, but by shaping a repertoire or 'tool kit' of habits, skills, and styles from which people construct 'strategies of action' " (Ann Swidler, "Culture in Action: Symbol and Strategies," *American Sociological Review* 51 [April 1986]: 273).

32. The term "gendered actions" is used, instead of "gender roles," to connote that all gendered behaviors are relational constructs, and to challenge assumptions about the mutually exclusive bipolar notion of "gender roles."

33. Gordon, 1983.

34. Arliene S. Skolnick, and Jerome H. Skolnick, *Family In Transition*, 5th ed. (Boston: Little, Brown & Co., 1986).

35. Although a feminist tendency in documenting gender oppression has been based on its multifaceted understanding of patriarchy, Elisabeth Schüssler Fiorenza coined the term "kyriarchy" to denote the hierarchal reign of the master/lord. She states that her intention in coining the term "kyriarchy" is to "underscore that Western patriarchy has been and still is kyriarchy; i.e., ruling power is in the hands of elite, propertied, educated, freeborn men" (Elisabeth Schüssler Fiorenza, introduction to *Violence Against Women*, in *Concilium* ed. Elisabeth Schüssler Fiorenza and M. Shawn Copeland, [Maryknoll, N.Y.: Orbis Books, 1994], xxii).

36. Tamara K. Harven, "American Families in Transition: Historical Perspectives on Change," in *Family In Transition*, ed. Arliene S. Skolnick and Jerome H. Skolnick (Boston: Little, Brown & Co., 1986).

37. Shaun Assael, "Judge Defends Sentencing Wife-Killer to Probation: Pincus Accepts Immigrant's Novel Defense," *Manhattan Lawyer* (4 April 1989): 4, 17.

38. A Report of the United States Commission on Civil Rights, *Civil Rights Issues Facing Asian Americans in the 1990s* (Washington D.C.: Commission on Civil Rights, February, 1992), 177.

39. Shaun Assael, "Wife-Killer May Get Probation," *Manhattan Lawyer* (14 March 1989): 1, 11 as cited in *Civil Rights Issues Facing Asian Americans in the 1990s.*

40. The stance of "cultural defense" argues that "someone raised in another culture should not be held fully accountable for conduct that violates U.S. law but would be acceptable in the country or culture where s/he grew up" (Office of Attorney General and Community and Consumer Affairs Office, *Attorney General's Asian and Pacific Islander Advisory Committee: Final Report* [Sacramento, Calif.: n.p., 1988], 71).

41. The term "1.5 generation" is a political identity for denoting people who were born in Korea and migrated to the U.S. at an early age, not by their own choice, but by their parents' choice. The term is often used to set them apart from both first generation immigrants and second generation Korean-Americans. Sometimes the term "knee high generation" is used to denote 1.5 generation Korean-Americans (See Kitano, *Race Relations*).

42. According to the *Attorney General's Asian and Pacific Islander Advisory Committee Report*, only 10 percent to 50 percent of Asian/Pacific Islander Americans nationwide report crimes against them, and those who "persist in obtaining victim assistance will be a fraction of that," (67).

43. Young I. Song-Kim, "Battered Korean Women in Urban United States," in *Social Work Practice with Asian Americans*, ed. Sharlene Maeda Furuto, Renuka Biswas, Douglas K. Chung, Kenji Murase, and Fariyal Ross-Sheriff (Newbury Park, Calif.: Sage Publications, 1992).

44. Song-Kim, "Battered Korean Women."

45. Chow, "The Development of Feminist Consciousness."

46. Hazel Rose Markus and Shinobu Kitayama's "Culture and the Self: Implications for Cognition, Emotion and Motivation" describes differing conceptions of individuality in the West and the East. The fundamental difference is "the difference between a construal of the self as independent and a construal of the self as interdependent" (Hazel Rose Markus and Shinobu Kitayama, "Culture and the Self: Implications for Cognition, Emotion and Motivation," *Psychological Review* 98: 2, [1991]: 224).

47. Carol B. Stack, *All Our Kin: Strategies for Survival in a Black Community* (New York: Harper & Row, 1974).

48. bell hooks, *Feminist Theory: From Margin to Center* (Boston: South End Press, 1984)

Shakti And Sati

*Women, Religion,
and Development*

IVY GEORGE

This chapter is a brief survey of the interactions of women, religion and development on the Indian sub-continent. Because of the vastness and complexity of this topic, I have chosen to focus on the religious resources available to women in the Chipko movement[1] as they resisted the destructive forces of development for the sake of their families and communities, their natural environment and culture. In order to place this discussion in its proper context I refer to related discussions on the subjects of women in India, women in Hinduism, the socio-historical background of the Indian women's movement and the development experience in India.

The Study of Women in India

India is a wonder. Those familiar with India know that there is no "typical" Indian woman. Women in India exist in the vortex of diversity determined by gender, ethnicity, language, religion, region, age, education, class, occupational status, family structure, lineage, and much more. Moreover, every woman is influenced directly or indirectly by the interaction of all these distinguishing factors. The enormity and complexity of such diversity defies comprehension, especially by academic theoreticians wanting to fit these gargantuan realities into preconceived categories and causal relations. But the formidable scope of this subject has not deterred the study of Indian women by Indian and other scholars. The magnitude of the field has been managed by the adoption of various approaches to the study of Indian women.[2] Earlier studies of women's social roles involved examining the ideals of femininity laid out in the Hindu sacred texts and folklore.[3] More recent studies have addressed the role and status of women from the standpoint of social movements and social legislation.[4] The life of the westernized urban Indian elite woman has been the focus of still other studies.[5] Another approach has addressed the conditions of poor and illiterate women, urban and rural women, professionals and housewives.[6] There are also issue or place specific studies of Indian women otherwise known as micro-studies. These studies focus on women of a particular geographic or social territory,[7] or are issue specific, such as those concerning women and ecology.[8] Lastly, there are macro-studies that undertake an overview of issues related to social change and development among women.[9]

Despite the overwhelming diversity among Indian women, researchers show that there are some shared features to the female experience in India. Scholars attest to the characterization of Asia as a continent ravaged by gender inequalities.[10] Political economist Amartya Sen shows how, despite worldwide statistics indicating the longer life expectancy of women over men, the reverse has been the case in South Asia.[11] In comparison to Europe and North America, there is an 11 percent negative ratio of females to males in South Asia. Such disproportionality is also present in female infant mortality and illiteracy rates. These general observations are qualified by factors such as religion and public policy, as in the case of Sri Lanka and the Indian state of Kerala. Suffice it to say that this diversity among Indian women calls for caution as one proceeds to examine the dynamics surrounding women in India.

Women in Hinduism

I turn now to a partial exploration of femaleness as it is depicted in Hinduism. While the Indian population adheres to various religions, the majority are Hindu; hence my choice of Hinduism.[12]

Hinduism is an ancient religious system that predates many of the other great world religions. It is an expansive philosophical whole that contains several established written and oral traditions. Since Hinduism is an evolving tradition, it is quite likely that beliefs and practices found among one group may be absent among groups elsewhere. Further, Hinduism permeates all of the Hindu's daily life with its religious elements.[13]

Hinduism offers a plethora of gender images, roles, beliefs, and behaviors that have reverberated among Hindu women through the ages. Hence, it may not be assumed that there is *a* Hindu interpretation or tradition that stands out as a monolith, consolidating the diverse strands. As with all other religious traditions, Hinduism has both misogynic and emancipatory elements.

Carol C. Mukhopadhyay[14] draws out some central themes in Hinduism that support women's claims to power and significance: the presence of many female deities and protagonists displaying power and leadership capacities; the absence of a single essentialist female archetype embodying gender specific attributes; the presence of *role*-generated attributes and abilities rather than qualities intrinsic to *occupants* of the role; and lastly, a set of religio-ethical principles that are panhuman in nature. Thus, beginning in the Vedas (the ancient Hindu scriptures) and continuing into the epic Puranas, women have been portrayed as major and minor deities, and as powerful queens and consorts. Today, these outstanding depictions of women in Hinduism have not been relegated to an earlier Hindu orthodoxy. Contemporary Indian life is rife with the worship and following of these deities. These female role models of the sacred continue to inspire millions of women and men.[15]

What is the nature of "power" displayed in Hinduism? Power in the Hindu context is not about domination or the exercise of physical force; rather it involves the pursuit of knowledge, sacrifice, and transcendence of temporal reality through renunciation and surrender.[16] *Shakti* and *Sati* are *apparently* two paradoxical faces of Hindu womanhood that are set against this Hindu interpretation of power.

Shakti is the female generative force critical to all action and being in the Hindu universe.[17] Crucial to the concept of *Shakti* is the idea that all action and power are female. *Shakti* is primarily a moral and creative force, not an immoral and destructive energy. Moreover, *Shakti* stands for unity among women, between women and men, and with the entire universe.[18] The female deities who are manifestations of the Goddess Parvati are generally referred to as *Shakti*. Paradoxically, *Sati* (the virtuous one and an earlier incarnation of Parvati) is credited with beginning the practice of widow immolation. According to legend, *Sati* immolated herself in protest against her father's quarrels with her husband. It is said that the various spots in India where her ashes fell are now considered sacred for her followers.[19]

The practice of *Sati*, the self-immolation of a Hindu widow on her husband's funeral pyre, was held up as a cultural ideal for upper-caste women.[20] Theoretically this practice was voluntary, and high honor was accorded those widows who submitted themselves to death freely. They were admired and revered for their willingness to sacrifice their lives and rise above the world of illusion. One can understand how, when *Sati* is seen in the context of *Shakti*, it connotes power for the Hindu woman. Nevertheless, both *Shakti* and *Sati* have become elements of oppression and violence among Hindu women today. *Shakti* has been appropriated by men to control women, and by higher castes to dominate lower castes.[21] Similarly, *Sati* has been forced on many women throughout history. In other instances, due to poverty and social ostracism resulting from widowhood, many women went reluctantly to their deaths at their husbands' cremation. The practice of *Sati* was abolished in 1829. But among some conservative segments of the Hindu community today, *Sati* is being reclaimed as "a contemporary expression of a medieval Hindu Ideal."[22]

In light of Hinduism's use of female images like *Shakti* and *Sati* to demonstrate power and unity, how do we explain India's current wide gender inequities in social, economic, and political status? Contrary to the perception that Hindu women's disadvantaged position is attributable to Hindu cultural traditions, beliefs, and attitudes,[23] gender-activity differentiation is arguably a function of social-structural and preferential factors.[24] These social-structural and preferential factors involve the availability of means as allocated by a society's social, economic, and political institutions. These institutions provide the social means, that is, wealth, family and kinship networks, access to education and healthcare, laws, and so on, all of which open up opportunities to people. When religious beliefs run counter to social-structural realities or to personal preferences, usually beliefs are revised or reinterpreted to align the preferred behavior with the religio-cultural beliefs and traditions.[25] The implications of this argument for Hindu women is that it is not religion *per se* that is the source of their social disadvantage; rather, they are entrapped in patriarchal structures and systems that are oppressive to them.

The Socio-Historical Context of the Indian Women's Movement

In 1988 Madhu Kishwar, a prominent Indian activist and one of the founders of *Manushi: A Journal About Women and Society*, asserted that in India there was no women's "movement," there are only "mobilizations" and "sporadic struggles."[26] Nevertheless, scholars of social movements have been at pains to chart a women's movement in India.[27] The movement may be sketched in two parts: the movement *for* women that was undertaken by reformers during the nineteenth century when India was under British imperial rule, and the movement *by* women that began in the twentieth century.

In the nineteenth century Indian male social reformers who belonged to urban, upper-caste and upper-class groups advocated for women because of the challenges and demands presented by the British presence. It was in the interests of these men to prepare Indian society for the benefits of "modernity." Their role as advocates for women was in keeping with their perception of women as "dependents" and "recipients."

Such methods of reform merely perpetuated the prevailing system under the guise of attacking it. The reformers' psychology was complex: In part, the enhancement of women's image was caught up with their own image of themselves as "modern" and "civilized."[28] Further, these "enlightened" men sought social reform through legislation for women as a means of challenging the British administrators' charges of Hindu conservatism. They also wished to counter the indignation of Christian missionaries, who considered many of the social practices toward women "evil" and hence engaged in anti-Hindu propaganda.[29] The male proponents of this nineteenth-century reform movement examined the social conditions of women and campaigned against practices such as *Sati*, polygamy, child marriage, discriminatory inheritance laws, female infanticide, and other forms of violence against women. They enabled the passage of liberalizing legislation directed at women's welfare.[30] Some of these reforms affected men more than women. Attacking the practice of child marriage and advocating for women's education worked in the interests of the male social reformers. The reforms would not only enhance the personal lives and public images of the reformers, but they were crucial in facilitating the changing nature of the Indian state under British rule. Women's education was closely tied up with the "development" and "modernization" of India. Women as agents of social reproduction in the household and as custodians of culture were considered critical for the modernization project. This rationale for women's education was made clear in a speech made by Sarojini Naidu, an eloquent speaker and a prominent figure in the development of the Indian women's movement in the early part of the twentieth century, when she spoke regarding women's education to the Indian National Social Conference in 1914:

> We asked for nothing that is foreign to our ideals, rather we ask for a restoration. . . . We (women) ask only that we may be given that chance to develop our body and spirit and mind in that evolution that will reestablish for you . . . *ideal womanhood that will make noble wives who are helpmates, strong mothers, brave mothers, teaching their sons their first lesson of national service.*[31]

Several women's organizations sprang up at the national and the provincial levels in the early twentieth century, including the Women's Indian Association in 1917, the All India Women's Association in 1926, and the National Council of Women of India in 1925. Their objectives were twofold: reform and resistance. In keeping with the spirit of the social reform movement of the previous century, these women's organizations served the special interests of women and children through the provision of social services. The women also engaged in resistance against British imperialism by joining forces with the more political movement—the Indian National Congress (INC).

The Women's Indian Association (WIA) was made up of elite women and perceived itself as presenting the interests of all Indian women when it took up the issue of women's franchise with the British. This concern complemented educated Indian men's demand for self-government expressed by the INC. After prolonged negotiations with the British, women's right to vote was granted in select Indian states in 1921. Other states followed sporadically. Since franchise was tied to property ownership, however, enfranchisement was affected by gender and class, making millions of women ineligible to vote. It was under the 1950 Constitution of independent India that all citizens over 21 years old were granted the right to vote. Interestingly, women's entry into education and politics was always accompanied by a reminder and reassurance about the different spheres of men and women. In fact, references to Hindu ideals elevating woman as mother, wife, and helpmate were put forward by proponents of women's rights demanding education, enfranchisement, and legal rights.[32] Such an approach to women's issues without a critical evaluation of the power determinants inherent in the traditional gender roles led to the continued preservation of gender inequalities.

Since the adoption of the Indian Constitution in 1950, which guarantees gender equality, legislation to further this goal has been enacted. Laws have been directed at improving the position of women by attacking polygamy; raising the age of marriage to 18 for females and to 21 for males; allowing women the restitution of conjugal rights, marital separation, and divorce; the abolition of dowry; and providing for equal remuneration in the workforce. Laws have also been enacted to provide for maternity benefits, punishment for sexual violence, and so on. It should not be surprising to learn, however, that it was mainly the educated middle and upper middle-class women who could use these laws to their advantage. Low literacy rates, lack of knowledge of the law, and the adherence to traditional gender roles that enforce dependence on father, brother, husband, and son leave a large majority of Indian women outside the pale of the law. The scope of the laws is biased in favor of those women who are urban, educated, and middle-class. Issues like widow remarriage, inheritance rights, and equal remuneration pertain to socially and economically advantaged women, whereas deforestation, famine, rising prices, rape, materialism, dowry murders, and sexual harassment affect all women to some degree regardless of their social standing.[33]

The emergence of these latter issues marked a turning point for Indian women in the 1970s. The workings of the Indian political economy that led to declining standards of living, rising food prices, the commercialization of agriculture, the globalization of the Indian economy, and rising unemployment generated a gendered response, resulting in the organization of women as protesters, picketers, and demonstrators. The Women's Anti-Price Rise Committee formed in Bombay in 1972 drew attention to the basic connections between women, food, and employment. Tens of thousands of women took to the streets in protest against the government, store keepers, and underground marketers. They demanded price cuts, unadulterated grains, and increased food rations.[34] The Anti-Price Rise movement raised the consciousness of many women about women's problems in the areas of culture and tradition. All over India, women's groups emerged in protest against rape, sexual harassment, dowry murders, and the exploitation of sex in the media. This movement of urban women's groups was made possible by their associations with women's organizations and political parties already in place.[35] Voluntary organizations with the express purpose of providing poor women economic empowerment through loans and employment are yet another kind of women's group that caters to both urban and rural women.[36] Another facet of the women's movement in India is seen in peasant grassroots movements, in which women have played leading roles. The Chipko movement (which will be discussed later) is an example of this mobilization among rural women.

This brief overview of the origins and the status of the women's movement in India shows a shift from women's interests and rights being named and addressed by upper-caste, westernized males over a century ago to the present day, when women are claiming their agenda by and for themselves.

Women And Development

The discourse on development was conceived in the post–World War II West as a national alternative for the newly independent countries in the tripartite postwar order that these countries entered—that of the capitalist West (the first world), the socialist East (the second world), and the "underdeveloped" South (the third world).

Development thought and practice became a means of devaluing indigenous systems of knowledge and social arrangements outside the western hemisphere. Western economies, political systems, and social institutions were deemed the foundation for progress in these societies, and local western-educated elites were initiated into this paradigm for progress. Economic indices became crucial measures of development. Increased production and consumption were seen as hallmarks of development. Such theory led to remarkable shifts in worldview: concepts such as growth, needs, poverty, community, freedom, and rights all underwent radical changes in meaning. The Rostowian modernization theory viewed local tradition and natural systems as an obstacle to progress and modernity.[37] Conversely, it was assumed that the bounties of development would bring about an automatic improvement of women's economic and social position. The United Nations Decade for Women was predicated precisely on such an assumption of women's improved choices under development programs. Yet the Decade ended with the following statement: *"the almost uniform conclusion of the Decade's research is that, with a few exceptions, women's relative access to economic resources, incomes, and employment has worsened, their burdens of work have increased, and their relative and even absolute health, nutritional and educational status has declined."*[38]

Indian activist and environmentalist Vandana Shiva argued that the exploitation or exclusion of women and the exploitation of nature and indigenous culture are inherent to the dynamic of western development.[39]

In the 1950s and 1960s women were invisible in the schemes of development planners and organizations. Maria Mies suggests that this exclusion of women is in keeping with the epistemological status of "development" in which notions of "good" and "bad," "civilized" and "savage," "tamed" and "domesticated," "developed" and "underdeveloped" take on new meanings.[40] Paradoxically, women were valued for their capacity to birth and nurture the waged workers of the coming generation, and were expected to provide hearth and haven for the adult waged workers who came home for comfort. Yet the worth of women's contributions in the domestic sphere did not factor into the development economists' calculation of production values. That women's contribution in the home was vital to the program of development is to be seen in the kind of women's development programs offered during these years: family planning and population control, maternal and child welfare programs, nutrition, home economics, and so on. In a few instances "cottage industries" were set up for women. Knitting, sewing, weaving, and handicraft production were confined to "female domains" in the cottage.[41] Development projects reduced the significance of women to their biological functions and grossly overlooked their roles as primary producers of the means of subsistence in the production of food, clothing, transportation of water and fuel, of home building, making kitchen implements, and so on. India has one of the largest female populations of the world, and in a country where 80 percent of the people live in the rural areas, large numbers of these women are involved in subsistence agriculture. Ester Boserup documented the significant contribution women have made to the productive sectors of the third world, especially in agriculture. Boserup and others have shown that women's conditions actually deteriorated under development programs.[42] Boserup's and others' research on women's contributions to economic development led to policy and program formulation among development planners. The concept of Women in Development (WID) was coined in the early 1970s with the objective of integrating women's contributions in the development process. Research in the 1970s and 1980s, however, showed that integrating women into development thinking and programs whereby their participation and benefits could be increased was not sufficient. Women were still trapped in unequal social and gender relations and were far from being free agents in the engine of development.

Independent of the patriarchal nature of Indian society, researchers provide ample evidence that women suffer specifically from the ills of development. While statistics from around the world indicate a higher average ratio of women to men (105:100), in the Indian states of Punjab and Haryana (which were the prosperous Green Revolution states) the ratio is 84:100.[43] The commercialization of agriculture under the Green Revolution led to a high view of the market economy controlled by men, and a devaluation of the subsistence economy sustained by women. The displacement of women in agriculture was no accident in the minds of the planners and implementers of the Green Revolution. In 1959, when a Ford Foundation mission of North American agronomists came on an assignment to India, they were opposed to the idea of integrated rural agricultural development for all of India's villages; instead they recommended subsidies to the well-irrigated areas. Invariably this meant that the technical inputs went into the hands of privileged male farmers, who became known as "progressive" farmers. The rest of the population (large numbers of women and peasants) were forced to move for lack of land (since the Green Revolution technology required large tracts of land) and access to finance and credit. Consequently these groups of people became marginalized. The market devaluation of women, combined with newly added burdens of work (for sustenance rather than surplus) led to the reduction in women's entitlement to food, health, and life itself. Women came to be seen as social burdens and hence socially dispensable through femicide, dowry murders, and harassment. With increasing commercial prosperity in the regions of the Green Revolution and the resultant devaluation of women, there came an increase in dowry demands, which led in turn to the murders of women and female infants. These regions were also the first to turn to reproductive technology for the gender selection of their children through amniocentesis and abortion.[44]

Throughout the third world, economic development (according to the capitalist model) and the integration of local industry into the global market frequently begins in a setting where the subsistence labor of large numbers of marginalized women can be exploited and where the ideology of woman as housewife can be kept intact. The male entrepreneurs who market the women's products are the real beneficiaries of such employment structures, although they explain their role as benefactors by providing employment to women who would otherwise starve.[45] Development thus upsets the pattern of sex-specific division of labor that existed in subsistence communities by establishing systems that promote male dominance and control.[46] When systems of production for surplus and exchange value are introduced, it is the men who are usually recruited as laborers; the women are expected to carry on with the maintenance of the family. When local market systems are replaced with larger market systems, women who have thus far been engaged in the local selling and buying are marginalized by the men who take on the new capitalist market relations. Mies suggests that the polarization of gender during development is a function of an overall polarization that takes place under commercial agriculture.[47] Based on observations in the Indian context, Mies puts forward the tentative argument that with increasing class stratification there may be increasing sexism and sexual violence. When some members of "backward classes" move up to the status of middle or rich peasants, their women (who are engaged in agricultural labor) are now subjected to seclusion and retirement as "housewives." Among rural classes the implicit expectation is that the women of the upper classes recline in leisure, while those of the "inferior classes" may bend over and labor in the fields. Similarly, many of these "lower" classes who did not previously participate in the dowry system prove their new higher social status by demanding exorbitant dowry amounts from prospective fathers-in-law, mimicking the fashion of the upper-class men. In such instances, the daughter becomes a social liability.

The employment of men and the exclusion of women from the monied production sphere results in the women's increasing dependence on their husbands' income, and leads in turn to household violence. Modernization and urbanization have led to the transformation of the traditional family, with men migrating to the cities in search of employment and leaving their wives to fend for their broken families.

Frequently the women themselves travel to the cities and take up employment as domestic servants, hawkers, prostitutes, and beggars, or work in the informal sector for less than minimum wage. Further yet, the reproductive capacities of women and men become a target for state planning and programs, especially when the state is uncommitted to the subsistence needs of the masses of marginalized people it creates. Thus, "family" planning and population "control" is a major policy focus in India, which resulted in state coercion and violence in the 1970s.

The use of the *family* or *household* (usually implying a male head) as a unit of analysis in development planning is problematic. Research shows the multiplicity of experience that exists among the various members of the family unit, based on gender, age, class, and other social characteristics. When the economic status of the household is seen only in terms of the adult male's income, it overlooks the lower economic status of the women and the children. Instead of the household as a representative measure, it is the experience of individual women, children, and men (without negating their mutual relationship to the household) that should be assessed. Development planners' concern for social welfare should move beyond the "household" denoted as a homogenous category and step into the household itself in order to assess the internal dynamics at work.[48] The gendered inequities in access to and control of resources that pervade the labor market are likely to be played out in the home. Amartya Sen describes the household as the locus of several bargaining units where members engage in "cooperative conflict" to seek their own ends.[49] The interaction between family and society is mutually reinforcing. Thus women's lower pay makes it difficult to challenge existing gender-based family dependencies; another result is the easy appropriation of the women's wages by male or senior family members.

These inegalitarian family dynamics in turn influence women's capacity to compete in the labor market. Married women may be confined to certain sorts of work by pressure from family members, in order to preserve their respectability by undertaking only those jobs "suited" to women. Mothers of young children are similarly constrained by family and childcare, and settle for poorly paid home work or low-skilled jobs outside the home. Employers take advantage of the availability of such women and exploit their services.[50]

Ownership of land and resources allows women a relative degree of control.[51] But Hilary Standing shows that this degree of control does not necessarily lead to increased personal autonomy for women, since they come up against mitigating circumstances in their social matrix.

Culturally constructed notions of needs and rights based on gender constrain such women from amassing personal savings or from spending on themselves.[52]

In sum, my research on women and development shows a growing polarization and inequality between the sexes, with the added introduction of new elements of patriarchy.

In the late 1980s there was a shift in thinking from the Women in Development (WID) paradigm to Gender and Development (GAD).[53] GAD represents a transition from earlier attempts merely to integrate women into development, to examining how development programs might address social and gender inequalities and empower women. But the GAD approach has been criticized for not questioning the fundamental assumption of the development model, which is still firmly entrenched in the logic of modernization and western-style growth and is thus necessarily patriarchal.[54]

The environmental degradation brought about by development, and the response of many third world women's groups to this crisis gave rise to the Women, Environment, and Sustainable Development (WED) debate in development discourse. Vandana Shiva, a physicist, philosopher, and women's activist, was influential in shaping WED. Shiva's thinking and writing has been influenced by the Chipko movement. This is a grassroots movement that got its name when women hugged trees to protect them from being felled. I shall devote the next section to the influence of Hindu ideals on women's resistance to environment-hazardous development.

The Chipko Movement:
The Interplay of Women,
Religion and Development

The Chipko movement of the 1970s[55] was born in the mountainous region of Uttarkhand in the North Indian state of Uttar Pradesh. This region had experienced intense resource exploitation, which led to the degradation of the natural environment and the destruction of local peasants' livelihood. Uttarkhand is noted for its rich forest, mineral, and hydroelectric resources, as well as the scenic beauty of its location in the Himalayan region, which draws tourists and pilgrims. Uttarkhand is the only region in the Himalayan range without local self-government. It is governed by bureaucrats located 200 miles away, who have little understanding of local life. In the last thirty years the area's timber, forest, and mineral resources have been extracted; the land has been cultivated for commercial crops; and dams have been constructed in areas with river networks. Such development has led to soil erosion, landslides, pollution, and other ecological crises, resulting in serious economic and social displacement of the local people. Further, the local people were overlooked in the planning or implementation phases of these "development" programs, and they were not beneficiaries of the profits. Due to the ongoing depletion of the local resources, there is a continuing emigration of local men from the mountains to the plains in search of employment. Thus many of the village communities contain only women, children, and the elderly, leading to a dual economy of remittances from the absentee males and meager earning from local subsistence agriculture.

The vast majority of the population depends on agriculture and on the forests. The significant contributions of women in this traditional economy (planting, weeding and harvesting, looking after the cattle, transporting the crops from the fields, cooking, collecting fuel and water, childcare) provided sufficient impetus for the launching of the Chipko movement, which protested the deforestation and development process directly threatening their livelihood and culture.[56]

The significant catalysts of the Chipko movement were women who had been disciples of Mahatma Gandhi[57]—Mira Behn, Sarala Behn, Bimala Behn, Hima Devi, Gauri Devi, Gunga Devi, Bachni Devi, Itwari Devi, Chamun Devi, and others. Men like Sunderlal Bahuguna and others joined the Chipko movement to support the women. Bahuguna was accustomed to saying, "We are the runners and messengers—the real leaders are the women."[58]

The women in the movement were motivated by two attitudes toward the forest. First, from the standpoint of Hindu cosmology nature (Prakriti) is an expression of Shakti (the feminine and creative principle of the cosmos). Prakriti, through its interaction with Purusha (the masculine principle), creates the world. Purusha-Prakriti (person and nature) are not separate but related entities. Prakriti is an integral aspect of the Hindu's daily life and provides a significant dimension from which the women of Uttarkhand viewed the deforestation of their sacred forests. Second, to the women the forest was the protector of and provider for their families, their cattle, and their soils (an extension of their cosmic family).[59] Such moral/religious conviction about their cause gave the women confidence in dealing with their adversaries. At various points in their protest, the women read from the Hindu scriptures and sang folk songs that expressed their conviction about the interrelatedness of the world of humans and nature. The women sometimes tied the rakhi (a sacred thread) around the trees, symbolizing sacred protection of the forest. Interestingly, rakhi is customarily given by a sister to a brother as a symbol of her shakti (power).[60]

The Chipko movement may be seen fundamentally as a conflict in worldviews between the Chipko perception of the forest as a source of "life" and "nurturance" and the developer's perception of the forest as potential "product" and "profit." The Chipko movement has been able to affect government forestry policy to a limited degree, but, more important, Chipko's success lies in its moral power to challenge the state's notion of development, and in its lesson that nature is indispensable to survival. The example of Chipko women has spread all over India in various forms and has been a source of inspiration for ecological movements elsewhere in the world.

In December 1987, the Alternative Nobel Prize was awarded in Stockholm to honor the Chipko women.[61] Their movement is a good illustration of what "women's issues" mean to women in the third world. Concerns over alcoholism, unemployment, food, deforestation, drought, and development have occupied the center stage of women's activism.

The Road Ahead

A general survey of the development literature shows an insular and specialized approach on the part of theorists and practitioners. Orthodox development theorists approach development primarily as economic development, and family as the male-headed household. Religion has been at best a peripheral variable in their consideration, and at worst ignored completely.

These trends have been changing over the last two decades, however, during which planners and activists have perceived "economic" as belonging to the category of "social," and "gender" as an integral part of "family" and "society." Religion comes under serious consideration when the realm of the social merges with values, beliefs, traditions, cultures, and ethics, which often have their underpinnings in various religious traditions. Insight into religious matters is especially important when understanding development issues. For religious traditions provide a society, both overtly and covertly, with icons and images of social relations that encompass the economic and political, the public and the private workings of a society. Religion plays a significant role in furthering and deterring development. This is illustrated in the earlier discussion of *Shakti* and *Sati* as being alternately empowering and enslaving forces for Hindu women.

Religion does not have a unilateral impact on public welfare; rather its influence is mediated by the roles of the state, the cultural context, community participation, and other factors in a given society. Thus, the role of religion in community development will vary within and across regions, even under the umbrella of the same religion, leading in some instances to the emancipation of some people and the subordination of others.

The significance of women's participation in development is another factor that has come under study. That women are agents and not just targets of development has been increasingly recognized. Development analysts have begun to see gender and class as critical variables in the design and implementation of their programs. In India the interaction of region, religion, ethnicity, occupational status, household structure, and other variables further complicate the relationship between development and women. To neglect any of these components in development analysis is to engage in distorted and partial analysis.

In spite of the movement in development discourse in the last two decades there are still some serious anomalies in development theory. First, development continues to be seen as a third world issue. In reality, all societies are developing, thus development is a global subject. Second, development cannot be seen in isolation from the global military market and economic relations. Changes are needed from micro-communities to the macro-world of international finance and politics. Third, from third world feminists' perspective a development paradigm that is unwilling to examine its epistemological assumptions in light of the situatedness and specificities of human struggles everywhere is increasingly untenable.[62]

Last, I restate the need to reexamine the multiplicity of variables that affect the postmodern human condition of our day. Understanding the influence of cultural history on social conditions is crucial. India is a country highly stratified by caste, class, and gender. Scholars like Amartya Sen link the Hindu worldview with Indian elitism,[63] pointing to countries like Sri Lanka and Burma, under the less elitist Buddhist tradition, which have improved social welfare conditions over that of India. While Sen's argument has much merit for national conditions, there are other variables at work that bring about different outcomes even in the same country. The southwestern Indian state of Kerala is a case in point.[64] The per capita income of Kerala is lower than that of the rest of India, yet on development indicators such as literacy, life expectancy, infant mortality, and birth rate, this state is closer to the United States than it is to the rest of India or other low-income countries. In Kerala, the divisions based on gender, caste, region, and class have been under pressure for a long time. Kerala has a unique place in Indian history in terms of its cosmopolitan nature, from its participation in international trade dating back to 3000 B.C. to its first elected communist government in 1957. These are regarded as factors contributing to Kerala's enlightenment. Nevertheless, the role of Kerala's women in social change has also been cited as a significant factor in Kerala's development in the absence of much economic growth.

In summary, the location of all societies in the overwhelming scale of free market capitalism is indisputable. But in addition, research and experience lead me to see remarkable parallels in power relations between the countries of the rich North and the poor South, and those between men and women in all of these societies. The paradigm of patriarchy is inescapable. The patriarchy of what passes for "development," through its impact on the family, has brought about gender subordination where none existed, or has reinforced gender subordination where it was previously sanctioned by religion and culture.

While one witnesses the many faces of development fallout (such as increased poverty, violence against women, a rise in religious fundamentalism, etc.) one also sees the rise of resistance and organization for change. The relevant social movements display a whole range of ideological and political positions, sometimes convergent and in other instances divergent; yet it seems to me that the recognition of religion as a relevant factor in understanding social crisis represents an opportunity to explore and suggest egalitarian and holistic means of social and economic change. Existing illustrations such as the religious impulses that activated the Chipko women provide a hopeful example of an imagined universal future.

NOTES

1. A grassroots women's movement in India that came to public attention in the 1970s.
2. Joyce Lebra, Joy Paulson, and Jana Everett, eds., *Women and Work in India—Continuity and Change* (New Delhi: Promilla & Co. Publishers, 1984).
3. Nancy Falk and Rita Gross, eds., *Unspoken Worlds: Women's Religious Lives in Non-Western Cultures* (San Francisco: Harper & Row, 1980); and Doranne Jacobson and Susan S. Wadley, *Women in India: Two Perspectives* (Columbia, Mo.: South Asia Publications, 1992).
4. Arvind Sharma, ed., *Today's Woman in World Religions* (Albany, N.Y.: State University of New York Press, 1994); and Leslie Calman, *Toward Empowerment: Women and Movement Politics in India* (Boulder, Colo.: Westview Press, 1992).
5. Rama Mahta, *The Western-Educated Hindu Woman* (New York: Asia Publishing House, 1970); and idem, *The Divorced Hindu Woman* (Delhi: Vikas Publishing House, 1975).

6. Rehana Ghadially, ed., *Women in Indian Society: A Reader* (Newbury Park, Calif.: Sage Publications, 1988); Haleh Afshar, ed., *Women, Work and Ideology in the Third World* (London: Tavistock Publications, 1985); Elisabeth Bumiller, *May You Be the Mother of a Hundred Sons—A Journey Among the Women of India* (New York: Ballantine Books, 1990); and Lourdes Beneria and Shelley Feldman, eds., *Unequal Burden: Economic Crises, Persistent Poverty, and Women's Work* (Boulder, Colo.: Westview Press, 1992).

7. Manisha Roy, *Bengali Women* (Chicago: University of Chicago Press, 1975).

8. Vandan Shiva, *Staying Alive: Women, Ecology and Development* (London: Zed Press, 1989).

9. Dilip K. Basu and Richard Sisson, eds., *Social and Economic Development in India: A Reassessment* (Newbury Park, Calif.: Sage Publications, 1986).

10. Aruna Rao, Mary B. Anderson, and Catherine A. Overholt, eds., *Gender Analysis in Development Planning—A Case Book* (West Hartford, Conn.: Kumarian Press, 1991).

11. Ibid., 1.

12. I realize the problematic nature of such a choice, as this chapter is one more contribution to a large bank of studies on Hindu women. More than 11 percent of India's population are Muslim, and Muslim women are significantly further down the scale on education, health, and workforce participation and are as affected by class, ethnicity, region, and other factors as their Hindu sisters. Sikhs, Jains, Christians, and Buddhists also form large numbers of the Indian population. While this chapter highlights the particulars of one group, the hope is that it illustrates some principles about women, religion, and development that are relevant for other groups also.

13. Susan Wadley, "Women and the Hindu Tradition," in Ghadially, *Women in Indian Society*, 23–43.

14. Carol C. Mukhopadhyay, "*Sati* or *Shakti*: Women, Culture and Politics in India," in *Perspectives on Power: Women in Africa, Asia and Latin America*, ed. Jean O'Barr (Durham, N.C.: Duke University Center for International Studies, 1982), 15.

15. Ibid.

16. Agheananda Bharati, "*Sadhuization*—An Indian Paradigm for Political Mobilization," in *Aspects of Political Mobilization in South Asia*, ed. Robert I. Crane (Syracuse, N.Y.: Syracuse University Press, 1976), 109–28.

17. See Susan S. Wadley, introduction to *The Powers of Tamil Women*, Foreign and Comparative Studies/South Asian Series, no. 6, ed. Susan S. Wadley (Syracuse, N.Y.: Maxwell School of Citizenship and Public Affairs at Syracuse University, 1980).

18. Ibid.

19. Mukhopadhyay, "*Sati* or *Shakti*," 16.

20. Margot I. Duley, "Women in India," in *The Cross-Cultural Study of Women—A Comprehensive Guide*, ed. Margot I. Duley and Mary I. Edwards (New York: Feminist Press, 1986), 167.

21. See Sheryl B. Daniel, "Marriage in Tamil Culture: The Problem of Conflicting 'Models,'" in Wadley, *The Powers of Tamil Women*, 61–91.

22. See Katherine K. Young, "Women in Hinduism," in Sharma, *Today's Woman in World Religions*, 119–23.

23. Alfred DeSouza, *Women in Contemporary India* (New Delhi: Manohar Book Service, 1975); David R. Kinsley, *The Sword and the Flute: Kali and Krsna, Dark Vision of the Terrible and the Sublime in Hindu Mythology* (Berkeley, Calif.: University of California Press, 1975); and Prabhati Mukherjee, *Hindu Women: Normative Models* (New Delhi: Orient Longman, 1978).

24. Mukhopadhyay, "*Sati or Shakti*," 22.

25. Ibid.

26. Bumiller, *May You be the Mother of a Hundred Sons*, 129.

27. Calman, *Toward Empowerment*; Kamaladevi Chattopadhyay, *Indian Women's Battle for Freedom* (New Delhi: Abhinav Publications, 1983); Suresh T. Renjen Bald, "From Satyartha Prakash to Manushi: An Overview of the Women's Movement in India," in Basu and Sisson, *Social and Economic Development in India*, 194–214.

28. Deniz Kanidyoti, introduction to *Women, Islam and the State* (Philadelphia: Temple University Press, 1991).

29. Young, "Women in Hinduism," 79–80.

30. Ibid.

31. Quoted by Bald in Basu and Sisson, *Social and Economic Development in India* (Naidu's italics).

32. Ibid., 201–203.

33. Ibid., 208.

34. Calman, *Toward Empowerment*, 47–49.

35. Bumiller, *May You be the Mother of a Hundred Sons*, 130–31.

36. The Self Employed Women's Association, or SEWA (the acronym means "service" in many Indian languages), is a model voluntary organization that is widely acclaimed for its empowerment of poor women. See ibid., 135–46.

37. See Rossi Braidotti et al., eds., *Women, the Environment and Sustainable Development—Towards a Theoretical Synthesis* (London: Zed Press, 1994); and Shiva, *Staying Alive*.

38. Gita Sen and Caren Grown, *Development Crises, and Alternative Visions* (New York: Monthly Review Press, 1987), 28 (italics added).

39. Shiva, *Staying Alive*.

40. Maria Mies, introduction to *Women: The Last Colony*, ed. Maria Mies, Veronika Bennholdt-Thomsen, and Claudia Von Werlhof (London: Zed Press, 1988).

41. Braidotti et al., *Women, the Environment and Sustainable Development*, 78.

42. Ester Boserup, *Women's Role in Economic Development* (New York: St. Martin's Press, 1970).

43. Rao, Anderson, and Overholt, *Gender Analysis in Development Planning*, 4–5.

44. Shiva, *Staying Alive*, 94–178.

45. Annette Fuentes and Barbara Ehrenreich, *Women in the Global Factory* (Boston: South End Press, 1988).

46. Mies, Bennholdt-Thomsen, and Von Werlhof, *Women: The Last Colony*.
47. Ibid., 41.
48. Rao, Anderson, and Overholt, *Gender Analysis in Development Planning*, 4–5.
49. Ibid., 5.
50. Hilary Standing, "Resources, Wages and Power: The Impact of Women's Employment on the Urban Bengali Household," in *Women, Work, and Ideology in the Third World*, ed. Haleh Afshar (London: Tavistock Publications, 1985).
51. Joan P. Mencher, "Women Agricultural Laborers and Land Owners in Kerala and Tamilnadu: Some Questions about Gender and Autonomy in the Household," in *Gender and the Household Domain—Social and Cultural Dimensions*, ed. Maithreyi Krishnaraj and Karuna Chanana (Newbury Park, Calif.: Sage Publications, 1989), 117–39.
52. Standing, "Resources, Wages and Power," 234.
53. Braidotti et al., *Women, the Environment and Sustainable Development*, 82.
54. Ibid., 85.
55. Shiva traces the beginnings of Chipko to a time three centuries ago when members of the Bishnoi community, led by a woman, sacrificed their lives to save the sacred khejri trees by clinging to them (*Staying Alive*, 67).
56. Paul Routledge, *Terrains of Resistance* (Westport, Conn.: Praeger Publishers, 1993), 74–118.
57. Shiva, *Staying Alive*, 281.
58. Ibid., 70.
59. Ibid., 97.
60. Routledge, *Terrains of Resistance*, 103; and Shiva, *Staying Alive*, 75.
61. Shiva, *Staying Alive*, 218.
62. Braidotti et al, *Women, the Environment and Sustainable Development*.
63. Amartya Sen, "How is India Doing?" in Basu and Sisson, *Social and Economic Development in India*, 35–36.
64. Richard W. Franke and Barbara H. Chasin, *Karala: Radical Reform as Development in an Indian State* (San Francisco: Institute for Food and Development Policy, 1989).

Final Reflections

ANNE CARR

Because our wide-ranging authors employed various methods and genres in dealing with the issues presented in this volume, and because some perspectives are missing that we had hoped to include, our collection is something of a mosaic rather than a single argument for a particular point of view. Nevertheless, the variety of approaches and the absence of some topics enable the reader to make necessary connections and cross-references in assessing the complicated subject of "religion, feminism, and families." We note that the variety offered here is mutually corrective in its diversity of views. And perhaps that is appropriate in an attempt to deal with three subjects that are each inherently many-sided and are seldom treated together. This volume thus serves as an index of the complexity of all three subjects under review.

Yet there are important connecting links in this mosaic; not least is that a challenge is presented to each of the three conversation partners. Like the connecting colors of stones that comprise a full mosaic pattern, certain issues emerge in different areas of discussion, which are both historical and contemporary. These issues remind us of abiding themes in the current debate: the interaction of gender with the private and the public spheres; the historically and geographically conditioned shape of the family; and the patriarchal assumptions and generational imbalances at play in different contexts and the way these "cash out" concretely in various situations. We note especially how diverse religious perspectives in different periods have influenced the shape of the family in history and continue to influence it in the present.

A major theme of several of the authors is that, despite the prevalence of the popular view that today's "family crisis" is the result of feminist-influenced women moving out of the home and into the paid work force, much of both historical and contemporary feminism is decidedly pro-family. Many first-wave American feminists in the nineteenth century were biblical and domestic feminists who claimed special female virtues and women's moral superiority. Their goal was to bring the power and goodness of women, home, and family into the public arena. And much contemporary feminist thought suggests that feminist perspectives indeed serve to strengthen and democratize family structures by offering women and girls strong, positive role models and enhanced life possibilities. But has secular feminism acknowledged the significant role of religion and the churches in its efforts to win broader support for these very goals?

Regarding the religious aspect of our three-sided subject, several authors have underscored a historically Christian problematic: An early antisex and antiwoman orientation served to make virginity the ideal in Christianity's formative theological period. Marriage and family therefore were second-best options and of less significance in the early Christian scheme. When family was considered important, earlier patriarchal notions of the subordination of women were maintained, and it was often the birth families of both mother and father that were central. While it has been argued that because of its requirement of free consent in marriage, Christianity implicitly placed increased importance on the new family created by husband and wife, old loyalties to the birth family (especially the maintenance of its property) perdured. Has Christianity, either in church policy or theology, acknowledged or dealt with practical family issues that are "up front" for people today in a way that affirms the best ideals and goals of feminism? These very ideals and goals often coalesce with Christian ideals and goals—such as mutuality, equality of all individuals, the importance of embodiment.

A further issue concerns the way Jesus apparently relativized the (patriarchal) family in announcing that his followers comprised a new family (Mark 3:35). Hence, the organic "body of Christ" might be understood as religiously and theologically superior to, and a replacement of, the natural family. This position holds that by denying the central importance of the family, Jesus was in fact releasing women from traditional family obligations and bonds, thereby affirming women's personal dignity and religious autonomy. The chapters on ethics and on fatherhood place the family within the wider horizon of Christian love in a way that may appear to subordinate it to the larger concern; in fact, these approaches also invigorate the significance of the immediate family. Several writers point out problems in Christian ideals of sacrifice and humility, both of which have been especially enjoined on women in the family context. They argue for the secondary character of sacrifice within the wider context of mutuality (a common feminist theme), deal with the complexity of maintaining this perspective through the stages of the life cycle, and integrate family love within the broader notion of Christian neighbor-love. Chapter 13 on the important links between family and society and the need for a "home-like society" is set in the context of an historical dialogue about the emergence of the welfare state, highlighting both economic and religious factors in discussion of the current "feminization of poverty."

The vivid description that is presented of a contemporary mother's attempt to "have it all" in both love and work suggests the particular complexities that emerge in that attempt. One factor is the continuing impact of traditional socialization that encourages feminist women to take on too many "family" obligations, in addition to emerging public ones, while only a few men have really changed their traditional patterns of behavior by assuming more domestic responsibilities. This pattern is confirmed in chapter 16, which discusses fatherhood. Moreover, issues of racism and classism can often be intertwined with feminism in the (mostly middle-class) desire to "have it all."

Racism and classism continue to be critical questions within feminist reflection on the family. In the African-American context, womanism specifically includes the whole community and thus has special concern for the family in its formulations. At the same time, qualifications need to be made about the stereotyped idea of the "cohesive" Asian-American family that is sometimes held in American thought, as well as the important role of religion in such "minority" cultures. Our single contribution about a non-western situation illustrates well how religion can either help or hinder the promotion of gender justice, especially in family relations.

A model of justice that respects both gender equality and gender difference clearly remains an ideal to be fulfilled. It surely is the goal to be sought in future discussion and action, as "family friendly" feminism comes to influence analysis in the churches as well as social-scientific research and public policy debate. It is our hope that such a model presents us with an ideal religious horizon that takes the ideal and the concrete dimensions of family life seriously as we plan for the future.

Our mosaic of chapters suggests the "ripple effect" that several women's movements have had on women (and on men) generally and especially on the family, in itself, and in its various relations with the churches. Whether individual women would call themselves "feminist" or not, the lives of most women and of the men to whom they relate in families have been touched and changed by the cultural assumptions and expectations that have emerged in the wake of the women's movements. Even prior to the explicit movements of the last centuries, our historical chapters demonstrate the long resistance of women to the asymmetrical, imbalanced shape of family life for women. But especially in recent times, the impact of the feminist movement on family life is patent. And it calls for reconsideration and reformulation in all areas of our threefold subject—religion, feminism, and families.

Our suggestion is that this reformulation toward new understanding calls for increased attention to the family and to feminism on the part of churches as they account for and assess the changes that have occurred for the family in our culture. It also calls for new attention on the part of secular feminism to religion, its traditions, and institutions. Finally, it calls for serious consideration of feminist theory and theology on the part of family and cultural theorists, as they explore the changing character of the family and come to appreciate and eventually, perhaps, to advocate the ideals of equality, mutuality, and respect for embodiment that are central to feminism.

Although our volume represents no single theory or perspective on the range of issues it treats, we suggest that the very complexity of these issues within different racial, class, and geographic contexts calls for an open acceptance of the ideas and broad goals of feminism—especially the equality of women and girls—on the part of the churches, as they attempt to address the many crises in contemporary family life. This complexity also calls for feminist theory and theology to attend more explicitly to family issues. A few decades ago, at least one commentator suggested that the failure of the Equal Rights Amendment was due to the wide perception that its women backers, and feminists generally, failed to take account of the issues of children and family, issues which were crucial to many women. It was assumed that feminism was inherently antifamily, a position clearly belied in the foregoing chapters. Lastly, our collection calls for a new family theory (or theories) that appreciates and accepts the significant advances that feminism has entailed for girls and women, rather than implicitly or explicitly blaming feminism for the current troubles of the family.

Our suggestion is that, both practically and theoretically, the groups delineated as religion, feminism, and families are compatible, but their compatibility requires reassessment and reformulation on the part of each. Such reformulation would acknowledge and seek to correct the historical imbalance of the place of women and girls in family life, as well as the negative cultural effects of this assymmetry, and would affirm the ideas and goals of feminism, especially equality and mutuality. It would acknowledge both the positive and negative elements—and thus the ambiguity—of ideals of "sacrifice" within the family, particularly within a Christian framework. It would also heed the importance of historical, geographical, racial, and class contexts in making such an assessment.

It is our hope that the preceding chapters encourage new thinking on the parts of the three institutions central to this volume. Such new thought in religion and the churches, in feminist thought and theory-building (including theology), and in family theory, would incorporate positive appreciation of the important values represented by the others. Rather than as mere reflex blaming feminism for current problems, there would be recognition of the positive gains for women and girls that feminism has entailed, of the important human contribution of family life to society, and of the significant role that religious tradition and institutions do or can play in encouraging authentic family values. This new thought would honor all three components—religion, feminism, families—not subordinating any, but integrating the inherent value of each.

In some ways, our authors already attempt this integration. However, their conjoined work needs broad dissemination and discussion in family discourse, in feminist debate, and in religious and church contexts. We hope our volume contributes to the advancement of a discussion that will mark a new stage in practical experience and thought about religion, feminism, and families.

Index of Names and Subjects